HETEROSEXUALITY / WILLIAM H. M

DATE DUE

OC 14 '94	JY 29 '99		
DE 23 '94	SE 22 '99		
FE 17 '95	OC 20 '99		
MR 31 '95			
JY 20 '95	NO 24 '99		
DE 15 '95			
	DE 18 '99		
MR 29 '96			
	AG 2 '00		
DE 17 '96	OC 6 '00		
	NO 27 '00		
FE 12 '96			
MY 7 '97			
OC 30 '97	NO 15 04		
AP 9 '98			
MY 7 '98			
MR 10 '99			
AP 9 '99			

DEMCO 38-296

Heterosexuality

Heterosexuality

WILLIAM H. MASTERS, M.D.

VIRGINIA E. JOHNSON

ROBERT C. KOLODNY, M.D.

HarperCollins*Publishers*

An earlier version of Chapter 14, "HIV Infection and AIDS," appeared in Masters, Johnson, and Kolodny's *Human Sexuality*, 4th edition, HarperCollins Publishers, 1992.

HarperCollins books may be purchased for educational, business, or sales promotional use. For information, please write: Special Markets Department, HarperCollins Publishers, Inc., 10 East 53rd Street, New York, NY 10022.

FIRST EDITION

Designed by Irving Perkins Associates

Library of Congress Cataloging-in-Publication Data

Masters, William H.
Heterosexuality / William H. Masters, Virginia E. Johnson,
Robert C. Kolodny.
p.   cm.
Includes bibliographical references and index.
ISBN 0-06-019041-8
1. Sex. 2. Sex (Psychology) 3. Sex (Biology) 4. Sexual
disorders. I. Johnson, Virginia E. II. Kolodny, Robert C.
III. Title.
HQ21.M46156   1994
613.9'5—dc20   92-56197

94 95 96 97 98 PS/RRD 10 9 8 7 6 5 4 3 2 1

Contents

Figures

Acknowledgments

The creation of a new book rarely occurs in a vacuum. Throughout the various stages of this project, we were especially fortunate to have the input and assistance of several highly talented people without whose guidance and advice we would have been at a signal disadvantage.

The original idea for this book grew out of detailed discussions with Aaron Asher, a knowledgeable, talented publisher and editor who believed in the importance of what we had to say and helped shape the way we should present it. Through numerous meetings and planning sessions as this book progressed, Aaron consistently impressed us with his insightful publishing instincts and his precision with words. In addition, Aaron's flair for line editing strengthened our manuscript in numerous ways.

We are also indebted to two other individuals whose love for the craft of writing is matched by scholarly acumen, a sharp eye for mixed (or slightly off-the-mark) metaphors, and the unfailing energy they bring to the tricky task of ensuring clarity in the presentation of highly technical scientific material. Glea Humez, our copy editor, was enlisted to work with us on this book at our specific request, since we had been remarkably impressed by her editorial talents and judgments in prior projects. Once again she provided us with invaluable counsel; her editing skills and general readerly inquisitiveness are evident throughout these pages. What is not evident is Glea's sprightly sense of humor, which gently nudges authors into agreement with most of her various corrections and suggestions. We are also grateful for the guidance of Joy Johannessen, our editor at HarperCollins, whose thoughtful input throughout this project has been invaluable.

Special thanks are also due to Nancy Kolodny, M.A., M.S.W., who brought a sharp critical eye to numerous early drafts of the entire manuscript, suggested rewrites and revisions, and offered encouragement when the writing seemed to be dragging.

Finally, we owe a major debt of gratitude to the patients, research subjects, and colleagues who have made our work possible over the years.

One

Love and Intimacy

Love is not love
Which alters when it alteration finds,
Or bends with the remover to remove.
O no! It is an ever-fixed mark
That looks on tempests and is never shaken.
—WILLIAM SHAKESPEARE,
Sonnet 116

But love . . . it's only a story one makes up in one's mind about another person, and one knows all the time it isn't true. Of course one knows; why, one's always taking care not to destroy the illusion.
—VIRGINIA WOOLF,
Night and Day

Love means vastly different things to different people. Even if we restrict our discussion to what most of us call romantic love, leaving aside the complexities of familial love, brotherly love, platonic love, and other nonromantic expressions of this elusive emotion, the word "love" remains extremely hard to define.

For one thing, it is often difficult to draw a line between liking and loving. Although various researchers have tried to measure love,[1] not everyone agrees on whether love is a distinct, separate entity. Some psychologists believe that "the only real difference between liking and loving is the depth of our feelings and the degree of our involvement with the other person."[2]

1

On the other hand, the psychologist Ellen Berscheid has observed that "it seems quite clear that more and more liking for another does not, in the end, lead to romantic love; more and more liking just leads to a lot of liking."[3] We too believe that liking and loving, while interrelated, are quite distinct phenomena.

Psychologists have studied love intently over the past 25 years, but the clearest definition of love that we have seen was penned by the novelist Robert Heinlein, who observed, "Love is that condition in which the happiness of another person is essential to your own."[4] Despite its clarity, this description doesn't begin to hint at the passionate intensity of romantic love, its ardent yearning for sexual as well as emotional union, or the stormy anguish that usually follows when romantic love dissolves.

You don't have to be able to define the exact nature of romantic love to envision what happens when romance isn't working right. Unrealistic expectations about love and romantic relationships lead to monumental pain. (Just look at the soaring divorce rates of the past 40 years and you can see this in rather stark quantitative terms.) We may want to fall in love quickly and effortlessly, have love be unconditional and last forever, be embraced by love as a haven of safety and permanence against the world, but we may be unprepared for the trickiness and challenges when it comes down to real-life implementation of our good intentions.

Even more realistic expectations aren't enough by themselves to sustain a love relationship over time. It takes work—often hard work—and conscious efforts to shape and reshape communication and understanding. Many people are oblivious to this point, believing that true love will always flourish no matter what obstacles appear in its path. But romantic love does not sustain itself effortlessly, just as its passion can dwindle away if neglected or taken for granted. Likewise, even the most passionate loving relationships have no guarantees of permanence. As a sociologist, Morton Hunt, noted, "Formal promises to love are promises no one can keep, for love is not an act of will; and legal bonds have no power to keep love alive when it is dying."[5] Such difficulties aside, love's allure is powerful, exciting, and energizing. Romantic love can seem to be a panacea for many of life's problems: a source of intense, heady, enrapturing feelings, love makes us feel good about ourselves, boosts our self-esteem, and bolsters our sense of connectedness and self-realization. So the tireless search for love in the hope of finding "the" right person to hook up with for life is a high priority for many people—and well it should be, because love expresses an essential optimism about our human potential.[6]

Unfortunately, love's inherent glamour and the premium our culture places on being successfully coupled lead some people to see love through a filter that obscures reality, creating a view of romance that has a fairy-tale quality about it. This is the "and they lived happily ever after" version of relationships that views falling in love as a passive, inexplicable event that somehow just *happens* and believes life falls into place rather effortlessly after finding true love. People with this view of love may spend the better part of their young adult lives waiting for the sudden magical encounters that will sweep them off their feet. But if and when they do manage to fall in love, they are almost invariably disillusioned as soon as love gets beyond the initial stage of intense emotional bliss. Real life means that along with the romance and sex come inevitable shock waves of power struggles, arguments, frustrations, jealousies, and boredom that routinely test any human relationship. It can be a rude awakening to discover how different reality is from the sense of what love should be.

Other people expect love to be shaped primarily by intense, passionate attraction. This view of love downplays its durability or its ability to grow and flourish over time and rates it in an essentially one-dimensional, quantitative way: by the strength of the attraction. Those who think like this misunderstand the complex underpinnings of love, ignoring such important variables as the personal maturity each partner brings to the relationship, how partners react to being loved, how flexible each partner is, and how loyal and trustworthy the lovers are. No matter how passionately two people are attracted to each other in the "falling in love" stage of a relationship, there is no guarantee that it will turn into a long-term commitment. Passion, lust, sensuality, and sex are parts of love but not all there is to loving and being loved. That's why it is counterproductive to have all-or-nothing notions about love, why set definitions miss the point.

Love can be an elixir, a panacea, a rush. Love can be a dream, a quest, an ideal, a goal. Finding someone to love can seem to solve many problems in one's life (especially if one finds a person whose strengths enhance one's own and help one neutralize or overcome what one defines as one's deficiencies), but it can also cause problems one has yet even to imagine. The point is that love is a *subjective* experience, and subjective experiences are intrinsically personal. Who is to say that his or her concept of love is better than yours? Who is to say that his or her concept of love is more authentic, more rewarding, or more meaningful than your own? Each person's perception of love and personal definition of love is as valid for that person as any other person's is for him- or herself, for, as Virginia Woolf tells us, "It's only a story one makes up in one's mind."

If love is to get beyond being a self-made-up story, if it is to emerge from fantasy and illusion, if it is to achieve a foothold in reality and flourish, the lovers must be willing to examine the hopes and fears each of them has about the commitments inherent in a love relationship and develop a framework for discussing and dealing with the changes that will inevitably occur as their relationship matures. Not everyone is willing to do this, however, because for some couples, silence is blissful and change is unimaginable.

Characteristically, when people fall in love, they overlook or minimize flaws and personality quirks in one another. (This is what the ancients meant when they said love was blind.) But self-deception about love extends to a variety of other situations. In some cases, relationships become caricatures of love. This can happen when one or both lovers are emotionally immature or selfish; when one partner is generally unresponsive to the other's needs; or when what seems to be love is actually a dependency relationship. Two social psychologists, Stanton Peele and Archie Brodsky, developed the latter idea in detail in 1976, in a book called *Love and Addiction*, in which they argued that some people who believe they are in love are actually caught in stultifying relationships in which the other person serves as their narcotic. Such relationships are driven by uncontrollable urges to find a source of security that can simultaneously provide a "quick fix" for the problems of everyday living (such as loneliness, boredom, and the need for predictability) and wipe out the pain of internal psychological conflicts or scars. Peele and Brodsky stressed that these addictive relationships impeded mutual growth and were generally incapacitating, in contrast to nonaddictive love, which they saw as a productive, beneficial experience.[7]

In the 1980s, a growing number of books dealing with problematic love relationships made it onto the national best-seller lists—for example, Robin Norwood's *Women Who Love Too Much*, *Smart Women/Foolish Choices* by Connell Cowan and Melvyn Kinder, *Men Who Hate Women and the Women Who Love Them* by Susan Forward and Joan Torres, and Steven Carter and Julia Sokol's *Men Who Can't Love*. Partly as a result of this publishing trend (and the attendant TV exposure such books received on the talk show circuit), many people were able to see more clearly that not all love relationships are the idealized, perfect unions we'd like them to be. In reality, some are exploitive, desperate, or simply unfulfilling.

Our focus here will not be on such problematic relationships but on the everyday love patterns we all try our best to find and maintain. In order to do this, we will begin by examining some general theories about the nature of romantic love and then discuss some specific guidelines for keeping love blooming.

GLOBAL THEORIES OF LOVE

STERNBERG'S TRIANGULAR THEORY OF LOVE

Psychologist Robert J. Sternberg of Yale University has devised a three-part theory of love that can be shown in the form of a triangle (see Figure 1.1). The three components of love, according to this theory, are intimacy, passion, and what Sternberg calls "decision/commitment." Briefly, here is a summary of what these components encompass.[8]

The intimacy component includes giving and receiving emotional support, as well as other behaviors that foster a feeling of warmth in a loving relationship. These include communicating openly and honestly, sharing, experiencing happiness together, understanding each other, and valuing the loved one.

The passion component includes both sexual passion and other needs that elicit a passionate response. For instance, needs for self-esteem, affiliation with others, dominating, or being dominated may be more of a source of passion than plain old sex for some people. Consider the following example that Sternberg provides:

> Debbie grew up in a broken home, with no extended family to speak of, and two parents who were at constant war with each other and eventually divorced when she was an adolescent. Debbie felt as though she never had a family, and when she met Arthur, her passion was kindled. What he had to offer was not

FIGURE 1.1
STERNBERG'S TRIANGLE OF LOVE

The assignment of components to specific corners of the triangle is arbitrary. (*Redrawn from* The Triangle of Love: Intimacy, Passions, Commitment *by Robert J. Sternberg. Copyright 1988 by Basic Books, Inc., Publishers.*)

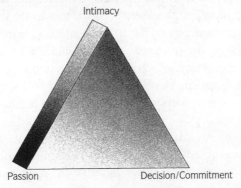

Intimacy

Passion   Decision/Commitment

great sex but a large, warm, closely knit family that welcomed Debbie with open arms. Arthur was Debbie's ticket to the sense of belongingness that she had never experienced but had always craved, and his ability to bring belongingness into her life aroused her passion for him.[9]

The decision/commitment component of love has two parts. The short-term part is the decision that a person loves someone. The long-term part is the person's degree of commitment to maintaining that love. If you think about it, you will realize quickly that the short-term decision to love someone doesn't always go hand-in-hand with a major long-term commitment, although there are certainly times when the two are absolutely linked.

The involvement of each partner in a love relationship can be compared by seeing how closely their love triangles fit each other, as shown in Figure 1.2. In well-matched involvements, the two triangles can almost be superimposed. In mismatched relationships—where one person's needs greatly exceed the other's, or where the two partners' needs are widely divergent—the triangles are far from being congruent. Thus, the comparative size and shape of the partner's love triangles depict two dimensions of love that can be termed the intensity and the balance of the relationship.

Sternberg suggests that it is both the match between the two partners' real love triangles and the match between each individual partner's real love triangle and his or her ideal love triangle that determine satisfaction in a love relationship. For example, whenever there is a substantial mismatch between a person's ideal love triangle and the triangle that actually describes a current love relationship, the person is apt to be dissatisfied. Likewise, a major discrepancy in the love triangles of two partners implies that they are out of phase with each other and probably have difficulty in reciprocating each other's needs.

Love triangles are neither static over time nor independent of the loved one's behavior and feelings. For example, passion tends to peak fairly quickly in a love relationship and then settles down to a lower level, in what can be called the habituation phase. With habituation, a partner is no longer as stimulating as he or she once was. (This is like the habituation that occurs with regular use of many substances such as caffeine, alcohol, or cigarettes, although the habituation Sternberg describes is probably not due to physiological factors. Once habituation occurs, even increased amounts of the substance do not stimulate the arousal that occurred at first. Similarly, if a lover loses her or his partner, withdrawal symptoms such as depression, fatigue, restlessness, and inability to concentrate may occur, which closely mirror what happens when other habituating substances are withdrawn.) Likewise, it would be a mistake to neglect the influence one partner has on

FIGURE 1.2
HOW LOVE TRIANGLES "FIT"

The "match" of two people in a love relationship can be depicted diagramatically by showing how well-matched in size and shape their individual love triangles appear. (*Redrawn from* The Triangle of Love: Intimacy, Passions, Commitment *by Robert J. Sternberg. Copyright 1988 by Basic Books, Inc., Publishers.*)

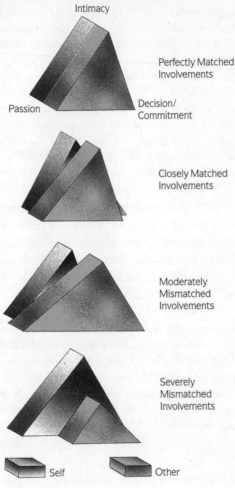

the other in a love relationship. Since each person's needs may change from time to time, it is important to be flexible in order to let love continue to flourish. As Sternberg notes:

> Perhaps the most important use of the triangular theory is to help people recognize that relationships are, almost inevitably, dynamic. "Living happily ever after" need not be a myth, but if it is to be a reality, the happiness must be based upon different configurations of mutual feelings at various times in a relationship. Couples who expect their passion to last forever, or their intimacy to remain unchallenged, are in for disappointment. The theory suggests that we must constantly work at understanding, building, and rebuilding our love relationships. Relationships are constructions, and they decay over time if they are not maintained and improved. We cannot expect a relationship simply to take care of itself, any more than we can expect that of a building. Rather, we must take responsibility for making our relationships the best they can be.[10]

Sternberg's theory has not yet been tested by others. However, some critics have claimed that the triangle image is overly simplistic, failing to distinguish between various nuances of passion, commitment, and intimacy, and not taking into account the influence of third parties—or the real world—on a love relationship.[11] In fact, Stanton Peele, who originated the "love as addiction" concept mentioned above, notes:

> Evaluating a love relationship in the larger framework of a couple's psychological functioning and connection to their environment often yields a picture different than that of an idyllic love affair. What is most lacking in the ostensibly social-psychological perspective is this sense of context, so that the research focus on the intensity of the lovers' experience of each other supports the notion that love can be isolated from the rest of the lovers' lives.[12]

LOVE AS ATTACHMENT

An unusual theory views adult love relationships as remarkably similar to attachment behavior between an infant and its parent.[13] Common dynamics found in both love pairings include reliance on the loved one to fulfill basic emotional and security needs, fear of rejection, distress at separation, powerful empathy between the two people in the relationship, and a great deal of nonverbal communication.

According to Phillip Shaver, Cindy Hazan, and Donna Bradshaw, the authors of this theory, all love relationships in a person's life, including those with lovers and spouses, mimic the type of attachment found in early mother-infant (or other primary infant-caregiver) relations. Clearly, not all mother-infant relationships are perfect. If a mother is consistently slow in responding to her infant's cries, or if she regularly interferes with the infant's spontaneous actions, the baby often becomes anxious.[14] And if a mother ignores her baby's attempts to have physical contact with her by cuddling, or touching, or other similar behaviors, the baby will probably learn to avoid her.

Shaver, Hazan, and Bradshaw use precisely the same categories to describe adult love relationships. They differentiate between *secure* lovers, who don't worry about being abandoned or about having someone get too close to them, and *avoidant* or *anxious/ambivalent* lovers. Avoidant lovers are uncomfortable in being too close to someone else and have trouble trusting a lover completely. Anxious/ambivalent lovers, on the other hand, are insecure about their relationships. They tend to worry that their partners don't really love them or won't want to stay with them; they are often so intense and overbearing in their love that they scare partners away.

Shaver, Hazan, and Bradshaw analyzed 620 responses to a questionnaire they published in a Denver newspaper. They found that a little more than half of adult love relationships could be categorized as secure (see Figure 1.3), while one-fourth were avoidant relationships, and 19 percent were anxious/ambivalent ones. Similar results were obtained in a later replication study in a university population, which is intriguing because these numbers match reasonably well with the proportions previously reported in a major study of mother-infant attachment.[15] In addition, there were no sex differences found in any of these studies.

Some psychologists believe that the attachment theory of love is an exciting new development. Observers have even noted that nonhuman primates seem to demonstrate this same attachment behavior in infancy,

FIGURE 1.3
THE FREQUENCY OF VARIOUS ADULT ATTACHMENT TYPES
IN LOVE RELATIONSHIPS

(*Adapted from Shazer, Hazan, and Bradshaw, 1988, from data in Table 4.2.*)

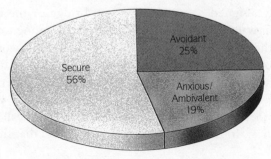

implying an evolutionary imperative for this theoretical viewpoint.[16] Others, however, are more critical. For one thing, to say that the nature of adult love relationships is determined largely by events during infancy is to ignore the pivotal development of thinking patterns, moral and social responsibilities, and experiential input during childhood, adolescence, and adulthood.[17] In a sense, if the attachment theory is right, we are more or less doomed (or at least, preordained) to our own particular love style before we are even out of diapers, which effectively pushes the concept of free will right out the window. (On the other hand, many psychoanalytic thinkers would be fairly comfortable with such a deterministic notion; it is very much in keeping with their view of behavioral causation.)

Another problem with attachment theory is that it doesn't adequately explain cross-cultural observations about love and love relationships: these are very different in India or Japan or the Fiji Islands from the patterns we take for granted in America. Despite such criticisms, attachment theory nevertheless offers an interesting opportunity for long-range research. What seems to be needed to assess this theory properly is a study that initially evaluates a large sample of mother-infant attachments and then determines the love styles of the former infants 20 or more years later.

LOVE AS AROUSAL

Some men believe that taking a date to an emotionally evocative event, like a horror movie or a boxing match or a ride on a rollercoaster, will stir up the woman's romantic feelings. There is now some experimental evidence that such an arousal effect does indeed occur.

The best-known example of this effect is a study by Donald Dutton and Arthur Aron in which they compared the reactions of young men crossing two bridges at a scenic tourist spot in north Vancouver.[18] One bridge was a 450-foot-long, narrow, wobbly structure that swayed back and forth 230 scary feet above a rocky gorge. In contrast, the second bridge was a solid, safe, immobile structure not very high off the ground. Male test subjects were randomly assigned to walk across one bridge or the other. As they completed their walk, they were met by an attractive young woman who was an assistant of the psychologists conducting the study. The woman explained that she was conducting a class project and asked each man to answer a few questions and write a brief story in response to a picture. After this was done, the woman offered to explain her project in more detail and wrote her home telephone number on a piece of paper so the men could call if they wanted more information. Intriguingly, the researchers found that the highest level of sexual imagery in the stories the men wrote was provided by the men who had crossed the anxiety-provoking suspension bridge. In addition, 9 of the 33 men who had crossed the suspension bridge called the research assistant later on, whereas only two of those who had crossed the solid bridge called her.

While it is possible to interpret these results in different ways—for instance, perhaps the men who called the female research assistant may really have been interested in her project—the most plausible explanation is that emotional arousal seems to trigger sexual attraction.

A second experiment by Dutton and Aron also explored the role of fear in provoking sexual arousal. College-age men were recruited for a learning experiment. When they arrived at the testing facility, they found that the partner they would be working with was an extremely attractive young woman. At the same time, they were informed that the experiment they were about to begin was designed to test the effects of electric shock on learning. Some of the men were told that they would receive strong, painful electric shocks as part of the experiment. Others were told that they were assigned to a control group and would receive very weak electric shocks that would barely cause a tingling sensation. (None of the subjects actually received any shocks. The shocks were mentioned just to cause anxiety in some of the men as part of the *real* experiment.)

Before the sham experiment was supposed to begin, one of the investigators spoke with each man in private and asked him about his feelings toward the attractive young woman who was to be his partner. Not surprisingly, the men reacted just as the researchers predicted they would—those who were frightened found the woman much sexier than the calmer men did and were much more interested in dating her.

Now it has become evident that other types of arousal, including intense physical exercise, can fan the flames of passion, at least to a limited degree. In one experiment, running in place for 2 minutes intensified the reactions of male subjects to videotapes of either an attractive or an unattractive woman.[19] Men who had exercised vigorously found the pretty woman even more appealing than did those who had only exercised for 15 seconds; by the same token, they had more intensely negative reactions to the unattractive female than the men who had not become physiologically aroused. (There may be a message here about coed gyms or health clubs as places to find a lover, but we're fairly certain the reality is quite a bit more complicated than the experiments described above.) Other studies also support the concept that emotionally neutral physiological arousal can stir up passion.[20]

LOVE MAINTENANCE

Although the reasons why we fall in love are often difficult to identify, what is clear is that the fires of passionate, romantic love do not burn forever. Over time—usually within a few years—passionate love either evolves into a different, more stable and mature form of relating, or simply dissolves into bickering, second-guessing, boredom, power struggles, and frustrations that eventually lead to a dissolution of the relationship. The more stable form of love is often called companionate love in the research literature, which unfortunately makes it sound about as rewarding as an old pair of shoes—comfortable and familiar, but not much more. We prefer thinking of this phase as a time of a new, more solid equilibrium in which passion is replaced by mutuality, enhanced intimacy, and a broader repertoire of problem-solving skills.

The nature of love changes over time for a number of reasons, not just because passion fades away. For one thing, individual growth and development are not suspended the moment we fall in love. As a result, two lovers are not the same people 5 or 10 years into their relationship that they were when it began, and unless they are able to accommodate to these changes, they are apt to drift apart. For example, one partner may have become considerably more assertive at age 33 than at age 23, and the other person may have become much more cynical about life. Or, child-rearing responsibilities may have significantly changed both partners' views of their priorities and commitments. Similarly, as time and circumstance change, needs and expectations shift as well, sometimes in quite dramatic fashion. As the psychologist Nathaniel Branden puts it, "Our greatest chance at permanence lies in our ability to handle change. Love has the greatest chance to endure when it does not fight the flow of life but learns to join with it."[21]

The trick is, of course, to build and maintain a more deeply rooted love in the face of a host of various obstacles that can be daunting. For instance, there is a clear danger that as the intense passion of a love relationship drops to only occasional flickers, the relationship can slide into a state of drabness and routine. This can obviously involve the sexual side of a relationship, but it can also reverberate through all aspects of a couple's interaction. Likewise, everyday tensions and pressures—financial problems, child-rearing problems, job pressures, health concerns, and other issues—can slowly erode a couple's love if they don't take deliberate preventive steps. Here too, the impact is apt to be felt on the sexual side of the relationship as well as in other arenas of day-by-day existence.

Here are some suggestions that may help to keep love blooming over time.

1. *First and foremost, don't expect perfection.* When we're caught in the throes of passionate, head-over-heels love, we tend to idealize our loved one. "Love is blind," Chaucer reminded us, and that is true . . . up to a point. When passionate love begins to be transformed into a more stable, deeply rooted type of love, there is a danger that we suddenly become aware (and critical) of the many shortcomings in our partner that we overlooked before. Expecting perfection in a love relationship is one of the surest ways to doom it, because a consistent degree of disappointment is practically guaranteed.

2. *Be flexible.* While we like to pay lip service to the constancy of love, truly lasting love is not so much a result of stalwart loyalty and devotion as it is a testimonial to the ability to cope successfully with life's ups and downs. The fine art of compromise is an important part of keeping love alive. Another key skill is adaptability: shifting one's behavior (and even one's attitudes) to deal with changing circumstances. People who mistake rigidity (and an insistence on always being right) for strength are usually not people who are well loved.

3. *Recognize that love cannot be a substitute for anyone's personal identity.* There are several ramifications to this important point. First, don't try to engulf your lover; be certain that you leave enough room for your lover to be his or her own person. Second, don't make the mistake of giving up all of your outside interests and friendships in the belief that doing this will somehow strengthen your love. The fact is, if you allow your own identity to be subsumed by the relationship, the chances are that the relationship will be diminished. (Over the years, we've found that the strongest, most durable loves are usually those in which two individuals retain and foster their individuality.) Third, while your love may be a great source of strength, stability, and support, don't lose sight of the fact that your relationship is no more than the sum of the ingredients you and your partner each bring to it. If you allow your personal life outside your relationship to fade away, you lose an important source of vitality as well as an opportunity to fulfill needs that may not be met in your love relationship.

4. *Don't forget about romance.* When it comes to romance, it's usually the little things that count. Romance is not so much buying her a diamond on her birthday as it is dozens of little things on varied occasions: calling to say "I love you," bringing flowers home for no special reason, tucking a

handwritten love letter in her suitcase if she's off on a business trip, whisking him off to a fancy dinner or a show when he's least expecting it, or coming up with tickets to the big game he was going to watch on TV. We should recognize that even small romantic gestures carry a great deal of weight because they are symbols of feelings and intent.

5. *Be sensitive to your partner's feelings.* This is not an admonition for you to become an accomplished mind-reader. It's really a reminder to pay attention to what your lover is saying, either in words or in nonverbal communication. In addition to paying attention, don't belittle your partner's feelings just because they're not the same ones as yours or because you don't understand why they are there.

6. *Don't let anger undermine your interaction.* Although it's often possible to prevent misunderstandings and frustrations from escalating into anger if you're willing to talk about your feelings openly and in a nonaccusatory manner, realize that it isn't humanly possible to keep anger completely out of your life. When anger erupts, instead of letting it fester and color your entire interaction, bring it out in the open and search together for ways to defuse it. Solving a conflict can be a challenge, but it can also be a creative, growth-enhancing process. If you aren't always able to do this in a calm, rational way; if you find that you're arguing and fighting with alarming intensity; if you've both said hurtful things in the heat of anger (maybe even deliberately)— relax and remember that while it takes two people to have a fight, it usually takes only one to end it. Learning to say "I'm sorry" is one of the simplest ways to defuse anger. Without having to give in to your partner unilaterally, there are a number of ways to restore much-needed equilibrium to a situation when anger distorts feelings. You can both agree to table the issue until a later time, when you're able to discuss it more rationally. (Letting a little time pass is one of the simplest ways to defuse anger.) You can reach a compromise solution to whatever problem precipitated your disagreement. You can decide to analyze the problem in some detail and come up with possible options for solving it. You can also turn to others for help. Discussing a delicate situation with good friends or with professional counselors (for example, a member of the clergy, a marriage counselor, or a psychotherapist) may be just what you need to get things back on track.

7. *Be a considerate sex partner.* Most people seem to think good sex is a matter of passion and performance. Actually, good sex is more often a matter of being attuned to your partner's feelings and preferences. In fact, in some ways, good sex is as much related to knowing when *not* to do certain things

as it is to knowing exactly what to do. Here are three examples. (1) If your partner is fighting a cold and had a bad day at the office, this is *not* a good time to try out your new sensual massage oil and the new technique for improving your orgasmic potential that you've just read about. (2) If you are really feeling sexually tense and your partner agrees to a "quickie" just to help you out, don't try to make this into a marathon lovemaking session. That your partner doesn't need or want sex in the same way you do at this precise time is no sign of a problem and shouldn't be seen as some sort of challenge for you to rectify with a virtuoso erotic performance. (3) Be careful about saying no to sex too often. Even when you're not exactly or completely in the mood, if this is the third day in a row you've rebuffed your partner's romantic overtures, you run the risk of triggering a sense of rejection that is preventable if you simply make yourself available. This sort of modest accommodation to your partner's sexual needs strengthens the bonds of any relationship far beyond the bedroom.

8. *Don't take your partner for granted.* Complacency is one of the deadliest enemies of love. As Robert Solomon, professor of philosophy at the University of Texas, has noted, "The waning of love can be attributed, in many cases, to lack of attention—lack of attention to the person, lack of attention to the relationship itself."[22] Not paying attention is certainly one way of taking someone for granted, but other, more subtle forms also exist. Condescension, for example, is one of the most insidious underminers of love. Neglect—as in forgetting to call your partner when you promised to, or showing up an hour and a half late for a dinner date, or generally being unreliable—is also a sign of trouble in paradise.

9. *Maintaining love isn't automatic.* Many people are astounded to find that love doesn't sustain itself effortlessly. In order to make love work, you have to work at loving. This requires time and energy. We know of no substitute for this formula: in love, unless you give of yourself, you are unlikely to get much in return.

INTIMACY

Intimacy is a process of caring and closeness that differs from love in important ways. For one thing, it is not an emotion or a feeling; for another, unlike love, it requires reciprocity. Most notably, perhaps, intimacy is different from love because the happiness of the other person is not its main object. Since it is an ongoing process, intimacy fluctuates in intensity at

different times in a relationship. This sometimes leads to the intriguing
paradox of relationships in which the level of intimacy increases as the
intensity of love declines. Furthermore, most people are likely to have a
much larger number of intimate relationships than romantic love relationships in their lives. In fact, it is precisely because we all juggle a number of
intimate relationships—with friends, with family, and with lovers—and
because intimacy is often influenced by factors outside our direct control
(time spent at work, the impact of an illness) that we sometimes run into
difficulty in devoting the time and attention to our primary relationship that
is required to maintain or enhance its intimacy in a way that allows for
growth and pleasure.

Just what *is* intimacy? If you asked a dozen different people, you'd probably get a dozen different answers. But there is a consensus among behavioral
scientists and clinicians that intimacy consists of certain "core" ingredients.
Although they are not always described in the same words, these are mutual
caring and a willingness to translate that caring into commitment; sharing
freely with each other; communicating with openness and depth; valuing a
relationship enough to imbue it with vulnerability and trust; tenderness; and
making a consistent effort to empathize with each other.

The caring and commitment that many people yearn for do not happen
automatically in relationships. They develop gradually—sometimes so gradually that the entire process seems to be agonizingly slow. One reason why
intimacy can't be rushed is that its components are not easily manufactured
or assembled. Another factor to consider is the reciprocal nature of the
process. A certain degree of symmetry is required as both parties feel
intimacy beginning to stir; they each make deliberate decisions to reveal
themselves (more swiftly or more gradually), to be receptive or guarded, to
move eagerly but cautiously through the fits and starts of what is at its essence
an organic, unpredictable form of creativity: forging a unique relationship in
the face of uncertainty and hope. Perhaps for these reasons, intimacy often
grows out of friendship—in the context of liking, rather than loving—
instead of bursting forth magically at the outset of a new relationship.
Furthermore, when intimacy does begin to develop, it usually takes a very
tenuous, fragile form at first. This happens largely because the caring and
commitment that are necessary to solidify intimacy are unlikely to appear
(except in small amounts) until the other necessary components have been
added to the equation, since truly becoming committed to one another is
making a promise about future intentions, about being in it for the long haul.
Few people, for example, are willing to make a commitment to someone
until they believe they know a fair amount about the other person. Commitment usually requires enough time for meaningful self-disclosure to occur.

(There are exceptions to this generalization, of course. A common example is that when a couple has very pleasurable sex soon after meeting, they may be willing to "care" for/about each other more readily than in other circumstances because they imbue each other with certain idealized expectations. If these expectations turn out to be reasonable approximations of reality, the relationship is likely to continue; if, on the other hand, these expectations are too far off the mark, the relationship is apt to come to a quick demise.) In a sense, then, caring and commitment are usually the factors to be added last, precisely because they are largely dependent on the presence of the other components. That is, unless you trust someone fairly thoroughly and unless you have spent a good deal of time together talking about each other, you really don't have much basis (or motivation) for caring a lot about the other person.

Caring about someone usually comes about because you find that he or she is interesting and likable. (It may also happen if you find someone who is appealing because of his or her wealth, power, or attractiveness.) In general, people distance themselves from individuals they distrust or fear, as well as those they find dull, boorish, or spiteful. They are more likely to allow themselves to become closer to individuals they regard in a positive light. The result is that developing closeness (when it occurs voluntarily) often leads to caring because the very basis for becoming closer is the existence of a certain minimal set of positive factors.

To expect commitment to come before caring is unrealistic and illogical, but commitment has become something of a buzzword in recent years. Commitment is not simply deciding to be there for each other early in a relationship (although that decision is a prerequisite to a deeper level of commitment). The real test of commitment comes when the initial rush of a relationship subsides and its problems begin to surface. It's true that any couple feeling head-over-heels in love will say that they are committed to each other, but this may be a charade caused by their passions. The first *real* test of commitment is this: when the passion dies out, is the commitment still there? Beyond this, when time together becomes heavily tinged with negatives—financial problems, health problems, family pressures, and so forth—is the relationship still valued enough for its own sake that the commitment remains in effect? After all, it's easy to be committed when times are good and everyone's having fun; the character of a relationship is tested in the crucible of conflict and despair.

The sharing component of intimacy operates at several different levels: behavioral, emotional, physical, and cognitive. Sharing at the behavioral level involves togetherness that fosters closeness and includes the entire gamut of everyday activities. A point some couples misunderstand is that sharing mundane tasks—from cleaning the garage to doing the dishes—is just as much a source of intimacy as sharing in pleasurable, playful activities. (We are not referring here to sharing in the simple sense of splitting the chores—"You do the dishes and I'll take out the garbage"; we mean actually doing them together.) In some ways, the process of sharing the not so pleasurable chores is an even more important source of intimacy than other forms of sharing, because it builds a couple's sense of mutual involvement and co-responsibility. When partners demonstrate a willingness to share only in having fun, their intimacy may be a sort of "fair weather" way of relating.

Many men derive a sense of emotional closeness from shared activities with another person. What is not generally understood is that these activities, including work and sports, are not simply a matter of sharing (as in passing time together) but also of assessment. Men watch and evaluate how adept their companions are at problem solving, strategic analysis, dealing with stress, handling teamwork, and deflecting insults, attacks, and incursions into their territory. A woman might be puzzled that her boyfriend views a two-hour session of mixed doubles on the tennis court as intimate time together, whereas he may have garnered a great deal of information about her from the experience. (He may be equally puzzled that she considers a dinner party an intimate activity, but chances are that she is just as evaluative and judgmental in assessing his participation and "fit" there as he was on the tennis court.)

Sharing at the emotional level is one of the hallmarks of intimacy. Unless two people are willing to reveal a good deal of information about themselves—not only biographical but also in terms of what they feel, what they fear, what they worry about, and what they hope for or dream about—it is unlikely that any meaningful intimacy can exist. It is actually in this process of communication that the essence of intimacy is expressed. As the social psychologist Elaine Hatfield says, intimacy is a process in which a couple "attempts to move towards complete communication on all levels."[23] While this certainly includes nonverbal dimensions of communication (including sex), it is clear that the verbal expression of feelings within a relationship is the actual bedrock of intimacy. This holds true for nonromantic relationships as well as for romantic ones.

A substantial body of research indicates that, from childhood on, females are more adept than males at self-disclosure and verbal expression of emotions. As Kate Millett noted acerbically, "Women express, men repress."[24] This reflects differences in socialization between males and females rather than any innate biological difference: in general, males and females are reared to see the world differently and to deal with it with different styles. Males, for example, are taught that showing feelings doesn't fit the masculine ideal; it is no accident that Arnold Schwarzenegger achieved megastardom as the virtual embodiment of the tough, no-nonsense hero—the male ideal whose attitude is as hard as his biceps. Boys who display their emotions too openly are often taunted or belittled; they may even be accused of being "crybabies" or "sissies" (terms that are often surrogate cultural markers for a label of impending homosexuality), since showing one's feelings too clearly (or being highly sensitive) is regarded as a "feminine" trait.

In a marvelous book called *You Just Don't Understand*, Deborah Tannen has written with great insight about the resulting discrepancies in the styles of communication between men and women. Here is an especially cogent point that she makes on the subject of intimacy needs and male-female stylistic priorities.

> *Intimacy* is key in a world of connection where individuals negotiate complex networks of friendship, minimize differences, try to reach consensus, and avoid the appearance of superiority, which would highlight differences. In a world of status, *independence* is key, because a primary means of establishing status is to tell others what to do, and taking orders is a marker of low status. Though all humans need both intimacy and independence, women tend to focus on the first and men on the second. It is as if their lifeblood ran in different directions.[25]

Along the same line, Helen Fisher, an anthropologist, believes that women's emphasis on verbal intimacy stems from "their long prehistory as nurturers."[26] Whether this is true or not, it is not that men lack the capacity for either verbal expression or intimacy, but simply that they have been less programmed to use it.[27] As a result, women have often been left with the burden of attending to the emotional side of relationships, with men regarding nonphysical intimacy as one of the less important aspects of their lives. In one of the ironic twists of fate of the past decade, the HIV/AIDS epidemic may have made intimacy more fashionable (and healthier) for heterosexual men. In fact, as intimacy and commitment have become more important as means of gaining access to a sexual relationship (with less casual sex available), it may be that males are actually learning to become better communicators (albeit for somewhat different reasons than those of females).

Sometimes, however, couples can take the process of sharing too far. If a couple tries to do everything together, directing virtually all their time and energy to mutual activities, the relationship not only can be emotionally smothering but its growth potential can actually be lessened. Similarly, there can even be too much verbal communication in a relationship: one or both partners may have a tendency to analyze ad infinitum every one of their feelings and interactions, or openness in communication can become obsessive, ruminative communication. Sometimes an avalanche of words can be counterproductive because it blocks feelings and even creates a smoke screen around deficiencies and problems.

In an intimate relationship, trust comes from the underlying assumption that neither person intends to hurt the other. This is not to say that inadvertent hurts will never occur; injured feelings are inevitable in virtually all relationships, whether between friends or lovers. Conversely, if there is evidence that one person is deliberately trying to hurt the other, it is exceptionally difficult for intimacy to be maintained except at the most superficial levels. This is not only because the implicit trust in the relationship is undermined but also because the one who is afraid of being wounded must begin to adopt a protective stance, which involves having to close up emotionally, be more guarded in what he or she says or does, and constantly assess the meaning and intent of the other. A corollary of this observation is that if dishonesty creeps into a relationship, it also significantly erodes the intimacy of that relationship.

A climate of trust in a relationship sets the stage for building one of the most important foundations of intimacy, the condition of each partner's permitting himself or herself to be vulnerable to the other. To be vulnerable is to be willing to expose your weaknesses, your fears, your shortcomings and anxieties and inadequacies and embarrassments, without worrying that these will be used as weapons against you. A person can agree to this sort of vulnerability only in a very special type of intimate relationship.

There is an additional aspect of intimacy that brings a special dimension to romantic relationships: the free (and frequent) exchange of tenderness. Tenderness, as we use the term, can be expressed both by word and by deed. In fact, nonverbal expressions of tenderness, especially as conveyed by a type of touch that signifies a couple's connectedness and regard, are probably at least as important to fueling romance as verbal expressions of love and affection. It is particularly striking to us that in happy long-standing relationships, there is a good deal of handholding, close physical proximity, and snuggling. In contrast, in a sex therapy clinic or marital therapy office, where couples often are unhappy and conflicted, they tend to maintain their distance and rarely touch casually. (In our experience, one of the better, if unscientific, indicators of successful therapy is seeing a couple gradually move closer when they are sitting in a therapy session or when they are entering or leaving the office.) When tenderness disappears from a relationship, it is a definite sign that the level of intimacy is dropping and that the stability (and longevity) of the relationship may be in jeopardy.

The last aspect of intimacy that we will mention here is the empathetic attention partners show when they are genuinely concerned with each other's feelings and needs. Part of this involves the effort to be a good listener, which is crucial to a couple's overall process of communication. But an equally important component is not just listening accurately to what is being said, but listening nonjudgmentally, which is admittedly much harder to do. Not belittling your partner's feelings or fears, even though they don't match your own (or somehow seem illogical or even mistaken), is a cardinal aspect of intimacy, but one that is ignored more often than not when experts stress the process of getting in touch with and verbalizing feelings as though that is the major goal of intimacy.

A cautionary note about intimacy has been sounded recently. The psychiatrist Carol Anderson points out, for example, that we may set our expectations for intimacy in our relationships at such a high level that it becomes unattainable.[28] Anderson notes that this may be related to our search for intense forms of intimacy while assigning less value to such forms of intimacy as loyalty, steadiness over time, and a sense of family. She traces this trend, in part, to the emphasis that arose in the 1960s in the encounter group movement on "getting in touch with feelings" and then expressing these feelings verbally. The implication is that too much emphasis on verbal intimacy as the "premium" or most meaningful variety can make it difficult for a person who cannot easily verbalize to be accepted as a caring, committed partner in an intimate relationship.

Another relatively common problem is that if intimacy is demanded or expected constantly, it is likely to diminish. In fact, intimacy occurs most reliably "when it emerges spontaneously within a context of basic, well-functioning relational processes."[29] Couples who have tried to force themselves into intimacy are probably already conversant with how such attempts can be counterproductive. When you try too hard to share things, to reveal your innermost feelings and thoughts, and to demonstrate tenderness in direct response to your partner's repeated requests, there is always the danger that the whole effort collapses under its own weight. When intimacy is turned into a homework assignment, to be successfully completed under the threat of getting a failing grade, its spontaneity and effervescence are likely to be missing, and whatever closeness occurs may seem counterfeit or forced.

There is another sort of intimacy problem that crops up with some frequency in newly formed relationships. We call this "intimacy impatience." Because intimacy has so much cachet these days—because it has come to be seen as the ultimate marker of authenticity, commitment, and honesty—there is an understandable push for developing intimacy sooner rather than later as a relationship is getting underway. (We are not referring to sexual intimacy here, but rather intimacy in its broadest nonsexual sense.) This has a number of ramifications, including a definite tendency to end some relationships prematurely if a suitable amount of intimacy isn't forth-coming early on—without regard to how comfortable both partners are with self-disclosure, moving toward intense levels of personal vulnerability, and being willing to make an emotional commitment to the other. Another outgrowth of intimacy impatience is the practice of "rating" your partner on some imaginary intimacy scale to judge how well he or she is measuring up to your expectations (as well as how much long-term relationship potential you can hope to discover). Just as it may not be wise to rate your partner's sexual skills too early in a relationship, for a variety of reasons, trying to judge someone's intimacy potential too quickly doesn't make allowances for important situational elements (is she just getting over the breakup of a long-term relationship with someone else?); personality differences (is he pro-ceeding cautiously because he's shy?); and other variables that may mean nothing in the long haul.

Finally, we should point out that there is such a thing as *too much* intimacy. Marriage therapists are well aware of this problem. For example, one partner may use intimacy as a manipulative tool in a power struggle, or too much sharing and togetherness become stifling and eventually seem to suffocate a relationship. Furthermore, intimacy does not always lead to the warm, fuzzy feelings that most people think it will. Consider, for example, the oppressive nature of intimacy with a highly neurotic person who insists on detailed, voluminous self-disclosure. Or how about intimacy with a person who is fundamentally hostile, bitter, and defeatist? In real-life situations, relation-ships are considerably more complicated than they are in books or magazine articles. Intimacy, for all its pleasant sound, is no guarantee of happiness.

Two

Sex and Sensuality

If words are the currency of poetry, and color is the currency of art, touch is the currency of sex. But somewhere in the evolutionary process, modern civilization has lessened our awareness of this important fact, and sex has been recast as a type of action. This has reduced it from a sensual and sensory phenomenon to a set of reflex responses that happen to meet together from time to time. However, ignoring our sensual side inevitably lessens our sexual involvement and our sexual gratification. As the noted anthropologist Ashley Montagu put it, "Without tactile communication—what the body feels and says nonverbally—the experience of sex can only be at most incomplete."[1]

Trying to talk about sensuality and how it can be a part of sex is difficult. For example, some people think of sensuality primarily in pictorial terms: the famous photograph of James Dean with a cigarette dangling jauntily from his lower lip; a young Brigitte Bardot in one of her pouting, sex kitten poses. But there are many ways to be sensual and sensuous. The ways we will explore in this chapter all involve awareness of our sensations and how we interact at a physically intimate level, not how someone looks.

If this were a book about music, we would stress the sensual side of listening. If this book were about food, we would instead put the emphasis on gustatory sensations, along with an appreciation of color and visual appeal, and more than a passing nod to the olfactory side of appetite and food appreciation. But this is a book about sex, and when we talk about the sensual side of sex, we are referring primarily to our tactile sensations, for it is largely (although not exclusively) through skin-to-skin contact that we experience sex.[2]

Here is a point raised by Montagu in his classic book, *Touching*, that explains part of the link between tactile sensations and sex.

23

Interestingly enough the fingertips are erogenous. Reciprocal stimulation of the fingertips between two mutually sexually interested persons can be quite sexually arousing. During coitus [intercourse] breathing is deepened, and this has the effect of washing the CO_2 from the blood; this, in turn, changes the ionic balance of the body fluids, with a resulting increase in nerve excitability, expressed in a tingling of the skin especially at the fingertips.[3]

In fact, many different regions of skin are supplied with rich sensory innervation; the activation of these nerve fibers often starts how we get "turned on" with sexual arousal. The electrical analogy of the phrase "turned on" is apt: neural impulses are a form of electrical activity coursing from the peripheral sensory fibers to the spinal cord and from there both upward to the brain and back to the periphery in local reflex loops. Although these neural signals are not always interpreted as sensuous or sexual—depending on their context, they can be irritants or intrusions— under the right circumstances they can certainly serve as erotic activators in part because of the physiologic mechanism Montagu described above. (Montagu's description is somewhat oversimplified, since part of the tingling sensation felt in various body parts with sensual stimulation is a result of alterations in local patterns of blood flow, and hormone changes also play a role in sexual arousal.) Moreover, since breathing is actually deepened and accelerated during any form of sexual excitation, the biochemical changes that Montagu points to as potentiating nerve excitability affect the skin of most regions of the body, from scalp to toes, increasing neural activity whether or not intercourse occurs.

It would be a mistake, however, to think about sensuality as "only" a by-product of heightened nerve excitability. While sensuality is certainly largely a physical process, it is experienced and interpreted in a matrix of mental receptivity, mood, and attitude. In the rest of this chapter, we will examine how these aspects of sensuality fit together and provide specific suggestions for focusing on and improving your sensuality.

SENSATE FOCUS

It's one thing to talk about sensuality in the abstract and quite another to put it into action. Some couples have an intuitive grasp of what being sensual is all about; others seem baffled, as though they've been asked to read a document in Sanskrit. From our work as sex therapists, we know very well that telling couples to just go home and touch doesn't usually do much to rekindle their sensuous cravings. In cases where passion has turned to indifference, or where a couple is having fundamental problems with unfulfilling sex, it often takes careful orchestration to get things back in tune.

One of the key approaches we have devised to accomplish this is a set of at-home exercises that virtually any couple can employ. These sensate focus exercises, as we call them, provide a framework for individual self-discovery as well as a vehicle for a creative reawakening of a couple's sensuous impulses and interaction. When used in the course of sex therapy, sensate focus has a number of different purposes. For example, a couple's reports about their sensate focus experiences provide important diagnostic information to the therapists. Sensate focus is a key part of the treatment arsenal for reducing or eliminating performance anxieties (which are ultimately the cause of many sexual dysfunctions). As therapy proceeds, reports of what has happened during sensate focus also help the therapists judge a couple's progress in solving whatever problems they are facing. But the utility of the sensate focus approach is much broader than these points convey. Because sensate focus restructures and reorients how people ordinarily approach sexual interactions, letting them move away from old, familiar habit patterns that they have fallen into, it allows any couple to reinvent the physical side of their relationship.

Sensate focus is about touching and being touched. Many couples think that this sounds about as exciting as wet sand, but the truth is that the art of touching and the art of being touched have a lot more to them than most people realize. One of the ways of maximizing the potential of sensate focus is to begin without any preconceived notions of what you will feel, how good it will be, or how much pleasure it will produce. In other words, even if the idea doesn't seem thrilling, you need to start out with an open mind about it, because otherwise your expectations tend to color your experience and feelings.

You also need to reorient your thinking away from being judgmental and evaluative to simply being and experiencing. In sexual matters, judgmental thinking almost always boxes us in: Was it good? Was it boring? Was it ecstatic? Evaluative thinking—which we define as a form of judgmental thinking that occurs as something is happening, not after it's over—is even more self-defeating in erotic moments. Just as being a restaurant critic changes the experience of dining out, being evaluative as sex is happening invariably puts you in the position of being an observer as well as a participant. The part of your mind that is observing is blocked from experiencing, with the all-too-common result that you think too much and feel too little.

The judgmental/evaluative posture also forces us to pigeonhole what's happening in terms of loaded words and concepts. Sex gets rated as good or bad, boring or sizzling, explosive or tame in an artificial way. Part of getting into the sensate focus experience is to avoid judging or evaluating what's happening and to concentrate instead on *noticing* what's happening in terms of physical feelings. By noticing whether your partner's skin feels smooth or warm or moist, you avoid having evaluative, judgmental thoughts and simply focus on the experience.

In order to set the stage for a new type of touching that puts the emphasis on sensuality, rather than sexuality, we instruct couples to abstain from any type of sexual activity during the first step of sensate focus. This means that no matter how turned on they might become, touching the genitals (or the woman's breasts), having oral sex, having intercourse, or having any other type of sexual involvement is off limits. This prohibition is partly intended to set a clear focus on the sensual side of touching as a distinct entity in its own right. (Of course, learning to be sensual has something to do with being sexual, too.) It also serves to remove any pressures on either partner to need to respond in some particular way—getting an erection, becoming sexually aroused, or responding in a certain manner to a partner's needs. In addition, this approach is likely to be very different from the way couples usually approach touching, and this is exactly the point: it allows for new discoveries and avoids ingrained behavior patterns that may have gotten stale and unrewarding.

We will now describe a version of sensate focus that is slightly modified from the form we use in sex therapy, having been designed especially for use on your own.[4] Many couples will find that time spent on the sensate focus process can be a useful and pleasant way to reawaken their own sensual (and sexual) feelings.

We suggest that you try these exercises when you and your partner are both relaxed, well rested, and affable toward one another. (Trying to start at a time when either one of you is tense, tired, or grumpy is not advisable: the chances are that you'd just be wasting your time.) In the privacy of your own home, at a time when you won't be interrupted by children, telephone calls, or other distractions, and when you have at least 30 to 40 minutes to yourselves, you can begin. As a practical matter, we suggest that it's best to decide in advance who will pick the time for the first touching session; after that, alternate who chooses, so you don't have to deal with the problem of "Are you ready to start touching now?" queries and unnecessary negotiations or guesswork.

STEP ONE: NONGENITAL TOUCHING

There are two parts to this step, which we call A and B. For illustrative purposes and grammatical simplicity, assume that it is the woman who decides when to begin in part A. (Second-guessing her timing isn't very useful and can get things started on a sour note, so don't turn down her invitation unless you're really tired, distracted, or emotionally wrung out.) From the beginning, both partners should be completely undressed. We also suggest the removal of earrings, watches, necklaces, and rings, and it also helps to be sure that you're not sweaty or dirty, so a preliminary bath or shower may be in order. It isn't necessary, however, to be obsessive about cleanliness, and it's best, too, not to pour on perfume or cologne or after-shave lotion. If nudity distresses either partner, or if overwhelming hostility is a fact of life in your relationship, it is advisable to get professional help before trying these exercises.

The one who issues the invitation to begin is the active participant in part A. Her partner lies flat on his back on the bed (or even on the floor, if he likes); his role, for now, is simply to take in the sensations he is feeling as he is touched by his partner, not to reciprocate her touch (or comment on her touching, or what he is feeling) in any way. Remembering that the man's genitals are off limits, the woman is free to begin exploring her partner's body in any other way that interests her in order to discover what she feels as she does this. Because starting can be awkward, some women prefer to begin at one spot on the man's body—say, the neck or feet—and work their way up or down from there. Other women don't need a definite plan of action and simply explore the various textures and temperatures and contours of their partner's body without any preconceived idea of how they will pro-ceed. Whichever way you choose, the point of this exercise, as the term sensate focus implies, is to zero in on the sensations you are experiencing as you touch. There is no right way or wrong way to do this, and the point of this touching opportunity is *not* to try to turn your partner on, or to make him feel good, or to give him a massage: the point is to try to live through your fingertips, taking in each and every physical sensation they provide, while doing whatever happens to interest you at the moment.

Some women become fascinated by the fine detail in the contours and angles on their partner's face. They may never before have taken the oppor-tunity to trace their fingertips lightly along his lips, or to feel the difference in texture between an ear and a cheek, or to notice that the hair at the nape of his neck is softer than the hair on top of his head. Other women move from one region of the man's body to another more quickly, comparing the smoothness of the skin on his thigh to the rougher palm of his hand, or to his toes. Again, there is no right way to do this exercise other than allowing yourself the opportunity to focus on your physical awareness of sensations in a nonevaluative way. At any point during the touching, the woman can ask her partner to turn over so she can touch his back and have easier access to the backs of his legs and neck.

The man's role in part A is primarily to focus on his own sensations as he is being touched. For the moment, he is not expected to reciprocate by touching his partner. He should be noticing the sensations he is receiving not in terms of evaluating or analyzing them ("I like that," or "Why is she doing that?") but of allowing himself to *experience* them. His only responsibility is to protect his partner from doing something that makes him acutely uncomfortable, either physically or psychologically. If she is rubbing a sore spot on his back, he must tell her immediately. If her touch is so light that it tickles, he should let her know this as well. This permits the toucher to concentrate on her own feelings without having to worry about her partner's comfort.

Either partner can suggest going on to part B of this exercise. We recommend, however, that part A continue for at least 15 minutes—especially since we recognize that, at the beginning, it may seem a bit awkward or unnatural, and a few minutes might be needed to get past the strangeness. On the other hand, we urge touching not be prolonged to the point of boredom or fatigue for either partner.

Part B of this exercise simply reverses the roles of the man and woman, so that now the woman is the one who lies down and the man is the one who does the touching. Unless it's absolutely necessary—such as needing to use the bathroom—we strongly suggest not taking a break of any sort between parts A and B.

As in part A, the man is free to touch his partner's body anywhere but the genitals; in addition, he should not touch her breasts for now. His partner's only responsibility is to protect him from doing anything that makes her physically or psychologically uncomfortable. She, as he did, focuses on what her partner's touches feel like to her, avoiding any attempts to evaluate or judge what he's doing. (Helpful hint: neither partner should be comparing the man's touching style with the style the woman used in part A. There's no reason they should be taking the same approach or using the same touches or sequence; they are two different people with individual feelings and perceptions.) As the man explores his partner's body from head to toe, it is important that he not set out to try to touch her in a way that he thinks she's going to like, or in a way that he thinks she'll find stimulating. Again, the purpose of this exercise is *not* to set the erotic juices flowing; it is to let each partner feel her or his own physical sensations in a leisurely, unstructured, non-goal-oriented manner.

Unlike most women, many men aren't used to noticing the tactile sensations deriving from textures or temperatures, so they may need a little while to become acclimatized to this process. Here are some suggestions we've found helpful with regard to the various types of touching that can be explored.

• Play a texture awareness game with yourself. First, see if you can notice differences in the surface texture of skin on different parts of her body. How does the smoothness and softness of skin on her cheeks compare to the backs of her hands, her calves, or her neck? Are there areas on her face that seem silkier or more supple than others?

• Vary the firmness and tempo of your touching. Let yourself feel the difference between a long-drawn-out, feathery-light touch on your partner's arm (or face or leg) and a slightly firmer and quicker touch, using small circular motions, in the same areas. Switch to a staccato type of rhythm for a while, and then switch back to a smoother, more languorous touch. Does changing the tempo of your touch alter your tactile sensations?

• See how touching with your whole hand feels compared to touching just with your fingertips. Notice how touching with both hands at once differs (or *whether* it differs) compared to the tactile sensations you get from just using one hand.

Let us reiterate several points. First, the goal of this exercise is *not* to produce any kind of erotic response. Even if you find yourself becoming greatly aroused, *do not* turn this into a sexual encounter. Second, either partner can ask to end the touching session. Apart from the 15-minute minimum, as in part A, there is no need for part B to match or exceed part A in duration, but don't touch for so long that you become worn out or uninterested. (If you start to fall asleep while you're touching or being touched, it is not apt to be a positive growth experience, is it?) Third, the point of sensate focus is not to give your partner a back rub or massage (although either may be a perfectly wonderful and romantic thing to do on another occasion) or to touch her in a way that you think will make her happy. The point is very straightforward: to allow the person doing the touching to take in a variety of sensory experiences and to notice what they feel like, without any distractions or "shoulds" lurking in the background.

Some couples enjoy repeating this version of the sensate focus exercises for several days. Often they notice things a little differently each time, and they also try out variations in technique and timing that allow them to experiment—in a nonpressured way—with their sensual perceptions. But the decision on whether to repeat this exercise a few times or to move on to the next step is a flexible one: there's no test to pass before you "graduate" to the next level.

STEP 2: GENITAL TOUCHING

In this next step of sensate focus, the prohibition on touching the breasts and genitals is dropped, but you should still abstain from attempting sexual intercourse. As with the preceding step, one person should be designated to pick the time to begin. (If you don't simply want to alternate from whoever made this choice the last time, you can always flip a coin to decide. In this example, we will have the man begin.) The background details are also the same as before: privacy, nudity, cleanliness, and so forth.

In part A of this exercise, the man should begin exactly as in the nongenital touching, with general touching of his partner's body. It is often advisable for the woman to start out lying face-down on the bed to facilitate this process so the man doesn't become automatically fixated on her breasts and genitals. *Even though the ban on touching the breasts and genitals is no longer in effect, the man should be especially careful NOT to change the nature of the touching experience by rushing immediately and singlemindedly to "sexual" touching.* In fact, it is helpful to remember that this is not a torrid X-rated movie but a *sensate* focus exercise: the point is not to try to be turned on or to make something happen to or for your partner, but to pay attention to your sensations in the context of exploring your partner's body as a sensual, sensory tactile experience.

If the impulse toward action is overwhelmingly tempting, think back and try to repeat some of what you learned in the previous step of sensate focus. Slowly feel the curve of your partner's back and compare it to the contour of her hips; trace along the edge of her spine and see how this feels compared to the softer tissue on the back of her upper arms; run your fingers through her hair as though you were feeling its texture and thickness for the first time. After you are comfortable and feeling in the rhythm of the moment, as well as feeling as if you are connecting with the sensations that are registering through your fingertips, then shift into the position shown in Figure 2.1.

If there is no headboard on your bed, a few pillows behind the man's back will provide support for him as he sits with his legs slightly spread in a V. The woman leans back against his chest so that her head is resting on one of his shoulders. By reaching down or around her, the man can touch most of his partner's body (although he probably cannot reach her lower legs and feet in this position).

At this juncture, as the man continues his general exploration of his partner's body, a new twist is added in the form of a special technique to enhance nonverbal communication: the woman puts her hand on top of his as he is touching (as shown in Figure 2.2). The intention of this hand-riding technique is not for the woman suddenly to take the lead in directing the

FIGURE 2.1
A SENSATE FOCUS POSITION

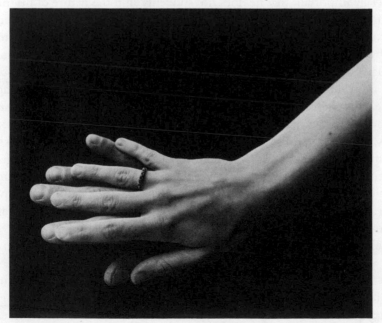

FIGURE 2.2
THE HAND-RIDING TECHNIQUE

action but rather to provide a simple, quick, effective way for her to transmit additional information to her partner as he touches her. He continues to touch for what he finds interesting, to distinguish and notice various sensations, and to do so in an open-ended, non-goal-directed manner, but she has the opportunity of providing him with nonverbal feedback about subtle preferences of her own. Although it is not his *job* to anticipate her feelings (in fact, she may not even be able to anticipate them herself), responding to her silent messages gives him a way to integrate her reactions into his actions.

With the hand-riding technique, the woman can show her partner where she'd like a firmer touch, where she'd like him to linger awhile, or where she'd like a lighter, silky sort of touch. She can show him when a slower sort of stroking might be especially sensual, or let him know when she'd like him to move from one part of her body to an entirely different spot. The man doesn't have to abide by these tidbits of information as though they were instructions from an airport control tower; with a little practice, he can learn how to combine his own feelings and needs with the messages provided by his partner. He should also recognize that a signal to move his hand is not a criticism of what he's doing; instead, it means, "Right now, I think I'd like to try this."

As we mentioned earlier, the man is free to incorporate genital touching into his tactile explorations in this exercise. (In part B, which we will describe shortly, the woman will have the same opportunity.) But it is especially important that he does not suddenly shift the nature of his touching into a relentless assault or a feverish push to make his partner quiver and melt in his arms. This means, for example, that it is usually best to touch briefly in or around the genital area and then move elsewhere on the woman's body for a while, returning to the genitals in the natural ebb and flow of exploratory touching. (For those men who may be wondering, "a while" means longer than 3 seconds.) If a man literally pounces on his partner's genitals and then concentrates his touching there almost exclusively, without regard to her feelings, it is understandably likely to make her feel like a sex object and not much more. If, instead, the man adds gentle, light caresses of the breasts and genital area (including the lips of the vagina, the clitoris, and the region between the vagina and the rectum) to a broader repertoire of touching that includes all of his partner's body, he extends the range of the sensual experience both he and his partner are having.

Here are a few additional pointers to keep in mind.

1. The couple should feel free to move whenever they would like into a position different from the one suggested (although many women report feeling especially comfortable and relaxed in the position illustrated).

2. The woman should be especially careful to give her partner signals while he is touching her genital area so he doesn't need to guess at what type of touching she prefers. It isn't necessary that she know in advance exactly what will feel pleasing or interesting, only that she provide him with feedback as he's touching her.

3. So that you don't lose sight of the fact that this is a sensate focus opportunity, not just a preamble to sex, we suggest that you abstain from kissing while you are doing this exercise. Kissing often seems to push people into cruise control when it comes to sensual/sexual behavior, and what you are trying to accomplish here is to break old habit patterns, not solidify them.

4. If the woman finds that her feelings are aroused enough that she wants to be orgasmic, it is perfectly appropriate to let orgasm occur either by manual stimulation from her partner (with some hand-riding guidance from her) or by using the reverse approach: letting her partner put his hand on top of hers and follow her motions and touches as she stimulates herself to orgasm. (Men: if you try either of these methods, this is *not* the time for an analytical discussion of why a particular type of touch feels a certain way.) There is no point, however, in working to make orgasm happen. If it gets to feeling like a job, either partner should call "time out."

As in step 1 of the sensate focus exercises, either the man or woman can say "I'd like to switch." There is no specific time requirement or limitation, although once again, our general suggestion is that the touching should not last so long that either person becomes bored or tired.

The procedure for part B should parallel the steps that are outlined above. We suggest that the woman begin with a period of general body touching, permitting herself to flow into the experience by focusing on her tactile sensations. As in the previous phase of sensate focus, she should take time to notice subtle variations in surfaces and contours, textures and temperatures of her partner's body, and she should explore his body in a way that interests her, not in order to make something happen to or for him.

At some point when she is feeling reasonably comfortable and absorbed in the experience, the couple can move into the position shown in Figure 2.3. (This is not a mandatory part of the exercise, but many couples have found it useful.) In this position, where the man is lying on his back with his head pointed away from his partner's body, and his legs bent at the knees and draped over her waist while she is sitting close to him, she is able easily to reach forward with access to most of his body. At this juncture, the couple can again use the hand-riding technique, this time with the

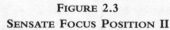

FIGURE 2.3
SENSATE FOCUS POSITION II

man's hand placed on top of his partner's as she touches and explores his body.

The woman can now extend her touching to include her partner's genital area as well as other regions. We recommend that the woman simply incorporate genital touching into her general explorations with no specific goal (such as trying to get her partner aroused) and without parking her hand indefinitely in this area. The man may or may not develop an erection, and whether he does or not is unimportant. If he does become erect, the woman should make a point of stroking the penis for a bit and then deliberately moving her hand to a different area, rather than staying focused on his sexual organ. In addition to touching or stroking the penis (whether or not it is erect), the woman might also want to use her fingertips to explore the scrotum, feeling the texture of the skin of the scrotal sac, gently cupping the testicles in her hands, and running her fingers along the perineum, the sensitive region of skin between the base of the scrotum and the rectum. These are not meant to be suggestions in the how-to-turn-your-partner-on mode: they are meant to provide a greater degree of awareness of your partner's body.

As this touching and exploration continues, the man can use the hand-riding technique to send subtle messages to his partner about the types of touching he finds most comfortable and pleasurable. It's important for both partners to realize that when they receive a message of this sort suggesting they move to a different spot, it doesn't mean they should never return. Both men and women find that what is comfortable or pleasing changes with time; a touch that is just perfect right now may be too much, or too little, or off target, in just a few moments. (Here's a perfect case in point. If you've ever tried to have your partner scratch an itchy spot on your back because you couldn't reach it yourself, you know how elusive getting that itch can be. One moment he or she is at exactly the right spot, but then the itch shifts just a little higher or a little lower or a bit to the left, and you've got to ask him or her to move a little to relieve the itch precisely.)

As the woman's exploration of her partner's body continues, the man may well find himself becoming sexually excited, which is perfectly fine and natural. The woman doesn't need to direct her attention immediately to penile stimulation, as though an erection requires emergency care, but if her partner feels that he wants to receive further penile touching and possibly go on to ejaculation, either she can provide this type of stroking for him (with his hand riding on hers to guide its tempo and firmness) or she can instead put her hand on his and follow his motions as he stimulates himself. Either choice is a matter of personal preference at the moment, not a reflection of the state of your relationship. As in part A of this exercise, if either partner starts to feel that the touching has turned into some sort of job or obligation, it's advisable to stop. (If necessary, the man can ejaculate by self-stimulation even if his partner needs to call it quits for now.)

STEP 3: ADDING LOTION

One of the ways of enhancing sensory awareness is to alter the medium of touch a bit. Since we don't have volume control knobs on our fingertips, the next best thing is to try the same sensate focus exercise described in step 2 with the addition of a lotion or oil to add a slicker, silkier dimension to your touching. We suggest using a nonalcoholic, hypoallergenic lotion, but many couples find that baby oil or even suntan lotion is convenient, inexpensive, and fun.

If you try this step (which is completely optional), it's best first to warm the container of oil or lotion in a basin of hot water. Another hint to prevent the lotion from feeling chilly is never to drip it onto your partner's body. Putting some lotion in the palm of your hand and then rubbing it briefly also helps to warm it up.

Some couples like to begin touching *without* the lotion and then add the lotion partway into the experience for contrast. Other couples experiment by using the lotion on one hand and not the other, comparing and contrasting sensations between the two hands. Other couples find it easier to use the lotion from the very beginning of their touching. Whichever approach you choose (and you might want to try each on different occasions), be sure that you don't let the lotion inadvertently turn you into a massage artist. The point of the exercise is still to focus on your sensations.

STEP 4: MUTUAL TOUCHING

So far, we have deliberately structured the touching exercises so that you were always in a "your turn/my turn" mode. Now, it's time to extend the scope of the touching experience by removing the artificiality of separate turns. This gives each of you the opportunity to use your newly improved sensory awareness to focus simultaneously on your fingertip sensations from touching your partner *and* on the physical sensations your body registers from being touched and held.

We suggest that the first time or two you try this version of sensate focus, you still refrain from kissing and from attempting intercourse. These simple steps help to prevent you from just reverting to your old, tried and true sexual behavior patterns. Remember, what you are trying to achieve here is a way of adding a new sensual dimension to your lives.

When you become involved in mutual touching, it's useful to view it as a continuation of the earliest sensate focus opportunities, not just another way of getting around to sex. If you decide that you are becoming too sexually (as opposed to sensually) focused, it's perfectly fine to lie back and let your partner do the touching for a while. It's also useful to direct your attention to decidedly nonsexual areas, although it's amazing how absolutely sensuous (and stimulating) your partner's hair or neck or lips can be. Another way of avoiding the problem of turning this into pure sex is to keep yourself from sexual fantasies as the touching is going on. (While we are enthusiastic advocates of sexual fantasizing in lots of other situations, it does have a way of distracting your attention from sensual matters because your brain has to focus on your mental erotic imagery.)

One possible variation in the mutual touching opportunities is to incorporate oral-genital stimulation as part of your sensual play. This doesn't mean using oral sex to make something happen to or for your partner; it means using your lips and tongue as a way of sensually exploring your partner's body. There is a big difference in these two intentions. Especially if you've done oral sex a lot before, see how different it can be when you approach it as sensual exploration instead of a way of servicing your partner.

Another variation you might want to try is changing the scene of your sensate focus activities from the bedroom to the shower or bathtub. Some couples find that the slippery feel of warm water and soap suds (or with bath gel) gives them a special set of sensations. While this might not be an everyday event, it can provide an interesting change of perceptions.

STEP 5: SENSUAL INTERCOURSE

Almost everybody knows what sexual intercourse is, but have you ever thought about *sensual* intercourse? If you haven't tried it, you probably don't know what you're missing.

Sexual intercourse is often a very mechanical act, with an emphasis on thrusting and pushing toward orgasm. In this version of sensate focus, you extend the gains you have already made in emphasizing your awareness of physical sensations into the realm of penile-vaginal contact to find a stylistically different type of intercourse. Here again, there is no right way or wrong way of doing things; instead, the goal is to find out what feels interesting and pleasurable.

As with all of the previous phases of sensate focus, which build on the same foundation, we suggest starting this exercise with a period of general body (nongenital) touching. Allow yourselves to get into a comfortable rhythm and focus: be aware of what your fingertips are telling you and don't worry about whether or not you or your partner is becoming aroused.

Gradually extend the scope of the touching to include exploration of the genitals. Don't be shy about using the hand-riding technique to show your partner what you like, but don't try to be a traffic cop and direct every move he or she makes.

When you are both comfortable, move into a position where the man lies on his back and the woman moves astride him, positioning herself so that her vaginal area is close to his penis (see Figure 2.4). Once you've gotten to this point, don't rush things. Use the same principles of sensate focus you've been using all along to continue your touching, but now extend the touching so that it is not only done by your fingertips, but so your genital areas can touch each other, too. It is usually easiest for the woman to take hold of the man's penis (which, after all, is fairly easy to find) and move it against herself, rubbing it against her clitoris, or along the lips of the vagina, or playing with the penis around her vaginal opening. The man doesn't need to be a passive participant as this is happening. In addition to focusing on the sensations he is receiving through his penis, he can be actively touching the woman anywhere he finds interesting or pleasurable, whether this involves stroking

FIGURE 2.4
A POSITION FOR GENITAL PLAY

her hair, fondling her breasts, running his fingers up and down her spine, or reaching up to trace gently the curves of her cheekbones.

When the woman feels ready, she can hold the erect penis at an angle of about 45 degrees (pointed toward the man's head) and slide back slowly on the penis, letting her vagina snuggle around its head without attempting to insert it any further.[5] Once in this position, resist the urge to start thrusting right away. Instead, let the penis rub very gently and slowly in and out of the opening of the vagina, noticing the sensations you both are receiving from this type of contact. After a few minutes, the woman can slide a bit more onto the penis, letting about half of it inside her. Again, instead of immediately establishing a vigorous thrusting pattern, stop to feel the sensations of warmth and contact. Hold absolutely still for a few seconds, and then the woman can squeeze her legs together (or contract the muscles around her vagina) to see what different sensations these movements produce.

Here again, instead of moving right away into the old, familiar thrusting pattern, continue your sensual intercourse experience by slowly withdrawing the penis from the vagina and playing with it at the external genital area again briefly—for 20 or 30 seconds. Then the woman can slide back onto the penis, repeating any of the above steps that seem interesting or pleasurable, until either partner decides that some deeper thrusting would be desirable.[6]

Once you've tried such sensual variations, you may certainly want to move to a quicker type of thrusting, and you may also instinctively move into a deeper thrusting pattern. Some couples find that it's very enjoyable to establish a quicker, *shallower* thrusting pattern for a while. (In fact, women find this especially sensual, since nerve endings in the vagina are more heavily concentrated in the outer portion than deep inside, as we will discuss in more detail in the following chapter.) However you proceed, try to keep your focus on your sensations as much as possible, and give yourself the opportunity to enjoy your "new" way of having intercourse.

One final point: if you enjoy sensual intercourse and want to use this approach from time to time, you've got to let your partner know in advance what you're thinking about. If one person is having good old lusty sexual intercourse while the other wants a more leisurely sensual experience, it could be like playing a record at 33$^1/_3$ and 45 rpm at the same time.

A woman once wrote us a letter in which she referred to "sense aid" instead of sensate focus. In a way, she was absolutely right. The point of these exercises, after all, is to help your senses: to restore the feeling side to sex.

TEN WAYS OF BLOCKING SENSUALITY

Over the years, we've learned a good deal about what interferes with the sensual side of sex. Here are the most common barriers we've encountered. Not listed in any particular order, they are self-evident enough to require no further explanation.

1. The "wham, bam, thank you ma'am" approach.
2. Children who pop into your room whenever they want to.
3. Time constraints, including always leaving sex for the last thing at night when you and your partner are both tired out.
4. The "it's my job to make my partner happy" attitude.
5. The notion that sex is serious business.
6. The idea that sex is solely for the man's pleasure.
7. Inattention to your partner's sensibilities, as demonstrated by cigar breath, a headful of hair curlers, or unrelenting body odor.
8. The mistaken belief that fulfilling sex is only for young and attractive people.

9. Thinking (and worrying) too much during sex.
10. Being angry with your partner, but keeping your anger to yourself.

Obviously there are many more sources of sexual problems. (We will discuss many of them in the remainder of this book.) But it is certain that if a couple manages to maintain a healthy sensuality in their relationship, they will be well on the way to a sexually satisfying life together.

Three

Patterns of Sexual Response

Sex can be a source of profound pleasure but it can also be the cause of frustration, embarrassment, and pain. Part of this ecstasy or agony is psychological in origin, but an important part reflects the biological underpinnings of sexual feelings and responses. Necessarily, these components of sexual function are inextricably intertwined, each influencing the other. Nowhere is this better demonstrated than in the events of the human sexual response cycle.

Our primary understanding of the physiology of human sexual response stems from laboratory observational studies conducted by William H. Masters and Virginia E. Johnson 3 decades ago.[1] On the basis of detailed testing of 382 women and 312 men in more than 10,000 episodes of sexual activity, Masters and Johnson gathered an unprecedented array of information about the physical processes and manifestations of sexual arousal during various types of sexual stimulation. They also were the first to devise a four-stage model to describe and explain these natural physiological changes.

Many of the findings of these studies were startling in 1966, when *Human Sexual Response* was published. For example, the discovery that vaginal lubrication did not come either from secretory glands in or around the vagina or from the cervix was contrary to the prevailing medical belief at the time. The identification of the point of ejaculatory inevitability in the male's sexual response cycle—a point at which the process of ejaculation is triggered internally, and thus cannot be stopped—was also a totally new notion, as was the concept of a male refractory period—an interval after ejaculation when repeated sexual stimulation cannot trigger ejaculation again. Detailed proof of the continued capacity for sexual functioning in older adults ran counter to even the most progressive medical thinking. And perhaps most startling of all were descriptions of the phenomenon of multiple orgasms in women.

At a conceptual level, Masters and Johnson established a major philosophical beachhead for the feminist movement by showing the essential similarity of male and female sexual response. In fact, the revelation that women, unencumbered by a refractory period, and physiologically capable of multiple orgasms, actually had a physiologic capacity for sex *greater* than that of men virtually turned the world upside down, authoritatively deflating the myth of male sexual superiority.

It is also important, of course, to recognize that sexual response does not occur in the physical realm alone. Our sexual reflexes and feelings are virtually always activated and experienced in a psychosocial matrix. Since our emphasis in the next five chapters will be on the psychosocial side of sexual function and dysfunction, here we will emphasize the physical events of the sexual response cycle and consider how it is normally felt and interpreted.

SEXUAL DESIRE: PRELUDE TO SEXUAL RESPONSE

Sexual desire is influenced both by physical factors (such as sex hormone status, general health, and degree of fatigue) and other, nonbiological, elements. Among these are emotional aspects such as anxiety, self-confidence, overall mood, and tension levels that interact in the complex equation of determining the level of sexual desire. Similarly, cognitive elements—including sexual attitudes, beliefs, and expectations; attraction to one's partner; preoccupying thoughts or schedules; and past sexual experiences, to name just a few—operate either to foster sexual desire or to dampen it. Situational aspects also influence sexual desire. You would probably react very differently to an opportunity to make love when your in-laws are about to arrive for dinner as opposed to a leisurely Saturday morning when the kids have just left the house for the next 2 hours. Other situational factors include ambience (noisy vs. quiet; public vs. private; comfortable vs. not-so-comfortable, and so on), the prospective sexual partner you are with and whether you've had sex with this person before (and if so, how often, and how pleasurably), and what sort of relationship you have with this person (both overall and at the moment).

Motivation also plays a key role in sexual desire. This is not simply a matter of physical need or a need for orgasmic release. Other elements, such as the need to feel connected, the need to feel loved, the wish to be held, the desire to combat loneliness, the wish for a sense of security, and even the need to be dominated or to make a conquest can all play a part—although not at precisely the same moment. The need for excitement (and even the need to take risks) is another facet of the sexual desire equation.

The frequency and stimulative quality of a person's sexual thoughts and fantasies also contribute to this complex process. Just as thinking about a favorite food (or seeing an appealing feast on television) can fuel your hunger, an enticing sexual fantasy or a provocative visual cue can be a source of sexual turn-on. Sexual fantasies can either be willfully conjured up as a sort of self-administered aphrodisiac or they can pop into awareness seemingly unsummoned. Sexual dreams also can be catalysts for sexual desire, although relatively little is understood about the role dreams play in subsequent sexual behavior.

Physical stimuli of various sorts frequently trigger sexual feelings, although we may not always be aware of this happening. These range from the obvious, such as skin-to-skin touch, to less straightforward cues, such as a fragrance, a texture, or even a particular type of mood-setting music. (One woman we interviewed told us that she always became aroused when she heard Joan Baez recordings: it seems that at age 16, she and her boyfriend petted passionately almost every night while listening to this folk singer, and even thirty years later, Baez's crystal clear singing voice still evoked what was left of a conditioned response from her first experience with being in love.) Some people find that the languorous warmth of a hot bath gives them a relaxed, sexy feeling; others are aroused by a motorcycle ride, a lazy hour or two of sunbathing, or a vigorous jog followed by a shower.

These various components of sexual desire are interactive both in the sense that one can be influenced by another—being tense may make you feel fatigued and anxious—and in the sense that they push and pull at your libido like vectors in a complex mathematical equation. The vector/mathematical model is, in fact, useful for visualizing the way in which these various elements (and many other possible ones) combine to produce a state of sexual desire at a particular moment. Figure 3.1 shows a simplified version of such a model.

If you imagine the various positive and negative factors that affect sexual desire as three-dimensional, with time the third dimension, you will quickly see that although sexual desire is indeed the sum of input from all of these elements, various combinations of vectors and small changes in the intensity and direction of a particular vector will alter sexual desire in a virtually infinite number of ways. Furthermore, some of the factors that influence sexual desire, such as mood, are subject to rapid changes over time so that an individual's level of sexual desire typically fluctuates from one time to another.

Of course, there are those who claim to be *always* ready for sex. But this does not so much reflect a high level of sexual desire as it does a particular

FIGURE 3.1
THE VECTOR MODEL OF SEXUAL DESIRE

A schematic, simplified way of conceptualizing the elements that shape sexual desire and how they interact. No attempt has been made to offer a complete listing of the hundreds of vectors that contribute to this process in positive and negative ways; only a representative sampling has been depicted for illustrative purposes.

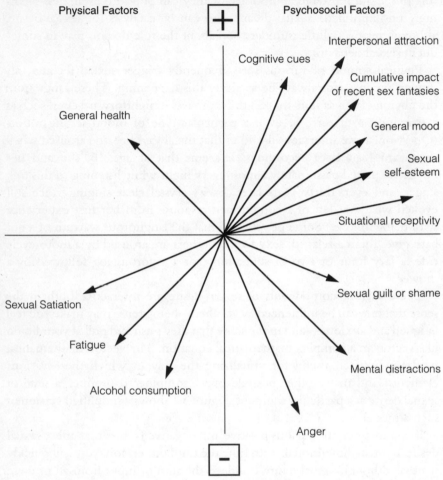

mind-set. Hunger and eating, in many ways analogous to sexual appetite, provide a parallel. Many people will eat whenever there is an opportunity, regardless of what their actual appetite at the moment may be. For them, the act of eating (which may be imbued with important psychological meanings or may just be an ingrained habit) is separate and distinct from actual hunger; they would no more dream of missing dinner because of lack of appetite than they would agree to give up a week's sleep. In much the same way, there are men and women who would never pass up a sexual opportunity, regardless of the level of their sexual desire. They may even try to instigate sexual activity at times when they really don't care at all about sensual or sexual gratification per se: they may do this to preserve a particular sort of reputation, or to attempt to dominate their partners, or even to convince themselves that they are sexually normal.

There are also people who claim never to feel any stirrings of sexual desire. Such sexual apathy can result from a medical condition, such as a severe hormone deficiency, or may reflect a psychological or relationship problem effectively blocking the build-up of sexual desire or the person's recognition of sexual desire. (The common problem of low sexual desire is discussed extensively in Chapter 4.) Some people who have deliberately chosen a life of celibacy also claim to have virtually no sexual desire, but whether this is a triumph of willpower or a matter of self-deception (in the sense of refusing to recognize any sexual stirrings) is not always clear.

For the great majority of individuals not at either of these two extremes— always ready for sex, never ready for sex—there is considerable variability over time and circumstance as to how they experience and interpret their own state of sexual desire. Some people are so tuned in to their sexual feelings that they are able to identify a sense of being ready for sex—in the vernacular, being "horny"—with great accuracy. Others have little recognition of this feeling but are aware of being more receptive to sexual overtures from their partners at certain times and being unreceptive at others. Of course, being sexually receptive doesn't simply reflect the intensity of a person's sexual desire; sexual receptivity may be triggered by guilt or a sense of obligation (or by not wanting to risk the consequences of refusal) as much as by thoughts of pleasure or physical gratification. And some people who are vaguely aware of feeling horny would never dream of initiating sex because they believe that is strictly the prerogative of their partner.

One thing is very clear to us: sexual desire is not a steady, unvarying state. A corollary is that sometimes sexual desire can be turned up almost instantaneously, even when a person least expects this to happen. This is not usually a volitional act (although it can be). Becoming suddenly interested in sex—even when sex seems to be the last thing on your mind, and the situation isn't "right" for it—can take you by surprise, as though the sexual urge sneaked up on you.

Although there is no precise way of reliably quantifying sexual desire, it can be useful to think about the vector model we have proposed as leading to a final product, reflecting the pushes and pulls and deflections of each of the positive and negative influences on a person's sexual appetite. This product may be in the neutral zone, where there is neither a strong tendency toward sexual readiness nor a marked state of avoidance of or resistance to sexual opportunities, or it may be in either the positive or negative zone.

These are not absolute states, of course, both because they are easily changeable and because they may be overridden by conscious decisions to accept or reject a sexual invitation or a sexual opportunity. For example, a man may be horny but turns down a chance for sex with his partner because he's angry at her for some completely nonsexual reason. Or a woman may be completely uninterested in sex because she's tired, fighting the flu, and has just spent two hours working on her tax returns, but she agrees to have sex with her partner because he's going out of town the next morning and will be away for a week. In real life people accommodate each other and infuriate each other with some regularity, which further complicates the process of viewing sexual desire as an isolated entity.

Despite this complexity, it is certainly true that sexual desire serves as a springboard for subsequent sexual arousal. If levels of sexual desire are high, the intensity and tempo of a person's sexual responses are apt to be accelerated. In contrast, when levels of sexual desire are in the negative zone, not only does it typically slow a person's arousability, but it may sometimes prevent arousal from occurring at all. Because of this, it is useful to view sexual desire as the first phase of the human sexual response cycle, as has been suggested by psychiatrist Helen Singer Kaplan.[2]

No matter how appealing it is to attempt to describe a working model of the various components of sexual desire, this exercise winds up being a little like trying to construct a human brain from a batch of computer chips and circuits: what is missing is the subtlety and spirit of real life. We can analyze vectors, talk about negative versus positive inputs, and even seek to measure blood levels of hormones that might play a role, and we still don't know exactly what distinguishes old-fashioned lust and passion from other tamer varieties of sexual desire.

SEX PARTNERS AND SEXUAL CHEMISTRY

The various physiologic changes of sexual response are essentially the same whether arousal occurs as a result of watching an erotic movie, reading a provocative book, fantasizing, masturbating, or having sex with a partner. This doesn't mean that they are *subjectively* the same, experienced and interpreted in the same way by everyone, or even experienced and interpreted identically by the same person on all occasions. Clearly, just as you may eat a meal with great relish and enjoyment when you're famished and have a dining experience that is more routine when you're not particularly hungry or when the food isn't out of the ordinary, you can also have quite different sorts of sexual experiences at different times. But just as the process of chewing and swallowing your food and then digesting it is the same, physiologically speaking, whether you're dining on sumptuous lobster tails or a greasy chili dog, the underlying physiologic patterns and processes of sexual functioning are the same under widely different sexual scenarios.

This is not to say that all erections are the same, because any male can vouch for the fact that they're not. Some erections seem to poke their way into existence gradually, while others virtually spring into action like a rocket being launched into space. Some erections are rock-hard, throbbing, and seemingly possessed of a mind of their own; others are firm and steady; still others seem to be operating at only 50 percent of peak efficiency in terms of size, rigidity, and passion. Likewise, most sexually active females are well aware of considerable variability in their own sexual responses. There are times when a woman's vagina or clitoris feels intensely hot and pulsating and when her vaginal juices are flowing copiously; there are other sexual episodes when her vagina may simply feel warm, moist, and mildly aflutter. On still other occasions, even though she may be a willing, interested partner who is highly involved emotionally in the sexual action, her vagina may feel vaguely detached from her, as though it's half asleep, and her clitoral sensations are minimal. This degree of physiologic variability is certainly not unique to sex: for example, on some occasions you may digest a meal quickly, while on other occasions it sits heavily in your stomach for hours. Likewise, one night you may sleep very soundly for 9 or 10 hours, while another night you toss and turn fitfully, only managing a few hours' sleep.

We do not intend to focus this discussion on subjective aspects of sexual response, since we will consider this topic in various other parts of this book. Instead, our focus in this chapter is on the general physiologic patterns of sexual functioning, which will provide a framework for understanding many of the problems, such as sexual dysfunctions, that we will deal with in detail later on. There is, however, a factor which might be considered subjective by some that we want to mention briefly since it is a significant part of the interpersonal sexual experience. Since there is no precise terminology to describe this process, we have chosen to call it partner reciprocity.

Partner reciprocity refers to the chemistry or complementarity of two people engaging in sex together. It is both a physical process and a psychological one: these two dimensions are invariably intertwined. For instance, it should be obvious that while a portion of one person's sexual turn-on comes from his or her unique feelings and sensations, part of the arousal is dependent, as well, on his or her partner's responsivity and arousal. When your partner becomes highly aroused, your own level of excitement will usually increase; conversely, if your partner seems to be uninvolved and uninspired during a lovemaking interlude, there will often (but not invariably) be a drag on your own passions and responses.

Partner reciprocity is not the same as partner synchrony. Just as lovers may not be hungry at exactly the same moment and can still dine together, it is not necessary for two people to make love as though they were in a synchronized swimming exhibition, doing exactly the same thing (and experiencing exactly the same feelings) at precisely the same time. Partner reciprocity involves being tuned in to one another's feelings rather than being locked into them in a tandem duet.

There are certainly a number of different reasons why partner reciprocity is important. At the strictly physical level, partners who are reciprocally involved each contribute to the pleasure and increasing sensual passions of the other. You can think of this as being a bit like two singers harmonizing together, since sexual reciprocity involves awareness of the other person's tempo and volume and pitch. If one person's touch is too rough or too insistent or too monotonously focused in one spot, the other feels out of synch and unsure of how to remedy the situation. If one partner rushes ahead to intercourse before the other is ready, it also usually detracts from the experience: Instead of harmonizing, they wind up with the sexual equivalent of cacophony. At the psychological level, when there is a high degree of sexual reciprocity and resonance—including adjustments to pacing and touch and the accompaniments (such as kissing)—the partners are comfortable because they feel that they are attuned to each other's experience and needs.

Sexual reciprocity is in part the result of two people's having a mutual awareness of and sensitivity toward each other's needs. For this to succeed, there usually has to be a willingness to adjust one's own sexual impulses when necessary to coordinate them to a certain extent with one's partner, as well as openness to devising effective lines of communication to allow these adjustments to be made.* Words don't always work well in this regard, because verbal requests may be both distracting and taken as commands or directives, even if they're not meant that way. If a woman says "Slow down" to her partner, he may take this as a form of criticism rather than a constructive

---

* If sexual reciprocity is forced to depend on guessing what your partner needs, it usually doesn't work very well. Sometimes, of course, couples discuss their sexual preferences when they're *not* in the midst of sexual activity, and the information gleaned from such conversations can be an important source of guidance for subsequent sex play. It helps to know that your partner likes to have his or her earlobes fondled while you're kissing, or to be told that she or he doesn't like to be clutched tightly around the neck during intercourse. Such general directives or suggestions, however, aren't always effective, since people's feelings and needs are highly variable.

suggestion or a request to let her catch up. We have found that many couples do better with nonverbal messages during lovemaking, although there certainly are exceptions to this generalization.

Sexual selfishness is one of the biggest obstacles to sexual reciprocity. In the most blatant examples, one partner uses the other like a masturbatory aid. In less extreme cases, one partner is so self-absorbed that he or she shuts out any attempts at communication from the other, making sex seem like two solo performances that happen to be occurring on the same stage. Regarding sex as work is another common impediment. In couples with this problem, genuine sexual reciprocity is limited because one partner feels that it's his or her job to satisfy the other. Couples who approach sex as a matter of pushing the right buttons also have great difficulty developing any true reciprocity, in part because they are constantly worried about what they *should* be doing and whether they're doing it right. A related difficulty is that sex for some couples is more like following a recipe than a creative, interactive process. ("Hug for 30 seconds. Kiss for one minute. Feel for her vagina; rub his penis. As soon as penis is erect, insert. Thrust vigorously for one to two minutes. Roll over and go to sleep.")

As with most good things, taking sexual reciprocity to extremes has its drawbacks. In the 1950s and 1960s, striving for simultaneous coital orgasms was all the rage. The notion was that timing one's sexual response so that both partners reached orgasm at precisely the same moment during intercourse was the ultimate peak sexual experience. Couples who could not consistently achieve this coordination were made to feel that their proficiency as lovers was lacking and that they were settling for a "second best" version of sex. Now, virtually all sex therapists and counselors disparage the idea of simultaneous orgasm as a specific goal of lovemaking. (This is not to imply that simultaneous orgasm is a bad thing; when it happens, it can be exhilarating. But working to make it happen and being disappointed if it doesn't is something else entirely.) What the cult of simultaneous orgasm also missed was that most people get so wrapped up in their own orgasm that they are relatively unaware of their partner's orgasm if it happens at the same time. His or her orgasms occurring separately give each partner an opportunity to savor fully both experiences.

PHYSICAL ASPECTS OF SEXUAL RESPONSE

Although sex is not merely a physical process, the physical changes that typically occur during sexual response are well worth knowing about and understanding. For convenience and clarity, we will describe these events as part of the overall pattern of the human sexual response cycle (Figures 3.2 and 3.3). In real life, however, there is no single, automatic, invariable model of sexual response, and there is no reason to enshrine "the" sexual response cycle, or *a* particular pattern of response, as sacrosanct. Variations from the general pattern occur from one individual to another and in any one individual at different times and circumstances. For instance, being with a new partner may produce pronounced changes in sexual functioning, not only because adrenaline is pumping more than usual but also because of unfamiliarity, embarrassment, heightened sexual desire, or dozens of other psychological reasons. Likewise, physiologic responses may be sluggish as a result of too much alcohol, fatigue, physical stress, or recuperation from a previous illness. Furthermore, sexual satiation or deprivation can also alter sexual response patterns: someone who has gone without sexual release for weeks is usually more likely to have a turbo-charged response in his or her next sexual encounter rather than a leisurely, slowly unfolding response pattern.

Sexual response is not just a genital event. With increasing levels of sexual arousal, many different body systems are involved in subtle and less subtle changes in functioning. The neurologic system serves as the central coordinator of these processes, gathering sensory input from peripheral sources and integrating it with thoughts, feelings, and perceptions in the brain (the central repository for controlling neurologic events), then relaying messages encoded in electrochemical form back to end-organs throughout the body, from fingertips to lips to blood vessels in and around the genital organs. The most automatic of these messages govern our basic sexual reflexes. Sensory awareness as we ordinarily experience it also undergoes sharp alterations during sexual arousal. Certain types of tactile stimulation become magnified in intensity as sexual involvement heightens; other types of sensory awareness such as vision and hearing are commonly diminished when sexual arousal is especially high. If the telephone rings when you're hovering on the brink of orgasm, you may not even realize it because your brain has focused on the sexual matter at hand. (This alteration in sensory awareness at high levels of sexual arousal explains why one person may be surprised to discover that he or she had been scratched or bitten during sex. Pain awareness is dulled during sexual excitation, along with visual acuity and auditory perception.)

The various physiologic changes that occur during sexual arousal reflect two underlying processes. Changing patterns of blood flow produce vasocongestion, an increased amount of blood, in various parts of the body, especially the penis and the outer portion of the vagina. Changing neural messages also produce heightened levels of neuromuscular tension through-

FIGURE 3.2
THE MALE SEXUAL RESPONSE CYCLE

(*a*) The most typical pattern of male sexual response. The dotted line shows one possible variation: a second orgasm and ejaculation occurring after the refractory period is over. (*b*) Male sexual response in a situation of prolonged arousal at the plateau level not going on to orgasm and ejaculation. Note that there is no refractory period in this instance, and resolution occurs considerably more slowly. (*c*) Male sexual response pattern showing erratic initial arousal and a relatively brief plateau phase prior to orgasm.

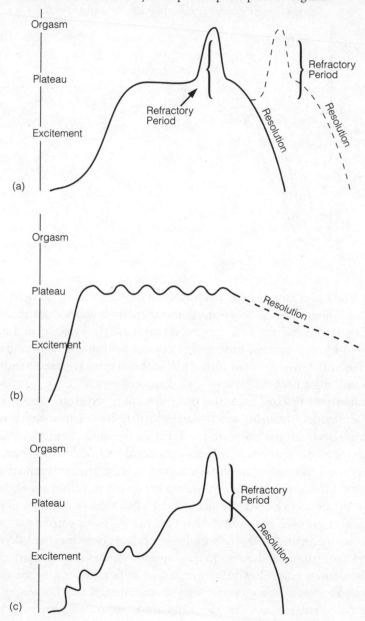

FIGURE 3.3

THE FEMALE SEXUAL RESPONSE CYCLE

Three representative variations of female sexual response. Pattern 1 shows multiple orgasms; pattern 2 shows arousal that reaches the plateau level without going on to orgasm (note that resolution occurs very slowly); and pattern 3 shows several brief drops in the excitement phase followed by an even more rapid resolution phase. Also note that, unlike in males, there is no refractory period in the female sexual response cycle.

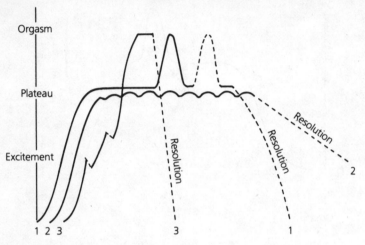

out the body as sexual arousal mounts. The term "tension," as used in this physiologic sense, doesn't mean anything negative; it refers to an accumulation of energy in the nerves and muscles that results in a heightened state of activation. How these two processes—vasocongestion and the build-up of neuromuscular tension—lead to the physical reactions we experience during sex will soon become clear.

It's important to emphasize that although there are clearly some fundamental differences in male and female sexual response, in many ways the similarities between the sexes are greater than the differences. For much of the twentieth century, female sexuality was vastly misunderstood because it was rated as an inferior version of the authentic male article. (Freud may not have started this notion, which was already present in earlier times, but his concept of penis envy certainly advanced it.) Now we realize that in physiologic terms, women have an infinitely greater orgasmic capacity than men do, that women commonly have multiple orgasms (whereas men do not, if being multiorgasmic is defined in the same way), and that women are not sexually aroused more slowly than men and in fact sometimes are aroused more quickly. Sex is not a speed contest between men and women, nor is it exactly fair to suggest an Olympic competition to see which sex has bigger or more frequent orgasms. There is a huge amount of individual variability, but there is a remarkable overall similarity between men and women in the physical patterns of their sexual responses.

EXCITEMENT

As we have already noted, sexual excitement can arise from a variety of different sources, from thinking about sex to reading an erotic novel to watching someone undress to direct physical stimulation. No matter what the exact source of the initial stimulation, the basic physiologic mechanisms of sexual arousal (in the physically healthy individual) are relatively straight-forward and predictable.[3]

In men, the first visible sign of sexual excitation is usually erection of the penis. Erection occurs because of changing patterns of blood flow. As a result of neural signals, an increased amount of blood flows into the penis, where it is trapped in three spongy cylinders that run the length of the organ. The resulting fluid pressure is what causes the penis to increase in size from its flaccid state and to become rigid.

Some men get erections as soon as they can unzip their pants (or even before), whereas for others it takes a few minutes of touching and kissing. (Young men tend to get erections more quickly than men in their sixties and beyond, but there is considerable individual variability in this process.) While it may be psychologically satisfying to have an instantaneous erection—and it may even convince your partner how virile you are and how attractive you find her—there is nothing inherently "better" about erections that appear like a flash of lightning. In fact, because most men find that erections quite naturally wax and wane during sex, the quickness with which an erection appears isn't very meaningful.

Since this waxing and waning seems to be a common cause of concern to both men and women, it's important to emphasize that erections come and go quite naturally during sexual play—they do not progress from firm to large to colossal in nonstop fashion. Sometimes an erection fades a bit when the man is concentrating on pleasing his partner; sometimes it recedes if there is a distraction (a noise from the next room; a barking dog outside); sometimes an erection slackens when there is a lull in the sexual action, or when a couple changes positions, or when there is too much of a particular kind of touch. (Any type of touch or caress can lose its stimulative or pleasure-inducing properties if it is continued too long. Not only does it tend to become boring, it may actually be a result of loss of sensory input, since repetitive stroking of the same area of skin eventually dulls tactile awareness.) Whatever the reason for some loss of firmness of an erection, or even its complete disappearance, one thing is certain: if you take this as a sign that there's a problem, you vastly increase the odds of this becoming a self-fulfilling prophecy. If you take things in stride and continue to touch, caress, and play together, the odds are high that the erection will naturally reappear.

Since the question of penis size seems to be of major concern to many men and women, we should point out that a relatively large penis in the flaccid state enlarges less during erection than a smaller flaccid penis does. This doesn't mean that all erections are identical in size, but it does point to the fact that despite what you might have seen in X-rated movies (which not only preselect well-endowed men but use deceptive camera work to make their erections loom larger than life), erect penises are much more alike, sizewise, than penises that are just hanging around doing nothing.

There is more to excitement, physiologically speaking, than just what's happening to the penis. (The various physical changes of the sexual response cycle are summarized in Tables 3.1 and 3.2 and Figures 3.4, 3.5, and 3.6.) About 40 percent of men experience nipple erection during excitement, whether there is any direct physical stimulation of the nipples or not. (In some men, nipple erection begins during the plateau stage; in another 40 percent of men, nipple erection doesn't usually occur.) The skin of the scrotum (the sac of skin holding the testicles) begins to thicken and the testes themselves are drawn up closer to the body than in their normal "hanging" position. Late in the excitement phase the testes increase slightly in size as a result of vasocongestion. In addition, the heart rate increases, blood pressure rises modestly, and there is a generalized increase in neuromuscular tension throughout the body.

In women, the excitement phase entails similar processes. The earliest physical sign of sexual arousal is usually (but not always) vaginal wetness, which can result from the anticipation of sexual activity, sexual cues or fantasies, or direct physical stimulation. Vaginal wetness (technically termed vaginal lubrication) is the direct result of increased blood flow into the pelvic region. Vasocongestion in the walls of the vagina causes fluid to seep through the permeable tissue lining the vagina. At first, only a few droplets of moisture randomly appear on the inner vaginal surface. As the number of moisture droplets increases, they begin to coalesce into small rivulets of fluid, like raindrops dripping down a windowpane.

When vaginal lubrication first begins, the amount is usually so slight that it may go unnoticed by either partner. As it becomes more copious, which can happen within seconds or take considerable time, lubrication often trickles out of the opening of the vagina and produces a sensation that some women have described as "gushing." The physical properties of vaginal lubrication are also variable. Although this fluid is usually colorless or slightly

TABLE 3.1
PHYSICAL CHANGES IN THE MALE DURING THE SEXUAL RESPONSE CYCLE

Desire Phase	No specific physical changes
Excitement	Erection begins
	Scrotum begins to thicken, scrotal folds disappear
	Testes begin to elevate
	Nipples may become erect (may be delayed until plateau phase)
	Heart rate and blood pressure increase
	General neuromuscular tension increases
Plateau	Rigidity of erection increases
	Head of the penis enlarges modestly
	Testes become enlarged and pulled up closer to the body
	Preejaculatory fluid may appear
	Sex flush may occur (about 25 percent of males)
	Heart rate and blood pressure increase further
	Breathing may become more shallow and rapid
	Voluntary contraction of rectal sphincter used by some males as a stimulative technique
	Further increase in neuromuscular tension
	Visual and auditory acuity are diminished
Orgasm	Onset of powerful involuntary rhythmic contractions of the prostate, seminal vesicles, rectum, and penis
	Ejaculation occurs shortly after prostatic contractions begin
	Testes pulled tightly against the body
	Sex flush, if present, reaches maximum color and spread
	Peak heart rates, blood pressure, and respiratory rates
	General loss of voluntary muscular control; may be cramplike spasms of muscle groups in the face, hands, and feet
Resolution	Rapid loss of most of the penile erection, followed by slower return to normal size
	Testes drop to their normal position and return to normal size
	Scrotum loosens and scrotal folds reappear
	Refractory period occurs during which another episode of ejaculation is not possible (duration of refractory period is highly variable, generally being shorter in younger males and increasing in duration with age)
	Loss of nipple erection
	Rapid disappearance of sex flush
	Irregular neuromuscular tension may continue, as shown by involuntary twitches or contractions of isolated muscle groups
	Heart rate, respiratory rate, and blood pressure return to baseline (preexcitation) levels
	General sense of relaxation is usually prominent
	Visual and auditory acuity return to usual levels

TABLE 3.2
PHYSICAL CHANGES IN THE FEMALE DURING THE SEXUAL RESPONSE CYCLE

Desire Phase	No specific physical changes
Excitement	Vaginal lubrication begins
	Inner two-thirds of the vagina expands
	Color of vaginal wall becomes darker
	Outer lips of vagina flatten and move back from the vaginal opening
	Inner lips of the vagina thicken
	Clitoris enlarges
	Cervix and uterus move upward
	Nipples become erect
	Breast size increases modestly
	Sex flush appears (late and variable)
	Heart rate and blood pressure increase
	General neuromuscular tension increases
Plateau	Vaginal lubrication continues, but may wax and wane
	Orgasmic platform forms at outer third of the vagina
	Cervix and uterus elevate further
	Inner two-thirds of vagina lengthens and expands further
	Clitoris retracts beneath the clitoral hood
	Lips of the vagina become more swollen and change color
	Sex flush intensifies and spreads more widely
	Further increase in breast size; areola enlarges
	Heart rate and blood pressure increase further
	Breathing may become more shallow and rapid
	Voluntary contraction of rectal sphincter used by some females as a stimulative technique
	Further increase in neuromuscular tension
	Visual and auditory acuity are diminished
Orgasm	Onset of powerful involuntary rhythmic contractions of orgasmic platform and uterus
	Sex flush, if present, reaches maximum color and spread
	Involuntary contractions of rectal sphincter
	Peak heart rates, blood pressure, and respiratory rates
	General loss of voluntary muscular control; may be cramplike spasms of muscle groups in the face, hands, and feet
Resolution	Clitoris returns to normal position within 5–10 seconds after orgasm
	Orgasmic platform disappears
	Vaginal lips return to normal thickness, position, and color
	Vagina returns to resting size quickly; return to resting color may take as long as 10–15 minutes
	Uterus and cervix descend to their unstimulated positions

TABLE 3.2 (*cont.*)

Resolution (*cont.*)	Areola returns to normal size quickly; nipple erection disappears more slowly
	Rapid disappearance of sex flush
	Irregular neuromuscular tension may continue, as shown by involuntary twitches or contractions of isolated muscle groups
	Heart rate, respiratory rate, and blood pressure return to baseline (preexcitation) levels
	General sense of relaxation is usually prominent
	Visual and auditory acuity return to usual levels

whitish, its consistency can range from runny to slippery to somewhat sticky. The odor of vaginal lubrication, too, is variable, in part because the fluid produced during sexual excitation mixes with other secretions containing microorganisms that naturally inhabit the vagina, as well as occasional interlopers. When there is a vaginal yeast infection, for example, it may produce a foul-smelling or acrid odor, and if a woman is using broad-spectrum antibiotics that alter her normal vaginal microbial mix, there may also be a different smell to her vaginal secretions than at other times. The odor can also be affected by diet: for example, women who consume a lot of garlic may have a slightly garlicky odor (and taste) to their vaginal juices.

When vaginal lubrication begins in the excitement phase, other internal changes are also occurring. The inner two-thirds of the vagina begins to expand from its resting state in both width and depth, as shown in Figure 3.5. (In the sexually unaroused resting state, the vagina's walls are collapsed, so that there is no real cavity inside it. Functionally, the vagina is a potential space that can expand like a balloon, changing its size and shape.) The walls of the vagina undergo a color change from their ordinary purplish red hue to a darker purple as a result of vasocongestion. The uterus is tugged in an upward direction, away from the bladder, and as the uterus is elevated, it pulls its lowest end—the cervix—along with it.

Externally, the lips of the vagina (the labia) begin to swell slightly and move gently away from their ordinary position in the midline of the body, where they cover the opening of the vagina. The clitoris enlarges somewhat as a result of vasocongestion in a pattern similar to erection in the male. (Some women can feel the erection of their clitoris during sexual arousal; others notice increased warmth and sensitivity but no marked change in size.) In most women, nipple erection occurs during the excitement phase along with a modest increase in breast size, the result of blood pooling in the breast tissues.

Stimulation of the clitoris is intensely arousing to many women, but most men are far from expert in this art. Here are a few suggestions that may be

FIGURE 3.4
EXTERNAL AND INTERNAL CHANGES IN THE MALE SEXUAL RESPONSE CYCLE

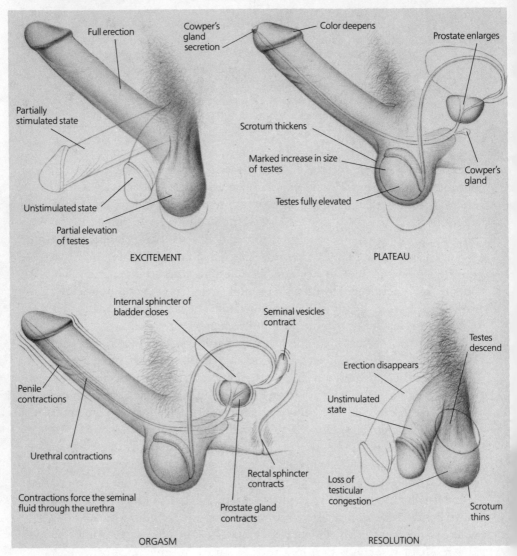

Full erection

Cowper's gland secretion

Color deepens

Prostate enlarges

Partially stimulated state

Scrotum thickens

Marked increase in size of testes

Cowper's gland

Unstimulated state

Testes fully elevated

Partial elevation of testes

EXCITEMENT

PLATEAU

Internal sphincter of bladder closes

Seminal vesicles contract

Testes descend

Erection disappears

Penile contractions

Unstimulated state

Urethral contractions

Rectal sphincter contracts

Loss of testicular congestion

Scrotum thins

Contractions force the seminal fluid through the urethra

Prostate gland contracts

ORGASM

RESOLUTION

helpful. In the tens of thousands of interviews we have conducted with women about what pleases them sexually and what doesn't, one of the most common complaints is that many men (even—or especially—those who fancy themselves skillful lovers) search out the clitoris almost immediately and then, once they've found it, stimulate it vigorously and almost continuously in a determined effort to fire up their partner's passion. What

FIGURE 3.5
INTERNAL CHANGES IN THE FEMALE SEXUAL RESPONSE CYCLE

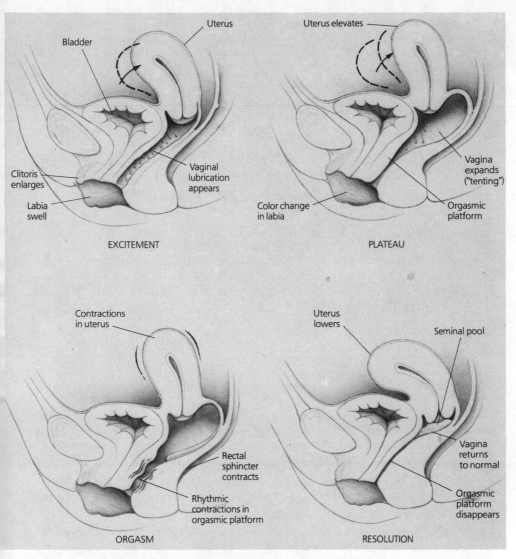

they don't realize is that (1) most women don't enjoy having the clitoris stimulated before they've begun to get physically involved through cuddling, caressing, and kissing; (2) what men construe as vigorously enthusiastic touching is perceived by many women as too rough; (3) few women like the "find-it-and-stick-with-it" approach, preferring that their partners move away from the clitoral area entirely, after fondling it for a little while, and then return to it; and (4) *direct* clitoral stimulation is often so intense that it

FIGURE 3.6
BREAST CHANGES DURING THE FEMALE SEXUAL RESPONSE CYCLE

After orgasm, the rapid reduction in swelling of the areola often makes it appear as though the nipple has again become erect.

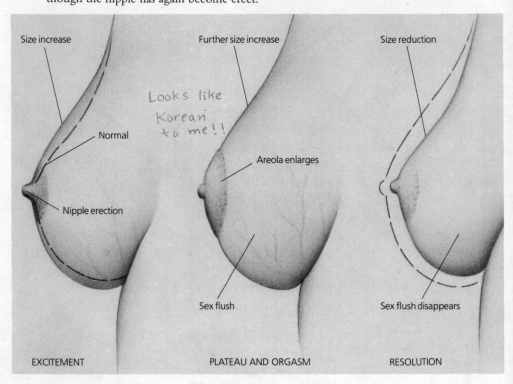

can actually be unpleasant; many women prefer being touched or rubbed in the area around or above the clitoris. Moreover, because there is no source of lubrication close to the clitoris, touching it (especially with dry or rough fingertips) may be physically disagreeable. An easy way to give clitoral touching a silky, smooth feeling is to use either saliva or an artificial lubricant like skin cream or hypoallergenic massage oil. Another possibility is to bring some of the vaginal lubrication to the clitoris. (Many men who try these methods marvel at the increased erotic sensations they are giving themselves as well; as with other seemingly altruistic actions during good sex, it isn't just something they are doing for their partners.)

Late in the excitement phase, a measleslike reddish rash called the sex flush may appear, beginning on the skin of the upper abdomen and spreading to the breasts and chest. (We estimate that only 50 to 60 percent of women have this skin flush, and even among these women, it doesn't always appear. Since it seems to be more common in well-heated settings, you are certainly less likely to observe this phenomenon if the air conditioning is blasting away.)

As in males, the heart rate increases, blood pressure rises modestly, and there is a generalized increase in neuromuscular tension throughout the body.

The excitement phase can be exceptionally brief, with passions rocketing straight up to the plateau level of arousal (we'll describe it shortly), or it can be a much more languorous time, with an ebb and flow of arousal levels. Sometimes, in fact, the excitement phase starts with a rapid trajectory but then slips back as a result of a momentary distraction, a lull in the action, or a problem with technique. For instance, many women are discomfited, both physically and psychologically, when their partners immediately rush to insert a finger in the vagina as virtually the opening arpeggio of a sexual concerto. It feels like too much too soon. Likewise, many men complain that their partners are too timid about stroking the penis, not grasping it firmly enough, as though they feared they might hurt or injure the man with too much pressure or too vigorous a motion. These men complain that the women's light, feathery touch on the penis is annoying or distracting rather than stimulating. Other problems with pacing can occur while partners attempt to coordinate with each other's state of arousal and erotic preferences. Sometimes a couple works out the flow of their initial sexual interaction smoothly and quickly, but on other occasions it may take the same couple a few minutes to get into a rhythm they find congenial.

Plateau

The hallmark of the plateau phase is a relatively high level of sexual arousal sustained within a fairly narrow range. Physiologically, the changes that began during the excitement phase (primarily the result of vasocongestion and increasing neuromuscular tension) intensify during the plateau phase but then level off rather than continuing to accelerate.

In the male, the rigidity of erection increases slightly during the plateau phase, and the head of the penis (the glans) enlarges in diameter and develops a deeper color as a result of greater pooling of blood. The testes also typically swell (with size increases of 25 to 50 percent over the resting state) and continue to be drawn upward more closely to the body, rotating in position as this happens until their back surfaces are pressed against the perineum (the region between the scrotum and the rectum). When the testes are fully elevated and held tightly in this position, it becomes a certainty that ejaculation is about to occur, although not in the plateau phase but in the next phase of the sexual response cycle.

Some men emit anywhere from a few drops to a quarter-teaspoonful of preejaculatory fluid during the plateau phase. (This mucoid fluid is not identical to semen, but it may contain a small number of live sperm.) Preejaculatory fluid can be produced even if no ejaculation occurs. This fluid is thought to come from Cowper's glands, two pea-sized structures, located just below the prostate gland, that drain into the urethra (the tube that in the male carries both urine and semen).

About 25 percent of men occasionally develop a sex flush during the plateau phase, as previously described. In the later stages of the plateau phase, some men use a technique of voluntary repetitive contraction of the rectal sphincter as a means of heightening their stimulation. This maneuver effectively provides indirect massage to the prostate and seminal vesicles, where internal pressure is building up toward ejaculation. The basic effect is well known to prostitutes, with their financial interest in a relatively quick end to a sexual encounter: many of them vigorously rub the man's perineum when he seems to have arrived at a high level of arousal, knowing that such indirect stimulation of the prostate often will trigger ejaculation.

In women, the hallmark of the plateau phase is a marked vasocongestive swelling in the tissues surrounding the outer third of the vagina, forming a cufflike region called the orgasmic platform (Figure 3.5). Becoming engorged with blood, the tissues of the orgasmic platform expand inward, narrowing the tunnellike interior of the outer third of the vagina. Because of this narrowing, the width of a man's erection is less important to a woman's sexual stimulation than it is often thought to be. In fact, the orgasmic platform effectively grasps the shaft of the penis, accommodating to almost any penis width. Because the region of the orgasmic platform is relatively well endowed with sensory nerve endings, sensations from stimulation in or around this area are, for most women, especially pleasurable.

Vaginal lubrication continues during the plateau phase and may even increase in quantity, but if the phase lasts for more than a few minutes, the production of fluid may wane noticeably or may seem to stop. (This is exactly analogous to the waxing and waning of erections in men; it is a good illustration of the fact that physiologic processes, such as vasocongestion, are not static but subject to minute-to-minute fluctuations.) For this reason, some couples find it helpful to use an artificial lubricant when they are ready to have intercourse, although using saliva as a lubricant is often more natural and convenient.

During the plateau phase, the uterus elevates to a higher position, and the inner two-thirds of the vagina expands further in width and depth. This region of the vagina is less well endowed with sensory nerve endings than the outer third, so this size expansion is not particularly meaningful in terms of sexual sensation. As a result of this sparser supply of sensory nerve endings, relatively fewer vaginal sensations come from deep penetration than from friction against the walls of the outer third of the vagina (especially when they have swollen to form the orgasmic platform). This is another reason why the size of the man's erect penis is not as critical to a woman's sexual pleasure during intercourse as most people seem to think it should be.[4]

During the plateau phase, the clitoris enlarges further as a result of increasing vasocongestion, but it pulls back against the pubic bone, which action, combined with swelling in the vaginal lips, makes it seem to disappear beneath the clitoral hood. (This can be disconcerting to the male if he is trying to locate the clitoris visually, because now the budlike clitoral glans is nowhere to be seen.) Vasocongestion causes the inner lips of the vagina to double or triple in thickness and to undergo a color change that has been dubbed the "sex skin" color change. In women who have never been pregnant, the inner vaginal lips turn a bright red at the height of the plateau phase, while in women who have had children, the color is usually deeper in hue, like a deep wine red, because of a more highly developed blood supply in this area. (In more than 7,500 cycles of female sexual response during intercourse, masturbation, and oral sex, Masters and Johnson noted that orgasm was invariably preceded by the "sex skin" color change in the inner lips of the vagina.)[5]

In addition, the sex flush (if present) intensifies in color and spreads more widely over the breasts and chest. As a woman nears orgasm, the sex flush may even spread over her lower abdomen, shoulders, thighs, and buttocks. Generally, the intensity of the sex flush is indicative of the physiologic intensity of the orgasm that it foreshadows. This doesn't mean that a well-developed sex flush is *always* a sign that orgasm will occur. Any sort of major interruption of sexual stimulation or psychological distraction can certainly block a woman's orgasm, no matter how aroused she has been up to that point. Furthermore, it also is important to point out that orgasms can certainly occur when there is no visible sex flush, and that these orgasms aren't doomed to be less intense or physiologically (or subjectively) inferior in any way to the orgasms that occur during sexual experiences in which a sex flush is present.

The plateau phase is also a time when the areolae (the dark skin surrounding the nipples) become prominently swollen. This may create the visual illusion that the nipples are no longer erect, because the areolar enlargement partly obscures them. A further increase in breast size is also typical of the plateau phase. In women who have never breast fed a child, a size increase of 20 to 25 percent is commonly seen, whereas the increase in breast size is less dramatic in women who have nursed.

In both women and men, heart rate and blood pressure increase further during the plateau phase, and breathing often becomes more shallow and rapid. Like some men, some women use a technique of voluntary, rhythmic contraction of the rectal sphincter late in the plateau phase; they do so as a means of pushing themselves towards orgasm.

Not everyone always experiences a distinct plateau phase leading straight to orgasm. On some occasions, the plateau phase is only a brief moment between excitement and orgasm which seems to fly by like telephone poles viewed from a speeding car. (This is more likely to happen when a couple begins intercourse while still in the excitement phase and their levels of sexual desire were high to start with; it is also common when an electric vibrator is used, either in sex with a partner or during solitary masturbation, particularly if a person has frequently used one.) At other times, especially when a sexual episode is more than just a quick one, a couple's passion rises to the plateau level for a while, only to drop back at irregular intervals to excitement levels again, from which it may or may not rebound. In situations where sexual play lasts for 15 minutes or longer, this irregular pattern is probably much more common than the classic form of the sexual response cycle shown in figure 3.2.

It is important to realize that sexual partners may not be particularly coordinated in terms of their physiologic response patterns. This isn't necessarily good *or* bad. There are situations in which one person becomes quickly aroused and reaches orgasm almost instantly while his or her partner is just getting warmed up, and there are times when one partner may not be particularly interested in sex but agrees to make love as a favor. There are also situational factors that may explain a temporary discrepancy in the level of each partner's arousal. For example, in oral sex, the person receiving the stimulation may experience an accelerated response, while the response of the person providing the stimulation may be at a lower point. In couples who have come to recognize that one usually reaches orgasm much more quickly than the other, deliberate alterations in their sexual routines may be called for to compensate for this discrepancy in timing. We know of many couples in which the man had ejaculated very rapidly during intercourse but made sure to stimulate his partner to orgasm manually or orally (or with a vibrator) before making coital connection, thus accommodating her pleasure as well as his own. There is absolutely no reason for sexual partners to be concerned about being exactly at the same point in their sexual response patterns. And, as we discussed earlier, there is no reason partners should strive for simultaneous orgasm. This not only sets up an almost unavoidable artificiality to their lovemaking, but is likely to leave them feeling shortchanged and inadequate if they fail in their quest.

ORGASM

If vasocongestion and myotonia (increased muscular contractility) build sufficiently in intensity as sexual stimulation continues, eventually neuro-muscular tension reaches the orgasmic threshold. This is the point at which a complex set of reflexes is triggered, both in the sex organs and elsewhere in the body, that collectively are known as orgasm. However, orgasm is certainly not an inevitable consequence of sexual arousal. Like all reflexes, it doesn't occur if its threshold isn't reached. And there are innumerable factors that can interrupt the buildup of sexual arousal even when it has gotten within a hair's breadth of the orgasmic threshold. As always, an outside distraction can cause either or both partners to lose sexual focus: anything from an untimely muscle cramp to a distasteful or annoying or physically uncomfortable act by either partner can deflect erotic feelings and therefore stop the progress toward orgasm. There is also a host of common problems (discussed in detail later in this book) that can interfere with the natural flow of sexual response: a man may lose his erection or ejaculate too rapidly; a woman may be afraid of "letting go" because she worries about losing control of her bladder or even of losing consciousness; an unrecognized sexual phobia may be an insurmountable obstacle. And in some cases, a person may simply be trying too hard to make orgasm happen; concentration on reaching this goal—with its self-monitoring to check on progress—effectively blocks the very response that is being sought.

There are also situations in which one or both partners are not particularly interested in reaching orgasm, as when one partner has agreed to sex simply to accommodate the needs of the other, or when sex is more ceremonial than passion-driven. At times, sex *without* orgasm can be highly pleasurable and stimulating. Nonorgasmic sex can produce tremendous warmth and closeness, as well as passion, and under some circumstances it may be satisfying and fulfilling in its own right. As one woman told us, "When I want an orgasm, I masturbate. When I want to feel close and loved and cared for, nothing beats intercourse, even though it rarely makes me come."[6] Except when a woman is attempting to conceive, where the need for intravaginal ejaculation is self-evident, there is certainly no reason that sex *always* has to end with orgasms. In fact, nonorgasmic sex is seen positively by some couples because of its staying power, while others find it an opportunity to make sex playful (and creative) rather than goal-oriented. However, as one woman in Shere Hite's survey remarked, "Whoever said orgasm wasn't important for a woman was undoubtedly a man."[7] This is not precisely true, since there are a fair number of women who have *never* had an orgasm and are not terribly concerned about it: they do not try to learn how to be orgasmic via masturbation, nor do they enter sex therapy seeking a cure, and in many instances, they do not think of themselves as abnormal or deprived. Other nonorgasmic women (or women who have infrequent orgasms) place a far higher premium on what they are missing and actively seek to rectify this situation, sometimes by experimenting with a change of partner as well as more traditional potential solutions.

Clearly, while many men downplay the importance of regular orgasm for their female sex partners or ignore it altogether (either to avoid making themselves feel inadequate or because they don't view orgasmic release as a woman's prerogative or requirement), almost all men feel that being orgasmic is integral to *their* sex lives. Although nonorgasmic sex might be all right once in a while, on a regular basis it would be viewed by most men as unsatisfying, frustrating, and incomplete. In the past few decades, more and more women have begun to demand equality between the sexes in this regard, but it appears to us that there are still substantially more women than men who see their own orgasms as optional accessories to their sexuality rather than the central focus.[8] We will discuss this matter in more detail in Chapter 7.

In the male, orgasm actually occurs in two stages, although the sequence is so brief that most people miss the distinction. The first stage is the initiation of emission, which takes about two or three seconds. Emission is started by a series of rhythmic reflex contractions in the prostate gland, seminal vesicles, and the vas deferens (the tubes that carry sperm from the testes) that begin at 0.8-second intervals and push the semen into the base of the urethra just below the prostate. As the semen collects in a pool and the urethra expands, the male has a clear-cut internal premonition that he is about to ejaculate. This is the point of *ejaculatory inevitability*, meaning that although external ejaculation has not yet occurred, the internal process of ejaculation has already begun and cannot be held back under any circumstances.

As emission occurs, the opening between the urethra and the urinary bladder clamps down firmly, preventing the semen from flowing backward into the bladder (and also keeping urine from mixing with the semen). Almost immediately thereafter, a powerful series of rhythmic contractions in the bulb of the urethra and the muscles at the base of the penis, as well as the shaft of the penis itself, pump the semen forward along the length of the urethra to the end of the penis, where it spurts out. This is the actual ejaculation. Although these contractions begin at regular 0.8-second intervals, after the first three or four strongest contractions, both the rate and intensity of contractions begin to fade. For this reason, the first few spurts are the most powerful; after a few seconds, there may be some continued seepage of small amounts of semen, but the expulsive force is significantly reduced.

Most men are aware of three somewhat different sensations during orgasm. The first, which corresponds to the start of emission, is a deep internal wave of diffuse warmth or throbbing pressure. This quickly leads to the powerful pumping action of the rhythmic orgasmic contractions described above, which most men describe as the most pleasurable part of orgasm. These contractions are felt both internally, in the region of the prostate, and externally, involving the entire penis. The third sensation is that of semen rushing through the urethra: men generally experience this as a warm spurting or shooting sensation.

The physiological process of orgasm in females is similar to that in males, except that most females do not have a sensation that corresponds exactly to the point of ejaculatory inevitability in men. In fact, a woman who is quite literally at the brink of orgasm can be left hanging with her orgasm blocked or foiled by any sort of interruption or cessation in stimulation. In contrast, once a man reaches the point of ejaculatory inevitability, the entire process of orgasm has been initiated: a herd of wild horses running through the bedroom wouldn't stop it.

No matter how an orgasm is produced (by masturbation, oral sex, vaginal intercourse, anal intercourse, or use of a dildo or vibrator), most women describe their subjective orgasmic sensations as emanating initially from a sudden burst of warmth and pleasure in the clitoris.[9] In fact, it is usually either direct stimulation of the clitoris or friction produced in the clitoris by a rubbing action of the clitoral hood that causes overall sexual tension to build to the point where the orgasmic threshold is reached. This, in turn, triggers a process of involuntary muscular contractions throughout the body which rapidly release the accumulated neuromuscular tension and pump blood from the vasocongested areas of the pelvic region and genitals back to its normal pattern of distribution.

As its name implies, the orgasmic platform provides the anatomic focus for the most intense physical responses during orgasm, as Masters and Johnson discovered. Physiologically, female orgasm begins with a series of involuntary rhythmic contractions in the orgasmic platform (at the outer third of the vagina) and in the uterus. Exactly as in men, these contractions start at 0.8-second intervals. After the first three to six contractions, the time interval lengthens and the intensity of the contraction diminishes. In a mild orgasm, there may be only three or four short, fluttery contractions, whereas a stronger orgasm may have ten to twelve contractions that are far more intense. Some women describe their strongest orgasms as torrid, ecstatic experiences in which they virtually lose awareness of themselves or even have an out-of-body experience; these same women note that their typical orgasms are less intense and more sensual, although these are still exciting and fulfilling experiences. In general, women's orgasms tend to be more variable than men's are in terms of physical intensity, duration, and subjective perception.[10]

Women have one sexual advantage over men: with continued stimulation immediately after orgasm, they can have additional orgasms within a short period of time without ever dropping below the plateau level of sexual arousal. This ability to be multiorgasmic seems to be unique to women. There have been isolated claims of multiorgasmic males,[11] but this usually involves nonejaculatory "orgasms" that follow an initial orgasm/ejaculatory experience. In our experience, most men who claim to be having multiple orgasms are actually producing orgasmlike contractions by voluntarily contracting the rectal sphincter. But other signs of physiologic arousal, such as testicular elevation and engorgement, are typically not present during these "multiple" orgasmic sequences.

Although all healthy women have the *capacity* to be multiorgasmic, not all women are. And among those who have occasionally been multiorgasmic, most report that this has occurred more often during masturbation than during sexual activity with a partner. (One explanation for this difference is that women may be distracted from their own needs during sex with a partner; another relevant point is that many women are more adept at stimulating themselves than their partners are at stimulating them.) Furthermore, many women tell us that it is easier for them to be multiorgasmic during oral sex than during intercourse, which may indicate that more direct clitoral stimulation is an important factor in this pattern. Overall, we suspect that only a quarter to a third of women have ever been multiorgasmic during sex with a partner, although there are no reliable scientific surveys to document this impression. One possible explanation has been posed by Avodah Offit, a psychiatrist:

> Women are not as eager as one might imagine to learn how to have multiple or sequential orgasms. The women who do inquire about increasing their potential are often wary. "Will my lover be threatened if I can have more than one?" "What happens when he gets tired, or has already come, and I still want to go on?" "Can multiple orgasms ruin a relationship?" Women are often sensitive to the possibilities of losing the lover who fails in an orgasmic competition, just the way they may respond to men who don't like to be beaten at Ping-Pong, cards, or academics. And it's quite true that men do become threatened by women capable of multiple orgasm.[12]

Most women do not ejaculate during orgasm. There is some controversy over the exact number who do, what the source of the fluid they produce might be, and whether what has been described as female ejaculation is a normal physiological variant or a sign of pathology. Since we have discussed this issue in detail elsewhere,[13] we will not address it further here except to say that our fundamental view is that only a small percentage of women consistently release fluid simultaneously with orgasm and that this often turns out to be a form of urinary stress incontinence, a condition in which urine is expelled from the urethra due to physical straining such as occurs with coughing, sneezing, or sexual arousal.

In both sexes, there are usually sharp increases in the heart rate, respiratory rate, and blood pressure during orgasm. In addition, muscles throughout the body often tense up in tandem with the rhythmic contractions of the orgasmic response, and the body may stiffen momentarily at the penultimate height of orgasm, as though the intense neurological bombardment of sensations had overwhelmed all systems and everything had suddenly frozen. Sometimes the discharge of all this neuromuscular energy during orgasm also leads to cramplike spasms of the hands and feet or involuntary facial grimaces, although often a person doesn't realize that this is happening.

RESOLUTION

The resolution phase is the body's return to a baseline, unaroused state. The primary difference between the male and female resolution phase is that for men, the initial portion of this phase is a *refractory period* during which ejaculation is physically impossible. Although some men maintain semierection during the refractory period, and a few men are even able to maintain a full erection with continuing stimulation, the ejaculatory reflex is out of commission during this interval, no matter how aroused the man may feel psychologically or physically. The duration of the refractory period is highly variable. In general, the refractory period is shorter in younger males and lengthens considerably in men over the age of fifty. It may also be shorter if there has been no ejaculation during the previous few days, whereas if a man has ejaculated several times in the past 24 hours, the refractory period tends to lengthen. At times, the refractory period can be as short as a few minutes, but a more typical range is from 30 minutes to several hours. For older men, the refractory period may last a day or longer.

The rapid loss of full erection is a direct result of the orgasmic contractions that reflexively pumped blood out of the penis. The slower, second stage of receding erection is a result of a combination of decreased inflow of blood to the penis, as compared to the rate during arousal, and relaxation of the veins in the penis that drain blood away from the organ. At the same time, the testes rapidly shrink to their normal (unstimulated) size and drop away from the body to hang loosely again in the scrotum, which itself changes its appearance and position as it reverts to the resting state.

In women, unless stimulation continues, the orgasmic platform disappears very rapidly immediately after orgasm. This is a direct result of the pumping action of the orgasmic contractions in the muscles surrounding the outer portion of the vagina, as shown in Figure 3.5. The clitoris also returns swiftly to its resting position within a few seconds after orgasm, although its return to its nonstimulated size takes a few minutes to occur. Many women find that the tip of the clitoris is so sensitive to stimulation during the early portion of the resolution phase that any direct touching in this area is uncomfortable or annoying. Internally, the uterus also returns quickly to its resting position and the vagina begins to collapse inward, shrinking in its overall dimensions to reverse the expansion that occurred with sexual arousal. If breast enlargement occurred during the excitement and plateau phases, this change also reverses itself. Because the areolar tissue returns to its flattened nonstimulated state faster than the nipples do, it may look as if a woman's nipples had "suddenly" become erect again at this point, but this appearance is misleading. It is simply a case of nipple erection taking a little longer to disappear.

In both sexes, the sex flush (if it has been present) disappears quickly after orgasm. Some people also develop a profuse sweating reaction at this time, as though they've just finished a workout (which, in fact, they have). This is typically accompanied by a pounding heart and rapid respiration, but all of these changes gradually revert to baseline levels unless sexual activity continues.

Contrary to what some people think, there is no reflex reaction that makes the male roll over and fall asleep after orgasm, although some men behave as though this is an automatic, biologically determined event. In the glow of postorgasmic relaxation, many women want to have continued physical contact with their partner—being quietly cuddled or caressed—as well as conversation, but a surprisingly large number of men are either unaware of or simply choose to ignore this desire. This, unfortunately, creates the (often justified) impression that the man is interested in the woman only for his sexual pleasure, and once that's been obtained, he has little or no further interest in her, leading many women to say that their lovers are selfish and insensitive.[14]

If orgasm doesn't occur, vasocongestion in the pelvic region doesn't resolve as quickly, especially if there has been a lengthy period of plateau-level sexual arousal. Here is a brief description of this situation:

Although certain changes occur quickly (such as disappearance of the orgasmic platform in women and the erection in men), there is sometimes a lingering sensation of pelvic heaviness or aching that is due to continued vasocongestion. This may create a condition of some discomfort, particularly if high levels of arousal were prolonged. Testicular aching ("blue balls") in men and pelvic congestion in women may be relieved by orgasms that occur during sleep or by masturbation.[15]

Not having an orgasm can also lead to annoyance, disappointment, or even anger, although these reactions are not physiologically determined. Indeed, how any individual reacts to sexual situations is another matter entirely, which we will explore in detail in the next five chapters.

Four

Low Sexual Desire

It's only in the movies that couples always have burning passions ignited at precisely the same moment. In everyday life, there are far more times when a man's mind is on his big sales presentation the next morning or how he's ever going to come up with the $4,000 for the kids' orthodontia bill rather than sex, so he misses his wife's subtle overtures to make love, and she goes to sleep unhappy and unfulfilled. It's only in the movies that when couples start disrobing, kissing, and caressing one another, it invariably flows into flaming (and satisfying) sex. In everyday life, you may start to disrobe and kiss and the kids come to the bedroom door having an argument . . . or you suddenly remember an important phone call that you have to make . . . or your partner is trying to rush things when you want to take the slow, leisurely approach. In everyday life, you may be bursting with the need for sexual release, and your partner couldn't care less—and tells you so. In everyday life, there are arguments to contend with, uninspiring (even boring) sex, and partners who don't always look like movie stars.

In other words, people aren't always ready for sex at the drop of a bra, nor is sexual desire an ever-burning flame. Which brings us to the topic for this chapter: the various forms and causes of low sexual desire.

THE BIOLOGICAL SIDE OF SEXUAL DESIRE

There are many ways to conceptualize sexual desire. Freud defined it in terms of libido, an innate urge for sexual expression, which he saw as both instinctive and biological at its core. Other theorists, such as Havelock Ellis, Margaret Mead, and Albert Ellis, moved away from Freud's libido model and reconceptualized sexual desire in terms of a more purely psychological force that could be situationally and environmentally shaped. In the last chapter, we examined some of these psychological forces and how they serve as a springboard for sexual arousal. However, there is also a strong biological component to sexual desire. To summarize its nature, we need to take an excursion into several realms of intriguing medical phenomena that many readers will not be familiar with.

For example, there are a number of sex chromosome disorders that are inextricably linked to low or absent sex drive. The most common examples are Klinefelter's syndrome, in which males have an extra X chromosome, giving them a 47XXY pattern (compared to the normal 46XY male pattern), and Turner's syndrome, in which females have one, rather than two, X chromosomes (giving them a 45X pattern rather than the normal 46XX female karyotype). In men with Klinefelter's syndrome (which occurs about once in 1,200 male babies), testicular development is stunted because of the chromosomal aberration, with the result that testosterone production is severely impaired. Sperm production is also almost invariably nonexistent or at grossly subfertile levels. The characteristic finding is that these men have very low sex drives, which they do not consider a problem at all. They rarely masturbate as teenagers or adults; they have few spontaneously occurring sexual fantasies; and they do not usually get turned on by watching erotic films or reading sexually explicit novels. If they marry, however, their wives may see the situation as problematic, although in many instances, it appears that the wife may have selected her Klinefelter's male as a mate at least partially on the basis of his totally nondemanding, even invisible, sexual nature. Not surprisingly, the Klinefelter's male's sexual desire is apt to be magnified to virtually normal levels by adequate testosterone replacement therapy. In other words, treatment that restores the man's missing testosterone to near-normal primes the pump of his sexual drive even in the face of a decades-long history of quiescent sexual interest. Furthermore, it can readily be demonstrated that this is not simply a learned response that needed an initial boost hormonally: if testosterone maintenance therapy is withdrawn for a period of just a few weeks, the Klinefelter's man who had been enjoying a relatively average amount of sexual activity suddenly returns to his monastic ways—almost invariably, his sex drive fades away. (There is, of course, a subtle difference in this new situation compared to his previously untreated state: now he knows what he's missing.)

In Turner's syndrome (which occurs about once in 2,500 live female births) there is a more complex situation, hormonally speaking. Because of the missing X chromosome, most females with Turner's syndrome do not develop normal ovaries and only have nonfunctional strands of tissue where their ovaries would ordinarily be. As a result, they do not have normal production of estrogen during adolescence or adulthood (estrogen is primarily made in the ovaries in women), and they do not have spontaneous menstruation or breast development because of their estrogen deficiency. However, they *do* have almost as much production of testosterone and related androgens as other women do, since 90+ percent of female androgen production occurs in the adrenal glands. The result is a little different from Klinefelter's syndrome. Women with Turner's syndrome tend to be somewhat less interested in sex than normal women are—but not much less. Here is support for the idea that androgens, rather than estrogens, are the primary endocrine determinants of libido in females. The example is not as pure as it might appear to be at first, however, since most females with Turner's syndrome are diagnosed with this problem during childhood or adolescence and thus begin receiving estrogen therapy early in their teenage years in order to stimulate breast growth. Furthermore, since they are also usually told that they are infertile and incapable of spontaneous menstrual cycling, there are possible confounding psychological variables that make it harder to evaluate exactly what's going on.

There are many other examples of how conditions that cause deficiencies of androgens in both men and women are commonly linked to a low sex drive.[1] One of the best examples can be drawn from the treatment of male sex offenders, where various antiandrogens are commonly prescribed to suppress the aberrant sex drive.[2] In parallel fashion, when even weakly antiandrogenic drugs are given to women to treat conditions such as hirsutism (excessive facial and body hair), a drop in libido is a frequent, and annoying, side effect. Another interesting example of the opposite sort is that when androgens are administered to women for various nonsexual medical problems (e.g., in the treatment of certain forms of cancer), increased libido is a commonly noted side effect.

The point we are making is simply this: there is an important biological element to sexual desire that should not be overlooked.

That said, we should quickly point out that hormones aren't the whole story. There are strong psychosocial determinants of libido, and exactly how they interact with our sex hormones isn't well understood at present. On balance, the best we can say is that in the absence of a marked androgen deficiency (or a serious chronic illness) in either men or women, sexual desire is more a reflection of psychosocial forces than biological ones. For the remainder of this chapter, we will examine what these forces are and how they express themselves in situations where sexual desire is impaired.

Before reading any further, you might want to take a few minutes to complete the following self-assessment quiz.

Self-Assessment Quiz: Could I Have ISD?

Rate how well each of the following statements applies to your life on a scale of 1 to 9, where 1 = doesn't apply at all, 5 = applies moderately, and 9 = fits me to a "T."

1. I don't think about sex very often.
   (1) 2   3   4   5   6   7   8   9   (circle one)

2. Sex usually isn't very satisfying for me.
   (1) 2   3   4   5   6   7   8   9   (circle one)

3. I never initiate lovemaking.
   (1) 2   3   4   5   6   7   8   9   (circle one)

4. I frequently turn down my partner's overtures to make love.
   1 (2) 3   4   5   6   7   8   9   (circle one)

5. Even when my partner tries to be romantic, I have a hard time getting in the mood.
   (1) 2   3   4   5   6   7   8   9   (circle one)

6. I generally feel unattractive and undesirable.
   1   2   3 (4) 5   6   7   8   9   (circle one)

7. I never masturbate.
   (1) 2   3   4   5   6   7   8   9   (circle one)

8. When I'm making love, I usually feel distracted or detached.
   1   2 (3) 4   5   6   7   8   9   (circle one)

9. I'm not a very passionate person.
   1   2 (3) 4   5   6   7   8   9   (circle one)

10. My partner's sex drive is a lot stronger than mine.
    1 (2) 3   4   5   6   7   8   9   (circle one)

11. I would be perfectly content to leave sex out of our relationship if I thought it wouldn't cause problems.
    1   2   3   4   5   6   7   8 (9) (circle one)

12. I never have sex fantasies.
    (1) 2   3   4   5   6   7   8   9   (circle one)

Self-Assessment Quiz: Could I Have ISD? (*cont.*)

13. Disagreements about our sexual frequency are common in our relationship and often lead to arguing or hurt feelings.

    1 2 3 4 (5) 6 7 8 9 (circle one)

14. It's not unusual for me to invent excuses (e.g., "I'm not feeling well") to avoid having sex.

    1 2 3 4 (5) 6 7 8 9 (circle one)

15. Sometimes at night I pretend to be asleep so my partner won't try to get me to make love.

    1 2 3 4 (5) 6 7 8 9 (circle one)

The key for scoring your answers can be found at the end of this chapter.

SEXUAL AVERSION

Sexual aversion is a severe phobia about sexual activity or the thought of sexual activity. As with most phobias, the victim generally recognizes that it is an irrational fear, but nevertheless, despite that intellectual realization, is largely powerless to face the phobic situation directly.

This problem, which lies at one end of the spectrum of disorders of sexual desire, is more than a simple matter of appetite. The dilemma is not just one of absent or deficient sexual desire: instead, the difficulty is attributable to an intensely focused fear about a particular situation (sexual intimacy) calling for a particular type of involvement—one form or another of physical sexual contact. The intensity of the fear, and the characteristic anticipatory dread that the fear evokes, is so strong that it can precipitate a full-fledged panic attack even when there is no practical possibility of having to engage in or confront the anxiety-provoking activities at that moment or in the near future.

Sexual aversion occurs in both men and women, although in its clinical presentation it involves women two to three times more frequently than men. Whether this is a real sex difference, as is found with other types of phobias, or whether it means that women are more likely than men to seek therapy is unclear at present. It is possible, for instance, that more males with sexual aversion may remain single than females with this disorder, which allows them to avoid the need to seek treatment for their phobia and may even permit them to virtually ignore the existence of the phobia, instead labeling it, for example, as lack of interest in sex. Furthermore, even if we consider cases of sexual aversion that arise during marriage, it may be that when females are affected, couples are more likely to seek therapy as the husband is less willing to accommodate his partner's phobia by either sexual abstinence or by seeking gratification outside the marriage.

Almost all of the cases of sexual aversion that we have seen have occurred in adults between the ages of 20 and 40. This is not to imply that sexual aversion doesn't exist among teenagers or middle-aged or older adults. Adolescents who are sexually aversive are not likely to be diagnosed as such; instead, they will probably be told their problem is one of nervousness or lack of experience. In a few instances, we have worked with adults in their twenties who had lifelong histories of sexual aversion and had been told by a previous therapist or counselor during adolescence that they had a gender orientation problem. The most likely reason middle-aged adults do not present clinically with sexual aversion is that they have already made adjustments in their lives to accommodate their phobia. Such adjustments include never marrying, opting for a life of celibacy, getting divorced (to escape uncomfortable, anxiety-provoking sexual demands), or choosing a mate who is comfortable with an asexual or nearly asexual existence. An example of the last type of relationship provided a fascinating case for us 15 years ago, when we had not yet seen a large number of such couples:

> Doris and Larry G. were both successful academics with doctoral degrees in library sciences and economics, respectively. They had each attained the rank of associate professor at a large state university on the West Coast and were active, healthy, and well liked by their peers and students. Doris was an avid tennis player and acted in several amateur theater productions each year; Larry was a jogger who was also an accomplished bridge player. They had been married to each other for 11 years: at the time of their marriage, Doris was 25 and Larry was 27.
>
> They came to see us complaining of an almost nonexistent sex life. They embarrassedly related that it had taken them almost two years to consummate their marriage. (Before marriage, they had agreed to wait until after the ceremony before having sex, and each took that agreement not only quite literally but also as a tremendous relief. The result was that their premarital physical contact consisted exclusively of holding hands and good night kisses—nothing more.) Not only were both husband and wife completely inexperienced sexually when they were married, their past attempts at marital sex had been fumbling, awkward, and unsatisfying. As Larry put it, "We both just used to close our eyes and hope that we could get the whole thing over with in a hurry." As a result, they had discussed their mutual discomfort some years back and had come to an agreement: they would have sex only twice a year—once on their anniversary (which came in July), and once on New Year's Eve. Not only did

they both come to dread the approach of these two dates on their calendar, they devised identical ways of dealing with it: they fortified their resolve to fulfill their obligations as man and wife by getting fitfully drunk before disrobing. They were both convinced that only by overcoming their inhibitions by the use of alcohol could they actually go through with the distasteful task of sex. Alcohol was, for them, clearly a kind of self-medication. Sex was, for them, as Doris wrote in one of her diaries, "like a visit to the dentist."

Fortunately, we were able to help Doris and Larry overcome their difficulties. By the end of therapy, they were having sex together three to four times a week. A few weeks later, Doris and Larry sent us the following note:

We know that you have repeatedly told us that you didn't have a magic wand to wave, that the progress we made was of our own doing. But we came to you in a state of fear and confusion, struggling with personal demons that had haunted us all of our lives. With your guidance, a huge weight was lifted from our shoulders, and we have found the gift of loving each other physically and experiencing the joyous intimacy of passionate, deeply gratifying sex. If that's not magic, we don't know what it is.

Not every case of sexual aversion has a history that is quite as dramatic as this one, but many have a remarkably similar ring. And clearly, most cases of sexual aversion do not involve a marriage with both parties so afflicted. Nevertheless, a person with sexual aversion may be able to get his or her partner to agree to a virtually sexless life under a variety of circumstances: one might fake a health problem, call on the partner's sensitivity and compassion, ascribe the discomfort with sex to religious principles, or simply select as a mate a person with little interest in sex.

Sexual aversion needs to be differentiated from what may at first appear to be similar problems that actually involve either aesthetic distaste for sex in general or an intense dislike, on moral or aesthetic grounds, for a particular sex act. For example, if a man cannot bring himself to perform cunnilingus on his wife because he finds the odor or taste repellent, but has no difficulty having other forms of sexual contact, including intercourse, this is not a case of sexual aversion. If a woman finds the very idea of anal intercourse degrading and physically repugnant, this strongly held preference or belief is not equivalent to sexual aversion, even if the thought of the undesirable activity is loathsome, shocking, and anxiety-provoking to her. Sexual aversion is not involved unless there is a consistent phobic component to the reaction.

As with phobias in general, there is often a physiologic element to thinking about or being confronted with the phobic stimulus. Profuse sweating, a pounding heart, dizziness, faintness, nausea, and a dry mouth are typical symptoms. Interestingly, the severity of a person's physiologic reaction is not always linked to the proximity of the dreaded contact; there are many people with sexual aversion who manage to internalize their responses in a manner which may make them feel as if a psychological vise were tightening about them but in which external signs of physical symptoms are not apparent at all. The physiologic symptoms of sexual aversion (as with any phobia) are quantitatively different from the milder symptoms of nervousness that can also occur in a sexual context, particularly in sexual encounters with a new partner.

One intriguing feature of sexual aversion that is somewhat different from most other phobias is that anticipation of the dreaded situation is often more intensely anxiety-provoking than being in the actual situation itself. As we have previously reported,[3] some people with sexual aversion tell us that they have more difficulty with the preliminaries of a sexual encounter—getting undressed, kissing, or caressing—than they do actually having sexual intercourse. Along the same line, it is notable that sexual response is not necessarily impaired in people with sexual aversion. Many men with this condition have completely normal erections and little or no difficulty ejaculating, and most women with sexual aversion have normal patterns of vaginal lubrication and do not have true vaginismus (spasms of the muscles surrounding the entrance to the vagina that make intercourse painful or even physically impossible). While many women with sexual aversion are not regularly orgasmic during sex with a partner, most of them have orgasms with masturbation.

Sexual aversion appears in several different varieties. Primary sexual aversion, which appears to be the least common form, is a lifelong condition in which a person has never enjoyed a period of sexual experience unfettered by the phobic block that characterizes this condition. In secondary sexual aversion, which typically has its onset during young adulthood, the affected individual gives a history of having previously had a relatively normal sex life. Situational sexual aversion is a category that we have seen almost exclusively in men who are either (1) comfortable with solitary sex (e.g., masturbation or watching erotic movies) but phobic in situations involving sex with another person, or (2) anxiety-free in male-to-male sex but intensely phobic in having or thinking about sex with a woman.

CAUSES

The causes of sexual aversion are not always easy to decipher. One category of cases that has become increasingly visible in the past decade consists of people who were traumatized by sexually abusive situations. Included in this category are survivors of incest or other forms of sexual abuse during childhood.[4] Many of these adult men and women have repressed their recollections of these events so effectively that they are virtually unaware of this highly pertinent background until the catharsis of therapy somehow serves to unlock the psychic closet in which their feelings of betrayal, remorse, guilt, and victimization have been stored. In other instances, sexual traumas of adolescence or adulthood can trigger sexual aversion as an acute defense mechanism. Particularly dramatic cases we have seen involve women who develop sexual aversion after being raped. (We should point out that lasting sexual aversion is an infrequent part of the aftermath of rape; however, the rape trauma syndrome, which is quite common, usually involves a time-limited period during which the rape survivor may be extremely anxious about sex and understandably is relatively sexually unresponsive.)

Sexual trauma doesn't derive only from rape or child sex abuse. We have also seen cases of sexual aversion that have had their origins in what psychologists would term a classical operant conditioning model. Here, as a result of repeated unpleasant sexual experiences, the man or woman develops a pattern of avoiding sex in order to steer clear of painful, embarrassing, or anxiety-provoking sensations. If avoidance by itself is enough to buffer them from the unpleasant results, the situation never progresses to a phobia about sex, although it may take on the form of inhibited sexual desire, which we will discuss later in this chapter, or possibly evolve into depression (which we discuss in Chapter 12). When avoidance isn't protective enough—when, for example, a spouse is so insistent on having sex that the person's feelings are ignored or overridden—the more extreme means of avoidance that the phobia provides is brought into play.

In cases where sexual trauma is apparently not involved, there are several other categories to consider. Some instances appear clearly connected to problems with adolescent sexuality. For example, individuals who had serious body-image problems during adolescence seem to be at a generally heightened risk of later sexual problems. Sometimes these body-image problems are directly linked to sexuality, as in the case of a boy who is distraught over having excessively prominent breasts or in the case of a teenage girl who is ashamed of too little breast growth. In other examples, the body-image problem may be less sexual, but still impacts on the teenager's self-perception of attractiveness and masculinity or femininity. Obesity is probably the most common problem of this sort, but others, including severe acne, excessive facial and body hair growth in females, and even problems with excessive sweating, can all set the stage for a scenario of social ostracism and withdrawal, fear of physical intimacy, and poor self-esteem contributing to a view of sex as unnecessary, undesirable, and even frightening. After years of internalizing such programming, the adolescent becoming a young adult does not automatically come to regard sex in a more positive light even if he or she succeeds in becoming slimmer, growing into a more pleasing physique, or otherwise moving beyond the original source of the sex-negative feelings. A particularly good example is seen in many cases of teenage anorexia nervosa, the self-starvation disease, which is a precursor of adult sexual aversion far more frequently than would be expected by chance alone.[5]

In a small number of cases we have seen, sexual aversion proves to be part of a constellation of multiple phobias. One example of this unusual pattern involved a woman who, along with sexual aversion, had a pronounced fear of both flying in airplanes and riding in elevators. Her psychiatrist was convinced that if she could overcome her fear of flying, it would cause her other phobias to fade away, but after two years of working unsuccessfully on this issue, she was no better off than at the start of treatment, according to her own assessment. When she and her husband came to see us in a last-ditch attempt to save their marriage, we completely ignored her airplane/elevator phobias and worked solely on the issue of sexuality. Her sexual aversion, happily, was resolved, but her elevator phobia and airplane phobia remained firmly entrenched, which they continued to be for the five-year follow-up period during which we stayed in touch with them.

Treatment

Phobias are, generally speaking, among the psychological disorders that are most successfully treated, and sexual aversion is, happily, no exception to this rule. At the Masters & Johnson Institute, we have seen 215 cases of sexual aversion in the past two decades, and our overall success rate is above 90 percent even in cases of startlingly long duration.

The key to successful treatment is virtually always to empower the person with the aversion by putting him or her (temporarily) in control in any situation of physical intimacy. In order to begin this process, any form of direct sexual contact is deliberately put off limits until the couple can approach nonsexual skin-to-skin contact through a series of exercises that gradually desensitizes and reconditions the phobic response. By allowing the person with the aversion to develop personal comfort with the fact of his or her control, combined with the patience of the nonaversive partner (which may require therapeutic attention of its own), it is usually possible to progress fairly quickly to the trickier parts of therapy. This involves encouraging the person with aversion to develop the ability to tolerate mild discomfort (e.g., anxiety) if it comes in small, measured doses, which they can control by deciding exactly when they're ready to stop, with no pressure exerted by the partner to go on any further. Once this begins to happen, it is not too difficult to help the aversive person first acknowledge the level of his or her anxiety (without feeling foolish or incompetent for having such anxiety) and then find ways to reduce or eliminate it. This is also largely done through sensate focus exercises, which are specially tailored to the needs of the individual couple and generally progress more slowly and in finer gradations than is typical of most other sex therapy cases.

The desensitization procedures are reinforced by reminders to both partners that what is unfamiliar is often uncomfortable. As they allow themselves to become more familiar with touching and caressing, and eventually with genital stimulation and intercourse, the comfort level of the previously aversive person usually improves by leaps and bounds. This dramatic change helps to keep the nonaversive partner interested and involved and motivated enough to continue to permit the person recovering from aversion to stay in control.

While the actual process of therapy is considerably more complicated than we have indicated here, the general outline presented above works rather quickly in the vast majority of cases. In virtually all of our successes, we have been able to reach a positive outcome with 2 to 3 weeks of intensive, day-by-day therapy.

INHIBITED SEXUAL DESIRE

How to define what "inhibited" means when talking about sexual desire is the source of considerable professional controversy. The dilemma is in attempting to quantify something that is subjective and not easily measured. The commonest practice is to equate sexual desire with the frequency of engaging in sex. However, this creates lots of problems, both conceptually and practically: for example, if a man doesn't really have any desire for sex but has intercourse with his wife twice a week to accommodate her needs, is the situation normal or abnormal? If a woman has sex with her husband only once a month but masturbates almost daily, how should her sexual desire be described? If both partners in a relationship are completely comfortable with having sex once every 2 weeks, is it appropriate to "diagnose" them as having inhibited sexual desire (ISD), or is it more practical to consider this a well-adjusted couple who happen to fall at the lower end of the frequency distribution for normal sexual appetites? Likewise, if a man had sex with his wife, on average, three times a week in his twenties, twice a week in his thirties and forties, but only once every 2 to 3 weeks now that he's 55, is he suffering from ISD? Or is he just getting older?

These and other questions lead many sex therapists to take a stance akin to Supreme Court Justice Potter Stewart's famous dictum regarding pornography: "I know it when I see it." While it may not always be easy to define ISD operationally and precisely, it isn't usually too difficult to recognize it in real life situations, because ISD is problematic only when it creates conflicts for a couple on a consistent, long-lasting basis.

Frequency doesn't provide the sole key to determining if a low sex drive is present. Consider, for example, the person who has a great deal of interest in sex but no available partner. Other situational factors obviously enter the equation as well: if a woman finds her mate physically unattractive, her lack of sexual interest may not indicate a low libido, but a partner-specific problem. (Arnold Lazarus wryly notes that some apparent "desire disorders" actually stem from one partner's "neglect of basic hygiene." He goes on to say, "I have had to urge many a spouse to take a bath or a shower before even considering making sexual overtures. Compliance in such cases has usually led to an immediate increase in the formerly reluctant partner's sexual desire.")[6]

Distrust or hostility can also take a decided toll on sexual feelings toward a particular partner. If a man discovers his wife has been sexually involved with his business rival, he may be so angry and hurt that he completely rejects the idea of sexual intimacy with her, but this would not be an example of inhibited sexual desire at all. Hostility stemming from almost any source can lead one spouse into withholding sex as a means of both exacting retribution and controlling or manipulating the other. The most destructive patterns occur in relationships marred by chronic hostility; while occasional episodes of hurt and anger can certainly lead to sexual rejection or avoidance, these are apt to be temporary snags in a couple's life rather than an ingrained pattern that is typical in cases of inhibited sexual desire.

One of the key issues that arises in discussions of sexual desire is the automatic assumption that male sexual interest is virtually always greater than female desire. In fact, no such generic difference exists: overall, men and women are relatively similar in the strength of their libidos (although individual men and women vary considerably). This overall similarity is remarkable in light of the incredible differences in how males and females in our society are socialized in regard to sex. Given the persistence of a strong double standard toward sexual behavior in America for at least the past half century, which, in its simplest version, gives the male permission to be sexual while disapproving overt female sexual behavior outside marriage,[7] it is astonishing—and probably something of a testimonial to the fortitude of the underlying biological forces at work—that women do not have a more constricted sexual appetite than men do.

It is quite possible that what is really meant when people say that men have a stronger sex drive than women is that men are more goal-oriented when it comes to sex: they know what they want and they work at getting it quickly. But while women may be less narrowly focused on intercourse and orgasm than men are—although research on this point is far from certain—it seems to us that women have a more sensible goal for what they want out of sex: for many women, closeness and cuddling and attentiveness are more important than rockets-bursting-overhead orgasm.[8] Still, for both genders the desired end point seems to be sexual satisfaction. And while differences may arise in the process of reaching for such satisfaction, or even defining what that satisfaction might be, the quest for sexual satisfaction is more similar than disparate for men and women overall.

To return to our consideration of inhibited sexual desire, let us examine for a moment the statement that ISD is problematic only when it creates conflicts for a couple on a consistent, long-term basis. First, it is important to recognize that no matter how loving and caring a relationship might be, the two individuals in it are not going to have absolute synchrony in their sexual appetites any more than they would always be hungry or thirsty or sleepy at exactly the same times. Despite this obvious and fundamental fact, couples are often surprised and even hurt when they discover the existence of such discrepant desires: expecting to fulfill one another's needs and wanting to share in a passionate relationship, they come up against a reality that doesn't match because it includes too many individual, noncouple, variables. (She's had a bad day at the office. He didn't get much sleep the last two days. She's coming down with the flu. He's feeling very tense and wants sex to help him relax. She's in a bad mood.)

Second, wide discrepancies in the desire for sex between two people in a relationship don't always imply that ISD is present (although the more desirous partner may try to convince his or her partner that this is the case): for example, if one person wants sex every day and the other is quite satisfied with sex twice a week, there may be a problem and there may even be conflict, but there is no ISD. At the Masters & Johnson Institute, such a situation is defined as disparate levels of sexual interest rather than incorrectly formalizing it with a diagnosis of ISD.

Third, it is very common when there are differences in sexual interest in a couple for one person involved to have a tendency to see him- or herself as normal and to label the partner as being either over- or undersexed. This view frequently turns into a self-fulfilling prophecy: the person labeled as oversexed makes more and more insistent sexual demands and thinks about sex more and more frequently, while the person labeled as undersexed falls into a pattern of rejecting almost all sexual overtures and virtually never assumes the role of sexual initiator. Such self-fulfilling prophecies entrench problematic behavior and worsen what are probably already strained relations well beyond the bedroom walls.

Most often, people with ISD have little or no difficulty with sexual functioning per se. In about one-third of cases, however, there is a coexistent sexual dysfunction: for men, a problem with erections or ejaculation; for women, a problem with arousal mechanisms or with orgasm. In a portion of these cases, it appears that the ISD develops secondarily as a means of coping with the previously existing sexual dysfunction. In a sense, by gradually diminishing his or her interest in sex, the dysfunctional individual avoids what had been a psychologically painful or embarrassing situation: he or she is no longer confronted very frequently with evidence of sexual failure, and when subsequent failure (dysfunction) occurs, it can be easily blamed on "not being in the mood" or "not being interested." In other words, there can be significant psychic gains from being uninterested in sex.

CAUSES

Individual Factors

There are numerous medical problems that can cause ISD, which we summarize in Table 4.1. (Many of these conditions are discussed in detail in Chapter 12.) However, in our experience, only about 15 percent of cases of true ISD are attributable to organic problems other than alcoholism or drug abuse. Nevertheless, it is important to realize that almost any chronic medical condition can take its toll on sexual desire, although the mechanism involved may not be strictly physiologic. Sometimes it is the psychological adaptation to the illness, rather than its physical symptoms or effects, that changes a person's sexuality. In any event, if ISD is purely situational—for instance, if a person shows little or no interest in sex with his spouse but actively maintains an outside sexual liaison—it is strong evidence that the problem is not a medical one.

There can also be relatively "pure" psychological factors that impair libido, although these cases may not always be as simple as they might at first appear. As with sexual aversion, ISD can be a reaction to various forms

TABLE 4.1
MEDICAL CONDITIONS CAUSING LOW SEXUAL DESIRE

Addison's disease (adrenal insufficiency)
Alcoholism
Anemia (severe)
Anorexia nervosa
Chronic active hepatitis
Chronic kidney failure
Cirrhosis
Congestive heart failure
Cushing's syndrome
Depression
Drug addiction
Drug ingestion:
   antiandrogens
   antihypertensives
   digoxin (in men)
   estrogen (in men)
   tranquilizers
Excessive prolactin secretion (drug- or tumor-induced)
Feminizing tumors (in men)
Hemochromatosis
Hypothyroidism
Kallmann's syndrome
Klinefelter's syndrome
Male climacteric (with testosterone deficiency)
Multiple sclerosis
Myotonic dystrophy
Nutritional deficiencies
Parkinson's disease
Pituitary insufficiency
Pituitary tumors
Testosterone deficiency
Tuberculosis

SOURCE: Adapted from Kolodny, R. C., Masters, W. H., and Johnson, V. E., *Textbook of Sexual Medicine*, Little, Brown, 1979, p. 566, table 22.1.

of sexual trauma, particularly to child sexual abuse.[9] In addition, ISD can be a direct by-product of gender orientation ambivalence: a married man who is struggling to suppress his homosexual urges may not have much appetite for heterosexual activity, even if he genuinely loves his spouse; likewise, a woman who discovers in married mid-adulthood that she is more attracted to women than to her husband is unlikely to have much sexual desire if it is measured solely along the heterosexual axis. Similarly, ISD can seem to result from various paraphilias: some transvestites and fetishists, for example, have incredibly low sex drives except for the powerful urges toward their preferred (or required) erotic stimulus. However, in cases like these the problem really isn't with flagging sexual desire—the problem is that the desire is directed toward an object or activity that is outside the relationship.*

Low sexual desire can also be a prominent feature of depression. Fortunately, this symptom responds well to treatment of the underlying depression and generally does not require specific sex therapy at all. In fact, it would be a mistake to treat the low sex drive caused by depression with sex therapy alone. However, there are some instances in which depression develops as part of the aftermath of ISD, particularly when marital tensions escalate and the person who feels very little interest in sex perceives himself or herself as sick or dysfunctional. In these cases, sex therapy is not only indicated but is the treatment of choice.

There is one other relatively common element in many cases of ISD. It's the "I don't feel anything when we're making love" response, which serves both as an excuse for not finding sex interesting or pleasurable and an explanation of why someone's sex drive has disappeared. Usually, "I don't feel anything" means that a person isn't *noticing* his or her feelings. This occurs for a variety of reasons. For example, some people are so focused on what they expect sex to feel like—whether it's a pulsating surge of electrical energy; hot, throbbing, tremors; or the Philadelphia Symphony playing the *1812* Overture with fireworks going off overhead—that their personal reality can't match their expectations. Other people are so busy rating their feelings as good or bad (or quick enough, passionate enough, or sincere enough) that they block out the experience of the physical sensations they are having, in a decided case of overinterpretation. Still others have their sensual and sexual feelings submerged in a sea of anxiety. For one last example (because the list could go on for dozens of pages), some people have become so dependent on the rational side of their brain that they have actually forgotten how to feel: they ignore sensory input because they overwhelm it with cognitive activity.

* Some couples make adjustments to this type of situation by incorporating the paraphilic object or activity into their sex play, effectively providing a means of harnessing at least a portion of the husband's sexual energies. For example, the wives or girlfriends of some transvestites not only tolerate the men's cross-dressing activities, but actually help them put on makeup, style their wigs, and otherwise accommodate the transvestite impulse. More typically, though, the paraphilic (almost always a man) goes to great lengths to keep his paraphilic obsession strictly private and hidden from his spouse or partner.

Relationship Factors

The exact causes of ISD are not always clear, and in many instances there are probably several causes interacting with and amplifying each other. At times, ISD seems to evolve out of a pattern of negative conditioning that can occur even when a relationship seems otherwise healthy and intact.

In a common scenario, one partner begins to avoid sexual interactions when he or she finds them to be either unrewarding or a source of stress. (The exact cause of the original sexual problem may be a relatively simple one, but it is unlikely to be precisely deciphered years later at the time most such couples might enter therapy.) The sexual withdrawal, whether intentional or inadvertent, starts a reciprocal chain of events within the relationship. The person with the higher level of sexual desire feels cut off and neglected; eventually, as the situation escalates in intensity, feeling neglected gets transformed into feeling rejected and unloved. The natural reaction that feeling elicits is that this partner begins to ask for sex more and more frequently, almost inevitably leading to a higher rate of rejection, and thus further escalation in the feelings of being deprived, rejected, and unloved. The other partner is caught in the proverbial quicksand. To begin with, he or she feels misunderstood and unfairly accused. As tensions mount, the more frequent demands for sex become an annoying sort of power struggle, so that even on those occasions where the less interested partner agrees to comply with the demands, sex becomes a form of obligation rather than a source of closeness and pleasure. This further reinforces the less interested partner's avoidance of sex and may create an additional degree of ambivalence, possibly leading the person to question whether or not he or she is still in love. To complicate matters even more, the less interested partner often experiences guilt, further clouding any chance for erotic fulfillment. What happens next is quite variable. In some instances the couple reaches a virtually total sexual impasse: the power struggle spills over into other areas of their relationship and things continue on a progressively downhill course. The partner who is more interested in sex may venture outside the relationship for sexual fulfillment, sometimes doing so as much to exact revenge for the perceived wrong that has been done to him or her as for the sexual gratification involved. In other cases, the partner who feels rejected and unloved slips into a downward spiral of depression and self-doubt.

Other relationship factors that cause ISD range from the simple and straightforward to the more complex. At the simple end of the spectrum, there are many relationships in which one person feels little, if any, sexual attraction toward the other because of physical appearance. A common example is when one spouse gains a lot of weight some years into a marriage.

Although issues of weight and attractiveness in marriage are not always simple, it is not difficult to see how—given our cultural messages that "slim is in"—severe obesity can be an obstacle to sexual desire. Another obvious cause of inhibited sexual desire is the case of the bumbling lover. In an era where we have come to expect a certain level of sexual proficiency as a mark of sophistication, not everyone has a feathery touch or an active interest in pleasing his or her partner. As one woman told us, "When Walter tries to make love to me, he's so clumsy that I can't wait to get done. He pinches my nipples and thinks that's a turn-on; he always manages to stick his knee into my crotch; and he pins me down to the bed so hard I can scarcely catch my breath." Other problems involving sexual style include situations where one partner (usually the woman) is physically hurt during sex, either because intercourse itself is painful (a condition called dyspareunia) or because sex play is too rough. It's not surprising that when sex turns out to be a source of distress rather than pleasure, people devise ways of avoiding the distress: not being interested or available in these situations is actually a means of coping.

More complex relationship issues also take a toll on sex interactions. One common example is when sex role stereotypes dominate a couple's behaviors so rigidly that the wife is unwilling ever to initiate sex because she sees doing that as the man's exclusive role, or when a man feels upstaged or even demasculinized if his female partner not only takes the lead in initiating sex but tries to set the tempo, suggest new positions or activities, or otherwise becomes the "conductor"—a role that he believes should be his and his alone. A variation on this theme is that the husband may feel personally diminished if his wife becomes more successful than he is in her career, particularly if she earns substantially more than he does. This situation can sometimes be accentuated if the husband loses his job while his wife is still working.

Power struggles outside the bedroom characteristically lead to power struggles in bed, and this category provides one of the most prevalent patterns contributing to ISD. (Admittedly, it can be difficult to figure out which came first: the power struggle or the sexual problem. One doesn't always precede the other.) Unlike most relationships, where either party can initiate sex and where there is a reciprocal give-and-take that allows for sexual expression even when both parties may not feel simultaneously in the mood, when ISD exists, there is an absence of such flexibility. Almost invariably, the person with the low sexual desire is the one who controls what happens sexually. Recognizing this, some individuals seem to "choose" ISD as a means of coping with a domineering spouse. By withholding sex, they exercise a sort of primal control that they can't get away with in any other aspect of the relationship. In this situation, the ISD becomes a means of manipulation, a way of exacting revenge or retribution for actual or perceived wrongs.

A common variation of how sex gets caught in the middle of a couple's power struggle is when sex becomes the currency for obtaining other desired behaviors from a partner. For example, many women complain that their mates always want sex without providing them with much love or attention; the men counter by saying that it's hard for them to be loving without frequent opportunities for sexual gratification. In another version, women complain that their male partners are noncommunicative, especially when it comes to expressing feelings, which results in the woman's believing she is "locked out" of the man's life. Perceiving this state of sparse communication as a barrier to closeness and intimacy, the women don't feel in the mood for sex very often. The men caught in this impasse claim that they actually do communicate directly with their partners: the problem is, they point out, that the feelings they communicate are not always the ones the woman wants the man to have. (It's amazing how often the man thinks he's communicating effectively when he tells his wife, "I'm feeling pretty horny now—how about jumping into bed?") In addition, many of these men are not very adept at identifying their own feelings, and when it comes to verbalizing the feelings they do manage to recognize, they are uncomfortable and often at a loss for words. In these and similar situations, there is a downward spiral over time in which the woman's initial sexual withdrawal becomes so habitual and automatic that it is transformed into sexual apathy and then into inhibited sexual desire.

Another dilemma in a couple's interaction that may lead to ISD is when one party feels like a sex object. It is usually the woman who has such a perception, voicing concerns such as "He just wants me around to service him," or, as one unhappy 36-year-old told us, "He'd be happier with an inflatable rubber sex doll as long as it could give him head." In some relationships there is a role reversal when it comes to sex: if the woman persistently wants sex more than the man, the man often feels threatened and may retreat into a pattern of avoidance that is at least partly rationalized by the claim that his mate makes him feel as if he's useful only when he's got an erection. Here is another instance of how this role reversal sometimes plays out.

At age 42, Charles M. had been divorced for 3 years before marrying Sarah, a stockbroker who was 9 years younger than he was. Their relatively brief courtship was a whirlwind of sexual passion and experimentation, which Charles found exciting and invigorating in contrast to the unenthusiastic sex that had marked his first marriage. However, after 6 months of marriage, Charles's interest in sex began to drop off considerably, and he and his wife suddenly found themselves making love only once or twice a week, rather than every day as they had done when they were dating. Sarah began to complain that Charles didn't find her attractive anymore and made it plain that she wanted sex much more often. Charles, in turn, found Sarah hard to please in many ways, not just sexually. When they first came for sex therapy, one of the major complaints that Charles voiced was that his wife never gave him a chance to initiate sex because she brought the subject up so frequently, he almost always had to be the "bad guy" by saying no.

This vignette illustrates a common set of problems in relationships that are trying to resolve a major discrepancy in libido between the two individuals involved. Disagreement over differing sexual appetites typically leads one person to be labeled as "sick" or "undersexed." To make up for that person's lack of sexual interest, the "healthy" partner resorts to constant verbal reminders and references to sex, burying his or her partner in an avalanche of mixed messages. There is a dual purpose to this pattern: at the surface level, the deprived partner believes he or she is signaling a continued sexual interest and availability and interprets the frequent mentions of sex as a desire to gently remind the less-interested partner that he or she hasn't forgotten the matter. At a deeper level, there is a more sinister motive. These constant references to sex are a not-so-subtle way of inducing guilt. Instead, the barrage of sexual messages winds up inducing resentment, impatience, and anger. "That's all he ever thinks about," or "That's all she ever wants to do" is a common complaint from a person contending with ISD.

Not all couples with major power struggles or with communications problems fall into a pattern of sexual combat, and for some couples who adhere to rigid sex role expectations, the predictability they confer is a valuable asset rather than a problem. In some marriages, conflict and tension get resolved by the couple's coming together sexually. Some couples actually fight because the best sex they ever have is when they make up with each other. The point we are making is that the mechanisms we cite as causal elements in many cases of ISD do not always lead to sexual distress or dissatisfaction. While this may partly be a testimonial to the resiliency and adaptability of sex, it is as much an indication of the vagaries and idio-syncrasies of the human animal.

Intimacy issues abound in the thicket of problems that can cause ISD and often operate in tandem with several of the patterns previously described. For some couples, getting too close is threatening and anxiety-provoking, so they find subtle ways to regulate the degree of closeness that develops by picking fights, burying themselves in work, or withdrawing from sexual interplay. When they have created enough of a buffer by this distancing, their worries lessen and they begin to move closer together in a cycle that repeats itself over and over. Other couples have intimacy problems of a different variety: they distrust one another, or they have difficulty maintaining personal independence if they share too much with each other, or they become so codependent or enmeshed that sexual desire may actually be repressed.[10] Margaret Nichols has written extensively on the latter point and its applicability to lesbian couples, where, she notes, couples may exist happily for years with little or no genital contact.[11] Nichols suggests that too much closeness develops in many of these relationships, smothering or ignoring individual differences and needs, with the result being a reduction in the mystery and unpredictability needed to maintain sexual tension and desire.

GETTING THERAPY FOR ISD: A CAUTIONARY NOTE

Except for those cases where low sexual desire is caused by a medical condition or a problem such as depression, the chances for treating it successfully depend most on the motivation of the person whose libido is impaired. If that person is dragged into therapy reluctantly and has little or no interest in changing his or her situation, therapy is doomed from the start. If, on the other hand, a couple seeks treatment because both partners are distressed by the problems ISD is causing in their relationship, the chances for success in therapy rise exponentially. *However*—and this is a *big* however—we have found that when a couple comes for therapy ostensibly because both partners have agreed to seek help, it is important to look beneath the surface of their accord. In a good number of cases, the more-interested-in-sex partner has got her or his mate's cooperation by threatening divorce or separation, not exactly an enthusiastic wish to find lasting behavioral change.

Another recurring problem that will throw a genuine monkey wrench into any couple-oriented therapy process is when one partner just doesn't like the other very much. (Although good sex therapists can work wonders in helping people's sex lives, they aren't magicians.) Since there are many reasons why a person who has fallen out of love with her or his spouse might choose to remain married—for the children's sake or for economic self-preservation, for example—this situation is hardly unusual.

A related issue that doesn't necessarily prevent therapy from being effective but that certainly complicates matters is when the supposedly sexually apathetic partner is actually leading an active sex life with partners outside the marriage. Likewise, if ISD is just a mask for a condition such as pedophilia or exhibitionism, it needs to be dealt with in a conceptually different way and will usually require individual psychotherapy as well as sex therapy for the couple.

Finally, we believe that sex therapy for ISD is unlikely to be very effective if it involves only the individual with low desire. Because of the tremendous importance of relationship dynamics in this situation—even if relationship factors aren't the primary cause of ISD, there are certainly apt to be relationship repercussions—treating the individual in isolation from the relationship is a little like watching the musicians at a concert but not listening to the music.

DISCREPANCIES IN SEXUAL DESIRE

There is a wonderful scene in Woody Allen's film *Annie Hall*, in which the camera shows Woody in his psychiatrist's office while simultaneously showing his lover (Diane Keaton) in session with her psychiatrist. Each person is being asked how often they make love.

"Hardly ever," Woody says plaintively; "maybe three times a week."

"Constantly," Diane intones; "I'd say three times a week."

In real life, actual disorders of low sexual desire are nowhere as common as they are in sex therapy clinics. Yet, as this bit of dialogue from *Annie Hall* shows, more couples complain about disparate sexual needs than any other single category of sexual problem. How, one wonders, did two such mismatched people ever get together in the first place?

The answer isn't all that complicated. When two people first become seriously attracted to each other—whether they're dating, living together, or have just gotten married—they seem to have remarkably similar appetites for sex. This is partly because major discrepancies in sexual desire work selectively in the courtship process to weed out mismatches, and partly because in the early going, both parties are trying their best to be sensitive to their partners' needs and to be romantic, sensual, and sexy. Once this initial halo effect wears off, once the newness and excitement of sex begin to tarnish and the wish to accommodate a partner gives way to thinking about oneself (or the children) first, sex not only becomes more routine but also frequently becomes less rewarding—and for some people, more of a job. The natural by-product of these factors is that the couple's frequency of sex decreases.

When they finally reach a new steady state of sexual relations, it is quite possible that it will, by mutual consent, be entirely satisfactory. But for millions of couples, the new rate of sexual activity leaves one partner feeling deprived, while the other often feels put upon and even overwhelmed by the perceived voraciousness of the opposite's sexual needs. Further compounding the dilemma is that the person who feels sexually deprived typically experiences an artificial exaggeration of libido, so that it often sounds as if he or she is preoccupied with sexual thoughts and feelings. This emphasis can have a markedly negative effect on the person whose sexual appetite is lower, because this one sees the partner as having insatiable sexual demands.

The normal give-and-take of people making ordinary decisions ("Would you like to rent a movie tonight?" "Can we go out with the Hammonds for dinner?") becomes distorted by an intensified scrutiny of motivations or the lack thereof when it comes to contending with markedly different sexual appetites. Just as the less interested person is convinced that his or her partner thinks about sex all the time, the more highly sexed person is convinced that the other never thinks about sex at all. Even worse, the sexually deprived person begins to feel that his or her partner is deliberately avoiding sex to torment him or her. Thinking about sex as often as he does (as a starving man thinks and dreams about food), he cannot conceive of the possibility that she isn't thinking about sex, too. So when he wakes up and showers and has a little time before breakfast, he already has sex on his mind, and he is puzzled and upset when she isn't interested because she's busy getting dressed and preparing for a hard day at work. When he calls her at her office to say he'll be home early, he has sex on his mind, whereas she hears an invitation to an early dinner and a relaxing time. No wonder, then, that he is angered when she isn't ready to jump into bed as soon as he walks in the door at 6:00 P.M. At the end of the day, he has already been thinking about how maybe things wouldn't be so bad if they could just make love. She is tired, or preoccupied, or deep in a novel, and not feeling very interested. "Maybe tomorrow," she says hopefully. He hears this as just another put-off and resolves to get back at her for her insensitivity to his needs.

In all probability, neither person in the above example intends to hurt the other. Neither one is likely to see things from the other's point of view, because if they did, the odds are that the problem would get resolved. Even though long-term relationship problems like this become so deeply ingrained that it feels like being stuck inside a revolving door in perpetual motion, the basic approach we take is to point out to people that if they just stop the door from revolving, it's easy to get out. And, to continue the revolving door metaphor, if the people trapped inside stop pushing, the door stops revolving.

PRACTICAL POINTERS FOR DEALING WITH DISCREPANCIES IN SEXUAL DESIRE

As the above examples show, when one partner wants sex more than the other person does on a consistent, persistent basis, severe tensions are created within the relationship. Here are some suggestions for improving the situation without having to resort to therapy.

1. *Communicate clearly*. We are amazed at how often this simple edict is ignored by otherwise intelligent, creative people. More often than most couples realize, missed communications (or muddled communications) contribute mightily to the sexual impasses that occur in their lives. Consider the case of Betty M., an attractive 37-year-old realtor married to Bill, a district sales manager for a well-known national corporation. When she wanted sex, she went through a particular preparatory ritual: taking a bubble bath, shaving her legs, and putting on what she thought was her sexiest nightgown. The trouble was that Bill often didn't respond to her overtures, leaving her incredibly crabby and feeling neglected. It took many sessions of marriage counseling before it became clear that Bill had no idea of what she was doing in the bathroom and really never noticed what nightgown she was wearing. ("They sort of all look the same to me," Bill said.) What she had interpreted as lack of interest on his part was, instead, more a case of being unaware of her sexual signals. "If you'd just tell me when you want to make love, there'd be a lot less confusion," said Bill, and thereafter the frequency of their lovemaking picked up to a satisfactory level for Betty.

It's not always this simple, of course. For some people, a direct invitation to have sex makes it somehow less romantic and spontaneous. But this situation can often be handled by developing a useful code language to transmit clearly one party's sexual interest without making it sound like ordering from a Chinese restaurant. The code language needs to be agreed on in advance, of course, entailing an effort to sit down together and talk things over; a means of allowing the "invited" party to clearly turn down the sexual invitation must also be devised. For example, one couple used a musical metaphor for their erotic invitations: "Do you want to go dancing tonight?" became their code phrase for bedroom activities. Another couple picked a more literary allusion, coding their sexual interest in the question "Can I read you some poetry?" Be sure to pick a code that is mutually agreeable and not likely to transport you quickly into gales of laughter. "How would you like to wrestle tonight?" just might set the wrong tone for many couples.

2. *Differentiate between an invitation and a demand*. With a few exceptions more in the realm of sex fantasies than reality, no one really likes to be pushed into something. When it comes to sexual interactions, it is almost axiomatic to say that making demands on a partner is likely to be a turn-off: the partner of whom something is demanded (rather than requested) usually feels hassled, becomes stubborn and uncooperative, and is unlikely to respond with passion—or even nonpassionate, lukewarm compliance. Most couples realize this tendency and avoid making sexual demands as demands; if one

person has something he or she really wants, they bargain, beg, or sweet-talk to get the partner's cooperation. In couples with a major discrepancy in levels of sexual desire, though, this natural dynamic is thrown out of kilter for two reasons. First, the person being invited to a sexual interlude often doesn't hear an invitation at all, but hears a demand. The fact that it is perceived as a demand immediately makes it seem one-sided, inconsiderate, selfish, and imposing; invitations do not have such negative baggage attached to them because they are offered as a more genuine choice, with the person being "invited" not being treated as a villain if the invitation is declined. Second, the tendency for the not-so-interested-in-sex person to hear an invitation as a demand is not always as unreasonable as it may sound at first. Past experience—in fact, *many* past experiences—may have told them that what is advertised as an invitation ("It's up to you") is actually a demand: it is a demand in the sense that if the invitation isn't accepted right then and there, the degree of disappointment and resentment that the other partner shows makes it plain that it wasn't, in fact, an invitation at all, but a poorly masked form of demand that over time becomes more odious exactly because it is made to seem innocuous and nondemanding.

3. *Try to let sex simmer on low instead of expecting it to come to a boil.* What we mean is this: if the expectation is for sex to heat up rapidly, the not-so-interested person may tend to check his or her initial responsiveness and say, "Hmmmm, I'm not really very turned on—so that must mean I'm not interested." That sort of "preflight inspection" turns out to be self-defeating, because it doesn't allow for the possibility that sexual feelings (and responses) can get stirred up by simply allowing oneself to be in the situation with no automatic performance checklist (or timetable) to signal success or failure.

4. *Understand the difference between rejecting an activity and rejecting a person.* Here is one of the major sources of trouble when it comes to individual differences in sexual appetites. How you turn your partner down when you're not in the mood or preoccupied has a great deal to do with how your partner reacts to your message. If he or she feels rejected as a person, almost invariably he or she will feel hurt or angry. If, on the other hand, you make it clear that there's a reason why sex doesn't fit your needs right now (and leave open the possibility that the situation may change soon), your partner doesn't feel as if you've just slammed the door in his or her face.

The flip side of this equation is that if your partner turns away from your preludes to making love, don't leap to the conclusion that he or she is turning away from you. If you can't help feeling rejected—especially if you have a very strong need for sexual togetherness or release—talk things out instead of just rolling over and stewing about it.

5. *Learn to employ the art of compromise.* In sexually "together" relationships, usually each partner is willing to be available sexually when the other one needs him or her. You don't have to promise to be at your most passionate peak of performance in order to make things work. In fact, often a "quickie"—not necessarily involving intercourse—may be enough to assuage your partner's need, just as a snack will sometimes be a good way of substituting for a bigger meal when someone is hungry. Women can almost always accommodate their partners without too much physical difficulty (assuming the absence of out-of-the-ordinary conditions such as severe PMS, a vaginal infection, or the like); anatomical reality dictates that unless a male becomes at least moderately aroused, he will have to provide sexual stimulation to his partner by some means other than a fully erect penis. *There is absolutely nothing wrong with this!*

6. *Don't approach every lovemaking session as though it has to follow the numbers.* If you are flexible in allowing for options in your sexual togetherness, you may find it paying more dividends than you imagine. Consider the marriage of Dave and Mary L. After 14 years and three kids, Mary was chronically tired and not particularly interested in sex. Dave not only wanted sex more than Mary did, but (as so often happens in these situations) became more and more obsessed with sex the more he was stymied in his approaches. The solution they found, after a one-hour consultation with us, was stunningly simple. Mary agreed to "service" Dave even when she wasn't particularly in the mood, as long as Dave would respect her wishes to decline when she was really frazzled. But she had the option of *how* she would "service" him: by hand, by mouth, or by intercourse, which gave her more choices . . . and more control. Dave was amenable to this arrangement initially because, as he put it, "Half a loaf is better than none." He quickly discovered that the half loaf kept replenishing itself, as Mary's willingness to be available on her terms, rather than his, apparently freed up something inside her and she began gradually to find sex more interesting and inviting. At the same time, as Dave found himself with a partner who was available to him more often than before (even though not as the wildly turned-on partner he would have liked), his own sexual appetite began to become less pressing. The moral of the story is simple: if you'll meet each other part way when there are different sexual appetites, the differences often disappear or become inconsequential. Part of the agony felt by the person whose sexual needs are not being met in a relationship is fueled by

the lack of willingness to *attempt* to deal with his or her needs—no one likes to feel neglected or ignored.

7. *If you're not interested in sex at the moment when your partner "invites" you, but you might be later on, convey this clearly.* If your wife is starving at 4:00 P.M. on Sunday afternoon but you don't want to eat then, there's no reason to say, "I'm not going to eat today." Why not take the same approach to sex? While you may not both be interested in sex at exactly the same time, if you keep your options open for the possibility of more convergent appetites later in the evening, you haven't shut her out completely. What's more, even though your wife was the one who offered the initial invitation, the opportunity is now there for either of you to flash a green light if the feelings are even mildly favorable.

8. *Expand your sexual repertoire.* If boredom is the bane of satisfying sex, following the same sexual script over and over again is not the wisest way to kindle dwindling sexual interests. In nondysfunctional couples, one reason for sex losing its allure and creating desire discrepancies is that it simply becomes too routine. In your sex life, doing the same thing over and over again in the same way, in the same position, even at the same time of day, can become predictable and stale. The solution is straightforward: try something a little different. We're not suggesting that you run out and recruit another partner so you can have a threesome (although that would certainly be one way of expanding your sexual repertoire). Instead, we're suggesting that you should try to implement some changes within your present relationship. If you're used to always having a cold appetizer, try a hot one. If you always have shrimp cocktail instead of soup, once in a while, go with the soup instead. In other words, try some things you haven't done recently, or maybe never before; try varying the timing or setting for sex (a motel room, or the living room floor); consider using a vibrator or some flavored massage lotion to add a new dimension to your erotic existence.

9. *Use sex fantasies to help turn yourself on if your level of passion is only lukewarm.* Sex fantasies are incredible catalysts to setting the sexual juices flowing. However, people with low sexual desire often don't spend much time thinking about sex and don't have many sexual fantasies, either.[12] Anyone can change this pattern by deliberately calling up erotic fantasies to enrich (and jump-start) their sex lives. And if you don't have some favorite fantasies of your own, you can find various books that will help you get started with short descriptions of many common fantasy scenarios. As we've

said before many times, sex fantasies are probably the best aphrodisiacs around—and they don't cost anything, either.

10. *Identify obstacles to your sexual opportunities and come up with practical ways to get around them.* As incredible as it seems, kids are one of the principal problems when it comes to flagging sexual desire. For example, young children may tire their parents out so badly that hitting the pillow is more important than melting into your spouse's arms with passionate abandon. Even older kids have a funny way of being unintentionally intrusive just when you're trying to make some time for yourselves to have a little romance—and few things can botch up foreplay more than a 15-year-old's knock on the bedroom door just as you're beginning to be aroused. Possible solutions to these problems are not hard to devise, but they are sadly neglected, as though putting your sexual needs before the needs of your kids might somehow damage their development. Tackle problem Number 1, wornout parents of young children, by the judicious use of a babysitter to allow you and your partner to get away, rest up, or recharge your sexual batteries. Problem Number 2, intrusive older children, can be dealt with in various ways. A DO NOT DISTURB sign on the bedroom door can work wonders, for example. In any event, take time with your partner to draw up a list of problems of a similar nature that interrupt or inhibit your sexual togetherness and then implement specific action plans for handling each one.

Scoring Key for Self-Assessment Quiz: Could I Have ISD?

Step 1: Add together your point totals for the answers you gave to questions 1 to 10. Enter this number on line A, below.

Step 2: Add together your point totals for the answers you gave to questions 11 to 15. Enter this number on line B, below.

Step 3: Double the number on line B and enter it on line C.

Step 4: Add the numbers on lines A and C to get your total score.

Line A _____ 19   57
Line B _____ 26   44
Line C _____ 30   88
A + C _____ 145   129   Total Score

Here is how to interpret your results.

A total score below 90 indicates it's unlikely that you have ISD. A score from 90 to 120 raises the possibility that ISD may be present, but cannot be clearly determined from your responses. Total scores from 121 to 140 are strongly suggestive of ISD, but not absolutely diagnostic. Scores above 140 indicate that you have ISD, although a definitive diagnosis cannot be made from a paper-and-pencil test alone. For people whose scores fall in the last two categories (121 and higher) and whose lack of interest in sex is at all problematic, we strongly urge consultation with a qualified sex therapist or marriage counselor.

Five

Ejaculatory Problems

Ejaculatory problems were poorly understood for most of this century. One reason for this situation was that surprisingly little pertinent research had been done on this subject by the medical community through a combination of scientific reticence, societal taboos, and factual misunderstanding. It was assumed that ejaculatory disorders were simply subtypes of impotence. This misclassification necessarily made the possibility of successful treatment rather bleak. Fortunately, once it became clear that these conditions were in a class of their own, quite separate and distinct from most cases of erectile difficulties, the development of new treatment approaches used to reprogram the ejaculatory reflex led to stunningly high levels of cures.[1]

In this chapter, we will discuss both ends of the spectrum of ejaculatory problems: the very common condition of ejaculating too rapidly and the relatively rare situation of retarded ejaculation. Although these conditions are at opposite ends of the spectrum in functional terms, both can produce intense frustration and psychological anguish not only for the man who is affected but also for his partner.

PREMATURE EJACULATION

Premature ejaculation is one of the most unsettling of all sexual dysfunctions, but fortunately it is also one of the easiest to conquer. Although there are no exact statistics on the prevalence of this problem in the general population, it appears that premature ejaculation is the most common male sexual dysfunction, affecting tens of millions of American men.[2]

The core problem in premature ejaculation is that the man ejaculates too fast. In the most severe cases, ejaculation consistently occurs before the penis can even be inserted in the vagina; in less extreme cases, ejaculation characteristically occurs as insertion is being attempted or a few seconds after the penis actually is contained in the vagina. Other men with milder forms of this dysfunction manage to hold off from ejaculating long enough to begin having intercourse, but lose control after a few intravaginal thrusts no matter how desperately they try to distract themselves from becoming too aroused too quickly. As one 33-year-old man told us, "As soon as my wife starts moving, I shoot off like a half-cocked pistol."

Rapid ejaculation isn't *always* a problem. Some couples prefer having quick, passionate sex, and others are happy just to have sex be quick. In some cases, the couple devises ways of taking care of the woman's sexual needs before vaginal penetration is attempted (for example, with manual or oral stimulation, or the use of a vibrator), and some women are able to accommodate to their partners' lack of ejaculatory control by learning to reach orgasm very quickly themselves. However, millions of couples are unnerved by this problem, which can be a never-ending source of embarrassment, arguing, and sexual frustration.

While experts have long debated over the precise definition of premature ejaculation, almost every man with this problem knows he's got it: splitting fine semantic hairs doesn't add much to our understanding. Older definitions that specified a precise minimal time period (say, 30 seconds) for determining what was premature have now been tossed out in favor of a more flexible (and sensible) view of this problem. (Some men actually tried to time their coital longevity with a stopwatch, which didn't exactly make for a relaxed, romantic interlude for them or their partners. This fact certainly illustrates how commonly males subject themselves to performance pressure.) The American Psychiatric Association defines premature ejaculation as follows: "Persistent or recurrent ejaculation with minimal sexual stimulation or before, during, or shortly after penetration *and before the person wishes it* [italics added]."[3] Of course, what constitutes "shortly after penetration" is subject to debate. Some couples think that intercourse is supposed to be over in 10 or 20 seconds and are perfectly happy with that situation, while other couples are distressed or disappointed if the male doesn't manage to last for 15 minutes of vigorous coital acrobatics. The italicized portion of the "official" definition is also problematic because ejaculation is, after all, a reflex response that is not usually subject to strict voluntary control, so despite the fact that many males *wish* to have more staying power in sexual interludes (just as they also wish for bigger and quicker erections, bigger and more frequent orgasms, and bigger and faster cars), in this case the wish or desire doesn't do much to define whether a problem exists.[4] Most men will never have the degree of voluntary control of ejaculation that they have in terms of their bladder function, and some men seem no more able to control ejaculation than they are able to control their heart rate or how much they sweat.

Having a consistent pattern of overly rapid ejaculation is the hallmark of premature ejaculation. For this reason, males who have trouble controlling the rapidity of ejaculation only in certain circumstances do not really suffer from this dysfunction. For example, it is very common for a man who has little or no difficulty maintaining ejaculatory control with his regular sexual partner to ejaculate at almost breakneck speed with a new partner. The greater psychological arousal of being with someone new undoubtedly contributes to the precipitous response; heightened performance anxiety usually plays a role in this pattern as well. Another instance in which very rapid ejaculation is so common that it's actually normal occurs when a man first attempts intercourse after not having had sexual activity for a prolonged period of time—generally, a period of several weeks or longer.

Another confusing aspect of premature ejaculation is that most males with this problem are unable to control the urgency of their ejaculatory response only in situations involving coitus. During solitary masturbation, many men who are premature ejaculators can actually maintain high levels of sexual arousal without ejaculating for surprisingly long periods of time. Similarly, many men with dismal coital ejaculatory control have no such difficulty while receiving oral sex, although in the most severe cases this form of stimulation also provokes an almost instantaneous ejaculatory explosion.

A number of reports note that cultural, educational, and socioeconomic variables play a major role in determining whether a couple views the male's persistently rapid ejaculation as a problem.[5] In the lowest socioeconomic groups, it is not uncommon to find the view that sex is mainly something "for the male's pleasure," and rapid ejaculation may even be viewed positively, as a sign of virility. However, most couples find a persistent pattern of rapid ejaculation to be a frustrating, even painful, situation.

To deal with this frustration, couples try a number of different novel but generally unsatisfactory strategies. Over-the-counter topical anesthetic ointments may be used to dull the man's sensations, but these generally prove to be useless for two reasons: they don't usually cure the problem (except by the power of suggestion) and since the ointment rubs off on the wife, she winds up having her own genital sensations deadened, a situation hardly conducive to a pleasurable or satisfying sexual interaction. A somewhat better choice is using a condom, which may cut down on the man's sensations enough to improve his staying power. (Condom use can be helpful for men with very mild premature ejaculation, but it usually doesn't change things much for those with more virulent forms of this dysfunction.) Condoms at least offer the advantage of not otherwise interfering with the man's sexual response, unless the man tries to wear two or three condoms at once, something we have encountered in a few cases. The same cannot be said for techniques that involve the male's deliberately trying to distract himself from arousal by mental gymnastics such as trying to count backward from 1,000 or trying to recite the lyrics to the second verse of "The Star-Spangled Banner" in his head. (Not only is the "distraction" technique generally ineffective, it obviously puts an undesirable damper on intimacy in bed.) Likewise, disengagement techniques in which the female takes a "hands off" approach to sex—sometimes not even kissing her partner, but certainly avoiding any and all contact with his penis—while the male works furiously trying to get his partner turned on so she can signal him that she's ready for intercourse generally turn out to be a disaster.

There are two self-help techniques that many couples contending with this problem have found useful. The first is based on the fact that many premature ejaculators have far less ejaculatory urgency once they have already ejaculated. For those who can manage to become sexually aroused again within several hours after a first ejaculation, making love the second time around can be a relatively leisurely, unrushed event. (Some couples handle this together, while others let the male masturbate an hour or two before they expect to get together. As the saying goes, "Different strokes for different folks.") The second technique that some men find helpful is consuming a modest amount of alcohol—say, two shots of liquor, or a few glasses of wine—which may take just enough edge off the rapidity of the ejaculatory reflex to give them a greater sense of control and also reduce their intense anxiety in sexual situations. This works because alcohol is a depressant to the central nervous system, slowing things down just enough to diminish the abruptness of the reflex without blocking all sexual sensations. The downside is that some men may find that the amount of alcohol required to slow their ejaculation also impairs their erections, making intercourse impossible; other men shouldn't be consuming alcohol at all for medical or religious reasons, in which case such a solution isn't feasible.

There is no certainty regarding the cause (or causes) of premature ejaculation. Medical problems such as abnormalities of the prostate gland or inflammation of the genitals are rarely involved.[6] The older psychoanalytic notion that premature ejaculators harbor deep-seated unconscious hostility toward women (and thus "punish" their partners by ejaculating quickly, depriving them of the opportunity to enjoy sex) has now been largely discarded.[7] Instead, current thinking suggests that the most important elements in the development of rapid ejaculation may be a result of either (1) early sexual experiences that conditioned rapid responsiveness, or (2) anxiety that is activated in sexual situations.[8]

Since most boys have their first ejaculatory experiences as a result of either masturbation or wet dreams, it is not surprising that they have no reason to attempt to slow the tempo of their earliest adolescent interpersonal sexual encounters in order to accommodate a partner. In fact, boys who have participated in the common group masturbation contest known colloquially as a "circle jerk" epitomize the fact that ejaculatory speed is lauded as highly desirable and very macho. This conditioning of rapid ejaculation continues for many adolescent males both with private masturbatory experiences (in which they commonly push for speedy responsiveness to avoid getting caught by inquisitive parents or intrusive siblings) and with early sexual encounters with the opposite sex in which noncoital sex play (which used to be called "petting") also places a premium on swift ejaculation. (As one 30-year-old man ruefully recalled for us, "When I was sixteen and going steady, it would get to a certain stage of making out where I managed to get my hand inside her panties and she would put her hand around my prick. If I didn't come pretty quickly, she lost interest and decided we had to stop before we'd go too far.") Early coital experiences tend to repeat this pattern: many teenagers first attempt sexual intercourse in hurried or uncomfortable circumstances (e.g., the back seat of a car) where they are afraid of being discovered and where their anxiety, guilt, and anticipation combine to make fast ejaculation very commonplace. It appears that such early conditioning is one of the major ways in which a lifelong pattern of premature ejaculation evolves; many men with this dysfunction give histories of such experiences.[9]

Anxiety may also play a role in premature ejaculation. For one thing, anxiety triggers electrical and chemical changes in the nervous system that may accelerate the ejaculatory reflex.[10] At the same time, performance anxieties (Will I be able to satisfy her? Will I be able to keep from coming too fast so I don't make a fool of myself?) combine with frantic efforts to hold back the feeling of ejaculatory urgency in a futile and largely self-fulfilling prophecy: the anxiety actually seems to heighten the male's headlong rush into total loss of control. In fact, one destructive pattern that can be seen with chronic premature ejaculation is that the vicious cycle of performance pressures leading to performance anxieties leading to performance failures not only becomes self-reinforcing and escalating in severity, but often develops into secondary impotence as the effects of the anxiety become greater and more burdensome.

Men who have a good degree of voluntary control over ejaculation, who are virtually never troubled by ejaculating too fast, usually don't have an explanation for why (or how) they have acquired this control. While it's true that self-confidence may count for something, it doesn't seem logical to view it as the main factor. And differences in the frequency of sex, or masturbatory patterns, or age at first sexual experiences just don't have any predictive value in determining who will have trouble with ejaculatory control and who will function perfectly normally without much thought or effort.

Here is a brief explanation of the mechanisms leading up to ejaculation. When male sexual arousal begins, the earliest physiologic response is erection of the penis, which results primarily from extra blood flowing into the spongy tissues in the penile shaft. This initial excitement phase then progresses, with a combination of continuing physical and psychological stimulation, into the plateau phase, a time during which relatively high levels of sexual arousal are sustained. Men who have little or no difficulty with ejaculatory control generally are aware of the degree of internal pressure buildup in their pelvic region (which corresponds anatomically to swelling in the area of the prostate gland and seminal vesicles) and recognize when they are approaching the brink of ejaculation. Physiologically, this brink is known as the point of ejaculatory inevitability (see Figure 5.1a), because once it is reached, unstoppable reflex rhythmic contractions in the prostate begin the propulsion of semen from its temporary storage depot to the exterior.

Males with good ejaculatory control are able to recognize when their levels of sexual tension get close to triggering ejaculation and instinctively sense how to ease back from this point when they want to maintain their arousal without coming to an explosive conclusion. For some, it is a matter of slowing the tempo of coital thrusting just enough to take the edge off their ardor; for others, it is an adjustment made by a silent shift in cognitive attention or fantasy content. Still others control their degree of excitation by changing the angle or depth of penile penetration or by voluntarily slowing the tightening of their pelvic muscles. (Many men push toward ejaculation by alternately tensing and relaxing the muscles around the anus; the internal accompaniment of this movement is a sort of massage of the prostate gland that propels most males toward the point of ejaculatory inevitability.)

For men with premature ejaculation, these internal cues often seem to be missing, and there is a corresponding absence of instinctive compensatory strategies to avoid reaching the point where ejaculation begins. Often, the plateau stage is exceptionally brief: the anticipation of intercourse alone (coupled with the proximity of a willing partner) may be enough to push the man with severe premature ejaculation straight from excitement to ejaculatory inevitability without any discernible time spent at plateau levels of arousal at all (see Figure 5.1b). Other men with rapid ejaculation are able to get to plateau levels of arousal, and sustain them, as long as there is no attempt made at vaginal penetration. They may be able to continue noncoital play for lengthy periods, only to lose control abruptly once intromission occurs (Figure 5.1c).

FIGURE 5.1 (A,B,C)
GRAPHS OF VARIOUS FORMS OF EJACULATORY CONTROL

(*a*) The male sexual response cycle with good ejaculatory control. Note that plateau levels of arousal are maintained for a considerable time period after coitus is initiated before ejaculation occurs. (*b*) Severe premature ejaculation, with ejaculation occurring before intromission is achieved; note that there is no discernible plateau phase due to the rapid velocity of arousal. (*c*) The sexual response cycle in a man with premature ejaculation who has no difficulty maintaining ejaculatory control during noncoital sex play. Note the prolonged plateau phase, which ends abruptly within seconds after penile penetration of the vagina.

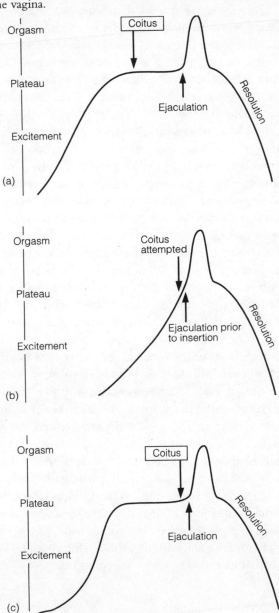

While part of the problem seems to be a conditioned response, the male's sense of helplessness and futility may also play a role in his lack of control. On the basis of interviews with more than a thousand men with premature ejaculation, we can say that it is striking how often their stories sound alike. Once the problem has been around for a while, the man tends to panic in the throes of sexual passion, one reason perhaps why he blocks out or fails to recognize the ordinary physical cues that other men use in gauging the level and velocity of their sexual arousal. Furthermore, the profound sense of panic that sweeps over him makes it harder to modulate his own participation in the sexual activity; instead of easing up slightly, as other men do, he tenses up, a feeling that seems to push him over the brink. "It's a feeling like I'm falling and can't stop myself," is how one 25-year-old man described it.

The repercussions of premature ejaculation can extend in several different directions. For single males without regular partners, this dysfunction can create such a low level of sexual self-esteem that dating seems to be self-defeating and even psychologically dangerous. The low sexual self-esteem sometimes translates into other psychological difficulties, including depression. Men in romantic relationships often find that premature ejaculation puts a serious strain on their liaisons. The woman may accuse her partner of being selfish and inconsiderate, or think that he's immature, or simply see him as an inept (and uncaring) lover. It is not unusual for the woman to turn to affairs both to make sure that *she's* not the cause of the problem and to find a more sexually satisfying lover. While certainly many women react to their partners' ejaculatory difficulties with love and understanding, there are many others who become angry and feel used. Indeed, while rapid ejaculation is a male sexual dysfunction, it often causes the female the greater sexual distress. For this reason, some women adopt a stance of sexual avoidance in order to minimize the magnitude of the problem, but this only worsens the situation because infrequent sex leads to even poorer ejaculatory control. Premature ejaculation has caused untold numbers of relationships to break up, including countless marriages where the woman may have believed initially that the situation would change over time but departed when she found that this wasn't the case.

As the psychiatrist Helen Kaplan notes, "Men who are highly achievement-oriented and competitive are particularly likely to overreact to their sexual 'failure' and are apt to try so hard to hold back that lovemaking loses its sensuous quality."[11] Other males develop a general sense of inadequacy as a result of their sexual shortcoming. Most of the time, premature ejaculation is a frustrating and difficult problem for a couple. Fortunately, it is also a problem that is relatively easily remedied.

OVERCOMING PREMATURE EJACULATION

There are a few situations so complex that we suggest sex therapy from the outset, rather than trying a self-help program such as the one we will present here. For example, if a man has premature ejaculation as well as erectile problems, it is virtually always advisable for him to get professional help. Similarly, for couples who have built up considerable hostility in sexual and nonsexual matters, marital therapy and/or sex therapy will be necessary to deal not only with the sexual distress but with nonsexual issues of trust, intimacy, communication, and general relationship problem-solving; dealing with the ejaculatory problem in isolation would have very little chance of working.

Many couples are able to cope successfully with reconditioning the man's ejaculatory response on their own so that sex becomes more relaxed and more fulfilling. The following techniques are drawn from methods we have found reliable in more than three decades of experience. One of the remarkable things about this approach is that it generally leads to significant improvement within a matter of days or weeks, so the couple don't need to commit to a months-long program before seeing any results.

The simplest and most effective way to reprogram the ejaculatory response requires the participation of a partner. (We offer some practical advice for men without partners in the next section of this chapter.) The partner's role is to learn to apply periodically a specific sort of nonstimulatory pressure to the penis from the earliest stages of sexual arousal on; the use of this method, known as the "squeeze technique," interrupts the male's headlong rush toward ejaculation by sending to the internal sex organs a new and unpredictable set of neural signals that seem to take the edge off the build-up of ejaculatory tension. In a fascinating (and unexplained) paradox of nature, most men do not benefit from trying to use the squeeze technique on themselves. In fact, the method seems to work only when the man doesn't try to direct the action or instruct his partner in when and how firmly to squeeze.

STEP 1: LEARNING THE BASICS

The basic squeeze technique, shown in figure 5.2, is done by the female partner putting the pad of her thumb on the frenulum of the penis, while positioning the first and second fingers of her same hand on the opposite side of the penis, with the first finger placed on the head of the penis just above the coronal ridge, and the second finger placed parallel to the first on the

FIGURE 5.2
THE SQUEEZE TECHNIQUE

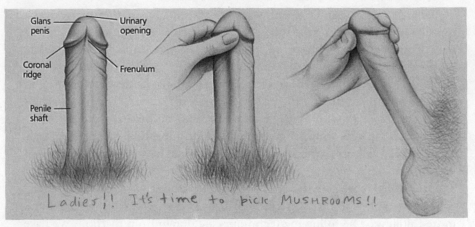

shaft, about a quarter of an inch below the coronal ridge. In this position, the female squeezes the penis with a firm pressure for approximately 4 seconds and then lets go cleanly.

It is important that the woman use the pads of her thumb and fingers for this maneuver, making sure to avoid either pinching the penis or scratching it with her fingernails. It is also important for the woman to be sure to apply pressure only in a front-to-back fashion, not from side to side. (The squeeze should not be done with the woman's fingers wrapped around the penis, as though she were gripping a tennis racket. Only the pads of the thumb and first two fingers should be in contact with the penis when the squeeze is applied.)

The amount of pressure provided by the squeeze should be proportional to the degree of erection that is present. When applying the squeeze to a completely flaccid penis, only a moderate degree of pressure should be used. When the penis is erect, however, a more forceful squeeze can be used, although it is never necessary for the woman to squeeze as hard as she possibly can.

When first experimenting with the use of the squeeze, it can be helpful if the male puts his hand on his partner's hand to show her how hard to squeeze, in case she is worried that a firm squeeze will be uncomfortable for him. Both partners can get a preview of the sensation produced by the penile squeeze by applying the squeeze to their own thumbs. To do this, place the pad of the thumb of one hand horizontally across the pad of the opposite thumb, while putting the pads of the first two fingers of the "squeezing" hand on the opposite side of the thumb being squeezed. (The first finger should be positioned horizontally with the pad directly on the thumbnail, while the second finger should be placed parallel to this just below the thumbnail.) Even with a very firm squeeze applied to the thumb, there is no discomfort—only a sense of pressure. Similarly, assuming that there are no medical problems of the penis or urethra (such as infection, ulceration, or rashes), while the penile squeeze produces a sensation of pressure, it doesn't cause pain or discomfort at all.

It is common to see a minor reduction in the hardness of an erection right after a squeeze is applied. This is not a sign that anything is wrong; in fact, it may actually be an indication that the squeeze is working properly. With continued sex play, the erection will spring back when it's ready to— becoming distracted by watching the size and rigidity of the penis is only apt to present a stumbling block to free-flowing sexual interaction.

STEP 2: USING THE SQUEEZE DURING SEX PLAY

When a couple first decides to begin a program to recondition the male's ejaculatory response, they should agree to forgo the opportunity of having sexual intercourse for about a week as part of the initial "training."[12] Instead, they should plan on spending a period of 30 to 40 minutes daily for several days embarking on the sensate focus exercises described in Chapter 2, incorporating the penile squeeze routinely into this activity. In the first phase of these exercises involving genital touching, in which the man and woman each spend 15 to 20 minutes exploring the other's body separately, the woman should begin by using the squeeze every 2 to 3 minutes when she is touching her partner *regardless of whether the penis is erect or not.* (Waiting for a good, strong erection before applying the squeeze will not work as effectively and may serve to put too much pressure on the male to have an erection "on demand.") It is not necessary to time things exactly; the idea is that it is simply desirable to make regular periodic use of the squeeze about six to nine times during such an exercise.

After completing 15 to 20 minutes of touching and exploration (incorporating regular use of the squeeze), it is perfectly fine to stop without going any further or, if the feeling is there, to permit either or both participants to go on to have orgasms. This can be done either by manual or oral stimulation (with the woman omitting the use of the squeeze), as long as it does *not* include any attempt at having intercourse. It makes no difference whether the man and woman reach orgasm together or separately, or whether one is orgasmic and the other isn't; orgasm is neither a requirement nor a problem for carrying out this program.

Here are a few additional practical pointers to cover situations that might arise in this first phase of reconditioning the male's ejaculatory response.

1. Some men may ejaculate while the woman is applying the squeeze or while there is penile stimulation shortly after a squeeze has been performed. This is completely normal in the early going and will almost certainly improve after three or four sessions of using the squeeze technique.

2. Although the squeeze should be released in a firm, clean manner after the 4 seconds of pressure are completed, there is no need for the woman to avoid touching or stroking the penis between squeezes. In fact, including the penis in the sensate focus touching with a variety of different types of touch—light touches, stroking motions, and other sorts of caress—is an integral part of the entire process. Most women who experiment a little with the squeeze learn to incorporate this seemingly "mechanical" procedure rather seamlessly into their lovemaking so that it just becomes a natural part of their physical interaction.

3. Using the squeeze is never an emergency. Although some men may be worried that their partner isn't squeezing often enough or hard enough, or that they are becoming too aroused too fast, the truth is that the squeeze is most effective when its timing and actual implementation are left completely up to the woman. There may well be some isolated episodes of premature ejaculation before the reconditioning process has taken hold, but this is to be expected. Panicking over such occurrences (or blaming your partner—"Why didn't you squeeze more often?") will be likely only to induce hostility and frustration. Once some familiarity is gained with the use of the squeeze, and the male begins to become more familiar with the signals of sexual arousal his body provides him with, he may occasionally ask for an additional squeeze (or signal his partner nonverbally to implement a squeeze) but this should be a refinement of the method, not the primary orchestration.

4. In the first phases of learning to use the squeeze, it is best to avoid the use of any form of lubrication—massage oils, skin lotions, and so forth—on the penis. Later on, such embellishments may be a source of variety and pleasure, but at the outset they may be counterproductive.

5. The woman doesn't need to use the squeeze in the first 2 seconds on every occasion when she is touching her partner.

6. The squeeze should always be kept as a separate and discrete type of contact, with a definite ending of its own. It is a mistake to extend the

squeeze into a type of caress or fondling of the penis. Instead, once the squeeze is completed, the woman should release the penis completely and move her touch away from the man's genitals for a period of at least 15 to 20 seconds.

STEP 3: USING THE SQUEEZE DURING MUTUAL SEX PLAY

After two to three days of the using the squeeze technique in the manner described in Step 2, the couple can move on to the next phase of sensate focus. This involves touching each other simultaneously rather than separating the touching into a "your turn"/"my turn" pattern. Here too, the ban on sexual intercourse should be strictly maintained no matter how hot and heavy things get. (Knowing that there is no possibility of attempting coitus takes the psychological pressure off the male, creating a better opportunity for the gradual reconditioning of the ejaculatory response to take effect.)

The woman should continue to incorporate the penile squeeze into her touching from the earliest stages on, even if there is no other direct stimulation of the genitals. As before, the squeeze should be used every 2 to 3 minutes, although it can be used slightly more frequently if the woman sees that her partner is getting exceptionally aroused. (There is a point of diminishing return to the use of the squeeze, however. Employing the squeeze more often than once a minute not only produces no further improvement but also may make things seem awfully mechanical and performance-oriented.) After 10 to 15 minutes of mutual stimulation and caressing, which need not always be marked by nonstop sexual action (there is, after all, no 24-second shot clock in sex), either partner or both may indicate that they've had enough and would like to stop, or either or both may let the other know (verbally or nonverbally) that they'd like to go on to orgasm. As long as intercourse isn't attempted, there are no other prohibitions on the forms of sex play that can be used; whatever seems comfortable, interesting, and exciting is perfectly in order. In this phase of the exercise, the woman can dispense with the squeeze completely and the man need not try to "hold back" in any way.

Couples should recognize that the male's sexual arousal may ignite more rapidly during mutual touching than it did in the previous stage of sensate focus, where he was being touched by his partner while he was an intentionally passive participant. This happens because with mutual touching, there are two separate sources of direct stimulation for the male: the sensations he receives from being touched by his partner, and the sensations he experiences while stroking and exploring his partner's body and noticing her responses. In addition, the male is more apt to get his psychological juices flowing from the dual interaction. As a result of these conditions, it is not surprising if the male ejaculates relatively quickly even while the squeeze is being used. Rome wasn't built in a day, and restructuring the male's ejaculatory pattern won't occur overnight, either.

We strongly suggest that couples continue the Step 3 exercise for a minimum of three different sessions. Ideally, these sessions should come within a day or two of each other. Skipping three or more days between sessions (unless it is absolutely unavoidable) makes it more difficult for the male to build up his ejaculatory control because the progress that is linked to the use of the squeeze is partially undermined by the natural male tendency to have greater ejaculatory urgency with longer periods of sexual abstinence. The goal of the Step 3 exercises is to allow the male to develop both physical and psychological comfort with prolonged noncoital sexual stimulation and to recognize that regular use of the squeeze helps to prevent him from rapidly pushing on to the point of ejaculatory inevitability.

STEP 4: GENITAL-TO-GENITAL TOUCHING

Once a couple has mastered the previously outlined steps, the man may begin to be nervous because he realizes that it's about time actually to try having intercourse, which in the past has probably been his major stumbling block. Step 4 is designed to help him ease into a situation of genital contact without actually having full-blown intercourse.

As in the previous step, a couple should engage in mutual touching for a period of 5 to 10 minutes, using the squeeze technique about every 2 minutes. If the man has a firm erection, and both partners are comfortable, the woman should then assume a position astride her partner reaching down to apply the squeeze just as she gets in this position, and then just resting quietly while the penis and vagina are in closer proximity than they've been during the previous days' exercises. After resting for a minute or two (during which time she may be stroking his chest, or kissing him, or engaging in any other nongenital contact that she finds appealing), she should again reach down to squeeze firmly, and then immediately position herself so that the penis is in direct physical contact with the lips of the vagina.

At this juncture, some men who have had very severe premature ejaculation may abruptly lose control. However, more often than not, even men who typically ejaculated with *any* contact between the penis and female genitals may now be surprised to find that they have developed some new staying power. In any event, whether or not the male ejaculates right away or feels a solid degree of confidence in not having his ejaculatory reflexes run amok, is not the point. The point of this exercise is just to allow the male to learn to feel comfortable with direct penis-to-vagina physical contact without putting any performance criteria into place.

If the male ejaculates unexpectedly, the couple needn't separate immediately and bemoan what's happened as though it were a disaster. In fact, it is often helpful to deal with such a situation by continuing to hold one another, keeping a degree of intimacy alive instead of acting as though intimacy and enjoyment are possible only when a man's penis is erect. The man can use the opportunity to provide his wife with additional sexual stimulation (if she's interested), which may allow her to reach an orgasm of her own.

If the male doesn't ejaculate after a few minutes of direct penis-to-external-genital contact, the couple should move out of the female-on-top position and decide whether or not to go on to orgasm by any noncoital form of sexual stimulation. (At this point, of course, the woman can stop using the squeeze for the remainder of the exercise.)

STEP 5: WOMAN-IN-CONTROL INTERCOURSE

The next step is to transfer the use of the squeeze to situations involving sexual intercourse. This is approached through unstructured touching and caressing in which the squeeze is used periodically, as in earlier exercises. After a few minutes of this type of sex play, the woman moves into a position astride her partner, where the couple continues their sexual activity. The woman should use the squeeze three to six times over the next few minutes before attempting insertion. She should be especially certain to use a squeeze just before inserting the penis into the vagina, and once vaginal containment is achieved, she should hold still so that both she and her partner can focus on their physical sensations. The male should also hold off from active thrusting during this process, since the point is to allow him to adjust to the new environment and new set of physical (and psychological) stimuli.

It is important that the woman be the one who is in charge of the entire process. This allows the man to concentrate on his own sensations, without having to fumble about trying to find where to place the penis; more important, since the woman determines the timing and frequency of the squeeze, she is in a better position to be the "instigator" of actual penile penetration. In addition, most men have a better degree of ejaculatory control when the woman is on top than they do in coital positions where the male is on top of the woman. While the exact explanation for this finding isn't clear, it may have to do with the fact that it is easier for the man to relax if he is lying flat on his back.

After about 10 to 15 seconds of quiet intravaginal containment of the penis, the woman should move off the penis, reach down and apply another squeeze, and reinsert the penis in her vagina. This time, after holding still for another brief period, the woman can begin a slow thrusting pattern. If the man feels that ejaculation is approaching, he signals his partner to dismount again and employ the squeeze. However, if a slow thrusting pattern continues for 3 or 4 minutes without any problem (with the woman dismounting and squeezing every minute or two), the couple can then move on to a more vigorous thrusting pattern and the man can be allowed to ejaculate.

Although this technique often works quite well the first time it is tried (after adequate "preconditioning" in the use of the squeeze, as we have outlined above), it is also possible that because of the very different sensations associated with intercourse—as well as the greater anticipation and anxiety that may be involved—the man may ejaculate very quickly the first time or two intercourse is attempted. This is not a "failure" nor is it a sign that progress hasn't been made. Because the reconditioning of the ejaculatory response is an ongoing process, it is quite possible that it may simply take a while for old patterns to be broken and new patterns to fall into place. It is often advisable to repeat this exercise for two or three days in a row. In fact, some couples find that a twice-a-day schedule is both pleasurable and confidence-building.

STEP 6: THE BASILAR SQUEEZE

Although it is important for a couple working to overcome premature ejaculation to continue to use the squeeze technique with some regularity, the need for the woman to interrupt the rhythm and flow of intercourse in order to dismount and squeeze every minute or two is something of a disruption to both parties. Fortunately, there is a solution for this problem. Once reasonable control has been attained using the methods previously described, the couple can begin to use a modified version of the squeeze technique that can be applied while the penis is still contained within the vagina. This is called the basilar squeeze.

In the basilar squeeze, which is shown in figure 5.3, pressure is applied to the base of the penis at the point just above where it joins with the scrotum. Unlike the other form of the squeeze, either partner can apply the basilar squeeze; in fact, it is often easier for the male to reach down and apply the basilar squeeze himself, since he always knows where the base of his penis is when the couple is in the midst of passionate intercourse. In the basilar squeeze, the thumb is placed on the base of the penis and the first two fingers of the same hand are positioned in parallel fashion on the opposite side of the penile shaft. Firm pressure is applied for about 4 seconds and then released; the pressure is always in the front-to-back direction, not from side to side.

FIGURE 5.3
THE BASILAR SQUEEZE

Unlike the squeeze at the coronal ridge, the basilar squeeze can be applied by the man during vaginal containment of the penis. Firm pressure is applied for about four seconds and then released; the pressure should always be from front to back (as shown by the arrows), never from side to side.

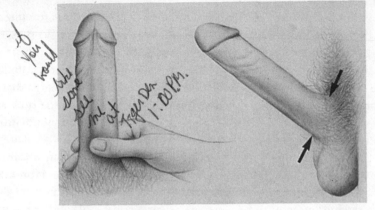

The basilar squeeze should not be used as a replacement for the "regular" squeeze during noncoital stimulation, since it is not quite as effective as the "regular" method. As ejaculatory control improves, however, the gains from continued reconditioning of the ejaculatory response are usually enough to compensate for this reduced efficiency, and in any event the trade-off of slightly lower efficacy in return for more pleasurable uninterrupted sex is almost always a desirable one.

ADDITIONAL CONSIDERATIONS

Maintaining and solidifying the gains made in ejaculatory control by the use of the method outlined above requires additional time and repetition. In general, it is useful to keep up a steady sexual frequency, using the squeeze at least six to eight times per episode at least three times a week. (While we can certainly say that this is a situation where more is usually better, this doesn't mean that a couple needs to turn their sex life into a form of work: daily sex is not mandatory.) If situations crop up where this isn't possible, either as a result of illness or prolonged geographical separation, for example, you should understand that the first few occasions of resuming your sexual interaction may revert to a pattern of less ejaculatory control and may even require a "refresher course" of a few days of repeating the exercises described above.

It's important to remember that every sexual experience won't be perfect.

You should expect that there will be times when ejaculatory control will be quite good and other times when—despite proper use of the squeeze— ejaculation occurs almost instantaneously. If you can take these episodes as minor setbacks with no inherent long-term significance, instead of regarding them as abject failures, you make it much easier for both of you to continue a growth process together.

Many couples will want to experiment with other positions for intercourse as they make progress with the male's ejaculatory control. We suggest that this be postponed for the first few weeks of successfully using the squeeze during intercourse. Here's a hint to keep in mind: many couples who have overcome premature ejaculation using these methods report that a side-by-side position is also one in which it is relatively easy for the male to maintain ejaculatory control. (You can shift into this position with little effort after starting out in the woman-on-top position.)

One other problem may crop up while following the program outlined here. In many cases where there has been a long-standing pattern of premature ejaculation, the woman has had very little opportunity to be sexually responsive during intercourse because of the time constraints and the anxieties involved. Once a man's ejaculatory control shows clear signs of improving, both partners may feel that it's time to pay more attention to the woman's sexual needs. This is completely understandable, and in fact even desirable, so long as the man doesn't take it to be his responsibility to be certain his partner is satisfied. In fact, if the man tries to take on this mission, he may find himself quickly falling back into a pattern of poorer and poorer ejaculatory control.

HOW MEN WITHOUT PARTNERS CAN OVERCOME PREMATURE EJACULATION

Some men with poor ejaculatory control lack the help of a sex partner to recondition their response. Others may be in the difficult position of having a regular sex partner who is unwilling, for a variety of reasons, to participate in the exercises outlined above. For example, some women believe that premature ejaculation is a sign of the male's innate selfishness; understandably, they may be angry and uncooperative in sexual matters unless they first see some indication that the man is trying to deal with "his" problem on his own. These women are often annoyed and frustrated because they have suggested repeatedly to their partner that he enter therapy to get help: they see his reluctance to commit to therapy as further evidence of his selfishness and lack of resolve to deal effectively with the situation.

Whatever the reason, the following approach has proven to be a useful beginning for many individuals with rapid ejaculation and does not absolutely require the cooperation of a partner. As sexual self-confidence (and ejaculatory control) improves, it will make it easier for a man to find and keep a partner who is right for him. This approach stems from a discovery made initially by Dr. James Semans of Duke University in the 1950s which has been developed extensively by the noted sex therapist Dr. Helen Singer Kaplan.[13] However, because this method involves masturbation, it may not be acceptable to everyone.[14]

The self-help exercises that follow are most useful if they are done with some regularity. We suggest that you do these exercises a minimum of four or five times a week, with each session planned to last for 15 to 30 minutes. Plan on a three- to four-week period to implement this reconditioning program most effectively. Since regularity helps reinforce the physiologic learning process, be aware that implementing this program sporadically (once or twice this week, once or twice a week or two later) is unlikely to produce any lasting benefit. In addition, it's advisable to try these exercises when you are not completely tired out at the end of a long day. Be sure that you have enough privacy to be comfortable. If necessary, take the phone off the hook so you won't be interrupted by an unanticipated call from a friend or business associate.

SOLO STEP 1: SELF-EXPLORATION

The first step in this program is an open-ended opportunity for the man to learn in an unpressured, unstructured manner about his own physical sensations. There is no one "right" way to do this, and other than trying to rush through it in a minute or two, or disregarding what you're feeling through your touches, there is no "wrong" way to do it, either.

At a time when you're feeling relaxed, rested, and unhurried, get undressed and lie down on your bed on your back. (Lying down is an important part of this exercise because it helps induce relaxation.) Run your fingertips slowly and lightly across your face, trying to notice differences in textures and surfaces. (Can you notice how the skin on your forehead is smoother than the skin on your chin? Try to see how your eyelids feel compared to your lips.) Dwell on your sensations, both in your fingertips and in your skin, letting yourself become aware of how slight variations in pressure or tempo produce different feelings. If your mind is filled with outside thoughts—worrying about something from the office, or thinking about a chore you have to do—try to refocus your attention to simply noticing the skin sensations you are having.

After a few minutes of touching your face, extend the touching to include your neck, shoulders, and arms. See how lightly you can touch yourself and how touching with just a little more pressure varies the sensations. Concentrate on little details: Does the hair on your arms stand up at all when you touch yourself with a long, light touch? Does a short, circular motion produce a different feeling? How does touching with the tips of your fingers differ from touching with the palm of your hand?

Now extend the range of the touching still further. Let the touching and exploration involve all of your body that you can reach. (Don't jump right to touching the penis: let your touch wander there naturally, as you also use a feathery touch on your chest, your nipples, your abdomen, and your thighs.) In the spirit of exploration, don't make this into a job. See if you can surprise yourself by moving your hands back to an area that you've already touched for a few minutes. (Does it feel any different from the way it did just before? Does touching your face with your right hand while gently caressing your inner thigh with your left hand feel different to you from just touching the same region of your body with both hands at the same time?)

Since the purpose of this exercise is simply self-exploratory, it doesn't make any difference whether you become sexually aroused in the course of the touching. If you find yourself having some genital stirrings, fine; if you don't find yourself becoming excited, that's perfectly fine, too. *If you do become aroused, don't try to make anything happen.* Just continue the touching for a while and see where it takes you.

As you stroke your penis and scrotal area, don't keep your touch focused there exclusively. Every 15 seconds or so (you don't have to count; just estimate roughly), move your touch to another part of your body for a while. Then return to touching in the genital region, seeing how many different types of touch and how many different rhythms or tempos you can use.

Here's a practical pointer for this exercise: don't just touch your penis the way you do when you masturbate (if you masturbate). Try running a finger around the rim at the head of the penis; try stroking the penis lightly on the underside; cup the scrotum in your hand, the way you'd cradle an egg, and just notice how the warmth of your grasp feels. Experiment with using your fingertips alone to touch your penis, and then perhaps change to grip your penis almost as if you were shaking hands. Use a firm touch; use a faster caress; and then suddenly change to a slower, lighter type of touching in which you see what it feels like to move your fingertips just a quarter-inch at a time every 4 or 5 seconds.

Even if you find yourself very sexually aroused with this exercise, we recommend that you not specifically try to masturbate right now. If you need to, you can masturbate later in the day, a while after you've completed this self-exploration, but sexual turn-on is not the point of this: getting in touch with your physical sensations is.

SOLO STEP 2: SELF-STIMULATION

Begin as you did with the previous exercise, getting undressed and lying down, taking 5 to 10 minutes to touch yourself in a general exploratory way. Try to focus on your fingertip sensations at first, letting yourself relax and getting attuned to your touching sensations. Don't just grab for your penis: in fact, it's useful to avoid touching the genital area entirely at first. Gradually, you can let your fingers wander to your genitals, touch for 15 or 20 seconds, and then move elsewhere on your body, repeating this pattern for 4 or 5 minutes.

Once you've begun to feel attuned to your body's sensations, you can reorient your touching to focus primarily in the genital region. At this point, *do not* try to push immediately into "masturbation" mode. That is, if you have a favorite way of stimulating yourself when you masturbate—a certain position, a certain way of grasping your penis, or a particular fantasy you use—leave those alone for right now. This is a time to extend your awareness of your body's sensations in general to include more of a sensory focus on what your penis (and genital region, including the inner parts of your thighs, your scrotal skin, and even the region around your anus) is feeling as you touch in an unhurried, exploratory way. As in the previous exercise, try to notice how small changes in the type or tempo of touch you use feels to you. (Hint: don't confuse the issue by labeling things as "good" or "bad"; this involves too much thinking and not enough feeling. Try to identify feelings in terms of physical characteristics—after all, you're trying to get in better touch with your body.)

Once you've had a chance to really notice the sensations you're experiencing, you can go on to a more deliberately stimulating type of touch. (For now, try to leave your favorite fantasies on the shelf, unless you find them absolutely necessary to get or keep an erection.) While doing this, focus on the actual physical sensations in your genital region. See if you can feel any internal changes (for instance, a sense of pressure building up, a feeling of tightening in your testicles). After a minute or two, deliberately slow the tempo of your touching for about 10 to 15 seconds, and then resume. Do this two or three or four times. Once you're comfortable and aroused, let yourself go on to ejaculate whenever you want to. Focus on noticing your physical sensations as your excitement mounts, especially noticing what it feels like just before you ejaculate. (This "peak" level of arousal just before you feel ejaculation occurring corresponds to the point of ejaculatory inevitability we discussed earlier in this chapter.) Most of all, let yourself enjoy what's happening. Don't worry about the exact timing or how "great" the whole experience was. You don't have to be your own critic; in fact, trying to be a critic right now is only apt to slow down your progress.

SOLO STEP 3: INTRODUCING THE STOP-START METHOD

After repeating the exercise described in Step 2 once or twice over the next few days, you're ready for a slight change in the procedure. This time, after again beginning with a 5- to 10-minute period of generalized body explora- tion and then moving on to genital touching, you're ready to begin using the stop-start method. Once you've gotten a firm erection (briefly using fanta- sies to help yourself get started if you need to), deliberately stop stimulating yourself *completely* for 5 to 10 seconds well before you're at your maximum level of arousal.

If you've stopped the stimulation before you've reached the point of ejaculatory inevitability, your urge to ejaculate will probably recede a bit. If you don't notice less urgency to ejaculate, adjust the "stop" to make it a little longer: 15 to 20 seconds, for example. (If you ejaculated right after you stopped, don't worry: it's just the beginning of a retraining process that will take some time to get accustomed to. What happened was that you got so close to the point of ejaculatory inevitability just before you stopped that your forward momentum carried you inadvertently over the brink.) You may lose part or all of your erection during the stop, although usually this isn't a major problem, since the erection will generally pop up again with just a brief resumption of stroking.

After your brief stop, resume manual stimulation of your penis. Don't try to wait to stop until the last moment before you feel yourself coming. Instead, stop your self-stimulation for 5 to 10 seconds twice more in the next minute or two relatively early in your sexual arousal cycle—in fact, at first, in order to help you get your sexual bearings, you should use a "stop" almost immediately after your erection appears.

Once you've used the stop-start method three or four times during one session, paying particular attention to focusing on both your penile sensa- tions and the cues of your internal sexual arousal, you should go on to an uninterrupted pattern of self-stimulation that lets you ejaculate whenever you feel like it. For right now, don't worry about exactly how long you lasted, because timing yourself is apt to be more a distraction than a help.

Besides, there is no reason to have to impose on yourself a pressure to perform in a particular way; you are still engaged in the early phases of a learning process.

SOLO STEP 4: CONSOLIDATING GAINS WITH THE STOP-START METHOD

Now you are ready to build on the beginnings you have already made by timely repetitive training. We suggest using the stop-start method with the slight modifications we will describe below on a daily or every-other-day basis for a week or two, until you begin to build confidence in identifying your personal pattern of sexual arousal *and* begin to gain a sense of exerting some control over your ejaculatory urgency. (Some people like to proceed relatively slowly here, feeling that it builds their self-confidence; others feel frustrated and foolish if they spend too long in one phase of these exercises. Each person should pick the pacing that seems right to him. Then, if the next step doesn't seem to be clicking into place, he can simply move back one level to allow himself to develop more comfort or control at a particular point in this sequence.)

Reminder: It is especially important to abstain from sexual intercourse during this phase of the program. No matter how tempting it may be to have sex with a partner at this juncture, either "for the fun of it" or to check out how much progress you've made (especially if you feel as if you've come a long way in defeating your premature ejaculating), don't give in to this impulse. At this point, continuity of the reprogramming process is especially important, and sex with a partner will only disrupt this continuity and jeopardize the results of your hard work.

Your self-stimulation exercises can now begin to use the pattern of manual stimulation you find most arousing; that is, if you had a "preferred" method of masturbating in the past, you can begin using that method again. (One exception: if your preferred method involved using any kind of lubrication on your hand or on your penis, don't try that just yet.) The only difference is, you should continue to employ the stop-start technique periodically during your self-stimulation, stopping yourself fairly early in your arousal pattern at first, and then letting your arousal climb to a slightly higher level the next time before stopping again.

As you experiment with letting your arousal mount before you use a stop, you may have some occasions where you don't catch yourself in time and ejaculate unexpectedly. There is nothing at all wrong with such experiences; in our opinion, the most effective type of learning is learning that involves ups and downs, not just a straight line up. After all, if you never, ever had a problem with rapid ejaculation, you wouldn't be following these exercises, would you?

The goal in Step 4 is to get to a point where you can genuinely say that you feel more ejaculatory control and where you can last for 5 to 10 minutes of self-stimulation (including your "stop" times) without ejaculating. (A practical note: If you have attained this goal after just a day or two spent on Step 4, we strongly suggest continuing with this phase for a few more sessions before moving on.)

SOLO STEP 5: THE "WET" STOP-START METHOD

Up to this point, the sexual stimulation you've experienced has deliberately been kept quite different from the physical sensations felt by your penis during sexual intercourse. One key reason for this, of course, is that when the penis is contained inside a lubricated vagina, the slippery sensation that is encountered is especially sensual and provocative for many men.

At this juncture, you are ready to move to the next step of reconditioning your ejaculatory reflex. The way to do this is straightforward: you use the same stop-start conditioning that was described above, except you supplement it by now using a non-alcohol-containing lotion or lubricant such as Vaseline or K-Y Jelly on your hand. This subtle change is an important one because it lets you gradually improve your control under conditions that much more closely simulate the natural feelings of sexual intercourse.[15]

Be sure to employ the "wet" stop-start method at least three or four times over the next week. The goal is to be able to masturbate in this fashion for 3 or 4 minutes before having to stop, but the exact time is less critical than the underlying principle.

SOLO STEP 6: "WET" STOP-START + FANTASY

Now it's time really to challenge yourself. In addition to using lubrication for your self-stimulation, in order to make the situation as sensuous and provocative as possible, you should shift your mental imagery into *highly aroused* mode by merging your favorite sexual fantasy scenes into your exercises. Once again, the objective is to be able to continue vigorous self-stimulation for 3 or 4 minutes while you are actively fantasizing *and* using a lubricant or lotion. Use the stop-start method as needed, recognizing that you may have to stop more frequently at first if your fantasies really provoke an intensely erotic response. (Remember, don't try to play the game of sexual brinksmanship: use the stop-start method well before you reach peak levels of sexual arousal, and pay close attention to the signals your body is registering about just where your arousal level is and how fast it is rising.)

SOLO STEP 7: THE VARIED STIMULATION SOLUTION

The next step involves moving away from exclusive reliance on the stop-start method (which can still be retained as a useful strategy) to developing enhanced ejaculatory control by varying the intensity and tempo of your self-stimulation. Start out as in the previous exercises, using lotion or lubrication for your self-stimulation and incorporating fantasies into your sessions as well. This time, instead of stopping the stimulation completely when you feel yourself getting highly aroused, just adjust the way you are stroking yourself. For example, change the type of touch you're using from a firm, grasping pressure to a looser, lighter touch. Or change from a rapid up-and-down motion to a slower, less demanding stroke. (You may have to experiment with these variations or adjustments to see which changes help you regulate your level of sexual arousal the best.)

The goal of this exercise is to develop comfort with an uninterrupted pattern of stimulatory action. This will more closely mimic the actual conditions you'll encounter in having sex with a partner than using the stop-start alone will, since even if you and your partner actually stop thrusting while having intercourse, holding completely still, there is still a good deal of penile stimulation as a result of the warmth and moisture of the vagina, as well as the sensations the penis receives simply from being contained and enclosed in the vaginal barrel.

Repeat this exercise two or three times to help consolidate the gains you are making and to give yourself a chance to experiment with different "slowing down" variations you can identify.

SOLO STEP 8: TRANSFERRING YOUR GAINS TO SEX WITH A PARTNER

For many men who have sailed through the preceding seven steps with little or no difficulty, the idea of transferring from self-stimulation to sex with a partner seems intimidating. Part of the problem often is that they are continuing to think of themselves as premature ejaculators, instead of recognizing the tremendous strides they have made in altering their underlying sexual responses through the retraining exercises. There are three things that can be done to minimize the anxieties of this situation. First, reorient how you view yourself, putting the emphasis on the new levels of self-awareness and control you have attained. In other words, think positively about yourself, because negative thinking often stacks the deck so that such thoughts become self-fulfilling prophecies. Second, communicate openly and honestly with your partner (or prospective partner) to explain your feelings, your concerns, and the program you have been following. While different women will react in widely different ways to this information, most will be supportive of your efforts and sympathetic to your needs. If you sense that a prospective partner is upset with the thought of helping you (assuming that you haven't described your expectations so it sounds as if you were hiring a therapist or giving her a work assignment), our best advice is—find another partner. (If this isn't a practical solution, you will have to be flexible in accommodating to your partner's needs and preferences, but you should recognize that this may require some innovation and experimentation on your part to solidify your gains in ejaculatory control.) Third, you can minimize your anxieties by proceeding slowly rather than plunging forward at full speed. For instance, you and your partner can agree to have sexual activity with intercourse off limits for a while. In this transition activity, you can show her how you use the manual stop-start stimulation method, and then have a few sessions where *she* provides the manual stimulation. (For the sake of reciprocity, be sure to include her in the sexual give-and-take. At first, it may be easiest for you to bring her to orgasm by manual or oral stimulation, or by using a vibrator, before she begins stimulating you. The negotiations over exactly how to structure such sequences should take her feelings and preferences as well as your needs into account.)

Whatever the exact details of your plan, it is often helpful to have a chance to apply the stop-start method to situations of sexual stimulation that put the penis in physical contact with the outer portion of the female genitals while stopping short of actual intercourse. We suggest using the woman-on-top position for this activity. You can simply lie back and let her play with your erect penis manually at first, while she is sitting over you at about the level of your waist. (If you begin to become very excited in this position, signal her, either verbally or nonverbally, to indicate that you need a brief stop.) Once you become comfortable with your level of sexual arousal, she can move back a bit so that she can rub the penis gently against her pubic hair, against the lips of the vagina, and even let the head of the penis rest for a moment or two right at the opening of the vagina. As these activities are going on, try to focus on the physical sensations you are experiencing, as well as keeping in tune with your level of sexual arousal and the direction in which it is moving. The goal is to stabilize your arousal at a moderately high level instead of letting it rush forward with a degree of acceleration that is too much for you to control. Gradually, you will be able to shift from having to stop to more subtle adjustments in the type or tempo of physical stimulation that is being provided. (For example, if your partner is rubbing the erect penis against her clitoris, and the sensations are becoming too hot and heavy for you, put a hand on her shoulder to signal her to slow down or to just hold still for a few moments.)

Once you and your partner are comfortable with the exercises described above, you can move on to extend the type of genital-to-genital touching you are doing to include short episodes of penile containment. You do not have to think of this as "having intercourse"; instead, you can look at it as an extension of the touching you've already been doing.

When you and your partner are both comfortable in the woman-on-top position, at a time when you feel moderate arousal but not any sense of supercharged, about-to-explode sexual tension, your partner can hold your erect penis at about a 45-degree angle to your body and can slide back, very gently and slowly, so that the head of the penis is contained inside the vagina. You should both hold this position for 15 or 20 seconds without moving. Instead of following your natural inclination to begin thrusting immediately, concentrate on noticing what your penis is feeling, while leaving your arms limp and inactive at your sides. This is not a time to be thinking about what's going to happen next, or to be using fantasies; it's a time to focus on the sensations you are experiencing, and to enjoy them for how they feel. (If you ejaculate immediately after insertion, it's no big deal. It's just a temporary setback as you're adjusting to a new situation. With practice, as you defuse the anxiety of trying this "new" activity, you'll become more comfortable and less likely to relapse toward your old patterns.) Sometimes the man will begin to lose his erection in this situation, which is perfectly okay. If this happens to you, your partner can easily slide off the penis and can reach down and provide enough manual stimulation to bring your erection back into action. (Sometimes a change in position is advisable here for a few minutes before attempting the same maneuver—inserting the head of the penis in the vagina—again.)

Once you've been able to keep the head of the penis in the vagina for 20 to 30 seconds without moving, your partner can slip back onto the penis a little further, so that half or more of the penis is inside her vagina. Again, hold this position quietly, with neither of you thrusting, for a period of 20 to 30 seconds. (Don't try to look at your wristwatch to get these time intervals exactly right—estimating them is perfectly fine.)

Now you can put your hands on your partner's hips and gently nudge her into a slow, shallow thrusting pattern. As you feel your level of sexual arousal rising, signal her to stop (or slow down) for 5 seconds or so. Try to do this *before* you get almost to the point of ejaculatory inevitability. The point here is to extend your range of control by initially being conservative and slowing things down earlier in your arousal pattern than may be necessary. As you gain confidence and experience, you will be able to adjust the timing and tempo in each individual situation to best suit your needs.

The stop-start (or "slow down") process doesn't need to go on indefinitely. In fact, the first time you've tried penile containment, if you've lasted for 3 or 4 minutes without ejaculating, it's fine to pull out all the stops and let yourself go. (If you come before your partner does, be sure to attend to her needs afterward, if she wants to be orgasmic, too.)

It often takes five to ten practice sessions in this transitional period for the man to gain enough comfort with his ejaculatory control to be consistently able to last for 5 minutes or more of vaginal containment and gentle thrusting. Once this point is reached, the man can become a more active participant in the thrusting, instead of lying there relatively passively, letting the woman do most of the work.

As the man gains self-confidence in his new degree of ejaculatory control, there often is an additional benefit that occurs. His self-confidence seems to shrink his personal anxieties about the situation, so that his successes become self-reinforcing. With less anxiety, he is apt to become a more spontaneous (and less self-centered) lover, a change that he may not notice until well after his partner does. In addition, with time, a couple can experiment with other sexual positions, since the woman-on-top position isn't absolutely required for good ejaculatory control. Many couples find a side-by-side position especially satisfying, since it gives each person a great deal of freedom of movement, and neither one is bearing the weight of the other.

As with retraining the ejaculatory reflex using the squeeze technique, there will always be a tendency for the male to revert to a pattern of rapid ejaculation in stressful circumstances (e.g., with a new partner) or after a prolonged period of sexual abstinence. He can minimize this problem by consistently using the self-stimulation exercises when a partner isn't available to him, for whatever the reason. Furthermore, he can learn early in a new relationship to be alert to the need to use the stop-start method with a partner more frequently.

IF THESE METHODS DON'T WORK

We have found that the vast majority of men who follow these guidelines with some diligence (sticking with the program and using it with regularity) are successful in overcoming their poor ejaculatory control. However, about 15 percent of men with rapid ejaculation aren't satisfied with the results they obtain from these self-help programs. In our experience, virtually all of these men can be helped by brief, time-limited sex therapy.

There are many different reasons why a self-help program may not work ideally. One common problem is that these exercises are designed for men who aren't having difficulty getting or keeping erections. For men who have erectile problems in most of their sexual encounters, along with rapid ejaculation, sex therapy is the only approach that offers a good chance of reversing the situation.

Similarly, there are couples for whom relationship issues—anger, power struggles, infidelity, alcohol or drug abuse, distrust, or physical abusiveness, to name just a few—are so central that working on a sexual problem in isolation without addressing these other matters is almost certain to be futile. Finally, men who are in need of individual therapy rather than sex therapy per se because of driving, compulsive, perfectionistic personalities may not always be successful using these self-help programs. But with these exceptions, we expect that most men having ejaculatory difficulties can benefit from trying the methods we have described above.

EJACULATORY INCOMPETENCE AND RETARDED EJACULATION

The inability to ejaculate inside the vagina, or ejaculatory incompetence, is the male sexual dysfunction seen least frequently in sex therapy clinics, generally accounting for under 5 percent of cases.[16] In the past 33 years, we have treated 145 men with this condition. Men with ejaculatory incompetence rarely have difficulty obtaining or maintaining erections even for lengthy periods of vigorous coital activity. Furthermore, most men with this condition do not seem to have any problem becoming sexually aroused; instead, the problem lies in the conversion of moderate sexual arousal to levels that are high enough to trigger the ejaculatory reflex.

Most men with ejaculatory incompetence have never been able to ejaculate intravaginally, although about 85 percent are able to ejaculate with solitary masturbation and about half ejaculate with some form of noncoital sex with a partner. (If a man is able to ejaculate normally with masturbation—that is, if it doesn't take lengthy periods of time and great effort—generally it is unlikely that a medical problem is the cause of his sexual difficulty.) Sometimes the man is able to ejaculate only after particularly prolonged, strenuous noncoital stimulation: simultaneous manual and oral stimulation involving intense friction, for example.

In a handful of cases we have seen, there has been a history of normal coital ejaculation that was somehow "lost." In one case, for example, coital ejaculation had occurred normally during late adolescence and premaritally, but had stopped abruptly when the man married at age 22 and his wife went off the pill so they could have a child. Although this man was able to ejaculate with masturbation, he was unable to ejaculate coitally for the next five years. Treatment revealed that the man was intensely ambivalent about starting a family, partly because his father had divorced his mother when he was 5, virtually abandoning him and his two siblings to a life of both economic struggle and considerable emotional emptiness. Once these issues were openly aired, and it was pointed out that his past history was no predictor that he and his wife would divorce, treatment proceeded smoothly. Not only did the man resume normal coital ejaculation, his wife became pregnant shortly thereafter. In another case, a 28-year-old man who had previously experienced no sexual difficulties developed complete ejaculatory incompetence after the accidental death of his oldest son. In a third case, a man had functioned normally until discovering that his wife was having an affair, at which point he abruptly became unable to ejaculate during intercourse.

There have also been instances of situational ejaculatory incompetence. We treated a 29-year-old stockbroker who had ejaculated perfectly normally with prostitutes but never with his wife. He confided in us that sex with his wife tended to be dull and mechanical, whereas he found that sex with a prostitute was far more exciting. As he explained,

> When I'm with a hooker, I feel like I'm in total control; I can do anything I want to her, or make her do anything to me I tell her to. I also get off on the feeling that the whole thing is sleazy and dangerous and not completely proper. In a way, I feel more relaxed and more aroused because I know she's a slut and I'm buying her.

Ejaculatory incompetence needs to be differentiated from retrograde ejaculation, a condition in which ejaculation occurs backward into the bladder rather than in the normal fashion. In retrograde ejaculation, the male experiences orgasm and ejaculation but there is no semen deposited in the vagina. In contrast, with ejaculatory incompetence, men do not experience orgasm or ejaculation during intercourse, although occasionally a man may fake having an orgasm in order to convince his partner that everything is okay. Retrograde ejaculation, which is discussed in more detail on pages 304, 338, 343, and 479, is typically a result of an underlying medical condition: for example, it is a common complication after certain types of prostate surgery; it occurs in about one percent of men with diabetes; and it is sometimes seen in neurological disorders such as multiple sclerosis. The diagnosis of retrograde ejaculation can be confirmed by microscopic identification of sperm in a urine sample produced shortly after ejaculation has occurred.

Ejaculatory incompetence also needs to be differentiated from sexual aversion, which we discussed in Chapter 4. Although the phobic component that is the defining feature in sexual aversion is usually readily apparent in that condition, there are a few men with sexual aversion who are enough able to mask their extreme discomfort in sexual contact with a partner to obtain erections and participate in intercourse by disengaging psychologically from the physical aspect of having sex. These men often insist on a relative "hands off" type of sexual relationship in which coital coupling is undertaken with virtually no foreplay; they may even avoid kissing during sex by telling the wife or partner that kissing distracts them or makes them self-conscious. One additional tip-off that the problem isn't a garden-variety case of ejaculatory incompetence is that such a man may consistently focus on elaborate ritualized fantasies of sex with another partner, such as forced sexual encounters or sex with a young boy or girl, which provides the "fuel" for his sexual arousal in the absence of any real erotic connection with his partner.

The related condition of retarded ejaculation is two to three times more common than ejaculatory incompetence and far more common if you include cases caused by drug or alcohol abuse.[17] In retarded ejaculation, the male is able to ejaculate intravaginally, but only after what seems to him (and his partner) to be an inordinate period of time. Most men with this dysfunction report that it usually takes them at least a half hour of extremely vigorous coital thrusting before they are able to ejaculate; in many cases, intercourse has to last an hour or more before ejaculation finally occurs. While this may sound appealing, the fact is that when such lengthy periods of sexual activity are *required* for orgasm and ejaculation to occur, it becomes frustrating and embarrassing to the man who is involved, and it typically turns sex into work for the couple, virtually eliminating any aspect of fun or enjoyment. Under such circumstances, the female is not only apt to become impatient with her partner (and not totally involved with the sex) but also she may develop physical irritation from the mechanical demands of prolonged coitus, especially if her vaginal lubrication dries up as her involvement diminishes.

Both forms of inhibited ejaculation pose psychological problems as well for the partner, who is apt to see the dysfunction as a personal sign of her own inadequacy. As one wife put it, "If he really found me stimulating, this situation wouldn't exist." In addition to questioning their technical proficiency and attractiveness as lovers, women whose partners have inhibited ejaculation often interpret it to be an indication of a fundamental flaw in the intimacy of their relationship. In cases of ejaculatory incompetence, if reproduction is a goal of the sexual partners, the matter obviously becomes even more complicated. The nature of the dysfunction also leads some women to question their partner's essential masculinity and sexual orientation: they may erroneously guess that the ejaculatory problem is an indication of latent homosexuality, for example.

Ejaculatory incompetence rarely has an organic basis, although congenital absence of the ejaculatory ducts or other anatomic abnormalities of the male genitourinary system (especially disorders of the prostate) should be excluded. Neurologic disorders, including tumors of the spinal cord, multiple sclerosis, Parkinsonism, and neurologic syndromes associated with uremia (chronic renal failure), alcoholism, and severe nutritional deficiencies should also be considered as potential causes, but are infrequently encountered, especially if there are no other neurological signs or symptoms. Various prescription medications can also block ejaculation, but these are more likely to lead to retarded ejaculation than to cause true ejaculatory incompetence. (In older males, these drugs are more likely to induce ejaculatory incompetence, especially at higher doses.) Severe testosterone deficiencies can also block ejaculation, but these conditions are almost always accompanied by erectile difficulties and often by low sexual desire. In a few cases, we have seen prolactin-secreting pituitary tumors cause a relatively selective ejaculatory incompetence, but usually the excessive prolactin levels produced by these tumors impair erections and libido rather than primarily affecting ejaculation.

Retarded ejaculation, as distinguished from ejaculatory incompetence, is more likely to be linked to medical causes, with heavy alcohol or cocaine use, narcotic addiction, and use of other psychoactive drugs, including various tranquilizers and antidepressants, as relatively common causes. Certain drugs used to treat high blood pressure—especially guanethidine, sold under the trade name Ismelin—also cause delayed ejaculation in a substantial number of users.

The psychologist Bernard Apfelbaum of the Berkeley Sex Therapy Group believes that the key element in many cases of ejaculatory incompetence (which he calls retarded ejaculation) is that the man finds only his *own* touch sexually arousing, in effect making him "autosexual" (in the masturbatory, or self-stimulatory, sense), rather than heterosexual or homosexual.[18] This produces a situation in which the male is inhibited (or at least not turned on) by his partner's touching, but manages to become sexually aroused by either touching himself or shutting his partner out of his mind, plowing on to the point of intromission by his autosexual momentum. However, at this point he cannot continue to stimulate himself physically, since the penis is now contained within the vagina; instead, he must become oriented to his partner because he depends on her for vaginal stimulation of his penis.[19] Apfelbaum contends that this sudden shift produces a compulsion in the man to satisfy his partner and a simultaneous detachment from himself that effectively blocks orgasm/ejaculation; as he points out, this shift is quite similar to what happens to many coitally anorgasmic women who seem to block their own feelings and responses by becoming unduly oriented to trying to please their partners. Apfelbaum also makes the interesting observation that the man with ejaculatory incompetence has a relatively insensitive (or numb) penis because even though it is erect, it is actually out of phase with his level of sexual arousal: it is, as Apfelbaum puts it, a "premature" erection in the sense that the penis is ready to proceed with intercourse before its owner is. This line of reasoning leads Apfelbaum to the otherwise unsupported view that ejaculatory incompetence is actually a type of sexual desire disorder.

The psychoanalytic explanation of ejaculatory incompetence is somewhat different: it views the symptom as resulting from unconscious fears of castration or injury from ejaculating during coitus. (Psychoanalytic writers have generally treated ejaculatory incompetence as a type of impotence rather than a distinct disorder, which is one reason why the same dynamics that supposedly cause impotence have been invoked to explain the origins of ejaculatory incompetence.) As Helen Kaplan points out, "reactivation of the patient's infantile fear of being abandoned by the primary love object (the mother), which now takes the form of an unconscious fear that his wife will abandon him if he should 'let go,' is also frequently a source of anxiety."[20] The conflict for the man arises from the fact that he *wants* to participate in the pleasurable act of intercourse (which "proves" his masculinity as well as providing him with stimulation) but unconsciously fears the consequences of going "too far" (i.e., ejaculating in the vagina); his neurotic solution is to engage in intercourse but block himself from the assumed danger associated with intravaginal ejaculation.[21] This "solution" is no real solution: it forces the man into withholding not only his own pleasure but withholding something his partner wants, which almost inevitably creates an emotional barrier for the relationship.

The behavioral view of this poorly understood dysfunction ignores the possibility of unconscious fears and generally views ejaculatory incompetence as a result of anxieties such as performance pressures (and their attendant antierotic response, being a spectator at one's own bedside), guilt resulting from religious prohibitions, and, in a few cases, earlier sexual traumas. Performance pressures may be particularly intense for a man whose partner wishes to become pregnant; here, the problem is not "just" a sexual one but one with ramifications that go far beyond the bedroom. We have found that in many cases of ejaculatory incompetence, conflicts or ambivalence over reproductive goals are major elements in the sexual dysfunction, although the couple may not realize this because at first the man often seems to agree with the woman's desire for achieving a pregnancy, and it is only after establishing considerable trust and insight into the couple's relationship and the man's own values and conflicts that the disparity is uncovered.

In the past 5 years, we have encountered a new category of cases of ejaculatory incompetence in which the predominant psychological conflict over intravaginal ejaculation for the man seemed to be his concerns that he would possibly expose his partner to HIV, the AIDS virus. These fears need not be based on actual knowledge of HIV seropositivity (in which case they would be absolutely appropriate and would, of course, mandate an honest explanation and warning to any sex partner); in fact, they usually were simply worries about the possibility in someone who had never even been tested for HIV, or whose only test was done indirectly (e.g., as part of the process of being a blood donor). The deeper-rooted psychological issue is linked to guilt over past sexual acts, especially sexual contacts with a prostitute or with another man, rather than being a matter of avoiding the transmission of an infection.

The importance of hostility in the genesis of ejaculatory incompetence has also been observed. As Helen Kaplan puts it, "it is often revealed that the man is really 'holding back' psychologically as well as physiologically with his orgasm. Frequently also a great deal of hostility to women is evident of which the man is unaware."[22] We have also found that hostility toward women is a relatively common feature of inhibited ejaculation. Furthermore, in our experience many of the men with this form of sexual dysfunction are high-achieving perfectionists who have a great deal of difficulty expressing their emotions openly or even getting in tune with what their emotions are.

In a small number of cases, either form of inhibited ejaculation may progress to another form of sexual dysfunction. For example, the intense performance pressures that build up as a result of ejaculatory incompetence can lead the man to almost continual spectatoring, in which his savagely critical self-scrutiny virtually wipes out his sexual arousal (and sometimes, his sexual desire), leading to repeated episodes of erectile dysfunction. As a result of continued failures to ejaculate when he wants to, or when he or his partner *thinks* he should, as well as the newly developed difficulty in getting or keeping erections (which many men would view, quite naturally, as a sign that their sexual functioning was deteriorating still further) he is likely to develop escalating fears of performance. Eventually, he learns to sidestep the anguish of this chain of events by avoiding sexual situations with his partner, which are, after all, the proximate source of failure. The result is that what began as a problem of inhibited ejaculation becomes more deeply entrenched in a combination of dysfunctions and impaired sexual desire. The avoidance feels good (and is thus reinforced) because it removes the burdens of anxiety and failure from his shoulders.

We believe that any long-standing problem of ejaculatory inhibition other than cases caused by temporary medical problems requires sex therapy for successful resolution. At the Masters & Johnson Institute, our overall success rate with this category of cases is about 75 percent.

Six

In Search of Potency

There is no sexual problem as devastating to the male ego as persistent difficulty in obtaining or maintaining an erection. The term "impotence," which has long been used to describe this condition, conjures up visions of inadequacy, weakness, and failure, and it is fair to say that these words accurately depict how many men with this condition view themselves. "I feel like I'm not really a man" or "I can't cut it anymore" is a comment that we've heard over and over again from men with erection problems. These troubles often have a pervasive effect on a man's life because they undermine his overall self-confidence. Indeed, many men dealing with long-standing erection problems are overwhelmed with shame, anxiety, and helplessness, and a good number feel that they are the only ones ever to have had this problem. On occasion, an intractable potency problem can cause such despair that it leads to thoughts of suicide or actual suicide attempts.

Isolated episodes of erectile difficulty are completely normal and have affected virtually every man at one time or another. These temporary bouts of failure to get a firm erection (or losing an erection once it's there) are typically a result of fatigue, illness, emotional stress, distraction, having too much liquor (or too much to eat), and similar mundane factors. Just as having an upset stomach may put your whole digestive system on the blink for a day or two, or the flu can play havoc with your normal breathing patterns for a while, brief disruptions of your sexual reflexes occur for perfectly logical reasons and ordinarily have no long-range impact or meaning.

However, millions of men have major difficulties with getting or keeping erections of enough firmness to allow them to have intercourse. In fact, according to some estimates, serious erectile problems may affect more than 10 percent of all adult men.[1] Although men with erectile insufficiency tend to be a silent and invisible minority, in recent years this problem has had considerable publicity as a result of the availability of new treatment methods, a greater number of hospital-based impotence treatment centers, more widespread advertising of products and services for affected men, and an increase in media coverage of this topic.

Men with erectile problems often try to place the blame for their problem on someone or something else. The "someone" who gets blamed is typically the wife or partner. For this reason, many impotent men seek out affairs in an attempt to find a more sexually appealing (or accommodating) partner and to try to discover who's to blame for the problem. Their premise is that if they can function properly with someone else, then it must be their wife's (or partner's) fault. Blaming his partner's looks, or lovemaking techniques, or even her occupational status[2] appeals to a man because it relieves him of a sense of personal responsibility for his condition. Deep inside, of course, he is afraid that his potency problem is indeed a sign of his own inadequacy.

Most of the thousands of men whom we have seen concerned about problems with erections also attribute their sexual difficulties to a physical problem at first. There are several different reasons behind this. First, if it's a physical problem, they believe there will be a higher probability that a pill or injection will cure it quickly and easily. Second, they believe that a physical explanation for their dysfunction automatically relieves them of being seen as psychologically disturbed or as having problems in their relationship. This is a key point to many men, because they are intensely embarrassed for their dilemma to have a psychological cause, as though this would mean that they were on the verge of being crazy or mentally unbalanced. (Even highly educated men are not exempt from this attitude. We have seen mental health professionals in consultation who refused to accept the fact that their problem was psychological and who sought medical treatment elsewhere for their sexual symptoms in order to preserve their pride.) Finally, many men are unwilling (or at least highly reluctant) to enter any sort of psychotherapy program, not just because of the possible stigmatization ("What if my boss finds out?") but also because they do not want to make a commitment to in-depth disclosures to a therapist about themselves and their sex life and active participation in a possibly time-consuming process of treatment.[3] In fact, many sex therapists are aware that a substantial number of men who come in for an initial consultation or evaluation never return for treatment if sex therapy is recommended to them, even if it is described as being a first step that can be followed by other approaches if it doesn't work.

Virtually all men with severe erectile difficulties, no matter what the cause, develop the pattern that we have previously termed performance anxiety or fears of performance.[4] Although this problem may affect women as well as men, and is also seen in other sexual dysfunctions, it is found in its most vivid version in cases of erectile inadequacy. Fears of performance can occur in a variety of situations—for instance, a man may be leery of how he will perform with a new sexual partner, especially on the first occasion on which they are together—but as we use the term here, it describes the end result of a cycle in which previous episodes of losing erections (or not getting them at all) begin to prey on the man's mind and influence his behavior and self-perception.

Here is what typically occurs. Fears of performance from previous failures usually lead to sexual avoidance, loss of self-esteem, and attempts to gain control over the anxiety by working hard to overcome it, in turn causing a loss of sexual spontaneity, making things even worse. As a side effect, problems often crop up in nonsexual aspects of a relationship, since the man's tensions don't make him any easier to get along with. But the most damaging aspect of fears of performance is that they characteristically lead to one or both partners' assuming a spectator role in the sexual interaction, in which they observe and evaluate their own or their partner's sexual response as a means of relieving performance anxieties. As one man put it, "It was like I was watching myself on closed-circuit TV." Here is what we have written previously about the spectator role:

> The almost preordained result of this spectator role is a reduction in the degree of involvement in the sexual activity, brought about by the distraction of watching and assessing the physical response patterns. The loss of intimacy that also occurs in such a situation, which is like having a third party in the bedroom to rate the sexual progress and activity, usually combines with the elements of distraction, heightened expectations, preexisting fears, and lessened personal involvement to dampen the sexual reflexes to the point where natural responsiveness is difficult if not impossible.[5]

In most sexual encounters, psychological and physical arousal occur in tandem, as we have already seen. The relations between these processes involve an interconnected series of reflex responses and brain-based excitation. A remarkable thing about this complex process is its ease of operation. For most people, most of the time, these responses occur automatically, partly triggered by neurophysiological forces and partly by conditioned responses that we all have acquired over our lifetimes—for example, culturally derived notions of what is pleasurable, what is attractive, and what is arousing. We don't usually have to think about these patterns of response since they happen so automatically. In a way, the automatic aspects of sex are similar to other activities we pursue. When eating, for instance, we don't usually have to think about the process of chewing our food, or check to see whether there is an ample flow of saliva, or worry about whether our swallowing mechanisms are intact, or focus on the adequacy of our digestive processes. When walking, we don't ordinarily have to concern ourselves with the matter of coordinating our legs, or stop and think which way we should move our arms to balance ourselves, or question whether we have planted our feet on the ground at an appropriate angle and spaced correctly. Having learned to walk, we walk automatically, letting our reflexes guide us and usually paying no particular attention to how we are accomplishing the rather complicated task we are engaged in.

For men with erectile dysfunction, all of this natural flow of sexual function disappears as a result of the distortions and distractions produced by performance pressures and spectatoring. For this reason, the success of sex therapy for erectile difficulties hinges not on teaching men new stimulative techniques but on helping them find ways to relieve their fears of performance and their obsessive need to self-monitor. If this is done, it is remarkable to see how quickly natural sexual function takes over again.

CAUSES

In the past two decades, a great deal has been learned about the causes of erectile disorders. It is now clear, for example, that physical problems play a much larger role than had previously been thought. Overall, we estimate that close to half of all cases of erectile dysfunction result mainly from organic factors. The most common biomedical conditions causing difficulties with erection are alcohol and drug abuse, which collectively account for some 2.5 million cases; diabetes mellitus, which accounts for another 1.5 to 2 million cases; vascular disease, which is the primary factor in another million cases; and half a million additional cases that occur as a result of unwanted side effects of prescription medications, especially drugs used to treat high blood pressure. We estimate that the remaining categories of organic problems, including a variety of endocrine disorders, neurologic diseases (such as multiple sclerosis, spinal cord injuries, brain tumors, or stroke), circulatory problems, and urologic disorders (including prostate problems and disorders directly affecting the penis), along with a large number of severe chronic illnesses (from cirrhosis to emphysema to collagen vascular diseases to certain types of cancer), collectively cause another one million cases of erectile dysfunction. (Since many of these problems are described extensively in Chapter 12, we will not attempt to discuss them in detail here.) If you add these together, you will see that medical problems alone are responsible at a minimum for 7 million cases of erectile dysfunction in the United States, yet sadly, few of these men get help for their problems.[6]

Organic factors may sometimes provide the initial trigger for erectile problems but then no longer play a role, although the erectile difficulties continue and worsen as the man becomes more and more anxious about his flagging sexual performance. A common example of this is when sexual functioning is temporarily impaired by excessive alcohol consumption, blocking the man's ability to get an erection. If the man becomes alarmed over what he labels as sexual failure, he not only becomes anxious but tries to work at making erections occur in an effort to prove to himself that everything is okay. As we have already discussed, trying to work at sex creates its own set of performance pressures, and the combination of mounting anxiety, spectatoring, and lack of sexual spontaneity add to these pressures over time to create still further problems. By the time the man seeks help for his problem, he may not even remember that what started his downward spiral was drinking too much at a friend's birthday party.

The psychosocial causes of erectile dysfunction include a broad spectrum of individual and relationship problems. For example, erectile difficulties are common in depression; they are also seen (but with lower frequency) in other psychiatric disorders such as posttraumatic stress syndrome, multiple personality disorder, obsessive-compulsive conditions, and with various types of phobias, including sexual aversion.

Occasionally, erectile problems are a result of other sexual dilemmas, as is the case in some men with a paraphilia (sexual deviation) such as pedophilia (preferential sexual attraction to children) or transvestism (sexual arousal that is dependent on cross-dressing). In these cases, the man may be able to function quite adequately in the deviant situation but has trouble getting or maintaining erections with his wife or adult partner unless he either gets her to cooperate in role-playing his desired "special themes" (for example, pretending to be a young child or helping him apply makeup and put on women's lingerie) or uses fantasies of these preferential themes to become aroused. Similarly, in certain phobias related to sexual or reproductive issues—for instance, a phobia about a partner's pregnancy, or about contracting a sexually transmitted disease—loss of erections is not only understandable but actually represents a sort of primitive defense mechanism: if you can't have erections, there is little chance you might inadvertently impregnate your partner.

Developmental factors also have been thought to be of importance. For example, a number of experts have noted that frequently backgrounds of rigid religious orthodoxy are associated with erectile difficulties.[7] In these cases, it is not the religious teachings per se that are the problem, but the often-associated family attitudes that are imparted to the child that sex is dirty and sinful. Childhood or adolescent sexual abuse is another pertinent cause of adult sexual problems, although this factor has been evaluated less systematically among men with sexual dysfunction than among women.[8]

Sometimes erectile difficulties arise in the context of sexual orientation problems. Clearly, a man who feels sexually attracted to other men but refuses to regard himself as homosexual may nevertheless have trouble functioning with a female partner. In addition, many men who recognize their homosexual orientation choose to marry in an attempt to avoid the appearance of living a homosexual life. It is not surprising to find that although they may manage initially to function sexually with women, as time goes by they often develop erectile problems.[9] In some cases, especially in young adults, ambivalence about sexual orientation is a source of considerable emotional anguish. In these situations, a man may not allow himself to consciously recognize his erotic attraction to other men and is puzzled by his lack of response with women. It make require some detailed digging before the source of the man's problem is uncovered and confronted.

Another common problem that leads to erectile difficulties is lack of information about sexual changes that accompany aging in men. Because most men have little or no understanding of how normal aging affects sexual functioning—for example, causing a slower erectile response and lessening the urgency to ejaculate—they may misinterpret these events as evidence that they are somehow becoming sexually dysfunctional. This fear in turn can produce considerable anxiety about performance as well as a sense of sexual defeatism. And if an older man stops having sex regularly because of these concerns, he compounds the odds of creating additional problems for himself. (We discuss in detail in Chapter 16 both the normal physiologic changes that accompany aging and many of the sexual problems that affect older men.)

Other individual factors that may play a role in erectile difficulties include problems with body image, self-esteem, and job-related stress. For example, a man who has been fired from his job, or has been passed over for an important promotion, may feel so threatened that his sexual self-confidence is undermined and he begins questioning his sexual prowess. Gradually (sometimes even suddenly) this process of self-doubt and worrying pushes him into a spectator role in his own bedroom, leading to disastrous results, as we have already discussed. Similarly, a man who is deeply troubled by some aspect of his physical appearance (such as hair loss or weight gain or concern about having a small penis) may question not only his virility but his potential attractiveness to a partner. Such concerns can also lead to erectile problems, although other elements usually contribute to the dysfunction as well.

Relationship problems are especially important factors in many cases of erectile difficulties, although it sometimes can be difficult to determine whether these problems are cause or effect. Certainly those situations in which a man isn't physically attracted to his partner present an obvious cause-effect dynamic. (Often the woman's weight is the key issue for the man, especially if he is in a marriage or other long-term relationship, and the woman has become considerably heavier than she was when they first were attracted to each other.) Another problem that some men face is that their partners may be relatively passive or inept sex partners. In one case we treated, the wife refused to touch her husband's penis (although she was willing to let him mount her and have intercourse), leaving him with a paucity of sexual stimulation, a sense of absolute uninvolvement on her part, and the entire burden of producing his own arousal. In other cases, a partner may permit sexual contact only on the most begrudging terms, making it plain that she has little or no interest in sex as a form of shared intimacy or pleasure.

Perhaps the largest category of relationship problems contributing to or causing impotence consists of couples who have high levels of conflict and anger. No matter what the source of the conflict—jealousy, infidelity, financial pressures, lack of respect for each other, in-law problems, drug abuse, compulsive gambling, or child-rearing conflicts, to name just a few—incessant arguing and bickering in a relationship rarely create a backdrop for good sex. Similarly, it isn't hard to see that if a man feels constantly criticized and put down by his partner, he may develop sexual difficulties. One thing we have learned over the years is that a couple's problems outside the bedroom inevitably carry over into their sexual relationship. The flip side of this process is that erectile problems can create their own tensions in a relationship, so it isn't always a case of conflict causing the sexual dysfunction.

There are also cases of erectile difficulty where the man seems to use a flaccid penis as a way of wielding power over his wife or partner. For instance, in cases where the woman prides herself on her physical attractiveness and having a healthy sexual appetite, the man may scorn her by repeated bouts of sexual failure, hinting that there is something wrong with her because she can't turn him on. (Blaming one's partner is a common defense mechanism for men having any sort of sexual difficulty; it allows the man to deflect responsibility for his problem to someone else.) In some other cases, men intermittently develop problems with erections when they feel that the degree of closeness in their relationship is getting too intense. (This pattern is especially evident in unmarried couples where the question of marriage looms on the horizon.) Although they may not realize what is happening, they are using their penises as weapons to guard against being smothered; as soon as they feel that a more comfortable distance has been created in their relationship, their erections magically return and they are able to have sex again until the relationship once more starts to seem too stifling.

In addition to those situations that seem to result from either physical or psychosocial problems, there are many cases that involve a combination of factors. For instance, a man with some impairment of his pelvic arterial supply may still be capable of functioning sexually, but when psychological stresses are added, they tilt the balance toward erection problems.

Finally, almost all sex therapists recognize that there are a fair number of cases in which the precise cause of a dysfunction is never found. This may be because the triggering conditions occurred so long ago that they are now virtually forgotten or overlooked, or it may be because the problem isn't actually attributable to a single cause. In fact, we have seen many cases where erectile dysfunction seems to be the result of an accumulation of minor factors acting in concert. No single factor ever emerges as the main one, but together they serve to undermine the man's sexual responsivity.

TREATMENTS

Today, there are so many options for the treatment of erectile difficulties that it is hard for the consumer to know where to begin. Since some of these options are widely advertised as "miracle cures," and others are rarely publicized, it isn't always easy to separate the wheat from the chaff.

The first thing to understand about treatment is that no single approach will work for everyone. The second thing to recognize is that there are never any guarantees that a particular treatment will be successful. If someone makes such a guarantee—whether that someone is a sex therapist or physician—we suggest you make a beeline for the exit.

Here is a rundown of the various treatment options available and their overall suitability and effectiveness.

Although just about every man who is dealing with erectile dysfunctions would like to find a pill or shot to restore his potency, there are relatively few situations in which such treatments are successful. If blood tests have documented the presence of a testosterone deficiency, testosterone replacement therapy can indeed work wonders, but meaningful testosterone deficiencies are found in fewer than 5 percent of cases of erectile dysfunction.[10] (In our experience, men with slightly subnormal testosterone levels don't usually benefit from testosterone replacement.)[11] Testosterone replacement is best accomplished by injections of a long-acting form of this hormone. In a typical treatment schedule, injections are given every three to four weeks and have a sustained effect. Testosterone pills are much less reliable because they are absorbed irregularly into the bloodstream. In addition, they sometimes cause liver damage. In any event, giving testosterone to men who do not have testosterone deficiencies doesn't improve the quality of their erections.[12]

A related hormone abnormality *can* be very successfully treated by pills. This is a condition in which a tumor of the pituitary gland causes excessive secretion of prolactin, a hormone that has no known function in men. If a high level of prolactin is identified in a blood test, treatment with a drug called bromocriptine can produce significant improvement in erectile functioning and sexual desire.[13] In cases where the pituitary tumor is large, surgical treatment (or radiation therapy) may be advisable.

Other pills or injections that have been proposed for treating potency problems have little to recommend them. The drug that is most widely marketed to physicians (and thus most widely prescribed, especially by physicians without any special training in sexual medicine, who are often at a loss for what to do when a patient complains of erectile difficulties) is called yohimbine. It is sold under the brand names Dayto Himbin, Yocon, and Yohimex. Despite the fact that its effectiveness has never been demonstrated in a well-designed study, it is widely used . . . although not by specialists in sexual medicine. Schover and Jensen note that the success rate reported for yohimbine is about what you would expect from a sugar pill.[14]

Some physicians believe in giving vitamin shots or supplements (especially vitamins B_{12} and E) for treating erectile difficulties, but there is no evidence at all that such treatments are effective. Likewise, a few physicians still give thyroid hormone to men with erectile difficulties, although unless a blood test has revealed a thyroid deficiency, this treatment is absolutely worthless.

A relatively newer type of injection is being used in the treatment of erection problems, but unlike the injections referred to above, this is not an ordinary shot. Certain types of drugs—including papaverine, phentolamine, prostaglandin E_1, and vasoactive intestinal polypeptide—can cause temporary erections after they are injected directly into the spongy tissue inside the penis.[15] These drugs act to dilate the arteries in the penis, which in turn increases the volume of blood flowing in. The result of the increased hydrostatic pressure is usually a good, firm erection (unless the man has "leaky" veins). Typically, such a drug-induced erection will last for one to two hours.

Although these penile injections have been highly praised by some urologists, who generally teach their patients to inject themselves at home, the truth is that they do not always work, they involve considerable risks, and they are not as painless to administer as they are claimed to be. For instance, one prominent U.C.L.A. urologist notes that 25 percent of the patients receiving such injections had no change at all in their erections and 14 percent had slight improvement but were still not able to have intercourse.[16] Another urologist, who specializes in male sexual problems, and his colleague point out: "There

is the possibility of permanent penile scarring as a result of priapism [pro-
longed erections] or of a local reaction from the needle or drug or of infection
or liver damage."[17] Priapism is a particular problem with self-injections,
affecting more than a quarter of men who undergo three months or more of
such treatment. Unless emergency treatment is promptly attained to release
the blood trapped in the penis, serious tissue damage can occur because of
oxygen deprivation.[18] Numerous cases of scarring of the penis at the local
injection sites have already been seen; what is less clear is what long-term
consequences there may be from these injections, including the possible risk
of malignancy.[19] Beyond these concerns, it has become apparent that many
men drop out of self-injection programs after a few months because they find
that injecting themselves is painful or that their erections are not as powerful as
they expected. While we believe that penile injections may be useful for some
men with organic impotence, we are exceptionally skeptical about using such
an invasive technique for treating erectile difficulties that are clearly psychological in origin.

Another innovation in the treatment of erectile difficulties is considerably
safer and simpler than penile injections. Several different vacuum devices
have been invented that allow for mechanically assisted erections. The
method involves putting a plastic cylinder over the penis and then pumping a
lever that pulls the air out, creating a partial vacuum inside. This draws blood
into the penis, producing an erection. Once the penis enlarges, a band is
wrapped tightly around its base to hold the blood in place. Although they are
simple in concept and execution, the major problem with these devices is
that the erections they produce are not as rigid as most men would like. Still,
a semirigid penis is better than nothing, as some men see it, so they are
reasonably happy to use this method. Among the men we have interviewed
who have tried this device, 32 percent said that the erections it produced
were so minimal and flabby that they gave up on it. There is no significant
risk involved, although the band around the base of the penis should not be
kept in place for longer than 20 to 30 minutes. ONE CAUTIONARY NOTE: *it
is DANGEROUS to try to use a vacuum cleaner on your penis. Serious injuries have
been reported from this activity. These vacuum devices are nothing at all like vacuum
cleaners; don't try to experiment and wind up in the hospital for surgical repairs.*

Another whole category of treatments for erectile problems involves various types of vascular surgery to repair blocked blood flow into the penis or
abnormalities of venous drainage that cause blood to leak out of the penis too
rapidly. A number of European centers have reported good to excellent results
with these demanding techniques, but American vascular surgeons have been
much less convinced of their efficacy. Relatively good results have been
obtained when there is blockage of a single artery supplying the penis; in

diffuse arterial disease such as arteriosclerosis (hardening of the arteries), the results tend to be quite poor. If you are considering the possibility of vascular reconstructive surgery, we recommend consulting with a major university medical center rather than having it done at a local community hospital.

One of the signal advances in the treatment of severe erectile difficulties in the past two decades has been the development of a variety of penile implants that permit a man who is otherwise impotent to engage in sexual intercourse. There are a number of different types of devices, from the more complicated inflatable implants that use hydraulics to produce realistic-looking erections, to flexible rods that are implanted within the penis and leave the man with a perpetual state of semierection. All of these devices must be surgically inserted by a urologist, and all of them are subject to the possibility of medical or surgical complications.

Although penile implants can be a great boon to men with otherwise irreversible erectile problems stemming from various medical conditions (such as severe neurological or vascular disease, diabetes, or anatomic deformities), they are not miraculous cures. In fact, what penile implants can accomplish is largely misunderstood by men with these difficulties, many of whom are desperately seeking an instantaneous solution to their sexual problem. For one thing, even the most successful penile implant cannot produce improvement in a man's sexual desire or in the quality of a man's orgasm. In fact, many of the conditions that cause severe erectile dysfunction also interfere with ejaculation, and a penile implant will not restore this to normal. Another problem is that although implants may stiffen the penis enough to allow for mechanical connection, they do nothing to enhance penile sensitivity. Thus, if part of the man's sexual frustration stems from reduced penile sensation, he will not find an implant helpful.

Furthermore, it is sometimes disconcerting for a man who has gone through an expensive and uncomfortable surgical procedure and recuperation in search of an improved sex life to find that his partner is largely turned off by the whole business. In many instances, in fact, couples do not resume sexual contact with much frequency because the wife feels that the man's sexual interest and arousal is purely artificial.

All of this is not to say that penile implants are ineffective. For men who place great personal value on being able to participate in sexual intercourse and who would otherwise be unable to do so, implants can produce considerable psychological satisfaction. They can also restore a significant degree of intimacy to a relationship that may have been sorely strained by long-standing erectile difficulties, and they may provide a major boost to a man's self-esteem. Clearly, penile implants have enhanced the overall quality of life for tens of thousands (perhaps even hundreds of thousands) of men and their partners. However, like any type of surgery they entail a variety of risks, including the possibility that they may have to be removed at some later date. In some series, in fact, complication rates as high as 54 percent with the inflatable devices have been noted.[20] Noninflatable penile implants, which are mechanically simpler, have lower complication rates, but postoperative infections and bleeding still occur in a significant number of cases. Nevertheless, these devices are enthusiastically recommended to many men with potency problems—too enthusiastically, in some cases.[21]

Here's the problem. Penile implant surgery is a big business today. The economic gains to a urologist who does just one such procedure a week are huge. This has created a situation in which, unfortunately, some urologists suggest implant surgery as an option—even the preferred option—to men who might well benefit from a different type of treatment, as well as to men for whom we believe such surgery is completely inappropriate. Furthermore, this surgery has sometimes been improperly recommended on the basis of shaky diagnostic information. For example, recent research shows that one of the most widely used diagnostic screening devices—the Dacomed Snap Gauge—which supposedly measures the rigidity of nighttime, sleep-associated erections, is so inaccurate as to be "uninterpretable."[22]

We do not mean to indict all urologists performing penile implant surgery as money-hungry opportunists. As with any profession, there are highly conscientious individuals working with absolutely impeccable credentials and principles, as well as a number of well-meaning but less conscientious souls who believe they are helping their patients by providing a service that the patient wants. There are also a few urologists who are running what can only be called implant mills. Their hospitals do not always act to weed them out because they produce huge amounts of revenue for the hospital's own coffers.

The final category of treatment options is sex therapy. Although this mode of therapy is not generally appropriate for erectile problems that are primarily medical in origin, it is clearly the treatment of choice for cases stemming from psychosocial factors or for cases of combined causes. (Even in cases where the problem is mainly a physical one, significant gains can be made by brief sex counseling that provides practical pointers for coping with an underlying illness and suggestions for maximizing whatever sexual potential is present.) The advantages of sex therapy are straightforward. It is noninvasive and poses no medical risks; it is ordinarily short-term; and it works in a high percentage of cases. As with virtually all sexual dysfunctions, much better results are obtained in treating a couple instead of just treating the man alone. In our own experience, which is primarily restricted to work with couples, our success rate for treating erectile dysfunction is close to 80 percent.[23] Other sex therapy centers have reported similar success rates.

Most sex therapists see their clients on a once-a-week basis. With this approach, if significant gains have not been made within 3 or 4 months, the odds of success drop substantially. However, in intensive treatment programs such as the one we have conducted at the Masters & Johnson Institute for more than 30 years, we usually see couples every day for a 2-week period, and in many instances therapy actually takes a little less time than this.[24]

OVERCOMING ERECTILE DIFFICULTIES

Here are some specific suggestions that can be followed by almost any man who is contending with difficulty in obtaining or maintaining erections. These steps are applicable whether the problem is of relatively brief duration or of a longer-standing nature.

Since the most effective ways of overcoming erectile difficulties hinge on the availability of a willing and understanding sex partner, it is important for any man undertaking this program to discuss it thoroughly with his partner before they start. Both partners should realize that it's not the woman's job to become a sex therapist in this endeavor, although her participation can be instrumental in making progress from step to step. Clearly, although the woman may not be doing anything "wrong," both partners in a committed relationship are certainly affected by any sort of sexual difficulty, so it is eminently logical for both partners to be involved in its solution. (In the next section, we provide a separate set of exercises for men who do not have a regular sex partner or a partner who is willing to help them.)

STEP 1: DECIDING WHETHER OR NOT TO GET A MEDICAL EVALUATION

We have already indicated that many cases of erectile dysfunction stem from underlying medical problems, many of which may have no other visible signs or symptoms. For this reason, we strongly suggest that a visit to either the primary care physician or a physician specializing in male sexual problems (typically, either a urologist or internist) is in order before going any further. This will provide an opportunity for identifying conditions such as diabetes, testosterone deficiency, vascular problems, prostatic disease, or neurological disorders that may cause erectile dysfunction and that require specific, targeted medical treatment.

However, there are some situations in which a man can be reasonably confident that his problems with erections are not primarily the result of a medical disorder. For example, if a man is able to get good, strong erections when he masturbates, and only has problems when having sex with a partner, this is a clear indication that the underlying difficulty is not organic. The same can be said if a man has no trouble with his erections during sex play with a partner until he tries to insert the penis in the vagina. Other situational problems with erection also make a medical checkup unnecessary. For instance, if a man gets firm erections during extramarital sex but not with his wife, or if he can function sexually with a prostitute but not his regular partner(s), the odds of a medical problem are virtually nil. Likewise, if a man notices that he wakes up with solid erections in the morning at least once or twice a week, this is reasonable evidence that the underlying anatomic, neurologic, circulatory, and hormonal components of sexual functioning are intact, and expensive medical testing is probably unnecessary.

In deciding whether to obtain a medical opinion, you may want to take into account your general state of physical as well as psychological health. If you've been feeling depressed (which is not an unusual reaction to a sexual problem), it is important to find out whether this is a condition requiring specific treatment or just a reflection of your worries and concerns. Likewise, if you're 30 pounds overweight and have little physical stamina, you need to recognize that your physical status may have something to do with your flagging sexual performance.

STEP 1A: DECIDING WHETHER OR NOT TO ENTER SEX THERAPY

Although you may have thought about this possibility fleetingly, you may be understandably reluctant to go this route until you've tried to solve your problem on your own. This is ordinarily perfectly sensible. However, there are a few situations in which self-help programs are unlikely to work well. If any of these apply to you, consultation with a sex therapist or psychotherapist is certainly in order.

- You have absolutely no sex drive; in fact, you hardly ever think about sex at all.
- You would have to characterize your relationship with your partner as angry, bitter, or full of conflict.
- You sometimes ejaculate through a flaccid (soft) penis. ("Sometimes" here means at least 10 percent of the time.)
- You are frequently troubled by feelings of sexual guilt.
- Your partner is very uptight about sex.
- You were sexually abused when you were growing up.
- You (or your partner) feel uncomfortable touching each other's genitals.
- You have obsessive sex urges that trouble you.

If none of these exceptions apply, you can move ahead with the knowledge that you have a very good chance of overcoming your erectile difficulties on your own.

STEP 2: TALKING ABOUT PERFORMANCE PRESSURES

Virtually every man who has problems with erection feels intensely pressured to measure up to how he thinks he should be performing. This usually means that he's expecting erections to pop up almost as soon as he puts himself in a sexual situation in an effortless show of his raw, unbridled sexual prowess. In addition to these self-inflicted performance pressures, there are others that stem from the man's concerns (real and imagined) about his partner's expectations.

Although these performance pressures are usually so pervasive that they can't be eliminated by any simple measures, there are definitely ways to minimize their impact. The first step along this path is to identify and talk with your partner about these tensions, and how they have affected you. This is not a time for recriminations or blame; performance pressures are no one's fault. But they can be defused considerably simply by acknowledging their existence and agreeing that it is okay for you to be having such feelings. They are, after all, a perfectly normal reaction to a frustrating situation.

Giving yourself permission to feel anxious about your performance ultimately helps you by making these pressures acceptable rather than objectionable. In addition, talking openly about your anxieties often helps to cut them down to size.

Here's a helpful hint for your partner. Don't belittle the significance or emotional intensity of a man's sexual performance pressures. These are likely to weigh heavily on his mind. While it's not up to you to solve these problems, lending him a sympathetic ear will let him feel less foolish and less like a failure for having anxieties that tear at the very core of his masculinity.

STEP 3: BASIC SENSATE FOCUS EXERCISES

One of the best ways of breaking up the fear of performance-spectatoring-failure cycle that is typically involved in erectile difficulties is to do something that sounds illogical at first: decide to give up sex absolutely for a while. We don't mean that you should avoid any and all physical contact in the hopes that sooner or later your erections will magically return by themselves. Instead, we will walk you through a carefully structured program for the enhancement of sexual function that we have used successfully in thousands of cases.

The foundation for this approach is the set of sensate focus exercises we described in Chapter 2. If you recall, the beginning premise of these exercises is to allow a couple to focus on their physical sensations without any performance demands whatsoever. This is achieved in part by actually prohibiting, at the outset, any form of sexual activity, including penile stimulation or attempts at masturbation, oral-genital sex, or intercourse. Without having to worry about whether or not you are getting an erection, you can easily step out of the spectator role and simply experience the sensations you are receiving through your fingertips (when you're doing the touching) and through your skin (when your partner is touching you) in a nonevaluative way. If you don't have an erection during these touching sessions, that's perfectly fine and understandable, since there is no reason that you should. However, you may be surprised to find that when you're least expecting it—in fact, when you can't do anything with it (if you are serious about following our advice)—you may actually have an erection or two even though there is absolutely no genital touching going on. If this happens, it is simply a sign that erections are natural reflex responses to sensory stimuli in a situation where you are reasonably relaxed and unpressured. If it doesn't happen at first, that's more than understandable, because it often takes more than one or two touching sessions to overcome habit patterns (and anxieties) that have been formed over many months or years.

At this point, both you and your partner should reread the instructions about sensate focus in Chapter 2 and plan to embark on a 3- to 4-week program, gradually implementing these exercises in your lives. You need to agree at the outset to abstain from sexual activity at any other times while you're following this program and to stick with the rules in terms of not trying to press on to intercourse or orgasm if you find yourselves becoming aroused. You also should be prepared to commit to setting aside private, uninterrupted time for each other quite regularly—45 minutes to an hour at a stretch, at least 3 days a week—in order to give this plan a chance to be effective.

When you utilize the initial sensate focus exercises (general body, nongenital touching), recognize that the man may be somewhat tense and tentative at first. Even though there is no real performance pressure here, since performance is not a goal of the exercise, the man may continue to feel some performance anxiety as a carryover from his past experiences. This is not a major problem. You can deal with it by spending 2 or 3 extra days on nongenital sensate focus until the man gets to the point that he feels more relaxed and more involved in touching for the sake of touching, not for the sake of trying to make something happen.

It would be wise to repeat this first set of sensate focus exercises at least twice before moving on. If you find that you're still more tense than you'd like to be, you can modify this procedure by adding the use of lotion (not as a sexual stimulant but as a facilitator of sensory awareness and different sorts of touches and textures), and continue these exercises for another few sessions.

STEP 4: GENITAL TOUCHING

The next phase of sensate focus exercises preserves the "your turn/my turn" approach of the previous exercises but extends the touching to include exploration of the genitals (as well as the woman's breasts). To some men, this automatically makes it into SEX, in capital letters. You and your partner should talk about this in advance, before beginning any physical contact, because the entire point of this procedure is for it to be a time of sensual and sensory awareness, not to have any sexual goal. In fact, we suggest that you agree on a nonverbal signal you can use if you find yourself starting to become anxious or feeling pressured; this can be a cue to your partner to slow down, to move her touch away from your genital area, and to let you set the pace for a while.

Either one of you can begin this touching exercise; it makes absolutely no difference who starts.[25] A key point to keep in mind is that having erections is *not* the goal of this activity. Before you start, you should reread the instructions about this type of sensate focus in Chapter 2 (see the section on pages 30–35).

At first, you may feel nervous, and you may start checking yourself to see whether your penis is showing any signs of excitement. This won't help your situation at all: you can't will an erection to occur. (If you need proof, just think of how many times in the past you tried to will an erection into existence, only to be disappointed.) In fact, erections often occur when you are thinking about them the least, which creates a sort of paradox for you. It's not easy to stop thinking about erections unless you find something to replace this thought. This is where the process of focusing on your skin-level sensory awareness comes into play. If you can allow yourself really to get involved with the physical sensations registering in your body, which is the whole point of sensate focus, you won't have time for checking on how your penis is doing. Besides, even if you get an erection, it's not something you need to celebrate. It's just a natural reflex of the body that will come and go, fluctuating as all body processes do.

Here are a few practical pointers for this part of the sensate focus exercises. First, while the man is touching the woman, he should studiously avoid trying to "cheat" by rubbing his penis against his partner. For now, the focus of the touching should be on fingertip sensory awareness, and trying to trick your penis into action only shortchanges your opportunities to take in these feelings. It also creates performance pressure for you, and you certainly don't need any of that. Second, when the woman is exploring her partner's body, she should avoid focusing her attention in the genital region. The point is not for her to work at producing an erection; in fact, *she* can't produce an erection at all. But she can facilitate the man's sensual/sexual awareness by adopting a nonpressuring pattern to her sensate focus touching. Even if the man develops a king-size erection while he's being touched, the woman shouldn't focus her touching on this organ exclusively. Third, if you don't get any erections the first few times you try out this procedure, that's perfectly fine. It often takes more than a few days to overcome patterns of impaired sexual arousal that have developed over long periods of time. If necessary, you can modify these touching sessions by incorporating lotion or oil into the touching, as discussed in Chapter 2.

Once you find that you've gotten erections a few times with this phase of the touching, it's time to move on to the next step.

STEP 5: DELIBERATELY LOSING ERECTIONS

Here is another one of those paradoxes we've been suggesting. Now that you've finally seen an erection or two, we're going to tell your partner to deliberately stop touching the penis once an erection occurs and to move her touch elsewhere on your body—for instance, stroking your face, or tracing the muscles in your arms—until your erection completely goes away. The reason behind this maneuver is simple: you need to discover for yourself that it's not a tragedy when an erection peters out because erections come and go pretty much by their own volition. If your partner continues touching you (and extends her touching to include, but not just focus on, the genital area), you will eventually see this for yourself.

It's important not to set yourself up for failure in this exercise by having a preconceived notion of how fast your erection ought to reappear once it has faded away. This sort of expectation is just the thing that produces performance pressure, almost as if you had a stopwatch in hand and were trying to time the speed of your erections. Since this isn't a race, and since it is still part of the sexual reconditioning process you are undergoing, give yourself a break and don't carry such baggage into your touching sessions. As you gain confidence in your ability to handle these situations, you will also be less likely to put performance pressures on yourself, because you'll realize more clearly that they just don't work. And since you are still operating on only a portion of your ordinary sensual input (as you will see shortly), this sort of expectation is unrealistic as well as counterproductive.

There's no need to spend more than a session or two on this step once you've seen that your erections can, if fact, reappear after they've flown the coop.

There is one other point we'd like to make here. Although you may find yourself becoming quite aroused with all of this touching, we suggest that for now you limit the number of times you go on to ejaculate. (Many men find that the more frequently they ejaculate, the lower their sexual appetite tends to be.) The point now is not for you to push for a certain type of sexual performance or release, but to become comfortable with new ways of approaching sensual opportunities.

Step 6: Mutual Touching

Up until this point in the sensate focus process, things have been deliberately kept somewhat artificial by dividing the touching into "turns." Of course, in real life things aren't usually structured this way, and now that you've learned more about your own sensual responses and your erectile patterns, it's time to eliminate this discrepancy. As we mentioned above, this can provide a considerable boost to your sensual input, because up until now you've been registering only half of the possible sensations at one time. That is, when you've been touching your partner, she hasn't been touching you; when she's been stroking or fondling your body, you haven't had the additional sensual input that comes from your fingertip caresses of her.

Now it's time to put the two pieces together. But just as before, the point of this sensate focus procedure is not to produce excitement; it's to produce sensory awareness. This doesn't mean that you should *ignore* sexual feelings you are having—they're not only perfectly acceptable; they can actually be fun. But to focus on your sexual feelings exclusively, to separate them artificially from your sensual feelings, is to run the risk of triggering those old bugaboos, fear of performance and its almost inevitable companion, spectatoring.

The odds are high that even having read the preceding discussion, you'll still have a tendency to revert to old patterns since this mutual touching opportunity seems a lot like what you used to call "having sex." Fortunately, there are some additional strategies you can use if you find this happening. Anytime you begin to feel as though part of you is perched at the side of the bed watching to see exactly how hard your penis is, or whether it is stirring at all, you can combat this reaction by getting lost in your partner's body. We'll explain how to do this in a minute. First, you need to understand that it doesn't help you much to say to yourself, "I won't be a spectator anymore," just as it's practically impossible not to think about food after someone has told you, "Don't think about food for the next five minutes." If someone gave you that directive, you probably couldn't keep from having images of chocolate cake, pizza, and ice cream sundaes marching through your mind. But if someone told you, "Don't think about food," and then gave you a short story to read, or a movie to watch, the odds are that you'd be more successful in keeping those ice cream sundaes out of your mind. Why? Because the human mind is constructed in such a way that negative suggestions are hard to displace unless they are superseded by a more immediate substitute.

In mutual touching, you have a highly effective way available for dealing with negative thoughts. You can literally become so involved with touching and exploring your partner's body that you don't have the time or the inclination to worry about how your penis is doing. This is what we mean when we say "Get lost in your partner's body": if you begin to feel like a spectator, pick out some aspect of her body to focus on closely and let yourself get so fully into touching, stroking, and noticing her body that what you are doing overshadows your spectator tendencies.

While we know that this technique is highly effective, it isn't always perfect. (In fact, it sometimes requires some practice before you can get the knack of getting lost in your partner's body.) If you feel that this isn't working in the sense that you are still having those spectatorish impulses, give your partner a signal, or tell her verbally, and stop what you're both doing, just holding and cuddling with each other until the feeling passes. It may help to talk about it right then, but a lot of times you might prefer just to be quiet and later to discuss what happened. If even stopping the action doesn't cause the spectator feeling to go away, simply end the touching session and try it again on another day.

STEP 7: MUTUAL TOUCHING + FANTASY

Even with the combination of touching and being touched at the same time, you still aren't using all of your sensual cylinders. You can turbocharge your erotic responses by the judicious use of sex fantasy themes, which you can call up in your mind privately and silently either as another antidote to spectatoring or as a means of boosting your turn-on. You can also use fantasy in some other important ways. For instance, if you sometimes feel that being with the same partner is boring, fantasies can let you spice things up considerably. Similarly, if your partner is a little pudgier and older-looking than your ideal lover would be, you can conjure up sex fantasies featuring you with a nubile young scorcher. Using such fantasies isn't cheating on your partner: everyone daydreams, and the chances are that she has sexual fantasies, too. In fact, using fantasies to enhance your arousal can actually make you a better lover.

What do we mean when we talk about the *judicious* use of sex fantasies? In a nutshell, we suggest using fantasies only as an occasional boost, not routinely. Here's why. First, fantasies can help to get things rolling if you're self-conscious about not getting an erection, but they won't be much good if you use them so often that they remind you that you're having erectile difficulties. Second, using fantasies all the time can cause them to lose their allure as a simple matter of satiation. In addition, the constant use of elaborate sex fantasies can actually distract you from a meaningful interpersonal closeness with your partner. The point of using fantasies, then, is not to have a steady stream of hot, steamy movies running through your mind as you and your partner caress each other but to have some reels on reserve in the back of your mind that you can call up virtually instantaneously if you need them.

A word of caution is in order. For now, it isn't advisable to discuss your fantasies with your partner. Doing this might lead to petty jealousies and arguments that might disrupt your progress and even distract you from this program. Keeping your fantasies private is not just judicious, it also helps to preserve their erotic potential. In our experience, many times after a couple has talked about their favorite fantasies together, the fantasies seem to have become less arousing.

STEP 8: NONDEMAND GENITAL CONTACT

By this point, you should be reasonably comfortable in understanding that if you simply give your body a chance to respond to the various sources of sensual input you can experience, nature takes over and erections manage to appear. You may not be able to predict just when this will happen or to will an erection to occur, but with the self-confidence you are gaining you are also getting further and further away from being a prisoner of your own performance pressures and tendencies toward distracting self-monitoring.

In this next phase of sensate focus, you can extend the gains you have made so far into a situation of penile-vaginal contact. Before your anxiety starts mounting at this prospect—since many men seem to see this opportunity as a test of their sexual prowess—let us hasten to add that this isn't the case at all. Since there is no test involved, there's no passing or failing grade, either. Instead of thinking of this as schoolwork, think of it as play. After all, what you've been doing so far with your sensate focus exercises is precisely that: play. And now you have the opportunity to extend the sensual play you have been doing to a new situation. Admittedly, some men find this new situation mildly uncomfortable at first, because things that are unfamiliar often seem uncomfortable. But as you gain familiarity with this type of genital play, the odds are that it will soon begin to seem not just more comfortable but even natural.

The important thing for this exercise is to continue building on the solid foundation of sensual exploration and sensate focus you've already developed. Start touching, then, as you've done before, in a nondemand, inquisitive manner. Let yourself become comfortable with focusing specifically on small details about your partner's body just as she explores your body with her touch. No special tricks are necessary, but as before, if you find yourself beginning to fall into the spectator mode, use one of the several methods we've suggested for changing this pattern. Whether or not you have an erection soon after you start touching is totally unimportant. If you let yourself get involved in the process, an erection will eventually occur.

After starting with some generalized body touching for a few minutes, and then moving gradually into the phase of mutual touching that includes some genital play, your partner should decide when she feels comfortable to move into a position astride you (with you lying flat on your back), so her genital region can be in close physical contact with your penis. Once she's in this position, *whether you have an erection or not*, she can reach down and hold your penis with one hand and gently rub it around the outside of her genital region. Let her handle things, quite literally; don't try to direct the action for her. She may want to see what the penis feels like rubbed directly against her clitoris, or what it feels like just held quietly against the lips of her vagina. Pay attention to the physical sensations you are having, but at the same time, you don't have to lie there like a bump on a log. Since your hands and your lips and tongue are free, you can certainly use this opportunity to continue actively touching her body as she plays with your penis in this position.

Even if you are erect and ready to go further, don't try it right now. The point of this exercise is strictly exploratory; it's a chance for you both to tune in to physical sensations and to become comfortable in a position that comes very close to sexual intercourse. And if you have erections part of the time but find that they occasionally fade away, don't be concerned: this is a natural pattern that is nothing to worry about.

STEP 9: SENSUAL INTERCOURSE AND BEYOND

After you've tried genital play in the female-on-top position a few times, the next step is a slight extension of what you've already been doing. At a time when you have an erection (even a partial one) when your partner is astride you, she can place the head of your penis directly at the opening of her vagina. While she's doing this, she might stroke the shaft of your penis a bit, or rub along the inside of your thighs; you can be fondling her breasts or her hair or noticing the smoothness of the skin on her face. She can also move her vagina up and down against your penis, but you shouldn't try to reciprocate by thrusting your hips forward right now.

Let yourself take in the sensations your penis is feeling without trying to evaluate them in any way and without suddenly trying to make something happen. The point is not to try to push on to further penetration but to acclimate to a new type of contact. Again, what is unfamiliar to you may feel a little uncomfortable at first, and there may be a tendency to lose your erection, especially if you start to watch yourself to see how things are going. If you find this happening, you can try the technique of getting lost in her body as one way of dealing with it; if this doesn't work, you can supplement your involvement by using a fantasy to carry you beyond the point of spectatoring.

If your erection continues while your partner holds your penis at the opening of her vagina, she can now slip the head of the penis just inside the vaginal opening. Does this mean you're starting to have intercourse? The answer is: only if you label it that way. Many men find that it's more comfortable for them to look at this as simply extending the genital play they've already been doing. After all, there's little difference to having the head of the penis right against the vagina and having it wander an inch or so inside. Again, focus on your sensations, trying to be aware of what your entire body is feeling.

There's no reason that you can't provide some manual stimulation to your partner's genital area as she is playing with your penis in this manner. You can either let her show you, with her hand on yours, how to rub her clitoris, or you can simply extend what you've already done on other mutual touching occasions to run your fingers around her vaginal area, stroking the lips of the vagina, or using a light, feathery touch to move across her perineum. But no matter how pleasant this all may be, don't try to rush things. Simply allow yourself to take in the sensations you are feeling.

Your partner needs to be the one to make decisions at this point, since she is certainly aware of how erect you are if she has her hand on the shaft of your penis. If there is a reasonable degree of erection present, she can gently slide back a bit further onto your penis. If your penis isn't erect, she can continue touching to see if the situation changes.

If you try this exercise on a few occasions, you will most likely be quite surprised to discover that suddenly you are actually having intercourse. Once the penis is slipped further into the vagina than just inside the opening, your natural instincts will take over and you can begin a thrusting pattern that feels comfortable for you. If you haven't ejaculated for a while, you may have a tendency to ejaculate fairly quickly in this new situation. This is perfectly normal and is no indication at all that anything is wrong.

You may also find yourself suddenly becoming alarmed if you think, "We're having intercourse now." The reason for this alarm goes back to old anxiety patterns. In a word, you still have concerns that you will lose your erection. Indeed, you *may* lose an erection if you suddenly become anxious, or if some unrecognized anxiety triggers your old spectatoring. So what? Even if you do lose an erection once in a while, you now know that your erections will return on their own. Here again, you should realize that reprogramming old behavior patterns isn't always done overnight, so it may take a little practice to consolidate the gains you have made over the weeks that you've been following this program.

STEP 10: MAINTENANCE AND PREVENTION

Once things are going reasonably well for you—which you will of course have to define according to your own criteria of improvement and satisfaction—it's very easy to become complacent about your new-found gains. Complacency poses a risk that you will start slipping back into some of the very problems that gave you trouble before. For instance, you may start to watch yourself to check on how fast you're developing an erection. You may also stop thinking about sensate focus and instead start thinking about having sex. The more you revert to old patterns, of course, the more you jeopardize the progress you've made and even risk temporary setbacks.

Here are several things to keep in mind in order to maintain the gains you've made and to prevent backsliding.

1. Remember that from time to time all men have episodes of not getting or keeping erections. This will happen to you, too. But the important thing is putting such an occurrence in perspective. What it probably means is that you're tired, or under a lot of stress, or just having a bad day. It can also occur if you forget that alcohol is a depressant to your sexual reflexes and have a few too many glasses of wine at dinner. If you blow this sort of episode out of proportion and allow it to bother you, then it serves as a trigger for the fears of performance that have troubled you before. One way you can defuse the situation is by talking about your worries and feelings with your partner. But the most important thing is not to talk yourself back into a state of feeling impotent.

2. Don't set yourself up for failure by having unrealistic expectations of how you should be able to perform sexually. These expectations create

impossible standards to live up to. If your expectations are realistic, they will include a recognition that there will be times where you just won't feel very aroused (as well as times where you feel you're exploding with passion), times when you temporarily lose an erection (or don't have one to start out with), and times where everything clicks together just as you'd like it to.

3. Keep the basic premises of sensate focus as a prominent part of your sex life. In fact, we strongly suggest that from time to time you and your partner go back to the very first steps in sensate focus for exploratory touching where the breasts and genitals are off limits, which can let you rekindle your facility to focus on tactile sensations with no performance demands or expectations. In fact, any time you feel that you're running into some trouble, sexually speaking, it can be useful to take a short "refresher course" in sensate focus as the immediate antidote.

4. Here's one last point to remember. Sex isn't just something that happens between your legs. The nature of your relationship has a tremendous amount to do with your sexual interaction. Even when things are going smoothly in bed, don't ignore your partner outside the bedroom. Good communication may be the single most effective aphrodisiac there is.

DEALING WITH ERECTION PROBLEMS WITHOUT A REGULAR PARTNER

Much of the advice we have already given for dealing with a wide variety of sexual problems hinges on enlisting the help and willing participation of a partner. In fact, in many cases, a partner's participation is a vital part of the solution, as we explained in the preceding section. However, there are men who don't have a regular sex partner, as well as men whose partners may be physically incapacitated or otherwise unavailable, and men whose partners—for whatever the reason—are simply not willing to cooperate with the self-help program we designed. (In some situations, a man's partner may be so eager to have him enter therapy that she's adamantly opposed to trying to improve things on your own. This is not always as unreasonable as it sounds; as one woman put it, "We'd been trying to conquer his impotence for three years, and we'd tried more different tricks than you could imagine. I finally felt it was time to confront the problem head-on, not try to squirm out of getting professional guidance.") Furthermore, some men have actually lost a regular sex partner who became so frustrated in dealing with his erectile difficulties that she ended the relationship. Last, but not least, is the

Catch-22 of this problem: many single or divorced men avoid getting involved with women precisely because they are embarrassed at the prospect of not performing adequately. Their lack of confidence and fears of performance can become not only self-fulfilling prophecies but also prevent them from developing any sort of intimacy in romantic relations.

No matter what the reason for not having a partner available, there are still a number of steps you can take to begin the process of overcoming your erectile insecurities. In the final analysis, though, whatever gains you make in following these guidelines will need to be solidified in opportunities to have sex with a partner. No matter what you might have heard or read, there is just no treatment available that will guarantee that your erectile difficulties can be cured *before* you try having sex with a woman.

SOLO STEP 2: ASSESSING YOUR A-B-C's

As we have already noted, if erectile difficulties occur for nonmedical reasons, they are usually linked to performance anxiety and lack of self-confidence.[26] But these problems tend to set off a whole cascading chain of attitudes, beliefs, and concerns (your A-B-C's) that may give you some hefty emotional baggage to carry around whenever you get into a sexual (or potentially sexual) situation.

Taking stock of just what attitudes, beliefs, and concerns you have about your sexual functioning is a very good starting point. After all, unless you identify where your problems are, you don't have much chance of solving them.

Use the following checklist to see which of the attitudes, beliefs, and concerns that are common among men with erectile problems are affecting you. (In column A, put a check mark next to any that seem to fit. After going through the whole list, look at the entries you've indicated, and designate your top three items [that is, the ones you experience most strongly] in column B.)

SELF-ASSESSMENT CHECKLIST

		A	B
Attitudes	I rarely feel very sexy.	☐	☐
	I expect in advance that any sexual experience will be a dud.	☐	☐
	I never seem to get rock-hard erections.	☐	☐
	I often feel guilty about sex.	☐	☐
	If I have an erection and lose it, I immediately feel that the party's over.	☐	☐

SELF-ASSESSMENT CHECKLIST (*cont.*)

		A	B
Attitudes (*cont.*)	Men should always take the lead in sex.	☐	☐
	My sex life is driven by my penis; if it's not doing anything, I know I'm not interested in sex.	☐	☐
Beliefs	Normal men get erections at the drop of a bra.	☐	☐
	Unless an erection is steel-hard, it isn't useful for much.	☐	☐
	Women are only satisfied sexually by a pile-driving erection, no matter what they might say.	☐	☐
	You can't be much of a lover if you don't have a good erection to work with.	☐	☐
	Not getting or keeping erections must mean there's something wrong with me.	☐	☐
	If I manage to get a firm erection, I have to rush it into action before it fades away.	☐	☐
	Intercourse is the main event in sex; everything else is just preliminary.		
Concerns	I worry a lot about lack of sexual desire.	☐	☐
	I think many times during the day about not being able to get or keep erections.	☐	☐
	Before I let myself get close to a woman, I worry a lot about how she'll react to my sexual problem.	☐	☐
	I often wonder if I'm having problems now because I masturbated too much in the past.	☐	☐
	I'm afraid I'm over the hill sexually.	☐	☐
	I don't think that any woman is very interested in being romantically involved with an impotent man.	☐	☐
	I feel like a failure in everything I do.	☐	☐

SOLO STEP 2: CHANGING YOUR NEGATIVE A-B-C's

On the basis of the answers you've given, you need to do some preliminary mental preparations before trying any physical techniques for improving your erections. These preparations, which will require about a week's time to implement, involve several key components. First, it's important to change your most negative attitudes and beliefs to more positive ones; as we've mentioned repeatedly, negative thinking about sex tends to become a self-fulfilling prophecy. The inverse is also true: positive thinking tends to lead to positive experiences. So, the object here is to replace negative A-B-C's with positive ones. For example, if you're particularly worried about having enough sexual desire and not getting aroused often enough, spend several minutes three times a day visualizing yourself feeling as horny as you can imagine. (Be quite specific in this self-imaging process. Close your eyes and try to see yourself in every detail. Be sure to focus on how energized and happy you are as you enjoy this feeling.) If you're worried about not having a strong enough erection, spend a few minutes several times a day constructing a mental scenario where you are sexually involved with a new partner and she tells you how delighted she is with your penis, both in terms of how nice it is to feel your erection and how nice it is for her to watch your erection appear. If being a sexual failure is what weighs most heavily on your mind, you can break this negative thought pattern by gradually replacing it with a more positive image. This doesn't mean just daydreaming about a great sexual experience, it means deliberately focusing on a detailed mental image of having great sex and being complimented about it by your partner. (When you repeat your "positive thinking" exercise at several points during the day, don't use the same script over and over again, try for some variety.)

SOLO STEP 3: SELF-EXPLORATION

This exercise, which was described in the last chapter (you should go back now and read over pages 119–21), is meant to provide a relaxed, unstructured opportunity for enhancing your tactile awareness in a totally open-ended situation without a goal of making anything happen. The whole point of the exercise, which you should repeat at least twice over a 3- to 5-day period, is to allow yourself to refocus your attention on your sensations instead of on what's happening to your penis. Whether or not you get any stirrings in your penis doesn't matter; in fact, if you get an erection, just ignore it and let your fingers roam over other parts of your body. The notion here is to let yourself realize that you aren't "wasting" an erection in this situation. Over time, you will see that it's perfectly natural for erections to come and go; sometimes this will happen several times in one sexual encounter. As you make progress in dealing with your problem, erections will appear more regularly than in the past, but right now, it's part of your attitude reconditioning to keep from panicking if you don't grab for any erection you get like a long-lost friend. Contrary to what you may have been feeling, erections are never emergencies.[27]

Even if you find yourself becoming highly aroused by your self-exploration, even if your penis becomes hard as a rock, even if you feel like a sheikh in the midst of his harem, *do not* masturbate or try to reach orgasm. And if you don't find yourself getting aroused or erect, that's perfectly fine: there was absolutely no expectation that this would happen at this juncture.

SOLO STEP 4: IDENTIFYING YOUR HIGHLY CHARGED FANTASIES

Almost all men understand intuitively that if their car stalls because the battery is dead, the thing to do is recharge the battery. But it's amazing how many men who are having sexual problems never think of checking the energy source for their own arousal. In a lot of ways, the energy for many of our sexual feelings comes from our sexual fantasies.[28] One reason for this, of course, is that there is a good chance that men with erectile problems are so preoccupied with their performance anxieties and spectatoring that they forget all about using fantasies during sex. Another reason for neglecting the use of fantasy is that many men with erectile problems begin to think in such a sex-negative way as a result of their repeated failures and frustrations that they stop having sex fantasies at other times, as well. This is partly because they forget that sex can be fun (since it certainly doesn't seem much like fun when you're failing), and partly because they don't want to turn up their desire when there is little or no likelihood that their performance will back it up.

To counteract these tendencies toward sexual inertia, we suggest that you set aside some time to identify several sex fantasy themes that work well for you. Some men with vivid imaginations will be able to do this fairly easily just by turning their attention to this matter. Other men may feel as though they're dealing with a mental block: they don't have a good idea of where to begin. In these cases, it may be helpful to read through a book describing a wide range of sex fantasy scenarios in order to identify which ones are most appealing, or to watch a few X-rated videos to aid your creative efforts. Whichever approach you choose, remember that fantasies are fictional, not factual. Even if your favorite fantasy runs toward scenes of group sex or bondage and domination, it is not a reflection of who you are or what you are looking for.

SOLO STEP 5: SELF-STIMULATION + FANTASIES

Fantasies provide psychological stimulation in a sexual situation to amplify the physical stimulation you are receiving. Now it's time to combine this powerful combination in your own sexual enhancement program.

For anyone dealing with erectile difficulties one of the key benefits in using sex fantasies is that they provide a wonderful way of drawing attention away from monitoring one's physical responses. As we have already noted, this self-monitoring process, or spectatoring, is a definite detriment to the natural flow of sexual feelings and responses, so anything one can do to cut down on watching oneself is apt to be beneficial.

To begin this exercise, for which you should set aside 20 to 30 minutes, get completely undressed and lie down on your bed, taking a few minutes to touch your own body in a self-exploratory way. As you do this—running your fingers along your cheeks, or up and down your neck, or brushing lightly against your nipples—don't think in terms of sex at all. You don't want to put yourself in a position where you're expecting something to happen. As you become comfortable focusing on the feelings coming in through your fingertips and the sensations registering all over your body through your skin, gradually let your touch wander down to your genital region. Be sure to make this a casual sort of touching, not the type of touching you do when you masturbate. At first, don't even touch the penis directly. Start out by stroking lightly along the inside of your thighs, or running your fingertips over the skin of your scrotum. Move your touch elsewhere on your body for a bit, and then return to the genital area again for a little while. After doing this three or four times, allow your exploration to extend to including the penis in your touches. After 15 or 20 seconds of stroking the penis, deliberately move to another spot.

Now that you've established a rhythm to your touching, bring one of your sex fantasies into play. Let your fantasy evolve gradually as a story line in your mind: don't just start thinking about having intercourse with the gorgeous blond you met last week. As your fantasy scene unfolds, return your touching to your penis, but don't focus there exclusively. Even if you find yourself starting to develop an erection, this is not a time to focus on sexual arousal. Instead, it's a time to let your body respond on its own, like a car on cruise-control.

Here is the tough part of this assignment. *Even if you find yourself becoming quite sexually aroused, don't try to push on to make anything happen.* In fact, even if you have the most colossal erection you've seen in years, don't let yourself turn into masturbation mode. This is still a time for exploring your sensations and getting in touch with your feelings.

If you don't have any erections the first time or two you try this exercise, that's perfectly understandable. Many men take a while to acclimate to a new approach to sexual feelings, and old habits can be hard to break. If one of the problems is that you can't help watching yourself to see whether your penis is starting to get hard, understand that you can't ordinarily deal with this by simply saying "Don't think about that anymore." You need to refocus your attention on something else in a positive way. Tuning in more intently to your sex fantasy is the most useful method for handling this problem when it crops up.

If you've tried this exercise on several occasions and still haven't had any genital stirrings, you may get a different result by adding oil or lotion to your touching.

SOLO STEP 6: DELIBERATELY LOSING ERECTIONS

We've already talked about the fact that in real life, as opposed to novels and movies, most men find that their erections wax and wane during a sexual encounter. But men with erectile problems often get alarmed as soon as their erection starts to fade, which makes it more difficult for their sexual arousal to build up in a natural, cumulative manner. To prove to yourself that erections do manage to return after having disappeared for a while, follow the procedures outlined in the preceding step, but this time, as soon as you get an erection, deliberately stop your sex fantasy (like hitting the "pause" button on your VCR) and move your touch completely out of the genital region.

It is not necessary to stop your touching completely, and just because we've asked you to stop your fantasy for a while, you don't need to dredge up distracting thoughts. In fact, after a minute or so, you can switch your fantasy back on (or switch to another favorite fantasy, if you prefer) and again return to touching in your genital area. If possible, repeat this procedure several times. What you'll discover ultimately is that losing an erection is no big deal. Another one will come along in a while to take its place. Knowing this intellectually and feeling it actually happen to you are two different things, so it's a good idea to repeat this exercise on at least two or three occasions.

SOLO STEP 7: TRANSFERRING YOUR GAINS TO SEX WITH A PARTNER

Once you've built up your confidence by knowing that your erections can come and go naturally and by learning how to incorporate sex fantasies as a boost to your arousal, it's appropriate to begin planning for non-solo activities. While we can't tell you whom to pick for this endeavor, we can offer a few words of advice.

First, it will probably be helpful to discuss your previous problems (and the steps you've taken to overcome them) with anyone you're about to have sex with. This isn't just a matter of courtesy; many men in this situation feel more comfortable (and less tense) if they openly acknowledge the fact that they've had some problems and they still have some uncertainties. Furthermore, if the woman you're talking with reacts with acceptance and reassurance, you know that it's sensible to proceed. On the other hand, if she seems unsympathetic or even caustic, it may be a valuable warning. An unsympathetic partner may not be willing to move gradually into a sexual relationship, and the last thing in the world you need at this juncture is a partner who demands instant performance.

Second, see whether your prospective partner will agree to trying some of the procedures outlined in the preceding section, from basic sensate focus exercises to mutual touching with no specific sexual goals in mind. This necessarily entails a willingness on her part to forgo the opportunity of having sexual intercourse for a while. Some women may be delighted to agree, whereas others may be highly skeptical.

Third, don't set yourself up for failure by having negative expectations. You can combat this tendency in several ways. For example, do some positive thinking exercises in which you visualize yourself having untroubled sexual interactions in a relaxed, comfortable atmosphere with an accepting partner. In addition, on the first time or two you have sexual contact with a partner, don't even try to have intercourse. (Letting her in on this decision in advance is advisable, of course.) Try out the nondemand sensate focus exercises described in Chapter 2 and in the preceding section and give yourself a chance to adjust. For example, if you find yourself starting to be a spectator during a mutual touching opportunity, try the technique of getting lost in her body to counteract this problem.

A NOTE ABOUT SEX SURROGATES

We are sometimes asked about the advisability of a single man's using a surrogate partner to overcome erectile difficulties. The idea of a sex surrogate was first introduced to a rather shocked world in 1970, when Masters and Johnson wrote about this in *Human Sexual Inadequacy*. In brief, a surrogate partner is a person who has been trained in the ins and outs of sex therapy and who temporarily becomes the paid partner of a sexually dysfunctional individual without a partner. As we originally conceptualized it, surrogates were *not* meant to be therapists, although they were knowledgeable enough, and experienced enough, to provide the therapist(s) with whom they were working useful feedback about a client's progress. Back in the 1960s and 1970s, using sex surrogates made a lot of sense to us in a wide variety of situations, including some involving physical disabilities and some involving sexual dysfunction that was so severe that it effectively precluded the affected man or woman's finding a partner on his or her own. However, there was no AIDS epidemic going on during those years. Once the AIDS/HIV epidemic started, we came to realize that the use of surrogate partners was no longer defensible or advisable on either ethical or practical grounds. Although it may be true that some sex surrogates are extremely careful about always using condoms during sex and having their clients screened by medical testing, it is also true that condoms are not foolproof and medical testing doesn't always reveal HIV infection. And it is also true, as we pointed out in a previous book, that having multiple sex partners tremendously increases any heterosexual's risk of HIV infection.[29] Since any sex surrogate is by definition not monogamous, we think it would be professionally unconscionable to utilize surrogates in our work any longer, although if a man hires a surrogate on his own and insists on having her come for therapy, we will view the situation a little differently (although we still may decline to work with a surrogate unless we are convinced the man fully understands the risks involved).

WHAT IF THESE PROGRAMS DON'T WORK?

Even if you've quite diligently followed the programs we've outlined above, it is possible that you haven't completely overcome your erectile problems. If you've made what you consider to be a good deal of progress, it may pay to stick with these exercises for another month or two. In this case, go back to the beginning and start completely over again: Sometimes things mesh together better the second time around.

But if you haven't made much progress—or if you're impatient and unwilling to try things on your own any longer—it is advisable to see a sex therapist. As trained professionals, they are often able to provide you with useful insights into the genesis of your problem as well as offer you a number of additional techniques, beyond those we have outlined here, that may be well suited to your situation and needs. In addition, it's one thing to try a do-it-yourself program of sensate focus, but you simply may not have been aware of particular problems or obstacles that cropped up as you were doing these exercises. Sex therapists are also able to provide relationship counseling that may be vital to reversing the sexual difficulties you are facing. And, needless to say, in more complicated cases, where there may be several different categories of problems and conflicts all brewing in the same cauldron, professional guidance is much more likely than a home study course to help you find solutions.

Seven

Female Sexual Dysfunctions

Imagine, for a moment, that men lost interest in sex when they became preoccupied with receding hairlines or bulging waists. Imagine just how much enthusiasm men who reached orgasms only once in every fifteen or twenty sexual encounters would muster at the prospect of erotic interludes with their partners—especially if the women involved had orgasms on every single one of these occasions. ("Was it good for you?" the women would ask in the mellow afterglow of their sexual release; the men would be left either to lie, to risk alienating their partners by telling the truth, or to reconstruct their notion of sexual fulfillment in terms of closeness, passion, or tenderness.) Almost inevitably, we could expect that many of these men would begin faking orgasms in order to convince their partners that they were responsive and enjoying something that they were *expected* to enjoy. Or imagine, if you can, a world in which men were socialized with the notion that they were to save themselves sexually for that special woman; that premarital sexual involvement might sully their reputations; and that marital sex was primarily a duty that they had to perform whether they liked it or not. Finally, think about how men would feel if they were constantly vulnerable to sexual victimization and assault at the hands of women, especially if they were walking outside alone, or wearing provocative clothing, or if they just seemed to be "asking for it."

If these situations seem preposterous, they are all-too-real versions of what sex is like for some women. This perspective makes it easier to understand why a substantial number of women have sexual problems. The fact is, many women experience sex in a very different way than men do, assign it different meanings in their lives, and think about sex differently than men do. While this doesn't mean that women are less interested in sex or get less pleasure from sex than men, it does mean that to think that there is absolute equivalence between the sexes is to miss the realities of how society shapes and limits all of our experiences of sexuality.

WHY THE DIFFERENCES?

All of us, male or female, develop our sexual attitudes from the matrix of the culture in which we are raised. A substantial part of this socialization occurs by a process called role scripting. As the sociologist John Gagnon explains:

> The idea of a script, a device for guiding action and for understanding it, is a metaphor drawn from the theater. Viewing conduct as scripted is a way of organizing our thinking about behavior. Scripts are the plans people may have in their heads for what they are doing and what they are going to do, as well as being devices for remembering what they have done in the past. Scripts justify actions which are in accord with them and cause us to to question those which are not. Scripts specify, like blueprints, the whos, whats, whens, wheres, and whys for given types of activity.[1]

The sexual scripts that girls absorb in contemporary America are quite different from the scripts to which boys are exposed. For example, consider the following scripts that are common in our society.

The *Don't Touch Yourself Down There* script discourages girls from touching their genitals and implies that the genital region is unclean. In adolescence, this script is reinforced by a secondary script about menstruation that says menstruation is a "curse" and that "sanitary" napkins are needed to prevent embarrassing accidents. The implicit message is hands off. In contrast, boys must learn to handle their penises in order to urinate, and thus they discover that their penises also provide sexual pleasure.

The *Nice Girls Don't* script teaches girls that all forms of sex (including masturbation) are dirty, sinful, and potentially dangerous. For reasons not specified in the script, these dirty, sinful acts should be saved for someone you love, when they are automatically transformed into acceptable and appropriate behavior. In contrast, boys learn that sexual experimentation is adventurous and acceptable (the *Boys Will Be Boys* script).

The *Romance Novel* script is a variation of fairy tales with Prince Charmings and happily-ever-after endings. Girls who buy into this script actually believe that the idealistic way sex and relationships are described in romance novels (and how relationship problems are revealed and resolved) are replicable in real life. While there is no precise male counterpart to this script, in preadolescence many boys are exposed to scripts derived from pornographic movies or books. These teach them that females are turned on by aggressive men and that sex is largely a matter of making conquests.

The *Sex Equals Intercourse* script conveys the idea that intercourse is the main event of sex. The term "foreplay," for instance, makes it sound as though anything other than intercourse is a preliminary, less valuable activity. Because intercourse is elevated to such lofty heights, women are led to believe that they should be especially responsive to intercourse itself and that sexual involvement without intercourse doesn't count or calls their sexual responsiveness as women into question. In contrast, the sexual scripts boys absorb are less hierarchical. Virtually *any* form of sexual activity with a member of the opposite sex is a notable and pleasurable achievement.

The *Modern Woman* script says a woman should be able to juggle all areas of her life with ease and pleasure, from home to career, from fun to finances. It implies that intimacy needs and sexual expression are just ordinary items in a busy woman's life that can be addressed easily and naturally, as if they could be checked off in a daily planner used to keep her commitments straight. This script suggests that there must be something wrong with a woman if she can't do it all.

As these scripts show, women really do receive different cultural messages about sexuality than men do. These messages are confusing and contradictory, setting up impossible and often outmoded standards with little attempt to separate the unrealistic or anachronistic from what is relevant to today's world. But there are other factors at work, many of which also involve cultural messages, that contribute to women's sexual difficulties.

From early adolescence on, females are indoctrinated by media messages attesting to the value of being thin as a key to attaining popularity and happiness. Conversely, to be overweight is to be abhorred. As the psychologist April Fallon has noted, "Women are more likely than men to equate self-worth with what they think they look like and what they believe other people think they look like."[2] The inescapable images of the advertising industry combine with a steady stream of photos in fashion magazines, television, movies, and a host of other media sources reaffirming slenderness as the icon and ideal to which women should aspire. Few females are able to ignore this process. Its programming power is so great that by age 18, most females—even those who are at or below ideal body weight—have tried some form of dieting, and most females voice dissatisfaction with their particular body-shapes.

For males, there is no bona fide counterpart to the tyranny of slenderness felt by females, which is primarily a culturally imposed phenomenon.[3] These pressures that equate thinness with attractiveness coincidentally denigrate any deviation from the thin ideal. Labeled as lazy, overindulgent, without motivation, and lacking impulse control, the millions of women who can't (or won't) achieve the ideal lithe body are left feeling personally inadequate. And all too soon they find that dieting to achieve the culturally mandated physique is an illusory and often self-defeating process. Dieting usually produces only transitory successes, even for the most diligent. Even in the ultradramatic cases where rigorous dieting for a year or more leads to profound weight loss for those who were severely overweight (e.g., weight losses of 100 pounds or more), virtually all medical research shows that the chances of successfully maintaining the new weight are quite poor. Those whose diets don't produce dramatic results see themselves as double failures: they feel unattractive and believe themselves to be weak-willed individuals who don't care enough about themselves to control their eating patterns. Those whose diets worked but who then slip back to their former weights feel equally bad, often stating that when they have escaped from their "prison of fat," regaining weight feels as if they've been recaptured and that such weight gain was a morally reprehensible act. Is it any wonder then that anorectic females, caught up in the vicious disorder of self-starvation, will state unequivocally that caloric restriction empowers them by giving them a sense of control? Is it any wonder that the feeling of power is enough to perpetuate self-starvation even when a person's health is severely threatened by this process? Bulimic women, with their binge-purge cycles, and women with other forms of eating disorders also typically report feeling obsessed with issues of control, which they view as a vehicle for personal validation. The flip side of this coin is that most females who are unable to control their eating behavior rigidly and reliably feel intense guilt and anxiety over their self-perceived transgressions. How to expiate the guilt is problematic—some become obsessive about exercise or work, others become so frustrated by their "failures" that they retreat from personal relationships and lapse into a cocoon of self-isolation. As Geneen Roth observes: "We'd rather lose weight than be close to another human being. We'd rather focus on our bodies than love or be loved. It's safer: we know where the pain will come from, we're in control."[4]

A vicious cycle of diet and exercise is established by some women in their attempts to deal with their sexuality/body image problems. The combination of too much exercise with too much dieting causes fatigue and sexual indifference even if weight loss is occurring. Conversely, straying from one's exercise schedule or being inconsistent in dietary vigilance produces feelings of failure and self-loathing, which are negative factors for sexual desire. Thus, the woman who is trying to overcome her self-perceived and self-labeled weight problem must walk a narrowly defined tightrope of "perfect" self-control and compliance, giving her little margin of error for the everyday ups and downs of life. Repeated dieting failures instill a sense of learned helplessness in many females: no matter how successful or articulate a woman may be in other aspects of her life, this intensely private sense of being too heavy is self-defining, deflating both the woman's self-esteem and her sense of her own sexual worth. In fact, the inability to monitor and control the consumption of food becomes a metaphor for the ability to control life in general, so that just as dieting successes can induce a temporary euphoria that is disproportionate to the gains in personal attractiveness or health benefits of the weight loss, diet failures become indelible markers of personal inadequacy. This sense of inadequacy spills over into many aspects of a woman's life, often contributing to depression, repeated bouts of anxiety, and relationship problems as well.

This raises yet another connecting point between eating patterns and sex. As any reader of the "Cathy" cartoon series knows, many women deal with food (at least at times) as a substitute for love and romance. The notion that a piece of chocolate cake can counterbalance loneliness or personal heartache may sound silly at first, but women often turn to food for solace, security, and immediate sensory gratification when under stress or when unhappy. For some women, food is the single most reliable source of pleasure, providing much more powerful and reliable gratification than sex does. In a sense, for these women eating becomes a substitute for masturbation or sex with a partner: it feels good, it is dependable, and it provides both an escape from drab reality and a quick, easy, and inexpensive way of relieving tension and producing a short but powerful spark of contentment. Other women use food as a form of self-medication: eating becomes a way of dealing with stress, and arguments with a husband or lover about eating patterns or weight are much more about issues of control and power than they are about personal health and fitness. It is not unusual to see such men use carefully targeted taunts about their partners' weight as a cunning weapon, a means of manipulating the woman and the relationship.

There is another side to this whole matter. As Richard Stuart and Barbara Jacobson point out:

> Being heavy and feeling unattractive can be as useful for keeping husbands at bay as for avoiding outside attention. Many women, consciously or not, put on weight to avoid marital sex. Weight gain usually serves a double purpose: it diminishes a husband's sexual interest, and it inhibits a woman's own sexual desire.[5]

Female body-image problems are not restricted to concerns about weight, however. The most ubiquitous example of how cultural conditioning imposes its negative sexual messages on females may be the way in which millions of women are tricked into dissatisfaction with the size of their breasts. Again, there is no directly comparable example of this phenomenon for males. Women are so thoroughly brainwashed with the notion that prominent breasts are sexy, desirable, and attractive that breast augmentation surgery has been a booming industry over the past 25 years. Regardless of the fact that many women experience relatively little erotic pleasure from having their breasts stimulated, and that many women who dream about having bigger breasts understand that their bra size may be more ornamental than of any functional significance, women from all walks of life and of virtually all ages share in the notion that "perfect" breasts are highly desirable.[6]

Body-image issues, while important, are not the entire source of the sex differences we are discussing. Here are some additional factors to consider.

The message conveyed by many women's magazines is that women's sexual dissatisfaction usually stems from problems such as an inattentive or inconsiderate partner, a partner who doesn't perform with sexual proficiency, or not being in love. But what has been overlooked is that the root causes of many female sexual problems are not intrinsically sexual. For every woman who is sexually inhibited because of a strict religious upbringing that equated sex with sin or because of sexual abuse suffered during childhood or adolescence, there are many more whose sexual difficulties stem from poor self-esteem, lack of mutuality and nonphysical intimacy in relationships, and from time and energy constraints that come from juggling responsibilities in the workplace and at home.

To understand these complaints better, listen to the voices of two women speaking about their concerns.

Betty W. was a 38-year-old legal secretary whose husband, Bill, complained that their sexual interaction was dull and infrequent. "Maybe that's because I don't like you very much most of the time," Betty said, stunning her mate with the possibility that her sexual apathy was a reflection of a larger nonsexual problem in their marriage.

Sonya F., a 42-year-old interior decorator, pinpoints a different problem with her sexuality:

> My husband and I spend relatively little time together. When he comes home at night, he's too tired out to do the things I want to do, and he buries his head in the newspaper rather than talk. Suddenly when it's bedtime he expects me to be rapturously aroused, and he's annoyed when I'm either not interested, too tired, or a passive participant in what is mainly a quick mechanical exercise of stroking his penis for a minute or two while he grabs my breasts, and spreading my legs as soon as he has a firm erection. I've told him over and over again that

if he only paid more attention to me *out* of bed it might help how I feel when I'm *in* bed, but he doesn't seem to get the connection for more than 15 minutes at a stretch.

Sonya's complaints are characteristic of those voiced by many women who indicate that the men in their lives seem to compartmentalize sex, regarding it as a required activity of living (something more like eating or shaving) rather than an outgrowth of closeness, sharing, and personal exchanges. These men want sex when *their* appetites are aroused and rarely pay attention to their mates' state of sexual desire. On the infrequent occasions when they do recognize the woman's needs—for example, by paying her a compliment or by taking her out to dinner—they often act surprised when she isn't able to turn on her sexual interest or arousal in as facile a manner as they do, which is to say something like flipping a light switch from off to on. The degree to which many men compartmentalize sex, separating its physical side from its emotional context, is perhaps best seen in the example of men who insist that the only way to end a marital fight is to "make up" in bed.

In the remainder of this chapter, we will consider some additional differences between women and men in the ways they experience their sexuality and explore how these differences can create or perpetuate sexual problems.

ORGASM PROBLEMS

While some women are able to have orgasms very easily, millions of women have never experienced orgasm, at least as far as they recognize. Alfred Kinsey and his colleagues reported that 10 percent of the women they surveyed had never had an orgasm.[7] Shere Hite's sample of 1,844 women found that 11.6 percent had never had an orgasm.[8] Seymour Fisher reported that 6 percent of married women had never been orgasmic by any means.[9] Other studies have examined the frequency of orgasm occurring during intercourse. Morton Hunt's survey of sexual behavior found that 53 percent of married women had coital orgasms "all or almost all of the time" and another 21 percent had coital orgasms about three-quarters of the time.[10] Only 7 percent of the white, married women in his study either had no coital orgasms at all or very infrequent coital orgasms. Similarly, in a survey of 100,000 women, *Redbook* found that 63 percent of married women had orgasm all of the time or most of the time with intercourse, and only 7 percent never had coital orgasms.[11]

Although there has been some disagreement in the past as to whether the absence of coital orgasms without concomitant manual clitoral stimulation is an abnormality per se, most sexologists today have concluded that this is not the case.[12] In fact, the American Psychiatric Association's definition of the diagnostic category of "inhibited female orgasm" notes that this pattern usually represents "a normal variation of the female sexual response" and does not justify a diagnosis of a sexual dysfunction unless there is a specific psychological inhibition present.[13] This distinction is often of little solace to a woman who is unhappy about not having orgasms with intercourse, however, even if she is vehemently reassured that she is completely normal.

Certainly, it is easier for most women to be orgasmic during masturbation than during intercourse.[14] The explanation for this difference is partly physiologic and partly psychological. With masturbation, a woman can focus sexual stimulation precisely where she finds it most arousing, making adjustments in the tempo, placement, and intensity of stimulation as required to give herself maximal pleasure. If she chooses, she can use a vibrator to provide an especially intense source of stimulation or take a leisurely approach to allowing her sexual tension to build to peak levels, something that is not always possible with a partner. For most women, masturbation involves some form of stimulation of the clitoris, whereas with intercourse, the clitoris is stimulated only indirectly, primarily by friction from the clitoral hood. As a sex therapist, Lonnie Barbach, notes:

> In reality, the clitoris is the female sex organ. Roughly comparable in sensitivity to the penis, the clitoris serves no other function than that of providing sexual pleasure. The vagina is comparable in sensitivity to the male testicles. Therefore, if instead of sexual intercourse, which directly stimulates the male's most sensitive organ, and only indirectly stimulates the female's most sexually sensitive organ, love-making were practiced by a male rubbing the clitoris with his testicles—then women would be orgasmic and men would be in groups of pre-orgasmic treatment![15]

In contrast, unless a woman's partner is exceptionally attentive to her preferred stimulatory patterns and the subtle adjustments that augment them, there is unlikely to be as much effective physical stimulation provided to the woman during intercourse as she can produce when she masturbates. Furthermore, the interactive nature of sexual intercourse means that a woman's sexual feelings are necessarily dependent, to a certain degree, on her partner's arousal and physical proficiency as a lover. Some women are distracted from attending to their own needs by concerns about their partner (especially if he is insecure in his erectile consistency, or if he ejaculates rapidly). Nevertheless, many women prefer intercourse to masturbation because it gives them additional sensual benefits such as being held and being kissed and also makes them part of a spontaneous give-and-take. Philip Blumstein and Pepper Schwartz call this "shared intimacy" and note that intercourse is a "central ingredient to [heterosexual] women's happiness," whereas for heterosexual men, intercourse is not always the preferred form of sexual activity.[16]

In our laboratory studies that involved physiologic measurement of people's sexual responses, the orgasms women had with masturbation were generally bigger than the orgasms they had during intercourse. However, most women enjoyed their coital orgasms more than their more intense masturbatory orgasms, which is consistent with Blumstein and Schwartz's findings. The subjective pleasure of orgasm consists of more than the intensity of its physical reflexes, just as the pleasure derived from listening to (or playing) a piece of music is more than a reflection of its volume, its length, or its tempo.

These laboratory studies involved women who were proficient in their sexual responses, a fact that undoubtedly played a role in their subjective interpretations and appreciation of their orgasms. Women who are worried about not being able to reach orgasm during sex with a partner (or not being able to have orgasms at all) see things from a different perspective. For example, they may have a more difficult time becoming aroused, and their lack of familiarity with personal cues that they are nearing orgasm may induce anxieties or a sense of awkwardness that itself interferes with sexual satisfaction. Performance anxieties and pressures to perform impede female sexual responsivity in much the same manner that they disrupt male sexual spontaneity, as we will discuss in more detail shortly.

Since orgasm for many females is more elusive or at least less consistent than it is for the vast majority of males, many women have engaged in faking orgasm on one occasion or another. While there may certainly be times when a bit of sexual deception may seem the better part of valor by allowing one's partner to save face or protecting a partner's feelings, problems often arise if doing this becomes commonplace or habitual. While women typically fake orgasms in order to accommodate or please their men (although some lesbians fake orgasms, too), the woman who fakes her sexual responses is usually sabotaging communication rather than doing her partner a favor. Although she may succeed in temporarily massaging his ego by making him feel like a great lover, her pretense convinces him that he's doing everything "just right." As a result, he will probably continue doing what he thinks she enjoys, having no reason to change his style and being unaware of her need for anything different. Furthermore, since he thinks she is being orgasmic, possibilities for discussing ways to improve lovemaking are severely limited: in this case, many men agree with the saying, "If it isn't broken, don't fix it."

CAUSES

The genesis of orgasmic problems in women is less well understood than most other sexual dysfunctions. As with inhibited ejaculation in men (which is the closest functional parallel), relatively few cases of orgasmic dysfunction seen by sex therapists prove to have a medical cause.[17] Conditions that affect the nerve supply to the pelvis (such as multiple sclerosis, spinal cord tumors or trauma, or diabetic neuropathy) and circulatory disorders affecting the pelvic region are capable of causing female sexual dysfunction (impairing arousal as well as orgasm), but these problems are not encountered very often in most sex therapy clinics. Endocrine disorders such as thyroid or adrenal insufficiency or pituitary tumors can certainly impair a woman's sex drive and her orgasmic responsiveness, and these disorders are seen more frequently by clinicians than those previously mentioned, but the most common endocrine disorders causing orgasmic difficulties are diabetes (discussed in Chapter 12) and estrogen deficiency (discussed in Chapter 16). Gynecologic factors such as severe recurrent vaginitis (discussed in Chapter 13) and anatomic abnormalities of the vagina, uterus, or pelvic support structures (including problems resulting from obstetrical trauma) can also lead to orgasmic dysfunction. Other important organic causes of orgasmic dysfunction include alcoholism, narcotic addiction, and severe chronic disease of virtually any variety. In addition, many drugs used in the treatment of hypertension and depression can interfere with normal female sexual response. Barbiturates and tranquilizers may also be a cause of orgasmic dysfunction in women, particularly when used in high doses on a regular basis. (Medical causes are more probable when a woman has previously been easily orgasmic but now finds that she is rarely or never orgasmic. They are especially suspect if there is a temporal relation between a specific physical problem—such as a back injury or starting to use a new medication—and the onset of orgasmic dysfunction.)

Because lack of orgasm can occur either as an isolated problem in a woman who has no difficulty becoming sexually aroused or as a secondary effect of impaired arousal (e.g., from a desire phase or excitement phase disorder), it is important to pinpoint the precise mechanism involved. Unlike the situation in men, where an excitement phase disorder is clearly visible in terms of poor erections, when excitement is impeded in women the problem is often misinterpreted as one of no orgasms. In actuality, inhibited arousal is quite different from being adequately aroused but not having orgasm and is much more likely to be the result of a negative mind set that the woman brings to a sexual situation, including components such as shame, embarrassment, resentment, conflict, guilt, and fear. Furthermore, tension in a relationship or hostility between partners clearly can undermine the unfolding of erotic encounters, blocking a woman's emotional and physical involvement. Similarly, depression often causes a drop in sexual desire that can masquerade as orgasmic dysfunction. In addition, past sexual traumas, from abuse suffered as a child to more recent sexual victimization, are now recognized as important elements in many cases of sexual inhibition. Each of these factors seems less prominent in cases of orgasmic dysfunction, although the line of demarcation is not always sharp, and the two categories are not mutually exclusive.

Women who have never had orgasms (a condition called primary anorgasmia or primary orgasmic dysfunction) are more likely than other women with orgasm problems to suffer from sexual guilt. The origins of this condition are complex, but in a significant number of cases the influence of a severely sex-negative religious upbringing seems implicated. Specifically, we have found that many women with primary orgasmic dysfunction were raised to feel that sex is inherently sinful and bad, that their genitals are dirty, and that masturbation is evil or perverted.[18] Indeed, many sex therapists have noted that negative attitudes about masturbation are especially common among women with primary orgasmic dysfunction, and defusing such beliefs is an important part of the successful treatment of this problem.[19] A closely linked contributor to orgasmic difficulties is that women with negative attitudes toward sex typically feel that sexual fantasies are loathsome or improper and actively fight off such fantasies when they occur. Since sex fantasies can serve a number of constructive purposes in enhancing excitement, defeating self-monitoring anxieties, and spicing up boring sex, blocking such fantasies rather than using them creatively poses another impediment to natural sexual release.

Body-image problems are another common cause of primary orgasmic dysfunction, although these appear to be less of an issue in women who are orgasmic in some forms of sexual activity with a partner. On the other hand, it is not unusual to find that women who have orgasms during solitary masturbation but not with a partner are troubled about issues of personal attractiveness and sexual self-worth, just as they are often conflicted about the relationship itself.

Tensions within a relationship are certainly not unusual and do not always lead to sexual dysfunction. In fact, some couples use sex as a common meeting ground to work out their other difficulties. (Good sex can defuse many tensions, and even mediocre sex can have the same effect, not only because of the physical release it produces but also because of its symbolic meanings.) Still, it is striking to us that in many cases, anorgasmia is a sign that all is not well beneath the surface of a relationship, whether the problem is one of power struggles, poor communication, gender-role conflicts, jealousies, or retribution for real or perceived injustices. It is not hard to imagine why a woman whose mate abuses her physically may have trouble letting herself relax enough sexually that her natural reflexes take over and trigger orgasm. Likewise, it should not be difficult to see why a woman whose husband drinks too much, or spends too much time at the office, or refuses to socialize with her friends, is guarded in sexual terms. Such relationship problems and a host of others—from conflicts over money to disagreements about child-rearing practices—do not exist completely outside the sphere of sexuality, although many men mistakenly think that one has nothing to do with the other. Even when there is no major problem within a relationship, what might seem like a minor issue (such as the man's always being the one to decide when to have sex) can create resentment or frustration that interferes with sexual enjoyment.

One other relationship issue has been postulated as a possible cause of anorgasmia. Seymour Fisher reported that many anorgasmic women have experienced their earlier male love objects, particularly their fathers, as absent or undependable; they also recalled more childhood memories with themes of separation and loss than do women who reached orgasm easily.[20] Fisher took this to mean that anorgasmic women (or women who have infrequent orgasms) may be anxious about losing the people they love, although exactly how this would translate into lack of orgasms was not clear. (This finding has not been substantiated by subsequent studies.)

Despite the existence of various contributing factors to a woman's lack of orgasmic responsiveness, the proximate cause of not having orgasms is remarkably uniform in women who have normal sexual arousal: performance pressures and the anxieties they produce. Regardless of whether these performance pressures are largely self-imposed or result from intense scrutiny or inquisitiveness from the male partner, the predictable result of performance pressures in the face of absent or infrequent orgasms is a pattern of spectatoring (i.e., detailed self-monitoring during sexual activity) which is difficult to overcome and which effectively reduces the spontaneity of a woman's involvement and almost inevitably inhibits her responsiveness. This inhibition in turn leads to the very sexual "failure" that is the source of the performance pressure, reinforcing a self-perpetuating cycle. As with men struggling to overcome such performance anxieties, most women attempt to deal with the problem at first by working harder to overcome these constraints, but turning sex into work (and making it goal-oriented, thus predefining criteria for success or failure) almost always dooms it to be joyless, unspontaneous, and unsatisfactory. Weeks or months later, when it becomes apparent that working at sex isn't effective, attempts to become more relaxed during lovemaking are hampered by the ubiquitous performance anxieties that by this point are often shared by both partners and that may well have been magnified from their original size. Furthermore, repeated unpleasant experiences with sex may also, quite understandably, reduce the woman's initial arousability, even when this was not part of the original problem. The net effect is often that it becomes harder for her to get turned on; once she begins to become aroused, she worries about how sustained her arousal will be; and if her excitement manages to mount high enough that she nears orgasm, she unwittingly blocks her own natural progression by intensifying her self-scrutiny and pushing to make orgasm occur.

As couples struggle with such a constellation of problems, they frequently attempt to change things by paying more deliberate attention to stimulatory techniques and setting up the most romantic, erotic encounters imaginable. While attending to technique may be fine for your golf game, and looking to enhance romance can be rewarding ordinarily, these strategies usually backfire in the face of sexual problems: each intensifies performance pressures. Furthermore, such "solutions" often seem contrived, reducing what little sexual spontaneity still exists and unwittingly placing the anorgasmic woman into the "sick patient's" role, further complicating the situation. Here is how one 33-year-old woman described it to us:

> Tom and I had been going out for 3 years and had finally decided to get married, but it was clear that he was unhappy about the fact that I didn't come when we made love. That I could have orgasms easily when I masturbated was no help, either; he seemed to take this as a blot on his masculinity, and so he determined that we would tackle my problem as soon as possible. At first I went along with him, because it seemed like a reasonable approach to solve a problem that bothered both of us. But as the weeks went by it became clear that candle-lit dinners followed by well-oiled massages followed by sex, or hot tub sessions followed by sex, or watching porn movies while we had sex, or acting out fantasy themes during sex all had the same result: making me feel like I was on display in a glass case in some museum of sexual oddities while the curator lectured to an attentive audience about my "condition."

Performance pressures can also be intensified unintentionally by detailed discussions of lovemaking techniques. While open communications about sexual needs and feelings are helpful in many circumstances, there is a difference between communication that informs and communication that primarily turns into a critique or analysis.

One last theory about what causes orgasmic difficulties in women should be mentioned. Several well-known sex therapists believe that a fundamental fear of losing control over feelings or behavior is often at the core of this problem. According to Helen Kaplan, for example, such fears are "highly prevalent" among anorgasmic women, and "the concomitant defense mechanisms of 'holding back' and over-control are probably crucial in the pathogenesis of the disorder."[21] Lonnie Barbach agrees, noting that the prospect of relinquishing conscious, deliberate control in the throes of orgasm can be quite anxiety-producing for some women, especially those without well-defined ego-boundaries:

> These women often express the fear that they will dissolve or merge with the partner as sexual sensations become intense. . . . If arousal mounts too rapidly, they can be overwhelmed by the strength of their sexual feelings and experience fears of exploding or even having epileptic fits.[22]

We agree that fears of loss of control are sometimes prominent in women with anorgasmia, although we have not found this to be a common problem. In addition to fears of losing consciousness, some anorgasmic women have a fear that they will lose control of their bladders if they become too highly aroused, which provides them with another reason to avoid letting go sexually.

THE MALE'S REACTIONS

Little attention has been paid to the man's reactions to a woman who doesn't have orgasms during sexual activity with him. We have found three basic patterns that are most common: obliviousness, concern, and anger. For a variety of reasons, it is easier for a man to be oblivious to his partner's lack of orgasms than it would be for a woman if the tables were turned. First, even in this supposedly sophisticated era of sexual awareness, some men have no idea (or only the vaguest notion) that women are capable of having orgasms. Second, men who know that women can have orgasms may have no clue as to what a woman's orgasm feels like or looks like. If a woman doesn't complain about the absence of orgasms (and a large number of women who have orgasms infrequently or never at all don't discuss this issue with their lovers), the man may simply assume the woman is orgasmic. Third, some men are completely fooled by a woman who fakes orgasms. These men may even take pride in the degree of passion they ignite in their partners, not realizing that it is simply an act. (Some of these men would not be oblivious to the problem if they were aware of it, but their ignorance is bliss.) Fourth, many men believe that women don't *need* orgasms. While they consider orgasmic release as virtually the whole point of sex for a man, they honestly think that women engage in sex for the warmth, closeness, and cuddling, *not* the passion. Because they have written off women's orgasms as trivial or incidental to women themselves, they are able to ignore the question of whether or not a woman was orgasmic with them. Finally, there are still men whose views of sexuality are throwbacks to Victorian attitudes: to them, women are meant to be the sexual vessels of men, and "good" women (as opposed to "wanton" women) do not have sexual passions.

The men who react to their partners' lack of orgasms (or infrequent orgasms) with concern reflect several different attitudes. Some see themselves as inept or lousy lovers, and to a certain extent, they may be right. For example, the millions of American men who have little or no ejaculatory control during intercourse certainly make it next to impossible for their partners to experience coital orgasm. (While they may have worked out a partial solution to this situation if the woman is able to have orgasm with other forms of stimulation, such as oral sex, this solution simply reminds some of them that they are to blame for the problem.) Other men who have no difficulty with their sexual staying power still label themselves as sexually inadequate if their partners are not regularly orgasmic. They may be under the impression that it is the man's responsibility to make his partner orgasmic; her lack of orgasms translates in his mind into a personal (or at least a performance) deficiency.

Another common male pattern is seeing the issue as a relationship concern, not a "his" or "hers" problem. This is a far more sensible view to adopt; in most instances, assigning blame only contributes to further difficulties rather than resolving them. Since genuine concern over the existence of a sexual problem can be a vehicle that motivates couples toward finding a solution—by seeking appropriate treatment, for example—men with this attitude are more likely to agree to participate in some form of couple therapy, which makes it more likely to overcome the difficulty.

However, there are also men who voice concern over their wives' or partners' lack of orgasms but still view it as "her" problem alone. They may be sympathetic, they may be interested in helping her, and they may even be relatively sensitive in their relationship overall, but they dichotomize the situation so that responsibility (and blame) for the sexual dysfunction is placed squarely on the woman's shoulders. (There is typically considerable rationalizing or intellectualizing supporting this stance; the man's defensiveness is aroused in part by the threat to his concept of his own sexual prowess.) Such men may agree to enter sex therapy or marital therapy, but when they do so they are actually taking their wives or partners to be "fixed." Other men who fall into this category refuse to participate in any type of couple-oriented therapy, sometimes telling the woman that she needs individual therapy to learn to overcome her inhibitions, to improve her self-esteem, or to uncover the psychological blocks to her orgasms. Many of these men inadvertently put a great deal of performance pressure on their partners. They may bring the women books and articles about female sexuality, or rent X-rated movies to help them get in the mood, or turn to a variety of sex toys or massage oils in their efforts to help. Sometimes these actions are appreciated, and sometimes they may even work, but many women feel them as pressure. Another way in which men in the "concerned" category unwittingly exert performance pressures on women having trouble reaching orgasm is by talking too much during sex. "Are you getting close?" is one obvious example, but queries such as "Do you like it when I do that?" are also apt to make the woman feel more like a specimen under the microscope than a participant in spontaneous, free-flowing sexual play.

Men who are angry over their partners' lack of orgasms are usually frustrated because they see this as an insult to their own macho proficiency.* In fact, many of these men have deep-rooted doubts about their masculinity, which they express in a number of ways, including exaggerated social flirting and rigid homophobia. Since anger rarely enhances erotic encounters, it is no surprise that the underlying problem generally becomes more firmly entrenched over time, and other aspects of such a couple's sex life may deteriorate considerably.

DEALING WITH AROUSAL DIFFICULTIES

One inadvertent effect of the sexual revolution has been the notion that sex is a test of adequacy. This view stresses the swiftness and magnitude of physical response while ignoring the feeling side of the sexual equation. It's little wonder, then, that women who don't warm up to sex as quickly as their partners do tend to see themselves as deficient or inhibited. Often, however, the problem lies more in their expectations and mind-sets than in their physical response per se.

Excluding specific physical problems that may impair sexual arousal, perhaps the most remarkable thing about sex is how effortlessly and automatically it can happen if it isn't blocked by extraneous factors. Since so much of sex involves reflex responses over which people have no volitional control, this

---

* The exception is when the man's anger comes from discovering that his partner has been faking orgasms: then it is apt to be anger at the deception, not at the sexual problem per se.

shouldn't come as a big surprise. For this reason, fostering sexual arousal is often mainly a matter of identifying the obstacles that prevent it from happening spontaneously, not concocting a recipe for instant turn-on.

Here are some specific suggestions for women to help identify and deal with common obstacles to sexual arousal.

1. *Don't shut off your erotic potential by locking yourself into negative prophecies.* Sex is as much a state of mind as a set of physical responses. Believing there isn't going to be any pleasure or pizzazz from a sexual experience not only limits your enthusiasm, it even changes your body's receptiveness so that touches, kisses, or other acts of tenderness aren't allowed to register their sensory messages in the brain. Since pleasurable sex depends in part on the cumulative, synergistic effect of such sensual messages—much as a symphony is built of thousands of individual notes and blended harmonies—obstructing your awareness of the building blocks of sensual/sexual feelings, tactile and otherwise, almost inevitably precludes sex from being a positive experience. To avoid such self-fulfilling prophecies and let yourself be receptive to whatever evolves doesn't mean you have to be wildly passionate or precisely in the mood: it's a matter of being a participant, rather than a self-critic, so that you can concentrate on your sensory awareness and let yourself experience the full range of physical and emotional sensations that occur during a sexual encounter.

2. *If there's something about your lovemaking style that doesn't suit you, take an active role in making a change.* Maybe the problem is that your partner rushes things. Or his touch may be too heavy or too light. Perhaps your sexual encounters always seem to unfold at 11:00 P.M., when you're so tired it's hard enough just to brush your teeth and get into bed, let alone think about participating in any kind of physical activity. This litany of problems, which could be expanded by hundreds of other similar examples, keeps many women feeling like sex doesn't hold much for them. The key thing to realize, however, is that these are not insurmountable stumbling blocks: they are minor stylistic glitches that each have simple and straightforward solutions. Finding solutions won't occur magically, though. To devise solutions, you need to begin by identifying what or where the problems are, breaking the problems down into their component parts, and then addressing the question of what might be done to change things. Sometimes the process of making a change—almost any change at all—will work right away, and sometimes it takes several tries to hit on the right combination of changes. But by giving yourself a chance to do things

differently with your partner's cooperation, you become an active agent in developing your options, which may help you view sex as more "user-friendly" than it's seemed before.

3. *Many problems with sexual arousal are a result of the tendency to think too much and touch too little.* Thinking about sex can be a turn-on for some women. But thinking about sex as it's happening can also lead women into negative self-appraisals: Did I shave my legs today? Maybe I should have showered again. Am I getting excited yet? Am I getting *him* excited? Is he rushing me again? Are we tuned in to each other? What am I going to do if he wants oral sex? As we've said before, this puts the woman into the spectator role at her own bedside, unintentionally inhibiting her own responses. One way of combating the tendency to think too much (or to dwell on anxious thoughts) is to luxuriate in the sensations and the action of a sensual/sexual encounter. As we discussed in Chapter 2, a good way to do this is to focus on a specific part of your partner's body and get lost in the sensations of stroking, touching, or holding him, thus taking the mental spotlight off your own response.

4. *Use fantasies to jump-start your sexual arousal or to boost your turn-on once it's underway.* Many women who are accustomed to using sex fantasies while they masturbate are hesitant to use them when they're with a partner, fearing that this is improper or immature or that it somehow detracts from the interpersonal nature of the experience. But avoiding the use of fantasy actually puts them (and their partners) at a disadvantage: without this customary stimulus, both their physical and emotional responses may lag. There is absolutely nothing wrong with using erotic fantasies as a private aphrodisiac. Fantasies can help a woman get in a particularly sexy mood as well as intensify or accelerate her arousal. Since using fantasies can aid women in becoming more responsive sex partners, and since most men are accustomed to using sex fantasies themselves, it's no wonder that most men have no objections at all to this practice. (If a woman is psychologically uncomfortable fantasizing about sex with a stranger, or sex with her old high school boyfriend, or sex with a movie star, she can usually feel very secure if she fantasies about sex with her current partner.)

5. *Emphasize the playfulness of sex instead of turning it into a chore or a mission.* Many women with arousal problems recall getting turned on very easily when they were teenagers necking in the back seat of their boyfriends' cars. This was probably not some accidental happening tied to adolescent hormones or sexual innocence; it's more likely to reflect the fact that at that age

they experienced sex more as a playful, unpredictable encounter than as a work assignment. Adults usually take things more seriously than teenagers do, but where sex is concerned, this can have its disadvantages. Reclaiming the playful, exploratory side of sex can help defuse performance anxieties and restore that sense of fun and adventure between partners.

6. *Don't be afraid to experiment with different types of sensual stimulation.* Many women with arousal problems become so intently focused on their difficulties that they lose sight of certain basic aspects of experiencing pleasure. One common problem is that too much sameness in sexual routines not only leads to boredom, it often triggers feelings of déjà vu that cause the woman to write off an encounter before she's even gotten into it. Another aspect of this problem is that many women are reluctant to experiment with sex, feeling that if they've tried something once and didn't like it, it means they will always react to this activity the same way. Nothing could be further from the truth. Experimentation can take many different forms. Try various positions for touching one another. Sometimes if the woman gets on top of her partner *without* any attempt to have intercourse, it opens new vistas of experiencing touches and kisses. Try exploring each other's body with your lips and tongues instead of your fingertips, doing so in a way that emphasizes the sensual side of this action instead of trying to produce a specific response. Have a sensual encounter while you're both fully or partially clothed. Once again, the point of experimenting is discovery. You may be surprised at how simple changes produce new or different feelings.

Women with arousal difficulties (but normal sexual desire) who find that the above suggestions are of little help should consider consulting a sex therapist for further evaluation and individualized treatment recommendations, especially if their problems seem linked to fears of sex, distaste for sexual acts, or recurrent deep-seated anxieties. In general, we suggest that if the woman is in a long-term romantic relationship, the couple should seek help together.

DEALING WITH ANORGASMIA

Many women who have never experienced orgasm are intimidated by their situation. The quest for orgasm seems daunting: instead of being a source of pleasure, sex is likely to be unrewarding, which may lead to avoidance, self-doubt, and low self-esteem. The accumulated frustrations of not being able to reach orgasm (and labeling oneself as a failure) may spill over into other, nonsexual areas of the relationships these women have, with dire consequences ranging from loss of intimacy to strained emotions or even divorce.

Fortunately, there is a high probability of reversing anorgasmia by following some simple, straightforward steps to enhance sexual feelings and responses. However, this is not an automatic process. It requires that a woman be willing to take an active role in devising her own solutions, and it demands a no-excuses, no-distractions commitment to participation in a series of sexual enhancement exercises that are not likely to be successful unless they are employed with some continuity over a period of 3 to 5 weeks. Without that commitment, the odds of success drop considerably.

While the anorgasmic woman may certainly have as her ultimate goal being orgasmic during intercourse, learning to be orgasmic is most easily done by oneself, without the presence of a partner. This is not a reflection on a partner's worth or intentions; it is simply a way to place the focus of the program where it belongs—on the person who is doing the learning. (In the next section, we will discuss ways of facilitating orgasm during sex with a partner, but that discussion is oriented toward women who have already experienced orgasms.)

STEP 1: TAKING INVENTORY

First, try to identify what the problem is. Start with some self-assessment to help you pinpoint the specific obstacles you are facing. Using no more than two sentences, write a succinct description of your sexual difficulties. Next, write a detailed description (of any length you wish) of what you would consider a perfect sexual encounter. Put these two items away in a safe place for later reference. Now, think about the sources of your sexual anxieties or inhibitions (if you have any). What are the three things about sex that make you most uncomfortable or that worry you the most? What are the most annoying or frustrating aspects of sex for you? How could these be changed? Make a list of your negative sexual attitudes, including those involving your appearance, your femininity, your relationship, and how you feel about various types of sexual activity. How many of these have you discussed with your partner? Do you feel that he has genuinely attempted to understand these matters, or has he brushed them off or belittled you for feeling this way?

Also take inventory of the positive aspects of your sexuality. What are your favorite sexual fantasies? What aspects of sex do you enjoy the most? When you're highly aroused, which parts of your body feel most energized? Have you ever felt absolutely wild sexual abandon? Do you ever have fun with sex? What are your three most positive sexual attitudes? What facets of your sexual relationship are most satisfying?

In considering these issues, you can begin to form some ideas about the sources of your sexual difficulties, along with a realistic assessment of your assets. Taking inventory is not the same as problem-solving, but defining a problem is the first step towards its solution. As you continue to follow this program, you may want to keep a personal journal of your feelings and thoughts. If you choose to do this, you should glance back periodically at the initial inventory you have come up with and see how your perceptions of your sexuality evolve over time.

STEP 2: BUILDING BODY AWARENESS

Problems or obstacles to sexual enjoyment that you may have uncovered in your attitudes, beliefs, and behaviors don't tell the whole story about anorgasmia because sex is not a purely cerebral event. One of the most useful means of enhancing sensuality and sexual response is to become more attuned to the feelings and messages your own body gives you. Yet many women with sexual problems are loath to do this because they disparage their bodies for not matching the glamorous ideal dictated by our culture. This attitude is antithetical to physical, sensual pleasure in several ways. If you believe you are unattractive and are unhappy with your body, the negative feelings create an aura that is very difficult to overcome and make it hard to feel sexy. Furthermore, if you are *not* in tune with your body and its messages, your sexual needs may be unfulfilled: your brain literally isn't recognizing what your body is telling it. Finally, women who are hypercritical of their bodies also tend to be hypercritical about many aspects of their sexuality; in addition to judging their own feelings and responses as inadequate, they assume that their partners' judgments mirror their own.

The following exercises are designed to help women become more attuned to their bodies' feelings and messages.

Exercise 1: Self-directed Sensate Focus

This exercise is similar in design to the sensate focus procedures described in Chapter 2, except that those were meant to be done with a partner. If you recall, the main purpose of sensate focus is to concentrate your attention on the physical aspects of your body's feelings and responses. In fact, the more you are able to focus on your sensations, the more you avoid the dual pitfalls of too much thinking and too much evaluation, both of which can be destructive to sexual self-awareness.

In self-directed sensate focus, you have an opportunity to explore as much of your body as you can reach with your fingertips. You will give yourself the chance to notice a range of tactile sensations and you will begin to distinguish between various types and tempos of touch and how they feel as they register in different spots. Does a light touch on the front of your thigh feel the same as a light touch on your neck? Does a circular motion at the base of your thumb feel different from the same motion on your cheeks? The intent is not to make something happen or to attain a specific objective; the point is only to allow yourself to notice minute details about your feelings.

We suggest that you try this exercise for a 15- to 20-minute period (with your genitals excluded from your touching) on at least two occasions. The first time or two, you may feel a little silly about touching your own body, as though it's impermissible or wrong. As you get beyond this initial awkwardness, you can augment your sensate focus experience in two ways. First, before you begin a session, close your eyes, try to clear your brain, and take slow, deep breaths for about 2 minutes. Then, while lying on your back with your arms at your sides, activate each of your body's major muscle groups by deliberately contracting the muscles, holding them in a clenched or contracted position for 6 or 8 seconds, and then letting them go absolutely limp. (It doesn't matter if you start out with you facial muscles and work your way down, or start with your feet and work up.) Both techniques aid relaxation and provide you with an enhanced body awareness.

When you have gotten beyond the initial sense of awkwardness and self-consciousness connected with the process of touching your own body, use the opportunity to develop your sensory awareness and to listen to the messages your body produces. You can change the physical sensations you are experiencing on different occasions by using powder, oil, or lotion before you begin.

Exercise 2: A Clinical Look in the Mirror

For a variety of reasons, but particularly because of the *Don't Touch Yourself Down There* script, many women have never taken a close look at their own genital anatomy. If you fall into this category, now is a good time to rectify the situation. Using a large hand mirror as a visual aid, take a few minutes to examine your genitals and identify the various anatomical structures. Use Figure 7.1 to assist you in this process, and understand that individual variation is normal—no two genital regions look exactly alike.

If you're squatting and looking down into the mirror, the entire area of the genitals that you can see is referred to as the vulva, or outer genitals. There are actually a number of structures in addition to the vagina and the clitoris that make up the genitals. Here are the landmarks you should identify. The mons (or mons veneris) is the area above your pubic bone which is usually covered by pubic hair. The labia (Latin for "lips") are two paired structures

FIGURE 7.1
THE VULVA

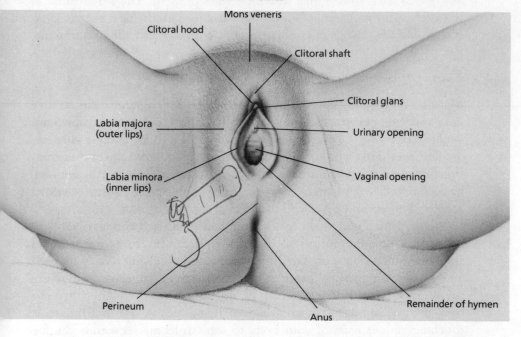

that surround the openings of the vagina and the urethra. The labia majora (outer lips) are large folds of skin that are covered with hair. The smaller labia minora (inner lips) are hairless structures that often look like curving petals. They are more delicate than the labia majora and also contain a richer concentration of sensory nerve endings (which you cannot see). The labia minora meet in the midline to form a hood of skin that covers the tip of the clitoris. The clitoris itself is mostly hidden from view, with its shaft located internally. The only visible part is the tip (also called the clitoral glans or head) which looks like a small, shiny button about the size of a pea. It is located just beneath the point where the labia minora meet, and in most women is exquisitely sensitive to touch or pressure. The urethral meatus, or urinary opening, is located in the midline between the clitoris and the opening to the vagina. (In some women, it is so small that it can be difficult to see.) In contrast, the opening of the vagina is readily visible. There may be small tags of tissue around the vaginal opening which are remnants of the hymen, the thin tissue membrane that stretched across this region during childhood. Finally, the perineum is the hairless area of skin between the bottom of the labia and the rectum. Although many women don't realize it, the perineum is also quite sensitive to touch and pressure because of its rich innervation.

It is not necessary to memorize these anatomical relationships or to run any tests to see if your genital structures work properly. The whole point of this exercise is simply one of visual familiarization. In the next exercise, you will extend this process of familiarization from the visual side to the tactile.

Exercise 3: Genital Exploration

Many women don't take the time to touch their own genitals unless they have a specific purpose to do so, such as inserting a tampon or diaphragm, washing, or trying to become sexually aroused. While any of these purposes are fine, they don't lend themselves to unhurried explorations of the sensations of your own genitals without the pressures to become sexually aroused, to accommodate a partner, or to go on to some specific form of sexual activity. This exercise gives you that chance.

Start at a time when you feel relaxed and unhurried and can spend 30 minutes or more by yourself. (Some women find it helpful to begin with a soothing bath or shower, but this is not a requirement.) Get undressed and find a comfortable position either sitting in an easy chair, lying on your back, or half lying, half sitting on a bed or couch with your back propped up against some pillows. Begin as you did in Exercise 1, touching various parts of your body to tune in to the sensations you are experiencing. After you get into the rhythm of the experience, shift the focus of your touch to your genital region. Run your fingers lightly through your pubic hair and allow the sensations to register in your brain. Trace the contours of your labia, noticing how your fingertips feel brushing up and down along these structures. If you wish, you can separate the inner labia, gently teasing them apart, or tugging on them with a slightly downward pressure. Slowly continue this exploratory process so that you stroke the area around the clitoris and massage the shaft and tip of the clitoris itself. See what sorts of sensations come from subtle movements of the clitoral hood as opposed to direct clitoral touching, and how these feelings contrast with the sensations produced by rubbing the palm of your hand across the area of your mons. Brush your fingertips around the opening of the vagina, and then let a finger creep just inside the vaginal opening, moving gently in and out. Compare how different types of touch—lighter or heavier, faster or slower, up and down or circular—produce different feelings. As you experiment with these and other types of touching, don't worry about whether you are becoming sexually aroused or not. The point of this exercise is not to turn yourself on; it is simply to notice and focus on what you're feeling.

If you feel odd about exploring your own genitals, you might want to repeat this exercise two or three times before going on. On the other hand, if you found that you felt comfortable with the experience, you can move forward to Step 3 as soon as you wish.

STEP 3: SELF-STIMULATION

The key to the process of sexual self-discovery for women who have never been orgasmic is learning to recognize and build on various sources of sensual pleasure. Certainly, sensual pleasure is not precisely the same as sexual pleasure (for instance, the aroma of baking bread may be quite sensual but not particularly sexual), but the two are often closely intertwined. Both forms of pleasure will develop naturally under relaxed circumstances if given a helping hand, and that is precisely what these self-stimulation exercises entail.

It's important to approach these exercises as a cumulative process of self-discovery and self-pleasuring, not as some type of school assignment on which you'll be graded. By emphasizing the cumulative nature of the learning experience, you can defuse your tendency to expect each session to be a wildly intense sexual experience and to view it with disappointment if it isn't. You can also do yourself a big favor by not anticipating that each new session will be better than the last. Learning rarely occurs in a completely linear fashion, and in sex, as with other types of learning, there are peaks and valleys, fits and starts, and days when just about everything seems to go wrong.

If you are concerned about whether learning to be orgasmic by yourself will somehow detract from your relationship, you should set aside that fear. What you learn through your own self-pleasuring can be used to enrich your relationship and give you more sexual self-confidence, which translates into you becoming a more turned-on partner. In other words, the gains you make on your own provide direct benefits to your partner.

Begin your series of self-stimulation exercises by setting aside a half-hour a day for this purpose. It's advisable to pick a time where you can feel relaxed and unhurried; it often helps to let yourself get into the mood by taking a shower or bath, or listening to some soothing music, before you begin. We suggest not leaving this for the very last thing you do in a busy day, because fatigue will work against you; similarly, this is not an activity to pursue immediately after a meal, when you may be feeling drowsy and your reflexes may be sluggish. Another practical matter to consider is how to preserve your privacy and avoid interruptions. If someone is walking outside your bedroom door, you will be distracted from focusing on your own feelings and sensations. It is also advisable, to minimize intrusions, to disconnect the telephone in your room before you start a session.

When you begin a session, start out by touching your body all over. Focus on both the fingertip sensations you are experiencing as you touch and the feelings your touches produce in various locations. For instance, stroke your forehead with a light, rhythmic, symmetrical touch, using both hands. Try massaging your breasts, or running a finger slowly around your nipples. Notice how touching with one hand compares to using both hands at the same time, or how varying your tempo produces different sensations. Gradually, as you feel comfortable about doing it, extend your touching to your genitals. Remember to let yourself experience what's happening without making judgments about it. And also remember that touching is never an emergency: you can not only take your time, you can also let your touch wander away from your genitals and then back. This can produce interesting contrasts in your sensations as well as prevent sensory overload when your arousal is still increasing.

While the point of this exercise is to help you identify ways of feeling sensual and sexual pleasure, there is no right way or wrong way to proceed. Many women find that the opportunity to experiment with different sorts of touching (without the pressure of having to deal with a partner) is liberating and informative. In addition, the chance to slow down the action allows you to identify the components of what feels good. Sometimes, in the headlong rush of sex with a partner, there is so much going on that it is difficult to notice these details.

Run your fingers along the lips of the vagina (the labia), and see how it feels when you stretch the labia apart or tug at them gently. Stroke your clitoris with different types of pressure and varying rhythms. Roll it gently between two fingers, rub it with an up-and-down motion using just one finger, and try pressing down firmly on it with your whole hand. Brush your fingertips across your pubic hair and against the inside of your thighs. Notice how the clitoris feels when you're first becoming aroused compared to when your excitement is rapidly mounting. Gently run your finger around the opening to the vagina, then let your fingertip move just inside, darting in and out.

It's often best to move away deliberately from the genitals once in a while so that too much stimulation doesn't lead to insensitivity. This doesn't mean that you have to call "time out," or that you have to let your sexual arousal drop to lower levels. Some women find that pressing their legs together or contracting their pelvic muscles produces pleasurable and arousing sensations when they're already turned on; others discover that nongenital stimulation can be just as sexy as direct genital touch.

Here is one caveat. Some women touch themselves for a few minutes and find that they are having little in the way of sexual feelings. Perhaps they feel awkward or embarrassed about touching themselves; perhaps their expectations overshadow their actual experiences; or perhaps they simply haven't given themselves a chance to relax and to acclimate to the sensory input that exists. So be aware that limiting yourself to a few minutes of touching is about as likely to lead to soaring sexual feelings as watching *Lifestyles of the Rich and Famous* is to make you into a millionaire. In order to give the learning process a chance to work, you must allow yourself the luxury of unhurried, free-flowing sensory experiences. Even if the touching seems unarousing or uninteresting, stay with it long enough to allow for the possibility that your feelings may change. Furthermore, remember that sexual feelings don't always move forward in a straight line. If you give yourself the opportunity, you may find that after 20 or 30 minutes of touching, you suddenly jump from a low-key flutter of sexual arousal to the red-hot zone on your erotic thermometer.

Once you've tried this type of self-stimulation for several days, there are a few variations to try. They will not push you into a particular type of sexual mold but they *will* let you discover what works to enhance your sexual potential. As you go through these exercises, try to focus on what consistently and reliably facilitates your sexual arousal, especially noting what techniques or methods feel most exciting when you're at relatively high levels of sexual response.

Variation 1: Experimenting with Different Forms of Touching

Part of the process of identifying what arouses you most effectively involves some comparative analysis. Try stimulating yourself using a water-soluble gel or oil on your fingertips to alter the smoothness of the touch. On another occasion, see what the use of other textures can do for your self-stimulation: stroke yourself with a piece of fur, a silk scarf, or a velvet glove. Some women find that using a hand-held shower nozzle directed at their genitals is especially pleasurable. (Nozzles that can adjust to various intensities of water flow, from a light spray to pulsating bursts, can be particularly useful for this purpose.) Others enjoy the relaxing warmth and security of a hot bath in a steamy bathroom, with the door locked for absolute privacy and security. (Bath gels are optional for such an exercise.) Discovery and inventiveness are your allies in this learning process.

Variation 2: Energizing Your Sexual Brain

As we have noted previously, sex is not just a physical process. Thoughts and emotions and subjective interpretations of our experiences all play a major role in driving our sexual responses. Yet many nonorgasmic women seem surprised to learn that they can play an active role in directing and coordinating this process, that they don't have to settle for whatever thoughts happen to be in their minds at the time. Although these women wouldn't hesitate to change the channel if a TV or radio show were bothering them, they haven't thought about doing just that with distracting thoughts or moods. As a result, their sexual responses are often held prisoner by their preoccupations.

Fortunately, you *can* see that your brain and your body are pointed in the same direction. One way of achieving this type of facilitating unity is to deliberately focus your mind on sexual matters. This can involve the use of favorite sex fantasies (or newly invented ones), recollections of passionate sexual encounters, or even acting out a sexual script complete with audible moans, groans, and dialogue. Some women have told us that 5 minutes of readings from erotic materials are a great prelude to these exercises, putting them in a sexy, focused mood. Sex fantasies, readings, or recollections are useful because they activate eroticism and effectively block extraneous or distracting thoughts and concerns. In this sense, sex fantasies are effective personal aphrodisiacs. Yet many anorgasmic women have been reluctant to use them.[23]

Variation 3: Role-Play Having an Orgasm

The power of positive thinking is remarkable. Many preorgasmic women have found that role-playing being orgasmic helps build their self-confidence and can be a prelude to the real event. For best effect, this should be done on several occasions a few days apart, rather than just as a single occurrence.

Role-playing is most effective if it is combined with self-stimulation that produces a high level of sexual arousal. The woman shouldn't worry about realism; she can employ considerable dramatic license to go through the motions of having an orgasm. This may involve a good deal of moaning and groaning and heavy breathing and thrashing around leading up to the magic moment. It may include intense gyrations and vocalizations ("Yes, oh yes, yes, yes, Yes, YES, Y-E-E-S-S-S-S") in the throes of the orgasmic experience. It may culminate in her virtual collapse as the orgasm shudders to an end. But her role-playing shouldn't stop here; she should play out her part by concentrating on what she will feel like after having had an orgasm, imaging the relaxation and the warm afterglow and the pleasure it will bring.

STEP 4: DEFINING YOUR ORGASM TRIGGERS

If you've already had an orgasm by now, congratulations. If you haven't, the odds are that you've gained a great deal of proficiency in getting in touch with your body, your sexual feelings, and your sexual response patterns. But sometimes it seems that although you are more proficient, you're still getting stuck at a point just before reaching orgasm. As one woman told us, "It feels like I'm pushing down on the gas pedal but the acceleration never picks up." This can be a frustrating situation because it may seem that even after a lot of effort, orgasms remain elusive.

In fact, this may not be the case at all. If you're consistently getting to high levels of arousal and then stalling right there, the problem may be that you simply haven't recognized some of the ways women trigger themselves into orgasm. For example, you can contract your vaginal muscles and the muscles in your rectal area in slow, rhythmic waves. These muscles are already primed for orgasm by changing patterns of blood flow in the region and by the buildup of neuromuscular tension, so that even a tiny additional stimulus may be just enough to push sensations to the orgasmic threshold level, triggering the full cascade of orgasmic responses throughout your body. Similarly, some women find that alternately tensing and relaxing their arms and legs, or pressing their backs into the beds, can also tilt them into orgasm.

There is no single maneuver that works as an orgasm trigger for all women. Some women find that talking "dirty" at peaks of sexual excitement helps to push them over the brink. Others deliberately change their styles of breathing (to a faster, panting pattern, for example), or save a particularly savory fantasy tidbit for this moment. Here again, the process of experimentation and self-discovery can stand you in good stead as you explore these and other possibilities to see how they work for you.

STEP 5: USING A VIBRATOR

By now you may have already had your first orgasm. But if you are among those who are still searching for that elusive event, you may be beginning to get nervous, with thoughts like "I *know* this won't work for me." Relax. If you've faithfully tried the exercises we've outlined, you've learned a great deal about your sexual arousal patterns and your sexual/sensual preferences, even if you haven't had an orgasm.

An almost sure-fire way of inducing an orgasm is to incorporate the use of a vibrator into your self-stimulation techniques. Vibrators have the advantage of being able to deliver a much more intense, focused stimulation to your genitals than your hand (or a hand-driven object) can produce. Since there are different types of vibrators, ranging from smaller, battery-powered models to larger, heavier, plug-in versions, as well as models with adjustable speeds and attachments of different sorts, you may have to experiment to find out which type is most pleasurable and arousing for you. Whatever model you choose, add the vibrator gradually to your pleasuring exercises. Don't just push the vibrator against your genitals; experiment with how it feels on various parts of your body, from your head to your toes, and learn how to vary its pressure and intensity.

You may want to spend several 15-minute sessions familiarizing yourself with this device before you attempt to use it in a deliberately sexual way. In fact, many women find that doing this allows them to determine which parts of their body are too sensitive for direct stimulation with the vibrator and to become acclimated to the physical sensations it produces. While most women are transported to new heights of arousal by the genital sensations a vibrator produces, others find that applying the vibrator directly to the clitoris is uncomfortable or painful. If this happens to you, experiment with using the vibrator in the mons area, a little above the clitoris itself. The sensations the vibrator delivers spread out in a ripple effect, with the ripples quickly losing intensity as they move away from the spot where the vibrator is applied. Many other women report that a vibrator that feels like "too much, too soon" on or around the unstimulated genitals is delightfully erotic when they've gotten to higher levels of sexual excitation. Another option is using the vibrator on the inner parts of your thighs and along your perineum as you rub your clitoris with your fingers. Remember, a vibrator is not a replacement for your own participation; it's an instrument to add to your overall orchestra.

Once you've completely familiarized yourself with the vibrator you've chosen, you can begin to use it creatively as part of your self-stimulation program. The emphasis should be on letting your sexual feelings unfold, rather than trying to force them into existence. For this reason, it is preferable to start out with general body touching, proceed leisurely to genital stimulation with your hand, and allow your excitement to build in intensity before you bring the vibrator into action. Try not to become so distracted by the vibrator that you forget the things you've already learned. That is, don't make having an orgasm your immediate goal. Use the vibrator as a way of exploring your sensual and sexual feelings, and don't forget to use fantasies or erotic daydreams to bolster the physical stimulation.

Some women are hesitant about using vibrators. They may see them as an artificial means of having an orgasm, or worry that they may get hooked on using the vibrator, making sex with a partner more difficult. Neither concern has much merit. First of all, an orgasm is an orgasm, no matter how it is produced. Orgasms that come from using a vibrator are physiologically identical to orgasms from any other source. Second, once a woman has learned to be orgasmic by any means, it becomes infinitely easier for her to have orgasms by a variety of other methods. After all, what she has gained from the vibrator-assisted orgasm is an appreciation of how her body responds during this previously unknown experience, and she has undoubtedly boosted her sexual self-confidence as well. Both of these gains translate into greater orgasmic facility as her learning curve expands. In the matter of women's becoming sexually dependent on vibrators, we will simply say this: while it can happen, it is usually a reflection of a particular woman's inability to appreciate the various stages of buildup to her release of sexual tension because the vibrator triggers almost instantaneous orgasms.[24] If you have followed the program of sexual awareness outlined here, this should not be a major issue because you will be using the vibrator as a bridge to a desired response, not because you see it as providing the ultimate sexual experience.

Although some women who have never had orgasms have them the very first time they use a vibrator, many others find that it takes a while before they become comfortable enough, and focused enough, to let their internal arousal synchronize with the external stimulus of the vibrator. Common obstacles that women in this situation encounter are expecting the vibrator to function magically, with no personal involvement of their own; placing such strong performance pressures (and expectations) on themselves that they actually make orgasms less likely to happen; and thinking negatively, which creates such an overwhelming flood of anxieties that sexual arousal is diminished and orgasms are blocked. If these (or similar) problems crop up and even seem to multiply, it can be useful to put the vibrator away for a few days and to return to steps 3 and 4 of this program in order to allow yourself to build up momentum again before returning to the use of the vibrator in your self-stimulation. If you still have not had an orgasm after resuming use of the vibrator for a 2-week period, it is advisable to seek professional help. A sex therapist may be able to help you pinpoint specific psychological or relationship issues that require treatment and can also tailor practical suggestions to your life and personal requirements.

One additional point: many women who have been troubled by anorgasmia for years find that the first orgasm they experience is disappointingly small. Expecting that orgasm will be an earth-shattering experience—and having anticipated the event (and its significance) with so much preoccupation that it would be hard pressed to live up to its advance billing—what these women often describe is an orgasm that feels more like a few quivers and a tingling sneeze than like a cataclysmic avalanche of shooting stars, earthquakes, and volcanic explosions. The explanation for this common experience is simple: first, most of these women have worked so hard to reach orgasm that the experience itself pales in comparison to the effort expended; second, first orgasms are apt to be less physiologically intense than later ones because the internal neuromuscular circuitry isn't yet burned in (to borrow a phrase from computer technology), so the reflexes are neither as smoothly coordinated nor as additive as they will be after being activated more often.

REACHING ORGASM WITH A PARTNER

For many women, the epitome of sex is being orgasmic with a partner. Some women, including those who have just learned to be orgasmic, make the transition from having solitary orgasms to having orgasms during partner sex quite easily and naturally. Others have discovered that all it takes is showing their partners how they have learned to be orgasmic in terms of what touches and positions they prefer. Although it may take a little practice for a partner to catch on and learn to coordinate his actions with the woman's needs, especially in picking up the fine nuances of the rhythms and pressures she prefers, this is time and effort that can pay considerable dividends to the relationship.

Not everyone manages to make this transition automatically, however. Various problems conspire to block a woman from having orgasms during sex with her partner. Self-consciousness is one major culprit. Being distracted by concerns about her partner's needs or reactions is another common difficulty. And the notorious problem of performance pressures—which can be self-imposed or partner-imposed, or both—is apt to rear its familiar face whenever sex doesn't flow along effortlessly.

Here are several options for women who either hope to be orgasmic with a partner for the first time or wish to increase the frequency of their orgasms with their partners.

If you have never been orgasmic with your partner, a logical starting point is to explain to him what you have discovered about reaching orgasm on your own. (While it may be hard to do this with words alone, make the attempt anyway.) Next, you can either stimulate yourself to orgasm while he watches, in order to show him how you do it, or you can use the sensate focus exercises outlined in Chapter 2 (especially the steps for genital touching and mutual touching), paying particular attention to the hand-riding technique as a means of "educating" your partner's touch. If you seem to be overwhelmed by the spectator role, the mutual touching exercises can be especially useful because they allow you to deal with this problem by getting lost in your partner's body. Please remember, however, that these exercises are not guaranteed to work automatically the first time you employ them. Unrealistic expectations can lead you to label yourself a failure if you aren't orgasmic right away, which is not only inappropriate but also one of those pressure-filled self-fulfilling prophecies.

Here's another option to consider. If you have been orgasmic easily and consistently with the help of a vibrator, try incorporating it into your sexual interaction. This doesn't mean making the vibrator the featured performer, but it can be used in several different ways. Some women prefer using the vibrator to reach very high levels of arousal and then finishing with manual stimulation of the clitoris provided by their partners or themselves. Other women use the opposite approach, allowing themselves to reach high levels of arousal from their interactive sex play and then adding the vibrator as the pièce de résistance. Still others use the vibrator for 10 to 15 seconds at a time in a sort of teasing pattern, switching back and forth between the vibrator and a minute or two of other types of love play. You can try each method and see which works best for you.

Oral sex can be another source of new and different stimuli. If you are comfortable with this form of sexual activity, it too can be incorporated into your lovemaking, although (like the use of the vibrator) it doesn't need to be the only form of stimulation used. In fact, options permit you to try out various combinations of sex play to see what is most appealing, most stimulating, or most provocative at any particular time.

While exploring these options, don't forget what you learned on your own. Specifically, be sure to use fantasies to boost your response if it seems to be stalled. Try to avoid the trap of deciding after just a few minutes of touching that this isn't going to work right. Most of all, don't let yourself get locked in to a rigid plan for making orgasms happen. Creativity and flexibility are valuable assets in your shared interaction; sometimes orgasms creep up when you're least expecting them.

Learning to have orgasms during intercourse is easy for some women but difficult for others. We have found that one key element that boosts a woman's odds of being orgasmic in this situation is using the woman-on-top position, which provides her with good control over the timing and depth of thrusting and frees her from the often uncomfortable burden of being pinned down by her partner's weight. Another advantage of this position is that either partner can provide manual stimulation to the woman's genitals while the penis is inside the vagina. (In the man–on–top position, this is more difficult to do.) Manual stimulation of the clitoris can be enhanced by bringing moisture up to this area from the vagina, by using saliva as another "natural" lubricant, or by using lotion or oil. Another possibility is using the vibrator to provide clitoral stimulation once the woman has reached high levels of arousal with intercourse. Many women have found that once they've experienced a few orgasms this way, they are able to be orgasmic during intercourse even without the vibrator, although they still may choose to use it from time to time.

Admittedly, not everyone with a sexual problem is able to solve it by following a home–study course. If you've spent a good deal of time following our suggestions and have not made any headway improving your sexual satisfaction, it is probably time for you and your partner to consult with a sex therapist.

VAGINISMUS

Vaginismus is a condition of involuntary spasms in the muscles surrounding the opening of the vagina. It can affect women of any age, but is particularly common in adolescents at the time of their earliest attempts at sexual activity and in the geriatric population, at a time when chronic estrogen deficiency may have caused the vagina to shrink in size and to have less elasticity. In its most dramatic presentations, vaginismus is so severe as to prevent penile penetration of the vagina entirely, making it one of the more common causes of unconsummated marriages. In cases of less severity, intromission is possible but causes the woman significant pain.

The exact prevalence of vaginismus in the general population has never been determined. Most of the professional literature suggests that it is a relatively uncommon condition, although this finding may reflect the fact that in most sex therapy clinics, vaginismus accounts for only a small percentage of cases that present for treatment. However, we suspect that the actual prevalence of vaginismus is somewhat higher than the sex therapy rosters suggest. We base this on our own clinical experience in gynecologic and infertility populations, where mild to moderate degrees of vaginismus were consistently found in about 3 to 4 percent of women, and on data from a large nonclinical sample of research volunteers aged 21 to 40 we examined at the Masters & Johnson Institute during the 1970s and 1980s, where we found that approximately one out of twenty women gave a history consistent with vaginismus and on pelvic examination had physical findings that confirmed this diagnosis.[25] One factor that probably

FIGURE 7.2
VAGINISMUS

The involuntary muscular spasms of vaginismus at the outer third of the vagina are shown by the arrows.

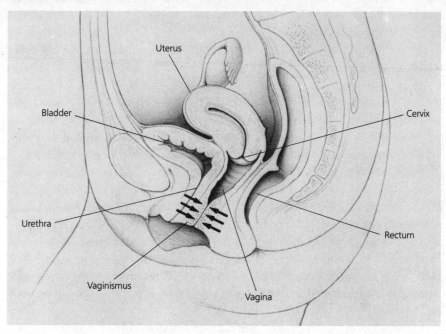

contributes to the underestimation of vaginismus in the broad population is that a substantial number of women with vaginismus choose a life of celibacy in order to avoid what is, for them, an anxiety-provoking and intensely embarrassing situation. These women are overlooked in surveys of patients undergoing sex therapy, although they are encountered in surveys of gynecology patients and nonclinical samples.

Although vaginismus occasionally coexists with sexual aversion or other conditions in which fear of sexual activity is prominent, in many cases (at least among those that present for therapy) what is striking is that the woman may have perfectly normal sexual arousal patterns. In most cases of vaginismus we have encountered, vaginal lubrication occurs normally, and noncoital forms of sexual activity are often pleasurable and satisfying.[26] In addition, women with vaginismus usually have normal sexual desire, and many of them are orgasmic with masturbation, oral-genital sex, or manual stimulation of the clitoris by their partners. In one study, 56 percent of women with vaginismus were orgasmic during noncoital sex play, 41 percent occasionally experienced orgasms during dreams, and 28 percent were orgasmic via masturbation.[27] Furthermore, it is interesting to note that nonsexual marital difficulties are far less prominent in couples where the woman has vaginismus than in most other problems that are seen for sex therapy. In fact, it is impressive to discover that most women with vaginismus feel strongly in love with their mates and report a high level of overall satisfaction with their marriages.[28]

Despite these patterns, it is remarkable that many couples put up with vaginismus for years before seeking professional help. In fact, we have seen more than a dozen unconsummated marriages that had lasted 10 years or longer before the couple finally came for help. Although these cases may be atypical, it is not at all unusual to find cases of vaginismus that have persisted for years before a couple finally tries to get professional help. Such delays may be more a matter of personal embarrassment than denial of the existence of the problem, although sometimes it isn't possible to be sure what the exact mechanisms behind such a lengthy delay might be. For example, while it is clear that the desire to become pregnant is what propels a fair number of couples to get help, it is also true that in some couples, vaginismus is just part of a broader constellation of sexual difficulties. We have previously noted that vaginismus is a very common component of unconsummated marriages—especially those of a year or more duration—and is accompanied by a higher incidence of primary impotence in the husbands of such marriages.[29]

Although vaginismus may be a lifelong condition, there are striking cases in which it arises as an abrupt secondary reaction to a traumatic event such as rape after a prior period of completely normal sexual functioning.[30] It may also appear as a conditioned response to physically painful intercourse. In cases of this sort, there is often an abnormality of the external genitals or the vaginal opening that is exquisitely tender. Sometimes, for example, a poorly healed episiotomy may be the initial source of physical discomfort. Other relatively common causes of local pain that may eventually trigger vaginismus include abnormalities of the hymen (including those caused by remnants of it that are stretched or irritated with attempts at vaginal penetration), ulcerations at or near the opening of the vagina, such as those caused by genital herpes, and atrophic vaginitis. Over time, repeated episodes of pain caused by such a lesion lead the woman, quite naturally, to an involuntary tensing and withdrawal from the actual or anticipated source of pain. This tensing proves to be protective, and what begins as a voluntary guarding effect is gradually transformed into a conditioned reflex. In fact, even when the original physical problem is successfully identified and treated, or simply heals spontaneously, the vaginismus may remain as a chronic condition.

In most instances, however, there is no physical cause that can be pinpointed as the proximate source of vaginismus. Among the various explanations that have been advanced for psychological causes of vaginismus, negative sexual conditioning due to rigid religious upbringing stands out as a particularly common background theme.[31] However, religion has no particular monopoly on antisexual attitudes, and we have been struck by the fact that there are many cases in which other forms of negative sexual messages have seemed to program a young female for a later case of vaginismus. To cite just one example from our files, a couple who came to see us after 5 years of an unconsummated marriage in which the wife was severely vaginismic related that the wife's mother had sent her weekly collections of news clippings describing every rape that occurred in her hometown during the 4 years that she was away at college. Further questioning revealed that from a young age on, the woman had been warned by her mother repeatedly that men were animals who wanted to use women only for their own carnal pleasure. The mother reinforced these warnings with repeated sightings of strange men supposedly lurking around their house late at night and also repeatedly warned her daughter about how painful and dangerous an experience childbirth was. (Perhaps the most remarkable thing about such a history was that the daughter eventually fell in love and decided to marry. However, her very genuine and enthusiastic love for her husband could not overcome the intense fears instilled by her mother's pronouncements, and when the daughter found her first attempt at intercourse on her wedding night was intensely painful and unsuccessful, it seemed to reinforce the truth of her mother's admonitions.)

Vaginismus is also encountered with some frequency as part of the unfortunate aftermath of situations of childhood or adolescent sexual abuse or sexual assault. Here, it may not be surprising that a defensive reaction to sexual contact occurs, especially in light of the fact that many female survivors of such traumas have never received appropriate counseling or, indeed, may have kept the burden of their personal ordeal completely secret.

Other factors that may cause vaginismus include a particularly traumatic experience with a first pelvic exam, as well as phobias about pregnancy, childbirth, or sexually transmitted disease. (It is interesting to note that in several cases we have seen of vaginismus caused by a pregnancy phobia, the woman was able to tolerate anal intercourse without pain or difficulty; thus, penetration per se didn't seem to be the major issue.) In many cases other than those involving a specific sexual trauma, it appears that several different elements contribute to causation, without any one factor being the specific key. We have frequently found that mothers' negative attitudes toward sexuality and reproduction, and toward female adolescent development in general, seem interwoven with other ingredients that create this condition. For example, many women with vaginismus recall that their mothers were distraught when the daughters began to menstruate and dealt with the daughters' monthly periods as though they were a type of illness. Some also remember that their mothers forced them to keep a written menstrual calendar (or a diary recording the exact dates of each menstrual period), which their mothers inspected regularly. In many cases, the mothers became close to hysterical if the daughter was even a day late in getting her next period. In addition, a substantial number of women with vaginismus have told us that their mothers were especially prudish and old-fashioned in their notions about sex: they were horrified if their daughters wanted to wear makeup before age 18, they absolutely forbade wearing tight-fitting sweaters, and they were quick to label the daughter's friends derisively as "sluts" or "whores" if they had boyfriends or dressed in what were simply everyday, ordinary teenage fashions.

Although cases in which vaginismus is so severe that intercourse is completely precluded are the most dramatic ones, these make up only a minority (less than one-quarter) of the 190 cases we have seen. The more common pattern is one in which a couple is able to have intercourse if the woman forces herself to tolerate the often considerable pain involved. While most couples seem to attempt this kind of sexual contact on very infrequent occasions, it may be psychologically important for the woman who wishes to conceive or for the woman who is trying to "reward" her husband for his patience in the face of their sexual tribulations. Here is how one woman described it to us:

> Every 3 or 4 months, I would begin to feel especially like an absolute jerk, a freak who couldn't have sex with her husband in the "normal" way. And so I would determine in my own mind, without consulting [my husband], that it was time for "real" sex. On those occasions, which usually took me 3 or 4 days of agonizing over before I could get up the courage to actually determine that this was *the* day, I would prepare myself like a maiden about to be sacrificed to the Aztec gods. I would lay out a sexy nightie, and chill a couple of bottles of champagne, and serve a candlelight dinner, and then I would consume about a bottle and a half of champagne so that I could get so sloshed that I barely knew what was happening. [My husband] was grateful for the effort, I suppose, and considerate of the fact that even under the influence of so much champagne, I was still in pain through the whole business. But he somehow would manage to get himself hard (I just couldn't bring myself to stroke his penis on these occasions, because my hands were usually grabbing a pillow so tightly that I once thought the feathers would burst out), and then he would push inside me, and I felt this searing, terrible pain that just

wouldn't quit, and finally it would be over and I felt beaten up and vio-lated. But I had done my duty, I would tell myself. I had proved that I really loved him.

Since conceiving a child is an important issue for many couples dealing with vaginismus, and since attempts at intercourse may be, as the woman quoted above described so vividly, extremely uncomfortable, it is not sur-prising that a number of couples resort to noncoital attempts at do-it-yourself forms of artificial insemination. Several couples have told us that they used plastic medicine droppers to attempt to insert the husband's semen (produced by masturbation) into the vagina or simply tried dripping semen onto the outside of the vagina while moving the labia away from the vaginal opening in the hope that this procedure might allow conception to occur. (In a few cases, pregnancies resulted from these practices.)

The uniquely frustrating nature of the physical difficulty posed by va-ginismus often produces complicated reactions in both partners. Many vaginismic women are deeply ashamed of their predicament and label them-selves as sick, unfeminine, and incomplete. Not surprisingly, these reactions often lead to low self-esteem, which may spill over into nonsexual aspects of the relationship. In addition, these women typically rate themselves as poor wives and woefully inadequate lovers, a negative self-assessment which sometimes leads them to try to compensate for their sexual shortcomings by becoming extremely deferential to their mates and smothering their own assertive impulses. At times, this behavior creates a situation in which the entire balance of the relationship changes so dramatically that the husband finds himself married to a virtual stranger, a situation that may lead to divorce. However, it is interesting to note that despite the extraordinary obstacles that severe vaginismus may pose for a couple, very few of the women with vaginismus we have worked with seriously considered divorce as an option: the couples were surprisingly dedicated to each other and to working through the sexual problems in their lives.[32]

In some cases, either as a result of entering individual psychotherapy or from their readings, women with vaginismus buy into the old (now largely discredited) psychoanalytic concept that vaginismus is a symbolic manifesta-tion of an unconscious hatred for men, which is expressed not only in the literal physical rejection of the male sex organ but also in the symbolic way the woman functionally castrates (desexualizes) her partner in revenge for her own castration (not having a penis; not being male). This notion implicitly—and mistakenly—casts women as envious of men, perversely retaliatory (after all, cutting a man off from sex is a rather low blow), and necessarily passive participants in acts of sexual union.[33] It leaves the woman, who is already all too willing to believe that she is both a failure and an abnormal person (unable to do what everyone else does easily and automatically), with virtually no psychological port in the storm of her psychosexual conflicts.

It is also common to find that after a lengthy period of repeatedly trying to overcome her condition, the woman gradually slips into a pattern of sexual avoidance as a means of coping with her self-perceived inadequacy by reducing the emotional pain of repeated failures. This avoidance is sometimes taken by the husband as a further indication of being rejected by his wife, but the truth is that rather than representing rejection, such behavior simply serves to provide the woman with a convenient psychological safe harbor in which she gains a degree of temporary respite from direct confrontation of her dysfunction and her husband's displeasure or anger. As we have mentioned elsewhere in this book, this is a common pattern seen in many different types of male and female sexual dysfunction; it is not unique to vaginismus and it is not the same thing as the phobic avoidance that is the hallmark of sexual aversion.

It is useful to understand that women react in diverse ways to their vaginismus. Some are able to keep the sexual symptom separate from their sense of self-worth; some attempt to deal with their problem immediately and directly and never go through the avoidance behavior noted above; and others who have only a mild dysfunction simply grit their teeth and make themselves sexually available to their husbands without realizing that pain-free sex is possible.

The histories of women with vaginismus often provide clues to the diagnosis. For example, women with severe vaginismus are usually unable to insert a tampon intravaginally during menstruation. (Among 75 consecutive women in their twenties and thirties giving such a history, we found vaginismus in 15, or 20 percent). Similarly, most women with vaginismus report having had painful and even frightening experiences with their first (and sometimes subsequent) pelvic exams. Commonly, the examining physician was unable to insert a vaginal speculum (the instrument used for conducting a pelvic examination) or was able to do so only after anesthetizing or heavily sedating the woman.[34] Other women with vaginismus report having had great difficulty in trying (or actually finding it impossible) to insert a vaginal suppository prescribed for the treatment of a vaginal infection. Notably, women with vaginismus do not use dildos or vibrators intravaginally during masturbation (typically, they focus their masturbatory stimulation on the clitoris) and they often report getting jumpy if their partner tries to insert his finger or tongue in the vagina, even if this is done gently and tenderly.

One aspect of vaginismus that is often overlooked is that it may gradually lead to sexual difficulties for the male. What happens is that an often sexually inexperienced man who is upset by both the difficulty in attempting to have intercourse and the apparent pain his wife (or partner) is suffering at his hands may compensate by both a gradual loss of interest in sex (which is, of course, a form of protective avoidance) and by a loss of ability to obtain or maintain erections. Typically, in the early stages of the evolution of this coexisting dysfunction, the male gets good firm erections during sexual play and has a firm erection at the time that he attempts penile insertion. However, as he is put off by his wife's evident physical and emotional discomfort with his erection's forceful pressures, his sexual arousal fades away and his erection quickly recedes. What happens next, in many cases, is an interesting form of sexual conditioning. The wife becomes distraught that her husband has gone limp in the face of her resistance, but at the same time she is greatly relieved by the removal of the threat to her most vulnerable region. Thus, putting aside her anxieties at the imminent threat of penetration (which has been obviously foiled for the moment), she becomes especially loving, tender, and solicitous, behavior that makes her husband feel good. Furthermore, in her guilt over having once again stymied the possibility of vaginal sexual intercourse, she may turn to another form of sexual stimulation to "do" her husband and relieve his sexual needs. Thus, failing at intercourse is rewarded with warmly and passionately delivered fellatio, which may well reinforce the husband's subsequent loss of erection in a similar situation of attempting coital connection. If this pattern is repeated with some consistency over time, the male gradually slips into a state in which he loses his erection—if any is present at all—as soon as there is an attempt at having the penis enter the vagina. In fact, in some cases of this sort, the man becomes erect only when his penis is in his partner's mouth or when his penis is being stimulated manually by his partner (sometimes with the assistance of a lubricating oil or lotion). In cases where the conditioned impotence becomes particularly severe, the man may lose the ability to have erections at all while with his wife; during noncoital sex with his wife, he may ejaculate through a completely flaccid penis, whereas with solitary masturbation (when there is no possibility of the threat of intercourse discomfiting his wife) he is still able to get erections with some degree of regularity.

Certainly, all the men who are partners of women with vaginismus do not respond in the same way. Some are accepting of and understanding about their partners' sexual difficulties, especially in cases where prior sexual traumas have been involved. Others are patient and understanding for a while, but then gradually come to see the primary symptom of the vaginismus—muscular spasms blocking the entrance to the vagina—as an almost willful way of avoiding intimacy, as though the woman is deliberately conjuring up this response as a means of foiling their sexual advances. Still others become misled by poorly managed attempts at therapy. Highly interpretive therapies, in which the precise "meaning" of the symptom is analyzed and dissected for long periods of time, are particularly apt to arouse the husband's ire and impatience. Other attempts at quick-fix solutions—ranging from hypnotherapy (which sometimes works) to pharmacotherapy (for example, attempting to use high doses of tranquilizers to help the woman "relax" and thus be more receptive to intercourse) are also apt to induce anger in the male if he has the sense that his wife really isn't trying, or really doesn't care about overcoming their problem. Coincidentally, there may also be a phase in which the male actively questions whether their relationship should continue, which sometimes includes one or more extramarital adventures that permit him to check up on whether he is functioning normally or not and whether what he is missing could provide him with as much excitement and erotic gratification as he thinks it can.

We believe that vaginismus is a condition that requires carefully directed treatment rather than something that should be approached by any sort of self-help program. For one thing, a proper medical evaluation is needed in order to determine whether any anatomic abnormalities exist that might be triggering the involuntary muscle spasms of this disorder. More important, in cases of vaginismus there are usually major psychological issues involving self-esteem, body image, and relationship dynamics that will not disappear by themselves even if a physical reconditioning program is successful. Fortunately, the success rate for treating vaginismus in sex therapy is excellent. At the Masters & Johnson Institute, we have successfully treated 98 percent of the cases we have seen, a fact all the more remarkable when you consider that many of these cases involved situations where the woman's partner was also sexually dysfunctional.

Eight

Compulsive Sexual Behavior

In the last three chapters, we discussed various types of sexual dysfunction. These conditions are clearly abnormal in the sense that they represent a statistical minority, a departure from healthy functioning, and (in many instances) actual physiologic symptoms or problems. But other sexual conditions that are not dysfunctions per se are also abnormal. Various types of compulsive sexual behavior fit in this category because the preoccupation with sex somehow exerts disruptive effects on a person's life. Our purpose here is not to catalog all these disorders, but to paint a broad conceptual outline of the processes and causes behind such difficulties.

THE PARAPHILIAS

The paraphilias are disorders of sexual behavior in which the compulsive element narrowly limits or focuses a person's sexual repertoire so that both arousal and satisfaction become dependent on what most people would view as abnormal or deviant forms of sexual fantasy or interaction. (In the past, the paraphilias were often called perversions or aberrations, but these terms became tinged with a moralistic tone that has led to substituting the more neutral-sounding label, paraphilia.) Some paraphilias involve a specific type of sexual object choice, as is the case in pedophilia (where children are the preferred sex objects), in fetishism (where an inanimate object, such as women's lingerie, or a body part, such as feet or hair, becomes the preferred or required engine for sexual turn-on), or in the very rare condition of zoophilia (where animals are the preferred sex object). Other paraphilias involve repeatedly and compulsively engaging in a specific sex act such as exposing oneself (exhibitionism), inflicting pain on a sex partner (sadism), or spying on people while they are undressing or engaging in sex (voyeurism).

211

In virtually all cases, the paraphilia is highly specific and static: exhibitionists do not generally become transvestites, for example, and voyeurs rarely if ever develop a taste for sadomasochism or having sex with animals.

The term "paraphilia" is not properly applied to situations where people engage fleetingly and experimentally in unusual or even obviously perverse forms of sex. (Of course, deciding what is perverse is not always as easy as it sounds: in certain quarters, oral-genital sex or anal sex is considered perverse even in the late twentieth century, and just a few decades ago, these same acts were even more widely labeled as "abnormal," "aberrant," or "morally repugnant.") Thus, a man who finds it stimulating or exciting to be spanked or whipped or tied up by his sex partner from time to time may be engaging in a statistically unusual behavior, a behavior over which many people would raise an eyebrow, and one that may raise questions about why he finds such an activity so erotically charged, but unless he *prefers* or *requires* this type of sex in order to become aroused and to obtain sexual satisfaction (or is, at the least, singularly distressed by recurring, persistent urges to be spanked or whipped), he is not an example of a paraphiliac. Likewise, a woman who has sexual contact with her German shepherd may be many things—including adventurous, "kinky," or even mentally unbalanced—but she is not suffering from a paraphilia unless she prefers her German shepherd (sexually speaking) to her noncanine (human) lovers.

We do not mean to sound flip in making these distinctions. The point we are trying to get across is that it is not just that these are somehow alternative scripts to "normal" sexual behavior: a true paraphilia is marked at its core by a combination of compulsivity and rigid focus. Like the person with compulsive handwashing, or the person who must constantly line up all the jars and boxes in the pantry into neat, perfect rows, the person with a full-blown paraphilia is preoccupied not by the pursuit of pleasure but by fleeing from psychic pain. Although the paraphilias seem to be about sexual choices, sex actually has less to do with them than does the ritualistic appeasement of personal demons.[1]

Some individuals with paraphilias are so driven by their compulsion that they choose an occupation or develop a hobby or volunteer activity that allows them to have direct, continuing contact with the desired erotic stimuli. For instance, a pedophile might become a Boy Scout troop leader or a Little League coach; a foot fetishist might become a lady's shoe salesman. More typically, though, the paraphilia is pursued on an extracurricular basis: a traveling salesman exposes himself to women from his car; an accountant makes obscene phone calls from his office between client appointments; a transvestite looks and acts completely masculine during the day, but dresses up as a woman at night.

In the most severe cases, the paraphilic urge is so intense and ever-present that it requires an almost ritualistic daily feeding, preferably through real-life enactment, but if this is not feasible, at least by fantasy-assisted masturbation. In fact, once-a-day enactments are not enough to keep some paraphiliacs from an overwhelming sense of anxiety or depression or spinning out of control. Connecting with the paraphilic urge is not always satisfying in the sense of orgasmic satiation and relaxation that nonparaphiliacs get from sex, but it *is* satisfying in suppressing these negative feelings, at least very temporarily, so they do not overwhelm the afflicted person. It is especially interesting that in this sense—in the personal gratification achieved by engaging in the desired action—the paraphilia is not always well-served by a totally willing partner. We have found, for example, that most sadists report far less intense gratification from sadistic sex with a cooperative partner than from someone they have forced into a sexual situation. (This may be why sadists are not always thrilled with having a masochistic partner; if the partner actually *enjoys* the pain, it definitely lessens the fun.)

In less severe cases, the paraphilic urge is not continually present but is triggered periodically by a specific stressful condition: for example, having an argument with a spouse or being slighted in some manner at work. In these situations, the need to engage in the paraphilic behavior lurks quietly beneath the surface of everyday life until it is stirred up by external events. Here, it is easy to see that the compulsion is much less intense than with more severe cases; in fact, the compulsion may exist only episodically rather than be felt on a virtually around-the-clock basis. In either type of paraphilia, the kinky sex acts are really not being used in the service of Eros but are rather primitive ego defense mechanisms that soothe an emotional wound, from loneliness to anxiety to a sense of shame or failure.

Many men with a severe paraphilia have difficulty becoming aroused in attempts at sexual activity that don't involve the paraphilic theme, so it is not surprising to find high rates of sexual dysfunctions, such as impotence or ejaculatory incompetence, in this population. These sexual dysfunctions may be exacerbated by the difficulties most of these men have in handling intimacy and interpersonal relations, as well as by concomitant psychiatric disorders, such as depression or personality disorders. Problems with substance abuse are also especially common in men with paraphilias, although sometimes in an effort to avoid prison these problems are invoked to give an excuse or explanation for deviant behavior when a man has been caught.

Reliable data on the frequency of true paraphilias are not available. However, most experts agree that unless kleptomania is considered to be a type of paraphilia,[2] males are much more likely than females to suffer from these disorders. While there are certainly isolated case reports of women with conditions such as exhibitionism, and there have clearly been more than a few female fetishists, along with a goodly number of female sadists and masochists, most of the paraphilias have at most a minuscule proportion of female practitioners.

This distinction leads us to make an important point. Just because a person engages in a particular activity, such as sadomasochistic sex, from time to time, it does not mean that the person is a sadist or masochist. Even if he or she *enjoys* the activity immensely, it still doesn't mean that a paraphilia exists. Unless the activity becomes the preferred, virtually required form of sexual outlet and arousal, it is a life-style choice (like opting to be a vegetarian) or a recreational choice (like playing golf instead of tennis) or an aesthetic choice (like preferring to listen to hard rock instead of modern jazz), but it is not a diagnosis of a sexual disorder. This is not just a matter of frequency; the essential element to a paraphilia is its compulsive urgency. When this compulsion is missing, the paraphilic act is simply an isolated behavior, not an integral part of a person's identity.

CAUSES

The "vandalized lovemap" theory, originated by Dr. John Money, traces the development of paraphilias to the period in early childhood when the first links among sex, love, and lust are formed. In Money's view, the formation of the child's lovemap, the brain's highly individual blueprint for what produces erotic arousal and what produces love, is traumatized or distorted in such a way that a paraphilic orientation is made more likely to occur.[3] This distortion typically involves a break in the natural link between romantic love and sexual lust during childhood, so that by adulthood the individual is unable to unite "pure" love and "dirty" lust in his (or her) sexual and romantic behavior. As a result of this inability to integrate love and lust, the lust is often expressed through highly specific paraphilic behaviors that are kept completely separate and apart from affection or intimacy.

Here are some ways Money suggests lovemaps can be inadvertently tipped in a paraphilic direction. (1) Parents who humiliate and punish a small boy for strutting around proudly with an erect penis, boasting and showing off to the females who watch him, do not realize that they are exposing the child to the risk of developing a lovemap of exhibitionism. (2) A pedophile who sexually abuses a young boy in an involuntary relationship in which the boy has no way of escaping creates a high probability of traumatizing the boy's lovemap so that he may repeat the pedophilic behavior when he becomes an adult. (3) Many transvestites report so-called "petticoat humiliation"—being dressed in girls' frilly clothes as a form of parental punishment—during childhood. According to Money's vandalized-lovemap theory, this form of negative conditioning about sex produces a distinct predisposition toward later transvestism in such persons by affecting their developing lovemaps at a particularly vulnerable age, although Money clearly acknowledges that not everyone so traumatized will wind up with a paraphilic lovemap.

Pedophilia has been studied more extensively than the other paraphilias in recent years, in part because it outrages people since it victimizes and traumatizes children, and in part because of the implications of the finding that the great majority—somewhere around 80 percent—of pedophiles have a history of having been sexually abused themselves when they were children.[4] (One implication of this finding, of course, is that if the incidence of child sexual abuse could be reduced significantly, theoretically the intergenerational "transfer" should be lessened for subsequent generations.) For this reason, we will discuss some of the theories about what causes pedophilia in more detail.

David Finkelhor and Sharon Araji proposed a four-factor model to summarize the various theories about why some adults become sexually interested in and involved with children.[5] The four factors they identified are emotional congruence, sexual arousal, blockage, and disinhibition.

Emotional congruence theories describe various reasons why adults may have an emotional need to relate sexually to children. This may arise from an adult's arrested psychological development, which leaves the adult with childish emotional needs, or from a generally poor self-esteem, which is improved (at least briefly) by being able to exert power and control over a child. Another aspect of emotional congruence is a concept called "identification with the aggressor," which refers to adults who were themselves the victims of sex abuse as children. By "turning the tables" when they get older, these adults become the powerful victimizers not only to gain revenge but also to combat their sense of having been victimized. In the same manner, fantasies about pedophilic sex can provide a symbolic mastery of the trauma that was felt by someone who was sexually abused as a child, helping that person to purge the sense of shame and powerlessness he felt when he was unable to do anything about it.

Sexual arousal theories try to explain why an adult finds children sexually stimulating. Among the possible explanations Finkelhor and Araji cite are that many pedophiles may have had early sexual experiences that condition them to be aroused by children later, when they are adults. These experiences may have been traumatic ones, perhaps become more indelibly conditioned because of the psychological pain associated with the experience, or they may have been incorporated into the child's fantasy life so that the scene of sex with a child was repeatedly used during masturbation, tending to reinforce (strengthen) the conditioning. Early modeling by others—that is, having as a role model a person who finds children sexually arousing—may also play a part in the origins of some cases of pedophilia.

Another group of theories is called blockage, the phenomenon in which some adults seem to be blocked from having their sexual and emotional needs met in more conventional adult-adult sexual relationships. Such gratification and fulfillment can be blocked as a result of poor social skills in adult heterosexual relationships, anxiety about sex, unresolved Oedipal conflicts, the unavailability of or conflict with a committed partner (such as a spouse), as well as repressive social-sexual norms.

The final group of factors is called disinhibition. The title refers to the reasons why our conventional inhibitions against sexual contact with children fail to operate in pedophilic adults. Disinhibiting factors include mental retardation, dementia, senility, psychosis, poor impulse control, drug or alcohol abuse, and failure of usual incest-avoidance mechanisms (such failure can occur, for example, between a stepfather and adolescent stepdaughter; because the stepfather was not in the family while the girl was an infant and young child, the ordinary inhibitions that would exist between father and daughter did not develop over time).

While the Finkelhor-Araji four-factor model of pedophilia does not offer a precise explanation for the dynamics of each case, it does provide us with a useful way of organizing our thinking about this problem. By allowing for the interactions of various factors, both individual and societal, that contribute to this type of behavior, we may be able to get closer to an eventual solution.

FOUR CASE STUDIES

Instead of providing detailed descriptive discussions of each of the paraphilias, which are beyond the scope of this book (and about which we have written elsewhere),[6] we believe that we can capture their essential flavor—especially as it relates to our discussion of compulsive sexual behavior—in a few brief case studies.

Case Study: The Underwear Bandit

Mr. Z. was a 27-year-old lawyer who contacted us because of occasional bouts of impotence in his four-year marriage. A personal interview revealed that Mr. Z. had a striking fetish for women's panties; without such a prop, his sexual excitement was marginal, and even fantasizing about panties did not always permit him to maintain an erection. Furthermore, it was not just any pair of panties that would do—only used panties with a female odor would excite him.

Mr. Z. was a middle child, with an older sister and younger brother. He recalled his childhood as happy and described his family as close-knit and well-to-do. At around age 6 or 7 he was occasionally involved in sex games with a few neighborhood children, but there was nothing remarkable that he could recall about these experiences.

At age 12 he began to masturbate. From time to time he tried to spy on his older sister (who was then 15) when she was showering or in the bathroom, but he was generally unsuccessful in these attempts. One day, however, his sister left her panties on the bathroom floor—he recalled vividly their appearance and the distinctly musky odor of the crotch—and he used these as a prop in his masturbation, with an accompanying fantasy of ravishing his sister while she was asleep.

Following this, his masturbatory fantasies sometimes revolved around female undergarments, while at other times they did not. At age 13, he stole a pair of his cousin's panties, which he kept hidden in his room and used from time to time for autoerotic stimulation. At age 14, when he began having a sexual relationship with a girlfriend, their activity consisted primarily of petting while still wearing clothing, which meant that his genital touching was done either through her panties or by slipping his finger just inside them. On one occasion, he talked his date into letting him have her panties, giving a reason he couldn't recall.

By age 16, he had begun to visit laundromats where he could conveniently "borrow" panties from a load of soiled clothing waiting to be put in the wash. His erotic turn-on was generally proportionate to the odor of the panties. On the few occasions when he could manage to steal panties only from a dryer, he found that they produced little sexual arousal.

This pattern persisted through college and law school. By his own estimate, he had stolen more than 500 pairs of panties over an 11-year period. His thievery had not slowed down at all after his marriage; even on his honeymoon to Hawaii, he had managed to slip away from his wife, visit a laundromat, steal some panties, masturbate with them, and discard the evidence.

Although he claimed to love his wife and professed a close relationship with her, she had no inkling of his fetish. In her view, his sexual difficulties were primarily a result of too much pressure at work. Mr. Z. had no desire to eradicate his fetish; he simply wanted to be able to function sexually with his wife. After a few days of therapy he terminated treatment because he became fearful that his "secret" would be unveiled.

Several years later, we learned that Mr. and Mrs. Z. had been divorced.

CASE STUDY: A MAN OF FASHION

The following letter was written to us by a 38-year-old married man seeking help because of his wife's growing discomfort with his cross-dressing activities.

I am asking for your help for only one reason—I'm afraid Sally will leave me if I don't take action now to deal with what she calls "The Problem." But "The Problem" isn't really a problem to me, it's a "Problem" only in how my passion for dressing up in feminine clothes has become a matter of conflict between us.

It wasn't always this way. When we became engaged more than 15 years ago, I realized that I needed to be open about my turn-on with Sally so she wouldn't discover my secret later on. After a lot of agonizing over it, I handed her a "True Confessions" letter one night. Although she was more than a little confused about the whole thing, she also seemed reasonably accepting. That is, she was as accepting as a woman in love could be, figuring that either she would change me eventually or that I would grow out of this obsession. I also realize that she was so touched by my embarrassment at making this disclosure to her that she misinterpreted my dilemma (should I tell her or keep it secret?) as an inclination to put this stuff behind me.

I never had any intention of abandoning my private passion; I simply wanted her to share in it. I knew that many other men had convinced their wives to be accomplices in their dressing up, even helping her husband put on makeup, select appropriate underwear, etc. I also had a strong desire to have sex with Sally while I was dressed up, because this was when I was the most aroused. And for many years, while Sally wasn't exactly enthusiastic in these circumstances, at least she went along with it, which was enough for me.

After we started our family, things slowly began to change. Sally began to nag me more and more about "The Problem," urging me to give it up—as though it was just some passing hobby of mine, like bowling, that I wouldn't miss much if I just found a substitute. Only after I convinced her that I was unable and unwilling to quit, after I did try a number of times to cut way down on my dressing up and just found myself becoming irritable and depressed and preoccupied with daydreams about what I was missing, did she start on her new tack: go get help.

So that's where we are now. Admittedly, it's been four or five years since she started pushing for me to go for help. Admittedly, I don't want help that is going to put an end to my private passion. It is simply too much a part of me to give up. The only kind of help I want is help to resolve the distance between us over "The Problem"—in other words, what I really want is to have you help Sally to learn to live with who I am and what I do as a legitimate form of sexual expression.

Although the letter-writer and his wife actually came for therapy, it was quickly apparent that there was such an impasse between them that no real "treatment" was possible. Instead, the therapists helped this couple find a compromise solution: the husband agreed to limit his cross-dressing to not more than twice a month in return for his wife's agreeing to stop nagging him to give up an activity that was intensely gratifying and not really harming anyone else. Considerable attention was also devoted to teaching the wife how to be more assertive by expressing her own needs and feelings in the relationship without making all of her happiness dependent on her husband's moods and actions.

The bottom line was that the paraphilia was not "cured," but it was repositioned in the couple's life. (This obviously couldn't work if the paraphilia had been dangerous to others, as with pedophilia.) Four years after treatment, the couple remained reasonably happy with the solution they had worked out.

Case Study: Telephone Sex

Mr. and Mrs. H. had been married for 7 years when they came to see us for treatment of a virtually nonexistent sex drive on Mr. H's part. Mr. H, age 33, was a successful computer consultant born and raised in Chicago. Mrs. H. was a kindergarten teacher from a small midwestern town.

They reported having an almost storybook marriage, with the only blemish in their lives being the absence of physical contact. They rarely argued, they had a close-knit circle of friends, they were relatively well-off financially, and they shared a strong mutual interest in skiing, bicycling, and traveling. But after an uneventful courtship and beginning to their marriage, when they made love without any problems (although only about twice a week), the frequency of their sexual contacts had gradually dropped to once every few months. This was especially disconcerting to Mrs. H., who took pride in being trim and attractive and couldn't understand her husband's lack of sexual interest.

In-depth conversations with Mr. H. finally gave us the information that was missing. From age 14 or 15 on, he had been obsessed with making obscene telephone calls, which provided him with his greatest erotic turn-on and, unknown to his wife, with a very prolific frequency of orgasm. By the time he was in college, he established a pattern of making at least a half-dozen obscene calls a day, and masturbated with almost all of them. At first, these calls were made at random to women he picked out of the phone book, but over time he developed methods for scouting out his victims in advance so he could see what they looked like (and sometimes, where they lived).

Although he tried to decrease the frequency of this activity when he first got married, he quickly found that sex with his wife began to seem overly tame in comparison to the intense thrills he got from his telephone adventures. For the past several years, he had spent 2 to 3 hours a day on his phone calls, and he typically masturbated to orgasm at least three times a day. He was certain that his wife had no idea of his extracurricular telephone activities, and he had never been caught by the telephone company or the police.

Because Mr. H. seemed motivated to try to change his behavior, which he admitted troubled him because it interfered with his work and made him feel foolish and guilty, we advised the couple (with his advance consent) that he needed individual therapy before we thought a sex therapy program would be effective. We did not inform his wife of the exact nature of the problem he was having, since it didn't appear to us that doing so would be particularly beneficial to either of them.

Mr. H. underwent a month-long program of daily psychotherapy, using several of the behavioral techniques described in the next section to extinguish his compulsive sexual preoccupations. By the end of this period, he was able to give up his obscene calls completely and found that fantasizing about such activities had lost its erotic thrill. As part of this process, he had also cut down the frequency of masturbating.

The next stage of his treatment shifted to a couples orientation, which drew his wife into conjoint therapy. After spending a short time with sensate focus exercises and simple communication training, Mr. and Mrs. H. suddenly found themselves having sex together several times a week . . . and liking it. There was no particular magic to this phase of the therapy, which generally followed traditional sex therapy lines. What seems to have happened was that by our creating a void in Mr. H's sexual universe by eliminating his paraphilic behavior, his natural sexuality reappeared after a twenty-year hiatus and he was able to make the transition to marital sex fairly easily. Our follow-up contacts with this couple showed that 2 years after completing therapy, their sex life continued to be pleasurable, as well as frequent—ordinarily, two or three times a week. In fact, Mrs. H. called us one day to tell us laughingly that the night before she had turned down an invitation to have sex with her husband because *she* was too tired.

This case illustrates an interesting point: not all paraphilias are equal in intensity. We have found that it is easier to eradicate certain types of paraphilias, especially exhibitionism, voyeurism, and obscene telephone calling, than it is to extinguish pedophilia, sadomasochism, or fetishism. (Transvestism falls somewhere in between.) While we cannot be certain of the explanation for this difference, since virtually all the paraphilias that clinicians see seem to be similar in severity and duration, the answer may well hinge on the fact that the paraphilias that are simpler to treat do not involve a physical interaction with a partner, whereas the other types do. In most cases of fetishism, the fetishist finds a way to involve his partner—if he has one—even if the involvement calls for a certain degree of deception. At the same time, the fetish-object can actually be seen as the fetishist's partner. As the late Robert Stoller observed, the fetish object is "safe, silent, cooperative, tranquil and can be harmed or destroyed without consequence."[7]

Case Study: A Marriage on the Rocks

A 26-year-old female law student was referred from the student health service of her university to a sex therapist because of sexual and marital problems. She had been married for four years to a college classmate; he was attending business school at the same university.

For as long as she could remember, she had become sexually aroused only if she was treated roughly, or if she fantasized about being ravished and abused. While her husband had initially been willing to go along with her requests to provide her with rough sex, he eventually found it both tiresome and demeaning. She felt cheated by his attitude and often tried to get him angry enough to hit her. When he more or less withdrew from her sexual demands, she began picking up men at off-campus bars and having sex with them in the back seats of their cars or in grungy motel rooms, as long as they would agree to slap her around as part of the sexual activity. While she was ashamed of her conduct, especially since she had hidden it carefully from her husband, she was also unwilling to stop because it was, as she put it, "the most intense, ecstatic feeling I've ever had."

Her history revealed that her first orgasm occurred at age 8 or 9 when she was being spanked by a neighboring kid as part of an "initiation" into a secret club. She was so taken by the experience that she deliberately broke club rules in order to be spanked as punishment over and over again, and she consistently found these spankings to be sexually provocative and experienced orgasm with virtually all of them.

As a young teenager, she whipped herself with a leather belt while she masturbated, using her vivid imagination to construct detailed fantasy scenarios of torture and punishment that drove her to peaks of sexual excitement. By the time she got to college, she had acquired a large box full of pornographic books about spanking, whipping, and other S & M activities and noticed that unless she fantasized about being sexually punished or brutalized she was unable to be orgasmic. She was particularly attracted to her husband because when they first met he showed considerable interest in her collection of erotica and seemed to enjoy acting out these fantasy scenes in their sex lives together.

Although she wanted to save her marriage, she was reluctant to disclose her extramarital sorties to her husband and insisted that treatment could begin only if the therapist agreed to keep this information absolutely confidential. After attending just a few therapy sessions, her husband announced that he was leaving her; they divorced shortly thereafter.

This case of masochism illustrates several points about the paraphilias. First, virtually all the paraphilias have their origins in a person's early sexual history. Second, the "victimless" paraphilias rarely create interpersonal problems if the sex partner is willing to cooperate with the required source of arousal. (For instance, a rubber fetishist may actually have a highly intimate, gratifying marriage if his wife participates enthusiastically in the wearing of appropriate paraphernalia during sex.) But when one party tires of the relatively exclusive focus on one form of sex—in the case above, the S & M component—then the relationship typically gets on much rockier terms. Although this deterioration is tied partly to the boredom of such situations, it is more apt to be a result of the sense of depersonalization about sex that the nonparaphilic partner comes to feel, as though he or she were simply a prop or an actor in the psychosexual drama required by the mate (with the insightful inference that, like a prop or an actor, his or her feelings don't really count much beyond providing the production required for the partner's sexual needs). Third, in a true paraphilia the preference for the specific act or object is so strong that it invariably leads to clandestine acts if the spouse or partner objects to it; in fact, in many cases, the person with the paraphilia will sacrifice a marriage in order to continue to pursue the pleasure-producing activity. In cases of sadomasochism, while therapists may be able to help people add new, nonsadomasochistic behaviors to their sexual patterns, attempts to eliminate the great turn-on power of sadomasochistic acts are usually only temporarily successful at best.[8]

TREATMENT OF THE PARAPHILIAS

There is considerable disagreement about the efficacy and reliability of various approaches to treating the paraphilias. Certainly, traditional psychoanalysis has fared quite poorly with these problems, and other approaches as well, including hypnosis and aversion therapy, have had spotty track records. Part of the dilemma is that paraphiliacs rarely agree to enter treatment unless they are forced to do so either in order to avoid criminal prosecution or to preserve a troubled marriage. In general, therapy works best with motivated individuals, so it is not surprising that attempts to treat someone who doesn't really want to give up what he or she deems to be a source of his or her most intense pleasure is likely to be fraught with problems. In fact, professionals who work with sex offenders are fully aware of how deliberately deceptive they may be. Telling your therapy group that you are no longer troubled by fantasies of having sex with young children may be exactly what is required to "graduate" (e.g., be released from prison) or to get off probation.

The most promising current therapy approaches involve behavioral techniques geared at eliminating sexual arousal resulting from illegal behaviors. These techniques are sometimes used in conjunction with treatment with antiandrogens—drugs that lower circulating testosterone levels—since this hormonal intervention typically reduces a man's sex drive significantly. In paraphiliacs, the effect is often very dramatic: the antiandrogens serve to take the edge off the compulsive urgency of the paraphilia to a great degree, opening the door for behavioral methods to work more effectively in reconditioning erotic impulses.

One reconditioning method being used with some success is a technique called satiation, which is used to break the connection between deviant sexual fantasies and orgasms. Satiation is achieved in a program that patients carry out in the privacy of their own homes on a daily basis. The patient must describe a nondeviant sexual fantasy scene out loud, while talking into a tape recorder at the same time as he masturbates to orgasm. (The use of the tape recorder allows the therapist to check that patients are following instructions exactly.) Immediately after orgasm occurs, the patient must begin describing aloud into the tape recorder one of his or her favorite paraphilic fantasies and continue masturbating while he or she does. The result is, of course, that with sexual responsivity at low ebb after the first orgasm, the paraphilic fantasy is far less effectively arousing than it would be on its own. Eventually, in fact, when this type of masturbatory reconditioning is carried out for 20 hours or so over a period of many weeks, the paraphilic fantasies that were once such a turn-on become boring and unrewarding, both physically and mentally. The result is that they get discarded, having lost their erotic appeal.

Other types of reconditioning exercises are also used to help cut down on the erotic fulfillment offenders get from their favorite paraphilic fantasies. For instance, an exciting paraphilic fantasy may be paired with thoughts of negative consequences (e.g., being caught by the police, catching AIDS) or with whiffs of a noxious odor like that of ammonia. Here is an example of such a scene that might be used in the treatment of an exhibitionist; the foul odor that was introduced at the indicated spot was valeric acid, which smells something like a combination of rancid butter and smelly gym socks:

You are going down Collins Avenue going to the laundry. You can feel yourself in the car, hands on the wheel looking out the windows. It's dusk and it has been raining. You can see the wet street and puddles. Just as you make that right turn on Andrews Drive by the ice cream parlor, you see this great-looking girl walking on your right. You slow down to get a better look. She is blond, about 16, and really stacked. You can see her breasts under her tight blouse, and her skirt is so short you can see her legs all the way up! You start to get excited just by looking and turn the car around to follow her. Now she is on your left and you slowly pull up to her as you start to play with yourself and your penis starts to get harder and stiffer. You can't help but think about touching and fondling her and you ache just to be naked with her, to see her be surprised and happy at how big your penis is [odor introduced], *but as you stop the car and start to take it out that bad smell and that sickening feeling in the pit of your stomach comes back. You really get turned off as your stomach turns over and over and pieces of your supper catch in your throat. You try to gag them back down but you can't. Big chunks of vomit gush out of your mouth, dribble down your chin, and drip all over you. The smell is making you even sicker. The blond can see you now all soft and vomiting all over yourself and she is starting to get your license number! People are starting to come out of the ice cream place to see and you've got to get out of there* [odor removed]. *You quickly clean yourself off and drive away, rolling down the windows to get some fresh air. As you get out of there you start to feel much better. That bad smell is gone and you can breathe deeply again. A fresh clean breeze comes in from the windows and you feel more comfortable and relaxed; your stomach starts to settle down and you begin to fully relax again. You're glad you're out of there, breathing freely and able to relax.*[9]

Other behavioral techniques are used to supplement the methods mentioned above, because blocking the turn-on value of the paraphilic imagery is hardly enough to return paraphiliacs to normal sexual relationships. Standard components of such treatment include the use of social skills training (e.g., how to communicate with women; how to express affection; how to deal with rejection or disappointment), correcting sexual myths, and cognitive therapy to help counteract the distorted beliefs that supported the sex-offending behavior in the first place.

Despite more than a decade of experience with these treatment programs, most workers in the field are not convinced that they have a high degree of success, and they definitely do not lead to reduced rates of recidivism.[10] Furthermore, because some cases involve severe abuse, many people would prefer locking up the sex offender to having him out in the community in a treatment program or on parole after the treatment has been completed.

SEX ADDICTIONS: FACT OR FAD?

In the last decade, a number of clinicians have suggested that compulsive sexual behavior is actually an addiction, like alcoholism, drug dependency, or compulsive gambling. The key features are (1) a lack of control over sexual impulses; (2) harmful consequences from the behavior, although this is characteristically denied by the addict; (3) unmanageability in other areas of life; (4) escalation in frequency over time; and (5) withdrawal symptoms with cessation.[11]

Ralph Earle and Gregory Crowe have described the overall pattern as follows:

> All of our sexually addicted patients get from sex the same things drug addicts get from drugs and alcoholics get from drinking: an intensely pleasurable high, comparable to nothing else in their lives; a means to anesthetize painful feelings such as sadness, anger, anxiety, or fear; and a way to escape the pressures and problems of daily living. The urge to escape and repeatedly recapture the high is extremely powerful, so powerful, in fact, that sex addicts, like alcoholics and other addicts, are virtually helpless to resist it. They *want* to stop. Time and again, they *promise* to stop. They even *try* to stop, but they cannot.[12]

According to the proponents of the sexual addiction thesis, most sex addicts are men, and sex addiction often involves unusual forms of sex, such as the paraphilias, but it can also include uncontrolled promiscuity, compulsive masturbation, homosexuality, rape, or incest, as well as more usual sexual conduct taken to extreme levels of ritualistic frequency. Patrick Carnes describes a typical case as follows: a married lawyer who had multiple affairs (often two or more at the same time), who habitually visited massage parlors for paid sex, and who also hung out in adult bookstores where he would have homosexual encounters with strangers in the private movie booths.[13] Earle and Crowe offer a more prosaic example of sex addiction: 26-year-old George, perfectionistic son of a workaholic father, who "longs for a normal intimate relationship with a woman" but has none, so instead he spends all his nonworking time alone devouring pornographic magazines, viewing X-rated movies, and calling fantasy phone lines to engage in erotic conversations with women.

In the case of one couple who came to the Masters & Johnson Institute for treatment, the husband insisted on having intercourse at least four times a day with his wife; the wife gave in to his demands because he threatened to have sex with prostitutes if she didn't "take care of his needs." Apparently, clinicians such as Carnes or Earle and Crowe would call this a case of sex addiction. We simply saw it as a case involving a domineering, manipulative man and a woman who was so unassertive that she let herself be a doormat in their relationship. If this is an addiction, the reason why escapes us.

In women, it is claimed that sexual addiction is most likely to appear as "frequent dangerous sexual encounters with strangers."[14] The sexually addicted woman, seeking a sense of personal power and self-worth, as well as an escape from pain and loneliness, uses sex as a way to feel in control and to grab for a momentary high, as described in the book *Women, Sex, and Addiction*:

> Sexually addicted women get caught up in a cycle in which their primary source of power is sexual conquest, and they fulfill their need for tenderness and touch through the sexual act. Beneath their addiction is a burning desire to escape feelings of worthlessness and shame. These women become addicted to seduction, to the hunt, to the feeling of having made a conquest. They long to bond but they don't know how.[15]

No matter what the specific type of sexual behavior, it is the element of compulsion and the utter disregard for consequences that purportedly make it an addiction. For this reason, it is important to realize that not all Peeping Toms or transvestites would be classified as sex addicts, although some of them (those most uncontrollably driven to peep or to cross-dress) would be.

Carnes identifies four core beliefs that characterize many sex addicts' negative views of themselves. (1) I am basically a bad, unworthy person. (2) No one would love me as I am. (3) My needs are never going to be met if I have to depend on others. (4) Sex is my most important need.

Charlotte Kasl identifies a similar list of core beliefs of female sex addicts.[16] (1) I am powerless. (2) I'll always be alone or lonely. (3) I'll always be abandoned. (4) My body is shameful/defective/repulsive.

These core beliefs (which are commonly found in people with all sorts of problems; women with bulimia or compulsive overeating, for example, have the same core beliefs that Kasl lists above as a sign of sex addiction) supposedly lead, in turn, to operational beliefs that translate into how a person acts. For example, the core belief that "No one would love me as I am" leads to a mistaken conception that equates sex with love: "I am lovable if someone wants me sexually" or "Having sex with someone proves I am lovable." And a woman's core belief that she'll always be abandoned is operationalized in the belief that "I won't be abandoned if I'm good at seduction."

Most treatment programs designed to help sex addicts and their partners are based on the Twelve Steps recovery program of Alcoholics Anonymous. Groups such as Sexaholics Anonymous (SA), Sex and Love Addicts Anonymous (SLAA), and Sex Addicts Anonymous (SAA) provide a self-help support network. Many experts believe that professional therapy—whether individual, couple, or group—is also needed to deal adequately with the addiction. Among the central tasks of such therapy are learning to alter the negative core beliefs that fuel the addiction, recognizing that there are effective alternatives to sex for dealing with anxiety or stress, and learning improved social skills. Better social skills help recovering sex addicts reduce their loneliness and isolation by successfully forming new relationships or by repairing the damage done to preexisting ones.

Not all experts (including ourselves) have embraced the sexual addiction model enthusiastically, however. Levine and Troiden claim that the definitions of sexual addiction and compulsion are "conceptually flawed" and that the criteria used to diagnose these conditions are "subjective and value laden."[17] They point out, for example, that sexual behavior that had been legitimized in the 1970s was reclassified in the 1980s as abnormal by "medicalizing" morality—giving it a scientific-sounding label (such as "sex addiction") and thus declaring it to be a disease. In this way, the mental health experts who advocate the sexual addiction model are functioning as "social control agents," in effect enforcing conformity to the sexual standards of the visible majority in our culture. Levine and Troiden claim that this push for conformity has been a result of the health threats associated with genital herpes and AIDS, as well as with the rise of politically powerful right-wing groups morally opposed to nonrelational sex. Furthermore, Levine and Troiden note that there are no true physiologic withdrawal symptoms (e.g., diarrhea, convulsions) when the "addictive" behavior is stopped.

John Money claims that the very idea of addiction to sex is inherently illogical.[18] Pointing out, somewhat wryly, that an alcoholic is not addicted to thirst but to alcohol, Money sees the sexual addiction camp as hell-bent on enforcing sexual abstinence as the "cure" for sexual addiction.

Finally, it should be pointed out that there is no research documenting that sex addiction is a valid or distinct entity. While this certainly doesn't mean that there is no reality to the concept—since it is entirely clear that there are people desperately driven by sexual compulsions—the main issue is whether labeling certain people as sex addicts provides a useful way of diagnosing or treating problematic sexual behavior or whether it is just another type of stigmatization. Because hospitalizing people for so-called sex addictions is big business today, sometimes commanding monthly fees of $25,000 and up (which are often reimbursed by insurance companies), this is not just a theoretical discussion but one with practical ramifications as well.

Nine

Conception and Contraception

One thing we have learned over the years is that very few topics in the broad realm of sexual health are regarded more casually than contraception. Most people, regardless of educational background, assume they have a pretty solid grasp of fundamental facts about various birth control methods. After all, what could be simpler than using a condom or taking a pill once a day? The reality is, however, that most people's birth control "facts" are often riddled with misinformation, partially correct information, and surprising gaps in knowledge.

Today, it is especially important for several reasons to have reliable knowledge about contraception. First, since the average age at marriage has risen substantially for both men and women in the past few decades, many individuals are sexually active for a longer time than ever before while wanting to avoid having children. (This trend is accentuated, of course, by today's adolescents becoming sexually active at a much younger age than several decades ago, a point which we discuss in detail in Chapter 15.) Second, there are more contraceptive methods available today than in the past. In order to make an intelligent choice between these methods, it is helpful to know something about how they work, how *well* they work, what their potential side effects are, and how they influence sexual feelings. Finally, there is a compelling health reason today for many people to consider using certain forms of contraception—condoms and spermicides—for a purpose that has nothing at all to do with birth control. The reason is that these contraceptive products offer some protection against the risk of many sexually transmitted diseases, including protection against infection with HIV, the AIDS virus.

In this chapter, before dealing with the various methods of birth control, we will briefly describe how conception occurs. The reason for doing this is simple: understanding the process of conception and the earliest stages of pregnancy allows for a better grasp of how each method of contraception works. The major portion of the chapter is designed to provide practical, comprehensive information for anyone who is thinking about using birth control. This is not just an exercise in cerebral gymnastics: an educated user is more likely than an ignorant one to avoid mistakes that can result in unwanted pregnancy.

CONCEPTION

In humans, pregnancy can result only when sperm meets egg. For this to happen, sperm must be deposited in the vagina close to the time of ovulation. In general, sperm retain their capability to penetrate the egg for 24 to 72 hours.

Although it may seem as though pregnancy happens almost instantaneously, fertile couples who are trying to have a baby or who have intercourse regularly without contraception take an average of 5.3 months for pregnancy to occur. Only 25 percent of women conceive after one month of unprotected intercourse. Sixty-three percent conceive by the end of 6 months, and by the end of one year, 80 percent become pregnant. Clearly, even when fertile couples time their intercourse to be near ovulation, there is an element of luck in whether a pregnancy occurs.

Ovulation itself is controlled by hormones secreted by the pituitary gland, an acorn-sized structure that sits directly underneath the brain. The pituitary gland, in turn, is controlled by a region in the brain called the hypothalamus. Two hormones produced in the pituitary act directly on the ovaries. One, called FSH (follicle stimulating hormone) prepares the ovary for ovulation. The second hormone, called LH (luteinizing hormone) serves as the actual trigger for ovulation to occur: a midcycle surge of this hormone, typically (but not always) around cycle day 13 or 14, causes one ovary to release an egg 12 to 24 hours later. (As we will see shortly, birth control pills act by blocking the secretion of LH and FSH, which prevents ovulation.)

After ovulation, the egg is gently drawn from the surface of the ovary into the Fallopian tube, where it is propelled toward the uterus by the movement of cilia (tiny hairlike outgrowths lining the hollow inner portion of the tube). If fertilization occurs, it is usually in the upper portion of the Fallopian tube, not in the uterus.

After ejaculation in the vagina, healthy spermatozoa swim rapidly into the female reproductive system in an arduous race that has few survivors. Although 100 million or more sperm are deposited in the vagina, only a few thousand get to the Fallopian tubes, and only about 200 actually get near the

egg. Most sperm never reach the cervix because they spill out of the vagina
or are immobilized by clumping together. Other sperm are damaged along
the way, and about half the sperm that swim into the uterus take a wrong
turn and enter the eggless Fallopian tube (except in rare circumstances,
ovulation occurs on only *one* side each month). The difficult journey is
probably nature's way of attempting to make sure that only the healthiest
sperm have a chance to fertilize the egg.

Sperm spend several hours in the female reproductive tract undergoing a
poorly understood process called capacitation, which enables them to penetrate the egg. Some sperm can reach the egg in an hour, but they must still
wait to undergo this process. The race to penetrate the egg then is not always
won by the swiftest; in fact, there are usually about 40 sperm clustered about
the egg at fertilization. After capacitation, sperm secrete a chemical that
dissolves the zona pellucida, the jellylike coating around the egg.

The egg is not just a passive participant in this process. It actually embraces
the sperm by extending tiny outgrowths, called microvilli, up from its
surface. Then, to avoid penetration by more than one sperm, the egg first
produces a brief electrical block on its surface (lasting only about 30 seconds), followed by a hard outer protein coat. The process has been neatly
described as follows: "The successful sperm is held down on the egg membrane in the tight grip of microvilli, while the coat rises above it, pushing all
other sperm away. It is rather as if the egg had opened an umbrella, holding
the crowd of spermatozoa at a distance."[1] Next, the egg pulls the sperm
inside itself and moves its nucleus (containing its key genetic material) to
meet that of the sperm. Once a sperm cell enters the egg, the zona becomes
impenetrable.

Fertilization is a complex process that lasts for 24 hours or longer, so it is
not biologically correct to speak of "the moment of fertilization."[2] The
process begins with the first contact of the sperm with the zona pellucida and
is generally considered to be completed when genetic material from sperm
and egg combine.

Fertilization produces a single cell called the zygote. This cell contains 23
chromosomes (strands of genetic material) contributed by the sperm and 23
chromosomes from the egg. These 46 chromosomes provide programming
for inherited characteristics such as blood type, height, skin color, and so
forth. Two of the chromosomes, called the sex chromosomes, combine to
determine the sex of the developing zygote. All eggs and half of the sperm
cells contain an X sex chromosome, while the remaining sperm cells have Y
sex chromosomes only. A zygote with two X chromosomes will ordinarily
become a female, and a zygote with one X and one Y will ordinarily become
a male. (There are rare exceptions to this general principle: certain hormone

abnormalities can cause a discrepancy between chromosomal sex and ana-tomic sex.)[3] Since eggs always have X chromosomes, the sex of the baby is determined by the contribution of the father, whether it be an X or Y chromosome.

Despite this biologic reality, some men mistakenly believe that the woman is responsible for determining the baby's sex, and in some cultures divorces have occurred when a wife "couldn't" produce a male heir for her husband.

The single-celled zygote starts to divide about 30 hours after the process of fertilization begins. It splits initially into two cells, then these two cells divide into four cells, eight cells, and so on. As this division occurs, the size of each cell becomes progressively smaller. This collection of cells, resembling a mulberry, is called a morula. During the 3 or 4 days after fertilization, the morula travels down the Fallopian tube and enters the cavity of the uterus. At this point, the morula has a hollow inner portion containing fluid; it is called a blastocyst.

The blastocyst undergoes further growth inside the uterus, receiving oxygen and nourishment from secretions of the lining of the uterus (the

FIGURE 9.1
EARLY DEVELOPMENT AFTER FERTILIZATION
The blastocyst implants in the lining of the uterus.

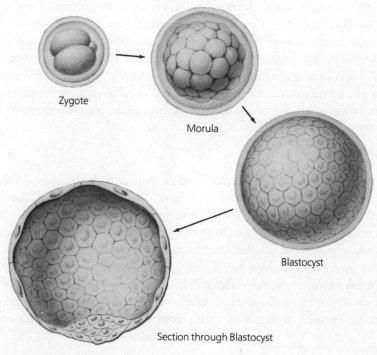

Zygote

Morula

Blastocyst

Section through Blastocyst

endometrium). After a few days, the blastocyst begins to attach itself to the lining of the uterus in a process called implantation. The endometrium of the uterus thickens and becomes richly endowed with blood vessels as a result of hormone secretions in the second half of the menstrual cycle. If fertilization does not occur, this hormone stimulation ceases abruptly and the thickened endometrial tissue is shed during menstruation. However, if fertilization does occur, the thickened, spongy endometrium becomes a "bed" for the blastocyst, which usually attaches to the upper portion of the back wall of the uterus. If implantation occurs outside the uterus (e.g., in the Fallopian tubes or in the abdomen), an ectopic (misplaced) pregnancy results.[4]

Implantation is completed about 10 to 12 days after fertilization. There are no physical sensations that accompany implantation, so it is impossible for a pregnant woman to know just when it has occurred. In some women, implantation is accompanied by bleeding that may be confused with a menstrual period. As a result, women sometimes miscalculate when pregnancy began, leading to a wrong estimation of the expected date of delivery.

CONTRACEPTION

Although there are many different methods of birth control, there is no single "perfect" method. This lack is reflected, in part, in current patterns of contraceptive use among American couples, which are shown in Table 9.1. Some birth control methods offer more convenience than others, some have very low rates of side effects, and some have particular advantages in terms of their aesthetic appeal, their reversibility, or their reliability. In the following sections, we provide a detailed look at these contraceptive options.

BIRTH CONTROL PILLS

Birth control pills were first introduced in the United States in 1960 and quickly became the contraceptive method of choice for millions. Their high level of dependability coupled with their ease of use provided the initial appeal for users, but by the late 1960s this surge of enthusiasm was tempered by reports of numerous side effects affecting pill users. Today, despite the fact that oral contraceptives have been more intensively studied than any other single form of medication, doubts still linger about the safety of the pill.

The most popular pill used today, accounting for 85 percent of the oral contraceptives used in America and Europe, is the low-dose combination

TABLE 9.1

PATTERNS OF CONTRACEPTIVE USE (PERCENTAGES) AMONG U.S. WOMEN
AGES 15 TO 44 USING BIRTH CONTROL, 1988*

Method	All Users	Married Users
Sterilization	39.2	48.7
Female	27.5	31.4
Male	11.7	17.3
Pill	30.7	20.4
IUD	2.0	2.0
Diaphragm	5.7	6.2
Condom	14.6	14.3
Foam	1.1	1.4
Periodic Abstinence	2.3	2.8
Withdrawal	2.2	2.3
Other[a]	2.1	1.9

* In 1988, 60.3 percent of women in this age range used contraception.
SOURCE: adapted from W. D. Mosher, Contraceptive Practice in the United States, 1982–1988, *Family Planning Perspectives* 22: 198–205, 1990, Table 3.
[a] "Other" consists of douche, sponge, jelly or cream alone, and other methods.

pill. Combination pills contain two different types of hormone: a synthetic form of estrogen and a synthetic progesteronelike hormone called progestogen. Today's combination birth control pills are strikingly different from pills of the 1960s: they have one-fourth or less the amount of estrogen and about one-tenth the progestogen that earlier pills contained. The lower hormone concentrations cause fewer annoying side effects; in addition, they are less likely than earlier, higher-dose forms of the pill to cause serious complications.[5]

Among the numerous types of low-dose combination pills on the market are some that have a constant dose of hormones in each pill and some that are *multiphasic*, meaning that the amount of hormone in each pill varies at different times in the monthly cycle. In biphasic pills, for example, the amount of progestogen increases around midcycle; in triphasic pills, the amount of hormone is changed three times. Women using the multiphasic pills should note that taking their pills in an incorrect sequence may considerably lessen contraceptive effectiveness.

There is also a completely different type of oral contraceptive, called the *minipill*. This pill contains no estrogen; its only component is progestogen. Because it doesn't contain estrogen, it has far fewer side effects than combination birth control pills, but it is also slightly less effective. (For clarity, throughout this chapter we will primarily be discussing combination pills; in cases where we are referring specifically to the progestogen-only minipill, we will say so.)

Birth control pills work by several straightforward mechanisms. Combination pills act on the hypothalamus and pituitary gland to suppress the midcycle surge of the hormones (called gonadotropins) that ordinarily trigger ovulation (Figure 9.2). In addition to blocking ovulation, the progestogen in the pill makes the cervical mucus thick and difficult for sperm to penetrate and also produces changes in the lining of the uterus that prevent implantation even if an egg should somehow be fertilized. (The minipill relies entirely on these progestogen-produced effects, since it doesn't contain estrogen.)

Birth control pills are taken daily for 3 weeks starting on the fifth day of the menstrual cycle. Although some brands provide seven hormone-free pills of another color to complete the 4-week cycle—with the woman then

FIGURE 9.2

SERUM LH AND FSH LEVELS DURING THE MENSTRUAL CYCLE AND WITH ORAL CONTRACEPTIVES

(a) Women not using oral contraceptives. (b) Women using combination oral contraceptives.

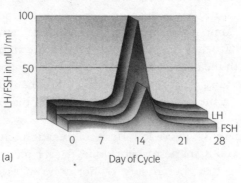

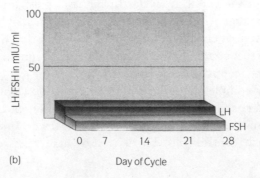

starting a new package of pills right away—with most brands the user must remember to begin taking her pills again at the appropriate point after a new cycle starts. Multiphasic pills also come in several different colors within each monthly packet, with each color corresponding to a different dose of hormones.

If a woman forgets to take a pill, she should take two pills the next day (or as soon as she realizes she forgot), but there is absolutely no need to worry, as the possibility of becoming pregnant from missing a single pill is virtually nonexistent. If she misses two pills in a row, the woman should take two pills as soon as she remembers and take two pills again the next day; after that, she should continue to take one pill each day. Since there is a chance the pill may not work properly in such a cycle, it is wisest to use an *alternative* form of contraception to be assured of preventing pregnancy. If a woman misses more than two pills in a row, or misses pills three or more times during one cycle, she should stop taking pills entirely and use another method of contraception for the rest of the cycle. She can begin a new cycle of oral contraceptives at the start of her next period. If her period is late, she should continue her other contraceptive method and get a pregnancy test before resuming the pill.

Birth control pills are the most effective reversible form of contraception available today. If combination pills are used perfectly, the failure rate is less than 1 percent per year, although the actual failure rate among pill users during their first year of using this method is 7.3 percent.[6] With continued use, the actual failure rate for combination pills declines to approximately one to 2 percent.

The minipill, which is taken on a daily basis for as long as protection against pregnancy is desired, is slightly less effective. When used correctly and consistently, only one or two pregnancies will occur in 100 women using the minipill for a year, but under real-life conditions, in which women sometimes forget to take a pill, the actual failure rate is 5 to 10 percent.

While safety concerns about the pill garner attention-grabbing headlines, what is often overlooked is that the use of oral contraceptives has a number of beneficial health effects. For example, birth control pills reduce the risk of ovarian cancer and cancer of the endometrium, the lining of the uterus. (This important protective effect of the pill is not just short-term, it persists for at least 15 years after a woman stops using oral contraception.)[7] The pill also reduces the incidence of noncancerous breast tumors by 75 percent and greatly lowers the risk of ovarian cysts and fibroid tumors of the uterus. In addition, women using oral contraceptives are only half as likely as nonusers to develop rheumatoid arthritis[8] and have a greatly reduced risk of iron deficiency anemia, ectopic pregnancy, and pelvic inflammatory disease.[9]

One very noticeable beneficial effect of the pill is that it fosters more regular menstrual periods and lessens problems like excessive menstrual flow, menstrual cramping, and pain (called mittelschmerz) around the time of ovulation. Thus the pill can be a tremendous boon to women who are incapacitated by such difficulties. Oral contraceptives alleviate PMS (the premenstrual syndrome) and often improve acne, as well.[10] Finally, the pill seems to cause an increased bone density, perhaps helping to prevent the thinning out of bone called osteoporosis that occurs in many women after the menopause.[11]

Minor but frequently annoying side effects of the pill resemble changes produced by pregnancy, but they have no real health implications. For example, a weight gain of 2 to 5 pounds—which usually reflects fluid retention—is common in the initial months of use, and some women complain of nausea, breast tenderness, or dizziness. These symptoms typically disappear spontaneously after several months; it is unusual for a woman to have to discontinue the pill solely because of such problems. Constipation, fatigue, minor elevations in blood pressure, edema (swelling), and skin rashes (including brown spots on the face, called *chloasma*, which may be increased by exposure to large amounts of sunlight) are other common minor problems. Other relatively minor side effects include spotting or breakthrough bleeding, an increased amount of vaginal secretions, and an increased susceptibility to vaginal infections.

Oral contraceptives can also cause more significant side effects, but these occur much less often than the minor problems cited above. These complications include gallbladder disease (especially a tendency to form gallstones), an elevated blood sugar (which infrequently turns into true diabetes mellitus), high blood pressure, a heightened risk of liver tumors (including cancer), migraine headaches, and depression. There also appears to be an association between long-term use of birth control pills and cancer of the cervix.[12] In addition, the pill can cause birth defects if taken during pregnancy and may interfere with the production of breast milk in nursing mothers. The minipill, which doesn't have such an effect, can be used safely during breast feeding.

One potentially serious side effect of oral contraceptives is that pill use may increase a woman's susceptibility to infection with HIV, the AIDS virus. Although at present there is no clear-cut answer on this important issue, several studies point to this possibility.[13] It is ostensibly for this reason that Japan has retained its longtime ban on the pill.[14]

The most serious risks to women using birth control pills are disorders of the circulatory system. Three different types of circulatory problem are involved. The most common is the formation in a vein (usually in the legs) of a blood clot, which typically results in only minor discomfort caused by inflammation and swelling. Infrequently, a piece of the clot may break off and circulate to the lungs or the brain, where it can cause serious damage or death. These problems, called thromboembolic diseases, were two to four times more common among pill users than other women in the 1960s and 1970s (occurring in about one out of 1,000 pill users in a year), but are thought to occur much less often now with the considerably lower dose of estrogen contained in today's pills.[15] The same observation (lower estrogen dose = lower rates of complication) applies to the other two forms of circulatory disorders linked to use of the pill: heart attacks and stroke. Earlier studies concluded that oral contraceptives increased the risk of heart attacks in women who smoked and/or women over age 35.[16] A heightened risk of stroke (bleeding into the brain, or blockage of blood flow in the brain) was also found in early research on pill users.

Data from these early studies tell us that the pill was not usually prescribed for women over age 35. More recent research indicates that use of low-dose combination pills by healthy, nonsmoking women up to age 45 does not cause any increased risk of serious cardiovascular disease.[17] In fact, one study found that in 54,971 woman-years of use of the pill, there was not a single cardiovascular death, while 11 cardiovascular deaths occurred in the age-matched control group of non-pill users.[18]

For several decades, there has also been a persistent concern that the pill may cause an increased rate of breast cancer. Most studies have not identified any link between birth control pills and breast cancer. For example, one recent investigation found no evidence that use of oral contraceptives, even over many years, increased the risk of subsequent breast cancer in women with a family history of the disease.[19] Likewise, a 10-year study of a total of 118,273 female nurses concluded, "Overall past use of oral contraceptives is not associated with a substantial increase in the risk of breast cancer."[20] The results of other studies have been inconsistent, however.[21]

An FDA panel convened in 1989 to examine all of the available evidence decided that there was no need for recommending changes in the use of birth control pills or in their warning labels (New York Times January 6, 1989, pp. A1, A13). The panel noted that the small number of studies suggesting a heightened risk of breast cancer in women who have used the pill are inconsistent with each other and plagued with methodological problems. (Since these problems have been thoroughly reviewed elsewhere,[22] we will not go into detail about them here.) More recently, a prestigious committee of the National Academy of Sciences and Institute of Medicine wrote:

> Oral contraceptives, as they have been used to date, have caused little or no overall increase in the risk of breast cancer in women in developed countries. Risks in women of all ages combined have not been appreciably enhanced by more than a decade of exposure or after a potential latent period of up to two decades.[23]

Nevertheless, because the risk of breast cancer occurring long after use of the pill (20 years or more) has not yet been conclusively examined, the final word on a possible relationship between the pill and breast cancer cannot be given at this time. As a practical precautionary matter, we suggest that people whose mothers or sisters have had breast cancer should probably avoid use of the pill until more conclusive studies have been completed.

The pill should also be avoided by women who are (or might be) pregnant, by women with a previous history of thromboembolic disorders, by women with a past history of stroke or coronary artery disease, by women with undiagnosed abnormal vaginal bleeding, by women with abnormal Pap smears, and by women who currently have an active liver disease such as hepatitis or infectious mononucleosis. In addition, we suggest that, although individual circumstances may differ, it is generally wisest for women with the following problems to choose a method of contraception other than birth control pills because of the risk that these pills may worsen their underlying difficulty:

1. high blood pressure (hypertension);
2. migraine headaches or recurrent, severe headaches of any cause;
3. sickle cell disease;
4. gallbladder disease, including a past history of gallstones;
5. heart disease;
6. diabetes mellitus with vascular complications;
7. jaundice during previous pregnancy;
8. frequent bouts of monilial vaginitis.

Nursing mothers should also use some other method.

Despite these health concerns, it is clear that today's low-dose birth control pills are safer than such pills have ever been by a considerable margin.[24] However, women who rely on the pill for contraception should recognize that it provides no protection at all against HIV, so any pill user who is not in a strictly monogamous relationship should also use condoms for maximal protection against HIV and other sexually transmitted diseases.

Most women find that the pill enhances their sex lives by freeing them from worries over unplanned pregnancy and by cutting down on unwanted gynecologic symptoms such as menstrual or premenstrual cramping or mittelschmerz. In fact, there may be other directly beneficial sexual effects as well. "When I started taking the pill, it really increased the sensitivity of my breasts," one 20-year-old woman noted. "Not only did my breast size increase pleasingly, I also found that I was more responsive to breast caresses or having my nipples sucked." Other pill users point to the fact that the pill is a totally unintrusive method of contraception: it doesn't require stopping the sexual action to do anything, thus in itself enhancing sexual spontaneity and enjoyment.

While there was some evidence that the original version of the pill commonly led to drops in sexual interest and responsivity, today's low-dose pills rarely have such an effect. Moreover, when sexual side effects occur, it is not always clear that they are pharmacologically induced; in some cases, for example, a woman may become less amorous while on the pill because she equates her femininity and attractiveness with her reproductive potential. Other women feel guilty if the pill goes against their religious tenets, which can also obviously lower sexual enthusiasm. Although there has not been any large-scale systematic research on the point, our clinical impression from working with thousands of women in the past decade is that today's oral contraceptives are much more likely to be beneficial sexually than to have any negative sexual effects.

THE INTRAUTERINE DEVICE (IUD)

The IUD, or *intrauterine device*, is hardly a new development. The ancient Greeks used a primitive form of such an apparatus: a hollow lead tube filled with fat was inserted inside the uterus as a form of birth control.[25] Purportedly, camel drivers used a similar method to guard against unwanted pregnancies in their beasts of burden on long desert journeys: they placed a large pebble into the camel's uterus for birth control purposes. By World War I, IUDs made from metal and catgut were introduced in Germany, although problems with infections after insertion were quickly evident and led to this approach's falling into general scientific disrepute. Subsequently, the German gynecologist Ernest Gräfenberg (the same man after whom the so-called "G spot" was named) devised IUDs made from coiled silver and gold, although he was persecuted by the Nazis, who were philosophically opposed to contraception. At about the same time, a Japanese scientist named Ota improved the functioning of the Gräfenberg ring by adding a strengthening midsection, but he too was politically unpopular, and awareness of both the Gräfenberg and Ota devices virtually vanished during the 1940s and 1950s.

Interest in alternative methods of contraception became intense after the invention of the pill, and the IUD was rediscovered. In its plastic reincarnations, the IUD quickly came into vogue as a safe, inexpensive, reversible form of birth control. By the early 1970s, IUDs were climbing in popularity among married women in the U.S. and were even more widely used around the world. In Scandinavia, IUDs were used by more than 20 percent of women of reproductive age; in China, the corresponding figure was above 50 percent. All in all, more than 50 million women around the world used IUDs.

Then, in the mid-1970s, the relationship between IUDs and infection again began to surface as problems with the Dalkon Shield—one of the most popular models available—became known.[26] The key finding was that IUDs (especially the Dalkon Shield) increased the risk of infection in the upper female genital tract, especially in the Fallopian tubes, where it was known as salpingitis or pelvic inflammatory disease (PID).[27] This is a particularly serious form of infection because it can cause permanent sterility, it increases the chances of having an ectopic pregnancy, and it can sometimes cause abscesses around the ovaries that might require surgery to be corrected. In 1974, A.H. Robins, the maker of the Dalkon Shield, had stopped production and distribution of its product. Nevertheless, women already using the Dalkon Shield were not adequately warned of its dangers until the early 1980s, and over the ensuing years, lawsuits against the company mounted, eventually forcing Robins into bankruptcy amid accusations of corporate greed and deliberate cover-up. By the mid-1980s, other major manufacturers of IUDs in the U.S. had withdrawn their products from the market because of concern over lawsuits. As a result of the crescendo of negative publicity and reluctance on the part of many physicians to recommend IUDs to new users, IUD use in America plummeted from 2.2 million in 1982 to 700,000 in 1988.[28] Although the older IUD devices have now been replaced by substantially safer versions, their popularity in the United States is still considerably lower than it had been a decade ago.

Today, there are only two models of IUDs available in the United States: a progesterone-releasing device (called Progestasert) and a copper-containing device (called the ParaGard T 380A). These are shown in Figure 9.3.

IUDs provide their contraceptive action mainly by blocking sperm from fertilizing the egg. This spermicidal action is thought to be primarily a result of white blood cells released inside the uterus engulfing or damaging sperm before they reach the egg. Chemical reactions caused by enzymes in the Fallopian tubes also create an environment hostile to sperm. In addition, IUDs containing progesterone thicken the cervical mucus, making it more difficult for sperm to swim up toward the awaiting egg; the progesterone also

FIGURE 9.3
IUDs

Insertion of an IUD (*a–c*) and photographs of the Progestasert and Paraguard IUDs currently in use in the United States.

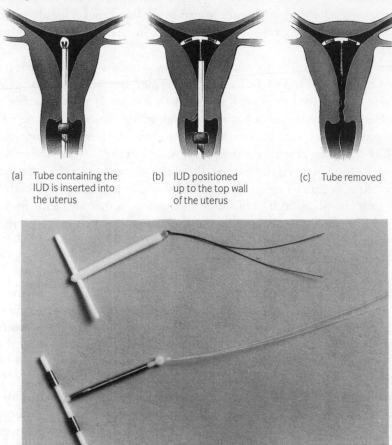

(a) Tube containing the IUD is inserted into the uterus

(b) IUD positioned up to the top wall of the uterus

(c) Tube removed

affects the lining of the uterus so implantation is unlikely even if fertilization occurs. The copper in IUDs appears to act on the lining of the uterus to provoke biochemical changes that tip the scales against sperm survival.

The best time to have an IUD inserted is during a menstrual period, since the cervical canal is more widely open at this time and it is certain that the woman isn't pregnant. However, IUDs can be inserted at any time during the menstrual cycle, although it may be necessary to dilate the cervical canal gently to allow the device to be positioned properly. Usually, a local anesthetic is used before inserting the IUD, although many women find the procedure relatively painless if they take several aspirin tablets an hour before insertion is done. (Women having an IUD inserted during their period will be, generally, better able to tolerate the procedure without any local anesthetic. Unless a woman is certain that she has a high tolerance for pain, insisting on the local anesthetic for insertion at other times is highly recommended. There is no reason to try to be a hero in terms of "natural" contraception.)

The insertion itself is accomplished using a hollow tubelike carrier, as shown in Figure 9.3. The IUD, which is loaded into the tube just before insertion, springs into its normal shape when it is gently pushed out of the tube inside the uterus and is positioned high inside the uterine cavity. The entire process takes just a minute or two. After the inserter tube is removed, the IUD "tail" that protrudes through the mouth of the cervix is trimmed so it won't be too long, and the woman should be shown how to locate the tail by feel. Any woman using an IUD should check its position periodically by feeling for the plastic IUD tail inside her vagina: if the tail seems to have increased in length, the IUD may be slipping out of its proper position. Likewise, if the woman can't feel the IUD tail at all, she should immediately have a checkup to see what the problem is, since this can be an early sign of uterine perforation, a serious complication described below.

In some women, contractions of the uterus push the IUD downward, causing it to be partly or completely expelled from the uterus. Expulsion rates for the copper or progesterone IUDs are about 7 per 100 women during a year, with most of the expulsions occurring in the first three months after insertion. Expulsion rates are higher in younger women and in women who have never had children.

Even though they may be expelled, IUDs are highly effective. A number of studies show fewer than 1 pregnancy occurring in 100 women using the ParaGard T 380A for one year, while the Progestasert IUD has a pregnancy rate of about 3 per 100 women in one year.[29] However, if women with expulsions and other IUD problems are included in the statistics, the actual overall failure rate for IUD use is 6 percent.[30] The Progestasert device must be replaced after one year of use because its progesterone supply is depleted by that time; the Para Gard T 380A is currently approved for eight years of continuous use.

The most serious complication of IUD use, perforation of the uterus (when the IUD pierces the wall of the uterus, usually migrating into the abdomen), is fortunately a relatively rare occurrence, with an incidence of about 1 in 1,000.[31] Perforation usually occurs at the time of insertion, although it does not always produce symptoms and may thus go undetected. More commonly, perforation is signaled by sharp, sudden lower abdominal pain and vaginal bleeding. Whether the IUD has penetrated partway into the muscular wall of the uterus or has actually broken through the uterus into the abdomen can be determined by either X-rays or ultrasound studies, which are simple, noninvasive, painless procedures that give almost instantaneous results. In either case, the IUD should be promptly removed by surgery. If perforation is undetected, copper-containing IUDs can cause adhesions and inflammatory reactions in the abdomen.

Although copper IUDs can cause heavier menstrual periods, spotting or bleeding between periods, and sporadic cramping in some women, progesterone-containing IUDs actually cause lighter periods and characteristically reduce menstrual and premenstrual cramping, so they are particularly well suited for women who have difficulties with such symptoms. Cramps and bleeding in women using non-progesterone-containing IUDs are problematic enough to require discontinuing this birth control method for about one out of ten women, but most users find that these symptoms subside considerably after the first several months of IUD use.

As we mentioned previously, concerns about a heightened risk of PID in IUD users fueled a mass migration in the 1980s away from this otherwise highly efficacious method of contraception. Now, a reexamination of research on this topic has uncovered a number of flaws in study design and the interpretation of data that accounts for an erroneous smear to the safety reputation of IUDs other than the now-infamous Dalkon Shield.[32] Our overall assessment is that while today's IUDs do slightly increase the risk of PID, most of this excess risk is due to the possibility of introducing infection into the uterus by pushing bacteria up from the vagina or cervix at the time of insertion. It is also clear that women with many sex partners—who are obviously at some risk of exposure to a sexually transmitted disease—have a higher incidence of PID with IUDs than other women do.[33] For women in monogamous sexual relationships, IUDs pose little risk of infection except in the first few months after they are inserted.[34]

If a woman with an IUD becomes pregnant, there is a 4 to 5 percent chance that the pregnancy will be ectopic (misplaced).[35] IUDs protect better against intrauterine pregnancies than against those that occur outside the uterus. Since pregnancies are very infrequent in IUD users, the rate of ectopic pregnancy is relatively low: less than 1.5 ectopic pregnancies per 1,000 woman-years of use.[36] (This is about one-tenth the rate of ectopic pregnancies overall, although it is higher than the rate in women who use birth control pills.)[37]

If an IUD user becomes pregnant, she has a 50 percent chance of aborting (usually in the second trimester) unless the IUD is removed. Removal of the IUD is associated with a miscarriage rate of about 25 percent, giving the woman a better chance to maintain the pregnancy if she wishes to do so. Removing the IUD is almost always the option for a pregnant woman to follow because leaving it in place runs a substantial risk of a septic abortion, which is a life-threatening miscarriage complicated by severe infection and shock.

IUDs are an excellent contraceptive method for women who want a high degree of effectiveness along with a method that requires no active involvement other than remembering to check the length of the IUD tail periodically. They are particularly well suited to women who can't use birth control pills for medical reasons and for those in monogamous sexual relations. Women who have previous histories of menstrual abnormalities (especially heavy or painful bleeding) and those who have never had a child should probably avoid choosing this method. Women who have previously had an ectopic pregnancy or pelvic inflammatory disease, or who have valvular heart disease, bleeding disorders, anatomical abnormalities of the cervix or uterus, or any disease that suppresses their immune system (including infection with HIV, the AIDS virus) should *not* use IUDs. IUDs are absolutely contraindicated in anyone who is pregnant or who has an active infection of the female reproductive tract.

IUDs generally have little or no effect on sexual feelings and specifically do not lower sexual interest in any way. A small number of women using IUDs find that their uterine contractions accompanying orgasm produce brief but severe abdominal cramping with an IUD in place. Occasionally, especially if the IUD is mispositioned, it may cause a searing, deep pelvic pain during vigorous coital thrusting, but this problem affects only one or 2 percent of women who are long-term IUD users. One other problem that is infrequently encountered (but that is very unpleasant when it occurs) is that the tail of the IUD can scrape or scratch the penis during intercourse.

Anyone using an IUD should realize that although it is highly effective as a contraceptive device, it provides no protection against infection with HIV, the virus that causes AIDS, or other sexually transmitted diseases.

THE DIAPHRAGM

The diaphragm was invented in Germany in the 1870s. Despite widespread use in Europe by 1900, it did not become popular in the United States until the 1920s, when it was brought to public attention largely through the efforts of Margaret Sanger and her colleagues. Today, after enjoying a surge of use during the 1940s and 1950s, the diaphragm has come to be largely regarded as a second-rate form of birth control since it generally has less than outstanding effectiveness and is among the most cumbersome birth control devices to use. However, it has no systemic health risks, which may make it suitable for women who cannot take the pill or use IUDs for medical reasons, and its effectiveness can easily be improved considerably by combining it with the use of condoms. Another benefit is that the diaphragm offers considerable protection against many sexually transmitted bacterial diseases, and thus seems to reduce the risk of damage to the Fallopian tubes from these sources.[38]

In brief, the diaphragm is a dome-shaped rubber cup with a stiffened but flexible circular rim. Coming in various sizes that require an individualized fitting by a health care practitioner, the diaphragm by itself is of little contraceptive value. In order for it to work, spermicidal jelly or cream must be placed inside the rubber dome and around the rim, with the diaphragm functioning primarily as a container for these spermicidal ingredients (Figure 9.4). Secondarily, the diaphragm also acts as a barrier to limit the number of sperm that gain access to the opening of the cervix, but in this regard it is a bit like an umbrella in a wind-driven rainstorm: it may work in a protective sense, but the user won't stay completely dry. Similarly, although the diaphragm's mechanical "shielding" effect may prevent a substantial number of sperm from reaching the cervix, some do get past . . . and "some" would be enough to lead to pregnancy if the spermicide weren't there to provide another form of protection.

Although failure rates as low as 2 percent have been reported among highly motivated couples using a diaphragm consistently and correctly, the method is generally not so effective. A failure rate of 8 to 12 percent among experienced users is more typical. During the first year of use, the actual failure rate for diaphragm use is 22 percent (see Table 9.2). The majority of failures are due to inconsistent or improper use of this method, including couples who sometimes gamble on the chance of getting pregnant by having sex without using the diaphragm. However, there are several specific problems with the diaphragm that can cause failures no matter how consistently it is used. These include the following:

1. *Improper fit*—If a woman has a substantial change in her weight (15 pounds or more), it is quite possible that her diaphragm will no longer fit her properly. Likewise, after pregnancy or after certain types of gynecologic surgery there may be anatomical changes that require refitting the diaphragm. A woman can also have a significant change in the size of her vagina as a result of certain sexual practices, especially as a result of repeatedly using

FIGURE 9.4
THE DIAPHRAGM

Proper use of a diaphragm: (*a*) After inserting spermicidal jelly or cream, the rim of the diaphragm is pinched between the fingers and thumb. (*b*) The folded diaphragm is gently inserted into the vagina and pushed backward as far as it will go. The front rim of the diaphragm should then be tucked up along the roof of the vagina so it is positioned snugly behind the pubic bone. (*c*) To check for proper positioning, feel the cervix to be certain it is completely covered by the soft rubber dome of the diaphragm. (*d*) A finger is hooked under the forward rim to remove the diaphragm after it has been worn for at least 6 hours, but no more than 12 hours, after intercourse.

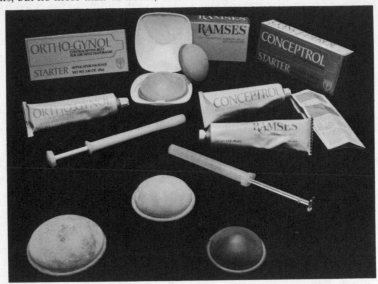

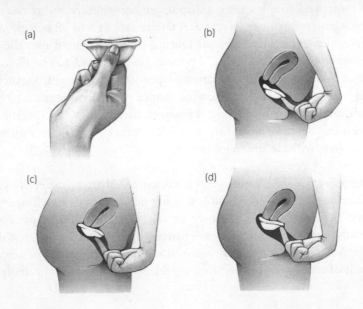

large dildos or engaging in "fisting" (where her partner inserts the whole hand inside the vagina to provide erotic stimulation).

2. *Displacement during sex*—Diaphragms may slip out of position during sexual activity as a result of vaginal expansion or movement of the uterus that occurs during the sexual response cycle. (During sexual excitation, the inner third of the vagina expands much like a balloon, changing the inside dimensions of the vagina considerably. In addition, the cervix and uterus are pulled upward from their resting position during sexual excitation.) Certain patterns of intravaginal thrusting can dislodge a diaphragm from its proper position as well, especially if the head of the penis pushes against the rim of the diaphragm behind the cervix, causing the front edge of the diaphragm to pop out of place.

3. *Time-related loss of spermicidal potency*—Spermicidal creams or jellies generally lose a portion of their sperm-killing capacity after 2 hours, but many women (and many health care providers who offer contraceptive counseling) don't realize this. It is common for single women to insert a diaphragm early in an evening in anticipation of later sexual activity, but by the time they get around to amorous activities, the effectiveness of the diaphragm may be tremendously reduced. The solution in this situation is to apply an extra application of cream, jelly, or foam shortly before having sex.

4. *Mechanical defects*—Diaphragms are made out of a relatively thin sheet of rubber, and like any rubber product, they can develop cracks, holes, or leaks. Vaseline or other oil-based lubricants can cause deterioration of the diaphragm rubber, so women must be especially careful to avoid these. Likewise, heat or light can damage the diaphragm.

The diaphragm should be left in place for at least 6 hours after intercourse. We emphatically advise that it should not be retained for more than 12 hours at a time in order to avoid the extremely small but real risk of toxic shock syndrome, a rare but sometimes fatal disease which is linked to an overgrowth of bacteria in the vagina and cervix.

Women who have allergies to latex rubber should not use the diaphragm for obvious reasons, and women who are allergic to spermicides will not be able to use a diaphragm, either. In addition, there is mounting evidence that diaphragm use predisposes to both urinary tract infections and changes in vaginal bacterial patterns that could have negative health implications.[39] Therefore, women who have had frequent urinary tract or vaginal infections would be well advised to use a different form of contraception. Furthermore, all diaphragm users should be aware that there is no evidence that the diaphragm provides meaningful protection against HIV or other viral STDs.

Many couples find that using a diaphragm is bothersome from a sexual point of view. For one thing, they point to the inconvenience of sometimes having to stop the action in order to allow the woman to get up, get her diaphragm and jelly, unpack it all, and put it in place. Understandably, this sort of interruption could douse anyone's passion. And since it is the "unexpected" sexual encounters that many people find to be most spontaneous, electric, and enjoyable, these are the precise times when a woman *won't* be wearing her diaphragm. Some women also complain that inserting a diaphragm feels awkward and uncomfortable, and they are never sure that they have it in exactly the right position. Other couples object to the fact that they can feel the diaphragm during intercourse, although most people have very little awareness of its mechanical presence.

THE CERVICAL CAP

A device related to the diaphragm is the *cervical cap*, which fits snugly over the cervix and stays in place by suction (see Figure 9.5). (Today's cervical caps are somewhat more advanced than those used by Casanova in the eighteenth century: he reportedly sometimes used a lemon half applied snugly to the cervix as a type of contraception.) After enjoying considerable popularity for the past three decades in Europe, the cervical cap was finally approved for use by the U.S. Food and Drug Administration in 1988 (*New York Times*, May 24, 1988, pp. A1, C8).

There are several types of cervical cap, although only one—the Prentif cavity-rim cap—has been approved by the FDA so far. This thimble-shaped version is made of soft, pliable latex and is a bit less than half the size of a diaphragm. Other types are made of a harder plastic material.

Like the diaphragm, the cervical cap is a mechanical barrier that blocks the mouth of the cervix so that sperm cannot enter. In fact, this blocking action is more efficient than that of the diaphragm because the cervical cap fits on the cervix more tightly than the diaphragm does.

The Prentif cap, made in four different sizes, must be fitted properly in order to be effective. It is somewhat more difficult for the user to learn how to insert the cap correctly than it is to master the use of a diaphragm. At the present time, the FDA has approved the cap for only 48 hours of continuous wear, although data suggest it can actually be worn for longer periods of time.[40]

The FDA recommends that a spermicide always be placed inside the cap

FIGURE 9.5
CERVICAL CAPS

The photograph shows three different types of cervical caps that are currently used for contraception. (*a*) Initial placement of the cap inside the opening of the vagina. (*b*) The cap must be positioned snugly over the cervix, the way a thimble fits over your finger. (*c*) Removing the cap.

(a)

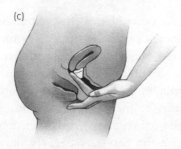

(b)

(c)

before use, but this is apt to be an effective "backup" only for the first few hours, since the action of spermicides decreases considerably after that. However, members of the National Women's Health Network, which led the drive to obtain approval for the device, believe that spermicide is unnecessary for the cap's effectiveness.

The cervical cap seems to be generally as effective as the diaphragm. In the results of several different studies, pregnancy rates ranged from 8 to 20 per 100 woman-years.[41] In the largest U.S. study of the cap, involving around 1,500 women who were randomly assigned to either the cap or a diaphragm, one-year pregnancy rates were roughly the same for both devices—17.4 per 100 women using the cervical cap, compared to 16.7 per 100 diaphragm users.[42]

There is only one major question mark about potential adverse effects of the cervical cap. The cap has been linked to abnormal Pap smears in a small minority of users. In one study, for instance, 4 percent of women who used the cervical cap for 3 months developed changes in their Pap smears, an incidence about twice as high as in diaphragm users (*New York Times*, May 24, 1988, pp. A1, C8). However, two other studies found no excess risk of cervical abnormalities among women wearing cervical caps,[43] so the matter is still uncertain. It is unclear if these cervical abnormalities are minor microscopic changes resulting from inflammation or if they may be precancerous.

There is also a small risk that if the cap is worn too long it may cause an overgrowth of bacteria linked to toxic shock syndrome. As with the diaphragm, a very few women may have an allergic reaction to the latex in the cap.

Women who have abnormal Pap smears or anatomical abnormalities of the cervix should not use the cervical cap.

One of the principal safety advantages of the cap is that it does not influence a woman's hormone production or cause any changes in the functioning of a woman's body.

Most women who have switched to the cervical cap after experience with a diaphragm say that it is advantageous in two ways: it permits more sexual spontaneity and it is considerably less messy. In a small number of cases, the cap has been reported to cause discomfort to the male during intercourse, but in our experience, this problem is quite rare. On the other hand, about one woman in five complains of the cap's causing vaginal odors, which can be embarrassing in intimate situations. One other drawback is that the cap can be dislodged from the cervix, especially during deep penile thrusting. In one large study, this occurred at least once in 40 percent of women using the cap.

CONDOMS

The Italian anatomist Gabriele Falloppio (Fallopius), after whom the Fallopian tubes were named, claimed to be the inventor of the condom, though its original purpose was to protect against syphilis rather than conception.[44] The earliest condoms were made out of linen (with a ribbon sewn into the open end in order to draw the device snugly around the shaft of the penis), but by the eighteenth century segments of sheep, lamb, and goat intestines (and sometimes fish skin) were used for this same purpose. The discovery of the process of vulcanization in 1843–1844 led to the production of a condom made of rubber, although the earliest versions were a far cry from today's prophylactic devices.

Although condoms (also called safes or rubbers) were relatively ignored in the 1960s and 1970s because they were viewed as cumbersome and old-fashioned, there has been a marked increase in their popularity in the past decade as they have come to be seen as effective protection against the spread of the AIDS virus as well as other sexually transmitted diseases. In addition to the positive publicity through numerous recommendations from governmental and scientific groups, condom manufacturers have increased their advertising, generating further consumer awareness and interest. Several brands are now being marketed primarily to women, and condom sales to women surged by an estimated 300 percent between 1980 and 1989 (in one ad for Lifestyle condoms, a young woman proclaims, "I'll do a lot for love, but I'm not ready to die for it").

Condoms work by providing a barrier that prevents sperm from entering the vagina. However, in order to work with maximum effectiveness, condoms must be used properly, requiring more attention to detail than most people imagine. Here are a number of practical pointers to keep in mind.[45]

1. Condoms in damaged packages or those that show obvious signs of age (e.g., those that are brittle, sticky, or discolored) should not be used; they are probably defective.

2. Condoms should be handled with care to prevent punctures or rips. In particular, fingernails and rings can tear them, and they can also be inadvertently ripped if the foil or plastic package they come in is torn open too vigorously.

3. Don't unroll a condom before using it. It's much harder to put on—and more likely to tear—if it's unrolled in advance of use.

FIGURE 9.6
THE CONDOM

The proper method of pinching the tip of the condom without a reservoir end to leave some room for the semen.

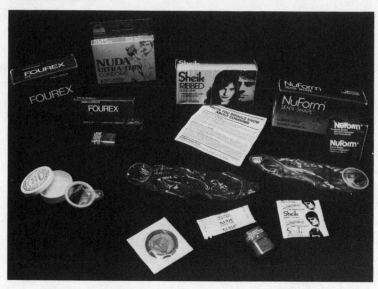

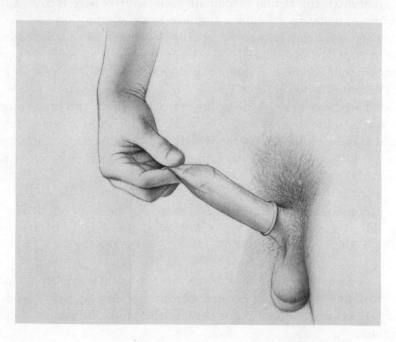

4. Condoms should be put on the erect penis *before* any genital contact to prevent exposure to fluids that may contain infectious agents as well as to prevent any drops of preejaculatory fluid (which might contain live sperm) from entering the vagina.

5. Don't put a condom on when the penis is flaccid, since this increases the likelihood that it will slip off as the penis becomes erect or once intercourse gets under way.*

6. When putting a condom on, first squeeze the air out of the tip. Then unroll the condom evenly onto the shaft of the penis, being sure to unroll it all the way down.

7. Only water-based lubricants should be used. Petroleum or oil-based lubricants such as Vaseline, baby oil, suntan lotions, cold cream, cooking oils, shortening, and most lotions should not be used because they weaken the latex and may cause breakage.

8. Use of condoms containing spermicides may provide some additional protection against STDs. However, vaginal use of spermicides along with condoms is likely to provide even better protection.

9. If a condom breaks, it should be replaced immediately. If ejaculation occurs after condom breakage, the immediate use of spermicide may be of some utility.

10. After ejaculation, care should be taken so that the condom does not slip off the penis before withdrawal; the base of the condom should be held throughout withdrawal. No matter how nice and cozy it feels to snuggle together after sex, the penis should *always* be withdrawn from the vagina while still erect.

11. Don't remove the penis from the condom while the condom is still inside the vagina.

12. Condoms should never be reused.

* As with most rules, there's an exception to this one. If you plan to put the penis into the vagina before it becomes erect, using a "stuffing" technique, then you'll have to put the condom on before having an erection. In this case, it's important to hold the condom firmly at the base of the penis, otherwise it is extremely likely to slip off.

13. Condoms should be stored in a cool, dry place out of direct sunlight. Despite its convenience, the glove compartment of the car isn't a good place for long-term storage because it gets too hot, causing condoms to become brittle and damaged.

14. It's inadvisable for men to carry condoms in their wallet; repeated bending and weight-bearing (from being sat on) is unlikely to be beneficial to the condom's life expectancy, although chances are you won't realize a condom has a leak until *after* you've used it.

Because these points are so important, we want to restate and expand on them here. Latex condoms deteriorate rapidly and are liable to break if they are in contact with oil-based lubricants such as Vaseline, baby oil, vegetable oil, many hand creams, or some of the exotic massage oils sold in sex shops. In one recent experiment, it was found that exposure of the condom to such products for just ten minutes at body temperature causes a significant weakening in the strength of the condom—a weakening that is pronounced enough to be "likely to cause [the condom] to fail during use."[46] Bruce Voeller reported that a large fraction of college-educated men who reported having condoms break on more than 10 percent of the occasions they used them mistakenly believed that because they washed off easily with water, these types of sexual lubricants were water-based.[47]

Unfortunately, despite all the enthusiasm that has been mustered for condoms as a means of protecting against sexually transmitted diseases and unintended pregnancy, the reality is that condoms—while highly useful— are far from foolproof. Most studies have found failure rates of 10 to 20 percent a year in couples using condoms for birth control.[48] Although better effectiveness rates may be attained by couples who are meticulous in their dedication to this method, it is irresponsible for health care professionals to convey the notion that condoms work all the time.

Under real-life conditions of use, one recent study found that 14.6 percent of the condoms used either broke or slipped off the penis during intercourse or withdrawal. The authors noted, "If they are accurate, these rates indicate a sobering level of exposure to the risks of pregnancy and of infection with HIV or other STDs, even among those who consistently use condoms."[49] Similarly, a study conducted at a family planning clinic in Manchester, England, found that 52 percent of the patients queried had experienced condom breakage or slippage during the preceding 3 months.[50] A number of other studies also have found that there are substantial rates of condom slippage and breaks even among experienced users.[51]

Despite these limitations, condoms *do* in fact confer a significant degree of protection against the risk of HIV or other STDs. However, latex condoms are much better at preventing STDs than those made from natural membranes: the latter sometimes have pores large enough to allow viruses such as hepatitis B or HIV (the AIDS virus) to pass through.

A recent experiment confirmed that latex condoms effectively block the transmission of HIV.[52] In this study, 30 condoms (20 of them coated with the spermicide nonoxynol-9) were mounted on hollow dildos and were then put into cylinder-shaped containers with a liquid culture medium. After a solution containing HIV was put inside each condom tip through a small hole in the end of the dildo, the dildo was pumped up and down in the container and the condoms were then deliberately ripped. Before the condoms were ruptured, none of the 30 allowed HIV to pass into the surrounding culture medium. After the condoms were ripped, 7 of the 10 without spermicide allowed HIV to leak out, but no leakage of HIV was detected in the 20 condoms treated with nonoxynol-9.

Condoms do not cause any significant side effects, although a small number of users may be allergic to either the latex of the condom or to the spermicide added to some brands. However, some male users complain that condoms cut down on pleasurable sexual sensations. In addition, using a condom is problematic for males who have difficulty getting or maintaining erections: it is not only awkward to put a condom on properly if the penis is flaccid or only partially erect, attempts to put the condom on call attention to the male's degree of erection and can actually inhibit sexual arousal by making men who are already dealing with fears of performance anxious and hesitant. On a more positive note, condoms can be beneficial for men with rapid ejaculation.

One of the most notable benefits is that a condom can help give a person in a new sexual relationship a sense of security about protection from sexually transmitted diseases such as genital herpes or HIV infection. For this reason, many women who use other methods of birth control such as the pill or an IUD insist for their own safety that their partners use condoms. For that matter, many males are also awakening to the fact that the use of condoms provides them with protection from infection at the same time that it serves as a form of birth control.

SPERMICIDES

The use of various chemical ingredients placed within the vagina for their spermicidal effects has a long history, although it is unlikely that the ancient physicians who invented these concoctions understood why they might be effective. Egyptian writings from ancient times advocated using crocodile dung in the vagina as a form of birth control. Along with its aesthetic drawbacks, it probably had little spermicidal effect, although its bulk may have blocked the entrance to the cervix.[53] An Egyptian papyrus earlier than 1550 B.C. suggested a less odiferous approach: a tampon of lint, honey, and acacia leaves. This recipe probably worked because when it fermented, it produced small amounts of lactic acid.[54] Soranus of Ephesus (A.D. 98–138), a physician who practiced in Rome, favored birth control recipes made from nuts and fruits, which may have also been acidic enough to have some spermicidal action. In fourth-century India, the *Kama Sutra* (also written by a physician) suggested using rock salt as a form of contraception. While this technique worked, it had serious (and painful) side effects, including sterility.

Today's spermicides are considerably safer and more reliable. In fact, spermicidal products are so safe that they are available as over-the-counter (nonprescription) items. These include vaginal foams, creams, suppositories, tablets, and jellies, as well as a vaginal contraceptive film and a specially constructed sponge permeated with a spermicidal agent. (Condoms containing the same spermicidal ingredient are also available, as well, but there the spermicide is simply meant to provide a "backup" in case the condom leaks.)

The major active chemical ingredient in virtually all spermicides in the U.S. is nonoxynol-9 or its close chemical relative, octoxynol-9. These agents are effective as contraceptives primarily because they damage the cell membranes of sperm. The inert material containing the spermicide may make a minor contribution to contraceptive effectiveness by acting as an absorbent barrier that at least impedes the access of surviving sperm to the opening of the cervix.

Since there are considerable differences in the mechanics and timing of using the various available spermicidal products, and since these may change if the product itself is altered in any way by the manufacturer, we will not attempt to explain the use of each product. This information is provided in the package insert that accompanies each spermicide, which you should be sure to read carefully. *For the best results, it is very important to follow the manufacturer's instructions exactly.* Or, to put it another way, if you *do not* follow the exact instructions for using a spermicide, you may wind up with an unplanned pregnancy. In addition, here are some practical pointers to keep in mind.

1. Don't make the mistake of assuming a product is a spermicide unless it says so directly on the package. K-Y Jelly is meant for lubrication rather than birth control, for example; it is *not* a contraceptive. Feminine "hygiene" products, which are often displayed right next to various spermicides, also

FIGURE 9.7
VAGINAL SPERMICIDES

Use of vaginal spermicides: (*a*) When contraceptive foam is inserted with a plastic applicator, it must be placed well within the vagina so it completely covers the cervical mouth. (*b*) Spermicidal suppositories must be removed from their wrapper and inserted high in the vagina; the manufacturer's instructions on the timing of intercourse must be followed carefully since these products may require up to ten minutes to dissolve.

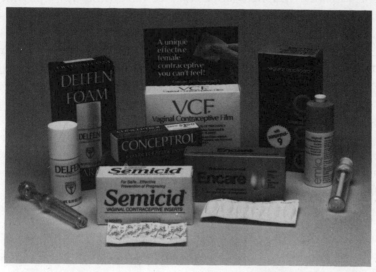

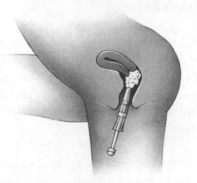

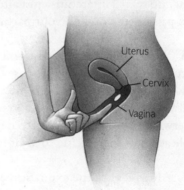

(a) Correct foam placement

(b) Correct suppository placement

have nothing at all to do with birth control. If you're not sure, ask the pharmacist or call your physician.

2. Although it may seem obvious, always unwrap the spermicide before using it. A plastic-wrapped suppository or tablet just won't provide any contraceptive action.

3. No matter which spermicide you choose, be sure to position it properly in the vagina. (The most common mistake women make is placing the spermicide close to the entrance of the vagina, rather than further back toward the cervix.)

4. For all spermicides except the sponge, protection is provided for only one episode of intercourse. Having intercourse a second time, whether it's 10 minutes or 4 hours later, requires using a second application of the spermicide—always.

5. Some spermicides—such as suppositories or foaming tablets—aren't effective for the first 10 to 15 minutes after they're inserted because it takes a while for them to become fully dispersed. This means that you can't jump right into sexual intercourse just after these have been put in place, no matter how passionate you and your partner might be.

6. Remember that most spermicides (except the sponge, which we will discuss in a moment) begin to lose their effectiveness 2 hours after insertion. This means that if you've been interrupted by a time-consuming phone call, or if your foreplay has turned into a marathon of massaging, cuddling, and otherwise engaging in intimate delights, you might need to use a second application of spermicide so as not to take any chances.

7. Always check the expiration date stamped on the package: an outdated spermicide should never be used, as it may be not much better than crossing your fingers while you're making love.

The contraceptive sponge, which is sold under the Today brand name, has certain properties that make it unique. It comes as a 2-inch-by-1-inch soft, round device that is permeated with nonoxynol-9. To activate the spermicide, the sponge must be moistened with water. (For additional use instructions and the correct method of insertion, see Figure 9.8.) Unlike most other spermicides, the sponge provides contraceptive protection immediately after it has been inserted (without having to wait for 10 or 15

FIGURE 9.8
THE CONTRACEPTIVE SPONGE

Proper use of the sponge: (*a*) Remove the sponge from the inner pack and hold with the dimple side up. The loop should dangle under the sponge. (*b*) The sponge will feel slightly moist. Wet it further with a small amount of clean water (about two tablespoons). (*c*) Squeeze the sponge gently to remove excess water. It should feel moist and soapy, but not dripping wet. (*d*) Fold the sides of the sponge upward with a finger along each side to support it. The sponge should look long and narrow. Be sure the string loop dangles underneath the sponge from one end of the fold to the other. (*e*) From a standing position, squat down slightly and spread your legs apart. Use your free hand to spread apart the lips of the vagina. You may also stand with one foot on a stool or chair, sit cross-legged, or lie down. The semisquatting position seems to work best for most women. Slide the sponge into the opening of the vagina as far as your fingers will go. Let the sponge slide through your fingers deeper into the vagina. (*f*) Now use one or two fingers to push the sponge gently up into your vagina as far as it will go. Be careful not to push a fingernail through the sponge. Check the position of the sponge by sliding your finger around the edge of the sponge to make sure your cervix is not exposed. You should be able to feel the string loop if the sponge is properly positioned.

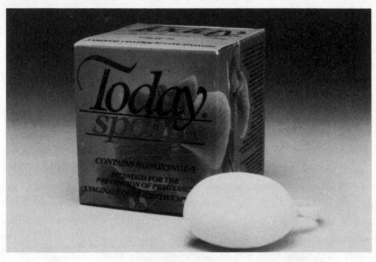

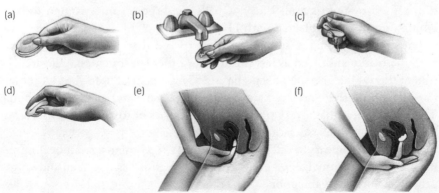

minutes) *and* it remains fully effective for 24 hours no matter how many episodes of intercourse occur. It should be left in place for at least 6 hours after sexual intercourse.

The actual contraceptive effectiveness for spermicides (excluding the sponge) is not too good, with 30.2 percent of women becoming pregnant in the first 12 months of using this method of birth control.[55] The sponge seems to have a similar effectiveness rate in women who have had children, but in women who have never given birth, the sponge has an average failure rate of 18 percent.[56] (This difference probably means that the Today sponge is too small for a woman whose birth canal has been enlarged by labor and vaginal delivery.) However, what should be emphasized here is that many studies show much better effectiveness for both spermicides and the sponge if the users are highly motivated and experienced. For example, one study of women in their second year of using the Today sponge reported a failure rate of only 5 percent.[57] There have been similar reports regarding spermicides. In addition, spermicides are very effective if their use is combined with condoms; used together consistently and correctly, this combination approach has an effectiveness rate as good as the pill's.

One decided advantage of the spermicides is that they have no major harmful side effects. (Minor allergic reactions such as genital burning, itching, or irritation occur in about 5 percent of users; these can often be eliminated by simply switching to a different spermicidal product.) There is also no evidence that spermicides cause birth defects.[58]

Another positive result is that spermicides reduce a woman's risk of developing certain types of vaginal infections (bacterial vaginosis and trichomoniasis, conditions discussed in Chapter 13) as well as certain sexually transmitted diseases, including gonorrhea and possibly chlamydia.[59] Despite preliminary laboratory evidence that spermicides containing nonoxynol-9 offer some protection against infection with HIV, field studies have not borne out such an effect, and concerns have been raised that vaginal irritation caused by nonoxynol-9 may actually predispose some women to becoming more easily infected with HIV.[60]

For most women the sponge is easier to use than a diaphragm and is enthusiastically endorsed as less messy than other spermicides. Mild irritation of the vagina or penis affects about 3 to 5 percent of users, but with one rare exception, there are no major health risks associated with this method. The exception is that a very small number of cases of toxic shock syndrome have been found in association with sponge use.[61]

The sponge appears to offer some protection to women against becoming infected with chlamydia and gonorrhea, although it has not been shown to protect against HIV infection.

Many men and women find that the sponge is a good solution from a sexual point of view because of its easy insertion, its tasteless, odorless character, and its 24-hour protection. In contrast, people who use other spermicides tend to complain about the messiness of this method and often find that oral sex is literally distasteful when the spermicide is being used. (If you're wondering why on earth they don't wait until *after* having oral sex to insert the spermicide, recall that many spermicides require a 10- or 15-minute waiting period after insertion. After your passion has been brought to near the boiling point by your partner's lips and tongue, would *you* want to sit there for 15 minutes before you could have intercourse?) One other common complaint about sex with spermicides is that it sometimes feels excessively wet or squishy. As one man said, "It felt like I was making love to my can of shaving cream."

PERIODIC ABSTINENCE

Periodic abstinence, sometimes known as the rhythm method or natural family planning, is the only form of birth control that is accepted by the Roman Catholic church. Actually consisting of several different methods from which features are often combined, periodic abstinence, as its name implies, depends on not having intercourse on days of the menstrual cycle on which conception is possible.

The simplest and most popular form of periodic abstinence is the calendar method, which identifies supposedly "safe" days in the menstrual cycle by calculations based on the length of previous cycles. Because many women do not have perfectly regular cycles, this method starts out on a somewhat flimsy premise. Furthermore, it assumes that ovulation will occur 14 days before the start of the next menstrual period, which is also not always true.

The calendar method requires recording the length of six consecutive menstrual cycles and then calculating when the "unsafe" (fertile) period begins by subtracting 18 from the number of days in the *shortest* menstrual cycle of the previous six. The end of the fertile period is calculated by subtracting 11 from the number of days in the *longest* cycle. For a woman who has cycles varying from 26 to 33 days, the unsafe days begin on the eighth day of her menstrual cycle ($26 - 18 = 8$), and will continue until the twenty-second day ($33 - 11 = 22$). This would require 15 consecutive days of abstinence from intercourse, which is one reason why many couples do not find this method particularly appealing.

Another version of periodic abstinence is the temperature method, which involves daily charting of the woman's basal body temperature (BBT)—her temperature before getting out of bed in the morning—to identify the time of ovulation. The premise here is that BBT rises by about 0.4 to 0.8 degrees F (0.2 to 0.4 degrees C) in response to the higher secretion of progesterone after ovulation.* Thus, intercourse is not permitted from the day menstruation ceases until there is a sustained temperature rise for 3 consecutive days. Unfortunately, ovulation is not always accompanied by a temperature rise; various infections or illnesses causing a low-grade fever can render BBT readings meaningless; and if there is no temperature rise, the couple, if they are truly sticking with this method, is unable to have intercourse for the entire menstrual cycle. (In addition, sleeping under an electric blanket can completely confound the usefulness of BBT readings. Imagine thinking that you've ovulated when your husband had simply turned up the blanket from medium to high.)

The most effective method of periodic abstinence is variously known as the ovulation method, the cervical mucus method, or the Billings method. It is based on the woman's observation of changes in cervical mucus during her menstrual cycle. The premise is that estrogen affects the color and consistency of cervical mucus at midcycle, near the time of ovulation: it changes from a tacky, thick, whitish substance to a clear, stringier, wetter form resembling raw egg white, a few days before ovulation occurs. Intercourse is permitted until the day the cervical mucus changes to the wetter, more slippery form, and can be resumed on the fourth day after the last day of wet, slippery mucus.[62]

The symptothermal method combines observations of cervical mucus changes and BBT patterns, sometimes adding other signs and symptoms of ovulation, such as breast tenderness or mittelschmerz. For those following such an approach, intercourse would be allowed until the cervical mucus changes consistency and color and can be resumed on either the fourth day after the last day of wet, sticky mucus or on the evening of the third day of the BBT temperature rise, whichever comes later.

The availability of a number of home-use ovulation detection kits, based on identifying the preovulatory LH surge in urine, may eventually prove to increase the effectiveness of natural family planning as a method of birth control by pinpointing the timing of ovulation more precisely, but so far there are no studies providing evidence on this matter.

The calendar method, used alone, is one of the least effective forms of birth control available, with a failure rate of approximately 40 percent. The temperature method is not much better: reported failure rates hover around the 30 percent mark and are probably somewhat higher. Detailed studies of

---

* Because it can be difficult to read small temperature differences on a regular thermometer, special BBT thermometers have been developed for this purpose. Electronic thermometers with digital readouts are also helpful in recording daily BBTs.

the ovulation method found that with absolutely perfect use, the failure rate was only 3.1 percent, but during imperfect use (e.g., sometimes having intercourse when the rules say one shouldn't), the chances of a woman's becoming pregnant are an astonishing 86.4 percent in a single year of use.[63] Since ordinary couples are less likely to follow this method perfectly than couples who volunteered to participate in a research program on its efficacy—and were screened to determine that they had learned the method accurately—the lesson seems clear: don't rely on this method unless you are absolutely, positively committed to it.

TABLE 9.2

ACTUAL CONTRACEPTIVE FAILURE RATES (PERCENTAGES) DURING THE FIRST YEAR OF USE*

Method	Failure (Percentage)
Pill	7.3
Condom	15.8
Diaphragm	22.0
Periodic Abstinence	31.4
Spermicides[a]	30.2
IUD[b]	6.0

* These figures are standardized by age, race, and marital status and are corrected to allow for underreporting of abortion. They refer to contraceptive practices in 1988.
SOURCE: Modified from E. F. Jones and J. D. Forrest, Contraceptive Failure Rates Based on the 1988 NSFG, *Family Planning Perspectives* 24: 12–19, 1992, Table 1.
[a] Spermicides reported on in this table do not include the contraceptive sponge.
[b] Data regarding IUD use are from 1982. Contraceptive Failure in the United States: Revised Estimates from the 1982 National Survey of Family Growth, *Family Planning Perspectives* 21: 103–109, 1989.

While couples who use periodic abstinence can continue to have noncoital sexual activity on days when intercourse isn't allowed, taking some of the austerity out of this approach to birth control, in the real world many couples are frustrated by the limitations and self-discipline periodic abstinence requires. The result is that they take chances: for example, they "cheat" by having intercourse a day earlier than they should, or by gambling that the probability of conception is low on a particular day, which it may or may not be. Human nature is such that what is off limits often seems especially alluring, and the capacity to resist sexual temptation—especially after having a few drinks, or to celebrate a special occasion like an anniversary or a birthday—isn't always firm and resolute. Although there are certainly enthusiastic advocates for periodic abstinence, and the method is, indeed, completely natural, there are some problems that go beyond simple risk-taking. We have encountered more than a few cases where a husband claimed that he was driven to extramarital sex (sometimes with a prostitute, sometimes in the form of an affair) by the rigors of periodic abstinence. While this may sound like a lame excuse for behavior that was probably motivated by numerous other factors, it should not be dismissed as completely outlandish.

One concern about the safety of periodic abstinence hasn't been definitively answered as yet. The issue is whether periodic abstinence heightens the risk of pregnancy's occurring with an older-than-normal egg, and whether this method may be associated with a greater risk of birth defects, chromosome abnormalities, and spontaneous abortions. Several studies have found some evidence of these problems.[64]

NORPLANT

In December 1990, the Food and Drug Administration approved the first subdermal implantable contraceptive, the Norplant System, for marketing in the United States. Norplant consists of implantable capsules containing a hormone called levonorgestrel, a synthetic progestin that has been widely used for years in birth control pills. The Norplant System had been in widespread use in Europe, Asia, and Latin America for some time before being approved in the U.S.; it has now been used by more than half a million women.

The Norplant System consists of six flexible, closed tubular capsules each about the size of a fat match. They are inserted beneath the skin of the upper arm in a procedure that takes about 10 minutes, after which they gradually release the hormone they contain for at least 5 years. Once they are in place they rarely cause discomfort, although they can be felt just under the surface of the skin and are often visible as bulges to the naked eye, especially in thin women. (The implants occasionally cause minor local itching or pain in the first month or two after insertion, but less than one percent of women stop using Norplant because of this problem.)

Norplant works by inhibiting ovulation[65] and by thickening cervical mucus, making it difficult for sperm to gain access to the Fallopian tubes. The effectiveness of the Norplant System is excellent: the failure rate is a low 0.3 to 0.6 percent for one year, with a total failure rate of only 1.1 percent for 5 years.[66]

Despite its high level of effectiveness and its convenience, there are several drawbacks for users. The most common one is that Norplant often produces

FIGURE 9.9
THE NORPLANT SYSTEM

abnormal menstrual bleeding.[67] This can take the form of very irregular periods (seen in about 40 percent of users), spotting or bleeding between periods (32 percent), or more frequent periods (25 percent). One woman in ten reports having consistently heavier periods while using Norplant, while 12 percent stop having periods entirely. Apparently many of these problems lessen after the first year of use, but there are no guarantees that this will occur. Other side effects of Norplant include headaches, acne, weight changes, increased growth of facial and body hair, uterine cramping, and breast discharge.

The other drawbacks of Norplant are mainly logistical ones. For example, it is important to recognize that it provides no protection whatsoever against HIV or other sexually transmitted diseases. Another problem is that discontinuing the use of Norplant requires a minor surgical procedure to remove the implants. While this may be an inconvenience (as well as a source of physical discomfort), the good news is that fertility is rapidly restored after the system is removed.

Since Norplant doesn't contain any estrogen, many of the risks that are associated with combination birth control pills do not apply to this contraceptive method, which is one of its biggest advantages. Norplant should not be used by women with undiagnosed abnormal genital bleeding, known or suspected pregnancy, active thromboembolic disorders, acute liver disease or liver tumors, or past or present history of breast cancer. In addition, women with high blood pressure or heart disease generally should not use this product (with few exceptions best decided by a woman and her physician), and other methods of birth control are apt to be more suitable than Norplant for women with a history of ectopic pregnancy, clinically significant depression, gallbladder disease, or severe migraine headaches. In addition, Norplant is not a good choice for women who weigh more than 154 pounds (70 kg). The reason is that the concentration of levonorgestrel in the blood is partly proportional to body weight, so that after the first year or two of use, blood concentrations of the active contraceptive ingredient may fall to unacceptably low—hence, ineffective—levels in heavier women.[68]

Most women who have used Norplant experienced no sexual changes. Of those who did report a change in sex life, almost two-thirds said that it had improved (usually because they were less worried about pregnancy and/or because sex had become more spontaneous). Only 11 percent of users found that their sex life had gotten worse, with some women indicating that this was because of menstrual changes, and a small fraction of women reporting that their sexual interest was lower.[69]

FEMALE STERILIZATION

Female sterilization is the most widely used method of birth control in the world, with an estimated 138 million women of reproductive age using this method today.[70] The appeal of this contraceptive method lies both in its high degree of effectiveness and its convenience and safety: once the sterilization procedure has been performed, no further action or apparatus is required, and virtually no long-term medical problems are encountered.

Most female sterilization procedures involve blocking the Fallopian tubes, thus preventing sperm from reaching the egg. Access to the Fallopian tubes can be gained in three different ways. *Minilaparotomy* involves making a small incision (about 3 to 5 cm) in the region above the pubic bone and then moving each Fallopian tube to the incision, tying each tube, and cutting out a small section of the tube to complete the procedure. *Laparoscopy* involves inserting through the abdominal wall a slender stainless-steel tube with a set of lenses and a fiber-optic cable connected to a light source. The laparoscope is usually inserted through a small opening to the side of the navel; inert gas, such as carbon dioxide or room air, is pumped into the abdomen to expand it and separate the internal organs from the abdominal wall. The surgeon can see the ovaries, tubes, uterus, and abdominal organs directly through the laparoscope and can easily move these organs about, using instruments inserted through a separate channel in the laparoscope. The tubes are blocked either by the use of special clips, occlusive rings, or electrocoagulation (using heat generated by an electric current) to destroy a portion of the tubes. In contrast, *laparotomy* is a more standard type of operation, requiring a longer incision into the abdomen. This approach may be used if the sterilization is being done in conjunction with a cesarean section or if there are medical reasons (such as obesity or pelvic adhesions) that make other approaches less feasible.

While hysterectomy (removal of the uterus) and ovariectomy (removal of the ovaries) both result in permanent sterility, these operations are not considered part of the contraceptive repertoire because they are usually performed for other medical reasons. However, before the 1970s hysterectomy was the most common method of permanent contraception for women in the United States.

Minilaparotomies and laparoscopies are relatively quick procedures, generally taking about 15 minutes to perform. In most cases, they can be done using local anesthesia and light sedation, eliminating the risks attendant to

FIGURE 9.10
TWO TYPES OF TUBAL LIGATION

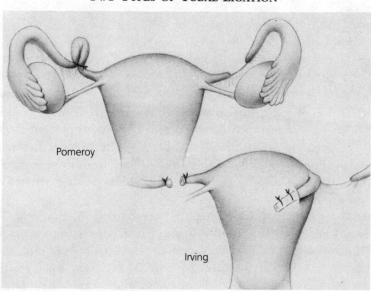

general anesthesia. When local anesthesia is used, complication rates are very low: major complications (hemorrhage, injuries to internal organs, cardio-vascular problems) occur in well under one percent of cases, while minor complications such as wound infection or slight bleeding occur in about 5 percent of women. Deaths due to female sterilization are quite rare—about 1 in 70,000 procedures.[71]

In contrast to standard practice in the 1970s, when tubal sterilization routinely required an overnight stay in the hospital, today's procedures are often performed in ambulatory surgical centers or women's health clinics and permit the woman to be up and about within hours. Postoperative abdominal pain is fairly common after a minilaparotomy, while after laparos-copy some women feel chest or shoulder pain resulting from the gas that was introduced into the abdomen.

Female sterilization provides a high degree of contraceptive protection, with an overall failure rate of approximately 0.4 percent (less than 1 in 200) during the first year. A significant number of these failures are a result of pregnancies that began before the tubal sterilization was done, so it seems advisable for a woman to have a pregnancy test just prior to the steriliza-tion. Other failures are a result of operative errors such as not destroying a large enough piece of one tube, or having spring-loaded clips come loose. Rarely, the cut ends of one of the Fallopian tubes grow back together (this reconnection is known medically as reanastomosis), which then of course can provide a channel for sperm to reach the egg. A dangerous situation, ectopic pregnancy, can occur following tubal sterilization, but fortunately it is very rare.

While female sterilization should be regarded as a permanent form of birth control, the fact is that some women (especially those who are sterilized at a young age, those who divorce and remarry, and those who have lost a child to death) subsequently have a change of heart and wish to have their fertility restored. Such reversal surgery is expensive and technically complicated, but in cases where there is enough of the Fal-lopian tubes left for reconstruction, there is a 40 to 80 percent chance of success.[72] Reconstruction involves delicate microsurgery that removes damaged portions of the tubes, aligns the healthy remaining sections, and sews them together using a technique that avoids putting stitches in the lumen of the tubes.

Female sterilization does not affect hormone production and doesn't create any long-term health risks. It also has no direct impact on female sexual functioning, although many women feel sexually freer once they are no longer worried about becoming pregnant. In a very small fraction of cases, women may become sexually apathetic after sterilization. The problem here is not a physiological one but rather that they still see sex as primarily linked to reproduction, so that when their reproductive capacity is eliminated, their sexual appetite declines precipitously. In some of these cases, it turns out that the woman really didn't want to undergo sterilization, but did so at the insistence of her husband or lover. Being pushed into such a decision is coercive, to say the least, which makes it all the more understandable why the woman's subsequent ambivalence or anger may make her feel uninterested in sex.

VASECTOMY

Vasectomy is a surprisingly neglected form of birth control, considering that it is one of the safest and most effective methods available. However, in the United States it has begun to enjoy some popularity as IUDs and birth control pills have fallen out of favor.

Today, as a result of improvements in surgical procedure, vasectomy usually takes no more than 10 to 15 minutes and has become a minor office procedure, which gives it a marked advantage over female sterilization procedures in terms of both safety and expense. Vasectomies in the U. S. are typically done in one of two ways. The conventional approach involves making a small incision (about 1 to 2 cm) in the skin of the scrotum to provide access to each vas deferens, which carry sperm from the testes to the prostate gland and seminal vesicles. The newer approach, called a no-scalpel vasectomy, substitutes a small (less than 1 mm) puncture for the incision, which lessens postoperative pain and complications. Both procedures are done using local anesthesia in an outpatient setting, and both involve blocking the passage of sperm through the vas deferens by mechanical means, such as tying the tubes after cutting out a small section, the use of electrocautery (burning the tissue with a carefully controlled electric current), or the use of clips. Following either type of procedure, the man is able to get up and go home without any major restrictions in his activities. Many men return to work the following day, although for those whose jobs involve considerable physical exertion, an additional day or two of rest may be in order.

Complications from either type of vasectomy are few. Bleeding or infections occur in about 3 percent of cases done by conventional methods, while with the no-scalpel procedure the complication rate is substantially under 1 percent.[73] Minor swelling and localized pain (usually treated by ice packs and use of an athletic supporter), along with temporary skin discoloration, while more common, usually resolve within a matter of a few days.

FIGURE 9.11
VASECTOMY

Drawing (*a*) shows the site of the small incisions in the scrotum used to perform a vasectomy; (*b*) shows the vas being cut with a surgical scissors; and (*c*) shows the cut end of the vas being burned with a controlled electric current so that scar tissue forms to block the passage of sperm.

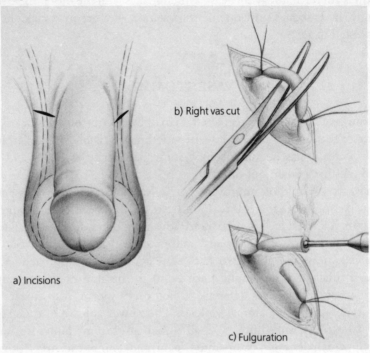

a) Incisions

b) Right vas cut

c) Fulguration

Following a vasectomy, it generally takes 6 to 8 weeks—or about a dozen ejaculations—to clear out sperm that have already moved above the blockade that has been put in the male's reproductive apparatus. Because this is a time where most postoperative failures occur, it is important to use a different method of birth control until at least two separate semen exams have shown that there are no sperm in the ejaculate. Very rarely, vasectomies fail even after one semen exam has been negative.[74]

Vasectomies are highly effective, with a failure rate of 0.15 percent, or 1 in 665 procedures. The most common failures involve not using another form of contraception during the weeks after surgery before the ejaculate is truly sterile. Apparently, some men just don't believe that after having had a vasectomy they are not completely foolproof and ready to go. Other men play a form of "postvasectomy roulette" in which the woman turns out to be the loser if her partner is not firing blanks. Other less common causes of vasectomy failure stem from errors in performing the procedure or from spontaneous rejoining of the separated ends of the vas.

In the 1970s, there was some concern that vasectomy might lead to later health problems, especially in light of research in monkeys that showed that vasectomy produces hardening of the arteries years after the operation. But several more recent large-scale studies provide convincing evidence that vasectomy does not lead to any long-term health problems in humans. Massey and his colleagues studied more than 10,000 vasectomized men and a matched nonvasectomized control group.[75] They found that vasectomized men had fewer cancers, fewer cancer deaths, lower rates of heart disease, and fewer deaths from heart attacks or strokes than the men in the control group, who had not had vasectomies. Perrin and co-workers, in a study with an average follow-up interval of 15 years, also found no indication that vasectomy predisposes to arteriosclerosis or heart disease.[76] And a 1992 study conducted at Harvard Medical School comparing more than 14,000 vasectomized men and a control group of nonvasectomized men found that vasectomy was actually associated with a lower overall death rate and a reduced rate of death from cardiovascular disease.[77]

Now, in what seems to be a case of déjà vu, concerns have been raised over a possible increased long-term risk of prostate and testicular cancer in men who have had vasectomies.[78] However, the scientific evidence on this matter is equivocal, and an expert group convened by the World Health Organization concluded that "any causal relation between vasectomy and risk of prostate or testicular cancer was unlikely."[79]

Vasectomies should be thought of as permanent, but improvements in modern microsurgery have in fact permitted vasectomy reversal to be successfully accomplished in a large number of cases, with pregnancy rates above 50 percent. However, reversal surgery is costly, complicated, and unpredictable, and the success rate declines considerably over time. Nevertheless, in an age where remarriage after divorce is commonplace, it is reassuring to some men to have the option of attempting to have a vasectomy reversed if their family situations change drastically.

MISCELLANEOUS METHODS OF CONTRACEPTION

Breast-feeding has long been noted to have a suppressive effect on fertility; the high levels of prolactin associated with nursing inhibit ovarian function. Recently, this effect was formalized into an actual method of family planning called the lactational amenorrhea method (LAM). In brief, this method relies on the principle that a woman who fully or nearly fully breast-feeds her infant and doesn't resume having periods for the first six months after having a baby is effectively protected from becoming pregnant during that time. Several studies have found that the failure rate using this method was 1.7 percent or less for this 6-month interval.[80] However, the method will not work once menstrual cycles return, and more than one-third of breast-feeding women resume menstruation within 3 to 4 months after delivery.

Withdrawal, sometimes given the fancier Latin name coitus interruptus, is a method of birth control that requires pulling the penis out of the vagina before ejaculation occurs. The method is somewhat ill conceived because it is a demanding, often frustrating, form of sexual brinkmanship and it doesn't always work even if done correctly. The reason is that the male's preejaculatory fluid often contains live sperm. (Men don't always produce preejaculatory fluid in noticeable amounts, and some men are never aware of producing any, but this doesn't mean that they are safe from this possible source of "method failure." The amounts involved may be more microscopic than visible.) In addition, withdrawal may not work because of various forms of "user failure": for example, the man may ejaculate just as he is attempting to withdraw; or even when ejaculation occurs outside the vagina, some sperm may be inadvertently deposited at or near the vaginal opening. The failure rate for the withdrawal method is in the range of 20 to 25 percent. For obvious reasons, this is not a method of birth control to be used by men who have difficulties with premature ejaculation.

Another method—douching, or rinsing the vagina with fluid—doesn't work effectively because millions of sperm swim up into the cervical mucus almost instantaneously after ejaculation, and rinsing the vagina won't disturb or affect them in any way. (Douching will, however, get rid of a large number of sperm that are still sloshing around in the vagina, outside the cervix. It serves no contraceptive purpose, though.) Few women rely on douching as their primary method of birth control; the failure rate is generally estimated to be more than 40 percent.

Another version of hormone-based contraception was approved for use in the United States in 1992, although it was already in widespread use in more than ninety countries around the world well before then. Depo-Provera, a long-acting, injectable synthetic form of progesterone, is given by injection once every three months and has an effectiveness rating comparable to the combination pill. Despite its high level of effectiveness, Depo-Provera has been the source of some controversy because of concerns that it might be linked to an increased risk of breast cancer or cancers of the liver or cervix.[81] However, a recent large-scale study found no evidence of a significant long-term risk of breast cancer, suggesting that this method is both safe and reliable.[82] Side effects with Depo-Provera include irregular menstrual bleeding, breast tenderness, weight gain, and depression.

Another new method of contraception, the female condom, was approved for use in the United States on May 10, 1993. This device, which is currently being marketed under the trade-name Reality, is sometimes also called a vaginal pouch. The 6½-inch-long pouch is made of polyurethane that is anchored by two flexible plastic rings, one at the cervix and one outside the opening of the vagina. The female condom, which is intended for one act of intercourse, is coated inside with a silicone lubricant. Unfortunately, female condoms are less effective contraceptives than other barrier methods, and considerably less effective than male condoms—their overall failure rate is more than 25 percent per year of use.[83] While there is hope that female condoms will protect against various sexually transmitted diseases (especially HIV), there are few data available documenting such an effect. Furthermore, the device is more than a little lacking in aesthetics. The majority of women we interviewed who have used this product have called it cumbersome or clumsy, and 17 out of 20 said that they would never consider using it as their primary birth control method.

Three methods of postconception birth control are also available. The first one, the so-called morning-after pill, involves using various types of estrogen in high doses starting within 72 hours after exposure—the sooner the better. The treatment actually involves taking *several* pills of estrogen (or several combination birth control pills containing both estrogen and progesterone); the estrogen is also sometimes administered in the form of injections. The estrogen prevents pregnancy by blocking implantation; the effectiveness rate is in the range of 98 to 99 percent, depending on timing and the exact hormone regimen used. The main side effects are nausea (sometimes progressing to vomiting) and breast tenderness. The morning-after pill should not be regarded as a routine method of birth control, but it has considerable value in situations such as rape, condom breakage, or obvious failure of another method of contraception (e.g., if a diaphragm becomes dislodged, or if it is discovered that a spermicide was outdated).

A second type of postconception birth control is less widely used. This involves inserting a copper IUD into the uterus within four to five days after unprotected intercourse. The IUD prevents implantation with a very high degree of efficiency (99+ percent) but of course will not prevent an ectopic pregnancy. This method generally should not be used for rape victims because of the risk of infection.

The third type of postconception birth control is a method called menstrual extraction. In this procedure, which is used just at the time when a woman expects her period, a thin, flexible piece of plastic tubing is threaded through the cervical canal into the uterus. Suction is applied to the tube, using either a hand-held syringe or a pump. If there is a pregnancy, something that can easily be determined by an at-home pregnancy test kit, the almost-microscopic preembryo is easily suctioned out. Menstrual extraction generally is done without any anesthetic and causes only minor discomfort such as cramping. However, there have been reports of infrequent but serious complications if the procedure is performed by anyone other than a trained health care professional.[84]

Ten

Abortion

Few issues in contemporary society are as contentious as abortion. And few people are neutral about this topic: the matter of abortion has fostered a sharp polarization of opinion and an often strident rhetoric from both the prochoice and the prolife camps. Yet a surprising number of men and women on both sides of the abortion issue—or somewhere in between, where the vast majority of Americans cluster—have never read the key legal opinions that govern our nation's abortion laws, have little idea of who actually *gets* abortions, and have only a smattering of knowledge about abortion procedures and their safety and side effects.

We do not feel that a condensed version of our personal views on the morality of abortion would add materially to the debate, so in this chapter we do not deal with the issue of whether abortion is always wrong or the circumstances under which it is ethically justifiable. Interested readers can consult a vast literature dealing with the ethics of abortion for information on this topic.[1] Instead, we have tried to present material that focuses on practical and personal aspects of abortion as a matter of sexual and reproductive health.

LEGAL ASPECTS OF ABORTION

HISTORICAL BACKGROUND

Although abortion has been common from ancient times on, legal attitudes toward abortion have varied considerably in different eras and different places. The Anglo-Saxon legal precedents that established the common-law right to terminate a pregnancy can be traced back to the fourteenth century.[2] The first restrictions on abortion in England were implemented in

275

1803 in the Lord Ellenborough Act, which made abortion illegal after quickening (the time of pregnancy at which the women first feels fetal movement). The justification for the Lord Ellenborough Act was not to protect the fetus, though; it was designed to protect the life of the woman, since the drugs that were used at that time to induce abortion were highly toxic.

In the United States, abortion was permitted without legal limitations in colonial times because the colonies followed the British common-law tradition. Although it is unclear why women's rights to abortions were not mentioned in the U.S. Constitution, many legal and historical scholars believe it was because this right was not a controversial issue at the time: it was "commonly accepted and fairly widespread."[3]

The first legislative limitations on abortion in America came between 1820 and 1841. These laws were enacted primarily at the urging of physicians who were trying to establish the medical profession as the sole provider of health care services in the U.S. At the time, midwives and pharmacists were the primary providers of abortions or abortion-inducing drugs. Thus, the restrictive abortion laws that were passed at that time did not really ban abortions but regulated who could perform them. As a result, the laws were aimed only against illegal practitioners; women who obtained abortions could not be charged with a crime. In addition, none of these laws placed limitations on abortions done before quickening. This may have been partly because there were no reliable pregnancy tests at the time to establish definitively that a woman was pregnant and partly because most abortions performed early in pregnancy were advertised as "menstrual regulation."

When the American Medical Association was founded in 1847, an anti-abortion campaign became one of its earliest focal points, and over the next half-century, physicians were among the staunchest advocates of antiabortion legislation. Public opinion was also mobilized by three other developments: a papal decree in 1869 that declared abortion sinful and banned it entirely for Catholics, an extensive newspaper campaign that provided readers with shocking details of cases in which women died from abortions, and a "morality campaign" led by Anthony Comstock, which was directed mainly against obscenity but had a certain amount of spillover into other areas dubbed as evil.

The result was not surprising. Every state in the Union except Kentucky adopted bans on abortion by 1900, and these bans were far more restrictive than those passed several decades before. As a result, in many states women could be charged as criminals if they tried to get an abortion, although actual convictions were few in number.

Despite the legal ban, women continued to obtain abortions, but now they were forced to go to illegal (and unregulated) practitioners. To say that among these abortionists there were many unsavory characters often more concerned with their money than with their "patients' " welfare is a great understatement; in many instances, these illegal abortionists were butchers who worked in unsanitary conditions, causing many deaths among their clientele. (In John Irving's novel *The Cider House Rules*, an exception is portrayed in a fictionalized account of a real-life obstetrician who provided abortions.)

By the middle of this century, concern began to mount among both the medical community and the public over the large numbers of women experiencing serious complications or death from illegal abortions. Since legal abortions had become especially safe as a result of improved techniques and the development of antibiotics (legal abortions were generally permitted when necessary to save the mother's life), many physicians and nurses began campaigning for a liberalization of abortion laws. They were particularly interested in broadening the reasons that would permit legal abortions to be done—for instance, allowing them in instances of rape or incest, or when pregnancy posed a serious threat to the woman's emotional or physical well-being.

In actual practice, so-called therapeutic abortions were done in many non-Catholic hospitals across the country if they were approved by special committees, although such approval was typically difficult to receive. Many women had to travel outside the United States to seek abortions (in Japan and Sweden abortions were relatively easy to obtain), so that as a practical matter, poor women needing abortions were discriminated against by existing laws. In addition, the first stirrings of the women's rights movement would soon put a spotlight on the abortion issue from yet another perspective.

Particular attention was riveted on the campaign to liberalize abortion laws when an epidemic of German measles struck San Francisco in 1966. Because women who come down with German measles early in pregnancy have a very high chance of having babies with serious birth defects, a number of San Francisco physicians had performed abortions for this situation even though they knew it was against the law. When the state's attorney general indicted twenty-one of these physicians, there was an intense public outcry and support was mobilized from the medical community across the nation.

By the late 1960s, several states changed their abortion laws as a result of legal challenges and public pressure. Colorado and California were among the first to do so, but only four states—New York, Hawaii, Washington, and Alaska—had legalized all abortions, regardless of the reason, during the first trimester. In another dozen states, abortion bans were liberalized considerably, although not to the point sometimes called "abortion on demand." The result was that the number of legal abortions done in the United States increased from an estimated 10,000 each year in the early 1960s to an annual 750,000 legal abortions by 1972. The stage had been set for a pivotal shift on the legal front, which we will briefly chronicle here.

THE ROE V. WADE STORY

In August 1969, Norma McCorvey was a 21-year-old divorcee down on her luck. Already the mother of a 5-year-old daughter, she was supporting herself by selling tickets to a carnival, only to have her belongings stolen by her roommates. Penniless, forced to call a friend to wire her money for bus fare to return to Dallas, her hometown, she had just managed to find a job as a waitress when she discovered she was pregnant again.

McCorvey asked her doctor about getting an abortion, but he bluntly informed her that under Texas law, abortions could be done only if her life were in danger—which it was not. He suggested she go to California, where the laws were more relaxed, but she didn't have the money to make that trip. Depressed, bitter, and more than a little frightened at her bleak prospects—including the likelihood that she would be fired when her pregnancy became apparent—she made up a story about being gang raped, thinking it might improve her chances of getting help. (Ironically, the fact that she lied about how she had gotten pregnant didn't come out until 1987, but the rape story played no material part in subsequent legal developments.)

McCorvey was introduced to two young Dallas attorneys, Linda Coffee and Sara Weddington, who were looking for a woman to be the plaintiff in a legal challenge to the strict Texas abortion law. McCorvey readily agreed to this. When they filed their lawsuit, which asked for an injunction preventing Henry Wade, the district attorney of Dallas County, from enforcing the state's abortion law as well as a declaration that the law was unconstitutional, they used the pseudonym "Jane Roe" to protect McCorvey's identity, so the suit became designated as Roe v. Wade.

The case was heard initially in federal court in Dallas. On June 17, 1970, the Court handed down a decision ruling that the Texas abortion law was unconstitutional. However, the Court refused to issue an injunction, which as a practical matter allowed District Attorney Wade to announce that his office would crack down even harder on illegal abortions. Eventually, the State of Texas appealed the decision, and the case went all the way to the U.S. Supreme Court.

While the entire legal process was slowly inching its way forward, Norma McCorvey turned down an offer from her attorneys to pay for a California abortion since she didn't want to do anything that might jeopardize their case. However, she had relatively little contact with Weddington and Coffee, mostly watching their legal skirmish from afar. When she had her baby, she immediately put it up for adoption.

The case was initially argued before the Supreme Court in December 1971, and as in many cases, McCorvey wasn't there. Weddington presented her side smoothly, despite her nervousness and youthful appearance, and while waiting for the Court's decision, entered the political arena by running for the Texas state legislature. Then, in a dismaying (but not unheard of) twist, the Court asked to have the case reargued. This was done in October 1972, a time when two new justices had arrived on the Court, adding to everyone's confusion.

When the long-awaited decision was finally handed down, on January 22, 1973, it was bumped from the front pages of most newspapers by coverage of the death of former President Lyndon Johnson on the same day. When Norma McCorvey read about the landmark decision in her evening newspaper, she burst into tears. A friend who was with her at the time said, "Don't tell me you knew Lyndon Johnson?"

"No," McCorvey responded, "I'm Roe."

ROE AND BEYOND

The Supreme Court startled many observers with its ruling in *Roe* v. *Wade* that legalized abortion on a nationwide basis. By a 7 to 2 vote, the Court held that the decision to have an abortion in the first trimester of pregnancy is strictly up to the woman and her doctor. This landmark decision also noted that the fetus is not a person and thus is not entitled to constitutional protection, while it defended the woman's right to an abortion in order to prevent a "distressful life and future." Other key points established in *Roe* v. *Wade* were the following.

• The right to have an abortion is grounded in privacy rights established by earlier judicial decisions as well as in the Ninth and Fourteenth amendments to the Constitution.

• States can impose certain regulations on second trimester abortions in order to protect the woman's health.

• In the third trimester, because the fetus may be viable, states may ban abortions except when they are necessary to preserve the mother's life or health.

Notably, the Court did not address all areas that concerned both sides of the abortion rights issue. Here is a telling excerpt from Justice Blackmun's majority opinion:

> We need not resolve the difficult question of when life begins. When those trained in medicine, philosophy, and theology are unable to arrive at any consensus, the judiciary, at this point in the development of man's knowledge, is not in a position to speculate as to the answer.[4]

On the same day that the *Roe* v. *Wade* decision was handed down, the Supreme Court ruled on a second case involving abortion rights. This case, known as *Doe* v. *Bolton*, challenged a Georgia statute that required that abortions could be done only in hospitals after approval by a hospital committee. In overturning such restrictions on a woman's right to an abortion, the Supreme Court was careful to make clear that it was not endorsing abortion on demand: it was still permitting states to play a role in regulating abortions done beyond the first trimester. This ruling would later serve as the basis for attempts made by many states to limit the circumstances in which abortions could be done.

For the better part of the next two decades, the *Roe* v. *Wade* decision governed more or less undisturbed over national abortion law. Nevertheless, there were numerous attempts by individual state legislatures to narrow the scope of abortion rights. In a few instances, these statutes were upheld by the Supreme Court. In 1979, for example, the Court implied that states are able to require a pregnant unwed minor to get consent from her parents before obtaining an abortion as long as there is also an alternative procedure available, such as getting approval from a judge (*Bellotti* v. *Baird*). In 1980, the Court ruled that the U.S. government and the individual states have no obligation to pay for abortions for women on welfare (*Harris* v. *McRae*). More frequently, though, abortion cases that reached the Supreme Court were decided in a way that seemed to preserve, rather than narrow, the *Roe* v. *Wade* ruling. For example, husbands were denied veto power over their wives' abortion decisions (*Planned Parenthood* v. *Danforth*, 1976), doctors were given extensive discretion in deciding when a fetus can live outside the uterus (*Colautti* v. *Franklin*, 1979), and regulations requiring that all abortions after the first trimester be done in hospitals were overturned (*City of Akron* v. *Akron Center for Reproductive Health*, 1983; *Planned Parenthood of Kansas City* v. *Ashcroft*, 1983).

This trend was brought to an abrupt halt on July 3, 1989, with a decision handed down by the Supreme Court in a Missouri abortion case known as *Webster* v. *Reproductive Health Services*. Here, in a closely contested 5 to 4 vote, the Court unraveled much of the substance of *Roe* v. *Wade* without actually overturning the decision. It did so by giving states the right to place sharp new restrictions on abortions, including (1) banning use of public facilities to perform abortions (even if the woman pays for the abortion herself); (2) prohibiting public employees (including doctors and nurses) from performing or assisting at an abortion unless it is required to save the woman's life; (3) requiring that medical tests be done on any fetus thought to be 20 weeks old in order to determine its viability; and (4) discarding the rigid trimester system suggested in *Roe* v. *Wade.*

The Court also upheld the language of the preamble to the Missouri law that declared that life begins at conception, while noting that because of the way in which this law was written, the preamble had no meaningful impact on the implementation of the legislation. The majority opinion of Chief Justice Rehnquist noted:

> Nothing in the Constitution requires States to enter or remain in the business of performing abortions. Nor . . . do private physicians and their patients have some kind of constitutional right of access to public facilities for the performance of abortion. Both appellants [the state of Missouri] and the United States [government] . . . have urged that we overrule our decision in *Roe* v. *Wade.* . . . The facts of the present case, however, differ from those at issue in *Roe.* . . . This case therefore affords us no occasion to revisit the holding of *Roe* . . . and we leave it undisturbed. To the extent indicated in our opinion, we would modify and narrow *Roe* and succeeding cases.[5]

In a dissenting opinion, Justice Harry Blackmun—the man who had written the majority opinion in *Roe* v. *Wade*—poignantly asserted:

> I fear for the future. I fear for the liberty and equality of the millions of women who have lived and come of age in the 16 years since *Roe* was decided. . . . [T]he plurality discards a landmark case of the last generation, and casts into darkness the hopes and visions of every woman in this country who had come to believe that the Constitution guaranteed her the right to exercise some control over her unique ability to bear children. . . . To overturn a constitutional decision is a rare and grave undertaking. To overturn a constitutional decision that secured a fundamental personal liberty to millions of persons would be unprecedented in our 200 years of constitutional history.

As the *New York Times* observed in an editorial about *Webster* v. *Reproductive Health Services*, the decision "produced remarkably little new law" (July 4, 1989, p. 28). But the real judicial test seemed to lie shortly ahead, as four Supreme Court justices signaled their intention to rapidly overturn *Roe* at the first available opportunity. However, many prochoice observers considered *Webster* a significant setback as it opened the doors for state legislatures to pass new laws regulating abortion.[6]

Another setback came on May 23, 1991, in the case of *Rust* v. *Sullivan*. By a 5 to 4 vote, the Supreme Court upheld federal regulations that bar employees of federally funded family planning clinics from all discussion of abortion with their patients, ruling specifically that such a restriction did not unconstitutionally infringe on First Amendment free speech rights. Even if a woman asked about abortion, physicians, nurses, or other clinic employees could only say that "the project does not consider abortion an appropriate method for family planning and therefore does not counsel or refer for abortion."[7] Although the constitutional status of abortion was not being contested in this case, prolife supporters received the decision enthusiastically, and prochoice advocates were dismayed, claiming the decision seriously eroded the doctor-patient relationship.

The following month, Louisiana (over the veto of its governor) passed the nation's strictest abortion law, banning virtually all abortions except those to save the life of a pregnant woman or, in limited conditions, when the pregnancy is a result of rape or incest. Under the new Louisiana law, physicians convicted of performing illegal abortions could be imprisoned for 10 years and fined up to $100,000. While this law has been legally challenged and thus has not yet been implemented, as it works its way up the ladder toward a possible Supreme Court hearing, it has had a chilling effect on abortion rights advocates across the nation, providing a glimpse of a nation that may be neither kinder nor gentler toward pregnant women in the future.

In the aftermath of *Webster* v. *Reproductive Health Services*, and in the shadow of the Louisiana law, legislation enacted by Pennsylvania took center stage on the Supreme Court's docket as the federal government, filing an *amicus curiae* brief, once again asked to have *Roe* overturned. Several provisions of Pennsylvania's Abortion Control Act were at issue: (1) a requirement that a woman seeking an abortion give her informed consent and be provided with certain information, including information about the risks of the procedure and the probable gestational age of the "unborn child," at least 24 hours before the abortion is performed; (2) a parental-consent provision for unmarried minors; (3) a requirement that a married woman notify her husband of her intent to have an abortion; and (4) certain technical reporting requirements for clinics or other facilities that provide abortion services.

On June 29, 1992, in a somewhat surprising decision, the Court found that "the essential holding in *Roe* v. *Wade* should be retained and once again reaffirmed" (the *New York Times*, June 30, 1992, p. A16). While preserving the notion of a woman's constitutional right to abortion prior to fetal viability, the Court's decision allowed room for the creation of new state laws creating procedural obstacles to abortion. Notably, the Court once again discarded *Roe*'s trimester framework that severely restricted a state's power to regulate abortion in the early stages of pregnancy, saying that it was permissible to regulate abortion at any point during pregnancy as long as it doesn't impose an "undue burden" on a woman's right to end her pregnancy. Under this newly defined "undue burden" principle, the Court rejected Pennsylvania's provision for marital notification, but upheld the 24-hour waiting period, the parental notification requirement, and the record-keeping requirements on clinics that perform abortion. As one legal expert noted:

> The Pennsylvania requirements for obtaining informed consent are based on the supposition that women who decide to have abortions do not think much about the decision and that if they had some additional information about the procedure and the development of the fetus, as well as 24 hours to think about it, many would continue their pregnancies to term. This view is extraordinarily patronizing to pregnant women, it is supported by no empirical data, and the consent requirements apply to no other medical procedure.[8]

While *Southeastern Pennsylvania* v. *Casey* clearly indicates that abortion laws as restrictive as Louisiana's will be overturned, this decision watered down the force of *Roe* v. *Wade* considerably, especially since *Roe* had held that the right to an abortion was "fundamental."

WHO HAS ABORTIONS: POPULATION PATTERNS

In 1988, there were approximately 1.6 million legal abortions performed in the United States.[9] This corresponded to a national abortion rate of 27.3 abortions done per 1,000 females aged 15 to 44. The national abortion ratio, which is stated in terms of the number of abortions per 1,000 live births, was 286 in 1988. Since 1972, the abortion ratio has declined for all age groups,[10] partly reflecting higher rates of childbearing for women in their thirties as well as better use of contraception by teenagers and young unmarried adults.

According to national data reported by the Alan Guttmacher Institute, teenagers had 25.6 percent of all legal abortions in 1988.[11] Women 20 to 24 years old accounted for nearly one-third of abortions, while women aged 25 to 29 had almost 22 percent and women 30 or over had 20 percent of the abortions that were performed that year.

Only 18.5 percent of women who had abortions were married. Close to two-thirds had never been married, while the balance were either separated (6.4 percent), divorced (11.2 percent), or widowed (0.6 percent). According to U.S. government figures, the abortion ratio was 11.7 times higher for unmarried women than for married women in 1988. A disproportionately high percentage of women who obtained abortions had family incomes of under $11,000 a year, while abortions were far less common among women whose family income was $25,000 or more.

Approximately two-thirds of the women who obtain legal abortions are white. However, the abortion ratio is much higher among minority women than for white women: 489 versus 259 abortions per 1,000 live births in 1988.[12] In addition, black women tend to have later abortions than white women, although age is a more dominant influence than race, especially for women who have abortions at 16 weeks of pregnancy or beyond. For all racial groups, the proportion of women having an abortion done at 8 weeks or less increased with age, while the proportion obtaining late abortions decreased with age. Educational level is also linked to the timing of abortion: college-educated women are more likely to have early abortions than women who have only completed high school.

Although 88 percent of legal abortions are performed in the first 12 weeks of pregnancy,[13] second trimester abortions are often chosen because of difficulty in coming up with the money for the procedure, which may partly explain why teenagers tend to have later abortions than older women do. Ironically, the later abortion is not only less safe but also more expensive and may require that the woman take more time off from work or school. Second-trimester abortions may be necessary under other circumstances, of course. For instance, women with irregular periods, who frequently go for months without any menstrual flow, may not realize they are pregnant until well into the second trimester. Women who take birth control pills don't always realize when they become accidentally pregnant, especially since the pill produces side effects that mimic symptoms of pregnancy. Similarly, women with IUDs in place also may not recognize the early stages of pregnancy because they think they are adequately protected by their contraceptive method; it may take months before they suspect something is amiss. Finally, there are also many instances in which a teenager in a state of massive denial simply refuses to admit the possibility that she might be pregnant, as well as other cases in which the teenager's worries about her parents' reactions lead her to hide her pregnancy, either hoping it will somehow disappear on its own, or actively try to miscarry by exercise, self-injury, or the use of drugs purported to cause abortions.

Looking at the religion of women who had legal abortions in 1987 reveals that 42 percent were Protestant, 32 percent were Catholic, 1 percent were Jewish, 3 percent were adherents of other religions, and 22 percent indicated that they had no religious affiliation.[14] These statistics are of interest since they show that many Catholic women are willing to disregard the church's teachings that prohibit abortion.

Another notable point made by the Alan Guttmacher survey was that half of all females who had abortions in 1987 said that they were practicing contraception during the month in which they conceived. This is in sharp contrast to the idea that most women who have abortions are either uninformed about contraception or unwilling to make an effort at practicing birth control, as the following comment makes clear:

> *A 23-year-old female graduate student*: When I was a college junior I was involved in a live-in relationship with a guy I cared a lot about. We had a great sex life, but we were careful about it, with me using a diaphragm and him using a condom. You can imagine our shock—and dismay—when I turned out to be pregnant. We had never "forgotten" to use birth control; in fact, we were using two separate kinds of birth control. Still, when I told my best friend about it, she insisted that there must have been one time we slipped up and forgot. "Maybe," she said, "you were both drunk and you don't remember it." I really resented that attitude and realized how easy it is to make assumptions about people's behavior that just may not be true.

As Table 10.1 shows, the majority of women who had an abortion in 1988 had never had a live birth. Likewise, most had never previously had an induced abortion. Fewer than one in 20 women who have abortions have had three or more abortions in the past. This strongly suggests that very few women rely on abortion as a means of birth control, although some who are opposed to legalized abortion claim that it is a common practice.

TABLE 10.1
DISTRIBUTION OF REPORTED LEGAL ABORTIONS,
BY NUMBER OF PREVIOUS LIVE BIRTHS AND BY
NUMBER OF PREVIOUS INDUCED ABORTIONS, U.S., 1988 (PERCENTAGES)

0	1	2	3	4	Unknown	Total
PREVIOUS LIVE BIRTHS						
51.0	22.8	15.6	5.5	2.5	2.6	100
PREVIOUS INDUCED ABORTIONS						
56.4	26.2	10.2	4.8	2.5	2.6	100

SOURCE: Modified from data in *Morbidity and Mortality Weekly Report* 40: SS-2, Tables 10 and 11, July 1991.

Many people seem to believe that most abortions are what are derisively termed "abortions of convenience," but these are tricky to define. As Anna Quindlen put it, "Semantics alone make it sound like a pregnancy ended because a woman wanted a child who was a Leo, not a Capricorn."[15] If a 13-year-old is impregnated by her seventh-grade boyfriend and has an abortion, is it fair to call this an abortion of convenience? If an unmarried, unemployed 24-year-old woman who is struggling to feed her four children with her meager welfare check becomes pregnant again and wants an abortion, is this also an abortion of convenience? Convenience, it might seem, lies in the eyes of the beholder in these situations.

In any event, what is certainly clear is that the 1.6 million women who have abortions each year in America (and the 37 million women around the world who have abortions each year) come from extraordinarily diverse backgrounds. While some are poor, undereducated women on welfare, others are law students, physicians, ministers, architects, housewives— women from virtually all walks of life. No matter how we view abortion as a moral issue, we should guard against prejudging these women and their biographies based on presumptive stereotypes about who they are.

ABORTION METHODS

There are a number of different procedures used to perform abortions, with the optimal method for any pregnant woman usually dependent on the length of time she's been pregnant. In general, the briefer the duration of a pregnancy, the simpler abortion is.

The commonest form of first trimester abortion is a method known as *vacuum aspiration* or *suction curettage*. This technique, which is usually done on an outpatient basis under local anesthesia (a paracervical block) or with no anesthesia at all,* now accounts for about 75 percent of all abortions in the United States and is in widespread use on a worldwide basis. The procedure involves first dilating (stretching) the opening of the cervix either by metal probes or by the use of small sticks of dried, sterilized seaweed (called laminaria tents) placed in the cervical canal a day before the abortion. As the laminaria sticks absorb moisture, their swelling causes the cervical canal to dilate gradually, which is often more comfortable than instrument-produced dilation. (Some women notice pressure or mild cramping with laminaria,

---

* Some women are so tense under local anesthesia that they require the use of a sedating drug such as Valium (diazepam) or a painkiller such as Demerol (meperidine) by injection during the procedure. If this is done, the recovery period is prolonged slightly in order to be sure the drug effects have worn off.

but many others experience no discomfort at all.) When the laminaria is removed, or when the cervix is dilated with instruments, a small plastic tube called a cannula is inserted through the dilated cervical canal into the cavity of the uterus. The tube is connected to a pump called a vacuum aspirator; as a result of the gentle suction provided by the pump, the contents of the uterus are quickly and easily evacuated. Most of the time, scraping the lining of the uterus (curettage, as in "D and C", for dilation and curettage) is not a necessary part of this procedure, and the entire process takes only 10 or 15 minutes.

After a vacuum aspiration abortion is completed, if the woman has Rh negative blood she is given a shot of RhoGAM to prevent the formation of antibodies and thus forestall the risk of Rh incompatibility in future pregnancies (unless it is known that her partner was also Rh negative). In most abortion clinics, she would then remain in the recovery room for about an hour while her blood pressure and pulse were monitored to be sure she was not hemorrhaging or having a reaction to the local anesthetic, if one had been used. Once discharged, she would be advised to rest quietly until the next day, when she can resume virtually all her everyday activities except for sexual intercourse or douching, both of which should be avoided for approximately two weeks. Normal periods usually resume some four to six weeks after abortion.

FIGURE 10.1
VACUUM ASPIRATION ABORTION

Vacuum aspiration for abortion involves suctioning the embryo and membranes within the uterus.

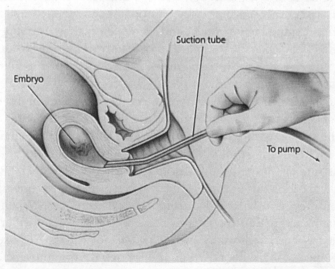

First-trimester vacuum aspiration abortions are generally very safe (see Table 10.2). They have no adverse effects on subsequent fertility, subsequent pregnancy outcomes, or the risk of subsequent ectopic (tubal) pregnancy.[16]

TABLE 10.2
COMPLICATIONS OF FIRST TRIMESTER ABORTIONS

Major Complications (hospitalization required)

Retained tissue	1 in 3,600
Severe infection	1 in 4,700
Uterine perforation	1 in 10,600
Hemorrhage	1 in 14,200
Incomplete abortion	1 in 28,300
Tubal pregnancy	1 in 42,500

Minor Complications (managed as an outpatient)

Mild infection	1 in 200
Cervical stenosis	1 in 6,100
Cervical tear	1 in 9,400
Convulsion	1 in 25,100

SOURCE: Modified from Hakim-Elahi, E., Tovell, H. M., and Burnhill, M. S., Complications of first trimester abortion: a report of 170,000 cases, *Obstetrics and Gynecology* 76:929, 1990.

Dilation and curettage (D and C) is the other method occasionally used for first-trimester abortions, although because this procedure requires general anesthesia and entails a greater risk of blood loss and other complications, it has distinct disadvantages. In a D and C, which is the same surgical procedure used as a diagnostic tool in cases of abnormal uterine bleeding or for removing uterine polyps, a sharp curette is used to scrape the lining of the uterus rather than suctioning out the uterine contents.

The techniques of vacuum aspiration and D and C are combined in the method generally used for abortions during the late first trimester and early part of the second trimester. This method, called *dilation and evacuation* (D and E), requires dilating the cervix more than for an earlier abortion because larger instruments must be used inside the uterus. (Laminaria sticks are frequently used for this purpose, since they expand by five times their dry size when they absorb moisture from cervical secretions. When needed, metal dilators are used to enlarge the cervical opening even further after the laminaria has been removed.) Following dilation of the cervix, a blunt curette is used along with a forceps and suctioning to remove the uterine contents. A drug called *oxytocin* is sometimes given to help the uterus contract after a D and E is done in order to slow down the amount of bleeding that occurs. The whole procedure, not counting the preliminary use of laminaria, usually requires only 15 to 30 minutes. However, since the uterus is softer and its walls thinner after the first trimester than earlier, D and E is a technically more demanding surgical procedure with an increased risk of complications such as bleeding or perforation of the uterus.

After the fifteenth week of pregnancy, abortions are usually performed by causing the uterus to contract enough to expel the fetus and placenta in a manner resembling natural labor and delivery. Such abortions are called *induction abortions.* Induction abortions can be thought of as chemically induced miscarriages; however, these procedures are riskier and more expensive than D and E's.[17] Although they were initially done with a hypertonic saline (salt) solution, which was injected through the abdomen into the amniotic sac after first withdrawing a small amount of amniotic fluid, it is now more common to use hormones called prostaglandins for inducing contractions of the uterus. Prostaglandins can either be injected into the uterus directly through the abdomen or infused through the cervix into the gap between the lining of the uterus and the amniotic sac. Solutions of urea (either alone or in combination with prostaglandins or oxytocin) have also been used in some centers, and prostaglandins can be used as vaginal suppositories.

No matter which method is used, midtrimester abortions are considerably riskier than abortions done during the first trimester: in fact, the complication rate ranges from 5 percent for D and E's to as high as 20 percent for induction abortions in some institutions.[18] Among the most serious, though infrequent, complications with saline abortion are hypernatremia (excessive salt levels in the blood), heart failure, and disseminated intravascular coagulation (a condition of widespread bleeding throughout the body). Cervical lacerations and uterine hemorrhage are more common, though less serious, problems. Common side effects of prostaglandin-induced abortion include nausea, vomiting, diarrhea, and headache, which affect more than half of women undergoing this procedure. Serious complications of prostaglandin abortion include a heightened risk of hemorrhage, a slight risk of seizures, and a risk of cervical laceration; in addition, the chances of having an incomplete abortion (requiring an immediate D and C) are somewhat higher with this method than with saline abortion. One other problem is that induction abortions don't always work: about 8 percent of prostaglandin inductions and 2 percent of saline inductions don't succeed on the first attempt and require a second injection. In addition, induction abortions take a much longer time (on average, about 24 hours), both in terms of waiting for contractions of the uterus to begin and then in the duration of chemically induced labor. One other problem with this method is that it may produce greater emotional stress for many women, particularly if they are awake when the fetus is expelled and the fetus is well-formed enough to have a very lifelike appearance.

Hysterotomy, which is an operation cutting into the uterus, is a method used infrequently for performing abortion. In addition to heightened medical risks to the mother, there is a chance that a live fetus will be delivered if this technique (which is essentially the same as a cesarean section) is used on an advanced pregnancy.

Hysterectomy, or surgical removal of the uterus, is possible until the twenty-fourth week of pregnancy without first evacuating the contents of the uterus. This is a method of abortion, infrequently used, that is generally reserved for women with large tumors (myomas) of the uterus that might interfere with other types of midtrimester abortion or for women who require a hysterectomy for other medical reasons. It is, of course, an irreversible procedure: not only is the current pregnancy terminated; no subsequent pregnancies will be possible.

One last form of abortion will be mentioned briefly. A small number of medical centers now perform an unusual type of abortion that is not aimed at ending fetal life, but preserving it. This seemingly paradoxical situation arises when women are pregnant with more fetuses than they can safely carry to term—a situation that occurs with some frequency when women have been given drugs to help them ovulate. For example, in one case a woman was carrying octuplets. Her doctors told her that all would die unless something was done. With her consent, the doctors performed what is called a selective abortion, eliminating six of the fetuses, thus reducing the number of fetuses to two. The woman was able to continue her pregnancy and she gave birth to healthy twins.

The selective abortion is performed using ultrasound to allow a miniature needle to be inserted into the chest cavity of a fetus when it is still smaller than a thumb. A chemical is injected through the needle that causes the fetal heart to stop beating. The dead fetus is eventually absorbed into the woman's body.

This octuplet case seems to offer few problems to most observers—after all, it is clear that all of the fetuses would have died if the octuplets were left undisturbed. But there have also been cases involving selective abortions as a matter of convenience for a couple—for example, reducing quadruplets to twins. (Ironically, such cases have sometimes arisen because of the practice of implanting multiple embryos as part of a GIFT procedure [discussed in Chapter 11], which is done very commonly on the theory that most of the implanted embryos will not survive.) If this is an ethically permissible practice, some wonder, where is the line drawn? What if a woman attending an IVF (in vitro fertilization) program conceives twins and then decides she wants only one baby—is it morally correct to abort one of the developing fetuses? What if a woman carrying twins or triplets wants to abort the female fetuses and give birth only to a male? While we don't claim to have all the answers to such questions, these are matters of some moral importance in today's high-technology world of medicine.

THE ABORTION PILL

The newest chapter in the abortion story involves a pill, developed in France, that can safely and simply induce abortions in early pregnancy. Known scientifically as mifepristone but more commonly referred to as RU 486, the name assigned to it during its developmental stages, this abortion pill has been approved for sale in France and China since 1988 and in Britain since 1991 but is banned in the United States. It is usually given in combination with a prostaglandin, which can either be administered vaginally or as an injection 48 hours after the RU 486 is taken.* Most often, abortion occurs within hours of the administration of the prostaglandin.

RU 486 works by opposing the action of progesterone, a hormone critical to implantation of the fertilized egg in the uterus and the maintenance of pregnancy. Although the exact mechanisms of its actions are not fully understood, it causes the lining of the uterus to slough off, shedding the small embryo and amniotic sac present in early pregnancy. It also blocks progesterone's calming action on the muscular walls of the uterus, leading to contractions that help to dislodge the embryo.[19] In addition, the combination of RU 486 and prostaglandin opens and softens the cervix.

The utility of RU 486 has been widely confirmed, with complete success in 96 percent of pregnancies of 7 weeks' duration or less.[20] The incidence of side effects such as headache, nausea, and pelvic pain is very low. Less than one percent of women who have used the drug have experienced heavy bleeding and even fewer have developed infections of the uterine lining. In cases where there is incomplete expulsion of the contents of the uterus, RU 486 is followed by surgical termination of the pregnancy.

Contraindications to the use of RU 486 include a suspected ectopic

---

* A new study in France has shown that an orally administered prostaglandin analogue is equally effective and easier to administer. [Peyron, R., et al., Early Termination of Pregnancy with Mifepristone (RU 486) and the Orally Active Prostaglandin Misoprostol, *New England Journal of Medicine* 328: 1509–1513, 1993.]

pregnancy (since the drug is not effective in terminating pregnancies that are outside the uterus), any concomitant medical problem requiring use of glucocorticoids such as cortisone or prednisone (since RU 486 interferes with the action of these steroids), and any contraindications to the use of prostaglandins, such as asthma or severe high blood pressure.

The inventor of RU 486, Dr. Etienne-Emile Baulieu, now spends much of his time engaged in a political campaign to increase the acceptance of this controversial drug. Although it currently is often called the "abortion pill," Baulieu objects to the connotation of this label, saying that the word "abortion" is automatically negative; instead, he suggests calling it a "contragestive"—a phrase he has coined to denote blocking gestation.

Although there are no indications of when, or whether, RU 486 will become available in the United States, it is important to realize that the drug has potential for many uses other than abortion. In addition to potential medical applications such as in treating breast cancer, Cushing's syndrome (overactive adrenal glands), and certain brain tumors,[21] RU 486 may also prove to be a highly effective contraceptive in the conventional sense. Taken during the first part of the menstrual cycle, RU 486's antiprogesterone action may be effective in blocking ovulation, which might eventually prove to be its most important use.[22]

THE SAFETY OF ABORTION

Although all surgical procedures have associated risks, deaths from legal abortion are very rare. According to U.S. government figures, the overall death rate for legal abortions for the years 1980–1985 was 0.7 per 100,000 abortions, which compared with a maternal mortality rate of 9.1 per 100,000 live births for the same time period.[23] Abortions done during the first 8 weeks of pregnancy are even safer: for these early abortions, the death rate is less than 0.2 per 100,000 procedures, or less than one in a half-million. Overall, 88 percent of abortions in the United States are done in the first trimester; death rates and rates of other complications for these abortions are approximately one-tenth those for abortions done after the twelfth week of pregnancy.[24]

There are several different reasons why the risks of later abortions increase. For one thing, second-trimester abortions often require general anesthesia, which carries its own risks, separate and apart from the abortion itself. In addition, later abortions are more difficult surgical procedures, with a greater chance of uterine hemorrhage and other major complications, including serious postoperative infection. Furthermore, the longer a pregnancy progresses, the more likely the woman is to develop associated medical problems that may interfere with having an abortion. Despite these factors, second-trimester abortions are still three times as safe as carrying a pregnancy to term. Furthermore, there are no indications that a woman's age has any effect on abortion safety, although increased age carries a definite risk of higher maternal mortality.[25]

A woman who undergoes a single vacuum aspiration abortion—the method used in more than 9 out of 10 abortions in the United States today—has no greater risk of subsequent infertility than a woman who carries her pregnancy to term. Similarly, a single vacuum aspiration abortion doesn't increase the subsequent risk of miscarriage, stillbirth, birth defects, or major complications during future pregnancies or deliveries.[26] And women who have had several induced abortions are no more likely than women who have never had an abortion to give birth to an underweight baby.[27]

As of the end of 1992, there has only been one death reported with the use of RU 486 and prostaglandin,[28] which makes it seem to be a particularly safe procedure. However, it may be too early to be certain of the relative safety of this drug combination compared to other methods of early abortion.

PSYCHOLOGICAL RESPONSES TO ABORTION

For most women, the decision to have an abortion is reached only after considerable anguish and ambivalence. In some situations—for example, when prenatal testing reveals a condition such as Down's syndrome or a severe hereditary disease—this anguish may be heightened by the fact that the pregnancy was desired, not unintended. In other circumstances, even when the choice seems clear-cut and necessary for the man and woman involved, it may still provoke considerable guilt and turmoil.

Despite the fact that the decision to have an abortion is often heavily laden emotionally, the emotional benefits of abortion outweigh the psychological risks for most women.[29] Except for case studies, which usually involve problem abortions, none of the scores of studies of women following abortion reveal a high degree of psychiatric distress.[30] In fact, serious psychological problems after abortions are far less common than postpartum depression. As the prestigious *Comprehensive Textbook of Psychiatry* puts it, "The emotional distress that is experienced by some women after abortion is usually mild and self-limited. Serious adverse sequelae are rare."[31]

Not surprisingly, many women report considerable relief after an abortion. As one woman explained to us, "When I found out I was pregnant, I felt like there was a dark cloud over my future. Once I had my abortion, I could feel the sunlight again." Nevertheless, short-lived feelings of guilt, sadness, and loss are common in women who have had abortions.[32] Pre- and postabortion counseling are usually effective in helping women deal with these reactions.

The right-to-life camp was dealt a serious and unexpected setback when U.S. Surgeon General C. Everett Koop (who personally opposed abortion) issued to President Reagan a letter on the health effects of abortion that failed to identify serious psychological aftereffects. Koop wrote, "[A]t this time, the available scientific evidence . . . simply cannot support either the preconceived beliefs of those pro-life or pro-choice."[33] Koop's basic position was that because of methodological flaws such as the absence of control groups, very low follow-up rates, and nonrepresentative samples, good scientific evidence was not available on the psychological or physical effects of abortion. However, it later became known that Koop's actual report had been more favorable in its conclusions about the relative safety of abortions, but had been censored by his superiors in the government.[34]

Partly for this reason, the American Psychological Association organized a blue ribbon panel to review studies on the psychological responses of U.S. women after legal abortions. The panel concluded: "[T]he weight of the evidence from scientific studies indicates that legal abortion of an unwanted pregnancy in the first trimester does not pose a psychological hazard for most women" and "[S]evere negative reactions after abortion are rare."[35]

Certainly, a woman's psychological reaction to an abortion doesn't occur in a vacuum; to an important degree, it depends on the social context in which the abortion occurs and the amount of emotional support she receives from significant others in her life. A woman who is made to feel guilty, as though her pregnancy were more important than she is, is obviously more apt to have a difficult time in her postabortion adjustment. In addition, an unpleasant abortion experience involving callous, judgmental clinic or hospital staff or ostracism by the surrounding community because of social or religious disapproval will be likely to have a similar effect. On the other hand, caring family and friends can be of tremendous importance in helping a woman over the turmoil of the abortion experience.

Eleven

Infertility

"Finding out that you can't have a baby when you want to is one of the most frightening experiences of your life."

In the past quarter-century, infertility has become a more frequent problem than ever before in America (and the world) for a variety of reasons. Clearly, changes in patterns of sexual behavior have led to higher rates of sexually transmitted diseases among teenagers and young adults, with major consequences on later fertility. Long-term exposures to environmental pollution and toxic substances may have also played a role, although on a much smaller scale. Most important of all is a fundamental change in the timing of attempted childbearing: simply put, there is more infertility today because the Baby Boom generation has delayed having children into the ages where they are more likely to become infertile.[1] As a result of these forces, infertility specialists are busier than they've ever been. In fact, more than a million couples seek treatment for infertility each year in the United States alone.

Here is the scope of the problem. In industrialized nations, one couple out of seven is infertile at ages 30 to 34, while in 35- to 39-year-olds, the incidence rises to one in five; for couples in their forties, the number rises further still.[2] Yet, except for splashy news stories about the high-tech end of treating infertility, this problem remains remarkably invisible in modern American society. Despite major breakthroughs in both diagnosis and treatment in the past two decades, infertility is often the source of considerable anguish and embarrassment, as well as a major cause of psychosexual stress in young adult couples.

MYTHS ABOUT INFERTILITY

There is more misinformation circulating about infertility than most people would believe. Take a few minutes to answer the following true-false questions in order to find out what your fertility IQ is.

1. Conception doesn't occur unless the woman has an orgasm.
2. Male sperm counts tend to be higher in the summer than in the winter because there are more hours of sunshine then.
3. One of the commonest causes of female infertility is psychological tension; if women would just learn to relax more, they'd have an easier time getting pregnant.
4. A woman is only fertile in the 12 hours before ovulation occurs; that's how long it takes the sperm to swim to the egg.
5. It is best to have sex only once a week when you're trying to get pregnant.
6. Seventy-five percent of all cases of infertility occur because of a female problem.
7. A majority of infertile men have subnormal levels of testosterone, the male sex hormone.
8. Many times shortly after an infertile couple adopts a child, the woman becomes pregnant.

Each of the above statements is incorrect. Here's a brief rundown of the facts that debunk these myths.

1. A woman's orgasm has nothing to do with whether or not she conceives.
2. Sperm counts are actually lower in the summer than they are in the winter.[3] In fact, even working in an air-conditioned environment doesn't reverse this trend. The probable explanation is that the process of sperm production is exquisitely sensitive to temperature, and higher temperatures slow down sperm production.
3. The "psychological tension" myth is one of the most insidious when it comes to infertility. While tension can certainly mount from the frustrations of being infertile, tension does not "cause" infertility. Still, well-meaning friends or relatives will often say, "Just get away for a vacation and relax and everything will be all right." They're wrong if they mean that conception will occur automatically.
4. The actual window of female fertility comes in the 12 to 24 hours *after* ovulation. Fortunately, sperm have the capability of penetrating the

egg for 24 to 72 hours after being deposited in the vagina, so it isn't
necessary to have a stopwatch in order to time things precisely.

5. Once a week *isn't* often enough for many couples trying to conceive,
   especially if the "once" doesn't come pretty close to the time of
   ovulation. While daily sex may actually reduce your chances of conceiving because it may lower the male's sperm count, a frequency for
   most couples of having intercourse two or three times a week will
   work best, as we will discuss in more detail below.

6. It used to be thought that 40 percent of infertility was due to a female
   factor and 40 percent due to a male factor, with the remaining cases
   representing either combined male/female factors or cases where no
   explanation could be found. Better diagnostic testing and understanding of the mechanisms of conception now indicates that a majority of
   cases of infertility are due to a combination of factors, with neither the
   male nor female the sole source of the problem. And even with all the
   advanced testing available, some 10 percent of cases of infertility
   remain completely unexplained. In any event, it is clear that infertility
   is not just a "female" problem: it is a "couple" problem.

7. Few infertile men have testosterone deficiencies, and testosterone
   pills have absolutely no place in the modern treatment of male
   infertility.

8. This myth is another variation on the "if they'd just stop trying so hard
   and relax" theme. A number of careful studies have failed to find
   support for the notion that fertility improves after adoption.[4]

IF YOU WANT TO HAVE A BABY: SOME PRACTICAL ADVICE

It has always been fascinating to us that people approach the process of
getting pregnant in the most haphazard ways, as though a baby will automatically fall into their lives. For some couples, of course, this works quite well.
But for many others, a little advance planning will go a long way toward
facilitating the entire process of conception and preventing them from
enrolling in the ranks of the infertile, or subfertile, population. Here is a list
of points that you might keep in mind.

1. *Don't use artificial lubricants of any kind if you're trying to have a baby.*
Substances like skin softeners, hand lotions, K-Y Jelly, and Vaseline may
make sex more exciting, but they all contain chemicals that may be damaging to sperm or may change the chemistry inside the vagina just enough to
make it slightly hostile to the sperm cells' attempts to swim up the female
reproductive tract.

2. *If you want to optimize your chances for success, both partners should cut out the use of marijuana, cocaine, or other so-called "recreational" drugs.* Contrary to what you may have heard, these chemicals can exert a detrimental effect on reproductive processes in both men and women. For example, chronic marijuana use suppresses sperm production and also temporarily lowers testosterone in men. In women, chronic marijuana use can cause a variety of hormonal changes that upset the balance of the normal menstrual cycle. While these problems are most evident with heavy drug use, why take a chance at all on something that's as important as a pregnancy? A mounting body of research also suggests that drugs like cocaine can cause abnormalities in sperm: why take the chance? One other caution is to young male athletes who may be using anabolic steroids: there is very solid evidence that these steroids suppress sperm production, so if you want to have a child, stop using them well in advance of any attempts at conceiving (ideally, at least 6 months before trying to achieve a pregnancy). (For more information on this topic, including a more detailed discussion of the health risks of anabolic steroids, see Chapter 12.)

3. *While there's no single "best" way to make love when you're attempting to conceive, there are some practical pointers to keep in mind.* Overall, there is little question that the mechanics of sexual intercourse have something to do with where sperm are delivered inside the vagina. With certain positions of intercourse, like rear entry or woman on top, it may be more difficult to achieve deep penetration and, more important, there is apt to be some spillage of semen out of the vagina as a result of gravity. If the man's sperm count is completely normal, these factors probably won't make any difference at all in conception rates. However, if the sperm count is reduced, or if there are other problems relating to sperm motility (the swimming ability of the sperm), then it makes considerable sense to maximize the odds of conception by using the man-on-top position for intercourse, with the woman remaining in a lying-down position, with her knees drawn up toward her chest, for 5 minutes or so after the man ejaculates.

4. *When it comes to conceiving, as with so many other things in life, timing is everything.* The way the female menstrual cycle works, there is only a rather narrow window of fertility each month. In fact, the egg can probably be fertilized for a period of only about 12 to 24 hours after ovulation. The bottom line here is that if you have intercourse at the wrong time, there is no chance of fertilization or conception. However, the odds aren't quite as bad

as they sound. For one thing, since sperm cells can survive in the woman's reproductive tract for 24 to 72 hours, you don't have to have intercourse at exactly the precise hour ovulation occurs. In fact, being within a day of the event is usually more than adequate to stack the odds in your favor. For another thing, you don't have to guess wildly as to when ovulation is likely to happen. For many women, the timing of ovulation is reasonably predictable. Especially for women who don't have much variation in the overall length of their menstrual cycle from month to month, it is relatively easy to pinpoint when ovulation occurs. This is because ovulation usually happens 14 days before the end of a cycle. Thus, if the woman's cycle is 28 days, ovulation would be expected around day 14. If her cycle typically lasts 32 days, ovulation is most apt to occur at day 18. To check on this (or for women who aren't so regular in their cycles), it is now possible to buy for home use a simple urine test kit that will let you discover when ovulation is happening. (Q Test, made by Becton Dickinson, is available at most pharmacies; Ovukit, made by Monoclonal Antibodies, Inc., can be ordered direct from the manufacturer by calling 1-800-622-5487; information about CLEAR-PLAN Easy, made by Whitehall Laboratories, can be obtained by calling 1-800-223-2329.)

5. *Determining the frequency of sexual intercourse that's best when you're trying to attain a pregnancy is simple.* This is a perfect example of when more isn't necessarily better. If the male ejaculates too frequently, his sperm count is lowered drastically, so most experts suggest waiting a minimum of 48 to 72 hours from the time of the last ejaculation before producing a semen specimen for a full laboratory analysis. (In one instance, we found that a young man who ordinarily had a sperm count in the range of 120,000,000 per cc suddenly appeared in the lab one day with a specimen that had a count of only 18,000,000. Concerned that our lab had mislabeled the specimen, we called the donor in for a confidential talk. We discovered that his fiancée had returned to town the previous weekend after 6 months overseas, and they had made love two or three times a day for the 4 days before he produced his subpar specimen.) On the other hand, having too much time between ejaculations also has a negative effect on sperm. In this instance, it is not just that the sperm count may be lowered: the real problem is that the motility of the sperm is likely to be impaired. Thus, the golden mean seems to be having intercourse every 2 days around the presumably ovulatory portion of the woman's cycle. For a woman with a 28-day cycle, this would mean having intercourse on cycle days 12, 14, and 16, with no intercourse (or ejaculation by any other means, including oral

sex or masturbation) between cycle day 8 and day 12. (After day 16, the couple can relax and enjoy themselves sexually: what they do is strictly for fun, not for procreation.)

6. *A special tip for women: avoid douching when you're trying to conceive.* Douching alters the normal acidity of the vagina, making the surroundings harmful to sperm survival. In addition, frequent douching can actually make a woman more susceptible to vaginal infections, as well as to pelvic inflammatory disease.[5]

7. *A special tip for men: avoid frequent or prolonged sojourns in hot tubs or saunas.* Excessive heat is detrimental to sperm production.

8. *Another special tip for men: avoid strenuous bicycle riding.* Apparently, a hard bicycle seat bumping against the scrotum isn't Mother Nature's way of coddling the testes, which are, after all, the factory for sperm production. If you're used to 15-mile daily bike rides as part of your physical conditioning regimen, find a different form of exercise (running, hiking, or swimming will do perfectly well) until you've gotten a pregnancy underway. Even men whose only biking is on a stationary exercise bike might do well to heed this advice, although there is certainly less mechanical pressure from this type of biking than from open-road riding.

9. *If you're trying to decide how soon you should get medical attention in the face of not getting pregnant when you want to, here are some specific guidelines.* If the woman had been taking birth control pills up until the couple decided to try to get pregnant, it pays to wait for a solid 15 months before getting a medical evaluation. (The reason is that it can take a while for women to resume normal ovulatory menstrual cycling after having been on the pill for several years; ordinarily, this is nothing to be worried about.) If the woman is over age 30 and was not using birth control pills, and pregnancy hasn't occurred within 6 months of trying, it's time to get medical help. This is because the longer a couple remains infertile, the worse their chances for an effective cure; in particular, treatment of most forms of infertility, including the most advanced forms of the new reproductive technologies, work far more efficiently in women under age 35 than in older women. Furthermore, the probability of conception declines from the woman's mid-twenties on (although this decline is more rapid after age 30), which further complicates matters.[6] For couples where the woman is still in her twenties, it seems wise to wait for a year of unprotected intercourse before deciding that medical help should be obtained.

CAUSES

Although typically the woman seeks medical help first, often both partners in an infertile couple have conditions that contribute to their inability to conceive. It is important that both the man and the woman be seen by a physician, since proper treatment and an optimal chance for pregnancy depend on accurate testing. In about 85 percent of couples with infertility, a specific cause can be found.

FEMALE INFERTILITY

The two major causes of female infertility are failure to ovulate and blockage of the Fallopian tubes. Lack of ovulation (or infrequent ovulation) can be caused by a variety of disorders. Problems affecting either the hypothalamus or the pituitary gland, including tumors and abnormalities in hormone feedback mechanisms, are more readily detectable today than in the past as a result of the availability of tests to measure the hypothalamic and pituitary hormones directly in blood. For example, it is now known that excessive secretion of prolactin, the pituitary hormone associated with milk production, is a common cause of infertility: in some studies, it has been found to affect approximately one-fifth of infertile women.[7] One special case of hypothalamic dysfunction causing blocked ovulation (and what is technically called amenorrhea, or not having periods) is weight loss. This condition is particularly common in women with anorexia nervosa (the so-called self-starvation disease; see Chapter 12), but it can also appear in women who are ardent long-distance runners, ballet dancers, or bicyclists—in other words, in cases where women train so emphatically that they reduce their levels of subcutaneous fat substantially.

Ovarian abnormalities make up another sizable category of cases of failure to ovulate. The commonest disorder of this type, affecting an estimated 3 to 5 percent of women in their reproductive years, is the polycystic ovary syndrome, which is typically marked by enlarged ovaries along with excessive facial and body hair (in about 70 percent of women with this disorder). Fifty to 55 percent of women with this disorder have amenorrhea, while 30 percent have irregular, heavy bleeding. The polycystic ovary syndrome is also marked by a relatively steady state of high circulating estrogen, androgens, and luteinizing hormone (LH), rather than the fluctuating levels of these hormones seen in the normal menstrual cycle. (Some women with this disorder ovulate on an irregular basis, while others do not ovulate at all.)

Ovarian tumors, ovarian infections, autoimmune disease, ovarian damage resulting from irradiation or chemotherapy, and genetic conditions affecting the ovaries (such as Turner's syndrome, a sex chromosome disorder in which the ovaries do not develop properly) are other causes of infertility due to anovulation. Certain types of chronic illness, including severe thyroid disease or disorders of the adrenal glands, can also be accompanied by infertility because of their negative effects on ovulation. Drug addiction or abuse also causes anovulation, although the ovarian dysfunction tends to resolve spontaneously within 6 months to a year after the drug use ceases. Rarely, ovulation is blocked by psychological stress.

Failure to ovulate may be detected by the use of basal body temperature (BBT) charts, hormone testing, or scraping the lining of the uterus to examine endometrial tissue under the microscope. The BBT chart is obtained by the woman's daily measurement of her temperature immediately after awakening, before getting out of bed. During the first portion of the menstrual cycle the BBT is low, but as progesterone production in the ovary increases just after ovulation, the temperature shifts upward and remains higher for 10 to 16 days. Theoretically, BBT increases just after ovulation. If no temperature rise is seen, it is a sign that ovulation didn't occur.

Although keeping BBT charts was, until recently, the primary method used for predicting the timing or occurrence of ovulation, new do-it-yourself urine tests allow users to monitor levels of LH in their urine to identify the LH surge that precedes ovulation by 12 to 24 hours.* Based on the same sort of monoclonal antibody technology used in some at-home pregnancy test kits, the LH tests are marketed under trade names such as First Response, Ovutime, and OvuStick. While the tests must typically be done on 4 to 6 days for best accuracy and are expensive (usually costing $40 to $60 for a kit that permits testing for one month), they are much more precise than BBT patterns in identifying whether and when ovulation occurs.[8]

Blocked Fallopian tubes may be caused by scarring after an infection in the pelvic tissues or abdomen. The commonest causes of such blockage are garden-variety lower genital tract infections with gonorrhea or chlamydia (discussed in more detail in Chapter 13), which affect some 3 million American women annually, with the heaviest concentration in the under-24-year-old group. An estimated 125,000 women become infertile each year due to these sexually transmitted diseases, which means that approximately 2 million reproductive-age women currently have infertility caused by blocked Fallopian tubes.[9] A majority of affected women have no

---

* Luteinizing hormone is produced in the anterior pituitary gland. In females, where it is secreted in a cyclic fashion, the midcycle outpouring of LH provides the hormonal stimulus to the ovaries that ordinarily triggers ovulation (the release of an egg).

history of symptoms of pelvic inflammatory disease (PID), which include lower abdominal pain, chills and fever, and a cervical discharge. According to one major study from Sweden, the risk of tubal blockage after PID increases with each episode: it is 11 percent after the first one, 23 percent after a second episode, and it rises to 54 percent after a third one.[10]

Blocked tubes can also result from endometriosis, a common disorder in which functioning endometrial tissue (the tissue lining the uterine cavity) grows outside the uterus in other pelvic or abdominal organs, often leading to scar formation. Endometriosis has its peak incidence in the 20-to-40-year-old age range, and is generally assumed to be a principal contributing factor in 15 percent of infertile women.[11] Its hallmark symptom is a deep-seated aching pelvic or lower abdominal pain usually beginning several days before a menstrual period starts and abating after several days, then usually subsiding completely toward the end of or just after the period. Less commonly, it can also cause pain during sexual intercourse. However, as many as 20 percent of women with endometriosis may be completely symptom-free, even in the presence of extensive disease. Endometriosis is being diagnosed more frequently today than in the past, perhaps because of a combination of greater vigilance for this problem and the trend toward childbearing at a later age than 20 or 30 years ago, rather than a true increase in its prevalence.

Endometriosis is usually diagnosed by inspecting the female reproductive organs through a procedure called a laparoscopy, in which a thin, lighted telescopelike tube is inserted into the abdomen through a small incision next to the navel. If endometrial implants or cysts are found, a small piece of the abnormal tissue can be removed and thoroughly analyzed under a microscope.

The Fallopian tubes can be checked for obstruction by either Rubin's test, which involves inserting carbon dioxide into the uterus and seeing if this gas passes into the abdomen, or by X-rays of the uterus and tubes, using a dye that outlines these structures. The X-ray method (called a hysterosalpingo-gram) is preferred by most infertility specialists because it is more accurate; it also has the advantage of showing the location of an obstruction if one is present.

Other less frequent causes of female infertility include abnormal cervical mucus that impedes the passage of sperm, birth defects of the reproductive organs, tumors, infections, and antibodies to sperm. In some cases, not having intercourse close to the time of ovulation may be a problem, and in other instances, the use of artificial lubricants like Vaseline or K-Y Jelly may be killing the sperm (but these preparations should not be considered as spermicides for birth control purposes).

MALE INFERTILITY

The primary cause of male infertility is a low sperm count. Less than 40 million sperm per cubic centimeter is below normal, but pregnancy is frequently possible with sperm counts of 20 million per cc or more. With lower counts, the chances of impregnation are considerably reduced, although not eliminated entirely. However, there has been a tendency to overemphasize the importance of the sperm count alone, without recognizing that it is really the functional capacity of sperm, rather than just the total number, that is most important in terms of fertility potential. These functional factors that determine male fertility include sperm motility (the ability of sperm to swim forward), the number of normal versus abnormal sperm forms, and the volume of seminal fluid. The ability of sperm to penetrate the egg is also an important factor, although it remains not well understood at the present time.

Low sperm counts can be caused by testicular injury, infection (especially mumps occurring after childhood, when it can spread to the testes), radiation, endocrine disorders, varicose veins in the scrotum, undescended testes, and birth defects. Drug use can also impair sperm production, with alcohol, cigarettes, narcotics, marijuana, and some prescription medications (especially cancer chemotherapy) potential sources of such a problem. Some reports indicate that long-distance bicycle riding or tight-fitting underwear can lower sperm counts.[12] Since sperm production is sensitive to temperature, prolonged and frequent use of hot tubs, saunas, and steam baths may have a negative effect. A high frequency of ejaculation can also lower the sperm count.

Varicose veins in the scrotum, a condition technically called varicocele, affects some 30 to 40 percent of infertile men, making it one of the leading causes of male infertility.[13] (The condition doesn't automatically cause infertility, however, since varicoceles are found in 10 to 15 percent of fertile men.) The exact link between varicocele and male infertility is uncertain, but a high proportion of men with this condition either have a low sperm count and/or abnormalities of sperm shape or motility. A varicocele can be detected during a physical examination. It generally feels like a "bag of worms" above the testicle within the scrotum when the man is standing, and it typically disappears or becomes much smaller in size when the man lies down (which is one reason a man's sex partner may never have detected the condition). Subclinical varicoceles, those that are too small to be detected by physical examination (but might be discovered using special studies, such as Doppler examinations, thermography, or special X-ray studies of the venous system), are claimed by some investigators also to cause male infertility, but this hypothesis is unproven at present.[14] The exact mechanism by which varicoceles cause male infertility remains unknown.

Hormone abnormalities present another important category of male infertility. Pituitary tumors causing elevated secretion of prolactin (which in turn suppresses testicular function, typically resulting in lowered sexual desire, potency problems, and impaired sperm production) are easily detectable today by measuring prolactin directly in a blood sample. Similarly, other types of pituitary or hypothalamic problems can be found by measuring levels of LH and follicle-stimulating hormone (FSH). Very high FSH levels in a man with low sperm counts (or azoospermia, the absence of sperm production) usually indicates testicular failure, which is not apt to be amenable to treatment. On the other hand, if LH and FSH levels are not elevated (as they should normally be in response to a low sperm count), it implies that the problem is a central one, at the level of the hypothalamus or pituitary, rather than at the testicular level.

Brief mention should be made of one other category of male infertility: sexual dysfunction can occasionally be the sole problem. Severe erectile problems can prevent placement of sperm in the vagina, unless the couple resorts to artificial insemination (discussed below). Likewise, cases in which the male gets perfectly normal erections but is unable to ejaculate intravaginally—called ejaculatory incompetence—are obvious causes of infertility, although they are fortunately infrequent in the general population. Another type of ejaculatory problem, called retrograde ejaculation, is marked by semen flowing backward into the urinary bladder instead of spurting out of the penis. This condition affects 1 or 2 percent of diabetic men and is also found in some men with multiple sclerosis or after certain types of prostate surgery. While it might seem at first that such difficulties are easily diagnosed, the sad fact is that many physicians never take an adequate sexual history from their patients, and the patients may be too embarrassed or uncertain to bring up the topic.

TREATMENT OF FEMALE INFERTILITY

Women who do not ovulate can frequently be helped by treatment with clomiphene, a pill that induces ovulation by stimulating the pituitary to secrete LH and FSH. About half of the women given this medication become pregnant. There is a modestly increased chance of having a multiple pregnancy (twins, triplets, etc.), which occurs about 8 percent of the time with clomiphene compared to 1.2 percent in routine pregnancies.

Women who do not achieve a pregnancy with clomiphene may be treated with HMG (human menopausal gonadotropins), which is given in a series of injections. This medication acts directly on the ovaries, bypassing the pituitary gland, and induces ovulation in more than 90 percent of women with functioning ovaries. Pregnancy is achieved in 60 to 70 percent of women receiving this treatment, and 20 percent of these pregnancies are multiple (15 percent are twins, and 5 percent are triplets, quadruplets, quintuplets, or sextuplets). Neither clomiphene nor HMG causes a greater risk of abortion or birth defects than in naturally occurring pregnancies. These drugs, however, can overstimulate the ovaries, causing them to enlarge (sometimes to the size of grapefruit) and to leak fluid into the abdomen. This condition, which is more common with HMG than with clomiphene, usually requires hospitalization because there is a danger that the ovaries may rupture.

Blocked Fallopian tubes can sometimes be treated by microsurgery. Using a microscope for visual guidance, a surgeon removes the obstruction and then sews together the healthy portions of the tubes with tiny needles and suture material. Microsurgery is no panacea, however: at the present time it is successful in only 30 to 50 percent of women with tubal problems. Women who have tubal damage that is not amenable to surgical repair or women without Fallopian tubes now have the possibility of being treated by various forms of *in vitro* fertilization, the dramatic "test-tube baby" procedure, which we will discuss shortly.

When endometriosis is the cause of infertility, it is usually treated by surgery. One promising development is the use of laser technology, in which the surgeon focuses a laser beam to burn away endometrial implants or adhesions. Since the laser beam actually seals off small blood vessels in the surgical area as it burns away diseased tissue, there is very little blood loss with this procedure. Pregnancy rates after laser laparoscopy are in the 40 to 65 percent range.

Severe cases of endometriosis, particularly those involving widespread adhesions or large masses, are not usually treatable by laparoscopic surgery. Here, the older form of surgical approach, called an open laparotomy, is often required so that the full extent of nonuterine endometrial tissue can be located and excised and adhesions can be removed. However, one recent study done at Stanford University School of Medicine found that pregnancy rates after laser laparoscopy were equivalent to those after the more conservative surgical approach, regardless of the severity of disease.[15]

Endometriosis can also be treated with drugs such as danazol or nafarelin. These drugs work by inhibiting the pituitary-ovarian axis, resulting in decreased estrogen production, which in turn causes the endometriotic tissue to shrink, since estrogen is ordinarily required for its growth. (One side effect of these treatments is hot flashes, which occur on much the same physiologic basis as they do during menopause: because of markedly lowered estrogen production. Vaginal dryness is a related side effect that occurs in about one-fifth of women using nafarelin.) Danazol, which is chemically related to testosterone, also commonly causes weight gain and acne, and in some women may cause distressing growth of facial and body hair. Either of these drugs is typically administered for 4 to 6 months, during which time pregnancy will not occur because ovulation is suppressed. (Danazol is taken by mouth; nafarelin is a nasal spray.) After the period of active drug administration is completed, pregnancy rates of 40 to 50 percent are attainable.

A practical observation about endometriosis is in order here. Mild forms of endometriosis usually do not require treatment; in many cases, pregnancy ensues once other treatable coexisting problems, if any, are dealt with. As with other medical conditions, it is possible for too much medical intervention actually to create problems or to cause unnecessary expense and worry.

TREATMENT OF MALE INFERTILITY

The treatment of male infertility is considerably less fully developed. Surgical repair of varicose veins in the scrotum can improve the sperm count substantially or can improve the quality of semen (i.e., better sperm motility, a lower percentage of abnormal or immature sperm forms), but at present it isn't possible to predict which men will be helped the most by this procedure. Generally, it appears that semen quality improves in about 60 percent of men after this operation, and about 30 to 40 percent will then initiate a pregnancy. However, the largest varicoceles are not always the ones that respond best to surgical repair, and sometimes dramatic results are obtained from correcting small and asymptomatic lesions. In any event, varicocele repairs should be undertaken only as part of the treatment of infertility if the woman's fertility is normal (or potentially so with treatment) and if the man's semen has one or more abnormalities.

When an endocrine problem is the cause of male infertility, the odds of correcting it are usually quite high. Excessive prolactin secretion is easily treated either medically, with the use of a drug called bromocriptine, or surgically, to remove the prolactin-secreting tumor. In either instance, there is usually a quick improvement in testicular function (although it takes 3 to 6 months for the improvement in sperm count and semen quality to become evident). Poor testicular function caused by a problem in the hypothalamus or pituitary is often treated successfully with the use of injections of HMG. In fact, in men with an isolated deficiency of LH or FSH, pituitary hormone replacement can attain a 95 percent fertility rate by stimulating sperm production.[16] One caveat about endocrine diagnoses causing infertility: years ago, it was thought that an underactive thyroid was a common cause of poor sperm counts, and many physicians automatically gave thyroid pills to almost all their male patients as a "therapeutic trial" (in other words, just to see whether it would work). It is now clear that such cases are very unusual: not only is there no reason at all for routinely prescribing thyroid hormone to subfertile men, but if your physician suggests this approach without an endocrine consultation, our kindest advice is *find another doctor.*

Less frequent causes of male infertility that are sometimes amenable to treatment include obstruction of the ejaculatory ducts, which occurs in about 5 percent of azoospermic men.[17] This problem may be correctable by surgery, but in many cases, as when the obstruction is the result of severe infection or severe injury, it is unlikely to be reversible.

Most other conditions causing male infertility respond poorly to treatment. The use of testosterone to achieve a "rebound effect" after first suppressing sperm production is rarely very useful, but the results obtained from using clomiphene in men have been inconclusive. (In our judgment, it is doubtful whether either technique works better than chance alone, and these treatments are certainly more expensive.) A diagnosis of male "autoimmunity" to his own sperm is also of dubious functional significance when it comes to being fertile: many of the men we have seen who were diagnosed as having this problem subsequently impregnated their wives without any specific treatment for the condition. Proper medical management of acute infections, anatomical defects, or hormonal disorders is definitely helpful, but such cases are relatively few. (Infertility as a result of chronic or long-ago infection is more common, but not apt to be treatable.) In men with borderline sperm counts, daily ejaculation can actually lower fertility by reducing the number of sperm, and the chances for a pregnancy can be improved by decreasing the frequency of ejaculation to a minimum of 48 hours from one time to the next.

Since many cases of infertility achieve pregnancy spontaneously, it appears important for physicians to perform careful diagnostic testing to determine whether treatment is required. Likewise, couples contending with infertility should realize that pregnancy is quite possible in many cases even if medical treatment initially doesn't seem to be effective.

ARTIFICIAL INSEMINATION

Artificial insemination means placing semen in the vagina or uterus by a means other than sexual intercourse. There are two basic types of artificial insemination: using semen from the husband (AIH) or using semen from a donor. For either method, the woman's fertility status must be relatively normal. AIH works by concentrating the husband's sperm at the mouth of the cervix (or higher into the uterus); with coitus, only a small fraction of sperm gets to this location. In other words, AIH is an attempt to improve the efficiency of sperm delivery.

AIH can be tried if the husband's count is low but not zero. For practical reasons, successful AIH is infrequent if the count is less than 10 million per cubic centimeter or if the sperm motility is low. AIH is best done by inserting a fresh semen specimen in the vagina at the mouth of the cervix, using a small plastic cap to hold it in place. Using frozen, thawed specimens reduces sperm motility (and actually kills some sperm), and combining several frozen specimens does not seem to improve the outcome, although this technique has been tried repeatedly.

Injecting sperm into the uterus (a technique called intrauterine insemination, or IUI) usually causes cramping and poses a risk of infection; generally, it offers no improved success over other methods, although it seems to be widely used at present.[18] IUI may be useful when cervical mucus problems are a contributing factor to the failure to conceive, since injecting sperm directly into the uterus bypasses what may be a hostile chemical or immunologic environment in this situation.

Attempts at using "split ejaculate" specimens, in which the first portion of semen produced during ejaculation is collected separately from the second half, so that the relatively sperm-rich first portion is used for AIH, have some theoretical advantages but in reality show results that are virtually identical to working with ordinary specimens.

Donor insemination is used when the husband's sperm count is zero or very low. A donor, selected on the basis of excellent health, good intelligence, and closeness of physical characteristics to the husband, provides a masturbated semen specimen (for which he is paid). The donor's identity is unknown to the couple. The legal status of donor insemination is uncertain in many states, although in California once the husband signs a consent form agreeing to use of a donor, he is the legal father of the baby. The pregnancy rate for donor insemination is about 60 percent using frozen semen obtained from a sperm bank. (In the past, fresh donor semen was typically used, since it offered the highest conception rates. Today, concerns over the possible transmission of HIV have led to regulations requiring the use of frozen specimens only.)

The decision to undergo donor insemination must be made jointly by husband and wife; clearly this type of treatment is not psychologically right for everyone for whom it might be used. Some people equate this procedure with adultery, others have conflicts with their religious values, and some fear that the husband will reject or dislike the baby because it is not "his." Despite the latter concern, almost all couples who achieve a pregnancy using donor sperm find that the experience brings them very close together and that the husband's excitement at fatherhood is genuinely felt. In some locations, donor insemination is also being used by single women who want to become pregnant.

IVF: *In Vitro* Fertilization

Late in the evening of July 25, 1978, a slightly premature 5-pound, 12-ounce baby girl was born by cesarean section to Lesley and John Brown of Oldham, England. They named their healthy, normal baby Louise, and since then her name and picture have made the pages of nearly every major newspaper in the Western world. The sperm and egg that united to conceive Louise met not in Lesley Brown's Fallopian tube, but in a test tube, *in vitro*, outside the mother's body. Louise Brown was the first baby ever born from *in vitro* fertilization techniques (see Figure 11.1).

The British doctors responsible for this remarkable achievement were Patrick Steptoe and Robert Edwards. Steptoe had been experimenting with *in vitro fertilization (IVF)* for more than a decade before meeting Lesley Brown, who was unable to conceive because of blocked Fallopian tubes. She had undergone surgery to unblock the tubes before coming to Steptoe. The surgery was not only unsuccessful, but when Steptoe did his exploration of her reproductive organs, he found the tubes so badly damaged ("Mere remnants," he said) that they were removed.

Lesley was first given hormones to stimulate the maturation of eggs in her ovaries. Steptoe and Edwards then made a small incision near her navel, and by using an instrument that magnifies and illuminates the tiny ovum, they withdrew a ripe egg and placed it in a laboratory dish. The dish contained a carefully mixed culture of nutrients designed to resemble the environment of the Fallopian tubes. As quickly as possible, John Brown's sperm (obtained through masturbation) were added to the culture, and the doctors waited for one of the sperm to impregnate the egg. After the sperm and egg united in the laboratory dish and the preembryonic cells began to divide, the blastocyst (a hollow sphere of 60 separate cells) was inserted into Lesley's uterus. In about a week, the doctors knew the preembryo had attached itself to a wall of the uterus and Lesley Brown was pregnant.

Steptoe and Edwards had made more than 30 attempts to implant eggs fertilized outside the mother before the success with the Browns. Two pregnancies had resulted, but both were spontaneously aborted—one because the membrane around the embryo ruptured and the other because of a genetic abnormality. This second case is typical of a cause of concern by doctors working in this area. Who is responsible for a child born with

FIGURE 11.1
THE STEPS INVOLVED IN THE IN VITRO FERTILIZATION (IVF) PROCESS

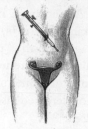

(a) Daily hormone injections stimulate egg production. About seven days later, a shot of the hormone hCG causes the release of eggs.

(b) A laparoscope is inserted at the navel to view the follicles, which hold the eggs. The eggs are retrieved using a hollow needle.

(c) Each egg is placed in a petri dish containing a culture medium that duplicates the chemical environment in the uterus. While incubation begins, sperm are collected.

(d) Sperm are added 5 or 6 hours later. Only the most active sperm are used, reducing the number needed for fertilization.

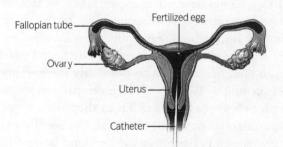

Fallopian tube

Fertilized egg

Ovary

Uterus

Catheter

(e) The fertilized eggs are replaced in the uterus after about 48 hours of maturation. There implantation may take place.

genetic damage? Did the damage result from handling the preembryo outside the uterus, or would it have occurred even during normal fertilization? Is destroying a fertilized egg in a test tube abortion?

Since the initial breakthrough by Steptoe and Edwards, a large number of IVF clinics have opened around the world, including more than 200 clinics in the United States alone. More than 25,000 babies conceived *in vitro* have been born as of 1993, including about 5,000 live deliveries in 1992 in America. Aside from a higher rate of multiple pregnancies and a very high cesarean rate (50 to 60 percent in many clinics)—reflecting both older maternal ages and the "premium" nature of such pregnancies—the overall obstetrical experience with IVF is largely comparable to that expected in a similar group of women who had conceived by natural means. In particular, there is no increased risk of birth defects or developmental difficulties for IVF children.[19]

The best candidates for IVF are women younger than 35 who have normal menstrual cycles and husbands with a normal sperm count. (About 50 percent of IVF programs will treat women 40 or older, and most will also proceed if the sperm count is mild to moderately reduced; if the sperm count is very low, or zero, then the couple can consider IVF using donor sperm.) IVF can overcome many of the causes of infertility, including blocked or absent Fallopian tubes, severe endometriosis, and immunologic infertility, that in the past were almost insurmountable obstacles to pregnancy for hundreds of thousands of couples.

As with any complicated medical procedure, there are some drawbacks. For one thing, IVF is expensive, generally costing $4,000 to $6,000 for each attempt at pregnancy. This has led to charges of commercialism (especially directed at private, for-profit clinics) as well as some rancor toward health insurance companies that refuse to pay for such procedures. Another problem is that not all IVF clinics have comparable results: in fact, some have never had a successful pregnancy resulting in a live birth. Since the IVF "industry" is essentially unregulated, even physicians involved in the field have been worried that there may be misleading claims and practices that may confuse, or even bilk, the public. This possibility is especially troublesome since couples turning to IVF are often emotionally overwrought as a result of their lengthy efforts to have a child, so they are not apt to be as objective as, say, consumers shopping for a new car. (A checklist of questions to ask to help you evaluate an IVF program can be found later in this chapter on pages 316–17.) In addition, since live deliveries result from only about 14 percent of IVF stimulation cycles, it is clear that not every couple going through this physically and emotionally arduous procedure will wind up with a baby. Some experts believe that ultimately only half the couples attempting IVF will be successful, with this success usually coming in the first four cycles in which IVF is attempted.[20]

To put all this in perspective, it is helpful to remember that despite the expenses and problems involved, IVF is in many ways a miracle come true. As one happy father said:

We had basically given up on ever getting pregnant after more than ten years of treatment. When an IVF program opened up at the university nearby, we decided to give it one more shot. Now we have two-year-old twins who are a testimonial to the skill of the team at the clinic. What better reward could persistence ever have?

OTHER ASSISTED REPRODUCTIVE TECHNIQUES

A number of related procedures have been developed as outgrowths of IVF. These are briefly summarized here.

GIFT (Gamete Intrafallopian Transfer) involves the direct placement of a mixture of sperm and eggs into the Fallopian tube. Fertilization takes place naturally, in the Fallopian tube, rather than in the laboratory, as it does with IVF. A woman must have at least one normal Fallopian tube to be a candidate for GIFT, but this procedure generally has somewhat higher success rates than IVF: an overall 23 percent live delivery rate was reported in the United States in 1991, with some centers having rates of 30 percent or more. GIFT is particularly useful in dealing with endometriosis and unexplained infertility (where the chemical environment of the cervix seems to kill sperm). It ensures that the ovum and a large number of motile sperm reach the physiologic fertilization site—the Fallopian tube. (GIFT can be combined with donor insemination if the male has a poor sperm count; this method has a high rate of success.) It should be noted that success rates with GIFT, as with other forms of treatment, are substantially better for women under age 40 than for older women. Women 40 or above had only a 9 percent live delivery rate per transfer cycle with GIFT in 1990.

ZIFT (Zygote Intrafallopian Transfer) combines IVF with GIFT. The wife's eggs are fertilized by her husband's sperm *in vitro*. The zygote (the fertilized egg) is then transferred to the Fallopian tube within 24 hours. The advantage to this procedure is that the medical team can be certain that fertilization has occurred. If fertilization doesn't take place, then the couple can decide if they want to try donor insemination. Approximately 16 percent of ZIFT procedures result in a live delivery.

Egg donors are used in a growing number of programs in the United States for women who are unable to ovulate or who don't have ovaries. (In some instances, egg donors have also been used to assist infertile women in their forties who are trying to conceive, since other treatments are not as likely to be effective as they are in younger women.)[21] Egg donation—although a relatively recent approach to treating infertility—resembles sperm donation in certain ways. The donor in some programs is completely anonymous but matched for physical characteristics with the recipient. In many other programs, no registry of egg donors is maintained, and only donors selected by the woman wishing to conceive are used. Most commonly, a sister or close relative is the egg donor, but personal friends and sometimes people paid for the egg donation serve as donors. (Donors are typically paid $500 to $2,000 per aspiration.) Egg donation may be particularly useful for women who want to avoid passing on a genetic disorder in the wife's family, like hemophilia, to their children.

Once the eggs are obtained from the donor, fertilization with the husband's sperm is usually done in the laboratory; the fertilized egg can then be placed by ZIFT into the Fallopian tubes or handled as a straightforward IVF procedure. (The recipient must be prepared by hormonal stimulation so her uterus is ready to accept a pregnancy.) Ethical and religious concerns about egg donation abound, as might be expected with a relatively new technology of this sort, but any discussion here is precluded by space limitations.

Results obtained with egg donation are about the same as with assisted reproductive techniques using the wife's own eggs, although since this procedure is a relatively recent one, relatively few centers have extensive experience with this technique. In fact, in a 1992 survey of the current status of egg donor programs in the United States, only five centers that had performed more than 100 embryo transfers using donor eggs were identified out of 63 clinics queried.[22] It is important to inquire about a center's experience with this technique because success rates tend to be significantly higher in centers that have done 100 or more procedures. Overall, 22 percent of the procedures using donated eggs result in live deliveries; of these, about one-third are multiple births.

Embryo transplant is a more controversial method, which uses the husband's sperm to artificially inseminate a woman who is not his wife. Five days later the embryo is flushed out of the donor's uterus, where it is in the earliest stages of implantation, and transplanted into the wife's uterus. If it implants successfully, a normal pregnancy typically ensues. (A key element to this procedure is synchronizing the recipient's menstrual cycle with the donor's by hormone injections so that the recipient's endometrium is properly "primed" to accept the transferred embryo and to allow it to implant.) Potential problems with this method include the need to be certain of the donor's health and guaranteeing that she abstain completely from using drugs or alcohol during the cycle in which she conceives. There may also be legal difficulties in some states, so couples should check with an attorney before undertaking this approach to having a baby.

Embryo freezing is another very recent development; the first human birth from a frozen embryo (actually, a frozen preembryo) was in 1985. One of the major reasons for freezing preembryos is to reduce the risk of multiple pregnancy when the woman has "superovulated"—produced a large number of eggs—in response to the hormonal stimulation given in an egg retrieval cycle as part of IVF. In addition, freezing the extra preembryos cuts down the costs of future treatment cycles, since it isn't necessary to retrieve more eggs.

Prior to 1989, approximately 2,000 patients had a total of more than 7,000 eggs and preimplantation embryos frozen at 25 clinics across the country, and 48 live births have already occurred after thawing.[23] Data from 1990 show a success rate of only 9 percent per frozen ET cycle at American clinics, which shows that thawing certainly doesn't always work. In addition, there are still some concerns that freezing and thawing might damage the fertilized egg, with unknown consequences; and ethical and legal questions abound. For instance, who "owns" the preembryo if a couple divorces, or if the couple dies? Who determines when, or if, to destroy the frozen preembryo? These are not just theoretical issues; parental custody disputes over frozen embryos have already occurred.

The amazing advances in treating infertility in recent years are, unfortunately, accompanied by some less publicized negatives. For example, it is clear that the consumers' expectations for success have been raised to a height where continued childlessness in the face of extensive expenditures of time, energy, and money is, for many, both unacceptable and shocking. Such high expectations are, unfortunately, out of synch with the realities of actual results. Even under the best of circumstances, in the most experienced, advanced infertility programs, a substantial number of couples will never realize their dream. The psychological toll on these couples is higher than has been acknowledged generally, as we will shortly discuss in more detail.

Another problem that is not widely known about is that each treatment episode in what may turn out to be a 2- or 3-year odyssey carries its own emotional peaks and valleys. The valleys are sometimes devastatingly low. For couples first embarking on an IVF program, failure of having an egg fertilized in their first cycle of IVF treatment is usually grim because it calls into question their ability ever to attain a pregnancy. As a result, a substantial number of such couples drop out of treatment, convinced they are preordained to be unsuccessful. The actuality is, however, that in subsequent IVF cycles these couples achieve pregnancies about as often as other couples do.[24]

Evaluating outcome statistics on the treatment of infertility is complicated. However, it is useful to look at some recent data on the overall probability of infertile couples attaining a live birth as a result of IVF, drawn from a British series of more than 5,000 consecutive IVF cycles.[25] For women up to 34 years of age, 45 percent will have a live birth as a result of five cycles of IVF treatment. For women between the ages of 35 and 39, 29 percent will have a successful pregnancy. For women in their forties, the rate of pregnancy resulting in birth of a living child is materially lower: 14.4 percent. The declines in successful pregnancy outcomes in women older than 34 were attributable to both a decrease in conception and a higher rate of pregnancies that failed (i.e., aborted or miscarried). It was also noted that successful outcomes were significantly lower in cases of male infertility or multiple infertility factors.

QUESTIONS TO ASK ABOUT AN IVF/GIFT PROGRAM

With any medical treatment, patients should ask questions to determine how appropriate the treatment is for them, how qualified and experienced are the personnel providing the treatment, what to expect in terms of costs and time, and perhaps most important, how successful the treatment may be. When it comes to highly technical procedures such as those involved in IVF or GIFT, the importance of these queries cannot be stressed enough when it comes to gathering the information necessary for an informed decision.

The following list provides 11 key questions to ask when evaluating an IVF/GIFT program. As a practical matter, if you don't get straight answers to these questions, or if the doctor or program director you're discussing them with seems annoyed at your inquisitiveness, it would be wise to find a different program. (Inquiries about the location of such programs can be directed to the American Fertility Society, 2140 11th Ave. S., Suite 200, Birmingham, AL 35205-2800; telephone [205] 933-8494.)

1. When was your program started?
2. When did the program perform its first IVF (or GIFT) procedure?
3. How many babies have been born as a result of this program's IVF (or GIFT) procedures? How many babies have been born from IVF or GIFT in the last 2 years in this program?
4. What is your clinical pregnancy rate per IVF (or GIFT) procedure? What is your clinical pregnancy rate for couples our age with our particular type of problem?
5. Do you freeze eggs or embryos as part of your program? If so, what is done with them after we've had a baby?
6. Do you offer an egg donation program? If so, do we provide the donor, or do you? If you provide the donor, how is she selected? How much is she paid? What steps do you take to screen the donor's health?
7. Does your program report its results to the IVF Registry?
8. Are any of your doctors board certified in Reproductive Endocrinology?

9. How much does the entire procedure cost per cycle, including the cost of drugs?
10. Do we need to pay in advance? (If so, how much?)
11. Do you have an age limit for patients?

SURROGATE MOTHERHOOD

Some couples composed of an infertile wife and a fertile husband have hired a woman to act as a surrogate mother. Such a stand-in is artificially inseminated using the husband's sperm and carries the pregnancy to term, at that point giving the baby for adoption to the couple who had hired her. In some cases, a surrogate mother has been implanted with an ovum from an infertile woman that was fertilized *in vitro* by sperm from the infertile woman's husband. In one such case, the infertile woman had previously undergone surgical removal of her uterus and Fallopian tubes and so was unable to carry her own pregnancy, but she still had functioning ovaries, which allowed one of her own eggs to be used for transfer to the surrogate mother after IVF.

It is currently estimated that thousands of surrogate mothers have contracted with couples to bear a child for them for pay (ranging from $2,000 to $20,000), with legal fees in the neighborhood of $5,000.

In January 1983, the public's attention was drawn to this previously little-known practice by headlines announcing "Surrogate Infant Left Unclaimed." As the complicated story unraveled, what became clear was that the 26-year-old surrogate mother, Judy Stiver of Michigan, had given birth to a deformed and probably mentally retarded baby, only to have 46-year-old Alexander Malahoff of New York, who had contracted for the child, reject the child on the grounds that he was not the father. Although medical tests eventually supported Mr. Malahoff, the entire episode was an unsavory one in many respects, including a tasteless, prearranged television confrontation between the Stivers and Malahoff in which accusations seemed more important than the welfare of the child. Although the Stivers eventually agreed to keep the baby, who may need to be institutionalized, this case raises a number of difficult issues about the ethical implications of our new reproductive technologies.

What would have happened if Malahoff, or some future Malahoff, had proved to be the infant's father? Could he, as one journalist suggested, try to send the child back and demand a refund?

Technological parenthood may have the trappings of a business, but it is not a business; it is the answer to someone's most personal prayers. So it should be seen and handled. If the answer to the particular prayer happens to emerge deformed, it is no less the prayer's answer; and, as so many parents of such "damaged goods" have discovered, they sometimes give more contentment to a family than whole and healthy children and thus provide answers to different prayers entirely.[26]

This viewpoint seems laudable, but in the real world, people don't always behave in kindhearted ways. What will become of deformed children born not only to surrogate mothers but to unmarried women using the services of a sperm bank? If a baby conceived by *in vitro* methods turns out to be defective, will lawsuits follow and financial repercussions ensue? Or are we on the verge of an era of government regulation of reproductive decisions along the lines envisioned by George Orwell in *1984* or Aldous Huxley in *Brave New World*?

Another twist in the surrogate story occurred in 1986, when Mary Beth Whitehead of Brick Township, New Jersey—who had contracted to bear a child for William and Elizabeth Stern, using Mr. Stern's sperm for artificial insemination—decided after the birth of the baby girl that she didn't want to give her up to the Sterns. Mrs. Whitehead and her husband fled to Florida with the baby, who came to be known as "Baby M." In a much-publicized trial in 1987, however, a New Jersey court awarded custody to the Sterns and upheld the legality of the contract Mrs. Whitehead and the Sterns had signed. Both the trial and the judge's decision provoked a great deal of controversy, with many observers feeling it was improper to enforce a contract that required Mrs. Whitehead to give up her baby. Subsequently, the New Jersey Supreme Court invalidated the surrogacy contract and found the payment of money to a surrogate mother "illegal, perhaps criminal, and potentially degrading to women," but still awarded custody of Baby M to the Sterns. Mary Beth Whitehead was given liberal unsupervised visitation rights, however.

Since the "Baby M" case, there have been several other notable twists to the surrogate mother story. In one, a 42-year-old grandmother acted as a gestational surrogate for her own daughter, who had been born without a uterus. She gave birth to healthy twins on October 31, 1991. In another development, when the biological father separated from his wife, a three-way custody battle developed in California over a child born to a surrogate mother. In still another case involving disputed custody between a surrogate mother and the couple who hired her, the surrogate mother sued the doctors and lawyers involved, charging them with malpractice and battery.[27]

Although legislation barring the practice of surrogate motherhood has recently been implemented in several states, and others are considering such bills, there is also growing acceptance of the practice among the public, physicians, and attorneys. A representative of the American Bar Association noted:

> The movement has to be seen in the perspective of the strong autonomy our society puts on the child-bearing decision. Legislation banning surrogate motherhood would be held unconstitutional, infringing on a couple's procreative autonomy under the right of privacy. So, we have to think about a public policy to make the experience a better one for everyone involved. We can't take an ostrich-like approach to this anymore.[28]

On the other hand, a report from an expert panel on ethics and reproduction from the American Fertility Society raised a number of questions about the ethical propriety of permitting surrogate motherhood and voiced "serious ethical reservations about surrogacy that cannot be resolved until appropriate data are available for assessment of the risks and possible benefits of this alternative."[29]

Opponents of the practice of surrogate motherhood argue that it treats babies as commodities, leading to a situation in which affluent people can afford to hire women to bear their children. Opponents also contend that surrogacy makes motherhood a contractual business decision that, by its very nature, may be driven more by the profit motive than by what is good for the parties involved. In addition, many feminists believe that surrogate motherhood promotes the exploitation of women, and some church groups argue that surrogacy is a dehumanizing, immoral practice that undermines the sanctity of marriage and the family. There is also concern that some surrogate mothers may be harmed psychologically by giving up a child that is genetically theirs after the bonding that occurs during a nine-month pregnancy and delivery, even if they originally feel they will be able to part with the baby unemotionally. As Phyllis Chesler argues in her book on the Baby M case, "[N]o citizen can ever sell or promise to sell any of her inalienable constitutional rights. For example, Mary Beth Whitehead may choose not to exercise her right to vote—but she cannot sell that right to Bill Stern. . . . Similarly, no woman, including one who signs a surrogacy contract, can sell her parental rights; they are also inalienable and constitutionally protected."[30]

Those in favor of the use of surrogate motherhood—including most couples struggling with infertility—see it quite differently, of course. They point out that for couples where the woman is irreversibly infertile or unable to bear a child because of medical problems, the use of a surrogate is the only practical way in which the husband can conceive and rear a child that is genetically "his." Advocates also note that surrogacy is a way of bringing a wanted child into the world and point out that it is not conceptually very different from adoption. They argue that rather than commercializing human reproduction or making babies commodities, the use of a surrogate motherhood arrangement is a profound act of love and creativity. In addition, they insist that although there are potential risks to the surrogate mother, these risks can be understood and consented to by the prospective participants, so that contracting to be paid for one's services as a surrogate is no riskier than many occupational choices a woman might make. Advocates of surrogacy also deny that the practice exploits women, claiming instead that women who voluntarily choose to become surrogate mothers are offered reasonable compensation for their services and inconvenience as well as the opportunity to provide a socially desirable service.

In 1992, the American Academy of Pediatrics weighed in with its own recommendations designed to walk a delicate tightrope.[31] In any surrogate parenting agreement, the surrogate mother should be in control up until birth and for a period thereafter, their policy statement said. In effect, the surrogate parenting agreement should be looked at as a tentative adoption agreement, specifying a period after the birth in which the surrogate mother could decide to keep the baby if she wished. The academy also recommended that the baby's health not be a basis for paying the surrogate mother, thus avoiding a potential quagmire if it turns out that the baby is not completely normal.

Despite all the debate, relatively little has been said about the child in such situations. The child can be affected by genetic defects the surrogate mother passes on (except for those infrequent instances in which the woman who hires the surrogate contributes an egg, which is fertilized *in vitro*, and implanted in the surrogate's uterus). Many of these conditions, unfortunately, cannot be detected by current screening techniques. The developing fetus can also be harmed if the surrogate mother is not careful during her pregnancy—for instance, if she uses drugs, or if she doesn't eat properly. Of equal importance, but unanswerable at present, are concerns about the psychological development of the child. If the child is told (or discovers accidentally) that he or she was born to a surrogate mother, will he or she have problems or psychological anguish? If the surrogate mother has continuing contact with the child after birth, as sometimes happens if the surrogate is a friend or a relative, what impact will this communication have on the child?

There are many unresolved issues surrounding the practice of surrogate motherhood. Legally, there may be some clarification in the next few years through a combination of legislative and judicial actions. Answers to the psychological questions that abound will doubtless require decades of careful data-gathering. The ethical quandaries surrounding surrogacy are, by their very nature, probably not subject to a true resolution at all; we suspect they will only linger about us until a public-opinion consensus emerges about the moral validity of surrogate motherhood. However, for many infertile couples, surrogacy remains an acceptable alternative—albeit perhaps a remote and last-ditch sort of alternative—that is not easily discarded as one of the various options on the road to having a child of their own.

THE IMPACT OF INFERTILITY

INITIAL REACTIONS

The millions of American couples living in a state of involuntary childlessness are a largely neglected and poorly understood silent and invisible minority group. Clearly, couples undergoing treatment for infertility experience a number of characteristic psychological problems as part of their ordeal. Not only is there often an initial loss of self-esteem and diminished sense of masculinity and femininity tied to the frustrations of being unable to conceive and the social stigma associated with involuntary childlessness, there appear to be longer-term psychological effects as well. For example, a number of studies have noted that depression and anxiety are common among infertile patients.[32] Others have found that frustration and anger are very common among infertile couples undergoing medical investigations or medical treatment programs. It's no wonder that infertility is considered by many professionals to be a psychological crisis.

The dynamics behind these reactions are not difficult to understand. In a society where adolescents and young adults are reared with the assumption that pregnancies occur almost automatically, it is little wonder that being unable to conceive after a few months of trying is an immediate source of consternation. Couples typically react by asking themselves, "What are we doing wrong?" In an effort to answer this question, they turn first to books and magazines, and then may talk with a close friend or even a parent for advice. Only after becoming convinced that they're not doing anything "wrong" do they then ask the next question, "Is there something wrong with us?"

The realization that there may be a problem is often met with denial. While they may discuss getting checked medically, along with a mental search for possible past health problems, most infertile couples have a strong tendency to avoid a medical evaluation during the first few months after they realize they are having difficulties. (The exception to this generalization happens when a woman who is trying to conceive is also having gynecologic symptoms, such as abnormal menstruation or pelvic pain; then she is much more apt to seek medical attention promptly, since it is harder to deny the probability of a physiologic problem.) It is also common for considerable tension to build up in a relationship during this denial phase. This happens partly because there is a natural tendency for each person to blame the other for their current difficulties: "If you were only more relaxed, you'd get pregnant." "If you hadn't had that abortion when you were nineteen, you probably wouldn't have this problem now." "If you'd stop drinking so much beer, maybe we'd have better luck." In addition, each person worries that he or she may be at fault; in the process, they begin examining various aspects of their lives and their bodies to come up with a possible explanation and solution. The result is that even in the early going of contending with infertility, couples question their sexual abilities, their health, and even their goodness of heart.

A number of researchers have noted that women take the initiative in obtaining medical care when pregnancy doesn't occur as quickly as they would like; men tend to be more ambivalent and likely to hold a "wait and see" attitude.[33] Similarly, once the infertility program is in full swing, men tend to be less active (and somewhat less enthusiastic) participants than their mates. While this difference in attitudes may be partially attributable to a male-female difference in motivation for having a child, we suspect that the dynamics are more complex. Part of the dilemma may be that men seem to view the state of infertility as more of a blot on their sexual prowess than women do; in addition, men seem to be generally more intimidated by the process of medical evaluation and treatment of infertility than women are, although it is clear that women have more "things done to them" (in terms of testing and especially in terms of invasive procedures).

We should hasten to add a qualifying point here. People don't react to problems in neatly stereotyped ways, and there is not always the "typical" pattern of male-female reaction that we have discussed above. Sometimes men initiate the process of medical investigation of infertility, and sometimes it is women who are the ones who are reluctant to be tested either because of embarrassment, deep-rooted fears, or ambivalence about pregnancy. There are many individual differences in coping styles, in biographical facts, and in cultural programming that all combine to determine how the situation is handled. In addition, of course, there is the particular chemistry of a given couple, including how they blend their individual ways of coping into a solution that fits them both.

LONG-TERM PATTERNS

It is clear that a sizable number of individuals contending with infertility become depressed: as a result, their interpersonal relationships may suffer, their work performance may falter, and they adopt a general attitude of helplessness and pessimism in regard to ordinary events and stresses that is qualitatively different from their previous patterns.

Even when depression doesn't enter the picture, there is often a major toll on the couple's relationship. For one thing, sex quickly becomes transformed from a source of pleasure and spontaneity to a goal-oriented task; this unfortunate transformation not only strips away the fun from sex, it deeroticizes it, too. Here are comments from several people who have spent more than a year in treatment for their infertility that illustrate what occurs.

• *A 36-year-old woman*: Sex used to be one of the best parts of our marriage, but sadly, having to deal with infertility has changed that more than I can explain. For months, we had to have sex virtually by appointment in order to catch me when I was ovulating. John sometimes had problems getting erections on those days, and I know that my impatience and frustration didn't help him any. I was so caught up in my own internal worries that I wasn't a very attentive or loving sex partner. In fact, sex just became a chore for us, like doing the laundry or raking the leaves. It had nothing to do with desire or romance except in the way being dutiful under stress is loving, too.

• *A 29-year-old man*: Here is what happened to our sex life because of our "problem." Jodie stopped ever giving me oral sex. She refused to make love getting on top of me, because she read somewhere that sperm get deeper in the vagina when the man is on top. I had days where I couldn't produce a sperm specimen, which led to arguments between us, and made me feel like an absolute jerk. All in all, sex became a mechanical event, with the constant question of "Did we do it this time?" overshadowing any sense of getting turned on or having fun.

• *A 41-year-old woman*: We went from having sex two or three times a week in the years before we started our infertility treatment to having sex maybe three times a month now. And those three times a month are all scheduled by the doctor. Sex is not only no fun for us anymore; it is a sort of constant reminder of our failures and disappointment.

Another problem for couples dealing with long-term infertility is that the stress to which they are subjected often leads to conflict. For example, in the early stages of attempting to determine whether the couple is actually infertile, the male is frequently unwilling to be evaluated medically until his wife is tested first. This recalcitrant male attitude (which is often tied to a sense of misplaced machismo) is usually seen by the wife as not taking the problem seriously; to the male, who rationalizes or intellectualizes his stance in various ways, it is a matter of protecting his ego. Later in the course of infertility treatment, there are numerous other times at which conflict is apt to appear. Just a few examples make the point. (1) There may be differences of opinion over a treatment option (e.g., the wife wants to consider donor artificial insemination, but the husband refuses). (2) The man and woman may have drastically different coping styles, which may lead them to act in ways which seem to bait each other. (3) Dealing with relatives often becomes stressful for couples struggling with infertility. (4) A couple may have serious disagreements about when to drop out of treatment or when to give up on a particular treatment method. Not only are many couples faced with conflict about whether to keep their infertility a secret because of their embarrassment, but normal interactions with parents and siblings are apt to be strained by offhand comments or questions that are especially painful to hear: "When will I ever get to be a grandpa?" "You'd better start your family now, or you'll be ready for the nursing home just when your kids are ready for college." "Listen, it's probably just all in your head. Just take a cruise and relax a little, and you'll probably come home pregnant."

The conflict and frustration that occur so commonly in response to the stress of infertility play out in various ways. Most often, the strong motivation to have a child serves to restore an equilibrium to the relationship. In fact, it is noteworthy that most infertile couples develop a finely honed sense of when compromise and caring are necessary to defuse the tensions and misunderstandings that have arisen in their relationships and become adept at providing enough support and encouragement for the spouses to help get past the stickiest moments. Along this same line, it is our observation (although this is strictly anecdotal, not supported by firm research data) that relatively few infertile couples divorce. In a way, the quest for a child seems to give them a common goal strong enough that even if they are ultimately unsuccessful, the shared experience and sense of being in it together binds them more tightly than might be expected.

On the other hand, the couple conflicts that occur do take a toll. It is not unusual to find that men in infertile couples turn to extramarital sex to bolster their masculine self-image and to reassure themselves that they are virile. (Virility is, of course, different from fertility, but the two concepts seem to be inexorably intertwined in the minds of most men, as though tuning up their virility will ipso facto enhance their fertility status.) It is much less common, but not unheard of, for the woman in a barren marriage to turn to extramarital sex, as the following example shows.

M. L., a 35-year-old housewife, had been through 2 years of treatment for infertility before being started on a program of artificial insemination with donor sperm because of male factor infertility. She had never had any sexual activity outside of her marriage, although prior to being married, she had three lovers. Finding herself impatient with the process of donor insemination, anxious to become pregnant, and perturbed by her husband's apparent aloofness from her plight, she began a carefully mapped-out campaign of extramarital dalliances. Unknown to her male partners, who were each selected on the basis of being married with children, she coordinated her afternoon activities to coincide with her fertile days. She firmly believed that her action plan had been successful when she became pregnant within 3 months of its implementation. "What my husband doesn't know doesn't matter," she said. "The important thing is, we're going to have a baby to love."

This woman's strategy was atypical but not unprecedented. There has been, so far as we are aware, virtually no research into the extramarital behavior of women contending with infertility. Thus, our impression that this is an infrequent coping mechanism must remain just that—an impression—until more definitive information is available.

For virtually all couples who become actively involved in long-term infertility treatment programs, there is an emotional rollercoaster ride of innumerable episodes of high hope that are quickly dashed by the realities of month after month of the failure to conceive. The start of the wife's menstrual cycle becomes, for many, a sign of failure and defeat. Basal body temperature charts (and cervical mucus patterns) are watched with anticipatory dread: even when they show progress (i.e., ovulation occurring), they are only temporary signposts on the highway to pregnancy. Not only are various medical procedures a source of intense emotional (and sometimes physical) difficulty, many couples find that attendant requirements— including the male's having to produce semen specimens by masturbation, the couple's having to practice timed intercourse, and the seemingly eternal waits for news of test results—all take an emotional toll that has a cumulative effect on their sense of autonomy and self-worth. The particularly plaintive anguish of a miscarriage or an ectopic pregnancy for such couples is difficult to imagine for most people who have not been in their situation already. In fact, even seemingly innocuous events—such as passing a pregnant woman on the street—can be a hurtful reminder of their plight.

For those couples who finally accept their infertility as permanent and untreatable (often after years of intense and expensive treatment), there is woefully little societal help or support. While we have elaborate social rituals to allow grief to be expressed for death, there are no funerals or wakes to commemorate the grief felt by infertile couples who have given up hope and given up trying. The couple's mourning is apt to be silent and isolated, and their grief is sometimes never actively expressed or resolved.

Fortunately, health care professionals have become more attuned to the emotional needs of infertile couples in recent years. Many programs include counseling as an active component, helping couples to identify key problem areas and offering useful suggestions toward finding solutions. In addition, there is a national self-help group for people dealing with infertility called RESOLVE: this organization provides a monthly newsletter, informational brochures, physician referrals, and telephone counseling in addition to local support groups in many cities across the country. We strongly recommend that anyone having problems with infertility join this group (their national headquarters is: RESOLVE, Inc., 5 Water St., Arlington, MA 02174; telephone [617] 643-2424).

Twelve

Sexual Aspects of Common Medical Problems

Millions of people with a variety of health problems experience sexual difficulties as a result of these conditions. In addition, drug and alcohol use and abuse commonly impair sexual functioning. Many people have a paucity of accurate information about such effects, however. In this chapter, we provide a practical overview of the most common sexual problems and concerns associated with various medical illnesses and with the use and abuse of prescription and nonprescription drugs.

ALCOHOLISM

Alcoholism and alcohol abuse pose a major public health problem today in the United States and Europe, as they have throughout this century. It is estimated that over 10 million American adults have major alcohol-related disorders,[1] with virtually all socioeconomic classes and cultural groups affected. Not surprisingly, there are a number of links between alcoholism and sexual disturbances that warrant examination.

Although everyone seems to know intuitively what alcoholism is, it can be instructive to consider the official revised definition of this disorder recently issued by the National Council on Alcoholism and Drug Dependence and the American Society of Addiction Medicine:

> Alcoholism is a primary, chronic disease with genetic, psychosocial, and environmental factors influencing its development and manifestations. The disease is often progressive and fatal. It is characterized by impaired control over

drinking, preoccupation with the drug alcohol, use of alcohol despite adverse consequences, and distortions in thinking, most notably denial. Each of these symptoms may be continuous or periodic.[2]

The adverse consequences of abusive drinking or outright alcoholism referred to in this definition span the spectrum from specific physical effects (e.g., liver disease, neurologic disorders) to problems with interpersonal functioning (e.g., marital problems, intimacy disorders, child abuse), and psychological functioning (e.g., wide mood swings, impaired thinking). Obviously, each of these adverse effects can spill over directly into the sexual arena.

Before turning to a description of the sexual problems associated with alcoholism, it is helpful to outline briefly the acute effects of alcohol on sexual response, because most people seem to believe alcohol is a sexual stimulant. Although this is certainly the impression created by Madison Avenue, the truth is that pharmacologically speaking alcohol is (as Shakespeare recognized some centuries back)[3] a depressant to the central nervous system, so that it generally has a dampening effect on sexual reflexes and sexual feelings.

Very low blood concentrations of alcohol have a mildly enhancing effect on men's erections, but at blood concentrations corresponding to two to three shots of liquor, erections are mildly suppressed and ejaculation is delayed. At higher blood alcohol concentrations, many males are unable to ejaculate and have marked difficulty obtaining or maintaining erections. Masters and Johnson recognized the clinical importance of this acute effect of heavy drinking in 1970, when they reported that in their large clinical population, excessive alcohol consumption was the leading cause of secondary impotence.[4]

In females, the situation is a bit more complicated. Very low blood alcohol concentrations seem to have minimal effects on sexual responsivity, but moderate concentrations (corresponding to two or three shots of liquor) cause a definite reduction in vaginal blood flow, a delayed time to reach orgasm, and less orgasmic intensity. High blood alcohol concentrations can block orgasmic responsivity and often interfere with vaginal lubrication. However (and this is a very interesting however), women tend to feel sexier the more intoxicated they become, and at high blood alcohol levels, women rate their sexual experiences as more pleasurable than when they are sober, *even though their sexual reflexes are clearly physiologically impaired*.[5] This reaction may well be an indication of how self-perception can be tricked by expectations and may also reflect the fact that many women feel freer to be sexual with a few drinks under their belts than when they're sober. This latter notion has been referred to at times as the "disinhibiting" effect of alcohol on sexual feelings and behavior. Certainly many teenage girls are quick to recognize that drinking gives them a perfect excuse to engage in sex without having to take personal responsibility for their actions, allowing them to experiment and yet in their own minds still maintain an upright moral posture.

In men, chronic alcohol abuse commonly causes sexual dysfunction. In various studies, 50 to 75 percent of alcoholic men have been found to have at least one sexual dysfunction.[6] Generally, 40 to 50 percent of alcoholic men have low (or sometimes nonexistent) sexual desire, and 30 to 40 percent are impotent. In addition, 10 to 20 percent report inhibited ejaculation. Although these problems can occur even in the absence of liver damage, the rates of sexual dysfunction are even higher among men with significant impairment of liver function.

These effects are largely the result of physical changes produced by the chronic use of large quantities of alcohol. Notably, alcohol is directly toxic to the testes, causing them to shrivel to a markedly reduced size in many alcoholic men, and greatly reducing the production of the male sex hormone, testosterone. (Sperm production is also frequently damaged by alcoholism.) The hormonal problem is compounded by the fact that the smaller amount of testosterone manufactured by the testes is actually broken down more quickly in the body because of changes in liver enzymes that metabolize this hormone. Neurologic problems are also very common in alcoholics, possibly creating another mechanism for sexual dysfunctions to occur. In addition, persistently high levels of alcohol in the bloodstream may alter neurotransmitter patterns in the central nervous system, including the brain, which could affect sexual reflexes as well.[7]

The sexual effects of alcoholism in women have been largely ignored in the scientific literature. While it is clear that chronic alcohol abuse is a direct cause of some female sexual disturbances, alcoholic women's sexual desire seems to remain intact more often than alcoholic men's.[8] We have found that 30 to 40 percent of alcoholic women report difficulty in becoming sexually aroused, and approximately 15 percent experience either loss of orgasmic responsiveness or significant reduction in the frequency or intensity of orgasm. However, it is clear that many alcoholic women have had sexual problems long before the excessive drinking began (and these may even have been a trigger mechanism for the heavy drinking), so it is difficult to interpret these data in terms of cause and effect. In one of the few controlled studies on the subject, no significant differences in the rates of sexual dysfunction were found between young married alcoholic women and age-matched healthy controls.[9] On the other hand, a separate report found that alcoholic women in a recovery program had significantly more sexual problems than nonalcoholic women, with more than 60 percent of the alcoholic women reporting impaired sexual arousal and anorgasmia (lack of orgasm).[10] There is evidence that heavy drinking may block ovulation and cause other hormone abnormalities in a minority of healthy women,[11] but detailed endocrine studies have not been performed on alcoholic women as yet.

Organic factors alone do not explain the entire gamut of sexual difficulties in alcoholics, of course, as the physical problems associated with alcohol abuse are just one piece in a complex jigsaw puzzle. Alcoholism is a multidimensional syndrome that is now recognized as having both genetic predispositions[12] and social learning and psychological components. These are especially complex issues, which we can only touch on briefly here.

Some people appear to turn to alcohol as a way of bolstering their sexual self-esteem. Frequently, teenagers get in the habit of using alcohol in this way; older adults who are dealing with sexual self-doubts and insecurities sometimes follow the same path. In some cases, the use of large amounts of alcohol seems to be an attempt at stress reduction—for example, for the man who is worried about his sexual orientation or his dismal sexual performance. In situations like these, alcohol becomes a kind of nonprescription tranquilizer that is particularly alluring because of its supposed added benefit as an aphrodisiac. The fact that its stimulant properties don't work (and indeed often have the exact opposite effect to the desired one) becomes lost in the relief over being less anxious (and more self-confident) sexually, and in the throes of the next morning's hangover, many a heavy drinker doesn't actually recall what happened in his or her previous night's sexual encounter, setting the stage for personal expectations to fill in what a hazy memory has not processed thoroughly. Often the net effect is that the recollection becomes a positive one, even when the actual encounter was a dismal failure.

In other instances, alcohol is used specifically because it reduces sexual desire, although the heavy drinker may not have any conscious awareness of this motivation. Many persons contending with a sense of sexual inadequacy are relieved to find that they're just not very interested in sex anymore. At times when they stop drinking heavily, they again become uncomfortable about sexual matters as their desire (and conflicts) return more vividly to the foreground of their awareness.

Another common problem is that alcoholics often have considerable difficulty in the capacity to develop and maintain intimate relationships.

The alcoholic is apt to misjudge ways in which intimacy is initiated and maintained; is likely to be manipulative, inflexible, and often hostile when things aren't going "just right"; and, in sexual terms, may show little regard for his or her partner's feelings or preferences. High rates of marital discord further complicate the picture when one spouse is an alcoholic; typically, as part of this pattern, the denying, blaming, and avoiding of responsibility that the alcoholic displays are apt to create anger and retaliatory measures from the spouse.[13]

BREAST CANCER

According to the most recent statistics, an American woman has a one-in-eight chance of developing breast cancer in her lifetime. In fact, breast cancer is now the most frequent female cancer and, after lung cancer, the second leading cause of cancer death in women. More than 150,000 new cases of breast cancer are discovered each year, and late detection seriously lowers the chances of survival.

Unfortunately, more than a third of women with breast cancer discover this condition only accidentally.[14] Most don't routinely examine their own breasts or have mammography (X-rays of the breasts), even though the medical evidence is strong that such procedures can be lifesaving. In fact, for the first time ever, eleven major medical organizations such as the American Cancer Society, the National Cancer Institute, and the American Medical Association have finally come to agree that all women age 40 or over should undergo mammography. Indeed, the evidence from several research studies shows that deaths from breast cancer can be reduced by 20 to 40 percent by the routine use of mammography.[15]

A mammogram, which costs about $100, can detect tumors as small as the point of a pencil—tumors that are far too small to be detected by a woman during a breast self-exam (or a physician during a physical examination). The actual procedure involves X-raying each breast separately while it is placed in a device that exerts gentle pressure on the breast, flattening it so that an accurate X-ray picture can be taken. A side view and a front-to-back view of each breast are usually taken, for a total of four X-rays. The great majority of women (88 percent) undergoing mammography report no discomfort or only mild discomfort with the procedure; only 2 percent report severe discomfort or actual pain.[16]

While experts agree that there is no need for women under age 35 to have a mammogram because breast cancer is unusual in this age range, many suggest that women between the ages of 35 and 39 should have one mammogram done to serve as a baseline to be compared to future screenings. Current recommendations are that women in their forties should have a mammogram every two years unless they have a family history of breast cancer, in which case they should be screened annually. From age 50 on, women should ideally have a mammogram every year.

In addition, recent studies by the Breast Cancer Detection Demonstration Project provide a way of calculating a woman's risk for developing breast cancer. The calculation involves an equation that utilizes four factors: age when menstruation began, whether her mother or sisters have had breast cancer, her age at the birth of her first live-born child, and the number of negative breast biopsies a woman has had.

A number of variables that are important predictors of breast cancer risk have been identified. Clearly, a family history of breast cancer is the single most important risk factor: if a woman's mother had breast cancer before age 60, the woman's relative risk is doubled, while if a woman has two first-degree relatives (mother, sisters, grandmothers) who have had this disease, her risk is three to five times higher than for women without such a history.[17]

It is hoped that by identifying women at particularly high risk for breast cancer, they can be encouraged to take steps geared toward both prevention and early detection. Possible preventive actions include, for example, losing weight if the woman is overweight, lowering fat consumption, and stopping the use of alcohol, since each of these factors has been tied to an increased risk of breast cancer. Early detection can be improved by regular monthly breast self-exams and by regular mammograms from age 40 on. The value of early detection is quite clear from this statistic: when found at a localized stage, 5-year cancer survival rates usually exceed 85 percent.[18]

In the past, breast cancer was typically treated by either radical mastectomy, an operation to remove the affected breast and lymph nodes adjacent to the breast, or by total mastectomy, which removed the entire affected breast itself. Since 1985, following the publication of a landmark study showing that less extensive (and less disfiguring) surgery was equivalent in effectiveness to these approaches,[19] many physicians (and many women) favor less drastic procedures such as "lumpectomy," which involves removing the tumor while conserving as much breast tissue as possible. While such breast-conserving surgery is suitable only for women with breast cancer in an early stage (and for best results is usually combined with radiation therapy), it is notable that this approach is used far less often than would seem to be warranted.[20] This practice is probably a reflection of several different factors. First, surgeons' attitudes toward their patients undoubtedly play a role. For example, surgeons seem to offer breast-conserving surgery more frequently to younger women than to older women.[21] (This age bias is accompanied by a second inherent bias among mostly male surgeons when it comes to treating breast cancer patients: from what we have seen [and this point has yet to be substantiated by formalized research], surgeons are more likely to recommend breast-conserving surgery to single women than to married women. As one male chauvinist surgeon explained to us, "A single woman needs to have her figure in order to find a husband; a married woman doesn't need to worry so much about her figure.") Second, many women who are presented with the option of breast-conserving surgery choose to have the more extensive procedures because of their inherent fears about the nature of breast cancer. Since it might *seem* to the uninformed patient that more extensive surgery is, if not always more effective, at least safer (especially in terms of eliminating the risk of recurrence of cancer in the same breast, if a good portion of that breast is left intact), it should not be surprising that so many women opt for what seems to them a "better" form of surgery. Sadly, most physicians have not made an effort to educate women well enough to counter this prevailing attitude. Certainly, evidence that women who undergo breast-conserving surgery have a better postoperative body image than those who have more extensive procedures should not be taken lightly.

Whatever type of surgery is chosen for the woman with breast cancer, concerns about subsequent sexuality abound. Although surgery of the breast does not directly affect a woman's sexuality in a physiologic sense, the breasts have been so enthusiastically enshrined as a cultural icon of a woman's femininity and sexual desirability that most women react to the prospect of breast surgery with dread. This reaction, which may express itself to different degrees in different women, encompasses several component parts. First, many women feel a primary threat to their physical attractiveness as a result of cancer surgery on the breast. This self-perceived loss of attractiveness translates for some women into diminished self-worth, a sense of helplessness, and (not surprisingly) an increased risk of depression. Second, many women faced with the prospect of a mastectomy worry about sexual rejection by their partners or prospective partners. These worries reflect fundamental anxieties about the nature of intimacy, the partner's reaction to the cancer as well as the surgery, and, in some cases, the woman's fear that she may become less sexual herself because of her illness. As one sex therapist has described it:

It almost goes without saying that the difficulties the woman might have in accepting and accommodating to the loss of a breast arise in large measure from her fears of how others will respond. The pain of rejection increases with intimacy, and the woman's greatest fears revolve around the man with whom she is most intimate. What many women fear is rejection not only in the form of aversion or denial but also rejection in the form of pity; for whereas empathy and concern imply an awareness of the woman's feelings of loss and fear, pity implies a belief that the woman has *really* been diminished, and involves not a sharing of her feelings but a reinforcement of her fantasies of incompleteness and worthlessness.[22]

Even in relationships where a woman has no reason to doubt her mate's love or dedication, it is common to find that she harbors secret doubts that her partner will still find her desirable after her surgery. And we have found that after a mastectomy, many women question their sexual partners to check on the authenticity of their sexual interest and enjoyment so often that the male may become exasperated with the repetitive nature of the interrogation. As one husband said, "I can understand why Mary was worried, but after the twelfth time I'd told her that I still thought she was sexy and I still loved making love with her, you'd think the matter could be put to rest." The fact is that simple rational answers do not always sink in immediately and are often not accepted at face value in the understandably emotional aftermath of a health problem of such consequence as breast cancer; furthermore, while the best reassurances are undoubtedly the behavioral ones (what you do, instead of what you say), verbal reassurances can be extraordinarily valuable in helping a person adjust to a situation that seems threatening and unpredictable at its very core.

It is notable that for many women the frequency of breast stimulation during sexual activity declines substantially after a mastectomy.[23] This reflects two separate facts: many men tend to avoid touching the uninvolved breast (fearing the woman will be reminded of her illness and her loss), while many women who have had mastectomies clearly prefer to put any form of breast play off limits for reasons of psychological security. In addition, it is fairly common to find that women who have had mastectomies are especially self-conscious about complete nudity during sex. For some women, avoiding direct reminders of the existence of their surgical scar extends to a change in preferred coital positions. The number of women who never use the female-on-top position, which is the sexual position that involves the most direct visualization of the missing breast for the male, triples after a mastectomy.

Although there is clearly no uniform response pattern among women, and past responses to stressful situations may not reliably predict how any particular woman will react to the news of breast cancer and the psychological traumas of a mastectomy (or partial mastectomy), there does appear to be some evidence that single, younger women are more apt to see their prognosis as a devastating one in social terms. (Fortunately, breast cancer is far less common among younger women than among those over 60.)

The following comment is typical of the reactions many women have.

After having a mastectomy at age 45, I was absolutely convinced my love life was over. After all, I thought, it was bad enough being single, but now with an ugly scar and a disfigured body, I could hardly be the target of anyone's ardent desires. For two years I moped around in this semidepressed state, feeling sorry for myself and feeling lonely, too. So when a neighbor asked me to his company's Christmas party, I was reluctant to accept at first. You can imagine my surprise when our date led to more invitations and the kindling of a romantic spark between us. Although I was acutely uncomfortable with the situation, I finally convinced myself to tell him about my "condition"—and was absolutely flabbergasted when it didn't scare him away, or even bother him. While we didn't wind up getting married, it wasn't because of any sexual problems we had—in fact, sex turned out to be the best part of our relationship, and it gave me confidence in myself to know that I could still be an attractive sex partner.

On the other hand, there are also single younger women who survive breast cancer with aplomb, allowing it to have as little impact on their psyches and sex lives as possible. "It was a question of giving in to a sense of being invaded and impaired or insisting on leading the active sex life I always had," one single woman told us. "Yes, there are some jerks out there who were put off by my mastectomy, but I would have realized these men were jerks even before my surgery."

As of this writing, the U.S. Food and Drug Administration's partial ban on silicone-gel breast implants because of safety concerns has made many breast cancer patients leery of reconstructive breast surgery even though the F.D.A. permits such devices (and similar implants filled with saline solution rather than silicone gel) if the woman receiving it agrees to participate in an F.D.A.– approved clinical trial.

HYSTERECTOMY

Hysterectomy, or surgical removal of the uterus, is one of the most common operations performed in the United States, with about 750,000 procedures done annually. There is a long list of reasons why such surgery might be done, ranging from the removal of benign or malignant tumors to treatment of endometriosis, severe recurrent bleeding from the uterus, and prolapse of the uterus. Whatever the reason a hysterectomy is performed, it is often accompanied by alterations in sexuality.

In some cases, hysterectomy leads to decided improvement in a woman's sex life, especially if the underlying pelvic problem that led to the surgery caused painful intercourse. Similarly, if a woman's presurgical sex life was negatively affected by symptoms such as lengthy menstrual periods or frequent episodes of uterine bleeding and cramping, it is not difficult to see how a hysterectomy can contribute to a healthier sexuality, both physically and from a psychological viewpoint as well. Furthermore, some women who were particularly worried about the possibility of developing cancer of the cervix or uterus (or were afraid of becoming pregnant) find that their sexual interest and responsivity improve significantly after a hysterectomy.

There are also many women whose experience is quite the opposite. Often, these are women who regard their surgery as a negation of their femininity. For some of them, a uterus is not just a reproductive organ but also a sexual organ; they may mourn its loss as a sign of aging and weakness and a threat to their vitality. In fact, the psychological impact may be so great that depression occurs.[24]

Women who have had their ovaries removed along with removal of the uterus may, no matter what their age, develop postmenopausal symptoms such as hot flashes and vaginal dryness, which may obviously complicate sexual matters. Although the absence of estrogen by itself doesn't seem to impair orgasmic ability directly, sexual arousal is sometimes adversely affected (for a fuller discussion, see Chapter 16), and estrogen replacement therapy is generally indicated in order to preserve genital health and optimize the chances for a healthy sex life.

One study of women who had undergone hysterectomy and removal of their ovaries reported that 37 percent described sexual problems after surgery, while 34 percent had improved sexual responsivity.[25] Notably, preoperative anxieties about developing sexual difficulties correlated strongly with the actual development of such problems, and for these women, postoperative estrogen replacement therapy didn't significantly improve sexual desire, the ease of vaginal lubrication, the ability to reach orgasm, or the woman's overall enjoyment of sex (although it did seem to reduce the occurrence of painful intercourse).

Some women complained that their orgasms felt different after they had a hysterectomy. There is a definite physiologic basis for such a claim, since the uterus (which is largely a muscular organ) contracts vigorously during orgasm when it is intact. However, it is hard to say why many other women never notice a difference in the quality or intensity of their orgasms after a hysterectomy, and some women actually report better orgasms after a diseased uterus has been removed, perhaps reflecting the fact that an abnormal uterus can produce orgasmic cramping and pain.

PROSTATECTOMY

The prostate, a walnut-sized gland that sits just beneath the bladder, is a source of a number of health problems and sexual symptoms for men. For example, among men, cancer of the prostate is the second most common cancer and the second most common cause of death from cancer; in 1992, an estimated 132,000 men were diagnosed with this disease and 34,000 were estimated to have died.[26] However, prostate cancer is unusual because in at least three-quarters of cases, it will not spread and will not result in death.[27] Nevertheless, vigorous forms of treatment for prostate cancer, including radical surgery, the use of estrogen therapy, and radiation therapy, have often been recommended in the past. Unfortunately, these treatments carry substantial risks of subsequent sexual dysfunction.

Prostate surgery done for cancer causes subsequent erectile insufficiency in a large number of cases, but the risk depends on the type of operation performed. In so-called radical surgery, where a wide operative dissection is performed (and the seminal vesicles are removed as well as the prostate), postoperative impotence is almost inevitable because of damage to the nerve pathways that control erection. In simpler surgical procedures also using the perineal approach (making an incision in the perineum, the area between the base of the penis and the rectum), there is still a 40-to-50-percent rate of postoperative erectile failure.[28] Men who have penile implants inserted after such surgery to permit them to function sexually are generally unable to ejaculate, because all semen-producing glands have been surgically removed. In some cases, so-called "dry" orgasms—no ejaculation, but normal rhythmic orgasmic contractions in the rectal and pelvic area—occur in these men postoperatively, but most men complain that these give them a very minimal sort of orgasmic sensation.[29] Radiation treatment of prostatic cancer, which is often combined with estrogen therapy, also produces high rates of sexual dysfunction. Estrogen, of course, reduces the man's sex drive considerably and may also be the key component in this treatment regime that causes impotence, as well.

Prostatic enlargement, a noncancerous condition which occurs in almost all men from their late forties on, is a completely different problem from cancer. This condition, which is called BPH (for benign prostatic hyperplasia), is usually detected by a rectal examination. It produces a number of annoying symptoms, especially urinary ones. The reason why this occurs is that as the prostate enlarges, it pinches the urethra (the tube that empties urine from the bladder), eventually causing problems like frequent urination, incomplete emptying of the bladder, difficulty starting to urinate, and a weak urinary stream.

In the past, BPH was aggressively treated by surgery to relieve the mechanical pressures from the enlarged prostate. Most frequently, this operation was a TUR, or transurethral resection, which does not require an open incision but involves inserting instruments through the urethra to shave off a portion of the prostatic tissue. In fact, it is estimated that some 400,000 operations are done for BPH each year in the United States, of which probably 95 percent are TURs.[30] TURs rarely cause erectile dysfunction, but they result in retrograde ejaculation (semen going backward into the bladder with orgasm) in about 90 percent of men because of damage to the internal sphincter (valve) of the neck of the bladder.[31] Now, however, the advisability of surgery for the routine treatment of BPH is being reconsidered for several reasons.[32] Most important, recent research has shown a higher death rate in the 5 years following TUR surgery than with open prostate surgery.[33]

Other forms of therapy are now being examined with renewed vigor, including the use of small balloonlike devices that can be slipped inside the urethra to dilate the prostate and the use of laser or microwave treatment to melt away part of the excessive prostate tissue.[34] The most intriguing new treatment is a pill called Proscar (finasteride) that actually can shrink the prostate. This pill, which needs to be taken for at least 6 months to determine if it will be effective, works by inhibiting the enzyme that converts testosterone into another form that specifically and preferentially supports the growth of the prostate. According to one large-scale study of Proscar, 5 to 6 percent of men using this drug develop a significant drop in their sex drive, 4.4 percent have inhibited ejaculation, and about 4 to 5 percent develop erectile failure.[35] However, we suspect that, following a pattern that is so common as to be almost inevitable, with further clinical experience reports of much higher rates of sexual dysfunction with this drug will appear in another few years. Nevertheless, as an alternative to surgical treatment, Proscar is certainly something men should consider.

SEX AFTER A HEART ATTACK

Every year there are an estimated 1.25 million heart attacks in the United States (about 800,000 of which are first attacks),[36] with more people surviving such episodes today than ever before. One of the primary issues for any survivor is the question of what impact his or her cardiac status will have on various everyday activities that had been pursued almost automatically in the past. High on the list of concerns for many people in this situation is a specific focus on how the heart attack will hamper sexuality. Unfortunately, few physicians are well enough informed in this area (or, for that matter, interested in this type of relatively personal counseling) to provide their patients with detailed guidelines. This leaves many men and women (and their spouses) filled with doubts and worries about their return to sexual activity in the aftermath of a heart attack. Often, the result is high levels of postcoronary sexual difficulties or unnecessary avoidance of sex as a default form of invalidism: the premise being, as many people have told us, "If the doctor didn't talk about this at all, it must be pretty bad."

For men in particular, there is a high rate of sexual difficulties following a heart attack. A number of studies have found that 25 to 45 percent of men develop impotence in the months after a coronary, and 30 to 70 percent of men develop a pattern of avoiding sexual activity as a result of self-doubts and concerns about their cardiac status. Notably, many men who have recuperated successfully from their heart attacks nevertheless have a significant drop in the frequency of sexual intercourse—in fact, men who resume sex as actively after a heart attack as before are in the distinct minority. This tendency can be viewed as an acceleration of the male age–related decline in sexual frequency, if one takes the position that the coronary event has made the male feel older physically and "think" older as well, but other factors are involved.

Of course, heart attacks don't occur in a vacuum, and there may certainly be medical factors that predated the coronary event (perhaps even heightening the risk of the heart attack) that can impinge on sexual functioning. Examples would include diabetes mellitus, high blood pressure, alcoholism, obesity, or hardening of the arteries (arteriosclerosis). In addition, medical complications, such as angina pectoris (chest pain with exertion), congestive heart failure, or irregular heart rhythms, may arise after the heart attack and complicate sexual matters. In these situations, or other examples of complicated heart attacks, advice concerning sexual rehabilitation needs to be tailored specifically to the medical profile of each person, including consideration of the prescription drugs he or she is taking, the amount of exercise or exertion he or she can tolerate, and the functional capacity of his or her heart and lungs.

In addition to these medical factors, psychological issues are very much involved in the recovery from and rehabilitation after a heart attack. For most men, a first heart attack presents the threat of imminent death with a harsh, unexpected reality—a reality that is dramatized by the high technology of a modern coronary care unit. But once the initial hours go by and the man's chest pain has been relieved by medications, he not only realizes that he will most likely survive but also begins to think long and hard about how the heart attack will change his life. At this juncture, issues of self-esteem come to the surface very quickly. Concerns about work ("How soon can I go back to work?" "Will I have to change the type of work I do, or my work habits?") and about sex ("Will the doctor tell me to abstain from sex?" "If it's all right to have sex, will I be able to?") are especially common. Fears that the heart attack will lead in one way or another to a major reduction in sexual activity often swarm in the man's mind while he is lying in the hospital, probably contributing in a significant manner to the depression that coronary patients commonly experience at this juncture. One reason for this depression (in addition to the sense of helplessness that overwhelms some men who have never before been hospitalized) is a major misperception of how life will be altered by the heart attack. The depression is, in part, grief for the loss of health and vitality that the coronary victim feels so powerfully.

Heart patients and their spouses or partners consistently voice a number of worries about sexual functioning. Some of these concerns are based more on myth than anything factual; others reflect exaggerated comments made by uninformed (or misinformed) friends. In general, these worries fall into the following categories: (1) fear that the excitement and exertion of sexual activity will produce sudden death; (2) fear that the doctor will ban sexual activity altogether, or that medical advice will be so restrictive as to make sex unenjoyable ("Well, it's okay for you to have sex—*as long as you don't move*. Got to watch out for too much exertion, you know. Weak ticker."); (3) concern that the heart attack will somehow cause physical problems with sexual function; and (4) anxiety that sexual arousal and orgasm may be so strenuous that it causes another heart attack. With such formidable worries, it is no wonder that a sizable number of people recovering from a coronary avoid sex after their heart attack or have sexual difficulties as they try to resume an active, satisfying sex life.

The best way to combat these common fears and concerns is with facts. First, it is important for anyone who has had a coronary to know that sudden death as a result of sexual activity is extremely rare. Despite occasional scare stories in the press, there is no evidence whatsoever that marital sex (or sex with a long-standing partner) poses a material danger of killing someone, unless you try it while you're driving a car. The one study that examined the link between sudden death and sexual intercourse actually found a very low incidence of such deaths (0.6 percent of all sudden deaths), with the vast majority occurring in association with extramarital sex, which may say more about mixing sex and alcohol than it does about the cardiac stress involved in coitus.[37]

The key fact about the physiologic stress of sexual activity on the heart in postcoronary men and women is this: careful electrocardiographic monitoring studies have shown that the cardiac stress involved in sexual intercourse is about the same as the cardiac stress involved in walking up two flights of stairs or in walking briskly around the block.* This means that a person who is

---

* It is important to remember that there are certainly individual exceptions to this statement, especially in cases complicated by other medical problems or by recurrent exercise-induced rhythm abnormalities of the heart.

able to walk up two flights of stairs or walk briskly around the block without experiencing any chest pain or shortness of breath can be reasonably confident that the physical demands of sex will not pose an undue strain on the heart. It also means that a person who is in reasonably good physical condition will often be able to return to an active sex life much sooner than someone who is overweight and completely out of shape. In fact, participation under medical supervision in a postcoronary physical rehabilitation program, involving regular exercise and dietary instruction, can be particularly beneficial to subsequent sexual functioning.

A few simple caveats are in order. There are obviously different styles of sexual activity, which—much like any other physical activity—can involve vastly different paces and levels of physical intensity. In the early phases of returning to sexual activity following a heart attack, using nonstrenuous positions for intercourse (rather than trying to have sex while hanging from a chandelier, for example) and avoiding marathon sessions of sex play would seem the better part of prudence. For many postcoronary men, it might be advisable to first try out sex using the woman-on-top position, since they then do not have to put forth the additional physical exertion of supporting their own weight with their arms (which can be almost like doing pushups). (However, if a man's wife is very heavy, a side-by-side position may be less strenuous than having to support her weight.) Likewise, it is usually advisable for the couple to experiment with nondemanding, low-key sex play (including intercourse) to be sure it is comfortable and well tolerated physically before attempting a more rapid-paced sex that involves vigorous thrusting, since more intense levels of exertion will produce higher heart rates and thus place a greater demand on the heart.

A few other simple and practical guidelines should be followed to minimize problems. For example, a person recovering from a heart attack should avoid sexual activity for at least an hour after eating or drinking, because blood flow is temporarily diverted to the stomach and intestines after a meal. In addition, people with any form of heart disease should avoid mixing sex and alcohol, because alcohol (even in small amounts) decreases the efficiency of the heart's pumping action. Finally, if symptoms of chest pain, chest tightness, or shortness of breath occur during sex, slow down or stop what you're doing, as your body is giving you an early warning sign that shouldn't be ignored. If the problem doesn't disappear right away with slowing your pace, it's wisest to stop entirely and notify your physician promptly of the situation.

For men or women with recurring chest pain (angina) during sex, it is often possible to manage the situation satisfactorily by the use of drugs such as long-acting nitrate preparations or the use of drugs called beta-blockers.

However, these drugs, particularly at higher dosage levels, can occasionally interefere with erections.

One other aspect of the return to sexual activity after a heart attack should be mentioned briefly: the role of the spouse. An overprotective spouse who is unduly worried about the risk of a repeat heart attack with too much exertion and who attempts to be overrestrictive in general can obviously present a significant obstacle to a smooth return to a loving sexual interaction. Being sure that the spouse participates in discussions of all aspects of the rehabilitation process and asking specific, detailed questions about resuming sexual activity is one good way of preventing this from occurring. We have also found that allowing the spouse to watch the heart attack victim during an electrocardiographically monitored exercise test (such as on a treadmill or a stationary bicycle) can be especially reassuring in convincing her (or him) that there is enough cardiac reserve to handle the moderate exertional demands of sex without untoward effects.

DIABETES MELLITUS

There are an estimated 7,000,000 people in the United States who have diabetes mellitus, a disease in which the metabolism of blood sugar is abnormal either because of a deficiency of insulin produced by the pancreas or a reduction in the biologic effectiveness of insulin or a combination of both. While only about 10 percent of these individuals require insulin therapy, virtually all diabetics are susceptible to a host of long-term complications that include hypertension, cardiovascular disease, and disturbances in eye and kidney function. Sexual problems are especially common in diabetes.

Erectile dysfunction affects approximately 50 percent of men with diabetes. This problem can occur at virtually any age and is found with about the same frequency in men who are insulin-dependent and those who are not.

In more than 90 percent of the cases, the erectile difficulties have a gradual onset, typically progressing from occasional episodes of erectile failure to full-blown impotence over a period of 6 to 12 months. As part of this gradual process, erections do not disappear entirely, but usually begin to become less firm and of briefer duration as time goes by. Many men with this condition complain of getting only partial erections rather than the fuller, more rigid erections they had been used to getting. Characteristically, the diabetic male's sex drive remains normal and ejaculation is undisturbed even when erections become relatively few and far between. The erectile difficulties caused by diabetes do not usually lessen the man's genital sensations.

There are two major causes of erectile dysfunction due to diabetes. The most common, affecting some 80 percent of men with this condition, is a poorly understood complication called diabetic neuropathy, which in this form involves microscopic damage to the nerves controlling erection.[38] Less commonly, abnormalities in the small blood vessels supplying the penis are the direct cause of impotence in diabetic men, causing a situation in which the amount of blood flowing to the penis with sexual arousal is insufficient to cause enough hydraulic pressure to build up for a firm erection.

In addition, it is important to realize that cases of impotence in men with diabetes may not be a result of the diabetes at all. For this reason, it is important for any man in this situation to undergo a thorough medical and psychological evaluation to identify other factors that might be the cause of poor erections, including drug use, depression, or coexistent medical conditions.

Approximately one percent of diabetic men develop retrograde ejaculation, a condition in which semen spurts backward into the bladder at the time of ejaculation. In diabetic men, this condition is usually a result of diabetic neuropathy affecting the nerves that supply the urinary bladder. In our experience, the appearance of retrograde ejaculation is a poor prognostic sign for the eventual development of diabetic impotence. In 30 cases of retrograde ejaculation in diabetic men aged 21 to 45, 22 progressed to full-blown impotence within 3 years after the retrograde ejaculation first appeared.

The treatment of diabetic impotence is problematic, since there is no means of reversing diabetic neuropathy. In cases of severe neuropathy, penile implants can be used to permit the diabetic male to have intercourse successfully, but this option is not always appealing. We have found that many men with no direct evidence of neuropathy respond well to traditional sex therapy.

The sexual status of diabetic women has been studied less extensively than that of diabetic males, and the picture here is less clear. The first report found that about one-third of diabetic women have secondary anorgasmia, with this condition usually developing gradually some 4 to 6 years after the diabetes is first diagnosed.[39] Although other studies have failed to confirm this high an incidence of orgasmic difficulties, several reports have noted a high rate of reduced vaginal lubrication in diabetic women,[40] and other studies have noted a higher incidence of sexual desire problems in diabetic women than in age-matched nondiabetic controls.

Sexual difficulties in diabetic women are sometimes exacerbated by chronic vaginal yeast infections, and it seems logical to believe that neuropathy in the pelvic region may also play a role. The latter point is supported by our observation that sometimes the problem with diabetic women who seem to have lost their capacity for orgasm is mainly a matter of the intensity of the sexual stimulus provided: using an electric vibrator during either masturbation or sex with a partner (which provides a more focused and intense stimulus than "ordinary" sexual activity) can produce orgasm in the great majority of these women. The explanation may be that with damage to the sensory nerves in the pelvic region, "ordinary" physical stimulation isn't enough to allow the woman to reach the orgasmic threshold (that is, the neurophysiological trigger point for the reflex of orgasm), whereas the more intense stimulation overcomes this problem of reduced sensory efficiency.

PSYCHIATRIC ILLNESSES

MOOD DISORDERS

The mood disorders, also known as affective disorders, are marked by a prolonged disturbance of emotion that affects a person's whole life. These disturbances generally take the form of either depression, euphoria (mania), or alterations of depressed and elevated moods. The latter condition has traditionally been called manic depressive illness but is now also called bipolar disorder (in recognition of the mood swings to each extreme state). Depression that occurs without accompanying bouts of mania is considered a unipolar disorder.

The core features of depression are depressed mood (sometimes described as feelings of sadness, hopelessness, or despondency) and/or loss of interest in or pleasure from all or almost all of a person's ordinary activities. The most typical symptoms are loss of appetite, weight loss, difficulty in sleeping, decreased energy, feelings of worthlessness or excessive or inappropriate guilt, difficulty thinking or concentrating, and recurrent thoughts of death or suicide.[41]

The core features of mania are inappropriate, sustained euphoria; hyperactivity; and "flight of ideas"—the rapid, often chaotic, jumping from one idea to another. In unbridled mania, a person's speech generally changes from its natural style to a fast, rushing delivery; it may also be filled with puns, rhymes, and jokes, as well as highly dramatic pronouncements. There is usually a decreased need for sleep and a great sense of restlessness—manic people have a very tough time sitting still or listening, without interrupting, to anyone else. The person typically feels sublimely self-confident and advises others about matters in which he or she has no special knowledge— like how to attain world peace, or how to run a world-class hotel. At the same time, manic persons often start, and then abandon, ambitious projects for which they have little or no background: for example, one minute announcing that they've started a novel, then calling friends to say that they've devised a new system for beating the stock market, then claiming that they've been hired to promote an Elton John concert. The hallmark of such actions is their grandiosity, their impulsivity, and their disorganization; these features carry over into other behavior as well, in which rash acts such as going on a major buying spree, driving recklessly, or resigning abruptly from a job occur.

Mood disorders are among the most common psychiatric conditions, with most studies reporting that more females are affected than males. The proportion of the adult population in the United States that currently has a mood disorder is thought to be approximately 5 percent. The lifetime risk of ever having a mood disorder has been estimated as 12 percent for men and 20 percent for women.[42] Mania occurs far less often than depression, but both conditions tend to recur. About 70 percent of people with a major depressive episode will have at least one additional bout of depression in their lifetime, and about 12 percent will have subsequent bouts of mania.[43]

The sexual effects of the mood disorders are varied. The majority of depressed persons experience a marked reduction in their sex drives, but overt sexual dysfunction occurs in less than a third of these cases. In chronic depression, inhibited sexual desire is not unusual, and the capacity for enjoying sexual fantasies is often lost. As we have noted elsewhere:

It is common to find that the depressed patient has few sexual fantasies or thoughts about sex; it is also common to find a significant decrease in initiatory sexual behavior, although the sexual receptivity of depressed persons is somewhat less affected. Mechanisms of sexual arousal (erectile function in the male and vaginal lubrication in the female) are more likely to be intact than to be impaired, but often the perception of sexual arousal is negatively affected.[44]

When a true sexual dysfunction occurs as a result of depression, it is sometimes masked by other problems. In one case, a married 42-year-old man suffering from depression withdrew from virtually all social interaction with his wife, even insisting on eating his meals alone; months later, it turned out that this self-imposed social isolation was in part his response to guilt over erectile difficulties that first appeared as part of the depressive symptoms. Similarly, because depression in one partner obviously has some impact on many aspects of a couple's intimacy, it is no surprise that it may interfere with their sex relations.

Infrequently, depression may trigger unusual forms of sexual behavior, such as incest, pedophilia, or exhibitionism. And in some cases, a depressed person may start an affair to stimulate both his or her mood and sexual performance.

Sexual behavior in mania is affected in a number of different ways, with the cardinal feature being its impulsivity. During a bout of mania (which typically lasts for weeks or months), hypersexuality is common. Ordinary social and sexual inhibitions may be loosened or shattered, with both male and female manics suddenly (and uncharacteristically) having sex with numerous partners, including partners who are total strangers, as the following case summaries show:

Case 1: A 28-year-old married female accountant who had a past history of psychiatric hospitalization for both manic and depressive episodes occurring sporadically since her early twenties called her husband from work one day to announce that she had taken all the money from their joint checking account and was off to the West Coast to see some friends. After flying from Boston to Los Angeles, she suddenly boarded another plane for Las Vegas. In four days there, she picked up seven different men at her hotel bar and had sex with them; the last two men agreed to a sexual threesome at her insistence.

Case 2: A 43-year-old Presbyterian minister who was revered by his congregation for his dedication and loyalty inexplicably began to frequent prostitutes and to show up at lunch hour at a seedy topless bar on the "bad" side of town, where he would sometimes climb up on the dance platform with the girls and try to lick their breasts. Despite his prominence in the community (or perhaps because of it), his mania was not diagnosed for almost two months, however, as his family physician mistakenly thought that his behavior was part of a "midlife crisis."

Case 3: A 37-year-old sociology professor was taken to a psychiatrist after she suddenly disrobed at a faculty meeting and began masturbating. The psychiatrist discovered that she had canceled all of her office hours for the past several weeks and had squandered some $25,000 from a research grant she had received earlier that semester. The diagnosis of mania was easily established.

Hospitalized manic patients often disrupt the psychiatric ward by similar displays of overt, inappropriate sexuality or by attempts to have sex with hospital staff members or their fellow patients. In addition, some manic persons show their hypersexuality by a frantic search for sexual partners or constant seductive behavior,[45] or by participation in forms of sexual activity that they had never tried previously, including bisexuality or homosexuality or group sex.

Mania is often treated with a drug called lithium carbonate. Although this is usually effective in controlling the manic episode and in preventing recurrences, lithium occasionally causes sexually difficulties in males, including erectile problems and decreased sexual desire.[46] One of the reasons for this effect may be that lithium decreases testosterone levels in the blood. Lithium produces negative sexual effects in females infrequently, although when used in combination with a tranquilizer like Librium or Valium it is more apt to cause drops in sexual desire and/or problems having orgasms.[47]

There are a number of different medications that are useful in treating depression; they are often combined with a program of cognitive psychotherapy. Virtually all of the antidepressant drugs can affect sexual functioning adversely in both males and females, although this problem occurs in only a small minority of patients.[48] (In males, the most common sexual difficulty is inhibited ejaculation, while in females inhibited orgasm is the most frequent problem.) As a practical matter, however, the sexual effects of antidepressant drugs are generally beneficial in the sense that as they bring about symptomatic improvement in the mood disorder, they usually boost a person's sexual interest back to its preillness level. In addition, if sexual dysfunction occurred as a result of the depression, then as the depression lifts, the dysfunction often disappears.

ANOREXIA NERVOSA AND BULIMIA

Anorexia nervosa, the self-starvation disorder, and *bulimia*, the binge-purge eating disorder, are related conditions marked by disturbances in body-image and obsessive-compulsive concerns focusing on food and eating. Both disorders characteristically start in adolescence or young adulthood and affect females much more frequently than males. There is mounting evidence that anorexia and bulimia have increased in frequency in the general population in the past two decades; the problem of bulimia appears to be especially acute on college campuses throughout the nation, where some studies have estimated that more than 10 percent of college females engage in bulimic behavior, which they learn from other females in what has been termed a "copycat" manner.[49] The increased occurrence may partly reflect the emphasis our culture puts on thinness as a way of proving attractiveness and personal self-worth—the "thin is in" mentality.[50]

The essential features of anorexia nervosa are: (1) progressive weight loss, to a point more than 15 percent below minimal normal weight for age and height (or failure to gain weight in a period of body growth); (2) disgust with food (often, paradoxically, accompanied by a preoccupation with thoughts about food); (3) intense fear of gaining weight or becoming fat, even when the victim is so thin that she or he looks like a concentration camp survivor; (4) distorted body image, so that the person "feels fat" even when emaciated;

and (5) loss of menstrual periods in females. The disorder, while treatable, is sometimes fatal and often requires hospitalization.

Although the cause of anorexia is not known, one frequently expressed viewpoint is that it is a form of rejection of developing adult sexuality. An early psychoanalytic theory was that, through starvation, anorectic females reject a wish to be pregnant; another thesis was that the anorexic's phobic-avoidant response to food results from sexual and social tensions generated by the physical changes that occur with puberty.

The anorexic female actually makes her body regress sexually by severely restricting her food intake. She can postpone the onset of menarche (if she hasn't yet started to have menstrual periods) or make her menstrual periods stop by losing a lot of weight; this effect occurs by suppressing the production of luteinizing hormone and follicle-stimulating hormone. By disrupting her ovarian functioning (estrogen production is kept at basically prepubertal levels in anorexia), the anorexic also can often postpone her breast development, or make her breast size shrink back to a less threateningly sexual degree of flatness. Similarly, testosterone levels are low in male anorexics, and the development of secondary sex characteristics such as facial hair and lowering of the voice are delayed.

Anorexic females typically show little or no interest in sex; in fact, they often appear frightened of sex. Most anorectic females avoid dating, do not masturbate, and have no desire to give up their much-coveted virginity. Adolescents with anorexia nervosa are often shy and withdrawn and appear childlike in their social interactions. In some cases, a history of sexual abuse or assault precedes the development of anorexia.[51] Even among married adult anorexics, avoidance of sex is common and sexual dysfunctions such as primary anorgasmia or vaginismus are frequently seen.

Bulimia is characterized by binge eating—the episodic consumption of large amounts of food in a relatively short time period (generally less than two hours)—usually followed by self-induced vomiting or abuse of laxatives or diuretics. The binges, which are usually planned, typically involve rapidly eating food with a high calorie content and a lot of sugar—such as ice cream, doughnuts, cookies, or chocolates—and are usually carried out in private, gobbling down the food with little chewing. The bulimic feels out of control during a binge and worries that she won't be able to stop eating. Immediately after the binge, there is often a depressed mood and self-deprecating thoughts. Sometimes, but not always, there is an anorectic eating pattern between binges; more commonly, the bulimic is preoccupied with her weight and pursues various diet plans and stringent daily exercising as a way of staying thin.

In contrast to anorectics, bulimics tend to be socially outgoing and sexually active at an early age. However, as the psychiatrist Domeena Renshaw points out, bulimics have a relatively high rate of sexual dysfunction as well as inhibited sexual desire.[52] Renshaw also notes that many bulimics feel guilty about masturbation, which she observes is "strikingly similar to their binge-guilt-purge eating cycle." On the other hand, some bulimic females lead very satisfying sex lives, so it is incorrect to assume that anyone with bulimia is automatically sexually dysfunctional.

SEX AND DRUGS

NARCOTICS

Addiction to narcotic drugs such as heroin is associated with a high rate of sexual problems in both sexes, although this reflects a number of factors such as preexisting psychological problems and difficulties with intimacy and relationships, as well as direct actions of the drugs themselves.

The extent of these sexual difficulties can be seen by considering the following statistics. In one survey of male heroin addicts, 63 percent were found to have low levels of sexual desire, 53 percent were impotent, and 79 percent had delayed ejaculation.[53] Another study reported that sexual desire was suppressed in 100 percent of the male heroin addicts surveyed as well as in 96.5 percent of male methadone users, with both groups also showing high frequencies of potency problems and ejaculatory impairment.[54] Similar effects have been seen in female addicts. One study noted decreased sexual interest in 60 percent of addicted women,[55] while another reported orgasmic dysfunction in 27 percent of female addicts and low sexual interest in 57 percent.[56]

These high rates of sexual disturbance are partly a reflection of hormonal effects of narcotics used in high doses over a period of time: the narcotics suppress testosterone production and also reduce LH output from the pituitary gland. Other medical complications of addiction, including high rates of infections such as hepatitis B, as well as poor nutrition, may also contribute to the sexual disturbances described above. Furthermore, many addicts use other drugs as well as alcohol (especially when they can't easily get their hands on heroin), and these combined pharmacologic effects may produce even more devastating sexual disruptions.

One practical aspect of narcotic use is that the stronger the addiction, the more the addict becomes preoccupied with finding his or her next "hit." Furthermore, after the initial "rush" of shooting up wears off, the addict then "nods off" for a while. Both situations leave less and less time available for initiating or maintaining sexual relationships even if the capacity for sexual functioning is relatively unimpaired. But the sex life of drug addicts is even more complicated than these facts would imply. An eloquently titled paper, "When Drugs Come into the Picture, Love Flies out the Window,"[57] describes the typical downward spiral as follows. Addicts often have partners who are also hooked on narcotics. In such relationships, the males usually have low sex drives and are sexually handicapped by various drug-induced dysfunctions, and often the women feel that the rush of heroin is far more intense and infinitely more pleasurable than orgasms ever were. (In addition, women who are in relationships with addicted males are often annoyed by the length of time it can take for their partners to ejaculate; the rush from shooting up is quicker, easier, and more dependable.) Typically, neither partner worries much about their diminishing sexual interaction, in part because each is apt to have a fairly low sex drive and because the woman is often forced into prostitution as a means of financing the drug habits of both of them. One former addict summed up her feelings this way: "For the three years I was hooked, sex was just a way of getting money. I had virtually no sexual feelings and no interest in sex; in fact, I don't think I was really interested in anything except feeding my habit."

COCAINE

For years, cocaine was touted among drug users as both an aphrodisiac and a potent stimulus to sexual performance, but the sexual effects of cocaine use are considerably more complex. As with virtually all drugs, both the frequency of use and the route of administration have a lot to do with the pharmacologic result; in addition, user expectations play an important role in personal perceptions of an experience as subjective as sex. Early studies with experienced drug users found that cocaine was consistently preferred over all other illicit drugs for its purported sexual enhancement.[58] Casual cocaine use was claimed to produce a noticeable increase in sexual desire (which some users said was like supercharging their sexual appetites), a general intensification of sexual feelings, and delayed orgasm in males, which allowed marathon sexual episodes with some regularity. Some males also found the temporary but powerful sense of aggressive mastery and invincibility that the drug confers a definite sexual enhancer, but interviews with couples who have used the drug together suggest to us that this is more a matter of individual perception than actual changed behavior. However, as with most drug effects, a different story was found in heavy users of cocaine. A number of reports indicate that sexual dysfunction is a common accompaniment to cocaine use in both sexes. For example, Siegel found that 20 of

23 men who were chronic cocaine users developed lack of sexual interest and situational impotence.[59] In another study, 62 percent of men who were addicted to cocaine and also drank heavily were found to have low sexual desire, and 52 percent suffered from erectile failure.[60] In a ten-year study of changing patterns of cocaine use, Robert Kolodny found that sexual difficulties were most pronounced with the use of the highly potent form of cocaine called "crack." Sixty percent of 70 female crack users were nonorgasmic, while 44 percent of cocaine "snorters" who used the drug at least three times a week and 28 percent of "occasional" users (women who used cocaine less than once a week) were nonorgasmic. Among male crack users, 65 of 90 (72 percent) had frequent episodes of erectile failure, whereas only 8 percent of "occasional" users had the same problem. Men who used cocaine heavily—three times a week or more—but didn't use crack had rates of sexual dysfunction midway between these extremes, with 24 percent reporting serious erectile problems.

Summarizing such studies, a recent report noted:

> At some point, nearly all chronic high-dose cocaine users become sexually dysfunctional (i.e., impotent and nonorgasmic). But despite their inability to perform physically, many chronic users find that their sexual feelings and fantasies are still heightened by cocaine, and their sexual acting-out behavior continues. At this point, however, sexual arousal and stimulation are often reduced to a purely mental (psychological) experience for the chronic user.[61]

Because crack use is often combined with the practice of bartering sexual services in exchange for the drug, females who become addicted to crack commonly have sex with a number of partners each day in order to feed their habit.[62] Partly because of this, crack use has been tied to soaring rates of sexually transmitted diseases (STDs) in the past few years.[63] In addition, Arnold Washton, a psychologist, claims that many people who become addicted to crack are also driven to compulsive sexuality.[64]

MARIJUANA

There has been a lot of controversy about the sexual effects of marijuana, which has been widely touted as a drug that strongly enhances sexual feelings and sexual performance. In fact, a good deal of the allure of marijuana use is its reputation as an aphrodisiac: the idea that not only does it intensify sexual feelings but that it helps turn someone on (thus making it the strongly desired seduction assistance for which many teenage males have been searching enthusiastically for eons). Street lore aside, there is absolutely no scientific evidence that marijuana is an aphrodisiac. In fact, what it mainly seems to do is accentuate the user's preexisting state of mind. If someone is feeling romantic, marijuana may indeed act as an erotic enhancer. But if someone is feeling tired, more often than not marijuana just puts them to sleep. Many people who have tried marijuana admit that it gave them the giggles or sent them on a "heavy" (and solitary) psychedelic mind-trip, or that it simply made sex seem like a slow-motion movie.

Casual, sporadic use of marijuana typically doesn't have significant sexual side effects for most users, although 10 to 15 percent of females complain that it causes vaginal dryness, which is similar to the dry mouth that most users report. This may cause pain with sexual intercourse unless an artificial lubricant is used. However, most marijuana users claim that the drug enhances their sexual experiences.[65] In interviews with more than 1,000 marijuana users, about 80 percent of whom endorsed this viewpoint, we have consistently heard that marijuana produces its erotic enhancement primarily by three mechanisms: (1) making sex less hurried and longer-lasting; (2) putting the partners in closer rapport with each other; and (3) providing greater tactile sensitivity all over the body (not just enhancing genital sensitivity). As one woman put it, "My whole body was eroticized; when my partner touched my face, it felt like it was directly wired into my clitoris."

The problem with these reports is that the subjective impressions of users are a bit at odds with some physiologic facts. It may be true that users "feel" more relaxed and unhurried with sex when they're high on marijuana than when they're not, but it's been clearly demonstrated that people who are stoned consistently misjudge the passage of time. This means that their sex play isn't likely actually to be lasting any longer than otherwise; it just *seems* to be. What's more, experienced users consistently note that when one partner is high on marijuana but the other is not, sex is almost always dysynchronous and unpleasant. Thus, however a marijuana high makes two people more closely attuned to each other, it works only if both are under the influence. Perhaps most telling, laboratory studies show that a person's sense of touch is either no different when high on marijuana than at other times *or* that often it is actually diminished (although people who are high claim consistently that their sense of touch is "better" than when they're not high). Adding up all of these facts suggests that what is happening is all in the mind of the user—not that this somehow negates what people *feel* is happening, but that it points out the problem in distinguishing which is real: a perceived effect or an actual effect.

The situation is somewhat different for people who become long-term heavy users of marijuana. Here, the drug can lead to decreased blood testosterone levels and suppressed sperm production[66] and may also have an impact on ovarian functioning in female users.[67] (These effects are quickly reversible once the drug is stopped.) Impotence occurs in almost one-fifth of men who are long-term daily marijuana users, although women who are chronic, frequent users of this drug do not seem to have increased sexual dysfunction.

ANABOLIC STEROIDS

Anabolic steroids are synthetic forms of testosterone that were developed in order to minimize the androgenic (masculinizing) effects of testosterone while amplifying its anabolic (growth-promoting) properties. While this class of hormone has some authentic medical uses as prescription drugs (e.g., in the treatment of osteoporosis, endometriosis, breast cancer, and some anemias), anabolic steroids have gained a degree of notoriety because of their widespread illicit use by athletes. Because the anabolic properties of the drug increase the body's conversion of nitrogen from protein food sources into muscle, the drugs are commonly used by athletes in "strength sports" such as football, wrestling, weight lifting, and some track and field events (e.g., shot put or discus) in which increased muscle size is thought to be beneficial. Whether anabolic steroids actually increase strength or speed, or otherwise improve athletic performance, or whether the performance enhancement is more apparent than real, is unclear at present.[68]

Although use of anabolic steroids has long been "athletes' darkest and best-kept secret,"[69] the world's attention was focused on this issue with the disqualification of the Canadian sprinter Ben Johnson, winner of the 1988 Olympic 100-meter dash, after he acknowledged that he had used anabolic steroids during training.[70] But it is hardly just elite, world-class athletes who use anabolic steroids: one recent survey found that 6.6 percent of twelfth-grade male students, a sample drawn from 46 public and private high schools across the country, had used anabolic steroids, with two-thirds of this group starting at age 16 or younger.[71] Another survey documented that high school females, as well as males, sometimes use anabolic steroids; one percent of the female high school seniors in this study reported that they had used these drugs during their athletic careers.[72] Among college athletes, use is both far more common and far riskier because of higher doses and the frequent practice of "stacking"—using two or more anabolic drugs at the same time.

There are a number of undesirable or harmful side effects associated with the use of anabolic steroids. In most cases, the frequency and severity of these untoward effects increases with the dose of the drug or drugs used; since it is not unusual for athletes who get anabolic steroids on the black market to use them in doses 10 to 50 times higher than the amounts used for medical purposes, the rates of harmful side effects are much higher than when the steroids are used for strictly medical purposes. In both sexes, there is a significant risk of liver abnormalities (including chemically induced hepatitis, jaundice, and tumors), high blood pressure, and endocrine and reproductive effects. In women, the most visible effects are masculinizing ones: growth of facial and body hair, male pattern baldness, and enlargement of the clitoris. Women are also apt to have menstrual irregularities and blocked or inhibited ovulation. In males, these drugs typically cause a sharp drop in circulating testosterone (because their weak androgenic action is enough to keep the hypothalamus from triggering the hormonal signals for more testosterone production) and atrophy (shrinkage) of the testes. Sperm production is seriously impaired with prolonged use, and the resulting sterility does not always improve after the anabolic steroids are discontinued.[73] Gynecomastia (enlargement of the male breasts) is another common finding.

Many males using high doses of anabolic steroids gradually develop low levels of sexual desire and erectile dysfunction—presumably as a result of their lowered testosterone production—but they are apt to ascribe their lack of sexual interest to "being in training," rather than to hormonal changes of which they are unaware. Because they are not particularly interested in sex, they may not discover that they are having difficulties with erection until many months after the problem first began.

There are also potential psychological effects from use of high doses of anabolic steroids. The most prominent is a form of increased aggressiveness known colloquially as " 'roid rage." Rapid mood swings are also frequently noted, and one report found that 12 percent of users had psychotic symptoms.[74] It has been theorized that the rapid mood swings and aggressiveness of steroid abuse may sometimes contribute to sexual assault committed by male athletes, although this is a complex issue in which blame should not be put entirely on the drugs.

Finally, since anabolic steroids are sometimes injected, their use in this manner entails an increased risk of infections associated with sharing needles, including hepatitis and AIDS.[75]

SEXUAL EFFECTS OF PRESCRIPTION DRUGS

Many prescription drugs cause sexual symptoms. Although a detailed discussion of this topic is beyond the scope of this chapter, we will briefly consider some of the most common culprits in this type of problem and what can be done when it occurs.

The largest single class of drugs causing sexual side effects contains those used in the treatment of high blood pressure. Virtually every drug in this category has been associated with sexual side effects, although fortunately the drugs that cause these problems with the highest frequency are less generally used today than in the past. For example, 15 years ago, when Aldomet (methyldopa) was the most widely prescribed drug to treat hypertension, it caused sexual problems for a considerable number of users. As with many medications, these side effects were dose-dependent: they tended to appear at higher dosage levels. For example, 10 to 15 percent of men taking less than one gram per day of Aldomet have depressed libido and/or potency problems, whereas at slightly higher doses (1.0 to 1.5 grams per day), 20 to 25 percent of men and women experience sexual difficulties.[76] (In women, the higher doses of Aldomet can cause orgasmic dysfunction as well as arousal difficulties and lowered libido.) Another example is a drug called Ismelin (guanethidine), which frequently blocks or inhibits ejaculation in men. At moderate doses of this drug, 50 to 60 percent have retarded ejaculation or lose the ability to ejaculate completely, and another 15 percent develop erectile difficulties. At high dosage levels, 85 percent of men have impaired ejaculation. (In many cases, this side effect is annoying enough to cause a man to stop taking his medication.)

Drugs that fall in the class known as beta-blocking agents, including Inderal (propranolol), Tenormin (atenolol), Lopressor (metoprolol), Corgard (nadolol), and Blocadren (timolol), have all been associated with erectile difficulties, although except at high doses, this problem only occurs in about 8 to 12 percent of men. (Many of these drugs are used in other conditions as well as high blood pressure; for example, in the treatment of angina pectoris.) Interestingly enough, when these drugs were first introduced, many of them were claimed to be free of adverse sexual effects, but time has shown otherwise.

Diuretics are sometimes called "water pills" because they remove excess fluid from the body. They may also be used for treating other medical conditions, including premenstrual syndrome and congestive heart failure. They are often combined, too, with another antihypertensive agent. Alone or in combination, they can be associated with sexual side effects. Aldactone (spironolactone) is the worst offender in this regard, causing decreased sexual desire and erection problems in 20 to 25 percent of male users.[77] Unlike other diuretics, Aldactone has actions that affect testosterone, and one of its other common side effects is breast enlargement in men. In women, Aldactone often causes menstrual irregularities, but it doesn't usually have a negative sexual impact. Other diuretics such as Diuril (chlorothiazide), HydroDIURIL (hydrochlorothiazide), Lasix (furosemide), and Hygroton (chlorthalidone) all have been shown, in carefully designed studies, to lower libido and cause erection problems, although these difficulties generally seem to affect less than 10 percent of users except at high dose levels.[78]

Calcium channel blocking agents such as Procardia (nifedipine) and Norvasc (amlodipine) generally carry lower rates of sexual difficulties, but in one study, amlodipine was found to have reduced the frequency with which almost 20 percent of men had sex.[79] In the same study, a new type of drug known as an ACE inhibitor, which had previously been regarded as relatively free from sexual side effects, was shown to depress libido in 16.3 percent of men. It does not appear that ACE inhibitors such as Vasotec (enalapril) or Capoten (captopril) produce erectile dysfunction with any frequency.

The other largest group of drugs that cause sexual side effects contains those used for treating psychiatric conditions. Almost all of the drugs used to treat depression, for example, have had some association with sexual problems. This issue is confusing, however, since untreated depression itself causes sexual difficulties—especially loss of sexual desire—and in the majority of cases, as a drug in this class helps improve a person's affect, his or her sexual interest and functioning are far more likely to improve than to deteriorate. However, drugs like Prozac (fluoxetine), Nardil (phenelzine), Zoloft (sertraline), Desyrel (trazodone), and Anafranil (clomipramine) are especially likely to produce orgasmic dysfunction in women and inhibited ejaculation in men;[80] in fact, Prozac has been suggested for therapeutic use in premature ejaculation because of this prominent side effect.[81] Erectile problems, however, are encountered less commonly with the antidepressants, in our experience.

Another class of psychiatric drugs, the phenothiazines and related compounds, which are primarily used in treating psychoses, tend to inhibit ejaculation more than they affect erection or libido.[82] These drugs, which include agents such as Mellaril (thioridazine), Stelazine (trifluoperazine), Prolixin (fluphenazine), and Thorazine (chlorpromazine), also can cause painful ejaculation. In women, these drugs also can block orgasm; they have also been found to reduce sexual arousal by interfering with vaginal lubrication.

Other prescription drugs can also create sexual problems. For instance, Tagamet (cimetidine), which is used in the treatment of peptic ulcers, can reduce testosterone levels and impair sperm production. It causes potency problems in approximately 12 percent of users.[83] Antihistamines, which act to dry up nasal secretions, also have a drying effect on the vagina and may impair vaginal lubrication. In addition, the drugs used to treat epilepsy (such as phenytoin [Dilantin] and phenobarbital) have sometimes been reported as a cause of sexual dysfunction and reduced sexual desire in both sexes, although there is disagreement on the incidence of this problem.

Whenever you begin treatment with a new prescription medication, you should ask your physician in advance whether there might be any sexual side effects associated with it. Then, if you experience any changes in your sexual feelings or sexual responses in the first weeks of using the medication (or after being switched to a higher dosage of the drug), you should notify your physician right away. It is often possible to find other drugs that will not produce the same effect (although it may not always be possible to predict in advance which ones will turn out this way) or to switch to a combination of several medications, each at a lower dose, to avoid this type of problem. Sadly, not all physicians are well informed about these subjects in pharmacology. In addition, in most areas of medical therapeutics, little systematic data has been collected on sexual aspects of specific drugs, so this information may not be available to a nonspecialist.

While you should never take it on yourself to stop using a medication on the suspicion that it might be affecting your sex life, because stopping could prove to be medically dangerous, you do have the right to a prompt and full discussion of this matter with your physician. If she or he can't help you, find another physician who can.

Thirteen

Sexually Transmitted Diseases

For many people, the topic of sexually transmitted diseases sounds forbidding either because it seems as if it must be too technical and uninteresting or because it is tinged with a moralistic, preachy tone, like old army V.D. movies in World War II. We have tried to steer away from these dilemmas in order to present some material that is timely, practical, and informative, because sexually transmitted diseases (STDs) are an important subject in modern society both because of their ubiquity and their consequences.

Here are two points to keep in mind while reading this chapter. In general, although we discuss STDs mainly from the viewpoint of their "classical" presentation in men and women, it is important to remember that (as with most medical conditions) not all cases of X, Y, or Z look—or feel—the same. Readers shouldn't expect to become absolutely proficient diagnosticians after reading this chapter. Making a correct diagnosis of anyone's specific problem is best left in the hands of a well-qualified physician, who has probably seen hundreds of similar cases before (and thus has a mental data bank adequate to the task). In addition, we have not provided specific drug dosages in sections where we discuss STD treatment. This is an intentional omission, since we believe that optimum dosage schedules should usually be individualized and should also be based on the most up-to-date recommendations possible.

GONORRHEA

Although the bacterium that causes gonorrhea was first discovered by Albert Neisser in 1879 (hence its name, *Neisseria gonorrhoeae*), the major clinical manifestations of this disease were described in ancient Greek, Roman, and Egyptian writings, as well as in the Old Testament.

Gonorrhea, which is also known as "clap," "a dose," or "strain," is transmitted almost exclusively by sexual contact. The risk of transmission is higher for females than for males and depends in part on the type of contact as well as the number of exposures. After a single unprotected coital exposure to an infected woman, a man has a risk estimated at about 20 to 25 percent; after four separate exposures, the risk rises to about 70 percent. A woman's risk of infection after having intercourse a single time with a man with gonorrhea is about 50 percent;[1] with repeated exposures, her risk rises to about 80 to 90 percent. The difference in risk is probably due to the woman's exposure to a larger number of infective bacteria as well as to retention of infected semen in the vagina, where the semen ordinarily pools around the cervix.

The risk of transmission is probably somewhat higher for rectal intercourse (either homosexual or heterosexual), although precise data are not available on this point. Likewise, anyone performing fellatio on a male with gonorrhea has a very high risk of developing gonorrhea in the throat, although the odds of transmitting this infection by cunnilingus are small.

Although almost 700,000 cases of gonorrhea were recorded in the United States in 1990, and 620,000 in 1991,[2] most authorities agree that fewer than half of all cases are reported, so there are probably actually about 2 million cases a year.[3] Despite the fact that this underreporting undoubtedly produces distortions in what is known about patterns of gonorrhea in the general population (e.g., cases seen by physicians in private practice are far less likely to be reported than cases seen by physicians in public health clinics, so there is a socioeconomic and racial bias in the available data), several points can be made. First, gonorrhea is principally a disease of teenagers and young adults: in 1990, 72 percent of cases occurred in persons 15 to 29 years old.[4] Second, more males than females are infected with gonorrhea: the sex ratio is about 1.5 to 1. Third, African-Americans are affected disproportionately by this disease, with rates substantially higher than those of whites.[5] In addition, the following generalizations can be made. Gonorrhea is found most often in persons with numerous sex partners. The risk of gonorrhea is partly linked to patterns of contraceptive use, with women who use the pill having an increased risk of this STD, while women who use spermicides or a diaphragm or sponge have a reduced risk of infection. Finally, gonorrhea often coexists with other STDs. Fifteen to 25 percent of men and 30 to 50 percent of women with gonorrhea have coexistent chlamydial infections, and many women also have *Trichomonas vaginalis* infections, as well.

Symptoms

Gonorrhea in the male typically begins with burning on urination along with a milky discharge from the urethra. These initial symptoms typically occur 2 to 4 days after infection. A day or two later, the urethral discharge becomes yellowish, thicker, and more copious and is occasionally tinged with blood. These symptoms are a result of gonococci attaching themselves to the mucosal surface of the urethra, usually producing a prominent inflammatory response as the body tries to fight off the invading microorganisms. However, about 10 percent of men with gonorrhea seem to have asymptomatic (silent) infections, a dangerous situation because without any warning of the presence of the disease, they do not seek treatment and continue to infect their sex partner(s).

With treatment, gonorrhea in males is usually easily eradicated, but if this condition goes untreated, the infection may ascend and involve the prostate and/or epididymis with acute, painful inflammation. (The epididymis is a tightly coiled network of tubing that is folded against the back surface of each testicle; epididymitis—inflammation of this structure—is often painful enough that it is sometimes called "great balls of fire," and it is common for the scrotum to become red and swollen with this condition.) These conditions are not innocuous, since they can occasionally lead to permanent sterility.[6] However, untreated gonorrhea in males usually resolves spontaneously over a period of weeks or months without causing other serious problems.

Women infected with gonorrhea have two distinct disadvantages compared to men. First, about half of all cases of gonorrhea in women are asymptomatic or have such mild symptoms that the women never notice them, which means that a much larger number of women have no early warning to indicate that they should obtain treatment. Second, women who are untreated tend to have graver consequences than males do, a point we will return to in a moment.

The most common symptoms of gonorrhea in women are pain or burning with urination, urinary frequency and urgency, and a purulent urethral discharge. Infection of the cervix also can cause a vaginal discharge and abnormal menstrual bleeding. However, none of these symptoms are very specific ones, and gonorrhea infecting the throat or rectum usually doesn't cause symptoms.

As we discussed in Chapter 11, a substantial number of women with gonorrhea develop pelvic inflammatory disease (PID), a condition in which the infecting organism ascends through the female reproductive tract to infect the Fallopian tubes. Although this complication is usually marked by fever, abdominal pain, and an elevated white blood cell count, its presentation is quite variable and it may sometimes be confused with appendicitis or other gynecologic conditions. PID is particularly devastating to women because it causes scarring of the Fallopian tubes, resulting in high rates of infertility, chronic pelvic pain, and a markedly increased risk of ectopic pregnancies. One authority states that involuntary infertility occurs in 15 percent of women who have had one attack of PID and 50 percent of women who have three such episodes.[7] PID is also problematic for a different reason: one careful analysis suggests that it accounted for health care costs of more than $4 billion annually in the United States.[8] (While gonorrhea is not the only source of PID, it is certainly one of the two major causes, the other being chlamydia, an STD we will discuss later in this chapter.)

Other serious but uncommon problems are associated with untreated gonorrhea in both sexes. In about 1 percent of cases, the infection spreads through the bloodstream and causes arthritis and skin rashes; it can also cause a mild form of hepatitis, an infection of one or more heart valves (gonococcal endocarditis), or meningitis (infection of the covering of the brain). Another potential problem is that gonococcal eye infections can occur by auto-inoculation—rubbing the eye with a hand that is contaminated. Newborns can also contract eye infections by direct contact with bacterially contaminated secretions in the birth canal.

Diagnosis and Treatment

The diagnosis can be easily established in men by microscopic examination of a specially stained smear of the urethral discharge, but such smears are often inconclusive for women. Cultures of pus or secretions are necessary to confirm the diagnosis in women and in men who have had homosexual or bisexual contact; swabs of cervical secretions and the rectum should be taken even if a woman has not had anal intercourse, because infected material from the vagina may have dripped onto the anus and caused infection there. (Anal infections are found in about 40 percent of women with gonorrhea.) If a woman has performed fellatio, a throat culture should also be taken. About 10 percent of women with gonorrhea have positive throat cultures.

Although penicillin used to be the treatment of choice for gonorrhea, this is no longer the case. Strains of gonorrhea that are resistant to penicillin now account for 9 percent of reported cases. As a result, the U.S. Public Health Service and the Centers for Disease Control now recommend that nonpregnant adults with gonorrhea be treated with a combination of an antibiotic called ceftriaxone (given by intramuscular injection) *plus* the use of doxycycline pills twice a day for one week. This regimen has the advantage of simultaneously treating the chlamydial infections that often coexist with gonorrhea.

It is also recommended that *all* people with gonorrhea should have blood tests for syphilis and should be offered confidential testing and counseling for HIV infection. In addition, anyone exposed sexually to gonorrhea within the previous 30 days should be examined, cultured, and treated as above on the presumption that they are infected.[9]

SYPHILIS

Syphilis was first recognized in the late fifteenth century when it produced an explosive and lethal epidemic across Europe. Whether an especially virulent form of the disease was imported from the New World by Columbus and his men or whether the disease was already present in Europe has been the subject of considerable debate. In any event, syphilis spread widely around the world in the next few centuries, although the virulence of the disease declined.

The bacterium that causes syphilis, *Treponema pallidum*, is a thin corkscrew-shaped microbe capable of infecting almost any organ or tissue in the body. It can enter the body through intact mucous membranes or through small breaks in the skin, so that it is especially efficient as an STD.

Although syphilis was a major public health problem in the early 1900s, when it was a leading cause of cardiovascular and neurologic disease, the introduction of penicillin in the 1940s—along with stringent public health measures used to combat the spread of this disease—brought syphilis largely under control. By the mid-1950s, there were fewer than 7,000 cases reported in the United States each year.[10]

Coincidentally with the sexual revolution, rates of syphilis began to creep upward in the general population during the 1960s and 1970s, reflecting changing patterns of sexual behavior as well as relative neglect of public prevention and education programs.[11] By the latter half of the 1980s, this trend began to accelerate still further. Many experts linked this sudden upsurge, which was found chiefly among heterosexuals, primarily to the use of crack cocaine (a smokable form of cocaine that is intensely addictive), since many women hooked on this drug traded sex with numerous partners for crack vials or for money to buy crack.[12] It was not unusual for women in crack houses to have sex with ten or more partners a day, often charging $5 or less for each encounter. The net result was that by 1990, more than 50,000 cases of syphilis were reported in the United States,[13] and in 1991, the total number of reported cases climbed still further, to almost 129,000.[14] This many cases had not been seen since the 1940s. (As with most other STDs, experts believe the actual number of cases is substantially higher.)

Although syphilis is mainly transmitted sexually, it can also be transmitted by blood transfusion or the sharing of needles by intravenous drug users. Both forms of nonsexual transmission are rare. Syphilis can also be transmitted across the placenta from an infected pregnant mother to her developing fetus. Very rarely, syphilis can be acquired by other nonsexual means, as when health care workers inadvertently come in contact with infectious lesions, or by contact with inanimate objects.[15]

Sexual contact with an infected partner leads to infection in about 30 percent of cases. Syphilis can be transmitted by vaginal or anal intercourse, by oral sex, by kissing, and by virtually any other form of sexual stimulation that involves skin-to-skin contact. Syphilitic lesions of the fingers, breasts, and even the nose are sometimes encountered as evidence of the versatility of the infecting organism. Typically, people with early syphilis are most highly infectious, while sexual contact with people who have had the disease for years is far less risky.

Symptoms

Although syphilis has sometimes been called "the great imitator" because of its protean manifestations of disease, most cases tend to follow a classic natural history. There are four distinct stages of infection: primary, secondary, latent, and tertiary (late) syphilis. Primary and secondary syphilis are sometimes referred to collectively as "early" or "infectious" syphilis.

Primary syphilis first appears after an incubation period that averages 21 days but can vary from 10 to 90 days. Generally speaking, infection with a larger number of treponemal organisms shortens the incubation period. The hallmark of the primary stage is a skin lesion called a chancre. The chancre (or several similar chancres) virtually always appears at the site of inoculation— where the infecting organisms first entered the body. The majority of chancres are painless and occur on or near the genitals or anus. The chancre initially appears as a dusky-red spot, which quickly changes into a pimple. The surface of the pimple erodes to form a round, painless ulcer, which is often mistakenly thought to just be a "sore." Typically, the borders of the ulcer are raised and firm, rather than soft or mushy, and over time the chancre enlarges to a diameter of 1 to 2 centimeters. If untreated, the chancre or chancres heal within 4 to 6 weeks, so almost always people are convinced that the problem has disappeared. This erroneous conclusion is unfortunate because it leads many people with early syphilis to postpone seeking medical attention and because it greatly increases the likelihood that they will be a source of infection to their sex partners.[16]

Several weeks after the chancre heals, an infected person usually passes into the stage of secondary infection. This is marked by low-grade fever, swollen lymph nodes, headache, sore throat, and skin rashes. The characteristic rashes can assume several different forms, including generalized symmetrical eruptions that have a blotchy reddish appearance; slightly raised round bumps of various sizes that frequently affect the face, the palms, and the soles of the feet (and often have a scaly surface); and flat, wartlike growths, called condylomata lata, that occur on moist areas of the skin, such as near the anus, around the vulva, or on the penis. On the scalp, there sometimes occurs an irregular pattern of hair loss that has been described as having a "motheaten" look, and patchy grayish ulcerations of the mucous membranes are also commonly seen, especially on the inner surface of the lips, on the tongue, in the throat, and on the penis or labia. These patchy lesions are easily confused with other STDs, particularly genital herpes. Both condylomata lata and mucous-membrane patches are highly infectious, as they contain large numbers of treponemes. A mild form of hepatitis occurs in about 10 percent of people with secondary syphilis, and other complications include meningitis, kidney abnormalities, and eye infections.

When the above symptoms disappear, after a few weeks or after many months, the infected person is said to enter a latent period. Although there are no symptoms during this phase, treponemes are widely spread throughout the body and may be producing damage that goes undetected, at least temporarily. Since an infected person remains infectious during the first year after the onset of syphilis, he or she can unwittingly transmit the infection to others without realizing that he or she is ill. About one-quarter of individuals have relapses of secondary syphilis during the latency stage, although this happens usually in the first year after infection. Latent syphilis is rarely infectious beyond the first year, except for the special case of transmission to a fetus during pregnancy, which can occur many years into the latent period if the disease is untreated.

After a time period in the latency phase that varies, about one-third of people with untreated infection develop tertiary syphilis, the most destructive stage of the disease. The most serious forms of involvement are damage to the cardiovascular system and nervous system, which each affect about 10 percent of persons with untreated infection. Among the consequences of these forms of involvement are heart failure (usually due to insufficiency of the aortic valve), sometimes-fatal aneurysms of the aorta (aneurysms are balloonlike weak areas in the wall of a blood vessel that can cause death by massive internal bleeding if they rupture), mental disorders, and a constellation of neurological problems called *tabes dorsalis*, resulting from degeneration of the spinal cord.

Diagnosis and Treatment

Syphilis is usually diagnosed with great accuracy by one of several blood tests. For those cases where a screening blood test is still negative during primary syphilis, either more specialized blood studies can be used or swabs of material taken from a chancre can be inspected microscopically to identify the spiral-shaped treponemal organisms directly.

Penicillin given by intramuscular injection remains the highly effective treatment of choice for most individuals with primary, secondary, or early latent syphilis. People who are allergic to penicillin can use tetracycline or erythromycin in pill form or can be given an injection of the antibiotic ceftriaxone. Higher doses of penicillin given over longer time periods are generally required to treat cases of late latent or tertiary syphilis.

CHLAMYDIAL INFECTIONS

The most common bacterial STD in the United States is neither gonorrhea nor syphilis, but rather infections caused by *Chlamydia trachomatis*. This STD, which generally mimics gonorrhea in its effects, is thought to have an annual incidence of 3 to 4 million cases in America. No one is exactly sure, though, since chlamydial infections—unlike most other major STDs—are, rather inexplicably, not reportable diseases at either the state or national level.

The widespread nature of chlamydial infections can be seen from several snapshot surveys of different at-risk populations. It affects 3 to 5 percent of women seeking routine gynecologic care, 9 percent seen in family planning clinics, and 20 percent or more of women attending STD clinics.[17] Chlamydial infections in males are found in 3 to 5 percent of those seeking routine general medical care, 11 percent of military personnel, and 15 to 20 percent of men attending STD clinics.[18] In adolescents, the prevalence is particularly high: 15 percent of teenage girls and 8 percent of teenage boys are infected with this STD.[19]

Chlamydial infections are generally sexually transmitted, except for a form called trachoma, a chronic eye disease that can lead to blindness, which affects millions of people in Asia and Africa but is rare in the United States and Europe. (Trachoma is spread by flies.) Although chlamydial infections are less transmissible than gonorrhea, they follow the same general patterns of sexual spread. Specifically, they are transmitted by vaginal or anal intercourse as well as by oral-genital contact. As with gonorrhea, women appear to be at higher risk for infection than men: 70 percent of females whose sex partners have chlamydial infections become infected themselves, whereas less than half of males whose female sex partners are infected develop chlamydial infections.[20] No studies are available documenting the risk to males or females from a single sexual exposure.

SYMPTOMS

In males, genital chlamydial infections cause several different syndromes. The most common is chlamydial urethritis, or infection of the urethra, which is thought to be some 2.5 times as common as gonococcal urethritis. With an incubation period of 1 to 3 weeks after infection, chlamydial urethritis typically manifests itself with a sense of burning with urination and/or a whitish urethral discharge that is visually indistinguishable from the discharge of gonorrhea. About one-third of men with chlamydial urethritis are completely asymptomatic—which obviously makes diagnosis difficult and spread quite likely—and another third have such mild symptoms that they are unlikely to believe they have a sexual infection.

C. trachomatis also commonly produces epidydimitis in young, heterosexually active males. This disorder appears as swelling, pain, and exquisite tenderness to touch of the scrotum on one side, along with fever, often (but not always) occurring coincidentally with urethritis. Chlamydial infections may also cause prostatitis, although the evidence here is inconclusive. In homosexual or bisexual men, chlamydial infection can lead to rectal infections (chlamydial proctitis) with rectal pain and bleeding, mucus discharge, and diarrhea. If C. trachomatis spreads throughout the body, it can cause Reiter's syndrome, marked by urethritis, conjunctivitis, arthritis, and characteristic inflammatory skin lesions. (This condition occurs in 1 to 3 percent of men with chlamydial urethritis.)

In females, chlamydial infections produce effects at virtually every level of the reproductive system but are often difficult to diagnose because they tend to be asymptomatic. Infections of the urethra (known as the urethral syndrome) are a prime example: they are symptomatic in females only about one-third of the time. Furthermore, the symptoms themselves (pain or burning with urination or frequent urination) are often so nonspecific that they are typically ignored. Most of the time, the characteristic signs of urethritis in males, such as a urethral discharge or inflammation at the urethral opening, are not experienced by infected women, which makes it even more likely that they will have no awareness of the existence of this infection. (This absence of symptoms is problematic for several reasons: not seeking treatment increases the odds of transmitting the infection to a woman's sex partner[s] and also makes it more likely the infection will become more medically complicated, as we discuss below.)

Likewise, chlamydial cervicitis (infection of the cervix)—which sometimes coexists with the urethral syndrome—tends to produce no noticeable symptoms. About one-third of females with this condition have a cloudy, milky-white cervical discharge, but this is such a common occurrence in adolescents and young adults that it rarely leads to suspicion of the existence of an STD. Such nonchalance of course increases the likelihood that the infection will spread further up the reproductive tract.

This higher involvement includes infections of the lining of the uterus (chlamydial endometritis), which occurs in about half of women with chlamydial infections, as well as pelvic inflammatory disease (PID), which occurs in 30 to 40 percent of women not treated for chlamydial cervicitis.[21] PID is particularly problematic because it can produce scarring of the Fallopian tubes, leading to female infertility. One episode of PID also increases a woman's risk of ectopic pregnancy by 700 percent compared to that of women who have never had this disorder.[22] PID also causes a host of other medical complications, including abscesses of the ovaries or Fallopian tubes, pelvic adhesions, and pain during intercourse. These problems, which occur in 15 to 20 percent of women with PID, often require subsequent surgical intervention.

In mild cases of chlamydial PID, there are often no symptoms at all. In more severe cases, there is typically lower abdominal pain, fever, nausea or vomiting, and irregular menstrual flow, as well as a vaginal discharge, but these are highly variable symptoms that are not always present.[23] Pain during intercourse is a common complaint during an acute episode of PID because the cervix is especially sensitive to movement of any sort: in fact, in a clinical examination, a marked tenderness when the cervix is moved slightly has been referred to chauvinistically as the "chandelier sign," meaning that the woman jumps up toward the ceiling because of her attendant pain. (In our experience, female physicians use this jargon just as often as males do. This isn't necessarily a sign of insensitivity, but it certainly comes across sounding like one.)

Infrequently, chlamydial infections spread from the Fallopian tubes to the surface of the liver. This condition, called perihepatitis, is marked by pain in the right upper abdomen, accompanied by nausea, vomiting, and fever. There may or may not be evidence of PID when this condition appears.

As with most STDs, chlamydial infections can be transmitted from a pregnant woman to her baby during childbirth. (Unlike syphilis, this infection does not seem to be transmitted to the fetus during pregnancy, either by being carried across the placenta or by ascending into the uterus.) Chlamydia causes conjunctivitis in about one-quarter of newborns whose mothers are infected; ear infections (otitis media) and infections of the nose and throat are also common. About 10 percent of newborns whose mothers are infected develop a mild form of chlamydial pneumonia.

One other form of chlamydial infection will be briefly mentioned. Certain strains of this bacterium cause an entirely different type of STD called lymphogranuloma venereum (LGV). This disease is common in tropical and subtropical areas of the world but is seen infrequently in North America and Europe. It affects males about five times as often as women. LGV typically starts out with a brief genital ulcer, which is usually painless and heals rapidly. Several months later, in the secondary stage of this infection, there is painful swelling of the lymph nodes in the groin (typically on one side, but on both in about a third of the cases) as well as fever, chills, headache, weight loss, and nausea. In women with this STD, the swollen lymph nodes that are so prominent in males are rarely found, so the disease is especially difficult to diagnose in females. In males, the swollen lymph nodes may coalesce and rupture through the skin, producing fistulas that drain a thick, yellowish pus for weeks. In either sex, LGV can cause abscesses in or near the rectum, and sometimes this STD produces enough scarring in the rectal region to cause partial blocking (called a rectal stricture) of the passage. There appears to be an increased risk of rectal cancer in people with LGV rectal strictures. LGV can also cause large swellings of the genitals years after the initial infection, a condition known as genital elephantiasis.

DIAGNOSIS AND TREATMENT

The presence of chlamydial infections is most accurately confirmed by special cell culture methods that attempt to grow these bacteria in the laboratory. However, because doing this is technically difficult and time-consuming, treatment is generally started on clinical suspicion of the presence of chlamydia. Antibody tests for detecting chlamydial bacteria in infectious secretions have also been developed and are generally simpler to perform, although they are somewhat less accurate than the cultures.

Tetracycline or doxycycline taken in pill form is the usual treatment of choice for chlamydial infections. Erythromycin is the drug of choice for pregnant women. In all cases, treatment should continue for at least a week. It is very important to treat sex partners of the infected person concurrently to prevent reinfection. Follow-up studies are also in order, because in about 5 percent of cases, chlamydial infections recur 3 to 6 weeks after treatment.

It is important to realize that drugs such as penicillin, ampicillin, and spectinomycin, which are often effective in single-dose regimens in treating gonorrhea, do not eradicate chlamydial infections.

CHANCROID

Chancroid is a sexually transmitted bacterial disease that until recently has been uncommon in the industrialized Western nations but is thought to be more common than syphilis on a worldwide basis.[24] Caused by *Haemophilus ducreyi*, a short, compact rod-shaped bacterium, this disease now affects an estimated 5,000 to 10,000 people annually in America, a startling increase over the fewer than 1,000 cases reported annually in the United States in the 1970s.[25]

Public health officials attribute the recent rise in chancroid in the United States to an increase in prostitution, tied to female drug use, since infected prostitutes make up the primary reservoir for this infection. A single infected prostitute may infect dozens of men a week. Increased international travel and shifting immigration patterns may also play a role in the rising incidence of chancroid and other previously uncommon STDs in the United States.

SYMPTOMS

The incubation period after exposure is short, usually between 4 and 7 days. The hallmark lesion is a painful genital ulcer (sometimes called a "soft chancre," in distinction to the "hard chancre" of syphilis) that begins as a tender pimple surrounded by a reddened area. Over 1 to 2 days, it becomes filled with pus and breaks into a sharply demarcated ulceration with ragged edges. Approximately half of those infected have more than one genital ulcer.

In males, the ulcers are most frequently on the foreskin, the frenulum, or the coronal ridge (the area separating the head of the penis from the shaft). Although the head or shaft of the penis can be affected, this site is much less typical.

In females, the ulcers are usually at or near the entrance to the vagina. They may involve the labia, the clitoris, or the area just inside the vaginal opening, as well as the region between the vagina and the rectum. The cervix can also be affected, and lesions involving the breasts, the fingers, the thighs, and the mouth have been encountered, although with far less frequency.

The other prominent clinical finding in chancroid is painful swelling of the lymph nodes on one side of the groin (the side that drains the infected region of the genitals). Although this occurs in only about half of chancroid patients, it is often a dramatic development, as the large swollen lymph nodes, called *buboes*, can rupture and exude a thick, creamy pus.

Chancroid does not appear to cause any major health complications beyond the symptoms mentioned above. However, it is important to realize that chancroid (as well as other diseases that cause genital ulcers) appears to facilitate transmission of HIV, the virus that causes AIDS.[26] *Haemophilus ducreyi* apparently does not cause disease at the time of delivery in babies born to mothers with this infection.[27]

DIAGNOSIS AND TREATMENT

No blood test is available to diagnose chancroid, so the diagnosis is usually made on clinical grounds after a physical exam. Cultures of material from a genital ulcer or ruptured bubo are useful if they can isolate *H. ducreyi*, but the test requires special materials and the results are not always reliable.[28]

The recommended treatment is either erythromycin, taken in pill form for a week, or a single injection of ceftriaxone. Fortunately, these treatments are highly effective; if improvement doesn't occur promptly (within a week after therapy), it is important to consider whether the diagnosis was correct, whether the person may also be infected with another STD—especially HIV[29]—or whether the strain of *H. ducreyi* is resistant to the antibiotic used.

Anyone who has had sexual contact with a chancroid-infected person within 10 days preceding the onset of that person's infection or during the infection should be examined and treated whether there are symptoms or not.

GENITAL HERPES

Ancient Greek physicians chose the term "herpes," from the verb meaning to creep or to crawl, to describe the spreading nature of skin lesions they observed that are today recognized to be of viral origin. Genital herpes, painful blisters on or near the genitals, is caused by infection with the herpes simplex virus. This STD, which affects an estimated 40 million Americans (with 500,000 new cases annually) is a chronic disease, incurable because the herpes simplex virus establishes a latent infection in humans, during which it persists indefinitely in an inactive state. Reactivation of the virus occurs at irregular and unpredictable intervals, and such reactivations often (but not always) cause recurrences of the genital blisters that are characteristic of symptomatic genital herpes.

Genital herpes can be caused by either of two different but related types of the herpes simplex virus (HSV). Herpes simplex type 2 accounts for 80 to 90 percent of cases of genital herpes; the remainder are caused by herpes simplex type 1, also (and more commonly) the cause of cold sores and fever blisters, which are manifestations of HSV infection of the lips or mouth.

A recently conducted national survey done on blood samples collected in the late 1970s showed that 16.4 percent of the U.S. population 15 to 74 years of age was infected with herpes simplex type 2.[30] The prevalence of herpes virus type 2 antibody increased from under one percent in the group under age 15 to 20 percent in the 30-to-44 age bracket and was significantly higher in blacks than whites.

Genital herpes is typically, but not exclusively, transmitted by sexual contact. Virtually any form of sex, including oral-genital sex, oral-anal contact, and even genital touching that does not include intercourse, can produce infection. HSV can enter the body either at mucosal surfaces (e.g., the mouth, the vagina, the urethra) or through tiny breaks or cracks in the skin. Since the saliva of infected persons can contain infectious virus during herpes attacks, transmission via kissing is more than a remote possibility. There is also a risk of transmission by contact with contaminated items such as clothing or towels, or by people sharing a sex toy such as a vibrator or dildo.

The infectiousness of this STD is especially high. A man who has a single sexual exposure to an infected, symptomatic woman has a 50 percent chance of becoming infected himself, whereas a woman's risk from one sexual exposure to an actively infected man is 80 to 90 percent.[31] As with most other STDs, the incidence of this infection correlates with the lifetime number of sexual partners: having a lot of partners (whether heterosexual or homosexual) materially increases the risk of developing genital herpes.

SYMPTOMS

The incubation period for genital herpes is 3 to 6 days after initial infection. A sensation of genital irritation or burning is common a day or two before the skin eruption actually appears. The characteristic pattern is for a group (or groups) of small, clear blisters to appear on or near the genitals. As the painful blisters break open, they leave superficial circular reddened erosions 1 to 2 mm in diameter that may either be clustered together or may appear in a slightly irregular row. Healing typically takes 10 to 20 days.

The severity of a first attack of genital herpes depends in part on whether there has been prior infection with HSV. This is because prior herpes infections (such as cold sores or fever blisters) result in antibodies that lessen the severity of symptoms with subsequent exposures. As a result, some people may be completely unaware that they have genital herpes. In fact, in one recent study, it was found that fewer than 20 percent of men and women with antibodies to HSV type 2 reported a history of genital herpes.[32] True primary infections are often marked by fever, headache, and muscle aches for the first few days, but the predominant symptoms are those at the site of infection. Pain and itching are nearly universal accompaniments of an outbreak of genital herpes, whereas a burning sensation during urination occurs in about 80 percent of women but only about half as many men. Eighty-five percent of women also have a vaginal or urethral discharge, and herpes infections of the cervix occur in almost 9 out of 10 women with primary HSV type 2 infections. Pain and irritation from the skin lesions typically increase over the first week of the illness and then gradually begin to decline, usually resolving fully by 14 to 16 days after they first appeared. Swollen lymph nodes may occur in the groin during the second and third week after infection.

About 5 percent of cases of primary infection with HSV are complicated by meningitis (inflammation of the covering of the brain) severe enough to require hospitalization. The symptoms are stiff neck, severe headache, and light sensitivity. Although this is usually a self-limited condition with no neurologic aftereffects, it can be life-threatening in people whose immune defenses are depressed from conditions such as AIDS or cancer chemotherapy. Other complications include herpes infections of the eye (1 percent) and of the throat (10 percent).

Although infection with HSV is lifelong, since the virus remains latent in the body, about one-third of the people with genital herpes never have another noticeable flare-up. Another third have just a few recurrences, while the final third experience repeat attacks with some frequency—more than three times per year.[33] Recurrences are more common in people whose genital herpes infection is with HSV-2. In general, repeat bouts are considerably less severe than the first episode of infection: skin lesions tend to be less numerous, less painful, and of briefer duration, and systemic symptoms are minimal. Recurrences also tend to diminish in frequency and intensity over time, although a small number of people with genital herpes are unfortunate enough to have frequent, painful flare-ups for 5 years or longer. Recurrences can be triggered by fever, illness, sunburn, physical exhaustion, and extreme climactic changes; however, whether emotional or psychological stress triggers these attacks is a matter of some debate.[34]

Recurrences are preceded by warning symptoms in about half of cases.

These range from mild sensations of tingling in the genitals or a burning sensation with urination to sharp, shooting pains in the buttocks or hips that occur a day or two before skin lesions appear. It is important to be alert for such warning symptoms, because they signal a strong likelihood that an infected person may be actively shedding virus even if there are no blisters or genital ulcerations visible.

It now appears that the pattern of repeat flare-ups is strongly influenced by the type of the infecting virus.[35] Recurrences affecting the mouth or lips are very common in type 1 infections but infrequent in those with HSV type 2, while genital recurrences are six times more common than recurrences in the mouth in people infected with HSV type 2.

One intriguing recent finding about genital herpes is that close to half of the people who were previously thought to have an "asymptomatic" recurrent infection can actually be taught to recognize genital lesions that don't have the classical appearance of herpes blisters, such as mild external irritation or small cracks or fissures in the genital skin.[36] Recognizing such lesions as herpes is important because it permits the person to avoid sexual contact during a time of increased transmissibility.

Another key point is this: there is now convincing evidence that people with genital herpes can actively shed virus (and thus are infectious) even when no herpes blisters are evident.[37] This "asymptomatic" shedding involves secretions such as saliva as well as vaginal and cervical secretions and seminal fluid. This means that if you or your partner have ever been infected with genital herpes, there is no time when it is safe to believe that there is absolutely no risk of transmission.

There are two other complications of genital herpes that should be mentioned briefly. The first is that there is mounting evidence that genital herpes may make people more vulnerable to infection with HIV, the AIDS virus.[38] One reason this occurs is that open genital lesions provide easier access for HIV to gain entry to the body. However, there may be other factors involved, including the fact, common to virtually all STDs, of there simply having been more exposures because the infected person had larger numbers of sex partners.

The second complication is that HSV can be transmitted from a pregnant woman to her fetus, a problem that is found in approximately 1 in 3,500 deliveries and that has increased significantly in incidence over the past two decades. While most such cases are a result of contact with contaminated genital secretions at the time of delivery, some result from earlier intrauterine infection, especially in cases of primary genital herpes occurring during pregnancy. HSV infection of newborn babies is a particularly serious condition because it can result in encephalitis (infection of the brain) or widespread infection throughout the body, although in milder cases it causes only skin, mouth, or eye infections. Fifteen percent of newborns with HSV encephalitis die and another 50 percent have severe developmental difficulties, including mental retardation and blindness; 60 percent of babies with disseminated HSV infection die, as well.[39]

Prior concerns that HSV causes cervical cancer have now been largely put to rest.[40]

DIAGNOSIS AND TREATMENT

Most cases of genital herpes are diagnosed by clinical appearance alone, although at times other STDs have presentations that are easily confused with this condition. Two clues are especially useful in making the diagnosis. (1) Unlike the primary chancre of syphilis, genital herpes lesions usually consist of a group of blisters or ulcerations. (2) Unlike the genital ulcerations caused by other STDs (including syphilis), the lesions of genital herpes are painful when touched.

Confirmatory evidence to pin down the diagnosis can be obtained by culturing the virus directly in the laboratory or by taking sequential blood samples to demonstrate rising levels in antibodies directed against the herpes simplex virus. Microscopic examination of cells in swabs taken of the lesions also can be useful, since it may show characteristic changes and is a rapid, inexpensive diagnostic method that doesn't require special equipment.

Although there is no cure for genital herpes, an antiviral drug called acyclovir is effective in reducing both the intensity and duration of symptoms in first attacks. Although acyclovir does less well in alleviating the severity of recurrences, it *is* quite useful in reducing the number of flare-ups in individuals with frequent or particularly symptomatic attacks. In 525 patients who used acyclovir continuously for three years after having had at least 6 genital herpes attacks in the year before being treated, 61 percent were completely recurrence-free in the third year of drug use, and no significant side effects were noted.[41] One potential problem with long-term treatment is that some strains of herpes simplex virus have become resistant to this drug, raising concerns that overuse of acyclovir may lead to a situation where a more virulent strain of the virus becomes widespread.[42]

Here are a few other practical pointers for dealing with episodes of genital herpes.

1. The use of a mild painkiller such as aspirin, or an aspirin substitute like acetaminophen or ibuprofen, or an over-the-counter topical anesthetic (best administered in spray form) can be helpful in alleviating local discomfort.

2. Wearing loose-fitting cotton underwear helps cut down local irritation. Women should avoid wearing pantyhose while they have any external lesions, and men should avoid wearing jockstraps or other tight-fitting athletic gear, as friction in the crotch area may worsen symptoms and slow healing.

3. Careful attention to proper hygiene is particularly in order. Wash the affected region several times a day, using mild soap and warm water (avoid soaps containing skin lotions and deodorants, since they can sometimes be irritants); dry the genital area gently but thoroughly, always using clean towels and a patting (rather than rubbing) motion. *Be sure that towels and washcloths that come in contact with herpes lesions do not touch other parts of your body.* (It's also advisable to launder them after a single use.) It may be helpful to use warm air from a hair dryer several times a day to keep lesions dry, especially if they are weeping. And after you've touched the affected area, always be sure to wash your hands carefully so you don't inadvertently spread the infection to your mouth or eyes.

4. Avoid wearing damp or wet clothing such as bathing suits during attacks of genital herpes.

5. Temporarily eliminate physical activities that may cause mechanical problems. For instance, avoid bicycling and long-distance running, as well as types of dancing that involve intense exertion. (Once lesions have begun to heal thoroughly, these activities can be gradually resumed.)

6. Use a disinfectant spray (we suggest Betadine, which is widely used in hospitals and clinics) several times a day to prevent secondary bacterial infections in the open lesions after herpes blisters burst.

In our view, it's asking for trouble to have any sort of sexual contact during an attack of genital herpes. In a first attack, you should abstain from sex until 10 days after all lesions disappear. In recurrences, abstain at least 2 days after complete healing occurs. People with genital herpes who experience burning, tingling, or itching sensations in the genital region *before* a recurrence is apparent should also temporarily avoid sexual contact, since the risk that they are shedding virus is particularly high at that point.

As we pointed out earlier, genital herpes is a chronic condition, and some people shed virus even when they are not in the middle of a symptomatic attack. This means that there is no way to be absolutely certain that there is no risk of transmission, which is why it is advisable always to use a condom for sex if you know you have this problem. Although condoms don't guarantee that your partner will be safe from infection, they certainly improve the odds considerably.

While treatment of pregnant women with genital herpes must be individualized on the basis of many biomedical considerations, there is no evidence at present that giving acyclovir in the weeks before delivery can prevent neonatal herpes. There is considerable disagreement about the preventive role of cesarean delivery in pregnant women with genital herpes.[43]

GENITAL WARTS

Genital warts, sometimes called *condylomata acuminata* or venereal warts, are soft, dry, usually painless warts that grow on or near the genitals and around the anus. Although genital warts were widely recognized in ancient times, neither their nature nor their significance was accurately understood until recent years. In the middle ages, for example, they were mistakenly thought to be a form of syphilis; later, scientists believed they were caused by gonorrhea. In fact, until 1954, the notion that these warts were infectious and easily transmissible by sexual contact was vigorously denied by many physicians. It took a study showing an outbreak of vulvar warts in the wives of GI's coming home from the Korean War to convince the medical establishment that this was, indeed, a sexually transmitted infection.[44]

Today, this once-neglected STD has begun to attract more attention because of both its widespread prevalence and its health implications. There are an estimated 12 million cases of genital warts in America today, with 750,000 new cases annually. They are caused by a sexually transmitted virus called the human papilloma virus (HPV) and are usually pink or grayish-white with a cauliflowerlike appearance.

Approximately two-thirds of the sexual partners of individuals with genital warts develop the disease themselves. The incubation period is 6 to 8 weeks. Although the infection is certainly transmitted by direct contact with the lesions, there is evidence that the virus is also transmitted by semen.[45]

When epithelial cells (cells that line the outer or inner surface of the body) are infected by HPV, they undergo a transformation in which they divide continuously,[46] causing a buildup of abnormal tissue that eventually becomes a wart.

Although genital warts were once thought to be more of a cosmetic nuisance than a health problem, it is now clear that the family of viruses that causes them is an important long-term cause of cancer of the cervix and other cancers of the anal and genital region, including cancer of the penis.[47] For instance, in one large case-control study in Latin America, cervical infection with HPV types 16 or 18 was found to be more than twice as common in cervical cancer cases as in controls.[48] While no one believes that it is the human papilloma virus alone that causes such cancers, scientists are now developing theories to explain what role these fairly common viruses may play in producing malignancies and why only some infected persons develop these cancers.

HPV was found in 29 percent of pregnant women in one study;[49] in the Latin American survey cited above, 32 percent of women in the control group had cervical infection with HPV; and in a recent survey of American university students, a sophisticated testing method found that an astonishing 46 percent of young women who called to make an appointment for a gynecologic exam were infected with HPV.[50] Male sexual partners of women with HPV infection are commonly infected too; in one survey, almost three-quarters of the males were found to have HPV in genital lesions.[51] In addition, since genital warts commonly coexist with other STDs, anyone with such growths should undergo thorough medical evaluation to check for the possibility of an asymptomatic case of gonorrhea, chlamydial infection, or syphilis. It is currently thought that genital warts are most likely to occur in adolescents and young adults—precisely the same age range as gonorrhea.

Symptoms

Although genital warts are, as the name implies, most often found on (or inside) the genitals, they can also be found in other locations, including the mouth, the eyelid, the lip, the nipple, and around the anus. (Genital warts are not the same as ordinary skin warts, which occur on most parts of the body.)

In males, genital warts can involve any part of the penis. Common locations include just inside the opening of the urethra (where they are apt to have a bright red appearance), on the frenulum, on the head of the penis or the coronal ridge, and on the inner surface of the foreskin, as well as along the penile shaft. The appearance of the warts can range in size from tiny, solitary, dotlike growths to large, irregular, rough-surfaced masses that protrude from the penis by a half-inch or more.

In females, genital warts commonly involve the labia, the opening to the vagina, the inner third of the vagina, and the cervix. In some cases, they appear as relatively isolated patches of grayish-pink tissue tags, while in other instances, the pattern of growth is distressing because extensive wart formation virtually covers the external genitals. (Rarely, genital warts can become so large as to block the birth canal at the time of labor, requiring a cesarean delivery.) As with males, genital warts in females may grow just inside the urethra.

While the primary problem with genital warts for most people is the embarrassment they cause, if they become large they may also create some mechanical discomfort (particularly during sex). In addition, large genital warts are more likely to become secondarily infected or to be ulcerated (often because of the rubbing of underwear against them). Infrequently, genital warts may be a source of bleeding, particularly if they are quite large.

DIAGNOSIS AND TREATMENT

The diagnosis of genital warts is usually obvious to a medically trained examiner. Because similar lesions (condylomata lata) can be found with secondary syphilis, a blood test to check for syphilis is, as we mentioned above, always in order when warts appear on the genitals. Currently, tests to detect the specific type of DNA that the HPV possesses are being performed in many centers, but at present it is not clear what practical influence doing this will have on treatment decisions.

According to the Centers for Disease Control, no therapy has been shown to actually eradicate HPV. Thus, the goal of treatment is simply to remove visible or symptomatic warts. The available treatments include (1) the use of a liquid containing podophyllin, a caustic chemical that erodes the warts when applied repeatedly for short periods of time (this must be done by a health care professional, not self-administered, and it should not be used for pregnant women); (2) use of trichloracetic acid applied to the warts on a weekly basis; (3) use of carbon dioxide laser surgery to burn away the warts painlessly; (4) use of liquid nitrogen to freeze the warts, which usually destroys them after one or two treatments; and (5) use of a protein called interferon injected into the base of the warts. Unfortunately, recurrences of the warts can occur after any of these treatment methods, and none of them eradicates the underlying HPV infection, since the virus remains in tissues next to a wart that has been chemically or surgically destroyed.

Anyone with genital warts should use condoms during sexual activity with a partner to cut down the risk of transmitting HPV. (For safety's sake, this is advisable permanently, not just when the warts are visible.) In addition, if your partner has been exposed, it is wise to have that person get a medical checkup to see if he or she requires treatment.

VIRAL HEPATITIS

Viral hepatitis is an infection of the liver caused by one of several different viruses, designated as hepatitis A, B, C, D, and E. The disease varies from a mild, brief form of infection to a virulent form that can be rapidly fatal. In symptomatic cases, the usual findings are fever, loss of appetite, nausea and vomiting, and flulike symptoms; jaundice (a yellowish appearance of the skin) and abdominal pain often develop as well. In most cases, the acute illness subsides over a period of 2 to 3 weeks, with recovery of normal liver function within a matter of months, although about 10 percent of hepatitis B patients and 50 percent of those with hepatitis C develop chronic liver disease, which can sometimes progress years later to cirrhosis and death.

Hepatitis A is primarily spread by the fecal-oral route; generally, it has been associated with crowding, poor personal hygiene, improper sanitation, and contamination of food or water, although it can also be spread by contaminated needles. Male homosexuality has been identified as a risk factor for this STD, largely because of oral-anal contact, although through most of the 1980s this accounted for less than 10 percent of cases.[52] In 1991, there was a sudden upsurge in hepatitis A among homosexual men, suggesting that there may have been a return to unsafe sexual practices that transmit this virus. Heterosexual transmission of hepatitis A is possible but broad-based population studies do not seem to indicate it as a significant risk factor. This may be largely because oral-anal contact is unusual among heterosexual couples. There are about 30,000 cases of hepatitis A reported annually in the United States.

Hepatitis B, which causes an estimated 200,000 cases a year in the United States, can be spread by a variety of mechanisms, but transmission by infected blood or blood products (either via transfusions, needle-sharing, or inadvertent incidental contact) is one of the major paths of infection. Since the hepatitis B virus has been identified in semen, saliva, vaginal secretions, and other biological fluids, there is also a significant risk of sexual transmission of this disease. Virtually any form of sexual activity, including kissing and oral-genital sex, can transmit the virus. Although homosexual males appear to have the highest rates of past or present hepatitis B, the proportion of cases in the United States accounted for by male homosexual activity decreased by 62 percent between 1981 and 1988.[53] In the same time period, heterosexual transmission became increasingly important, accounting for 26 percent of cases of this infection.[54] Recent data suggest that anal intercourse and failing to use vaginal contraceptives may facilitate sexual transmission of hepatitis B to women.[55] Having sex with multiple partners is another key risk factor for heterosexuals.

Many hepatitis B infections are completely asymptomatic or subclinical; they are so mild they appear to be brief bouts of a flulike illness. Approximately 5 to 10 percent of infected persons become chronic carriers who are infectious to others, although not usually ill themselves, for years; the remainder typically develop immunity. Chronic carriers not only make up a substantial reservoir for new infections, they also have a heightened risk of developing liver cancer or liver failure over time.

There are some 150,000 cases of hepatitis C a year. Fewer than one-tenth of cases result from transfusions, although hepatitis C accounts for more than 90 percent of all cases of posttransfusion hepatitis.[56] Needle-sharing among IV drug users is probably the most important mode of transmission. Heterosexual transmission plays a significant role in the spread of this form of hepatitis, as well,[57] although new evidence suggests that this sexual transmission is much less efficient than for hepatitis B.[58]

Delta hepatitis, also called type D hepatitis, is an unusual infection in the United States that was first discovered in the late 1970s. The hepatitis D virus requires the presence of the hepatitis B virus in order to multiply. In a sense, it "piggybacks" onto the hepatitis B virus, either at the same time acute hepatitis B infection occurs, or later on when it infects a chronic hepatitis B carrier. In both situations, it is often a very serious infection, with high death rates and serious permanent liver damage in many of those who survive. Unlike other forms of hepatitis, it is most likely to occur in prolonged, severe outbreaks in isolated communities. It is especially common in the Mediterranean and the Middle East, but relatively rare in northern Europe, the Western Hemisphere, China, and Southeast Asia. IV drug use appears to be an especially important means of transmitting the hepatitis D virus, but male homosexuals and non-IV-drug-using female prostitutes have also been found to be infected.[59] Detailed information is lacking on additional aspects of the sexual transmission of delta hepatitis at present.

Hepatitis E is seen in North Africa and Asia but not in the United States except for a handful of infections that have occurred in persons traveling outside the United States and returning with this infection.[60]

The presence of hepatitis may be suspected on clinical grounds either from characteristic symptoms, from a history of known prior exposure, or from physical findings such as jaundice, but it is confirmed from blood tests that reveal abnormal liver function and a pattern of characteristic antigen and antibody responses to the specific infecting virus. There is no specific cure for these viral infections; treatment is generally symptomatic, including bed rest during the acute phase and a gradual resumption of activities thereafter.

Fortunately, many cases of hepatitis can be prevented by the use of vaccines that have been developed in the past 15 years. A vaccine for hepatitis A was licensed in Europe in 1992 but is not yet available in the United States.[61] The vaccine for hepatitis B is widely available, however, and is quite safe and effective. It is currently recommended that anyone who is at high risk of acquiring hepatitis B, such as male homosexuals or bisexuals, heterosexuals with multiple sex partners, people who inject illicit drugs, all health care workers, and family members of hepatitis B carriers, be vaccinated.[62] There is no vaccine available for hepatitis C. Since hepatitis D depends on prior or simultaneous infection with the hepatitis B virus, it can effectively be prevented by the hepatitis B vaccine.

VAGINAL INFECTIONS

VAGINITIS

Vaginal infections are among the most common gynecologic complaints in postpubertal teenagers and adults; they are also a major source of sexual distress and personal embarrassment. While the term "vaginitis" is often used synonymously with "vaginal infection," there are also noninfectious types of vaginitis: vaginitis really refers simply to a condition of vaginal inflammation. Allergic vaginitis and vaginitis caused by chemical irritation are relatively uncommon problems. Atrophic vaginitis (caused by estrogen deficiency) is discussed in some detail in Chapter 16. Here, we will take up the two most common types of infectious vaginitis.

Trichomonas vaginalis is an unusual organism called a protozoon, which is in actuality a type of microscopic single-celled parasite. It is virtually always sexually transmitted and has a high rate of infectiousness. Eighty-five percent of the female partners of infected men and 40 percent of the male partners of infected women are also found to be infected.[63] While most men harboring this infection are asymptomatic (although a small percent have urethritis), trichomonal infection in females produces a vaginitis that is usually quite bothersome. The hallmark features are a profuse, often malodorous, frothy, yellowish or grayish runny vaginal discharge; intense vaginal itching; and pain with intercourse. The symptoms often begin or worsen during or immediately after a menstrual period. The diagnosis can be made by identifying the offending organism either by microscopic examination or by culture. Treatment involves the administration of a drug called metronidazole (Flagyl) in pill form simultaneously to the infected woman and her male sexual partner(s). Not treating the male increases the odds of a

Ping-Pong effect, in which the woman is temporarily cured, only to be reinfected by her partner. It is wisest to use a condom until the infection has cleared completely.

A second type of vaginitis, candidal vaginitis, is caused by various strains of the fungus *Candida albicans*. This infection, which is thought to affect three-quarters of all women at one time or another, is usually marked by vulvar and/or vaginal itching; a white, thick, curdlike, nonodorous vaginal discharge; and burning after vaginal intercourse. Sexual transmission accounts for only about 30 percent of cases. Other common factors that predispose to candidal infections are pregnancy, use of high-estrogen-content birth control pills, and diabetes.[64] Candidal vaginitis is also common during the use of various broad-spectrum antibiotics like tetracyclines and ampicillin, and is a particular problem in women who need to take corticosteroids like cortisone or prednisone on a long-term basis. Presumably, the antibiotics alter the natural microbial balance in the vagina, reducing the number of protective vaginal microorganisms that ordinarily prevent an invasion or overgrowth of candidal forms, while the corticosteroids alter the body's immune response as well as changing the microbial mix in the vagina.

The diagnosis of candidal vaginitis is made either by examining a vaginal smear microscopically to identify the characteristic fungus filaments and spores or by vaginal culture. Treatment can be accomplished with a variety of antifungal creams, lotions, vaginal tablets, or suppositories, including miconazole (Monistat), nystatin (Mycostatin), butoconazole (Femstat), clotrimazole (Gyne-Lotrimin, Mycelex), and similar products. For mild infections, good results are usually obtained with 3 to 5 days of treatment, but for more severe or recurrent infections, longer treatment schedules (7 to 14 days) are more effective.[65] Oral nystatin taken three times a day for several weeks may also be effective when other treatment regimens have failed.

Some promise for improved prevention may be contained in a recent study that found that eating 8 ounces of yogurt containing *Lactobacillus acidophilus* daily for six months greatly reduced the occurrence of candidal vaginitis.[66] Since all yogurt products do not contain this microorganism, it is important for a woman who wants to try this method to be sure that she is getting the proper type of yogurt, which is usually available at health food stores (not in general supermarkets).

While treatment of a woman's sex partner isn't usually indicated, in particularly recalcitrant cases this may be advisable. Because candidal species are common in the mouth, it may also be helpful to abstain from oral-genital sex temporarily to see if this is a potential source of reinfection.

BACTERIAL VAGINOSIS

Bacterial vaginosis is a vaginal infection that was previously known as nonspecific vaginitis or hemophilus vaginitis. The term "vaginosis" has been used in preference to "vaginitis" to indicate that signs of inflammation (such as redness and tenderness) are not usually present with this condition; commonly in medicine, the suffix "-itis" indicates inflammation. In addition the bacterial organism *Haemophilus vaginalis*, since renamed *Gardnerella vaginalis*, is now known to be only one of several bacteria that account for this disorder, although it can be cultured from the vagina in about 95 percent of cases.[67] The primary problem seems to be one in which the normal protective bacterial organisms in the vagina decrease drastically in number while the infecting bacteria overgrow. The result of the overgrowth is a grayish-white discharge that usually has a foul "fishy" odor and is accompanied by burning or itching, although the latter symptoms tend to be much less intense than with many other vaginal infections.

Bacterial vaginosis is very common in sexually active women. It occurs in about 15 percent of women seen at a university student gynecology clinic, in 10 to 25 percent of pregnant women, and in close to 40 percent of women seen at STD clinics.[68] However, many of these infections are asymptomatic, and their long-term significance is unknown. Simultaneous infections with *G. vaginalis* are typically found in the urethras of male sex partners of women with this disorder. Treatment consists of either metronidazole (Flagyl) taken in pill form or an antibiotic called clindamycin, used in the form of an intravaginal cream.[69] Treatment of the male partner does not appear to be necessary at present, although good data on this point are lacking. However, the male should definitely wear a condom during sexual intercourse, not only to cut down the risk of his becoming infected but also to prevent transmission of other pathogens (especially gonorrhea) to which the woman with bacterial vaginosis may be especially vulnerable.

PREVENTING VAGINAL INFECTIONS

Vaginal infections are a source of personal discomfort to millions of women because of their unpleasant physical symptoms, their often uncertain origin, and the emotional anguish they sometimes produce. Although most vaginal infections are relatively easily cured, this isn't always the case; chronic, recurrent vaginitis is a frustrating, sometimes infuriating, condition. Here are some practical pointers to help avoid vaginal infections.

1. Frequent douching can destroy beneficial bacteria in the vagina, leading to an overgrowth of pathological microorganisms that cause infection. In addition, frequent douching also reduces the acidity of the vagina, thus making women more susceptible to vaginal infections. Our advice to women is to avoid douching or to douche no more than once or twice a month.

2. Although this advice may sound trivial, wearing underpants or pantyhose made of nylon or synthetic fibers reduces air flow to the vaginal area and retains heat and moisture in a way that provides an ideal environment for bacteria and fungal organisms to thrive. Wearing cotton underwear and loose-fitting, well-ventilated clothing helps to prevent vaginal infections.

3. If possible, avoid long-term use of broad-spectrum antibiotics, since they may allow vaginal yeast and fungi to overgrow. Women with a history of recurrent candidal vaginitis may benefit from using prophylactic antifungal creams or suppositories if they require long-term antibiotic treatment for compelling medical reasons.

4. Heterosexual couples who engage in anal intercourse should never insert the penis into the vagina immediately after it's been in the rectum, since this can "seed" bacteria from the gastrointestinal tract into the vaginal environment. (Washing the penis may not be enough to prevent this from happening, because there may be bacteria scooped inside the urethra which escape the cleansing action of soap and water.)

5. After urinating or defecating, a woman should always wipe herself with a front-to-back motion so she doesn't inadvertently carry bacteria from the rectum or perineum into the vagina.

6. Avoid the use of feminine hygiene sprays, which can be irritating to the skin of the vulva and the lining of the vagina. Chemical irritation makes it easier for invading microorganisms to establish infection.

7. If you have more than one sexual partner, be sure they all get medical attention promptly. Many men who harbor organisms that cause vaginitis are completely asymptomatic, so don't be fooled by his saying, "I know I'm okay because I can tell if I've got a problem."

8. Temporarily abstaining from coitus may be advisable if a vaginal infection occurs. Doing this not only permits both parties to seek medical

attention, it also allows for a beneficial healing period for vaginal tissues. Sexual arousal and intravaginal thrusting may be associated with mechanical and chemical changes in the vagina that are irritating in the presence of an infection. Noncoital sex can be explored during this time, although some women find that any form of sexual arousal is uncomfortable for them while they have a vaginal infection because the increased blood flow to vaginal tissues may heighten symptoms of vaginal or vulvar burning and itching.

Fourteen

HIV Infection and AIDS

The newest and most frightening STD yet discovered was first documented in 1981. Known as *AIDS*—for *acquired immune deficiency syndrome*—this devastating illness is a result of infection with the *human immunodeficiency virus* (*HIV*). The hallmark of AIDS is a breakdown of the immune system, the system that ordinarily protects the body against infections. Because of the collapse of the body's defenses, people with AIDS get a variety of rare infections known as opportunistic infections, usually found only in cancer or transplant patients whose resistance is lowered by medications that impair their immune responses.

Because the earliest cases of AIDS were found primarily in gay and bisexual men and intravenous drug abusers, there was a certain amount of complacency toward the HIV/AIDS epidemic in many quarters—"This doesn't involve me."[1] As Harvard University's noted biologist Stephen Jay Gould put it, "If AIDS had first been imported from Africa into a Park Avenue apartment, we would not have dithered as the exponential march began."[2] In actuality, the HIV epidemic is driven by a virus that knows no racial, sexual, or class boundaries. Today it is clear that not only are more and more heterosexuals involved in the epidemic but also that HIV infection is not restricted to certain groups of people. It occurs on college campuses, in private high schools, in small towns and wealthy suburbs, and in the famous just as in the poor, the elderly, the unknown, and the homeless.

Today, HIV infection and AIDS are among the top three causes of death for males between the ages of 15 and 44 in the United States and are one of the major causes of years of potential life lost for both males and females, especially producing fatalities among people in their twenties and thirties.[3] In 1990, it was estimated that there were 212 cases of full-blown AIDS diagnosed each day and one death from AIDS every 12 minutes;[4] today, these numbers are substantially higher. However, because AIDS typically develops 7 to 10 years after initial infection with HIV, these numbers are only the tip of the iceberg. Since the cases of AIDS being diagnosed today are largely a result of HIV infections that occurred in the mid-1980s, the number of AIDS fatalities will continue to grow at an alarming pace unless a scientific breakthrough occurs. In the meantime, there are a number of measures we can each take to reduce our chances of becoming infected with HIV, which we will discuss in detail.

It is misleading to focus primarily on AIDS, the disease, instead of the broader spectrum of HIV infection. Thus, this chapter will emphasize the entire spectrum of HIV infection in terms of its biology, its clinical course, its social and emotional aftermath, and the public policy issues that need to be considered to turn the tide in one of the most serious epidemics our country, and the world, has ever faced.

It is particularly important to be careful about the language we use to discuss HIV infection and AIDS because it is easy inadvertently to create erroneous impressions and subtle prejudices by our choice of terminology. For example, calling AIDS a "plague" implies to some that this disease is a form of punishment for sinful behavior, whereas describing it as an "epidemic" sounds more scientific and less judgmental. Likewise, if we choose to declare war on AIDS, we must be careful to remember that the enemy is not the person infected with HIV but the virus itself.

Because new information about HIV and AIDS develops rapidly, the material presented here should not be considered the last word. Readers are urged to check with updates from other sources, especially information appearing in the publication of the U.S. Centers for Disease Control and Prevention, *Morbidity and Mortality Weekly Report*. The rapidity with which new discoveries are made is certainly one of the brightest rays of hope for an eventual cure for this problem: in one decade, we have learned more about HIV than about any other known virus. We have also learned a great deal about how to respond humanely to this challenge, helping set the stage for eventually overcoming what now seem like formidable obstacles in bringing this epidemic under control. The message that is most important to take from this chapter, however, is that this epidemic is treatable, preventable, and predictable. Each of us can play a real part in bringing it to a close.

EMERGING PATTERNS OF THE EPIDEMIC: AN OVERVIEW

According to the Centers for Disease Control, some 243,000 cases of AIDS had been reported in the United States as of year-end 1992. In Western Europe, AIDS is less common, but the situation is much worse in many major cities in East and Central Africa, where it is estimated that 10 to 20 percent or more of the adult population is infected with HIV.[5] In addition, areas that had previously appeared to be spared from this disease are reporting increased rates of HIV infection. In Thailand, for instance, HIV infection is expanding dramatically: among IV drug users in Bangkok the rate of HIV infection climbed from one percent in late 1987 to more than 30 percent in mid-1991, and growing numbers of female prostitutes are infected as well, endangering not only their own countrymen but the tens of thousands of foreign visitors who trek to Thailand for commercial sex vacations.[6] The threat of even larger epidemics is painfully evident in a number of other areas, including India and Latin America, where the epidemic seems to be establishing a strong foothold.[7]

These numbers hardly depict the full extent of the worldwide pandemic. For one thing, even in the United States, many diagnosed cases of AIDS are never reported to government centers that are tracking the disease.[8] In addition, in some countries statistics on the extent of the AIDS epidemic appear to have been understated because of political and/or economic concerns such as wanting to avoid a drop-off in tourism, or just as a matter of national pride. One other contributing factor to underreporting is that in some locations many cases of AIDS are never correctly identified. Thus, while "official" reports of AIDS cases worldwide totaled about 400,000 as of year-end 1992, the World Health Organization and the U.S. Centers for Disease Control estimated that the actual number was around 1.5 million.[9]

Even an accurate count of AIDS cases wouldn't tell the whole story about

FIGURE 14.1
WORLDWIDE PATTERNS OF HIV INFECTION AS OF MID-1993
(*Estimates made by the World Health Organization; see M. H. Merson,* Slowing the Spread of HIV, *Science 260:1266, 1993.*)

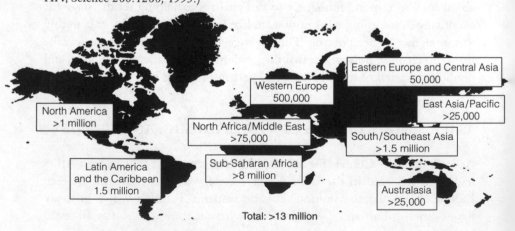

the extent of the HIV epidemic, however, since AIDS is only the final stage of HIV infection. According to the U.S. Public Health Service, 1.5 million Americans are infected with HIV and capable of transmitting it to others but have not yet developed any symptoms;[10] worldwide, the figure is thought to be 12 million adults and one million children.[11] (It is now projected that 40 to 110 million people worldwide will be infected by the year 2000.)[12]

Initially, it was hoped that only a small proportion of people infected with HIV but without symptoms would go on to develop full-blown cases of AIDS. According to current studies, however, it appears that almost all of those infected with HIV will eventually progress to AIDS if no effective treatment becomes available.[13] Since AIDS is, at present, almost always fatal, the implications are staggering. The U.S. Public Health Service has predicted that by the end of 1993 there will be a cumulative total of 450,000 cases of AIDS in America, with one million cases by 1998.[14] Other projections suggest that between one and 2 million Americans will have been diagnosed with AIDS by the turn of the century.[15]

Two different patterns of AIDS and HIV infection have been recognized around the world. In North America, parts of South America, Australia, New Zealand, and many Western European countries, most AIDS cases have occurred as a result of homosexual transmission or as a result of IV drug abuse. In contrast, in most of Africa and in the Caribbean, the vast majority of cases appear to be due to heterosexual transmission. However, in most of Europe, in South America, and in the United States, heterosexual AIDS constitutes the fastest growing category of new cases.[16] (In the United States, cases of heterosexual AIDS rose by 108 percent in women and 114 percent in men between 1989 and 1992, compared with increases of 21 percent in homosexual or bisexual men.)* Whether these two patterns will continue, or whether eventually most cases of AIDS will be a result of heterosexual transmission, is an unanswered question at the present time.

As shown in Figure 14.2, of the first 100,000 cases of AIDS in the United States, 63 percent involved homosexual or bisexual men who were not intravenous drug users, 19 percent occurred in heterosexual IV drug users, 7 percent occurred in homosexual or bisexual drug users, 7 percent occurred in heterosexual partners of people with AIDS or of people in high-risk groups, and 3 percent involved people who had received transfusions of contaminated blood products.[17] However, in Africa cases are divided almost equally between men and women. Elsewhere in the world, as the HIV epidemic has grown, there has been a notable shift in statistics:

* Haverkos, H. W., Reported cases of AIDS: An update, *New England Journal of Medicine* 329:511, 1993.

FIGURE 14.2

THE FIRST 100,000 CASES OF AIDS IN THE UNITED STATES*

*Note: The 100,000th case was reported to the Centers for Disease Control in July 1989.

(*Source:* CDC AIDS Surveillance Reports, *AMA/NET AIDS Information Service, September 1989.*)

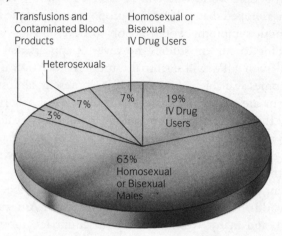

for example, in Central and South America, where earlier reports showed three to ten times as many men as women with AIDS, this ratio has now changed substantially, and in some regions men and women are affected equally.[18] In fact, it is now clear that heterosexual transmission is not only common but the predominant mode of worldwide transmission— accounting for some 80 percent of all new cases, according to the World Health Organization[19]—and that no single group can be singled out as "at risk" for developing this disease.

In the United States, it has become apparent that the nature of the HIV epidemic is shifting significantly from its early days, when the overwhelming number of AIDS patients were gay and bisexual men. In the past few years, AIDS has had a disproportionate impact on the poor, on blacks, and on Hispanics in inner-city populations, where the primary impetus for its spread has been needle-sharing by drug addicts, followed by the transmission of HIV to sex partners of infected individuals.[20] Notably, AIDS is particularly affecting women in these populations. In addition, the geographic nature of the epidemic is changing. What had initially been a problem of New York and California now affects every state and territory and is not limited to large metropolitan areas alone.[21]

This evolving view of the epidemic is buttressed by newly emerging data showing that HIV is spreading rapidly among some groups of teenagers and that among adolescents, equal numbers of males and females are infected.[22] A 1989 study by the Centers for Disease Control found that one percent of teenagers in cities like New York and Miami, where the HIV epidemic has been pronounced, are already infected with the AIDS virus.[23] Disadvantaged adolescents appear to be at particularly high risk of HIV infection, with the male-female ratio in this group an alarming 1.2:1.[24] Little wonder, then, that many experts agree with Dr. Gary Strokash, a specialist in adolescent medicine, who believes that HIV infection among teenagers is "dreadful and it's going to be devastating"; in fact, he states, it "is going to be the next crisis."[25]

THE ORIGINS OF HIV

Although there is no certainty at present about how the AIDS virus originated, many scientists believe that it began in central Africa.[26] One possibility is that a slightly different strain of the AIDS virus first infected monkey colonies there[27] and subsequently spread to humans. Viruses frequently cross over from animal species to humans; this is a natural part of the process of evolution that has been going on for tens of thousands of years. Today, in fact, our world offers many possibilities for exotic or previously undetected viruses to spread to new locales because of the efficiency and wide availability of modern transportation systems. It is likely that both the various types of HIV and the strains of the AIDS virus that infect monkeys arose from a common viral ancestor.[28]

Whatever the beginning may have been, one research study using long-stored frozen blood samples found evidence for the existence of HIV in central Africa in 1959.[29] From there, AIDS may have been carried across the Atlantic Ocean by Haitians who once lived in or visited central Africa. From Haiti, AIDS may have spread to the United States by two routes: Haitian immigrants and vacationing American homosexual males, who often traveled to Haiti. If this explanation is correct, the early clustering of AIDS cases in the United States in gay males may have been largely accidental. And if this scenario is true, it is likely that in the future far more AIDS cases in the United States will arise from heterosexual transmission.

The earliest known case of AIDS in the United States (not recognized as such at the time), based on the laboratory analysis of long-frozen blood and tissue samples, appears to have been in a teenage boy in 1968 in St. Louis.[30] There have also been retrospective reports of cases of AIDS in a Norwegian family during the 1960s[31] and a fatal HIV infection in a 25-year-old British sailor in 1959.[32]

THE HISTORY OF THE AIDS EPIDEMIC: A TIMELINE

1981   Five cases of *Pneumocystis carinii* pneumonia in young homosexual men in Los Angeles and 26 cases of Kaposi's sarcoma in young homosexual men in New York and California are reported to the CDC, arousing attention.

1982   New disease is named "acquired immune deficiency syndrome" (AIDS); case definition is first published by the CDC; first cases of AIDS detected in patients with hemophilia and in recipients of blood transfusions.

1983   U.S. Public Health Service issues guidelines for the prevention of AIDS; first cases of heterosexual transmission reported.

1984   A retrovirus, first called HTLV-III, is identified as the cause of AIDS; later, it is renamed the "human immunodeficiency virus," HIV.

1985   Blood tests to identify antibodies to the AIDS virus become widely available and are first used routinely to screen the nation's blood supply; AZT (zidovudine) is first used in clinical trials; the news that Rock Hudson has AIDS mobilizes worldwide media attention.

1986   *Surgeon General's Report on AIDS* is issued by Dr. C. Everett Koop; clinical testing shows that AZT can improve survival and quality of life for people with AIDS; cumulative total of AIDS cases crosses 25,000.

1987   FDA approves AZT for severe HIV infection; clinical trials of a vaccine against HIV begin in U.S.; President Reagan orders that all immigrants and federal prisoners be tested for HIV; the AIDS Quilt Project begins.

1988   President's Commission on the HIV Epidemic issues broad report urging focus on HIV infection rather than just AIDS, early diagnosis, and antidiscrimination measures; aerosol pentamidine found to be effective in preventing PCP pneumonia.

1989   National HIV prevalence study blocked by political pressures; FDA licenses aerosol pentamidine; cumulative total of AIDS cases crosses 100,000 in U.S.

1990   Recommended dose of AZT halved by FDA; first report of a dentist who may have transmitted HIV to patients published by CDC.

1991   Magic Johnson stuns the world by announcing that he is infected with HIV.

1992   Reports of AIDS-like illness without the presence of HIV draw worldwide attention.

THE BIOLOGY OF HIV

THE VIRUS

AIDS is caused by the human immunodeficiency virus (HIV), a virus discovered in the mid-1980s. HIV is so small that 16,000 could fit on the head of a pin. Typically, HIV gains entry to the body by sexual contact or by intravenous drug use with a contaminated needle. (It is believed that in most cases the virus must enter through a break in the skin or other tissue, like a cut, a sore, or a tear. This is one reason that drug addicts are at particularly heightened risk of infection.) Once inside, the virus selectively attacks two types of white blood cells, T-helper cells and macrophages. T-helper cells are the key coordinators of the immune system. They send out chemical signals that stimulate the production of antibodies and largely control the development of several other types of cells that make up the immune system, as we shall discuss in the next section. Macrophages, on the other hand, roam the bloodstream as scouts with two primary missions: to detect invading substances and to capture them, removing them from the circulation. Because they literally devour intruders, macrophages are classified in a group of cells known as phagocytes, from the Greek *phagein*, to eat. Macrophages not only search for invading microbes and engulf them, they also send an alarm to the rest of the immune system by secreting messenger proteins, called lymphokines.

After attaching itself to the outer surface of the T-helper cell by a biochemical process that is very much like a key fitting in a lock, HIV injects its core inside the cell, establishing a permanent infection. (The HIV core consists of two strands of RNA as well as a group of structural proteins and enzymes that are important for later steps in the life cycle of the virus.) Once this occurs, the virus copies its genetic information into the DNA of the host cell, actually becoming part of that cell's genetic structure.* In this form, it can remain inactive and hidden for years.[33] However, if the immune system is activated in response to another invader, infected helper T-cells proliferate, producing large quantities of new HIV particles that are then released from the host T-cell. These new viruses not only attack other T-cells but also other cells of the immune system and the brain.

---

* This is where the name "retrovirus" originated. Usually, the genetic material in cells is DNA, and when genes are expressed, the DNA is initially copied into messenger RNA which then functions as the model for the production of proteins. In a retrovirus, this process is essentially reversed: the RNA is converted into DNA before it can be expressed or duplicated. In other words, retroviruses reverse what had seemed to be the normal flow of genetic coding. (Haseltine, W. A., and Wong-Staal, F., The molecular biology of the AIDS virus, *Scientific American* 259 (4):52–62, October 1988.)

UNDERSTANDING THE IMMUNE SYSTEM

The primary strike force of our immune system consists of one trillion white blood cells that attack and repel our microbial enemies. Although the immune process is complex and multidimensional, here is a basic summary of the system's operations. Keep in mind that the same principles apply to how our bodies fight off any type of infection, from the common cold to serious, life-threatening conditions.

When a foreign invader manages to evade the body's first lines of defense—the skin and mucous membranes—it is quickly detected by macrophages, a type of white blood cell that acts like an armed scout roaming the bloodstream to clean up debris and sound the alarm when an enemy is encountered. One of the key duties of the macrophage is to search for antigens—chains of unique proteins attached to the surface of invaders that serve as identifiers, allowing the body to recognize what is "foreign" compared to what is "self." In addition to detecting suspicious intruders and engulfing them, macrophages also activate the main portion of the immune system by secreting messenger proteins, the lymphokines. In addition, some macrophages carry a fragment of what they've ingested as a type of biochemical flag to signal another element of the immune system, the helper T-cell. (This surface fragment is known as an antigen because it becomes an *anti*body *gen*erator.)

T-cells are manufactured in the bone marrow, as are all white blood cells. They are programmed for their work in the thymus, a butterfly-shaped gland in the upper chest. Here, one type of T-cell, the helper T-cell, is prepared to respond to specific "foreign" antigens and to recognize on every cell of the body a string of molecules that identifies it as self. A separate class of T-cells, called killer T-cells, serves as special troops that attack infected cells.

When macrophages engulf invaders such as HIV, the antigen they attach to their surface acts like a distress flag that summons help. This immunologic assistance comes first in the form of a backup army made up of helper T-cells. The T-cells travel through the circulation in specialized groups. Each group recognizes only a certain type of antigen. When the antigen displayed on the surface of the macrophage fits into the receptor on the T-cell's surface, the two stick together. This "key-in-the-lock" phenomenon causes the macrophage to release a chemical that activates the T-cells and sounds a general alarm to the immune system as a whole, particularly mobilizing the killer T-cells, which multiply and concentrate their attack on the invader, following their chemical programming.

Another part of the immune system is also activated in this process. It consists of a separate class of white blood cells, called B-cells, that ordinarily are stockpiled in the spleen and lymph nodes. B-cells have the primary task of manufacturing antibodies, protein substances that seek out and bind tightly to specific invader-antigens, marking the enemy for elimination. Many varieties of antibody are produced by B-cells. Each one binds to a specific antigen. Unless you have previously been exposed to an invading microbe, the body typically requires a number of weeks to generate a measurable antibody response. But if you've been previously exposed, either through a vaccination or by fighting off the actual microbe in question, the antibody response is much quicker because the body "remembers" the invader and is biochemically programmed to manufacture antibodies with greater rapidity. When antibodies stick to the antigen-surface of invading microbes, they usually prevent them from attacking other cells and make them easier targets for macrophages to capture.

With HIV infection, something in the body's immune process goes wrong. Although antibody production is stimulated quickly in most cases, the HIV antibodies that are manufactured seem to be unable to work effectively. The reduced effectiveness may be partly because HIV gets inside T-cells and macrophages, where it copies its own genetic code into the host cell's DNA, so that it actually becomes the part of host cell's genetic structure. In such a situation, any activation of the immune system actually stimulates production of the invading virus—the exact opposite of what should be happening. Over time—in fact, usually over a period of years—this insidious invasion wreaks havoc by destroying helper T-cells, so that the body's front line of defense is seriously depleted, and as the T-cell count drops drastically, the body is unable to respond appropriately to fend off the opportunistic infections and cancers that typically make AIDS a fatal disease.

HOW HIV IS TRANSMITTED

SEXUAL TRANSMISSION

In more than 78 percent of all AIDS cases the virus has been sexually transmitted.[34] HIV is not, however, as highly contagious as some other STDs such as syphilis, gonorrhea, and hepatitis B. Current estimates suggest that the risk of being infected with HIV from a single act of heterosexual vaginal intercourse with an infected person is 1 in 500 for a woman and 1 in 700 for a man.[35] The risk from a single episode of anal intercourse with an infected partner is considerably higher—probably on the order of 1 in 50 to 100.[36] This risk with anal intercourse is higher because the lining of the rectum is very delicate and tears easily during anal sex, readily allowing

FIGURE 14.3
THE IMMUNE RESPONSE

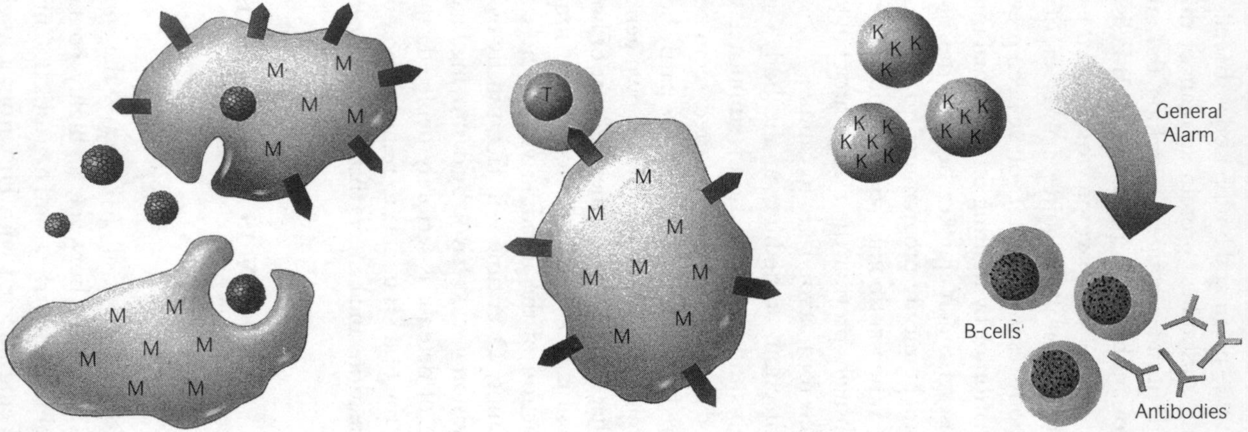

General
Alarm

Antibodies

B-cells

K K K
K K K

K K K
K K K

M M
M
M M
M

T

M M M
M
M

M M M
M M
M

1. When infectious microbes gain entry to
the body, macrophages [M] attack and
engulf them. Fragments of the ingested
microbes (antigens) are carried like flags
on the surface of some macrophages to
signal T-cells.

2. A helper T-cell [T] locks on
to the surface antigen and
is activated by chemical
messages from the
macrophage.

3. Once activated, the helper T-cell sounds
a general alarm, mobilizing killer T-cells
[K] and leading B-cells [B] to produce
antibodies.

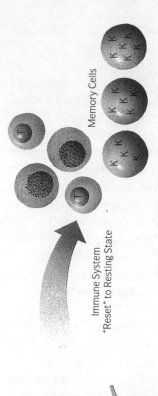

Immune System
"Reset" to Resting State

Memory Cells

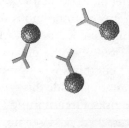

4. Infected cells are sought out and destroyed by killer T-cells, interrupting the disease-causing replication cycle.

5. Antibodies manufactured by B-cells bind to the invading microbes, inhibiting their infectiousness and targeting them for attack and destruction.

6. When the infection is controlled, an "all clear" is sent to the entire immune system via chemical signals. Specialized antigen-specific memory cells remain permanently to provide a swift response against another invasion by the same microbe.

infected white blood cells and HIV in the ejaculate to enter the tissue and bloodstream of the receptive partner (whether male or female).

Since the risk of catching gonorrhea from a single heterosexual exposure to an infected partner is 50 percent for women and 25 percent for men, and the risk of sexual transmission of hepatitis B appears to be more than 8 times greater than the risk of transmitting HIV,[37] it is clear that HIV is far less contagious. Nevertheless, anyone who engages in risky sexual activity has a small but definite chance, each time, of becoming infected with HIV—and the more chances taken and the more exposures, the greater the likelihood of infection. What's more, there have been numerous instances documented in which infection occurred with a single episode of heterosexual inter-course,[38] which means that even though the *average* risk may be only 1 in 500 per sexual encounter, there is still a chance that HIV can be transmitted with only one sexual contact.

While it is certain that vaginal and anal sexual intercourse are the primary means by which HIV is transmitted, it is also clear that it can be transmitted by other forms of sexual activity (see Table 14.1).

Oral-genital sex, which is known to transmit every other form of STD, has now been shown conclusively to be a means of transmitting HIV.[39] Earlier difficulties in proving that oral-genital sex could transmit HIV infec-tion primarily reflected the problem of finding people who had engaged exclusively in oral-genital contact and never in coitus or intravenous drug use.[40] Thus, one study of 45 married couples in which one spouse had AIDS found that the frequency of oral-genital sex correlated with the previously uninfected partner's becoming infected with HIV,[41] but this was not proof of a cause-effect relationship. (Correlational studies cannot provide this type of proof.) While it does not appear at present that the risk of transmitting HIV via oral-genital sex is as high as the risk during coitus, there has been no way based on current knowledge to quantify the risk precisely. It would certainly seem sensible in an individual set of circumstances to assume that the risk is higher if you or your partner have cuts or sores on the genitals, on the lips, or inside the mouth, but this doesn't help in determining the magnitude of risk for oral-genital sex when such conditions are not present. However, it is important to remember that oral-genital sex cannot "create" the AIDS virus if one person isn't already infected: if you are certain that both you and your partner are uninfected, there is no reason to abstain from oral sex.

There has been a great deal of skepticism about whether French kissing, or soul kissing (which involves exchanging saliva with your partner), can transmit HIV. While some reports claiming to document such transmissions have appeared,[42] there is also evidence that saliva inactivates HIV (at least in the laboratory setting). Furthermore, the concentration of HIV is much lower in saliva than in blood or semen. On the other hand, since it is very common to have minor cuts or abrasions of the gums, lips, or inner mouth that may provide a place for the virus to enter, it is a biologically plausible possibility. That it may be an actuality, under some circumstances, is suggested by one recent report that described the transmission of HIV infection from a 70-year-old woman who had been infected by a blood transfusion to her 72-year-old husband, who had had no sexual activity other than passionate kissing for many years.[43]

Absolute, incontrovertible proof that HIV can or cannot be transmitted by

TABLE 14.1

RISK ESTIMATES OF HIV TRANSMISSION FROM VARIOUS SEXUAL PRACTICES

SAFER—PROBABLY NO RISK FOR HIV TRANSMISSION

- abstention from sexual contact
- monogamous relationship, both partners uninfected
- self-masturbation
- touching, massaging, hugging, stroking
- dry kissing (social kissing)

LOW BUT REAL RISK FOR HIV TRANSMISSION

- anal or vaginal intercourse with proper use of intact condom
- French kissing
- fellatio without ejaculation in the mouth
- genital-genital contact without penetration
- contact with urine (exclusive of contact with mouth, rectum, or cuts or breaks in the skin)

UNSAFE—MODERATE RISK FOR TRANSMITTING HIV

- fellatio with ejaculation in the mouth
- cunnilingus (risk may be greater during menstruation when blood is present or if there are sores in the mouth)
- sharing sex toys and implements
- sex play (such as S/M activities) that causes bleeding

UNSAFE—HIGH RISK FOR TRANSMITTING HIV

- numerous sexual partners
- unprotected anal receptive sex with infected partner
- unprotected anal penetration with the hand (fisting)
- anal douching in combination with anal sex
- oral-anal contact (rimming)
- vaginal intercourse with an infected partner without a condom

SOURCE: Modified from T. Cohen, M. A. Sande, and P. A. Volberding, eds., *The AIDS Knowledge Base*, 1990, Chapter 11.1.4.

French kissing is not yet available and may be extremely difficult to obtain. Nevertheless, it is clearly possible that this type of transmission could occur. While this doesn't mean you should demand a medical certificate from your partner before embarking on a first kiss, or that kissing should be reserved only for long-term relationships, it would certainly be wisest to avoid French kissing a person you know to be infected with HIV.

Substantial evidence has accumulated showing that having another STD is an important risk factor for becoming infected with HIV via sexual contacts. (Such a risk factor is often referred to as a cofactor, a condition that plays a causative role, although it is not the sole cause of the infection.) This observation was first made in Africa, where the high rate of coexistent STDs (especially those causing genital sores or ulcers) is thought to be particularly important in the large proportion of heterosexually transmitted cases of HIV infection.[44] The association between other STDs and HIV infection has been noted in the United States as well. For example, researchers in Baltimore found an association between syphilis and HIV infection in men and a similar association with a history of genital warts in women.[45] Studies have also found that the risk of HIV infection is substantially higher in people with genital herpes than in others.[46] However, heterosexual transmission is possible even when there are no other STDs present.[47]

NONSEXUAL TRANSMISSION

Aside from sexual transmission, the major route by which HIV is transmitted is by intravenous drug users sharing needles or syringes that are contaminated by small amounts of infected blood. Once infected in this way, someone can then pass on the infection by sexual contact as well as by further sharing of needles.

Intravenous drug users may have a higher susceptibility than others to infection with HIV because their general health and nutritional status are often poor and their immune defenses may already be partly broken down by other illnesses.

The AIDS virus can also be transmitted by the transfusion of contaminated blood or blood products. In the 1990s, 2 to 3 percent of AIDS cases in the United States had fallen into this category, although the figure had previously been higher.[48] The routine use since 1985 of screening tests to detect HIV antibodies in donated blood and blood products (see pages 404–5) has substantially lessened the risk of using contaminated blood for transfusions. However, the blood supply is not completely safe because the screening tests are not foolproof, as we will discuss shortly. As a result, it is estimated that there are still about 1,000 cases a year in which the recipient of a blood transfusion is infected with HIV because of receiving a contaminated unit of blood.[49] To put this number in perspective, although the risk of HIV infection with a single unit of transfused blood is approximately 1 in 40,000, this is much safer than the risk of dying from general anesthesia (about 1 in 10,000).

Because of this small but real risk, some people having elective, non-emergency surgery have donated their own blood months or weeks before their surgery and have had it frozen and stored so it can be used if needed in a transfusion. This procedure has received strong endorsements from the medical community.[50] In addition to preventing any chance of inadvertently transmitting HIV, it also has the benefit of completely eliminating the risk of other transfusion-linked infections, such as hepatitis.

It is important to recognize that there is absolutely no risk to *giving* blood as long as a sterile needle is used, which is standard and mandatory procedure throughout the United States and Canada.

HIV can also be transmitted from an infected mother to her developing child during pregnancy or childbirth. Current research suggests that 20 to 50 percent of infants born to infected mothers will be infected,[51] although how many of these children will develop AIDS is not known at present. Because of the high risk that the baby will be born HIV-infected, women infected with HIV should not become pregnant if they can help it. Most experts also feel that a woman who is infected with HIV who becomes pregnant should consider having an abortion, although of course this is a complicated personal decision. The best solution is for women who are infected with HIV to avoid pregnancy completely.

HIV can also be transmitted from a sperm donor or an organ transplant donor to an uninfected person, although instances of this sort are rare.[52] Nevertheless, the possibility of transmission in this fashion has led several states to pass legislation requiring that all sperm donors be screened for HIV.

Another type of transmission happens during breast feeding. Since HIV appears in breast milk,[53] it can be passed from a mother to her nursing infant.[54] Furthermore, several cases have been reported from a Russian hospital where babies who had been infected by a contaminated syringe infected their mothers during nursing. Presumably, blood from sores in the baby's mouth entered the mother's body through cracks in the mother's nipples.[55]

HIV can also be transmitted by needle-stick injuries, which occur when doctors or nurses giving someone an injection (or drawing a blood sample) accidentally stick themselves with the needle after it has been used. It is currently thought that HIV transmission occurs in less than one-half of one percent of such injuries.[56] In contrast, the risk of infection with hepatitis B virus after such an exposure is estimated to be 23 to 43 percent, and the

CDC estimates that more than 10,000 cases of occupationally acquired hepatitis B occur annually in the United States.[57] At least one instance of HIV infection due to contaminated acupuncture needles has also been reported.[58]

HOW HIV IS *NOT* TRANSMITTED

Despite the finding of a low degree of infectiousness, many people have been so frightened by the AIDS epidemic that they worry that HIV infection might be transmitted by casual contact such as shaking hands with an infected person or coming in contact with the virus on a doorknob, toilet seat, or water fountain. Researchers agree that such fears are unfounded: there is no evidence at all that the AIDS virus is transmitted by casual contact of this sort.[59] While HIV has been identified in blood, tears, urine, saliva, semen, and vaginal secretions,[60] many studies have shown that people in close daily contact with persons with AIDS—such as a parent caring for a child with AIDS and nurses, doctors, and dentists working closely with AIDS patients—do not develop HIV infections from these contacts.[61] In many instances, of course, family members share drinking glasses or eating utensils with a person with AIDS, yet transmission of HIV by such acts has never been demonstrated.

Earlier concerns that the AIDS virus might be transmitted by insects such as mosquitoes now have been put to rest. Although HIV can survive for 48 hours in mosquitoes fed on infected blood,[62] there is no indication that the virus reproduces inside mosquitoes or any other type of insect. Furthermore, if HIV were transmitted by insect bites, there would likely be a high rate of infection in preadolescent children in Africa and other tropical areas, but there is no evidence that this has occurred.[63]

PROTECTING AGAINST HIV INFECTION: SAFER SEX GUIDELINES

Experts are somewhat divided on exactly what constitutes "safe" sex. Complete abstinence is one solution, but this option isn't appealing to most people. Another possibility is a mutually monogamous relationship with an uninfected partner. While there is no way to tell by someone's appearance if he or she is free of HIV, a blood test can be done to detect whether or not HIV infection is present (see pages 404–5). If you and your partner are both tested and are found to be uninfected and you remain sexually faithful to each other, you are effectively assured that you won't get AIDS (making allowances for the slim chance of becoming infected by nonsexual means such as a blood transfusion). If such an approach is either impractical or unrealistic in your circumstances, the following guidelines may be of some help.

1. *Completely safe sex is possible if there is no exchange of body fluids.* While this means cutting out oral sex and intercourse as options—because even without ejaculation there is a danger of transmitting HIV in preejaculatory fluid and vaginal secretions—techniques such as massage, use of vibrators, and mutual masturbation can be used. In addition, any sexual practices that can cause injury or rips in tissue should be avoided, too.

2. *Proper and consistent use of condoms will greatly reduce the risk of transmission of HIV as a result of sexual contact.* Studies have found that the pores of latex ("synthetic") condoms are so small that even viruses cannot pass through, and thus latex condoms, used properly, can prevent the transmission of HIV.[64] (So-called natural membrane or animal skin condoms do occasionally leak virus particles, and thus are not recommended.)[65] However, since improper use of condoms or a tear in the condom can certainly lead to leakage, this method is *not* a foolproof means of preventing infection (see Chapter 9). In fact, condoms fail more often than you might think. One survey found that 22 percent of heterosexuals and 31 percent of homosexuals had experienced condom failure in the preceding 3 months.[66] Remember, condoms are not perfect contraceptives, and they're not perfect barriers to HIV or other STDs, either.

3. *Use of spermicides containing nonoxynol-9 may offer additional protection.* Nonoxynol-9 kills HIV under laboratory conditions,[67] although under real life conditions it may not provide as much protection as a condom. The best solution seems to be to use *both* a condom and a spermicide with nonoxynol-9 during intercourse.

4. *Be selective in choosing your sex partners.* As we've already noted, it isn't possible to judge who's infected with HIV by any symptoms, since it can take years after becoming infected for symptoms to develop. Furthermore, the great majority of people who are infected with HIV don't realize they're infected, so don't rely on a potential sex partner to warn you that there may be a danger of transmission. Under current conditions, it is prudent to realize that people who have had a large number of sex partners and people who inject drugs are statistically more likely to have been exposed to and infected by HIV. Similarly, males who have had same-sex experiences in the past decade are statistically more likely to be infected with HIV. Selectivity regarding a prospective sex partner can be lifesaving.

5. *Learn as much as you can about someone before you have sex together, but don't blindly trust whatever you are told.* Research shows that people often lie about how many sex partners they have had.[68] *The Kinsey Institute New Report on Sex* notes, "Researchers suspect people are even more likely to lie about homosexual activity, sex with prostitutes, or the use of illegal drugs."[69]

6. *Stay away from high-risk sexual activity with a new partner until you have developed enough trust and rapport in your relationship to know each other fairly well.* While you shouldn't necessarily refrain from all sexual contact with a new partner for a period of months, it is perfectly sensible to start out slowly and to be forthright about which types of sex you'd prefer to leave until later in the relationship.

These guidelines need to be applied with a certain amount of common sense in order to be most useful to you. For example, we don't think it's advisable to have sexual intercourse (gay or straight) with a partner you know is infected with HIV, even if you use a condom. (We are sensitive to the problems this advice poses in long-term, committed relationships, including marriages, when one partner becomes infected and the other partner is not. Still, we stand by this position: condoms may reduce the risk of transmitting HIV, but they are far from fail-safe.) Likewise, if you suspect (but can't prove) that a prospective sexual partner has been an intravenous drug user, it may be most prudent to evaluate the situation cautiously and refuse to have any sexual contact without first having blood tests done.

DETECTING HIV INFECTION

Several different blood tests can be used to detect HIV antibodies. The most widely used test is called ELISA (for enzyme-linked immunoabsorbent assay); it was developed to screen blood used for transfusions. Like all biomedical tests, ELISA is not infallible, although the accuracy of current versions of ELISA, which is very high, is improved substantially from 5 years ago. ELISA tests fail to detect HIV antibodies in about 0.3 percent of samples known to be positive (a mistake known as a "false negative"). In addition, this test incorrectly "finds" HIV antibodies in about 1 percent of samples (in other words, using the ELISA test alone, 1 out of 100 tests will be mistakenly called positive when it actually is not—a situation known as a "false positive").[70]

Because of these inaccuracies, which may seem minor from a statistical viewpoint but which are certainly anything *but* minor if they involve *your* test, it is important to verify any positive result found by ELISA by using a different, more complicated (and expensive) test after repeating the ELISA test. This confirmatory test is called the Western blot test. When used together (ELISA test first, repeated if positive, and then confirmed by the Western blot test), the accuracy of testing for HIV antibodies is much better than most other medical screening tests, although even this method of screening is not perfect. In fact, several laboratories have reported false positive rates of less than 1 in 100,000 tests using these two tests combined.[71]

Testing is complicated somewhat by the fact that infrequently, a person may be infected with HIV for more than 2 years before antibodies become detectable by either ELISA or Western blot testing.[72] In addition, in rare cases a person who was initially seropositive (that is, had detectable HIV antibodies) may become seronegative (have no detectable HIV antibodies in the bloodstream), even though he or she is still infected with HIV.[73] In such cases, it appears that HIV "hides" in macrophages and monocytes, where it is somehow camouflaged from the usual testing. Fortunately, the incidence of disappearing HIV antibodies is low—0.4 percent (4 out of 1,000 persons tested)—and the phenomenon is still of uncertain significance.

A false positive test result can be caused by technical error in performing the test or a clerical error in identifying the blood sample. A false positive result can also occur if some substance in the blood reacts with chemicals used in the test so that a mistaken reading is given. (False positives are more common in women than in men and may be related to previous pregnancy.)

Despite these various possibilities and problems with testing, we should stress that a confirmed positive test *is* cause for concern and should be followed up by careful long-term medical evaluation. In addition, as noted emphatically by a panel of experts, "All persons who are antibody positive for HIV, whether they are symptom free or ill, must be considered to be potentially infectious to others by sexual transmission, by sharing of drug injection equipment, by childbearing, or by donation of blood, semen, or organs."[74]

It is important to realize that finding HIV antibodies in someone's blood does not, by itself, mean that the person has AIDS. Until 1993, the diagnosis of AIDS was made when a major disease such as *Pneumocystis carinii* pneumonia or Kaposi's sarcoma that signals an underlying deficiency in the immune system occurred in the absence of other conditions known to be risk factors for these illnesses. AIDS could also be diagnosed if a person had a positive HIV antibody test, evidence of a suppressed immune system (for instance, a low T cell count), and at least one disease from a list of some of the lesser infections associated with AIDS. As of January 1, 1993, however, the U.S. Public Health Service and Centers for Disease Control and Prevention revised and expanded the criteria used to diagnose AIDS to include all HIV-infected persons who have a CD4+ T-cell count below

200 and to add three "AIDS-defining" conditions—pulmonary tuberculosis, recurrent pneumonia, and invasive cervical cancer—to the previously established conditions.[75] The impact of this change will be discussed
shortly.

THE STAGES OF HIV INFECTION

As we have already noted, it is important to observe the entire spectrum of
HIV disease instead of simply looking at AIDS, because HIV is a slow-acting
virus. People who become infected today may not have any symptoms of
their infection for 10 years or more, although sometimes they become ill at a
much more rapid pace. Despite such variability, it is clear that HIV infection
is a chronic, progressive disease.[76] Full-blown AIDS is the end-stage of an
infection that begins long before we can recognize that people are physically
ill. Understanding this progression can help our understanding both of
people who are infected with HIV and of what we can do to avoid this
infection.

INITIAL INFECTION

No matter how someone is infected with HIV, when this virus enters the
bloodstream the person's immune system typically responds by producing
antibodies to the invading organism. Most people have no symptoms that
accompany the initial infection or the production of antibodies, but 10 to 25
percent may have a brief illness that occurs 2 to 5 weeks after the virus enters
the body.[77] Symptoms include fever, chills, aches, swollen lymph glands, and
itchy rashes, symptoms similar to those of infectious mononucleosis, or
"mono." Because of the nonspecific nature of these symptoms, which are
frequent accompaniments to many types of viral infections—including the
common cold—do *not* assume that a 2-day bout of swollen glands, a runny
nose, and fever means you've been infected with HIV! Antibodies to HIV
can usually be detected within 2 months after the initial infection, but there
are some cases in which antibodies do not appear for a year or longer.[78]

THE ASYMPTOMATIC CARRIER STATE

The infected person then passes into a phase called the asymptomatic carrier
state. (Asymptomatic means symptomless.) In this phase, a person looks and
feels perfectly healthy, but the infection is present and antibodies persist.
Many asymptomatic carriers also have a reduced number of T-helper cells in

their blood. *The presence of the live virus in the asymptomatic carrier state means that such a person can infect others without realizing that he or she is infected.* It is important to understand that asymptomatic carriers do not have AIDS (the illness), although they are infected with the virus that causes AIDS.

Here, from our files, are some personal reactions that illustrate the surprise and anguish many people who are asymptomatic HIV carriers express on learning of a positive test result:

A 23-year-old married woman: I was tested for HIV when I applied for an overseas job. When the results came back, I was absolutely sure they were wrong. There was no way I could have been infected, I thought. I never messed around, I never did drugs, and I never had a blood transfusion. Plus, I had never felt better in my life. But it turned out that my husband was positive, too, and that he had a bisexual affair when he was a sophomore in college. I was devastated, let me tell you.

A 28-year-old male rock musician: I found out I was infected when I went to donate blood for a friend who was having surgery. It sounds so simple now, but I was stunned when I heard the news. The counselor at the blood bank told me, "How can you be surprised? You've got about every risk factor in the book." Now that I've come to terms with it, I guess I had led a pretty wild life, but it's tough to think that I'll be dead in a few years unless they find some cure.

A 26-year-old gay man: When someone from the public health department called to tell me that one of my sex partners from a few years back had come down with AIDS, I had nightmares every night. I kept putting off the time to go get tested, because I didn't want to get the news. And I kept saying to myself, "Relax—you feel so good; you couldn't possibly be sick." But I finally went for testing and found out just what I didn't want to hear. What do I do now about my sex life? Do I tell someone "I've got it" just before we get it on? And what do I tell the people I've been with the past few years? "Oh, hey, I got it from Larry and now I've passed it on to you"?

It is uncertain how long infected people can remain asymptomatic before they develop signs of illness. Many individuals remain in the asymptomatic carrier state for periods of 5 years or longer before developing AIDS or related symptoms. Current evidence suggests that about 20 percent of asymptomatic carriers will develop full-blown cases of AIDS within 6 years,[79] and some data suggest that with the passage of additional time, as many as 99 percent may eventually develop AIDS.[80] The best long-term data now available, based on blood samples frozen and stored as part of a hepatitis study conducted in San Francisco in the late 1970s, show that 11 years after infection with HIV, 53 percent of subjects had progressed to full-blown AIDS, and under a quarter of the subjects were still symptom-free.[81]

Much remains to be done to clarify how and when HIV infection progresses to AIDS. Different groups may have different rates of progression. For instance, homosexual men seem to develop full-scale AIDS more rapidly than hemophiliacs do.[82] Similarly, adults over age 35 who are infected with HIV have been reported to progress more rapidly to AIDS than younger adults and adolescents.[83] Such differences may be a result of various factors. For example, repeated infections with HIV may reactivate the virus when it has been relatively dormant in the body. It is also possible that persons who have current or past infections with other viruses (for instance, the hepatitis B virus) may be most at risk for developing AIDS. Another theory is that use of certain illicit drugs—most particularly, volatile nitrites like amyl nitrite ("poppers")—may somehow set the stage for developing AIDS more easily by lowering natural resistance to HIV. Whether any of these theories will prove correct is uncertain at present.

It is also important to realize that there have been only relatively brief follow-up studies done on people infected with HIV, a fact that is understandable since this infection was first identified in the early 1980s. It is possible that 15 or 20 years after infection, unless a cure or other form of treatment is found, most people will progress to full-blown AIDS or will have died from other complications of HIV infection. On the other hand, since data from the 1980s is based primarily on HIV infection in homosexual males and in IV drug users, it is possible that this pattern may not accurately predict the experience that will be found in heterosexual, non-drug-abusing populations.

SYMPTOMATIC HIV INFECTION

In some people, HIV infection leads to symptoms that are less serious than AIDS itself. This stage was previously known as AIDS-related complex (ARC), but this term has now been generally discarded after the recognition that it was not a specific disease entity and had no special significance for treatment or outcome.[84] Symptomatic HIV infection should be understood as part of a continuum of effects. As HIV multiplies within the body over time, it slowly destroys immune defenses. As these defenses deteriorate, susceptibility increases to a variety of infections that the immune system normally holds in check. These include non–life-threatening infections such as *shingles* or *thrush* (a fungus infection of the mouth), as well as more dangerous infections such as tuberculosis.

Symptomatic HIV infection is also commonly marked by persistent swelling of lymph nodes in several locations in the body (for example, the neck, the armpits, just above the collarbones), which can occur alone or with other symptoms. The most common symptoms are diarrhea, weight loss, fatigue, and fever, but these tend to be episodic, not constant. In addition, neurologic problems are frequently encountered.[85] However, it should be emphasized that many people with symptomatic HIV infection are well enough to lead relatively normal lives much of the time, continuing to work productively, to participate in sports and other recreational activities, and to appear quite healthy. Here is how one person described it.

A 32-year-old male architect: I've been infected with HIV for more than 6 years now. Until last year I was completely free of any symptoms, but this year I've lost 12 pounds and have started to have occasional bouts of night sweats and fevers. But I still manage to jog three miles each day, play tennis on most weekends, and keep an active social calendar. My doctor tells me that staying in good physical condition will help my fight against this killer—and so far it has.

Unfortunately, people with symptomatic HIV infection do not always realize they are infected, either because their condition has been misdiagnosed, because they haven't gone to a doctor, or because they minimize the significance of the physical problems they are having. People in this situation may unknowingly and unintentionally expose their sex partners to HIV infection.

It is virtually inevitable that all people with symptomatic HIV infection will eventually develop AIDS.[86]

AIDS AND ITS SYMPTOMS

While no single pattern of signs and symptoms fits all cases of AIDS, some of the most common are similar to those of symptomatic HIV infection: progressive, unexplained weight loss, persistent fever (sometimes accompanied by night sweats), swollen lymph nodes, and slightly raised reddish-purple coin-sized spots on the skin. These skin spots often turn out to be a form of cancer of the small blood vessels, a condition called Kaposi's sarcoma (often abbreviated as "KS"). Kaposi's sarcoma was unusual in the United States before the start of the HIV epidemic. However, about one-quarter of homosexual males with AIDS in the United States have been found to have Kaposi's sarcoma, although KS is relatively rare in heterosexual IV drug users and hemophiliacs with AIDS.[87]

When symptoms of AIDS first appear they may remain unchanged for many months or they may be quickly followed by one or more opportunistic infections: that is, infections that occur when immunity is broken down. One of the most common of these infections is the unusual, often-fatal form of pneumonia caused by *Pneumocystis carinii*, the presence of which established the diagnosis of AIDS in almost two-thirds of the cases seen in the United States prior to 1993.

Among other common infections in people with AIDS are severe fungal infections (including a form that spreads to the covering of the brain, causing meningitis), tuberculosis, and various forms of herpes that are more severe and recur more often than usual. Encephalitis (inflammation of the brain) is another life-threatening condition that occurs with greatly increased frequency in people with AIDS. In fact, because HIV can directly infect brain cells, a variety of neurological disturbances are seen in an estimated 30 to 65 percent of AIDS patients.[88] These conditions include memory disturbances, psychiatric symptoms, severe mental confusion (dementia), difficulty walking, seizures, and coma. Although treatment can often temporarily fend off these infections, the typical course is for one after another overwhelming infection to occur until the victim finally dies because the depressed condition of the immune system becomes progressively worse, leading eventually to one final infection that cannot be overcome.

The human side of these symptoms is difficult to grasp unless you have been involved personally in caring for someone with AIDS. Here is a description offered by one man who took care of his brother for the last year of the brother's life, as they both dealt with this devastating disease.

> Tom was determined to handle his affairs with dignity. While he was a realist until the very end, he was also able to look at the cards life had dealt him without bitterness or a sense of defeat. "Everyone's got to die sometime" was a phrase he used over and over again, mostly to cheer his visitors out of their dismay at his appearance. Still, once he became so weak that he was unable to walk more than a few steps at a time, we both realized things were going downhill rapidly. What worried him most of all was that he might develop AIDS dementia. Fortunately, even through three hospitalizations and a ferocious bout of shingles, Tom's mind stayed sharp until he was done living. While this was an emotionally trying time for us all, it gave me a chance to get to know my brother on a level I never would have known him before.

At present, AIDS is almost always fatal within a matter of 2 to 4 years after it is first diagnosed.[89] (The median survival for AIDS patients in San Francisco is 12.5 months, with fewer than 9 percent of patients surviving for 3 years.)[90] Despite these statistics, many people with AIDS are able to lead relatively normal lives early in the course of their disease, although coping with the social, economic, and emotional aspects of their illness is especially difficult for many, as we will discuss shortly. As more treatments are developed and become available for AIDS and for the severe infections associated with it, both the quality and length of life for people with AIDS will improve substantially.

While some people with AIDS continue their employment and usual activities for 6 months or more after the diagnosis is established, eventually the weight loss, constant fatigue, and multiple infections take such a toll that even ordinary movement becomes a major effort and the person becomes an invalid. (In Africa, AIDS is often called "slim" because in its late stages its victims look as if they had been starving.)

TREATMENT OF HIV INFECTION AND AIDS

Although as of late 1993 no successful cure for AIDS or HIV infection has been found, there are some definite signs of progress against this disease. Most notable has been the identification of a drug called AZT (azidothymidine or zidovudine, marketed in the United States under the trade name Retrovir), which has proved to be an effective treatment. AZT was initially found to slow the progression of disease in patients with full-blown AIDS. Subsequent studies not only confirmed that AZT delayed the progression of disease in AIDS patients[91] and patients with asymptomatic HIV infection[92] but also showed that it could be effective in lower doses than were used initially.[93] By using lower doses, it is possible to minimize the serious side effects many people experience with this drug,[94] the most common of which is suppression of bone marrow function. Since the bone marrow serves to produce new blood cells, suppression of this function causes severe anemia (low red blood cell count, which causes severe fatigue) and lowering of the white blood cell count (further reducing the body's ability to fight infections).

The belief that AZT can prolong life for people with HIV infection was one major reason why AIDS experts began calling for early detection and treatment.[95] However, there is evidence that some strains of HIV develop resistance to AZT when they are exposed to the drug over long time periods.[96] If this resistance becomes widespread, the overall utility of using AZT will be reduced considerably. Furthermore, recent studies in Europe have found that the duration of AZT's benefits may be limited and that it may not actually prolong life to a meaningful extent,[97] raising additional questions about the overall utility of this treatment. Fortunately, additional drugs are available to be used in place of or in combination with AZT, including DDI (didanosine), which was approved by the Food and Drug Administration in 1991.[98]

Progress has also been made in treating some of the infections that are the actual causes of death in people with AIDS. For example, a drug called pentamidine helps to prevent *Pneumocystis carinii* pneumonia; other drugs are available for fighting encephalitis and other life-threatening complications of AIDS.

Additional interest is focused on a variety of experimental drugs that are being rapidly developed to assist in the fight against the HIV epidemic. Among the dozens of approaches that appear most promising are:

1. *Synthetic CD4.* CD4 is the receptor on the surface of T-helper cells that is unlocked by gp 120, a surface protein on HIV. By creating synthetic forms of CD4, which are infused into the bloodstream, HIV is lured to these "decoy" molecules and is thus prevented from attaching to as many healthy T-helper cells. While this approach has been found to work in the laboratory, it is not yet ready for full-scale testing in humans. The problem is partly that the synthetic CD4 doesn't live very long in the body.

2. *Enzyme blockers.* A number of scientists are searching for ways to block the key enzymes HIV needs to replicate itself. One of these is an enzyme called protease; if it could be blocked effectively, HIV would be unable to multiply within T cells or macrophages, and thus would be unlikely to seriously harm the immune system.[99] While progress with this approach is still in its early stages, many experts feel this offers the best possibility for effective treatment.

3. *Vaccines.* Vaccines can be used either to *prevent* infection from occurring or treat an infection after it has occurred. Dr. Jonas Salk, famed developer of the first polio vaccine, has tried the latter approach with some preliminary signs of success. First, he and his colleague, Dr. Clarence Gibbs, Jr., a virologist, developed an AIDS vaccine that contained killed HIV cells. Then they administered the vaccine to two chimpanzees who had already been infected with HIV. Both chimps had a sharp rise in HIV antibodies. A third chimpanzee, who was not infected with HIV, also had a sharp rise in anti-HIV antibodies after two immunizations.[100] Finally, Salk and Gibbs gave the vaccine to 19 people who were infected with HIV, all of whom had low T-cell count and other evidence of badly damaged immune systems. Although the vaccine did not eliminate the virus, only one of them had developed symptoms of AIDS within a year, and 8 had a notable improvement in their immune system.[101]

Progress has also been made in the search for a preventive vaccine, which, if successfully developed, would be a key element in actually halting the world-wide spread of HIV infection.[102] Researchers have recently succeeded in producing a vaccine that protected 8 out of 9 monkeys against simian AIDS (an AIDS-like disease caused by a retrovirus closely related to HIV).[103] On the basis of this finding, many experts now believe that it will be possible eventually to develop a safe and effective AIDS vaccine for human use, although most suspect that it will take 5 to 10 years to accomplish this task.[104]

One of the technical difficulties in devising a workable vaccine is that there are several different strains of HIV against which the vaccine must protect simultaneously. Another practical problem is that in order to be effective, a vaccine must have long-lasting protective effects—measured in years, not weeks or months. Whether such long-lasting immunity against HIV can be devised is uncertain at present.

Another difficulty is that vaccines work by triggering a person's immune system to produce antibodies that help to kill a virus. In HIV infection, however, the antibodies that are usually produced seem to be unable to kill the virus, which is why people with HIV antibodies eventually go on to develop AIDS. Overcoming this hurdle may be the primary stumbling block in developing an effective vaccine.

Finally, the matter of safety is also of paramount importance: in any vaccine containing killed virus, there is always a slight risk that some viral particles survive or get reactivated, so that once injected into an individual, they can cause the very disease they are intended to prevent. Despite such obstacles, development of the monkey vaccine is a major step forward in the fight against the HIV epidemic,[105] although progress is being made far more slowly than people had hoped.[106]

CARING FOR PEOPLE WITH AIDS

Because people with AIDS may have only minimal symptoms of their disease, may be struggling against acute, life-threatening infections, or may be anywhere on the spectrum between these two extremes, special care and support systems have been devised in many cities to provide a broad range of necessary services to those who need help. In San Francisco, for example, the following components exist:[107]

1. a walk-in clinic for everyone from the "worried well" to those who are dying;
2. a specialized AIDS inpatient unit for those requiring hospitalization;
3. an extensive array of community-based care, including the following services that are provided at the residence of the person with AIDS: assistance with shopping, housecleaning, meal preparation, special nursing services, legal assistance, and obtaining necessary medications;

4. volunteer organizations providing a variety of forms of support (the best-known of these groups in San Francisco is the Shanti Project, which assigns a trained volunteer counselor to every person newly diagnosed with AIDS and provides a wide range of services, from ongoing support groups to low cost housing for those who need it);

5. a hospice program for those in the terminal stage of illness. Hospices aim to make a dying person's last weeks or months more comfortable, both physically and psychologically, by providing a broad range of services. In addition to providing care aimed at minimizing the person's distress when no cure is realistically possible, hospices generally try to deal with many aspects of the lives of their patients, including spiritual needs, family matters, and legal and financial concerns. Hospices also help family members and friends deal with grieving and loss.

Across the country, community volunteers and both families and friends of people with AIDS are learning new ways of relating and communicating: of bringing caring, compassion, and dignity as powerful tools to deal with this epidemic. While it would be a mistake to believe that this action completely counterbalances the prejudices against people with HIV infection and AIDS that exist in many segments of our society, it is certainly a much-needed step in the right direction.

WHEN SOMEONE YOU KNOW HAS AIDS

When a devastating illness like AIDS strikes a family member or friend, it is natural to feel unable to offer much help or hope and to think you can't do anything that would make a difference. Instead of giving in to these feelings, here are some concrete suggestions for what you *can* do to make a difference.

• Simply being there as often as you've been in the past (or maybe even a little more often) is one of the best ways to convey your concern and caring. But be sure to call first. Let your friend decide if he or she wants a visitor right at that time.

• Offer to help out in various ways. Washing dishes, doing the grocery shopping, or picking up the cleaning may seem like small tasks to you, but such help is likely to be greatly appreciated. Your effort is tangible proof that you care, so it is much more than "just" cooking dinner or doing a few chores.

• You should realize that dealing with a fatal disease is not simple. You can get many helpful hints from AIDS groups in your area, but recognize that they don't make you an expert on the subject. So don't try to be one—you will only create conflicts with your friend's health care providers.

• Be aware that holidays are a time when loneliness can be particularly hard to deal with. (This is especially true if your friend is in the hospital.) A special visit that helps your friend feel included in the holiday spirit is a thoughtful act. And creative use of decorations, snacks, or gifts with the holiday theme—like a Christmas stocking stuffed with hard candies, paperbacks, and toiletries—is a concrete way of leaving a reminder of your feelings even after your visit is over.

• While it isn't useful to dwell on all the details of your friend or relative's medical condition and treatment, don't pretend the illness doesn't exist. Questions like "How are you feeling?" are certainly appropriate (just as they would be for someone with any other type of illness).

• Include news of the outside world in your conversations to help your friend avoid feeling completely isolated and uninvolved. Tell him or her about mutual friends and what's going on at work, discuss your favorite sports teams, and bring up current-event items from the national and international scene.

• Reach out and touch your friend. A hug, a kiss, or an arm around his or her shoulder means more than you may realize.

• Don't lie to your friend about how he or she looks or how he or she is doing. You don't have to blurt out everything you're thinking—there is a place for tactful gentleness in all human relations. If you try, you can probably find something optimistic to focus on, even if the optimism has to be put in terms of hope for the future: "I bet things will be better by the weekend."

• Don't give your friend lectures if he or she isn't dealing with the illness in the way you think is best. You don't know what medical, legal, or other advice he or she has been given, and you can't know exactly what his or her feelings are.

• Realize that from time to time, your friend or relative may get angry with you even though you've tried to be helpful. When this happens, don't take it personally. Anger may be a way of venting feelings of inadequacy and helplessness when dealing with illness. In a way, it's a compliment that your friend knows you care for him or her enough to get angry with you, knowing deep inside that such feelings won't be misunderstood.

• Try to be in touch with significant others in your friend's or relative's life. They can help you stay informed about progress (or complications) on the medical front, which allows you to offer help when needed—help your friend may be embarrassed to ask for. For example, your friend's spouse or lover may need a break from nursing duties. You can offer to take over for a Saturday afternoon, so he or she can get out and attend to his or her own needs for awhile.

• Do not confuse acceptance of AIDS with resignation from living. Accepting the reality of this disease may free your friend or relative from a sense of turmoil and uncertainty. Acceptance can also provide your friend with a sense of his or her own power.

• If you have been particularly close to your friend or relative, recognize your own needs for support or counseling. Many AIDS organizations have support groups you can join for just this purpose.

PATTERNS OF THE EPIDEMIC: A LOOK AT THE NUMBERS

Regrettably, 12 years after the first recognition of AIDS and 8 years after the development of tests to detect antibodies to HIV, no national prevalence survey has been done to establish definitively the exact dimensions of the HIV epidemic in the United States. (Prevalence denotes the proportion of a population that is currently infected.) In fact, former Surgeon General C. Everett Koop acknowledged this problem when he said, "How many are infected? That's our whole problem—we don't know that number. We use the number of a million or a million and a half, but it could be 400,000 or it could be 4 million. We just don't know."[108] Nevertheless, a substantial number of prevalence studies have been done in various segments of the population. By studying their range of results, it is possible to form a preliminary picture of the HIV epidemic as it currently exists.

Before considering these surveys, it is useful to look back at the evolution of the HIV epidemic from several different viewpoints. First, it is helpful to keep in mind that the early years of the HIV epidemic hit hardest in New York, New Jersey, and California. In fact, many scientists and politicians in the Midwest and in the South (outside of Florida) voiced doubts that AIDS would ever take much of a toll in their locales. While it is obvious today that this attitude of denial was incorrect, denial occurred in other ways as well. For example, as recently as the mid-1980s many scientists considered it unlikely that HIV could be transmitted by heterosexual intercourse, giving detailed explanations as to why the pattern in Africa and the Caribbean was somehow "different" from the United States. The AIDS epidemic was considered rather simplistically to be a problem of the gay community and of people who abused drugs. Even more recently, there have been many observers who contend that the epidemic is mainly a problem for minority communities—inner-city populations that are heavily black and Hispanic. This "ghettoization" of the problem also reflects a signal misunderstanding: HIV doesn't recognize skin color or social class when it invades a host.

PATTERNS AND TRENDS OF HIV INFECTION

Counting cases of AIDS only tells us what happened 7 to 10 years ago, because that is the average length of time from initial infection with HIV to the point where AIDS is diagnosed. Thus, to identify current trends in the epidemic, it is useful to examine information about the prevalence of HIV infection in various segments of the broader population. Here is a rundown on what is known.

Homosexual and Bisexual Males

In San Francisco and New York City, HIV infection among gay and bisexual men hovers around the 50 percent mark. Although it had previously been thought that communitywide education in these cities had resulted in careful adherence to safer sex guidelines, and thus no new cases of HIV infection were occurring in these groups, several recent studies have shown that a modest number of new infections are occurring in these groups annually.[109] Elsewhere in the United States, prevalence rates among homosexual and bisexual males are somewhat lower. For instance, in Milwaukee the figure recently stood at 24 percent, whereas in Albuquerque, New Mexico, it was 14 percent.[110] Similarly, a recent survey of homosexual men in 16 small cities across the country found that 9 percent were HIV positive.[111]

Intravenous Drug Users

Among IV drug users surveyed through treatment programs, hospitals, and drug treatment centers, HIV infection rates are considerably higher on the East Coast than on the West Coast. For instance, in New York City and northern New Jersey rates are in the 50 to 60 percent range,[112] and in Washington, D.C., one study reported a seroprevalence rate of 28 percent, which is similar to the rate reported from Baltimore. In contrast, in Los Angeles only a 3 percent seroprevalence rate was found,[113] and in Sacramento the seroprevalence rate in IV drug users participating in a drug treatment program was 2 percent.[114]

Heterosexuals

There have been relatively few studies of HIV infection in the general heterosexual population. One of the first studies (done in 1987) tested 800 heterosexual men and women in four locations (New York, Los Angeles, Atlanta, and St. Louis) and found that 5 percent of the men and 7 percent of the women with at least 6 sex partners a year for the preceding 5 years were seropositive.[115] (Having at least 6 sex partners a year would be considered by many to be an operational definition for promiscuity; we should also point out that only a small portion of the general heterosexual population would meet this criterion.) In contrast, none of the women and only 1 of 200 men in strictly monogamous relationships were seropositive.

A similar study of sexually active heterosexuals with no known risk factors for HIV infection was conducted by Margaret Fischl and her coworkers in Miami. Of 346 people they studied, 5 percent were seropositive, with the only potential risk factor identified being multiple sexual partners.[116] (This result was remarkably similar to that of our own study, described in the preceding paragraph, but Fischl's study has not been widely publicized.)

The appearance of HIV infection in middle-class heterosexuals, mainly as a result of sexual contact with IV drug users, is now being documented with increasing frequency.[117]

One interesting point to keep in mind is that in women, HIV infection appears to be linked increasingly to heterosexual transmission rather than to intravenous drug use.[118] For example, in New Jersey, the percentage of women who gave birth to HIV-infected babies whose only apparent risk factor was heterosexual intercourse rose from 14 percent in 1982 to 1985 to 43 percent in the time period from 1986 to 1988.[119]

AIDS SURVEILLANCE

AIDS cases have been reported in all 50 states, but the geographic distribution of cases—which has shifted over time—varies considerably from one region to another. In 1992, the annual incidence of reported cases of AIDS ranged from a high of 116 cases per 100,000 persons in Washington, D.C., and 46 per 100,000 persons in New York to a low of 0.9 per 100,000 persons in Wyoming.[120] Updated statistics are shown in Figure 14.4. Whereas before 1983 63 percent of all AIDS cases in the United States were reported from New York, New Jersey, and Pennsylvania, this proportion gradually dropped to below 30 percent of cases in 1992.

The U.S. Centers for Disease Control has noted that the reported cases of AIDS are underestimates because of incompleteness of reporting, delays in reporting, and the fact that not all persons with AIDS have access to adequate medical or diagnostic care, so that "reported AIDS cases may represent fewer than 80% of all cases of recognized or unrecognized severe morbidity associated with HIV infection."[121]

PERSONAL ASPECTS OF THE HIV EPIDEMIC

The HIV/AIDS epidemic has many faces. Thus far in this chapter, we have primarily examined its biologic side. But the epidemic also has intensely personal aspects.

SOCIAL AND EMOTIONAL REACTIONS

The impact of the HIV epidemic on our society has already been divisive and emotional. For many, the epidemic is a ready-made excuse for intensified prejudice against homosexuals, particularly among the misinformed, who think that shaking hands with a gay person or being served by a homosexual waiter could transmit a fatal infection. Some people have even suggested that everyone infected with HIV should be quarantined—a concept that is not only inhumane but also economically unfeasible since it would involve the enforced isolation for a period of many years of an estimated 1.5 million Americans now infected with HIV. Others are complacent about this major public health crisis because they mistakenly see AIDS as a problem confined to homosexuals, bisexuals, and drug users rather than a problem for American society as a whole.

Fortunately, our awareness of and sensitivity toward the HIV/AIDS epidemic has been heightened considerably in the past few years by a number of small steps that have succeeded in humanizing and demystifying the epidemic. One particularly noteworthy step in this direction was the creation of the AIDS Quilt Project, begun in 1987 by Cleve Jones. This project was started as a way of memorializing a friend who had died of AIDS. It has now grown to a giant quilt containing more than 11,000 panels sewn by friends and families of persons who have died.

Figure 14.4
U.S. AIDS Cases per 100,000 Population, by State,
July 1992–June 1993

(*Data from* Morbidity and Mortality Weekly Report *42: 587, 1993.*)

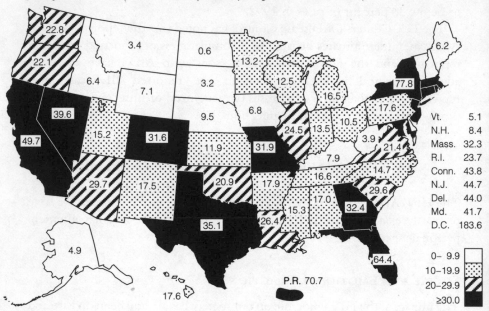

Vt.	5.1
N.H.	8.4
Mass.	32.3
R.I.	23.7
Conn.	43.8
N.J.	44.7
Del.	44.0
Md.	41.7
D.C.	183.6

0– 9.9	
10–19.9	
20–29.9	
≥30.0	

The Quilt Project has traveled around the country and been viewed by millions.

Other signs of increased awareness of the HIV/AIDS epidemic crop up in diverse places. In many cities, obituaries now routinely mention AIDS as a cause of death, in contrast to the situation just 5 or 6 years ago, when the topic seemed taboo. Fundraisers for AIDS research, hosted by well-known entertainers such as Elizabeth Taylor and Madonna, are frequent and successful. Even television soap operas have woven AIDS-related story lines into their scripts, although the same national television networks still refuse to air condom advertisements because of worries about the sensitivities of their viewers (and concerns about boycotts by right-wing groups).

In the gay community, which was clearly most directly affected in the first decade of the HIV epidemic, the initial fear and dismay quickly gave way to highly organized educational efforts combined with compassionate caring for people with AIDS and active lobbying for more government funding, antidiscrimination legislation, and streamlined guidelines for approving new treatment methods. Recognition of the realities of sexual transmission of HIV has generally led to widespread changes in the sexual behavior of this group: most gay men now avoid the bathhouse scene entirely and a large number have cut back to having sex with only a small number of partners who are well known to them.[122] In addition, a large majority of gay men have adopted safer sex practices, either by avoiding anal sex entirely or by carefully using condoms for anal intercourse.[123] As a result of these patterns, particularly the cutback in number of sexual partners, the incidence of other STDs such as gonorrhea and syphilis in gay men has also declined noticeably.

There are also some homosexual males who are so overwhelmed by fear of AIDS that they decide to be completely abstinent sexually until a vaccine or cure is found. In an occasional variation on this theme, a small number of male homosexuals and bisexuals have switched to heterosexual partners, at least temporarily. And, for reasons that are more than understandable, it is not unusual to find homosexual men who have developed such a degree of AIDS anxiety that they have become preoccupied with every minor physical ailment they experience. To these gay men, a sore throat, a skin rash, or a fever is a sign of impending doom, and they may even mistakenly tell their partners that they have AIDS before it is diagnosed. Among the very fearful it is common to see a sharp drop in sexual interest and sexual activity.

Anyone who discovers that one of his or her previous sex partners has AIDS or tests positive for HIV infection has definite reason for concern. So far in the epidemic, this situation has primarily affected gays and IV drug users, but heterosexuals are increasingly going to have to confront the same possibility as the HIV epidemic spreads into the broad population. Just how does it feel to be in such a situation?

A 28-year-old heterosexual man: I heard from a friend that a girl I used to date had come down with AIDS. At first I thought it was just a crazy story, something to try to scare me with, but when I checked it out I was horrified to discover it was true. God, I thought, we had sex together a couple of dozen times, and we never used a condom because she was on the pill. My doctor sent me for a blood test, which much to my relief came back okay, but in the 24 hours before I got that report I can only say that I had visions of a slow, agonizing death right before my eyes, and I was plenty worried. You can be sure that I'll remember this episode for a long time.

A 33-year-old divorced woman: I had been divorced for about three years when I found out my "ex" was in the hospital with AIDS. I knew he had messed around with drugs from time to time, but I never thought of him as addicted or anything like that. So this news shook me up pretty badly. When I was tested myself and the doctor told me I was positive, I broke down on the spot and cried. I have two kids, and I'm not ready to die. So far I've been lucky. My T cell count is pretty good and I haven't had any major problems, just some minor infections and stuff. But I am still furious that he did this to me, even though I know he didn't mean to.

For some heterosexuals, concern about AIDS is mounting as people become aware that AIDS is not just a homosexual disease. For instance, it is not unusual now for a person to ask a potential partner to have a blood test for anti-HIV antibody before beginning sexual relations. As one college-age woman told us, "It's not that I'm totally nervous about AIDS, but considering the stakes are so high, what's the purpose in pretending that everyone you'll meet will be honest? If someone doesn't care enough about me to have the test, the relationship isn't going to go anywhere anyway." But as we will discuss shortly, many heterosexuals continue to demonstrate complacency about their personal risks of encountering HIV or becoming infected with it.

Immediately after learning that they are infected with HIV or that they have AIDS, most people react with shock, anger, and denial. Here is how it is described by a counselor at one HIV testing center in New York:

> Typical responses have included crying hysterically, going blank and numb, ranting and shouting—"I'm going to die now!"—and questioning—"Did the test tell how long I have to live?" Some clients try to bolt out of the office. . . . Some clients report that they were prepared for this and have a plan of action/ treatment. Most clients, however, are "freaked out."[124]

These are perfectly normal defense mechanisms that can initially cushion the blow of receiving such a diagnosis. In the weeks or months after the diagnosis, this initial reaction typically undergoes a transition into guilt, sadness, and resignation to one's fate—a sort of unhappy acceptance of the situation. Of course, different people react in very different ways.

People who are diagnosed as being HIV infected or having AIDS are usually young adults who have generally been healthy, so they have relatively little preparation for facing a life-threatening disease with a very bleak prognosis. As if this were not difficult enough, those who are infected, whether gay or straight, must also face a hostile and fearful society. Many are ostracized at work, rejected by their family and friends, and put in a situation of social isolation.[125] It is emotionally difficult to find that your landlord wants to evict you, that your dentist refuses to take care of you any longer, or that your employer wants to fire you—all of which are uncalled-for discriminatory actions. Fortunately, federal legislation that prohibits discrimination against the disabled has been extended to apply to AIDS victims and people infected with HIV, but such legislation doesn't change people's attitudes quickly.

The scope of the emotional anguish people with AIDS must face is often even broader than the discriminatory problems just listed. Consider, for instance, the situation of a woman who knows she's dying from AIDS and has just discovered that her 6-month-old baby is also infected with HIV. Who will care for her baby after her death? How can she resolve the guilt she probably feels over transmitting this infection to her child? And who will care for her 4-year-old child who *isn't* HIV-infected? As another example, what about the personal turmoil in the life of a woman infected from a blood transfusion who has unwittingly transmitted her HIV infection to her husband?

Another problem you might expect is that people infected with HIV also are apt to have sexual difficulties. In a study of 120 gay men who were infected with HIV, Heino Meyer-Bahlburg and coworkers[126] found that two-fifths of their sample reported decreased sexual satisfaction, two-fifths had some degree of difficulty with erectile failure, and more than half had some degree of negative feelings during sex.

In addition to the emotional anguish caused by dealing with all of these issues, AIDS victims must face the prospect of numerous medical complications and hospitalizations, deal with concerns about the economic cost of their illness, and come to terms with their own identity and emotions as part of the ultimate task of preparing for death.

BEHAVIORAL ASPECTS OF THE HIV EPIDEMIC

Although it is clear that in the absence of an effective vaccine or cure massive changes will be required in patterns of sexual and drug-related behavior in order to stem the tide of the HIV epidemic, there is little evidence that such changes are occurring in the general population.

The gay community has been a major exception. It has been notably successful in implementing risk-reducing behavior since the exact nature of the AIDS epidemic became clear. While widespread changes have occurred, these changes have been "expectably incomplete,"[127] and concerns are now mounting that a "second wave" of HIV infections in younger gay men may be occurring.[128] Part of the reason for this is that widespread use of drugs and alcohol by young gay men may be altering their judgment and their planning for using safer sex practices. Another reason is that some people tire of following safer sex guidelines and relapse to risky behavior patterns.[129]

For example, in a longitudinal study done in San Francisco, it was noted that between 1985 and 1986 the average number of sex partners decreased by 20 percent for those men not in a monogamous relationship, but 37 percent of the men continued to engage in sexual activities that were "probably risky" (such as ingesting semen during oral-genital sex) and 38 percent still engaged in high risk activities such as anal sex without a condom.[130] Through the end of 1987, while almost a third of the subjects changed to and maintained low-risk behaviors, 16 percent relapsed to risky sex after an initial short-term behavior change.[131] A similar longitudinal study done in New York showed that 48 percent of the gay men studied continued to engage in risky sex, including sex with multiple anonymous partners, and that for every two men who shifted to safer sex practices over time, one slipped back from safer sex to riskier sex.[132] Continued high rates of risky sexual behavior have been noted especially among gay men in small U.S. cities, outside the original epicenters of the HIV epidemic. For example, 40 percent of one sample of such men reported more than one male sex partner in the previous two months, and nearly one-third reported engaging in unprotected anal intercourse.[133]

A number of other studies also show, collectively, that positive behavioral changes have occurred among gay and bisexual males, but that these risk-reducing changes are far from complete.[134] One review of 24 separate studies of changes in sexual behavior by gay men in response to AIDS found that overall, approximately 20 percent had not altered their unsafe sex practices and that a portion of this resistance to change was probably due to frequent use of recreational drugs.[135] For example, substantial numbers of gay men continue to engage in anal sex with multiple partners—even though these men know that they are infected with HIV.[136] About half of these men either do not use condoms at all or use them very erratically.[137]

Among heterosexuals there seems to be considerably less concern for safe sex in terms of changed behavior, although the matter has not been investigated extensively. For example, in San Francisco among patrons of bars, single heterosexual women were less likely to engage in safe sex practices than single homosexual men were.[138] In another study, it was found that only 6 of 200 heterosexual women who had at least 6 sex partners a year routinely asked their partners to use condoms during vaginal intercourse.[139] Likewise, a survey of Canadian college students reported that among those with more than 10 sex partners, only 21 percent of the men and 7.5 percent of the women used condoms regularly.[140] And a recent study of women in the military found that a growing number are becoming infected with HIV "through unprotected sex with bisexual or IV [intravenous] drug-using men" even though most of them reported having only one or two sexual partners.[141]

That lifetime monogamy is no longer the norm can be seen in data from a large national survey of U.S. women that found that two-thirds of all women aged 15 to 44 who had ever had intercourse have had more than one partner, and 41 percent have had four or more nonmarital partners.[142] A similar survey found that 23 percent of U.S. men aged 20 to 39 have had intercourse with 20 or more women in their lives.[143]

Although condom sales jumped dramatically in the late 1980s as a result of the public's awareness of AIDS, regular condom use has not become very common among heterosexuals, nor have heterosexuals in general shifted to strictly monogamous sex. A survey of the general heterosexual population in the U.S. found that only 17 percent of people with multiple sex partners and 12.6 percent of those with risky sex partners (e.g., IV drug users, bisexual men) used condoms all the time.[144] As a result of this complacency, rates of other STDs such as syphilis, chancroid, and hepatitis B in the United States jumped substantially in the past 5 years, with the rise attributable entirely to more cases in the heterosexual population. In fact, even among persons attending STD clinics, condom use is sporadic at best.[145] And only a minority of sexually active adolescents uses condoms at all.[146]

Other signs of a general lack of concern in most heterosexuals about the HIV epidemic are apparent, although no one has thoroughly studied them as yet. For instance, in most urban areas prostitution continues to thrive, despite considerable publicity about the possible transmission of HIV. (Since a majority of prostitutes are also IV drug users, there is an obvious danger of HIV infection with such sexual activity.) Furthermore, most male customers of prostitutes prefer not to use condoms; although few data are available on this point, one study showed that about half of the men who patronized prostitutes never used condoms, and many others used condoms erratically.[147]

Condom use is also very low in black and Hispanic groups who are at heightened risk of exposure to HIV infection because of widespread drug use in their communities.[148] In addition to this cultural bias, there is another relatively recent development contributing to the spread of HIV: the use of cocaine in a particularly powerful form known as "crack." The use of crack cocaine, which is highly addictive, is often done in "binges" of almost continual use over several days. In order to support their drug habit, many female crack addicts resort to prostitution (often with as many as 10 or more clients per day); since many of their clients have a history of IV drug abuse, and thus have a heightened likelihood of HIV infection, many observers believe this has become an important factor in the heterosexual transmission of HIV.[149]

Even in more "traditional" settings, there are many indications that inadvertent HIV transmission is not unusual in the heterosexual world at large. Walk through a singles bar on a weekend evening, or browse through the classified personal ads in many newspapers and magazines, and you will quickly realize that heterosexuals have hardly given up on the sexual revolution. Despite lip service to the notion of safe sex, many heterosexuals continue to behave sexually much as they did in the days before AIDS, which is certainly understandable since many have been led to believe that AIDS is "just" a gay disease. This misbelief was borne out in a national poll conducted by the *Los Angeles Times* in mid-1989 that showed concern about AIDS among the general public declining as well as a drop in people who say they have made substantial changes in their life-styles because of the epidemic.[150]

The following comments from interviews with single heterosexuals reflect this overall sense of complacency:

A 26-year-old woman: I don't want to sound like a fool, but I don't know anyone with AIDS, and I doubt that the guys I would date are shooting up drugs or anything like that. Maybe if I lived in New York or San Francisco I'd be more worried, but I don't want to live my life in fear.

A 29-year-old man: I think the papers made too big a thing out of the whole AIDS business. Last year I heard a government report that said the epidemic was leveling off. And even though I've had sex with five or six partners every year, I've never had a problem.

The same lack of concern is all too apparent on college campuses today, where despite well-intended attempts at preventive AIDS education, sexual behavior patterns are not much different from those of a decade ago. Several surveys of college students bear this out, showing that relatively few students are worried about personal exposure to HIV or are consistently using safer sex practices.[151] One of these studies, done in southern California with a sample of 851 students, found that 66 percent had not used condoms at all in the preceding 3 months despite being sexually active. In addition, students with 4 or more sex partners annually used condoms no more than students with fewer partners per year did.[152] Similarly, a survey of 350 students at a large East Coast university showed that most felt they had little or no risk of exposure to HIV, and also felt that they could somehow intuitively sense when a prospective sexual partner wasn't "safe." Many said that they did not use condoms at all, and "In general, students equated 'safer sex' with 'not-for-fun' sex."[153]

These attitudes are commonplace on campuses across the country. The medical director of the student health service at a large midwestern university recently described it to us this way, requesting anonymity so he could avoid getting embroiled in political problems from the administration:

Students here seem almost oblivious to the AIDS epidemic, as though it doesn't travel to this part of the country. We can see this from the soaring chlamydial epidemic we have going on, which is sort of a marker for sexual behavior. What no one realizes is that we had five HIV-infected students diagnosed here last year—but the president of the university has put a tight lid on the news, because he's afraid of the reaction from alumni donors and prospective freshmen if news leaked out about this problem.

The situation on college campuses is not unusual; in many ways, it mirrors the broader picture fairly accurately. As yet, we have not succeeded very well in implementing widespread behavioral change to fight the HIV epidemic because the American public has received mixed messages, watered-down messages, and often no messages at all about what needs to be done to turn the tide. Politicians and religious leaders have blocked many efforts at using public funds to develop educational materials about AIDS because of concerns that the materials would be too sexually explicit; school-based AIDS education programs have frequently foundered because of arguments over the "moral" way to teach about AIDS and HIV (for instance, some people claim it is permissible only to teach that abstinence is the sole way to avoid AIDS); on some college campuses, condom dispensers have been removed to avoid offending certain alumni groups. Until more effective HIV/AIDS education messages are sent to the public, this epidemic will probably continue to grow at a frightening rate.

PUBLIC POLICY ISSUES

The history of the early years of the HIV epidemic, thoroughly chronicled in Randy Shilts's book, *And the Band Played On* (1987), is in many ways a story of tragic dimensions. Lives were wasted and precious time was lost in combating a deadly disease because of homophobia, complacency, and the federal government's relative inaction. For instance, in 1983, *Time* quoted Donald Currie, then manager of the San Francisco Kaposi's sarcoma hotline, as saying, "If the same number of Boy Scouts had been dying of this, there would have been a hell of a lot more money for research."[154] Yet it was still almost 5 years before the government approved adequate funds for AIDS research.[155] Even as recently as 1990, Larry Kramer, founder of Gay Men's Health Crisis, has said, "I am so frightened that the war against AIDS has already been lost. It is beyond comprehension why, in a presumably civilized country, in the modern era, such a continuing, extraordinary destruction of life is being attended to so tentatively, so meekly and in such a cowardly fashion."[156]

Today there is still considerable complacency about the epidemic. Homophobia continues to play a major role in how people view questions about HIV infection and AIDS. There is another side to our ineffectiveness in dealing with the epidemic, however. For years, more emphasis was put on protecting individual rights to privacy than protecting public health. Furthermore, much-needed research on sexual behavior and other aspects of the HIV epidemic has been stalled or killed for strictly political reasons. Implementation of several federally funded national sex research surveys—studies that many believe are essential to a successful fight against the further spread of HIV—was blocked because a handful of politicians objected to asking explicit questions about private sexual behavior.[157]

Given this hodgepodge situation with different groups arguing for and against certain policy choices for their own self-interested reasons, it can be difficult to sort out the issues. The following discussion of a number of pivotal policy issues draws on the recommendations of the National Research Council, the Institute of Medicine of the National Academy of Sciences, the Presidential Commission on the HIV Epidemic, and the National Commission on AIDS, as well as other authoritative sources, to present consensus opinions emerging at the beginning of the 1990s on how to proceed in our efforts to control the HIV/AIDS epidemic.

EDUCATION AND RESEARCH

Since it is clear that science, by itself, cannot stop the spread of this epidemic (even if a vaccine were discovered tommorrow, it would take years of testing before it would receive approval and become widely available), it is important that every effort be made to implement widespread behavioral changes in our society to control the spread of HIV. To be effective, this type of education must go beyond simply informing people about facts—it must also motivate them to modify their behavior.

We have previously recommended the following steps for development of broad educational programs in this country.[158]

1. A comprehensive AIDS curriculum must be developed for widespread use in public schools. In order to be effective, such a program must begin well before young people begin to engage in sexual activity and drug use, which means such programs must begin no later than fourth or fifth grade.

2. Special education programs must be targeted at specific groups whose behaviors or situations place them at high risk of being exposed to HIV. These include intravenous drug abusers and their sex partners, homosexual and bisexual men, prostitutes and their customers, and heterosexuals who have multiple sex partners. Furthermore, special programs must be devel-

oped for groups that may have unique requirements in program design, including minority populations, the blind and the deaf, and people who cannot read.

3. A broad-based, multimedia general education campaign that encourages responsible behavior should be undertaken as soon as possible. This campaign should encompass the television and movie community (where scriptwriters can incorporate warnings about HIV into their prime-time shows or movies), celebrities from the world of rock, sports stars, and other "high visibility" spokespersons who have particular credibility with adolescents and young adults.

4. All colleges and universities should provide their students with extensive educational and counseling services related to prevention of HIV infection.

5. To coordinate and implement the entire educational effort, a special office should be created in the U.S. Department of Health and Human Services and it should be given enough budgetary support and administrative power to accomplish its mission.

In addition, it is imperative that the progress that has been made in the last decade in fighting the HIV epidemic be built upon and expanded by promptly and intensively increasing behavioral and biomedical research.

TESTING

Earlier in the course of the HIV epidemic, there was considerable resistance to the idea of widespread testing for the presence of infection because of concerns about the accuracy of the blood tests that were available, concerns about privacy and confidentiality, and a sense of futility: what good did it do to know that you're infected with the AIDS virus if there was no treatment available to prolong your life? Today, there is a vastly different perspective on this issue: most experts agree that virtually anyone at risk should undergo confidential testing on a voluntary basis.[159]

The reasons for this change are relatively straightforward. First, the accuracy of tests for HIV infection have improved significantly. Second, worries about lack of confidentiality of test results have been lessened considerably as many states have passed legislation specifically addressing this issue and as many states provide anonymous testing sites. Most important, however, early detection of HIV infection is the only way to ensure early medical treatment, and it is clear that early medical treatment can prolong life and prevent (or at least postpone) some of the serious complications of AIDS.

Widespread voluntary testing also leads to many personal benefits. For example, in many cases, people who have been tested will discover that they are *not* infected, which will not only be psychologically reassuring, but may also help them make important personal decisions about marriage, pregnancy, or other issues. On the other hand, people who discover that they are infected can: (1) protect their sexual partners from infection; (2) make arrangements for appropriate medical care; (3) avoid situations where they would have additional exposures to HIV; (4) make informed plans concerning careers, insurance, finances, and other related matters.

There are certainly some personal drawbacks to widespread testing. For one thing, positive test results may cause profound anxiety or depression. A second problem is the small chance of having a false positive result, which could certainly have a serious impact on a person's life. Another difficulty is that unless your test results are absolutely confidential (not all tests done in hospitals or doctors' offices are, especially if you sign a form authorizing the release of your medical records to an insurance company), you may find that you encounter problems. For example, military applicants who turn out to be HIV positive are denied jobs in the military. And someone who tests positive may have difficulty obtaining certain types of insurance coverage in the future.

Widespread voluntary testing also benefits the general public as well as individuals. For example, public health authorities would gain a better picture of trends in the HIV epidemic and would be better able to address broad policy issues such as educational campaigns and other prevention programs targeted at special population groups. Furthermore, this sort of information is essential to the economic planning that will be needed to deal with the epidemic in the future, as well as the planning for the delivery of health care services.

While mandatory testing of blood, organ, and tissue donors and the military population is currently in place in the United States, attempts at mandatory premarital testing for HIV proved ineffective in Illinois and Louisiana and have now been discontinued. Routine (but not mandatory) prenatal HIV screening has been advocated by some experts but has not yet been implemented in most locales.[160]

PUBLIC HEALTH MEASURES

Contact tracing and notification—tracking down the sex partners of people with a reportable STD and informing them that they may have been exposed, without revealing the identity of the "index case"—has been one of the most time-tested public health strategies.[161] In fact, public health statutes usually authorize contact tracing for STDs, but in an odd quirk, most states today do not classify HIV infection as an STD. (The reason for this is that these states wish to avoid the automatic contact tracing programs that would be triggered by existing laws if HIV infection was classified as an STD.) Nevertheless, a number of states (such as Colorado and South Carolina) and cities have implemented contact tracing and notification programs, with generally good results.[162] A few other states, such as California, have a voluntary contact tracing program.

By focusing on people with a high probability of exposure to HIV, contact tracing is efficient in detecting those with previously unidentified infection. This detection has important implications for prevention in two ways: (1) uninfected sex partners of an already infected person are warned that they've been exposed, which may lead them to behavioral changes that would reduce their risk of subsequent infection; and (2) identifying persons with a previously undetected HIV infection should allow them to take steps to protect their own sex partners, minimizing the risk of spreading HIV further.

There has been some controversy about the physician's role in contact tracing and partner notification. Concerns about protecting the confidentiality of HIV-infected persons have created conflicting opinions on this issue, but in many states, including New York and California, while protecting patient confidentiality is a legal obligation, there is also a responsibility to warn anyone who is in clear and imminent danger of becoming infected. This means that if an HIV-infected man refuses to inform his sex partners of his infection, a physician is authorized to disclose this information to the partners in order to protect their health and well-being.

Although public health laws in all jurisdictions in this country carry provisions for quarantine of persons with communicable diseases, and a few states have laws authorizing the compulsory isolation of persons with AIDS or HIV infection who are aware of this but continue to engage in high risk behaviors, there is virtual unanimity among public health authorities that quarantine is unnecessary—and inhumane—in the HIV epidemic.

Another possible public health measure that has stirred considerable controversy is the use of sterile needle and syringe exchange programs as a means of reducing the spread of HIV among intravenous drug abusers. While such programs have been operating successfully in Europe for years, in the United States they have been primarily restricted to small-scale pilot projects in a few cities such as New York, Seattle, and Portland, Oregon. The main obstacle in America is concern that providing sterile needles and syringes to drug abusers is condoning an illegal act and might lead to more widespread drug abuse. The available evidence suggests that this isn't happening in Europe, but needle exchange programs don't eliminate HIV risk behavior, either.[163]

ANTIDISCRIMINATION ISSUES

Because AIDS first appeared in this country in groups that were already stigmatized—homosexuals and IV drug abusers—society's response has been strongly shaped by bias, assignments of blame, and a disregard for the needs of those most directly affected by the epidemic. In addition, fears about casual transmission of HIV that were widespread in the early days of the epidemic (fears that have now been effectively proven to be unfounded) fueled many examples of discriminatory responses to people with AIDS or HIV infection. For instance, office workers sometimes shunned a colleague with AIDS because of worries that they might become infected by indirect physical contact with him. Landlords tried to evict tenants with AIDS on the grounds that they had an easily communicable disease that might affect other building occupants. In some particularly sad cases, infected children have been banned from attending school on the grounds that they posed a health hazard to their classmates.

Today we have made a good deal of progress in moving beyond these discriminatory practices, but fear of discrimination is still a major stumbling block to the acceptance of potentially effective public health strategies by gay rights groups and other AIDS activists. The federal Rehabilitation Act of 1973, Section 504, prohibits discrimination against "otherwise qualified" handicapped persons, and the courts have consistently found that HIV-related conditions are covered by this—but the coverage applies only to federally funded programs. To address this issue, legislative attempts to counter HIV-related discrimination have already been passed in many states. It will probably take a growing realization that HIV infects people from all walks of life (not just gay and bisexual men and IV drug abusers) to change attitudes toward the epidemic enough so that HIV-infected persons are regarded no differently than people with cancer, heart disease or high blood pressure.

ADDITIONAL CONSIDERATIONS

Society must face a large number of challenging issues as part of addressing the HIV epidemic. What can be done about the problem of HIV infection in the homeless? Who will care for HIV-infected babies whose parents have died of AIDS? How can we put an end to the patterns of drug abuse that contribute in major ways to the spread of HIV infection? How will we finance the health care requirements of the hundreds of thousands of people who are already HIV-infected? Unfortunately, it is clear that the answers to these challenges are not always easy or affordable, so choices have to be made in terms of budgets and allocation of manpower and other resources in this epic fight. One set of such recommendations is described in the section that follows.

The President's AIDS Commission

In 1987, President Reagan created a special commission to investigate the HIV epidemic and to make recommendations that could be used to protect the public health, assist in finding a cure for AIDS, and provide care for those already infected. (As a historical note, it should be pointed out that many observers felt that the commission should have been created years earlier; furthermore, there was initially considerable controversy over the makeup of the commission, with many groups dismayed that the gay community was not adequately represented and others worried that the commission was lacking in medical and scientific expertise.) At the end of a year of hearing expert testimony from some 600 witnesses, the commission issued a widely acclaimed final report. Among its key recommendations were the following:

• Early diagnosis of HIV infection is essential both for obtaining optimal medical care and counseling and for protecting others. This requires encouragement of extensive voluntary testing.

• "HIV infection is a disability and should be treated as such under federal and state law. . . . Infected persons should be encouraged to continue normal activities, such as work or school, and live in their own home as long as they are able."[164]

• Strong measures should be implemented for protecting the confidentiality of persons who are infected with HIV. At the same time, public health authorities should immediately begin a system of confidential partner notification so that all partners who have been exposed to an HIV-infected person can be counseled, tested, and followed up.

• States should begin to require the reporting of all HIV-positive tests, not just cases of AIDS, to track the course of the epidemic more accurately.

• Prevention and treatment of intravenous drug abuse should be made a top national priority. A new policy of "treatment on demand" should be implemented (at a cost to the government of about $1.5 billion annually), since the ability to control the course of the HIV epidemic depends to a large extent on being able to curtail IV drug abuse.

The commission also called for new federal and state funding to reverse the national nursing shortage, emphasized the need for developing comprehensive drug and alcohol education programs and "age appropriate, comprehensive health education programs" from kindergarten through grade twelve, and suggested that there is a responsibility for all citizens to treat HIV-infected persons with respect and compassion.

A Concluding Note

The HIV epidemic can be stopped in its tracks if people take personal responsibility for their behavior by abstaining from IV drug use and consistently following safer sex guidelines.

Medical science today is technologically equipped to solve the puzzles of HIV infection—although how long it will take to accomplish this is not entirely clear.

But what is clear is this: within the next few years, every single person in the United States will know someone who is infected with HIV. How we will respond to this challenge, both as individuals and as a society, cannot be known as yet. Yet one thing is certain: We are all in this together. As the novelist James Carroll puts it:

> Now no one is immune. Those things that have always cut us off from one another—sexism, homophobia, racism, hatred of addicts—have the additional effect of making this disease more powerful. However understandable the common impulse to blame is, however "human" it is, the fact now is that we indulge it at our common peril.
>
> The climate in which prevention thrives is marked not by blaming, but by caring. It is marked by the frank and open exchange of real information, even information that we once regarded as inappropriate for exchange. It is marked by willingness to consider, in the name of prevention, ideas and strategies that at first may offend us. We have to work constantly, in other words, at changing those attitudes that feed the infection, at keeping open minds as well as open hearts.[165]

Fifteen

Adolescent Sexuality

When we think about adolescent sexuality, the image that comes to mind is neatly captured in this dialogue.

FATHER: "I think it's time we had a talk about sex."
SON: "Sure, Dad. What do you want to know?"

The message is, however, a little out of touch with reality: teenagers don't really know everything there is to know about sex, even though many of them act as if they do. In addition to possessing incomplete, inaccurate, or misinterpreted information, many adolescents also lack personal comfort with sexual matters. Fourteen-year-olds are apt to worry about the "right" way to French kiss, or how to deal with a date's unbridled physical passion; 16-year-olds may be uncertain about how to "do" oral sex; almost all teens are concerned with the question, "Is my sex life normal?" The teenager's outward posture of sexual sophistication often hides an underlying sense of personal anxiety and confusion.

As adolescents grapple with their developing sexuality, a number of distinct themes come into play. These include:

1. the links among pubertal development, body image, and self-image;
2. the task of learning about one's body and its sensual and sexual responses and needs;
3. forging an identity, which includes dealing with issues of socially dictated gender role expectations and developing comfort with and certainty about one's sexual orientation;
4. learning about sexual and romantic relationships, including learning about sexual negotiation, intimacy, and commitment;
5. developing a personal sexual value system.

As we discuss each of these themes, keep in mind that all adolescents are not alike. Observations about the sexuality of 13-year-olds will not apply precisely to 17- or 18-year-olds. And not all 13-year-olds are alike: just as some are more physically mature than others, there also is considerable variation in their emotional maturity. In addition, teenagers in different communities (or even in different neighborhoods within the same community) are often subjected to strikingly different cultural values, peer group pressures, and social expectations, which combine with other variables—including socioeconomic and religious factors and gender role models—that shape the emergence and expression of their developing sexuality.

THE LINKS AMONG PUBERTAL DEVELOPMENT, BODY IMAGE, AND SELF-IMAGE

Teenagers are especially concerned with personal attractiveness, which is very closely linked to the way they see their own bodies—their body image. For better or worse, we live in a society that often measures personal worth in terms of how people look, and, influenced by movies and television, teens grasp this basic fact very quickly.

Whether you are male or female, if you think back to your early and middle teenage years you will probably recall many times when you stood in front of a mirror inspecting your face for pimples, checking out your body's physique from different angles, or worrying about your height, weight, or body shape. It's a sad but true fact that, for most of us, concerns about our physical attractiveness—am I too short? too fat? too gawky? too plain-looking?—have a lot to do with how we feel about ourselves.

For teenagers, these concerns seem to be magnified out of proportion to reality. The 15-year-old boy who hasn't yet started his adolescent growth spurt, and so is 6 inches shorter than the average girl in his class, or the 14-year-old girl who is 5'3" and 160 pounds are both likely to feel personally inadequate as well as self-conscious. The teenager's concern about physical appearance is usually of more importance to him or her than it is to other people. As a noted psychologist observes:

> Virtually any and all physical characteristics receive extraordinary attention and examination during this phase. This is a time when being different is to be avoided at almost any cost and when undesirable physical characteristics put the adolescent at risk for teasing, ridicule or exclusion.[1]

One reason for this central focus on body image is that the teenager hasn't yet identified a clear sense of his or her own identity as a person, so that, to the teenager, "what I look like" and "how others see me" equate very strongly with "who I am." Another reason is that most younger adolescents haven't yet developed a broad enough sense of self-esteem, based on their accomplishments, personal characteristics, and relationships with others, to counterbalance their perceptions of their unattractiveness.

The adolescent's concern with body image is made even more complex by the fact that his or her body is going through a metamorphosis of its own, changing size, shape, and other characteristics almost inexplicably as part of the process of puberty. Teenage girls are acutely aware of their breast development not only in personal terms but in comparative terms too: how do they stack up next to other girls in their grade or in their group of friends? (Teenage boys also notice—and sometimes rate—the girls' breast development; partly for this reason, being too well endowed can be just as embarrassing as being underdeveloped.) Teenage boys are less subject to sexual scrutiny on the basis of appearance, because their primary sex development is less visible; but their physical masculinity is rated by themselves and by others in terms of height, muscularity, the appearance of facial hair growth, and the development of lower-pitched voices. Slow-to-mature teenage boys are all too familiar with the terrors of the boys' locker room, where they must undress—and display themselves—in front of other boys who make fun of them for not yet having pubic hair or not having adequately developed genitals. Concerns like these lessen over time for most people as psychological maturation and physical development progress, but in the first half of adolescence these matters are understandably of central importance. And since there is a positive relationship between physical attractiveness and social acceptance during adolescence[2] the concern with body image has some logic.

THE TASK OF LEARNING ABOUT ONE'S BODY AND ITS SENSUAL AND SEXUAL RESPONSES AND NEEDS

In addition to focusing on outward appearance, teenagers also have to learn about their own bodies. This is not as easy as it seems because there are many aspects of puberty that no one bothers to discuss with them, and this lack of information creates predictable sources of anxiety. For example, most adolescent girls don't realize that the increased levels of circulating estrogen in their bodies typically produce a perfectly normal vaginal discharge, and they often feel embarrassed or worried when they notice their panties stained by it. Boys may react similarly to their first wet dreams if no one has explained that these are perfectly normal body responses. And the frequent occurrence of sudden erections at exactly the most inopportune moments—going to the blackboard to do an algebra problem, skinny-dipping with a bunch of guys, or even during the sermon in church—also creates an almost universal experience of confusion, embarrassment, and anxieties about normality for teenage boys. Here's how one college student described his most embarrassing moment in high school:

> I made the varsity swim team in my freshman year, which was a great accomplishment. The whole team wore these specially tight-fitting, low-cut racing trunks to cut down our resistance in the water. The only problem was, when I had to get up on the victory stand to receive my medal at the state meet, I got a gigantic boner. While I stood there at attention as the school victory song was being played, my crotch bulged out of my swimming trunks like there was an oversized cucumber inside.

One of the primary ways adolescents learn about their bodies is by physical inspection and exploration. Many young teenagers spend hours examining the intricacies of their genitals, sometimes aided by a hand-held mirror, sometimes (for boys especially) with the aid of a tape measure or ruler to check on exact dimensions. Young teenage girls are apt to inspect their breasts in great detail, worrying about size discrepancies between the two breasts, the presence or absence of hair around the areola, the prominence of their nipples, and the shape and size of these organs. Physical inspection typically extends to physical exploration, with teenagers of both sexes experimenting with how various types of touch feel and what sorts of responses they produce. As one 18-year-old girl put it:

> When I was 13 or 14, I would see what it felt like to put baby oil or hand lotion on my genitals, rubbing or stroking the surface with my hand or with various other objects, like a feather or a fuzzy stuffed animal. I didn't think of this as masturbation, and I wasn't trying to have an orgasm. I'm not even sure how I knew what an orgasm was back then. But I remember playing with my nipples, touching them real lightly one minute, pinching them, dripping warm water on my breasts, sometimes touching my clitoris at the same time I rubbed a nipple. It was like I was trying to find the right recipe—only I didn't know the recipe for what.

This type of learning eventually leads to more deliberate attempts at producing sexual arousal. Teenagers want to discover just how aroused they can become how quickly, how to integrate fantasy with physical response, how long they can stay aroused, how quickly they can regain their arousal after letting it flag, what orgasm feels like, and what it feels like to be aroused but not have orgasm. These experiences are partly a form of rehearsal for later interpersonal sex and partly a form of self-discovery and becoming comfortable with one's own body and its responses. In general, since we are comfortable with things that are familiar to us, repeated explorations lead to more familiarity and more comfort.

The process of learning about one's body is not the same for all teenagers, but there are probably few teenage boys who haven't, at one time or another, tried to put on a condom while they were in the privacy of their own rooms—just to "see what it's like." Similarly, the majority of teenage girls have probably tried to insert an object into their vagina to see what it felt like. Curiosity and a desire to "act grown up" are both normal components of early adolescence.

Learning about one's body occurs not only when teenagers are by themselves; it also occurs with touching or being touched, kissing or being kissed, undressing or seeing someone else undressed. Early adolescents, for example, usually don't plunge abruptly into sex but instead spend a lot of time holding hands, snuggling together (with the boy's arm around the girl's shoulder, slowly—perhaps over weeks—and casually dipping down toward its first "accidental" brush against the girl's breast). Later in adolescence, the ground rules may have changed considerably: for some 17- or 18-year-olds, oral sex on the first date is a distinct possibility.

FORGING AN IDENTITY

The psychologist Erik Erikson believed that the search for identity and the conquest of identity confusion are the central developmental issues of adolescence. This search is made more difficult for the teenager by a number of potential roadblocks, including rigid gender role expectations (cultural stereotypes about the appropriate traits and behaviors of males and females) and the related issue of sexual orientation. Adolescents who have no trouble fitting the "quarterback/cheerleader" expectations, in which males are supposed to be athletically inclined, emotionally controlled, and willing to take physical risks, while females are supposed to be attractive, vivacious, and supportive, usually have an easier time of it than those who don't fit these stereotypically defined roles. A teenage boy who is more interested in ballet than in baseball, or a girl who is a talented shotputter, may be unfairly labeled as a "weirdo" or worse unless he or she is able to establish firm proof of masculinity or femininity in other ways.

Much of the sexual behavior in early and mid-adolescence is motivated by expectations about gender-appropriate behavior and the related desire for peer acceptance rather than by actual sexual desire. Teenagers "prove" their masculinity or femininity in part by being seen going through the right heterosexual rituals or talking as though they have gone through them. A 16-year-old boy who's never had a girlfriend, who doesn't talk about the great centerfold in last month's *Playboy*, and who isn't seen wrapped around a female body in some starry-eyed "close dancing" at a class party may be suspect. Similarly, a 16-year-old girl who doesn't date may be socially ostracized as an "undesirable"; this negative labeling may be even stronger if she doesn't dress in a manner that is "in" for girls at her high school or if she seems too aggressive in her nonsexual conduct.

LEARNING ABOUT SEXUAL AND ROMANTIC RELATIONSHIPS

Learning about sexual and romantic relationships generally begins in early adolescence as boys and girls practice the social skills needed for group activities ranging from "hanging out" at the mall to dances, parties, and group "dates" to the movies. For most adolescents, these rehearsals of what will later blossom into more serious relationships take the form of heterosexual pairing off (a little later in this chapter we discuss adolescents who have a homosexual orientation). Generally, the degree of emotional closeness and sexual intimacy in these relationships increases as the adolescents become older and more experienced. Most adolescents have a series of such romantic relationships throughout the teenage years. There is considerable variation in this pattern, however: in some cases, young teenagers fall deeply in love and become sexually intimate by age 13 or 14, while more typically, sexual experimentation doesn't progress to intercourse until the late teenage years.[3] In some instances, sexual activity occurs outside romantic pairings: although few teenage boys have their introduction to sexual intercourse with prostitutes today (in contrast to the relative frequency of this way of losing their virginity back in the 1940s, as the Kinsey studies documented), sex is sometimes a more or less casual accompaniment to the use of illicit drugs or is simply "something to do" without having any romantic significance.

Despite the fact that many of the rigid old gender role "rules" differentiating what was acceptable sexual behavior for males and females have undergone massive change in the past 25 years, it is still true that sex is typically seen by teenage males as a form of "scoring" or "conquest," whereas for teenage females sex seems to be most important as a means of obtaining affection, caring, and intimacy.[4] However, what is particularly notable is that for most adolescents today, the old "double standard" that approved sexual experimentation by males, while insisting that teenage females remain virgins, has been discarded in favor of a more egalitarian outlook.

Whether in love relationships or in other social interactions, an important aspect of middle and late adolescence is learning the ground rules and the art of sexual negotiation. This includes learning how to set limits, how to communicate about sex with and without words, how to avoid misunderstandings (particularly, for females, how to avoid being considered a "cockteaser"; for males, how to avoid being too aggressive or insensitive), and how to show a partner what you like, as well as what you don't like. While many readers will have forgotten how important these issues seemed to be at age 16 or 17, the proficiency and self-confidence that adolescents develop in such sexual negotiations become important components of later sexual feelings. For example, a female who learns as a teenager how to say no to an insistent date—or how to disengage tactfully at a party from a guy who is "all hands" when she doesn't want him to be—is apt to be much more confident in her dealings with similar situations as a young adult. On the other hand, adolescents who feel that they have been ineffective in sexual negotiations may be cautious and guarded in future intimate relationships, an approach that can prevent them from being spontaneous and enjoying themselves.

DEVELOPING A PERSONAL SEXUAL VALUE SYSTEM

The process of developing a personal sexual value system is linked to the task of finding a comfortable identity. In answering the question "Who am I?" the adolescent is also looking for answers to questions like "What do I stand for? What do I believe in? Whom should I choose as role models?" Gradually devising a set of sexual values is partly an outgrowth of this important aspect of adolescence. For example, the teenager either chooses to be honest as a general way of behaving or decides that deceit is sometimes allowable in order to get something he or she wants. Similarly, teens must choose among sex as a means of expressing intimacy and affection, or as a more casual gratification with no strings attached, or as something reserved for a love relationship. These choices are not made in a moral or intellectual vacuum: family values, religious values, and the values of an adolescent's closest friends are undoubtedly important factors in the equation.

While no one knows exactly how any particular teenager's sexual value system will evolve from these various influences, family values play an important role in shaping subsequent attitudes and behaviors in two different ways. When teenagers have close relationships with their parents, they are more likely to have sexual value systems that are consistent with their parents' values;[5] however, when they are at odds with their parents on many fronts, they often choose to make sex a battleground for demonstrating their rebelliousness and independence by rejecting their parents' values and admonitions.

TEENAGE SEXUAL ACTIVITY

If the sexual revolution is over, today's teenagers haven't heard. Despite the realities of the HIV/AIDS epidemic, soaring rates of other sexually transmitted diseases, and an unremitting problem with unintended teenage pregnancy, American adolescents are more sexually active in the 1990s than they have been at any time in the past. The trend over the past 3 decades has been for participation in sexual activity at ever declining ages, perhaps mirroring a social climate in which sexual themes in movies, on television, and in music have become increasingly abundant and direct.

Throughout all ages of adolescence, males are more likely than are females to report having had intercourse (see Table 15.1).[6] This is nothing particularly new, since it was true in Kinsey's day and probably in earlier decades as well. What is new is that the gap in rates of coital experience between the sexes has shrunk notably since the early 1960s. However, males and females seem to take somewhat different attitudes toward their first experience with intercourse. As a recent report puts it, "Although they have equal levels of anxiety about first intercourse, girls are likely to be worried about whether they are doing the right thing, while boys are worried about whether they are doing the thing right."[7]

Boys and girls also have different motivations for becoming sexually experienced. For teenage boys, sex is first and foremost a badge of manhood:

TABLE 15.1
PERCENTAGE OF U.S. HIGH SCHOOL STUDENTS WITH SEXUAL EXPERIENCE, 1990

Category	Female	Male
RACE/ETHNICITY		
White	47	56.4
Black	60	87.8
Hispanic	45	63.0
GRADE		
9	37	48.7
10	42.9	52.5
11	52.7	62.6
12	66.6	76.3
Total	48	60.8

SOURCE: Data from Centers for Disease Control, Sexual Behavior among High School Students—United States, 1990, *Morbidity and Mortality Weekly Report* 40: 885–888, 1992, table 1.

becoming sexually experienced is part of the process of achieving maturity, acquiring social status, and regarding themselves as grown up. While teenage girls certainly also see sex as a marker of personal and social maturity (and thus desirable as a way of leaving childhood behind), girls are more likely than boys to view intercourse as a way of obtaining or solidifying love and commitment.[8] Teenage boys don't think about love and intimacy in the same romanticized way girls do: mirroring the practice of past decades, a boy is still more likely to give a girl a line in order to convince her to have sex, and one of the most common lines still in use is "If you loved me, you would."

There has been an interesting twist in historical patterns of male–female sexual relations in the last decade. Nowadays, it is commonplace for the girl to be the one who instigates a sexual relationship. This happens partly as a reflection of changing views of sex roles and partly a result of considerable erosion in the long-dominant double standard. (Today, very few males expect that the woman they marry will be a virgin; in fact, many young men would find this worrisome.) One corollary finding is that some boys are less enthusiastic about (or are even scared off by) this role reversal. Apparently, for them, part of the satisfaction from sex was the notion of conquest, and if they have been placed in the position of desired sex object rather than manly warrior, their preconceived notion of sexual symmetry is upset.

Reliable data on teenage sexual activity are few and far between. This is partly a reflection of a lack of sponsorship of such research by the federal government over the past several decades and partly a result of the difficulty of obtaining scientifically valid samples. In addition, statistics from the 1970s and early 1980s are now largely outdated, especially given the impact of the

TABLE 15.2

NEVER-MARRIED U.S. TEENAGE MALES WHO HAVE HAD SEXUAL INTERCOURSE, BY AGE (CUMULATIVE PERCENTAGES), 1988

Age	All Races	Black	White	Hispanic
13	5.4	19.8	2.9	3.9
14	11.0	34.6	7.1	6.3
15	21.2	47.8	16.2	19.4
16	37.8	63.5	33.0	37.7
17	57.5	78.4	53.0	63.2
18	67.4	84.7	69.8	60.9
19	79.0	95.8	75.9	80.5

SOURCE: Modified from Freya L. Sonenstein, Joseph H. Pleck, and Leighton C. Ku, Levels of sexual activity among adolescent males in the United States, *Family Planning Perspectives* 23: 162–167, 1991, table 1.

TABLE 15.3
WOMEN AGED 15–19 WHO HAVE HAD SEXUAL INTERCOURSE
(PERCENTAGE), 1988

Race/Ethnicity	Age	
	15–17	18–19
Non-Hispanic White	36.2	74.3
Non-Hispanic Black	50.5	78.0
Hispanic	36.1	70.0
TOTAL	38.4	74.4

SOURCE: Modified from J. D. Forrest and S. Singh, The sexual and reproductive behavior of American women, 1982–1988, *Family Planning Perspectives* 22: 206–214, 1990, table 4.

HIV/AIDS epidemic. However, we will briefly summarize the findings of some recent studies to provide a cogent snapshot of teenage sexual behavior.

• A study of 758 eighth-grade students from rural communities in Maryland surprisingly showed that 61 percent of the boys and 47 percent of the girls had already entered the ranks of nonvirgins.[9]

• A well-designed national survey of high school students recently found that 40 percent of ninth graders had had sexual intercourse and by twelfth grade, this percentage had risen to 72 (see Table 15.1).

• Data from the National Survey on Family Growth revealed that by age 18 or 19, three-quarters of females had had coital experience (see Table 15.3).

• A recent survey of heterosexual students at a large midwestern university found that undergraduate males reported having, on average, 11.2 lifetime sex partners, and female students reported an average of 5.6 different partners.[10]

These eye-opening statistics drive home what is common knowledge for today's teens: in a phrase, (almost) everybody's doing it. To be sure, there are still a substantial number of adolescents whose strict religious upbringing keeps them from experimenting with sex, and there are other teenagers who, due to shyness, lack of social skills, physical unattractiveness, and assorted other problems (or personal value systems) remain dedicated—or sometimes reluctant—virgins. But there is also no question that the survey data referred to above represent only a portion of the sexual activity that is going on among today's adolescents, since these surveys have primarily relied on yes/no answers to a few simple questions about sex.

Because of the lack of reliable data on noncoital sexual behavior during adolescence, we can only offer a few generalizations on this topic based on our own admittedly limited studies. One such point pertains to the incidence of masturbation during adolescence. According to Kinsey and his coworkers, male adolescents were much more likely than females to engage in masturbation at any age during the teenage years.[11] Studies done during the 1970s continued to report a considerable differential between males and females in teenage experience with masturbation.[12] However, data that we have gathered over the last 12 years suggests that this differential is shrinking: while close to 95 percent of teenage boys experiment with masturbation, for teenage girls the incidence has now risen to almost 80 percent. This convergence undoubtedly reflects a change in attitudes in society at large about masturbation in the past 20 years. Today masturbation is more likely to be seen as a healthy form of sexual expression than as a sinful, dirty practice.

Oral-genital sex is also more accepted by today's adolescents than it was in Kinsey's day. Several studies suggest that 40 to 50 percent of teenagers have tried oral-genital contact,[13] and our own surveys suggest that the figure may be even higher than this. Oral-genital sex serves as a good compromise for some teens who are seeking sexual gratification but want to avoid the risk of pregnancy or the moral confusion they may associate with sexual intercourse; for other adolescents, it is simply one of several different alternatives for sexual experimentation. As one 17-year-old girl put it, "Oral sex is a good way to take care of my boyfriend when I'm not in the mood for making love but he's really horny. I don't even have to take my clothes off and I can still get the job done."

The most notable change in adolescent sexual behavior in the past 20 years, beyond the trend toward becoming sexually active at younger and younger ages, is this: today's teenagers have intercourse with many more sexual partners than past teenagers did. While exact statistics are not available, think about this fact for a moment: according to a recent survey, the average sexually active 15-year-old American boy has had intercourse with at least four different partners![14] (An irreverent aside: and we wonder why College Board scores have been declining for the past two decades!)

These comments from teenagers help to explain why this all seems so casual to them.

A 16-year-old girl: The first time I had sex, I was 14, but I didn't really like the guy too much—it was just a matter of something to do. Then I tried it with two other boys the summer after eighth grade, and that was good because I enjoyed myself more and got to feel more confident. In high school, I started going out with a junior, and we had sex every weekend for most of the first half of the year, but then we broke up and my next boyfriend was also older, and by that time it was, like, having sex with your boyfriend was expected . . . you know, like you had to do it. On spring break, I met a guy in Florida and we had sex a couple of times, so I guess that now I've had sex with six different people. But I don't consider myself wild or anything—one of my friends told me that she's had 12 different guys this year alone.

A 15-year-old boy: I guess you could say that we were in love when we first started having sex. At least that's what Marcia wanted me to say, so I told her I loved her and that was the key. But I got tired of her after a while—I think we went together for a month and a half—and then I started going around with Sally, her best friend. Sally asked me if I had laid Marcia, and when I said I had, she had to have sex with me, too, and she wanted to know if she was better than Marcia was. Even though our sex was pretty good, I stopped going with Sally around Thanksgiving, and then I was just sort of hanging out without any one specific girlfriend. I think I had sex maybe with three different people between then and the spring. To me, it's no big deal. If a girl doesn't want sex, then she doesn't want to be with me.

The old concept of being faithful still applies for most of today's teenagers, who go to great lengths to explain how having sex with five different partners in a year can be done without having cheated on any of them. The operative principle seems to be that teenagers have a constricted view of what constitutes a long time: to most of them, a long time is from now until next Saturday. There is still a pattern of serial monogamy for the majority of sexually active adolescents, but the accent is on "serial" rather than on "monogamy."

As the above remarks show, many teenagers have discarded as a prerequisite for sex the standard of being in love in favor of simply feeling good about their partner. However, there are still adolescents who continue to see sexual intercourse as something to be saved for a love relationship and, ideally, for a premarital trial with the person they feel destined to marry. This points up another difference in sexual behavior for today's teenagers: adolescent participation in coital activity today is not "premarital" in the sense in which it once was.

Although it does occur before marriage, only some of it is in the service of the marriage institution. If, for instance, a young person's first intercourse occurs at 15 or 16 and first marriage in the mid-20s, with a number of affectional-sexual relationships (including intercourse) in between, the first experience and many of the later ones will have been undertaken for their own sakes, not in a search for marriage partners.[15]

In the midst of these various changes, teenagers today seem to be somewhat more conscientious about using contraception than in past decades. More than three-quarters of sexually active teenagers reported using some form of contraception during the last time they had intercourse.[16] However, since many teenagers use withdrawal (a notoriously ineffective method) as their primary form of birth control, this statistic is less positive than it might seem to be if taken at face value.

GAY AND LESBIAN TEENS

In a society that programs its children and adolescents for a heterosexual world, it can be a source of considerable emotional turmoil for a teenager to discover that he or she has a sexual orientation that's "different." For one thing, we continue to live in a society that is predominantly homophobic, and this negative attitude toward homosexuality spills over into rejection, hostility, and cruelty from numerous sources—including, at times, parents, friends, and church or synagogue—that makes the gay or lesbian teenager feel like a misfit. For another thing, since peer group acceptance is vitally important to most adolescents' self-esteem—far more important than at any other phase in the life cycle—lack of access to a readily identifiable peer group deprives the gay or lesbian teenager of both an important source of external support and a boost to feeling accepted and acceptable.

As a result, many teenagers who possess a strong same-sex attraction struggle against this impulse in an effort to make themselves fit in the expected heterosexual mold. Part of this struggle may involve telling themselves they are "just going through a passing phase," or withdrawing into a sphere of relative social isolation—sometimes becoming intensely involved in hobbies that can be pursued alone, like computers or art or music.

Relatively few lesbians actually identify themselves as such with certainty during their teenage years; many women do not admit their nonheterosexual orientation to themselves until a later point in their lives—especially after a failed marriage.[17] And relatively few women who later identify themselves as lesbians actually have a sexual encounter with another female during adolescence.

For teenage males who feel "different," there is more variability. Many have recognized this part of themselves since an early age and have already accepted their propensity as a given aspect of their lives. Others experiment hesitantly with their same-sex impulses: at first, they seek out books, magazines, and films to try out their reactions and expectations (frequently using such materials as masturbatory aids); later, especially if they connect with a friend who seems similar, they may seek to be initiated into the mysteries and attractions of male-to-male loving. (Teenage boys who live in cities with visible gay communities are at something of an advantage in the discovering-oneself process. They are usually able to make contacts and find information—not to mention partners—more readily than their counterparts who live in more isolated suburbs, small towns, or rural areas.) Still others, who may feel attracted to girls but have also been turned on in same-sex encounters with friends, are confused and worried about their sexual identities.

Many teenage boys who feel homoerotic urges fight against them in numerous ways: they may try to establish their masculinity (thereby obtaining peer acceptance) by participation in sports; they go through the motions of dating and otherwise trying to fit into the heterosexual scene; and most of all, they desperately try to hide the side of themselves that they consider shameful or even dangerous. However, a majority of gay males have an initial sexual experience with another male during adolescence, with many having a substantial number of partners by the time they graduate from high school.

It is clear that healthy psychosexual development for an adolescent who identifies himself or herself as gay is no easy task.

> There are no manuals, schools, institutions, or easily visible role models for guidance. In fact, the path is obscured by misinformation, fear, and shame. Sexual development for gay and lesbian people is a function of experiential learning; and mistakes are punishable by fatal sexually transmitted diseases, social ostracism, and other harsh penalties. The development of a healthy sexual identity against such odds is a testimony to the resilience of adolescents and adults who survive the crisis of "coming out."[18]

Today, many gay and lesbian adolescents find a ready-made support network when they get to college. A substantial number of colleges and universities now have active gay and lesbian societies that organize social events, work diligently to counter homophobia, and encourage students who have not yet become comfortable with their sexual identities. Still, we suspect that relatively few gays and lesbians actually identify themselves to their families until they are young adults. The natural identity confusion of adolescence is simply too fragile to permit most homosexual or lesbian individuals to undertake such a drastic step until they have solidified their own sense of who they are.

EFFECTS OF SEXUAL ACTIVITY

While most of the research about the effects of adolescent sexual activity has focused on teens who become pregnant unintentionally, there has been little attention devoted to the short-term social and psychological consequences of teenagers' early participation in sexual activity. One recent study shed light on this topic by examining data collected from 1980 to 1982 on a sample of teenage students in an urban area of Florida.[19] In 1980, the 1,405 students who were interviewed ranged in age from 11 to 17, with a mean age of 14.1; all were in the seventh, eighth, or ninth grades. Two years later, 1,182 of the original sample (82 percent) were reinterviewed; at this time, most were in grades nine, ten, or eleven, and the mean age was 15.9. There were several broad conclusions reached about the short-term consequences of early adolescent sexual involvement.

1. Contrary to what some adults fear, teenage sex does not usually lead to pronounced changes in the teenager's social psychological framework.

2. There generally tend to be more significant effects on the subsequent attitudes and behaviors of whites than blacks, most notably a negative effect on academic performance of white teenage males and a lessening of the importance placed among white females on going to college. (The reasons for these findings are unclear.)

3. Early participation in sexual activity produces more positive attitudes toward sex for all racial groups.

The biological side of this coin is worth examining too. For sexually active teens who do not experience unintended pregnancy, there are still some biological consequences. The most notable is the risk of contracting a sexually transmitted disease, which if undiagnosed or improperly treated may have a long-range impact on fertility and health (see Chapters 11 and 13). Evidence that rates of STDs have risen sharply among teens in the past two decades stands in contrast to the "it can't happen to me" attitude that many adolescents have about this aspect of their sex lives; in the United States, some 2.5 million teenagers contract an STD each year. Certainly, in the age of AIDS, it is imperative that teens be alert to the risks involved in engaging in sexual activity, although there is little evidence that knowledge about AIDS in teenagers has led to substantial changes in adolescent sexual behavior. In addition, there is considerable evidence that early participation in sexual intercourse and sex with multiple partners is a risk factor for subsequent cancer of the cervix in females.[20]

Beyond the health risks just noted, voluntarily engaging in sexual intercourse does not seem to pose serious personal or emotional problems for unmarried teenagers *who use contraception consistently and correctly*. In fact, "for the average adolescent sexual activity which is part of the ongoing attempt to relate to caring and supportive peers" doesn't typically cause problems.[21] However, not all teens who engage in intercourse do so voluntarily, and those subjected to coercive sex may have a variety of long-term psychological scars from the experience.

COERCIVE SEX AND ADOLESCENTS

One recent study found that 15 percent of students in grades six to twelve reported having had at least one unwanted sexual experience.[22] More than one-quarter of these episodes involved physical force, and another quarter occurred in association with drug or alcohol use. In another study, nearly 13 percent of white females reported having been raped or coerced into sex by age 20, while 8 percent of black females reported having such an experience.[23] The authors of the latter study, which utilized a nationally representative sample of adolescents, pointed out that their findings probably underestimate the actual figures because of the sensitive nature of the information.

One of the largely hidden problems of teenage sex in the past has been a remarkably high incidence of coercive sex, with date or acquaintance rape, rather than assault by a stranger, being by far the largest category of such cases. An extensive survey on 32 college campuses conducted by *Ms.* magazine showed that one out of ten women had been raped in the previous year, and one in six had been the victim of an attempted rape.[24] Fifty-seven percent of the actual rapes occurred on dates, and in 84 percent of cases, the victims knew their assailants.

Date or acquaintance rape is relatively common even among younger adolescents, including those in the junior high school age bracket. Although sometimes these rapes involve overtly aggressive behavior by the male, in which he uses threats or physical force to subdue his victim, at other times the male (or several males, acting in tandem, in a group acquaintance rape) pushes himself onto a not-fully-conscious female whose awareness or judgment is impeded by drugs or alcohol. In either event, it is rape, but the sad reality is that most teenagers who are raped never report the assault, feeling that they are somehow to blame for the incident or not even being sure if a crime has been committed.

One reason for this confusion is that weapons are almost never employed in date rape, and direct verbal threats are frequently not made. In addition, it's hard for many teenagers to define what has happened as rape, since the stereotyped image of a rapist in their minds is a stranger wearing a stocking mask and grabbing a woman as she walks past a dark alley. Victims of date rape also tend to put a lot of the responsibility for what happened on their own shoulders, questioning their own judgment, rather than placing the blame where it belongs—on the rapist.

If any common denominator among adolescent victims of date rape exists, it may be a lack of sophistication about males and dating. College women may be especially vulnerable to date rape because they are away from home—often for the first time—and may be uncertain of how to handle themselves in new situations. They may also be too trusting of males they are dating, assuming almost automatically that a fellow student wouldn't want to hurt or exploit them. This is particularly evident in cases where a college woman (or younger teenager) goes to her date's room and fails to recognize the sexual intentions likely to be present in such a situation.

Teenage females may also be victims of incest, although most commonly such behavior begins during preadolescence. Discussions of patterns of incest and its long-term consequences are beyond the scope of this book.

AIDS AWARENESS AMONG ADOLESCENTS

Data on adolescent awareness of the HIV/AIDS epidemic and on the impact of such awareness on actual sexual behavior are slowly emerging. Despite clear evidence that anal intercourse and vaginal intercourse with more than one partner put a person at risk of infection with HIV and that condoms reduce the risk of transmission of HIV, many teenagers seem oblivious to the need to exercise caution.

Several studies have found that fewer than 10 percent of sexually active adolescents consistently use condoms.[25] One report noted that 26 percent of teenage females had engaged in anal intercourse, with only one-third of them using condoms for this high-risk activity.[26] Approximately 40 percent of sexually active teenagers have multiple sex partners each year, and those who have the largest number of partners are least likely to follow "safer sex" guidelines.

A recent survey of seventh- and eighth-grade students (average age, 13.2) found that 25 percent were sexually active, and that those who were sexually active tended to be less knowledgeable about HIV, less afraid of becoming infected with HIV, and more likely to engage in risky behaviors than peers who were not sexually active.[27]

Even among teenage males with hemophilia—an especially high-risk group for infection with the AIDS virus—the reportedly "high level of factual knowledge" about AIDS did not seem to coincide with sensible behavior: only one of nine who were sexually active always used condoms, and 69 percent had not altered their sexual behavior because of concerns about transmitting HIV.[28] Remarkably, their knowledge of the AIDS risk did not predict whether teens would use condoms in their most recent episode of sexual intercourse.

On the other hand, data from the 1988 National Survey of Adolescent Males reported that levels of condom use rose substantially from 1979 to 1988: among 17- to 19-year-old males in metropolitan areas, condom use at last intercourse almost tripled (from 21 percent in 1979 to 58 percent in 1988).[29] At the same time, it was disturbing to note that male teenagers who had used drugs intravenously or whose sex partners had done so, or who had ever had sex with a prostitute, or who had five or more sex partners in the past year had significantly lower than average condom use. Since these groups totaled some 42 percent of the men in the survey, it is clear that AIDS prevention is hardly being implemented in a risk-related manner among most teenagers.

UNINTENDED TEENAGE PREGNANCY

Although the problem of unintended teenage pregnancy has been in the news for years, the actual scope of this epidemic is startling. Here are some pertinent facts.

• One out of 10 American teenage girls aged 15 to 19 becomes pregnant each year; of these pregnancies, five out of six are unintended.[30]

• In absolute numbers, in 1985 more than one million teenagers became pregnant.[31] These pregnancies resulted in almost half a million live births and more than 400,000 induced abortions (the rest ended in miscarriages or stillbirths).

• Less than half of teenage females use contraception the first time they have intercourse; not surprisingly, half of all first pregnancies occur within the first six months of first having intercourse.[32]

• In the United States, approximately 18 percent of sexually experienced teenage females aged 15 to 19 become pregnant each year, with substantially higher rates found among blacks than whites.[33]

• While it is true that since 1970 the birthrate among teens has declined significantly, most of this decrease has been due to the legalization of abortion in 1973.[34]

Overall, it seems that American teenagers are aware of the risk of unintended pregnancy, but many see little chance that this risk might apply to their own lives. As one sexually active 15-year-old girl explained, "We all sort of pretend that pregnancy is something that only happens to someone else." This attitude is unintentionally reinforced by parents who warn their adolescent children not to become pregnant but do nothing concrete to help their teens learn about or obtain contraception.

Although some teenagers are conscientious about using birth control—in part, out of concern for parental wrath or about sexually transmitted diseases such as HIV/AIDS—others steer away from contraceptives entirely, providing detailed rationalizations for their actions. Here are some of the comments we have heard from teens explaining why they don't use contraceptives.

A 17-year-old boy: Condoms are clumsy and cut down on your feelings. Besides, they make sex mechanical, like there's no intimacy involved.
A 16-year-old girl: I wanted my boyfriend to use something, but he refused, and then once we started, there didn't seem to be any point to it.
A 14-year-old girl: I'm too young to start using the pill, and if I carry around a condom, the guys will think I'm a whore.
A 15-year-old boy: I don't really know why we don't use anything. I mean, it's just that nothing's ever happened, so it doesn't seem like a big deal.

Although these explanations may sound empty-headed to adults, they apparently appear perfectly logical to many teens, which is one reason they have so many unintended pregnancies. (In fairness, we should note that there are millions of American teenagers who are more responsible with their sexuality. We don't mean to disparage them in any way: all teenagers are not alike.) Part of the reason for this contraceptive waffling is that many adolescents believe that planning for sex is wrong, that sex is somehow more authentic and meaningful if it occurs spontaneously, which precludes anything as nonspontaneous as purchasing a package of condoms or being fitted for a diaphragm. Again, this is a reflection of inadequate or nonexistent sex

education in the home; adolescents whose parents stress the need for contraception, rather than just talk about not getting pregnant, generally have
kids who *use* contraception. Another pertinent factor is this: many adolescent girls who get pregnant had no idea they were going to have sex. Here is
how one 14-year-old girl described it to us:

> It just sort of happened, you know, like one minute we were dancing close and
> kissing, and then the next minute our clothes were off and we were doing it.
> The whole thing happened so fast that I hardly realized what was going on.

Not using contraception, or inconsistent use of contraception—which
may be an even more common pattern among teenagers—is not the entire
explanation, however. Some teenagers regard having a baby as a sign of being
grown up and independent, although they are apt to change this tune when
the baby's a year old and they realize how much the baby actually cuts down
their freedom. Other teenagers see the risk of pregnancy as just one risk
among many that they encounter every day. As such, they mistakenly
trivialize this possibility because they assign it about the same probability as
other risks in their lives (e.g., becoming infected with HIV, being shot, being
hit by lightning) which are actually much less apt to occur. Teenagers are not
particularly good at risk assessment.

TEENAGE MOTHERS

Although statistics clearly show that nonwhite teenage females have a pregnancy rate twice as high as among white teenagers,[35] unintended pregnancies occur in virtually all racial groups and across all socioeconomic lines.

Teenage motherhood is problematic for a variety of reasons, but the
greatest concerns center about the fact that early parenthood almost inevitably puts the future of the young mothers and their children in jeopardy
socially, economically, and educationally. For one thing, most teenage
mothers have few financial resources available to them, which in combination with their poor occupational prospects places them at risk for becoming
dependent on welfare on a long-term basis. This welfare dependency is
exacerbated by the fact that teenage mothers don't usually stop with one
child: they have more children, more quickly, than their peers who don't
become mothers in their teenage years.[36] However, there is another way of
looking at this issue: it may be that girls who are weak academically and who
come from poor families see teenage motherhood as a more attractive option
than others do (seeing fewer available opportunities in their futures), thus
increasing their odds of becoming teenage mothers.

Teenage mothers are only half as likely to complete high school as females who delay childbearing until their twenties; for many of them this statistic translates into bleak prospects for jobs or breaking out of the poverty cycle. Fortunately, however, it now appears that a majority of teenage mothers are graduating from high school despite the obstacles in their paths, in contrast to the situation just a decade earlier.[37] On the other hand, a high school education doesn't go very far today compared to 25 years ago, so the significance of this newer trend may not be as positive as it sounds on the surface.

Teenage mothers who place their children for adoption do not appear to suffer more negative psychological consequences than those who choose to raise their children themselves.[38] In addition, they are more likely than those who keep their children to delay marriage and to be employed. Furthermore, teenage mothers who keep their children are more likely to become pregnant again while still teenagers than those who have put their children up for adoption.

The children of teenage mothers are also at a number of disadvantages that go beyond effects linked to poverty. Notably, they have higher rates of childhood diseases and more physical and cognitive problems than children of older mothers, in turn leading to a higher frequency of academic problems when they reach their school years.[39] These developmental difficulties may be partly due to the generally poor prenatal care received by pregnant teenagers, which is one of the most pressing aspects of the problem of unintended teenage pregnancy. In addition, two other factors may apply. First, younger teenagers have more medical complications in their pregnancies than women in the 18-to-30 age range have. These complications undoubtedly have adverse effects on the health of the developing fetus. Second, children who don't live with both of their biological parents have a higher risk of health problems such as accidents, injuries, and poisonings, which probably compounds their health problems.[40] Researchers who tried to discover why children of teenage mothers score lower on achievement tests than other children came up with another important finding. They found that the amount of cognitive stimulation in the early home environment—for example, whether or not a mother reads to her child, and whether children's books are available—is often sorely lacking.[41]

One additional point about teenage mothers bears mentioning. A recent study of a nationally representative sample of women found that those whose mothers had their first child while still in their teens were more likely to repeat this pattern than women whose mothers were older at their first birth.[42] Other studies also show an intragenerational transmission of teenage parenthood, although the exact explanation for this pattern is far from

clear.[43] Even though only a minority of children of teenage mothers actually
go on to repeat this pattern themselves, the situation is alarming because, as
one study noted, "the daughters have bleaker educational and financial
prospects than their mothers had, and are less likely to ever have married . . .
[and] may be less likely . . . to overcome the handicaps of early childbearing."[44] This self-perpetuating cycle of despair is of immense national importance, yet it has received remarkably little direct federal attention beyond
Band-Aid attempts at prevention programs.

TEENAGE FATHERS

Until very recently, little was known about teenage fathers or about which
adolescents were most likely to become teenage fathers. New research,
admittedly still incomplete, offers some interesting findings.

One important study used a sample of tenth-grade boys drawn from
1,100 high schools across the United States in 1980, with follow-ups done
in 1982 and 1984.[45] The researchers compared adolescents who became
fathers with controls who did not and concluded that there are three major
predictors of teenage fatherhood: (1) being black, which was associated
with an increased probability of fathering a child even when the effect of
socioeconomic status was controlled for; (2) going steady, which raised the
odds of becoming a teenage father by 50 percent; and (3) having nontradi-
tional, accepting attitudes toward out-of-wedlock childbearing. They also
noted that taking a sex education course in school had no relation to
teenage fatherhood.

These findings were consistent with other studies that showed that being
black increases the chances of teenage fatherhood.[46]

This racial disparity, which has been noted not only in the studies cited
above but in others as well, raises the difficult question of whether there is a
different outlook on teenage pregnancy and childbearing in the black community. This issue is highlighted by the fact that among all American teenage
males, blacks are twice as likely as Hispanics to father a child out of
wedlock, and more than four times as likely as whites.[47] (Of course, this
statistic is partly influenced by whether or not the pregnancy is ended by
abortion, so it is not as clear-cut as it might first seem to be.) In addition,
fewer black teenage males than either whites or Hispanics use effective
contraception in their first intercourse experience.[48] While a full discussion
of this issue is beyond the scope of this book, some experts have suggested
that lack of economic opportunity in the black community causes teens to
develop pessimistic outlooks about their educational and occupational prospects, setting the stage for fatalistic attitudes toward the inevitability of early

parenthood.[49] Others point out that black teenagers may have goals that are more compatible with early parenthood than those of their high school classmates.[50] In any event, there is no convincing evidence that black teenage males are sexually or socially irresponsible, although myths about teenage fathers abound.

The general stereotype about teenage fathers is well known: they are typically portrayed as irresponsible, interested only in their personal sexual gratification, and quicker to duck out the door than to assume any financial, emotional, or familial role in caring for their offspring. New research suggests that this bleak portrait is far from accurate. Instead, it shows that many teenage fathers are choosing not to abandon their babies, opting instead to contribute financially to the care of their children and showing more than passing interest in the responsibilities of parenting.

Much of the work on this topic done during the 1980s has been summarized in a book called *Teenage Fathers*, which identifies five common myths that have been applied to this group in the past.[51]

1. *Super Stud Myth:* The teenage father is worldly wise and more knowledgeable about sex, and more sexually experienced, than other teens.
   Fact: While teenage fathers tend to be sexually active earlier than other teens, they are relatively unsophisticated in their sexual knowledge— especially when it comes to knowledge about contraception.

2. *Don Juan Myth:* Teenage fathers prey on unsuspecting, innocent girls with their smooth banter and sexual demands; they are sexual exploiters, more interested in conquests than consequences.
   Fact: The available evidence indicates that there is relatively little exploitation in teenage sexual relationships where pregnancies occur. Indeed, some teenage fathers feel that *they* were exploited, rather than the other way around, especially if the girl claimed to be using contraception—but wasn't.

3. *Macho Myth:* Teenage fathers have poor impulse control and are bent on proving thaeir masculinity at all costs. Having sex with a girl lets them put a notch on their belt.
   Fact: There is no evidence that teenage fathers are more lacking in impulse control than other teenage males of the same age and background. Although the need to prove one's masculinity through sex may sometimes be present (as it is in many young adults and middle-aged men too), it could also be argued that teenage mothers are proving their femininity through their sexual participation.

4. *Mr. Cool Myth:* Teenage fathers typically have brief, casual sex with the girls they impregnate and have few emotional attachments to either the baby or the mother.
   Fact: In contrast to the notion of teenage fathers having brief, casual sexual relations, studies show that most have close, caring ties with their girlfriends and have strong feelings about the pregnancy.

5. *Phantom Father Myth:* Teenage fathers quickly detach themselves from the relationships once pregnancy occurs, leaving the mother and baby alone and on their own, with no support from them.
   Fact: In the past, a teenage boy who impregnated a girl often left town to avoid being forced to marry her, sometimes joining the army, sometimes just "disappearing." Today, things are different. Not only are forced marriages far less frequent, but teenage fathers frequently choose to marry the girls they get pregnant. (In one recent study, one-third of those responsible for a nonmarital conception married within one year, and half lived with their child shortly after the baby's birth.)[52]

Of course, exposing these myths and stereotypes doesn't mean that all teenage fathers are thoughtful, responsible individuals. Many are high school dropouts (although some may have dropped out of school before impregnating a girlfriend), therefore apt to be at a distinct disadvantage in the job market. By being undereducated, they limit their earning capacity, in turn hampering their ability to contribute financially to the upbringing of their child. Other teenagers who father children become involved in drugs, gambling, or other criminal activities either in pursuit of status and adventure or in pursuit of money. And some simply don't care about the girl they've gotten pregnant or the baby.

Those who marry as teenagers are not exactly destined for a happy future. Researchers have recently identified a number of long-range repercussions on their lives, regardless of whether they married because of pregnancy or not. In a nationally representative survey of more than 14,000 men in three different age groups, those who were married before age 19 were compared to those who married later. Men who married as teenagers had lower educational attainment (completing 11.8 years of school compared to 13.1 years for men who married later), lower family incomes ($22,950 compared to $25,700), and discernibly lower occupational status.[53] In addition, the men who had married as teenagers were twice as likely to get divorced as men who married later.

For the sake of completeness, it should be pointed out that the fathers of babies born to adolescent females are not always teenagers themselves. One recent study in Baltimore, which used data from birth certificates to analyze the age of fathers of children born to teenage mothers, found that 28 percent of the partners of black women and 45 percent of the partners of white women were 20 years of age or older.[54] Only 16 percent of the fathers in this study were living with or married to the mother of their child 15 months after the child's birth.

SEX EDUCATION FOR TEENS

It would be wonderful if we could say that effective sex education could solve the problems of unintended pregnancy and high rates of sexually transmitted diseases among teenagers, but there is relatively little evidence that this is the case. However, we want to be very emphatic in making the point that if parents don't provide their children with continuing doses of sex education well before their teenage years, they have largely missed the boat. The most important sex education for adolescents occurs during childhood on an ongoing basis, not just before a 14-year-old goes out on his or her first date.

It is clear that relatively few teenagers have had a meaningful type of sex education at home. This doesn't mean that most parents don't sit down for the dutiful "birds-and-bees" lecture; but it means that teens pick up most of their sexual knowledge from discussions with friends, from movies and television, and from books and magazines. Thirteen-year-old girls read articles like "What to Do When You Discover Your Man Is Bisexual" and "Ten Ways to Make Great Sex Even Better" with avid attention; young teenage boys pore over copies of various men's magazines with enormous amounts of enthusiasm. Even those teens who do talk to their parents about sex are more apt to get strict pronouncements than informative dialogue. Thus, most adolescents' parents don't serve as useful role models for them when it comes to sexual matters, because the teenagers aren't really sure what their parents feel or think about sex.

In the absence of much sex education emanating from the home, the messages about sex that teenagers get from television and the movies loom as increasingly important. Television programs, from popular daytime soap operas to prime-time shows, show glamorous actors and actresses hopping into bed with one another with no discussion of birth control, responsibility, or consequences. Since the average American teenager watches more than 30 hours of television a week, it's not too surprising that this lack of effective sexual role models may translate into impulsive, overromanticized views of what sex is all about. Despite pressure from groups such as Planned Parenthood, network executives have generally resisted balancing their programming by incorporating more realistic messages about sex into their scripts. This situation is compounded by the fact that advertisements for contraceptives have been widely banned by the TV networks on the grounds that they are too controversial and would be morally offensive to many viewers. We can only hope that both of these situations will change in the near future.

There has been a great deal of controversy on the topic of sex education over the years, particularly on the issue of sex education in public schools. One vocal faction made up of a small number of parents and some church groups opposes school-based sex education in any form, arguing that sex education should be done either in the home, where it can be placed in the context of family values, or in church-sponsored settings, where it can be taught within a proper moral framework. The vast majority of parents and teachers, however, believe that school involvement in sex education is both proper and necessary.[55]

In recent years, there has been a definite trend toward more sex education in public schools, although it appears that AIDS education is getting more attention and funding from both the states and local school districts than sex education. Currently, all but four states support programs for AIDS education, but only two-thirds of states require or encourage schools to teach about pregnancy prevention.[56] As a result, only one-third of American junior high schools and one-half of senior high schools offer sex education courses.

Unfortunately, sex education programs vary considerably from school district to school district in their timing, content, and community acceptance. Topics that most teachers believe should be covered by grades seven or eight, at the latest, frequently are not taught until ninth or tenth grades (or later), and many school-based sex education courses omit coverage of important topics, including sources of birth control, "safer sex" practices, and homosexuality.[57] When sex education is provided only to older teenagers, its preventive function is lessened considerably. Perhaps for this reason, there is very little evidence that school sex education programs are effective when measured in terms of actual behavior such as preventing unintended pregnancies. An exception to this is a study that showed that among unmarried sexually active teenage women, those who had had sex education had fewer pregnancies than those who had not.[58]

One school-based program, out of a handful, that *has* been conclusively found to be effective was conducted in inner-city Baltimore. Here, classroom teaching and individual counseling in junior high and high school settings were combined with educational, counseling, and medical services—including no-cost contraceptive services—provided in a store-front clinic located across the street from the senior high school.[59] The clinic was open after school every day until the early evening. While this program was effective in lowering rates of unintended teenage pregnancy by 30 percent over a 2-year period, it is a mistake to regard it as simply a sex education program. In fact, since only 22 percent of staff-student contact occurred in the classroom, to equate the results of this program with the more commonly encountered standard classroom-only sex education course is incorrect.

Another innovative program has been designed for use by eighth-graders in Atlanta schools.[60] The unique features of the program, which focuses on helping students resist peer and social pressures to initiate sexual activity, are (1) the use of older teenagers in male-female teams as session leaders and (2) practical exercises emphasizing skills like how to say no without hurting the other person's feelings. Among students who had not had sexual inter-course by the eighth grade, those who participated in this program were significantly more likely to continue postponing sexual activity through the end of the ninth grade than were students who did not participate in the program.

These two examples of successful programs highlight one of the major difficulties with current sex education curricula. There is little indication that transmitting information, by itself, alters adolescents' sexual behavior in a meaningful way, which is undoubtedly why most school-based sex educa-tion programs have not proved to be effective in reducing rates of teenage sexual activity or unintended teen pregnancies.[61] Furthermore, many sex education programs are so slanted toward the notion of sexual abstinence for teens that high school students are apt to disregard them entirely.

One possibly more effective approach represents a compromise position in which the role of abstinence is promoted, but not as the exclusive option available to teens. This can be accomplished by doing the following.[62]

- Encourage teens to make healthy decisions for themselves.
- Give straight facts about the health concerns of teenage pregnancy and STDs.
- Support those teens who have chosen abstinence.
- Strengthen communication between parents and their children.
- Support comprehensive sexuality education that involves parents and community leaders.
- Offer high-quality counseling and medical services to those teenagers who call for help.

There is also solid agreement that greater responsibility for contraceptive use by the adolescent male would be a major element in reducing the rate of unintended teenage pregnancy and curbing the spread of STDs, including AIDS. Evidence suggests that educating males about contraceptive options at an early age leads to better contraceptive use, but such education need not be confined to the classroom. Community-based programs, direct mail and media campaigns, and church-affiliated programs may all play a role in this undertaking. But the information given must be practical, not just informative: it must explain how and where to purchase contraceptives (and how to deal with embarrassment over the purchase), why it's important to discuss birth control with a partner, and why *consistent* contraceptive use is necessary.

Whatever the ultimate solution, we believe that it is particularly important to realize that sex education for adolescents cannot be successful if it focuses only on biological facts and negative consequences. Without including coverage of intimacy, interpersonal relationships, sexual decision-making, different sexual orientations, and coercive sex, to name just a few essential topics, school programs will be incomplete and, inevitably, ineffective. In addition, if sex education programs cannot acknowledge that sexual activity for adolescents is not inherently harmful, sinful, or destructive—if they cannot be honest enough to point out that sex for teenagers can be pleasurable, responsible, and caring—we are providing our teenagers with the wrong message.

Sixteen

Sex and Aging

A tremendous taboo surrounds the subject of sex in the geriatric years. It combines with general negative attitudes toward aging that create an unfortunate set of stereotypes: older individuals are widely believed to be rigid and incapable of growth or change; they are also commonly seen as hypochondriacs who are especially prone to depression; and they are often considered to be not only old-fashioned and unproductive but disengaged and more or less senile. Given the preceding stereotypes, it's little wonder that the elderly are seen as sexless. (After all, why would such awful people want to have sex?) Such ageisms help explain why Hollywood doesn't make many pictures showing elderly couples in bed with one another: the prevailing notion seems to be that the "golden years" are a time of neutered affection in which hugging, nuzzling, and maybe even a kiss or two are permissible, but anything more overtly sexual is perverse or unnatural—a sign of a dirty mind. (In the midst of the sexual revolution, the TV show "Laugh-In" had a Dirty Old Man as one of its regular mirth-provoking features.)

Myths about sex and aging abound in modern society; unfortunately, some of them are held by doctors and nurses who should be better informed about and less intimidated by the subject. Since the number of elderly persons in the U.S. almost doubled from nearly 17 million in 1960 to 32 million in 1991, and will reach a projected 51 million by 2020,[1] this topic takes on a particular relevance to all of our lives.

463

SEX AND AGING: THE PHYSIOLOGIC FACTS

There are certain changes in the physiology of sexual response that are hallmarks of aging. These alterations are no more signs of pathology than gray hair is, but because they constitute a different set of physiologic realities from those that apply at younger ages, they don't match the expectations most people have for how their bodies should perform. This gap between expectations and actuality frequently becomes the source of considerable emotional distress: convinced that something is wrong and that their sexual abilities are failing them, many older adults turn away from the physical side of romance under the mistaken impression that impaired sexual responsivity is the inevitable byproduct of advancing age. Armed with an understanding of just what is happening to their bodies, older persons can accommodate to the changes gracefully and happily, preserving the right to be sexual and intimate without using the wrong criteria as a yardstick of performance.

SEXUAL EFFECTS OF AGING IN THE MALE

The most visible sign of aging as it affects male sexual response is that erections no longer happen with the instantaneous ardor they seemed to possess at a younger age. To the man who was used to watching himself spring into action at virtually any sexual provocation in his twenties (and possibly in his thirties and forties as well), the notion of an erection unfolding slowly—taking minutes, rather than seconds, to poke into view—is often daunting and frustrating. For years, he measured his passion by the swiftness of his phallic response, and now he is puzzled by the discrepancy between the arousal he feels physically and the physical manifestation of his passion, often believing that his inner arousal is somehow suspect, a counterfeit feeling that is diminished by the absence of its matching external proof. He is, of course, confusing the speed of a physiologic reflex with its merit, as if faster always equals better. That doesn't hold true with sex any more than it holds true with the maturation of fine wine. To mix our metaphors up a little, faster doesn't equal better in sex any more than faster eating makes for a better meal.

Related to the concern over the swiftness of erectile response for the aging male is a second physiologic reality about erections. Most of the time, for most men, erections are not as rock-hard and throbbing in the sixties, seventies, and eighties as they were at younger ages. This doesn't mean that there is anything wrong: the penis engorges with blood, becomes enlarged and considerably firmer than in the flaccid state, and in most regards (save for a possible loss of dimension, from "gigantic" to just plain "big") is very much like erections of days gone by. True, some older men say that they notice a bit less tactile sensitivity in their erect penises than they remember feeling at a younger age. (This effect probably reflects a combination of a subtle change in the processing of sensory signals from nerve endings in the skin of the penis, and a mechanical effect in which the less taut skin on the shaft of the penis is not as sensitive to certain types of pressure.) But this slightly reduced sensitivity has its positive side, too; it undoubtedly contributes to a reduced urgency to ejaculate, which gives many men a greater degree of sexual staying power than they had when they were younger.

These two changes in the nature of erections with aging provoke considerable dismay. The unfortunate reality is that many men equate bigger with better, and faster with more aroused, more involved, more *ready* to have sex. Here are typical comments we have heard.

A 65-year-old attorney: I am slowly losing my sexual abilities, and it is especially distressing because I am otherwise in completely good health and see no reason for this deterioration in my functioning. The most worrisome thing, to me, is that I don't get erections quickly anymore, which is something that has developed over the past 5 or 6 years. The trouble is, when I don't feel hard, I don't feel like I'm participating, and my wife thinks I'm not interested. This causes her to give up on sex before we even get started. "You're not in the mood," she'll tell me, when in fact I am as horny as hell.

A 74-year-old retiree: I've sort of given up on my sex life because I've noticed that it seems to take forever to get myself worked up. Even when I masturbate, I have to conjure up elaborate fantasies and work at it before I get an erection, whereas when I was younger, my erections just sort of popped up as soon as I unzipped my fly—and sometimes even before I could get the zipper open. . . . And when I'm with my girlfriend, she has to play with me for 5 or 10 minutes sometimes before I can get it up, and sometimes even that doesn't seem to do anything—like the damn thing's gone to sleep.

It's not only men who are put off by this change in male sexual response that accompanies aging. Women frequently misconstrue the situation to mean either that their partners don't find them attractive or stimulating or that their partners are less interested in sex than they used to be. In addition, some women mistakenly decide that in the absence of a strong, swift erection, it's somehow better not to touch the man's penis, as though such avoidance will spare the man embarrassment or a sense of personal failure. The result of this assumption is all too often that there isn't enough physical stimulation to elicit an erection, so that the sexual episode ends in frustration or disappointment instead of pleasure. If, instead, a woman exhibits some patience in caressing the penis and scrotum playfully, in an exploring, rather than demanding, manner, the odds are quite good that an erection will blossom forth. In a fundamental law of sexual physics, we can say: lack of stimulus plus anxiety over an absent erection equal a missed opportunity and a lingering memory of failure, which, if reinforced by repetition, is apt to become raised exponentially to the level of a self-fulfilling prophecy.

In order to avoid any misunderstanding of the preceding point, we should hasten to add that we are not recommending that a woman direct all of her stimulative attention directly to the penis or genital region. Our advice, which applies equally well to younger as well as older couples, is that whenever erections are a bit slow to appear, there should be some attempt at nondirective stimulation: said another way, sex play should be just that—play—and should encompass as much variety as is pleasant and interesting to both partners. To focus one's stroking and touching exclusively or almost exclusively in the genital region is inadvertently to set the man up for failure. However, avoiding direct touching of the penis in such situations is one of the most common mistakes we encounter couples making. While the premise behind such a practice may sound logical—directly touching the nonerect penis only calls attention to its flaccidity, so it's sort of like rubbing salt in a wound—the logic is fundamentally flawed. Taking into account both the naturalness of sexual responsivity, when nature is allowed to take its course, and the reality of genital touching being stimulating, it is far more practical to adopt a "hands on" rather than "no hands" approach.

Here is a related point to consider. As we have said many times before, to view the presence of an erection as an absolute indicator of sexual passion and potential pleasure is a big mistake. It is certainly very possible to have great sex without having penile-vaginal containment. Intimate, tender, passionate sex can occur without a rigid erection, a semirigid erection, or any erection at all. Both men and women can be sexually satisfied in a variety of creative scenarios that involve myriad forms of oral, tactile, and/or frictional embraces. To think that there is only one "right" way to have sex is to lose the chance to multiply the fun a thousand times over. Besides, to miss the creative, playful, and highly stimulating sides of noncoital sex is to miss participating in the very passion-arousing acts that can spark an erection just when no one is expecting it to appear, which adds a happy bonus to the entire proceedings.

The other principal changes in male sexual functioning that occur with aging relate to ejaculation. Most men have a noticeable decrease in the amount of semen that is produced. (This diminution is the result to some extent of somewhat lowered production of testosterone and related hormones, which we will discuss separately.) Partly because of this reduced fluid volume, and partly because of changes in the intensity of neuromuscular signals to and responses in the prostate gland, which is itself affected by aging, the intensity of ejaculation is reduced. This diminished intensity is felt both as a less propulsive orgasm (corresponding to less vigorous rhythmic contractions by the prostate that initiate the process) and as a less powerful rush of ejaculatory fluid from the penis. This occurs because the fluid wave is started by less pressure generated by contractions internally, in the prostate and seminal vesicles (i.e., weaker pumping); in addition, a less powerful ejaculation is felt because there is actually less fluid moving through the urethra, the tube inside the body of the penis that carries semen to the exterior of the body.

Even though orgasm and ejaculation are not synonymous, many older men notice a reduction in the intensity of their experience of orgasm along with their altered sensation of ejaculation. This phenomenon is best understood by recognizing that the physical side of orgasm is primarily a neuromuscular event, and a certain amount of deterioration of neuromuscular function is a normal part of aging. Just as a man of 70 probably can't lift as much weight or run as fast as he did at age 25, so too there are more subtle changes occurring in neural transmission, blood flow to muscles, and the general coordination of physiologic responses that affect the intensity and duration of orgasm.[2] In addition, for many men, age-related alterations in the prostate gland itself, including the very common condition called benign prostatic hypertrophy (discussed in Chapter 12), contribute to the process by making the prostate less efficient as a mechanical pump.

Several corollaries of these physical changes involve ejaculation. For one thing, as we mentioned, there is usually less urgency to ejaculate associated with the buildup of sexual excitement: therefore, aging men usually have more sense of control over ejaculation, instead of feeling as if they were on the brink of shooting off in an uncontrolled manner. This change can, of course, be very positive for men who had a tendency to ejaculate too quickly at a younger age, and it is one that many female partners appreciate, as well. In addition, men feel less of a need to ejaculate at each and every sexual encounter. In fact, with aging, many men find that they are physically satisfied with ejaculating on occasion—for instance, once or twice a month—rather than at each opportunity. In general, we have found that the need to ejaculate diminishes with advancing age: a man who ejaculates twice a week at age 60 might ejaculate only once a week at age 75, even though he continues to have sexual activity as often at age 75 as he did at age 60.[3] Furthermore, in a related development, the refractory period is considerably longer in men over age 60 than in younger ones. That is, when he is older, it takes a man much more time to go through that phase of the physiologic resolution period during which he is incapable of ejaculating again, no matter how powerful the sexual stimulus. While a 70-year-old can perhaps get an erection again within a few hours after ejaculating (greater rapidity than this would be highly unusual for a man aged 70, but is certainly not impossible), the refractory period for men in their late sixties or seventies is apt to be measured in days rather than hours.

These changes relating to patterns of ejaculation are a common source of distress to aging men's female sex partners, who misunderstand what is happening. Instead of recognizing that not needing to ejaculate at every sexual opportunity is a reflection of a physiologic slowing down, many women assume that they are not providing their partners with enough stimulation or that their partners are not enthusiastic enough about the quality of their lovemaking. In either case, they may take the effect as a personal affront, which is apt to have a chilling effect on their own bedroom ardor. If, instead, they are aware of the underlying shift in the male's sexual responses that are part of the normal aging process, they can readily accept the situation without feeling that there is anything wrong with either one of the couple. Understanding these age-associated changes also allows both partners to enjoy their sexual interaction for its own sake instead of trying to rate its success in terms of one particular event: the male's ejaculation.

The primary mechanism underlying the various physiologic changes in male sexual responsivity seen with aging is a gradual decline in gonadal function. It is reflected in several different ways. Sperm production decreases in men with advancing age,[4] although (unlike the reproductive situation in women) the capacity to reproduce is not generally lost even at age 80 or 90. At the same time, there is a gradual reduction in production of testosterone and related androgens.[5] New research has elucidated the mechanism by which this change occurs, providing evidence that aging leads to changes in the central control of testicular function—that is, changes in the hypo-thalamus and pituitary gland that affect the secretion of LH, which in turn modulates androgen production at the testicular level.[6] The net result of a lowered production of testosterone is seen in the changes we have discussed above: erections are slower to occur, semen production is reduced, ejaculatory intensity decreases, and so forth. Theoretically, it would seem that lower testosterone levels would also lead to a reduced sex drive in elderly men, but it is fairly clear that in humans, at least, there is no simple equation describing this relationship, since there are important psychosocial determinants of libido that may outweigh minor changes in hormone production.

In our experience, about 5 percent of men over age 60 have a condition that can legitimately be described as a male climacteric. These men have clear-cut testosterone deficiencies (not simply low-normal levels of testosterone) and characteristically complain of listlessness, weight loss or poor appetite or both, low sex drive, usually accompanied by impotence, and weakness or easy fatigability. Since these are relatively nonspecific symptoms that could be seen with a variety of illnesses, including depression, cancer, or severe anemia, to establish the diagnosis accurately it is necessary to find a markedly subnormal testosterone level *and* to see significant improvement of the symptoms within two months of implementing adequate testosterone replacement therapy. (For most men, this requires injections of a long-acting form of testosterone every 2 to 4 weeks.)

SEXUAL EFFECTS OF AGING IN THE FEMALE

The changes in the physiology of women's sexual response that are associated with aging are less visible and less predictable than for men. By and large, as in men, these changes appear to be hormonally mediated: the post-menopausal decrease in estrogen production seems to be the primary culprit. However, there are undoubtedly a number of biological factors—including neurological and circulatory elements that are not well understood at present—that interact both at the cellular and at the systems level in producing these effects.

The most annoying physiological change in sexual response for many older women is that vaginal lubrication occurs more slowly and in diminished amounts than at younger ages. (This problem mirrors the changes aging men find in erections, not surprising since both physical responses reflect patterns of blood flow in the pelvic region.) While the relative slowing in vaginal lubrication is not by itself an impediment to sexual pleasure, it can become a problem if vaginal dryness produces pain or tenderness with intercourse. In addition, many women who have judged their degree of sexual arousal by how moist their vagina feels have problems with reduced vaginal lubrication: their self-monitoring tells them that they aren't sexually aroused or interested when they actually are.

Other physical changes that can affect women's sexual responses in the postmenopausal years include specific changes in the functional anatomy of the vagina. The lining becomes thinner and less elastic as a result of normal aging, sometimes appearing to be only of only tissue-paper thinness.[7] In addition to this thinning effect, the appearance of the interior of the vagina changes to a paler color, reflecting the decrease in its vascularity.[8] In some cases, this change is trivial, barely noticeable; in others, the thinning progresses to the point of actual shrinkage of the vagina (medically, this is called vaginal atrophy). The tissue lining the vagina sometimes becomes especially fragile when it thins out, with a tendency to bleed or become easily irritated or infected. When this happens, it frequently causes painful intercourse.

In contrast, the clitoris does not seem to be affected by aging. There is no loss of clitoral sensitivity with advancing age, and the clitoris continues to increase in size with sexual arousal as it becomes engorged with blood, just as it did at younger ages, although this enlargement is often not readily visible.

Likewise, the woman's capacity for orgasm is not impaired in any way by aging as long as there is no other health problem complicating the picture. In fact, many women report being more easily orgasmic in their post-menopausal years than they were previously, although this effect may relate more to psychosocial components of sexual responsivity (e.g., no worries about becoming pregnant) than to biological factors. In one study, the frequency of orgasm for sexually active women was actually found to in-crease in each decade of life through the eighties.[9]

While the ability to have orgasms does not decline with advancing age, many women over 60 note, as men do, that their orgasms are less intense than they were at younger ages. This probably reflects the physiologic realities of age-related deterioration in both the neuromuscular system and the dynamics of blood flow in both the pelvic region and perhaps the brain.[10] Notably, many postmenopausal women have fewer (and less intense) involuntary contractions of the outer portion of the vagina with orgasm. A noticeable reduction in orgasmic intensity—how orgasms feel—is partic-ularly common in women who have had hysterectomies. Whether the anatomical absence of the uterus alone is responsible, or whether there may be other factors involved (e.g., pelvic blood flow patterns, chemical sub-stances secreted in the uterus, etc.) is unclear at present.

Aging does not appear to have any predictable effect on female sexual interest. Probably, biologically speaking, libido is more dependent on an-drogen levels than on estrogen levels. Since in women androgens are made primarily in the adrenal glands and by peripheral conversion, with only a fractional production from the ovaries during the reproductive years, the cessation of ovarian function that accompanies the menopause does not significantly reduce the levels of androgens reaching the brain centers that control sexual drive. Nevertheless, some endocrinologists have advocated treating postmenopausal women who have low sex drive with testosterone. We believe this solution is usually unnecessary and liable to produce a number of unwanted side effects, including growth of facial hair, salt reten-tion, and enlargement of the clitoris.

It is clear, however, that many postmenopausal women will benefit mate-rially from estrogen replacement therapy (ERT). The specific sexual benefits that result from this practice are tied to countering the estrogen deficiency that occurs in the postmenopausal years: ERT helps to preserve the integrity of vaginal tissues, preventing atrophic changes from occurring; it also improves vaginal lubrication. In addition, some important nonsexual benefits result from estrogen replacement therapy in the postmenopausal years, the most notable of which are a reduction in the risk of developing osteoporosis (a weakening of the bones that leads to an increased risk of fractures) and protection against heart disease.

ERT reduces the risk of coronary heart disease by 40 to 50 percent overall in postmenopausal women.[11] This cardioprotective effect has been demonstrated convincingly in a number of large-scale studies.[12] It has been postulated that this result is due in large part to estrogen's favorable actions on serum lipids, especially increasing the amount of "good" cholesterol (high-density lipoprotein) in the bloodstream and lowering "bad" (low-density lipoprotein) cholesterol. In any event, an important study of 8,881 women found that older women who take estrogen tend to live longer than other postmenopausal women: among women who had used ERT for at least 15 years, there was a 40 percent reduction in the overall death rate.[13] Even among women with preexisting coronary disease, ERT produces major improvements in long-term survival.[14]

ERT's reduction in the rate of bone loss after menopause is particularly important because osteoporosis is a major cause of injury, disability, and medical expense worldwide.[15] In the U.S., osteoporosis causes more than 1,300,000 fractures annually, with hip fractures being especially common and dangerous. Here's why they are dangerous: 12 to 20 percent of women with hip fractures die within one year of the injury, and most hip fracture survivors have great difficulty with mobility and independent living. Spine fractures (technically called vertebral fractures) are another common problem among elderly women, causing pain, deformity, and disability.

Fortunately, osteoporosis can be effectively prevented by the use of ERT. When ERT is used for at least 5 years right after the menopause, the lifetime risk of hip fracture is cut in half and the risk of spine fractures is reduced by up to 90 percent.[16] While some experts advocate the concomitant use of supplemental calcium along with ERT in the postmenopausal years, not everyone agrees that taking calcium is necessary, and it is clear that taking calcium alone—without ERT—provides no protection at all against developing osteoporosis.

These effects are not the end of the story. ERT also controls hot flashes and other annoying vasomotor symptoms (like night sweats) in the postmenopausal years and helps to preserve skin texture and elasticity. In addition, many women report that ERT enhances their overall sense of well-being, which can certainly contribute to better sexual feelings and responses.

Given these highly beneficial effects, why is it that all physicians are not ERT enthusiasts? The drawback is this: there are indications that ERT may be associated with a greater risk of breast cancer and cancer of the endo-metrium (the lining of the uterus). While there are dozens of conflicting studies in the scientific literature, it appears to us that long-term estrogen use is associated with about a 30 percent rise in the risk of breast cancer.[17] For women with a family history of breast cancer, a much higher risk is involved. In our opinion, women with either a family history of breast cancer or a past breast cancer should not use ERT at all.

The situation in regard to endometrial cancer is better understood. This is a relatively uncommon cause of cancer, affecting far fewer women than breast cancer; in addition, women who have already had a hysterectomy don't have to worry about this potential problem at all. Although there is a three- to sixfold increase in the risk of endometrial cancer in post-menopausal women using unopposed estrogen, if oral progestins are used in the last 10 days of the estrogen cycle, allowing for a periodic shedding of the lining of the uterus, this risk is significantly reduced, although not eliminated entirely.[18] (Unfortunately, the addition of progestins to the hormone re-placement regimen means that women begin having menstrual periods again, which can be annoying.) Finally, it should be pointed out that since endometrial cancer is usually a slow-growing form of cancer, it is easily detectable in its early stages, when it is also eminently treatable.

PATTERNS OF SEXUAL BEHAVIOR

It isn't surprising that systematic data about sexual behavior in elderly individuals are not readily available. Much of the information that has been published is based on imprecise sampling procedures and questionable methods of gathering unbiased data. However, despite these deficiencies, what is clear is that people over age 60 continue to have sexual needs and feelings; what's more, they act on these needs and feelings far more often than many people might imagine.

There are three common themes that emerge from dozens of studies that have been done in the past 20 years on sexual behavior among older adults. The first is that patterns of sexual activity and enjoyment in old age depend, to a large extent, on the frequency and enjoyment of sex at younger ages.[19] Of course, common sense suggests that anyone who found sex distasteful or unappealing in young adulthood or middle age would be likely to adopt the mantle of a sexless old age as a comfortable way to avoid an unwanted activity. In addition, many individuals who tolerated sex as an expected part of their matrimonial responsibilities, but derived little pleasure from it, turn happily to abstinence in their older years. (In some instances, this attitude is tied to a view of sex as primarily having a reproductive purpose, but in many other cases it is simply retirement from a chore that is seen as no longer necessary, proper, or even dignified.) There are also many older men and women who mask their lack of enthusiasm for sex under the guise of health problems: they play out the role of being sick (usually with a chronic illness such as arthritis, heart disease, or hypertension) in a way that is disproportionate to the realities of their physical status. Illness thus becomes an excuse for abstinence, as well as a means of obtaining sympathy and perhaps other forms of special treatment in a relationship.

The opposite side of the coin here is that couples who found sex fulfilling and enjoyable as younger adults tend to continue active, fulfilling sex lives well into their sixties, seventies, and eighties. Not only does sexual activity continue for these individuals, it may even improve: some develop a broader repertoire of techniques and feel that they become better lovers; some relax more; some find greater freedom in not having to worry about pregnancy or interruptions by their children or in opportunities for having sex at different times of day. Here is how one 73-year-old woman described it.

> While it's true that our sexual reflexes may have slowed down a little, what's especially apparent to me is that sex has become more sensuous and more liberating for us at this point in our lives. For one thing, my husband and I spend much more time together than we ever did before, which results in us sharing in a lot of activities—including sex—that seem to me to bring us closer. For another thing, we communicate more openly about sex now than we ever did before, which has made it easier to match our actions to our desires. For me, that has meant more cuddling and caressing instead of just rushing into intercourse when we make love, which has improved my sex life by about 300 percent.

The second broad theme that applies to sex and aging explodes the myth of sexual apathy among the elderly: most older adults continue to be interested in sex as long as shaky health doesn't undermine their libido; furthermore, a majority believe that sexual satisfaction is an important component of the overall quality of life. Not only is sex seen as important in terms of the physical pleasure it produces, it is valued for its intimacy as well. This attitude shows clearly in data from the Consumers Union survey on sex and aging, involving 4,246 men and women over age 50: the great majority of happily married men and women saw the sexual side of marriage as important, while 54 percent of unhappily married wives rated sex as being "of little importance."[20] Notably, however, the enjoyment of sex with one's spouse was rated as more important than the actual frequency of sexual activity. (Quality, not quantity, proves to be more important for couples at younger ages, too.)[21]

Sex is important for many unmarried older adults, too. Nowadays it is hardly unusual for single senior citizens to embark on active dating careers, with sexual activity an expected—and generally desired—accompaniment. In many areas, it is common to see ads from men and women in their sixties and seventies in the "personals" section of a newspaper; these are sometimes quite direct in their sexual innuendos, as the following example shows. "Youngish 70 year old widow with petite figure and sensual style looking for a male companion who's energetic, romantic, and fun in bed. (Golf addicts need not apply.)" In fact, in some retirement communities, resentment builds up toward women who are seen as being overly seductive; some women develop "reputations"; and available men are dined and courted as very valuable commodities. As one 74-year-old man put it, "I feel a little like I'm a teenager all over again, only this time around, it's the females pursuing me . . . and I like it!"

Patterns of sexual behavior change for most people as they age, although an occasional couple maintains well into their later decades the coital frequency that they established in their thirties and forties. For most married couples, the frequency of sexual intercourse declines in a more or less linear fashion from about age 40 on, although there is often a much less drastic drop in overall sexual activity than might be imagined. This continuation is found because many couples experiment with forms of sexual activity other than intercourse as they get older[22] and also because the frequency of intercourse doesn't change as much as many people think (or fear) it will. In a longitudinal survey of 250 married couples we have followed over a 10-year period (in which the average age of the men was 61.8 at the beginning of the survey period, and the average age of women was 58.6), coital frequency declined only modestly, from 3.1 times per month to 2.6 times per month. (This finding is consistent with results from a longitudinal study done at Duke University, where it was recorded that a majority of men and women between the ages of 56 and 65 had stable levels of sexual activity over a 6-year period.[23]

Although it is a topic shrouded in silence, masturbation is far more common in the elderly than most people realize.[24] The Starr-Weiner report found that half of adults in their sixties masturbate, and in the 80-to-91-year age range, 46 percent of men and 35 percent of women masturbate as well. Besides being a convenient and pleasurable form of sex, masturbation provides a useful outlet for elderly persons who have no sexual partners (or whose partners are incapacitated by illness).[25] In addition, many married older persons masturbate, too. The Consumers Union survey found that 36 percent of married women over age 50 masturbate, and among married men, the figure was 52 percent. As one 76-year-old man told us:

I never really masturbated much when I was younger, except when I was a kid, but I've found that this is an easy way to take care of my sexual urges when my wife isn't interested. Besides, it gives me a good excuse to be selfish and just take care of my own pleasure, without worrying about whether or not she's enjoying herself.

On the other hand, there are many older people who are uncomfortable with the notion of masturbation in general and are particularly shocked by the thought of a married man or woman resorting to self-stimulation as a way of finding sexual gratification. For some, it is the old "masturbation is sinful" attitude, while others see masturbation as immature or unhealthy. If we realize that many of today's septuagenarians grew up at a time when masturbation was denounced in the *Boy Scout Handbook* as well as in many medical and religious texts, it is not hard to see where these views come from.

The third major finding related to sexual behavior in elderly couples is that declining frequencies of sexual contact are more linked to the health status of the male partner than any other single factor. A recent report noted that 35 percent of a sample of men over 60 had difficulty getting or maintaining erections, with more than half of the married men over 70 affected by this problem.[26] Many of these cases were tied to medical difficulties. The same conclusion has been reached in a number of other studies, suggesting that the real problem is not just declining sexual interest, but declining health.[27] One plausible explanation is that the health problems cause erectile difficulties—either directly, by a physiologic effect, or indirectly, by altering the male's perception of his vigor (possibly making him afraid of what sexual arousal will do to his health status)—and that male sexual interest wanes only after the erectile problems have been firmly established.

Data regarding sexual interest and behavior in a previously neglected subgroup of the aged, the "old old," have only recently become available. A 1988 study of 202 healthy men and women between the ages of 80 and 102 found that while 62 percent of the men and 30 percent of the women indicated that they were still having sexual intercourse, for both sexes the most common type of sexual activity was touching and caressing without coitus.[28] Notably, the importance and frequency of sexual activity earlier in life correlated significantly with the frequency and enjoyment of sexual intercourse and touching and caressing without intercourse in "old old" age. This same study also came up with several findings that debunk prevalent myths about sex and aging. For example, only one-quarter of the women who were 80 or older complained of low sex drive, and almost as many said that they didn't have enough opportunities for sexual encounters. Remarkably, only one-third of the men who were in good health and had regular sex partners reported having difficulties with erections, providing further evidence of a point we have made for decades.[29] A listing of the sexual problems of the "old old" who have regular sexual partners is given in Table 16.1.

We want to mention briefly one other aspect of sex and aging that often gets overlooked. Gay men and women grow old, too, and in addition to having to deal with cultural stereotypes about aging also have to contend with homophobic attitudes and stereotypes. These stereotypes don't come only from the straight community. As Berger notes:

> Many older gay men believe that younger gays react negatively to them. Most older gays feel that young people sometimes take advantage of them, do not welcome their company . . . , do not care to associate or form friendships with them, and think they are dull company.[30]

The situation with older lesbians seems to be somewhat more encouraging. Although many choose to remain in the closet, partly because they are afraid of causing pain to those they love by disclosing their sexual orientation, they are usually quite welcome among younger lesbians, where they are seen as both role models and potential sexual partners, as this passage shows.

TABLE 16.1

SEX PROBLEMS IN THE "OLD OLD" BY PERCENTAGE (MEN AND WOMEN AGED 80 OR OLDER, IN GOOD HEALTH AND WITH REGULAR SEX PARTNER OR PARTNERS)

Men (N=43)		*Women (N=20)*	
Fear of poor performance	37	Orgasms too infrequent	30
Inability to maintain erection	33	Partner's erection problems	30
Inability to reach orgasm	28	Lack of vaginal lubrication	30
Inability to achieve erection	28	Nonsexual worries	25
Not enough opportunities for sexual encounters	23	Not enough opportunities for sexual encounters	25
Partner's vaginal pain or lack of lubrication	23	Low sex drive	25

SOURCE: Modified from Bretschneider, J. G., and McCoy, N. L., Sexual interest and behavior in healthy 80- to 102-year-olds, *Archives of Sexual Behavior* 17:109–129, 1988, Table V.

Age differences aren't so important for a lesbian, and she may be less fearful [than heterosexual women] of aging and its physical changes. . . . Heterosexual women are by definition confined to men for the expression of their sexuality. As they age they face an imbalance of sexual interest. Male sexuality seems to be more fragile and more susceptible to the various infirmities of age. . . . No such problem arises for lesbians. We change and develop pretty much according to the same pattern, so our sexuality can be as varied and as satisfying as we want. We've long since discovered the fine nuances of lesbian loving, and they don't diminish with age.[31]

SEXUAL PROBLEMS AND AGING

WIDOWER'S SYNDROME

There is a common form of male sexual dysfunction that has a uniquely situational signature leading to the name we coined for it in the 1970s: widower's syndrome. The problem typically occurs after a loving marriage is dissolved by the death of the wife, usually (but not always) after a long chronic illness. On the resumption of dating or other types of social interactions that place the widowed man in a potentially sexual situation, he is distressed and surprised to find that although he never previously had difficulty with getting or keeping erections, he is suddenly plagued by a major degree of sexual ineptitude. Either he has great difficulty in becoming erect, or he finds that his erections resemble a flag flying at half-staff, or when he does manage to get a firm erection, it quickly and mysteriously withers away.

It would be easy to attribute these sorts of problems to a simple case of jitters: new partner, new situation, new demands. But this explanation is too superficial. The dynamic that seems to be the hallmark of these cases is that the man experiences a significant degree of guilt in forging his new sexual bond; it is as though he feels somehow unfaithful to his deceased wife and to the warmly monogamous relationship they had shared together.* As one 58-year-old widower put it, "The damnedest thing was that once I was undressed and got in bed [with his newly found partner], I had the strangest

* It is interesting to note that we have never seen a case of widower's syndrome in which during their marriage the husband had been unfaithful to his wife until the point at which her lengthy terminal illness set in. (Some of these men, however, had visited prostitutes or sought out other sexual companionship in the years of their wives' illness, especially if the nature of the illness more or less precluded marital sex.) This doesn't mean that such cases can't occur, but it does suggest that men who have been involved sexually extramaritally may be far less at risk for this particular form of sexual difficulty in later life.

feeling that my wife was there in the room with us, tsk-ing with disapproval. No matter what I did, I just couldn't get her out of my mind. I guess it was no wonder I was a colossal flop."

While returning to sexual activity after a prolonged period of abstinence in old age is fraught with its own set of problems, and when the situation is complicated by a new partner replacing a mate who has died, there is apt to be an emotional overlay for anyone, it is notable that women do not commonly seem to experience a "widow's syndrome." This probably reflects several factors. First, women do not require the occurrence of a single physiologic event as specific as erection in order to be able to have intercourse. Even if they are nervous, inhibited, and guilt-laden, they are often able to overcome these feelings by a combination of judicious role-playing and, if necessary, the use of an artificial lubricant to ease the necessary mechanical connection. They may not feel any sexual arousal under such circumstances and may not enjoy what they're doing, but if they are determined enough to return to a sexually active life, they can usually overcome these problems on their own with the simple passage of time. Second, many women who have been widowed after a long, loving marriage choose to be celibate rather than sexually active with one or more new partners. (Some men who are widowers also make this choice, of course, but widowers tend to remarry in much higher numbers than widows do.) These women never have to contend with the constellation of problems alluded to above; indeed, it is possible that some women choose celibacy because they didn't enjoy sex much when their husbands were living—even when they were younger— so widowhood gives them a welcome respite from an unpleasant chore. Finally, it is quite possible that a "widow's syndrome" is more common than has been previously identified because women do not complain about the problem as directly to physicians or other health care professionals.

OTHER SEXUAL PROBLEMS IN THE GERIATRIC YEARS

Two types of logistical problems stand out as particularly common obstacles to an enjoyable sex life in old age: those created by health problems and those resulting from not having an interested partner available. Many of the health problems that create sexual difficulties are correctable or at least manageable: for example, elderly persons with hypertension should realize that it is almost always possible to devise for hypertension a program of drug therapy that has little, if any, effect on sexual function, if the problem is dealt with by a knowledgeable physician. Likewise, if angina interferes with sexual activity, it can often be managed effectively by the use of either long-acting nitrates or the use of a skin patch that delivers nitroglycerin transdermally at a predetermined rate, as well as by the use of other types of drugs such as calcium channel blockers or beta-blocking agents. Other chronic illnesses create sexual effects that are less easy to resolve. For instance, sexual problems that occur in stroke victims often become permanent impairments unless there is good progress in the overall rehabilitation from the stroke; conditions like Alzheimer's disease are notoriously unresponsive to available treatments; and combinations of severe medical problems may be virtually insurmountable.

Sexual dysfunction is a common problem following many forms of prostate surgery. In particular, men who have had transurethral resections of the prostate (TURs) are prone to develop retrograde ejaculation, a condition in which semen spurts backward into the bladder instead of being propelled through the urethra in the normal forward fashion.[32] A man who experiences retrograde ejaculation often notices that it feels "different" from normal ejaculation: although his orgasm is unaffected, he misses the sensation of fluid (semen) passing along the length of the urethra. While this effect doesn't bother everyone, some men with retrograde ejaculation are so distracted or disenchanted that they subsequently develop erection problems by worrying over their impaired response.

However, conditions that were previously written off as virtually synonymous with impaired sexual enjoyment, including diabetes, heart disease, vascular problems, and many forms of cancer, can now be treated with some success. While a more detailed discussion of these situations is beyond the scope of this book (except as covered in Chapter 12), consultation with a specialist in sexual medicine is certainly in order to obtain an in-depth evaluation of an individual problem.

Although sexual desire remains intact in old age if a reasonable state of health is maintained, the practical matter of having an interested partner available for sexual activity poses a major obstacle for some. Women are most affected by this limitation, since married women tend to outlive their mates, and for those who are widowed past age 70, there is a decreased number of available men in the population in the same age bracket. (In fact, after age 65 there four times as many single women as single men.)[33] This limitation on partners is compounded by the fact that widowers frequently choose for sexual companionship or marriage women who are somewhat younger than they are.

Many an older woman who is without a sex partner for a prolonged time drifts into a state of sexual disinterest. This is often a way of coping psychologically with her circumstances: by turning off her interest in something she doesn't have and sees little likelihood of getting, she prevents herself from becoming frustrated or depressed. On the other hand, some older women without partners never give up hope and go to great lengths to make connections that will provide them with the male companionship they are missing.

Having mentioned depression, we should point out here that (as we discussed in Chapter 12), depression is often accompanied by a loss of sexual interest and can also be a cause of sexual dysfunction. However, the possibility of depression in the elderly is sometimes overlooked, as though being depressed is somehow normal for old people. Since depression is usually easily treated, if problems such as frequent crying bouts, difficulty sleeping, poor appetite, and general loss of interest in life crop up, along with the virtual disappearance of one's (or one's partner's) sexual appetite, one should be promptly evaluated for this condition.

One additional problem that we have observed fairly commonly but that has had little attention in print is this: many men develop sexual difficulties shortly after retiring from work on a permanent basis.[34] We suspect that the genesis of this problem comes partly from the fact that most males gain a considerable portion of their sense of self from their occupation; for some, being out of work is tantamount to a drop in self-esteem. In addition, if a man sees retirement as a sign of being "put out to pasture," he is effectively telling himself that others see him as too old to continue performing competently at work. As if these elements were not enough to create a special vulnerability around the time of retirement, there are several additional forces at work. (1) Many men who don't have outside interests or hobbies don't know what to do with their extra time and wind up being annoying to their wives by hanging around the house incessantly. (2) Except for men who are in the upper socioeconomic strata, retirement generally entails a sharp cut in income—and many men see their masculinity as tied to their "breadwinners' role." (3) Although most men report little difficulty adjusting to retirement, many dread this event as much as they would a major surgical procedure. Notably, men who are forced to retire unexpectedly seem to have particular problems coping with this situation.

For a man who has had little or no trouble with erections, the most frequent problem that occurs just before or after retirement is the rather abrupt onset of erectile difficulties. The flagging erections are emblematic of a crisis of self-confidence and, if not overcome quickly by a particularly sympathetic wife who practices a bit of homespun sex therapy on her spouse, they soon give way to a more ingrained pattern of performance anxiety, self-doubt, diminishing interest in sex, and sexual avoidance. Recognizing the source of the problem often goes a long way toward finding a solution, but in some instances, a few visits to a counselor or psychotherapist are in order.

What is particularly important to remember is that, counter to prevailing stereotypes, men and women over age 60 are hardly all alike when it comes to sexual preferences, attitudes, or behavior. To attempt to deal with statistical generalities and trends alone is to miss the rich individuality that comes from biographical background, components of personality, and socioeconomic circumstances, as well as the idiosyncratic quirks that determine the twists and turns of our lives.

PRACTICAL POINTERS FOR SEXUAL SATISFACTION WITH ADVANCING AGE

Here is some helpful advice for maintaining your sexual equilibrium through your sixties, seventies, and beyond.

1. *Use it or lose it.* This is the cardinal rule for preserving sexual vigor beyond middle age. Equally applicable to men and women, the message here is simple: staying sexually active helps prevent atrophic sexual organ changes that interfere with sexual response. Just as exercise helps promote muscle strength, flexibility, and endurance in numerous nonsexual physiologic processes such as running, jumping, or lifting, sexual reflexes that don't get a periodic workout become sluggish and weakened over time. In postmenopausal women, research has shown that those who are sexually active show less shrinkage of the vagina than those who have little or no sexual activity.[35] Furthermore, postmenopausal women who have regular sexual activity (whether masturbation or intercourse) have higher levels of androgens and pituitary gonadotropins than sexually inactive women do. Likewise, after age 60, men who are sexually active maintain higher blood testosterone levels than those who stop having sex.[36] The bottom line is this: if you become a sexual dropout after age 60, you are probably dropping out for good. If you remain sexually active, with or without a partner, you help to slow down some of the changes of the aging process. Who says sex doesn't have its benefits?

2. *Timing may not be everything, but it's important.* As strange as it sounds, many people try to have sex at precisely the worst time, physiologically speaking—at the end of a day, when they're fatigued, stiff, and still full from their pre-bedtime snack. Older adults in particular can benefit from a shift in timing: for many couples, sex in the morning (after a good night's sleep) may be just the right ticket.

3. *Watch your alcohol intake if you're interested in sex.* Contrary to the notion that it's an aphrodisiac, alcohol in any form (liquor, wine, beer) dampens

sexual responses by its depressant action on the central nervous system. Older individuals are particularly susceptible to this effect, so if you're feeling romantic, limit your alcohol consumption to a single drink—and be sure it's not a double. Better still, if you've been having any problems with sexual arousal, avoid alcohol entirely for a while. Why take any chances on its detrimental effects?

4. *Remember that good sex doesn't require breaking any Olympic records.* It's easy to lose track of what makes sex pleasurable and satisfying. For older adults especially, attempting to measure every sexual encounter against specific performance criteria, as though it were some kind of race, is an almost sure-fire way to make the fun disappear and to provoke an unnecessary chain of worries. Instead of watching to see how quickly an erection occurs, or whether vaginal lubrication is faster or slower than the last time, just go with the flow of your feelings.

5. *If problems crop up in your sex life, don't take them lying down.* You will find that almost every physical problem has an available solution, if you consult with a competent, interested physician. For example, vaginal dryness can be combated by estrogen replacement therapy or by the use of vaginal lubricating agents such as the relatively new gel, Replens, which not only moistens the vagina but keeps the acidity properly balanced so as to prevent unwanted vaginal infections. Once identified, drugs that cause sexual problems can be changed, but if your physician isn't aware that you're having a problem, she or he won't realize that there's a need to make any switch. Nonmedical problems also require (and can benefit from) attention: sometimes a brief counseling session or two can help you formulate a solution to what may seem like a very tricky problem. And keep in mind that seemingly small sexual problems can solidify, if left unattended to, into much bigger difficulties.

Seventeen

Affairs

Extramarital sex hasn't disappeared in the 1990s. In fact, there is little evidence that participation in extramarital sex has even slowed down a bit in the age of AIDS. Reflecting this reality, affairs are the regular subject of movies, television shows, and novels—from *Fatal Attraction* (and its real-life counterpart, the notorious Carolyn Warmus case) to virtually all of John Updike's books. In many ways, it seems as though America is obsessed with extramarital sex.

Let us start with a look at the different forms extramarital sex can take, from casual one-night stands to affairs that last for decades. We will then explore the motives behind nonmonogamy, especially focusing on the different factors that attract men and women to sex outside their marriages. We will conclude by examining the impact of such involvements as well as some of the myths about affairs that are prevalent in America today.

A TYPOLOGY OF AFFAIRS

There are many ways of looking at extramarital sexual involvement.[1] While we will suggest one framework for categorizing the social and psychological context of various types of affairs, it should be recognized that this is an artificially constructed framework that will not always neatly describe a particular person's extramarital involvement(s).

Situation-specific affairs are typically one-night stands or short-term liaisons that arise because the opportunity presents itself as convenient and alluring, rather than as a result of premeditation. This category includes the passionate two-night fling while attending an out-of-town national business meeting, the sexual encounter at an office Christmas party, the surprise telephone call from a former boyfriend or girlfriend that leads to an innocent lunch together and winds up in a hotel or motel room (but ends as abruptly as it began), or the short-lived but passionate cruise-ship (or Club Med or European vacation) romance that occurs when spouses opt for separate vacations. Hundreds of other variations on this theme exist, including the not-always-so-mythological one Erica Jong made famous in her novel *Fear of Flying*, the totally anonymous, just-fling-off-your-clothes "zipless fuck." While situation-specific affairs are usually measured in days or weeks, rather than months or years, there are exceptions to this generalization. For example, a summertime affair may be tied to a specific set of situational factors: a married couple rents a house on Martha's Vineyard for a 3-month season; while the husband works in the big city and commutes to the Vineyard for weekends, the wife meets a writer who is seeking occasional sexual companionship to help relieve the monotony of the book he is finishing.

In addition to the typical brevity, situation-specific affairs share several other common features. More than any other type of affair, they are kindled by alcohol use. The alcohol provides just enough loosening of ordinary social inhibitions that many individuals who were not actively on the prowl for extramarital sex acquiesce to the intrigue of the situation far more readily than they would have done while stone-cold sober. Another frequent element of situation-specific affairs is that they generally have a low probability of being discovered, which adds some obvious luster to their appeal. In large part, two facts account for the secrecy: these affairs usually involve strangers (or at least someone who isn't in the spouse's circle of friends or acquaintances) and they often occur at some distance from one's home. Another key feature of situation-specific affairs is that, in general, both parties seize the opportunity with an implicit understanding that their sexual interaction is a one-time (or time-delimited) matter. Not only is the convenience offered of a "no-emotional-strings-attached" affair—which certainly confers its own sense of psychic safety—also expectations are predefined and it is clear that there will be no long-term responsibilities for either party. For these reasons, the situation-specific affair carries less baggage than other affairs do: its simplicity allows it to fulfill whatever requirements the two participants bring to bed with them. For some people, these requirements are just for sexual adventure and variety or for combating temporary loneliness; for others, deeper psychological needs are involved, such as wanting to have one's attractiveness validated, wanting to attain greater social status, or wanting to get back at an unfaithful spouse.

While many people who seem to fall into situation-specific affairs are hardly newcomers to the extramarital scene, this is not always the case. From our research, we believe that at least a quarter of participants in these brief, unplanned affairs are either absolute neophytes or have had very limited previous experience with extramarital sexual involvement. Sometimes, as we hinted earlier, the person's ordinary marital-social conscience would prevent such an occurrence either by steering clear of potentially "dangerous" (i.e., nonmonogamous) situations such as going to a bar without one's spouse or by giving a cool, indignant and rather automatic rejection to any suggestive overtures made by a member of the opposite sex. But with these internal controls either materially disengaged by alcohol (or other psychoactive drugs) or by the intrigue of being in different, unfamiliar, and possibly even exotic territory (and even a motel in Nehawka, Nebraska, can seem temporarily exotic to a man or woman who is exhilarated by being momentarily spouseless), anything can happen. And frequently does. Consider this verbatim account from a repentant 30-year-old minister whose wife was home in Atlanta with the kids while he was attending a religious seminar in Washington, D.C.:

I have always been a person who tries to practice what he preaches, to put it in kind of trite terms, so I am very ashamed of what I'm about to tell you. After 8 years of a completely happy marriage, after having gently turned down seductive congregants on dozens of occasions, and after having sworn to myself that I could resist any temptation that was thrown my way, I was shocked to find out that I was much weaker than I ever could have imagined. Here's what happened. I went out to dinner with a group of six or seven people who were all at this seminar. When we came back to the hotel, we went into the bar for some more conversation. I guess, looking back, that I had had a few glasses of wine at dinner; at the bar, I probably had another drink or two. Suddenly, there were just three of us sitting there—a teacher from Oklahoma, a woman from Ohio, and me. The teacher got up and excused himself, and this woman—this very attractive woman—asked if I wouldn't keep her company while she finished her drink. Gallant person that I am, I agreed. Before I really even realized what was happening, she was rubbing my leg with her foot and running her very moist tongue around her lips over and over again. I was on fire and all I could think about was having her douse my flame. We got to her room in about 20 seconds, and we jumped on each other before I could even catch my breath. Now, I'm not blaming her in any way . . . I was a completely willing participant . . . but the next morning when I woke up, I felt like I had lost my head completely. I still have never gotten up the courage to tell my wife what happened. It's just something I chalk up to experience, and something I hope has taught me a lesson.

It is useful to point out the not-so-obvious for a moment. People don't usually decide at the outset whether an affair will be a brief fling or a long-lasting activity (or relationship). The time frame of almost any affair (with the exception of some of the situational affairs just discussed, which are

limited by geographic separation and similar logistic constraints) is determined by a number of factors that evolve as the two participants interact and
evaluate their returns not only in terms of the sexual gratification they
receive (which is sometimes secondary to other considerations, as we will
discuss a little later) but also in terms of their personal nonsexual chemistry,
their personal comfort, their mutual trust, flexibility, and ego-enhancement.
In other words, the equation is a particularly complex and not always
predictable one. Sometimes even the most attractive partner and the best sex
in the world aren't enough to overcome the other person's guilt or ambivalence about an affair, which may lead to its early demise. In other instances,
two people who seem to have little in common socially, intellectually, or
otherwise may provide just the right mix of ingredients to meet each other's
needs in a highly gratifying, comfortable manner, and the improbable pairing may last for years, or even for decades. For this reason, the typology of
affairs we are presenting is necessarily one that is, to a large degree, based on
an analysis of the dynamics of the affair after it has been in existence for a
while.

Having made that distinction, we can return to our main discussion by
suggesting that it can be useful to categorize other affairs according to several
contexts: their durability and their function. As a matter of convenience, we
will designate as short-term affairs that last less than 6 months. This doesn't
mean that all short-term affairs are equivalent, since there are apt to be both
major quantitative and qualitative differences between a one-night stand and
an affair that involves twice-a-week trysts for several months. But short-term
affairs, in general, operate with somewhat different dynamics from longer-
lasting affairs, especially in the sense that long-term extramarital involvements entail relationships in a much deeper sense than short-term ones do.
We are not suggesting that long-term affairs are always emotionally entan-
gled or somehow more serious in intent, since this is not true at all; but there
is a different evolution of relationship dynamics in these two sorts of affairs.

Other common types of short-term affairs (in addition to the ones that are
situation-specific) include those in the category of consensual extramarital
sex as well as those we can label as conquest affairs, anger/revenge affairs,
predivorce affairs, and male bisexual affairs (female bisexual affairs, as we will
see shortly, tend to be long-term rather than short-term, whereas male
bisexual affairs are much more likely to be quick and anonymous assignations).

Consensual extramarital sex encompasses both the "swinging" or "mate-
swapping" scene and the slightly different sort of consensual sex that is often
labeled as "open marriage," meaning that either spouse or both spouses are
free to seek sexual companionship extramaritally.[2] The mate-swapping ver-

sion of consensual extramarital sex is not always as consensual as it sounds. In quite a few cases, a woman is reluctantly pushed into agreeing to this form of sexual participation by a husband who makes it clear that without her acquiescence, he will venture into the swinging scene as a solo participant. The threat here is not just that the husband will be deliberately unfaithful (which might be threatening enough for some women), but that if she doesn't keep close tabs on what he's doing and with whom, she may be in danger of losing her man.[3] Even when mate swapping is truly consensual—and there are, certainly, instances in which the wife is just as enthusiastic about the activity as her husband, even to the point of being the one who initially suggests this possibility—it is apt to consist of a series of short-term involvements rather than to evolve into a long-term arrangement. The exception to this pattern is the largely secretive world of mate-swapping clubs. These clubs usually consist of a small number of couples who are able to satisfy their need for excitement, variety, and flouting conventional standards within an environment that they perceive as safe and trustworthy. Here, the element of safety may override the need for new partners, although this type of club may break up after the divorce or withdrawal of one or two of the "member" couples. One danger lurking in the wings for such clubs is that a particular swapped pair will find their match so enticing that they abandon their original spouses. Needless to say, this outcome generally crushes whatever aura of trust surrounded the group before.

Open marriage is not always the stale concept it is made out to be, although many participants who have tried it have found that it complicates their lives in more ways than they originally envisioned. However, some of the situations in which open marriage works best are not truly mutually open. For example, an open marriage may be a viable solution for a couple where there is a major discrepancy in sexual needs. If the wife views sex as an unenjoyable chore and would rather have her mate find sexual gratification outside the marriage than deal with the hassles of constantly arguing over their sexual frequency, she may be quite willing to let her husband pursue such activities without having any interest whatsoever in engaging in them herself. Likewise, there are some loving couples for whom a physical disability or illness precludes a fully satisfying sex life, where the partner with the physical limitation suggests that his or her mate find sexual companionship outside the relationship. There are also some semiopen marriages that work like this: for a couple that is separated geographically for lengthy periods, it's okay to have extramarital sex while apart, as long as it's done with no emotional attachments being formed. But these examples cover just a fraction of open marriages. The more common pattern is that open marriage generally turns out to be less than the utopian, have-your-cake-and-eat-it-too vision it seems to be at first. For every couple who finds that swapping stories of outside affairs is a turn-on, energizing the erotic side of their marriage, there are many more where the affairs create jealousy, anxieties ("Was his bigger than mine?" "Is she better than I am?"), and recriminations.

Conquest affairs are virtually always short-term because their appeal and excitement is in their initiation: the conquest gives the conqueror (usually, but not always, the male) a notch on his or her gun barrel, but once this has been attained and the challenge is over, the conqueror is already thinking about new conquests. Not surprisingly, many people who approach affairs primarily as conquests don't find the sexual activity itself particularly fulfilling or enjoyable. Instead, they derive a sense of power and self-worth from the process of seduction. The seduction, which they may have carefully plotted out and patiently pursued over a lengthy time period, energizes them and gives them a clear goal and focus. The sex that follows the seduction is usually a very weak postscript to their experience.

Anger/revenge affairs are also apt to be short-lived, although there are some notable exceptions that have considerable staying power. The latter can be seen particularly among women who have no real interest in the intricacies and logistical planning a string of affairs involves; for them, the convenience of a once-a-week or once-a-month lover is a good trade-off for one who might be more attractive or exciting. For anyone choosing an affair primarily as a means of venting anger at a spouse or "getting back" at him or her for real or imagined injustices, the sex itself has a different sort of meaning than in most other affairs. "Look at how I'm degrading myself" is often just a transparent means of saying "Look how I'm degrading you" to an inattentive or hostile spouse. Consider the following woman's plight—and her solution.

A 34-year-old artist: I'm just a normal sort of woman, with normal needs and wants. And I thought I had a pretty normal marriage. But my husband turned into such a fanatical physical fitness nut, with 2 hours a day of running and another hour a day at his office health club, that my place was more like the cook and trainer for the Olympic team than his wife. I had to make special vitamin–wheat germ–egg white concoctions; I had to wash the hamburger meat to eliminate fat; I had to get up at 5:30 in the morning so he could have his morning run. And with all of this training, he fell asleep by 9:00 every night—he was so exhausted. I became so angry when Bill escalated his training to 80 miles of roadwork a week that I wanted a divorce. Instead, I got back at him by starting an affair with one of his buddies . . . one who was happy to stay home and have sex instead of being out pounding the pavement in the pouring rain.

The inventiveness of the spouse who is angry or vengeful enough to seek justice (or at least retribution, which is sometimes sweeter than justice) through an affair may attain unusual heights of creativity. Take the case of Samantha G., who discovered that her husband had been carrying on for some while with a woman he had met at work. Samantha was absolutely furious at this revelation, but had no desire to get a divorce. What she wanted was revenge. After considering her options, Samantha first struck back by seducing her husband's best friend, but then realized that this ploy had limited potential, since it was unlikely the friend would own up to what had happened. So she then set out on a different course: over the next few weeks, she slept with her husband's boss, his lawyer, and his accountant. When she told her husband of her exploits—which she did with great pleasure—he was stunned. As Samantha put it triumphantly, "I beat him at his own game."

Samantha's case is unusual in that most anger/revenge affairs occur without any intention of overt disclosure to the spouse. A great deal of the satisfaction such affairs produce lies in their secrecy, as if the undetected act is a purer form of getting even. Additionally, many people intuitively realize that what begins as an anger/revenge affair may prove to be very sexually and emotionally satisfying and thus may be transformed eventually into a longer-term arrangement.

Predivorce affairs don't involve the same motifs as those we have just discussed. They are more like test flights—transient forays into the world of sex outside marriage as a prelude to making the final decision to terminate a relationship that is already on a shaky foundation. Predivorce affairs allow a man or woman to examine several critical issues: (1) Am I really missing something in my marriage, or is *everyone's* sex pretty much the same as mine? (2) Can I function adequately with a new partner? and (3) What are the sexual/relationship issues I will face after I get divorced? Predivorce affairs can either quickly offer some reassurance that ending a marriage is a good practical choice, if they go well, or can give the instigator pause to reconsider the whole matter, if they are fraught with anxiety, discomfort, or other negative ramifications.

Male bisexual affairs are more difficult to pigeonhole neatly. The label of bisexual is applied to such a broad spectrum of males that, in actuality, it probably encompasses several slightly different sexual orientations. At one end of the spectrum are those married men who are predominantly heterosexual but occasionally are drawn to the danger, variety, or intrigue of same-sex relations as a means of experiencing a different form of sexual excitement. At the other end of this spectrum are married men who might appear at first to be heterosexual (after all, they *are* married) but who are really tightly closeted homosexuals using the "cover" of a marriage to hide their true sexual proclivities. These men may manage perfectly well to have sex with their wives, or they may find various ways of largely avoiding marital sex. For instance, they may have married women who were not very interested in sex; they may claim to have very low sexual desire; or they may claim to be sexually dysfunctional. Somewhere in the middle of the spectrum of so-called bisexual males are those who indeed fit the conventional definition of bisexuality by actually being sexually attracted to people of both sexes.

Homosexual men who have conventional heterosexual marriages may either have very brief sexual encounters with other men or may, on occasion, get involved in long-term same-sex affairs that have extraordinary staying power. Indeed, some married homosexual men have both types of affairs. The other bisexual men we have described above, who probably comprise about 5 percent of all married males, tend toward one-time extramarital forays. Commonly, they meet their partners at public restrooms or gay bars and don't even know their names. However, anonymous assignations are not the only form of extramarital sex for bisexual men; they find male partners for themselves at work or at play, or in chance encounters, just as everyone else does.

The relatively few female bisexual affairs that fit into the short-term category of extramarital involvements can usually be explained by one of the following: (1) The affair was essentially a matter of sexual and psychological curiosity; after a short while, the experimenter decided either that she didn't enjoy the results or that the enjoyment wasn't worth risking her marital stability over. (2) The affair was a natural extension of a friendship that suddenly (possibly even accidentally) transformed itself into overt sexual contact. The new arrangement proved to be threatening or uncomfortable to one or both participants, which led to its conclusion—and a reversion to the previous style of friendship. (3) The affair occurred under special circumstances that put it into the situation-specific category. An example would be two women vacationing together who have a brief sexual fling but quickly drop this practice when they return home.

Long-term affairs serve a broader range of purposes and, in general, assume greater complexity than the brief affairs we have already discussed. For convenience in this discussion, we will group the most common types of long-term affairs into the following categories: marriage maintenance affairs, hedonistic affairs, cathartic affairs, intimacy reduction affairs, kinky affairs, and reactive affairs. This is not to imply that any particular affair will fit neatly and completely into a single one of these categories. In reality, blended versions of these categories exist, and the reciprocal nature of the relationships that evolve with and around these affairs is such that one person's experience of the affair may be quite different from, and serve very different purposes from, the experience and perception of her or his extra-marital partner. The picture becomes even more complex if one considers that any of these affairs may be conducted either with a partner who is also married or one who is single or divorced.

Marriage maintenance affairs are convenient arrangements that provide a key ingredient that is missing from one or both partners' marriages. By supplying this much-needed element, the affair actually stabilizes the marriage(s) and makes it less likely that a marital breakup will occur. The missing ingredient may be the same for both people involved in the affair—for example, it may be a willingness to experiment with sex—but frequently the affair provides different ingredients to the participants in a mutually beneficial exchange.[4] A common pattern is that the affair delivers a desirable and emotionally important type of sexual activity for the male (for instance, receiving passionate oral sex); the male reciprocates by providing his partner not only with sexual attentions (which may or may not be of more than marginal importance to her) but also, and more important, providing her with a good listening audience and a sympathetic ear. Another variation of the marriage maintenance affair is the arrangement of a man keeping a mistress. The mistress not only provides easy, reliable sexual accessibility—eliminating the man's need to go to the trouble of repeatedly seeking new partners—she is apt to serve other functions, as well. For instance, she typically gives her partner a sense of virtually unconditional acceptance and support, no matter how boorish or self-centered he may actually be. In return, she receives economic support in one form or another: her apartment might be paid for, he keeps her happy with a steady stream of expensive presents, and he may even take her on occasional trips that his wife thinks are strictly business. While marriage maintenance affairs may evolve into quasimarital relationships, with their own positive and negative scripts, if they last long enough (which they sometimes do), they may also be relationships of considerable intimacy without ever taking on the sorts of obligations or nuances that a marriage or a romantic attachment develops.

Although common wisdom has it that affairs often lead to marital dissolution, we have encountered hundreds of marriages that were held together and solidified by affairs. Generally, they fell in the category of marriage maintenance affairs. As several people have told us, these affairs are cheaper and more interesting than going to a marriage counselor, although they are certainly also riskier if they don't work out as planned.

Hedonistic affairs are rather narrowly focused on the sexual and sensual action. They are pure and straightforward demonstrations of Freud's pleasure principle at work: they rarely lead to emotional entanglements and they generally avoid the recriminations and ambiguities of other types of affairs that have a more driving focus. For those who are able to regard sex as a form of recreation—a term we do not use with negative connotations—these affairs fit the bill quite perfectly. The affair is an indulgence, a creative act of playfulness, an oasis of sensual energy in a world fogged over by trivial details of everyday life. Hedonistic affairs are, in one sense, relatively nonjudgmental. The participants often have happy and sexually fulfilling marriages of their own.

A cathartic affair allows a participant to vent feelings through the conduct of the affair (something that psychiatrists derisively call "acting out") as well as by having someone with whom to talk about troublesome or unresolved issues that are not adequately recognized or dealt with in his or her marriage. The extramarital partner in a cathartic affair often plays a pseudo-therapist role, whether he or she realizes it (or wishes to). Unlike a therapist's, however, the role of the partner is not meant to be objective: the person who is unloading his or her gripes and troubles wants a completely sympathetic listener, not someone to dispense advice.

Intimacy reduction affairs help individuals who are conflicted by ambivalence over the intimacy demanded by their spouses. The affair is a buffer against too much closeness in a marriage: sexual involvement outside the marriage creates a safety zone of emotional distance within the marriage. This safety zone can be adjusted to help regulate the degree of closeness (or the demands for closeness) that is felt within the marriage. When tension and anxiety over too much intimacy mounts, it can be defused by more involvement with the affair. In contrast, when enough emotional space has developed in the marriage for it to feel comfortable, rather than smothering, the affair may be ignored for a while, since there is (at least temporarily) a safe harbor at home.

Kinky affairs make up only a very small portion of extramarital relationships, accounting for well under 1 percent of such alliances. Here, the partners are complementary to or tolerant of each other's unconventional sexual needs. A prime example would be a dyed-in-the-wool masochist finding an attractive, compatible sadist for a partner. Likewise, two people who are willing to act out peculiar or ritualistic fantasies together may be a good fit, not so much because they have the *same* fantasies but because they are open-minded and accepting of each other's desires. In one case we studied, the male was especially aroused by being humiliated or demeaned by a woman; after a considerable amount of searching in which he was repeatedly rejected by women who wanted less bizarre behavior from their lovers, he managed to find a woman who combined his need for being ordered around with her own erotic impulses. The result was that she found a partner who would have sex with her in public places—at the baseball stadium during a game, in the stacks of the public library, or under a blanket on the beach, surrounded by hundreds of other couples—and the only worry either had was that they would run into their mates while in the middle of such an adventure.

Reactive affairs are triggered by a person's need to redefine or reassure himself or herself in the light of changing life circumstances. The male midlife crisis is a prime example: this is frequently a time when men question their vigor and attractiveness and attempt to "prove" their youthfulness to themselves by turning to younger sexual partners. A similar example that is also related to changes in self-perception comes when a woman whose life has been focused on being a mother suddenly confronts the emotional void created by the "empty nest syndrome," when her children have all left the home. With a great deal of free time on her hands, a lack of focus, and a wish to reexamine and redefine her life, it is not unusual for the empty-nester to discover her sexuality suddenly and to opt for the excitement and rejuvenation of an emotionally satisfying extramarital relationship. Sometimes the empty-nest syndrome occurs during the menopausal years, timing that itself may trigger a personal reappraisal and a search for a new identity, even if the identity is secretive and in some ways against the grain of the woman's previous sexual value system.[5] Reactive affairs can also occur at younger ages, as with women who find themselves rebelling against the role of "mommy" when their children are very young. Still another version of the reactive affair comes in response to unfortunate twists of fate such as the severe long-term illness of a spouse. Here, the affair serves to provide an equilibrium of sorts for the healthy spouse, not only in terms of sexual release but also by creating a temporary escape from the rigors of caring for the spouse who is ill.

When a married woman has a long-term affair with another woman, it often fits into the reactive affair category. Such affairs sometimes occur when a woman decides that she wants ultimately to divorce her husband and live in a lesbian relationship but prefers to maintain her marriage until the children grow up. And some women gradually shift to a bisexual philosophy as an extension of their personal beliefs. They may be perfectly content with a heterosexual marriage but view a long-term extramarital sexual relationship with another woman as both an ideological expression and a means of meeting a different set of emotional needs.

WHAT TRIGGERS AFFAIRS?

There is no question in our minds that the single greatest difference between men and women in the motivation for having affairs is this: men tend to seek sexual variety and excitement, while women generally are looking for emotional returns.[6]

Women enter extramarital affairs for numerous reasons, of course. But the vast majority explain their motivation in terms of a search for better feelings in the face of being emotionally dissatisfied with their husbands. For some women, it is a search for a sense of being wanted and needed; typically, these women report being taken for granted in their marriages even when they try their hardest to be sexually receptive, attentive to their husband's sexual desires, and attractive. In a word, these women feel unappreciated, both in sexual terms and in more panoramic relationship terms as well. Here's how one 38-year-old woman described it to us.

> Tom decided some years ago that I wasn't a good sexual partner. Whenever we had oral sex, he told me I wasn't doing it right. When we had intercourse, I was always too slow or too cold or too mechanical for his taste. On many occasions, he'd say to me, "You're lucky I'm your husband—no other man would ever be interested in you sexually." Little did he know that the three different men I'd had affairs with in the past few years sang a very opposite tune, telling me that my tongue was fantastic, my lovemaking the most exciting they'd ever had, and my overall sexual responsiveness was, as one of them put it, like a string of Chinese firecrackers.

Many women who are having affairs subconsciously barter their sexual favors for a sense of being desirable, valued persons. This doesn't mean that they are oblivious to the dynamics of their affairs; instead, the affair is usually a compromise they come to in order to obtain an ingredient that is otherwise missing from their lives. As one perceptive woman noted, "I trade 15 minutes in bed for a whole week of feeling wanted. I don't think that's such a bad trade-off." The extramarital partners of these women generally are quick to recognize the rules of the game (which are, incidentally, typically set by the women): their expected role is to be attentive, warm, and sympathetic listeners, even if their actual time together is severely limited. Men who fail to meet these needs for their extramarital partners are usually doomed to short-lived affairs; men who are adept at reading their partners' emotional requirements and providing them with what they want are, in contrast, able to sustain long-term affairs on their own terms almost indefinitely.

A substantial number of women also have extramarital affairs in order to gain revenge against their husbands, a motivation that seems to be almost exclusively female (at least among heterosexuals). In four decades of taking detailed sex histories from men and women from virtually all walks of life, we have encountered only a handful of instances in which men turned to extramarital involvements in order to "punish" a spouse, whereas the revenge motif figures prominently in a quarter to a third of women's extramarital forays.[7] Undoubtedly, the most common factor behind this type of revenge-seeking affair is the discovery of a husband's infidelity. Here are several explanations that women have given us that are typical of their reasoning:

A 29-year-old computer programmer: After 8 years of marriage, I had never even flirted with another man, and would never have dreamed of doing so. As far as I was concerned, almost everything about my marriage was good and solid. But then I found out that Dave had been having an affair with his secretary for more than 2 years. It made me so furious that I went out to a bar the first time he was away from home after that and let myself get picked up by a traveling salesman. I don't remember the sex very much, but I sure remember feeling, "I'm getting even with that son-of-a-bitch" the whole time the guy was on top of me.

A 33-year-old schoolteacher: I was brought up to think that extramarital sex was something that was sinful. With two daughters and a 7-year-long marriage, an affair was the very last thing on my mind. But after I discovered that my husband was messing around, I was madder than a bat out of hell. For revenge, I seduced his best friend and made sure he heard about it. I figured, what's good for the goose is good for the gander.

A 42-year-old nurse: I know that it seems startling for a minister's wife to be telling you this. I can still hardly believe it myself, because it's really out of character. But after John admitted to me that he had been sexually involved with several women in his congregation, something snapped inside of me, and I started to sleep around as sort of the ultimate act of revenge. I couldn't think of any other way to hurt him as much as he had hurt me.

Women also turn to affairs to extract revenge for other reasons. For example, some women use affairs to get back at their husbands for neglecting or ignoring them, as this example shows.

A 28-year-old librarian: I remember very clearly why I chose to start having affairs. Ted was on the fast track out of law school, working for a prestigious firm in L.A. In his quest to make partner, he became totally obsessed with his work. There were many days when he didn't come home until 2:00 or 3:00 A.M., and most Saturdays he was in the office all day long. No matter how many times we discussed it, and I made my unhappiness known, he refused to tone down his obsession. I dealt with it by having lovers come to my house, always thinking, "You jerk: while you're busy trying to make partner, your wife's getting fucked." The funny part was, Ted never made partner, and I never enjoyed my little trysts.

In other cases, married women have affairs to gain revenge for more serious injuries. It is far from uncommon for women who are physically abused by their spouses to have clandestine affairs in order to "even the score." (It should be noted, however, that this situation is potentially far riskier for the woman if her husband finds out, as the abusive husband may react swiftly and physically on discovering her act of rebellion.) In these instances, it is safe to say that the woman is not looking for sexual gratification at all: she is looking to mock or humiliate her spouse, to cut his masculinity down to size by taking control.

It is, by the way, a remarkable thing that in extramarital affairs involving two married people, the woman is virtually always the one in control. (In contrast, when a married man is having an affair with a single woman, the control is far more likely to be vested in the man: this is not only what we might term the "operational" control of the affair, but also the strategic control over the longer-term outcome, especially on the matter of whether or not the man leaves his wife.) Clearly, it is the woman who is most likely to decide if an affair ever starts, even if the man is the actual instigator. (And in a substantial number of cases, woman are the seducers, rather than the seduced.) Once an affair is a fait accompli, it is usually the woman who decides how often, when, where, and what the operative conditions for continuing the affair might be. Similarly, the types of sex permitted are virtually always governed by the woman rather than the man: the major exception here may be if the woman wants to indulge in full-scale sadomasochistic action and the man demurs.

The control element is a complicated one, to be sure. And the revenge factor as a motivation for extramarital involvement is sometimes murkier than in the case of physical mayhem. But the explanation given by this 33-year-old female psychologist addresses another fairly common aspect of how revenge plays out in the battle between the sexes:

I had been married for a dozen years when I discovered that my husband had methodically been moving money from his medical practice to an offshore bank account in his name alone. At first, I felt betrayed. After all, I had sacrificed plenty while he was in medical school and serving his medical residency: those were some pretty lean years, and now I deserved to reap the rewards of our improving position. Once I got beyond my initial reaction, I became outraged and angry. So I lashed out at him the easiest way I knew how: I seduced his partner and made sure that he found out about it. In retrospect, this may not have been a smart thing to do, or a mature thing to do, but at the time I wasn't trying to accomplish anything but make him cry out in pain.

While it is unquestionable that most men who seek out affairs do so because they are either sexually dissatisfied with their wives or are seeking a new type of sexual excitement, the search for sexual variety and excitement is uncommon among the motivations of women seeking affairs. In part, this may be because women seem to have a clearer understanding of the fact that, all in all, the sexual activity experienced in affairs is not too different from the sex in marriages.[8]

We do not dispute the fact that the extra thrill of an undiscovered affair may add a new quotient of excitement to a person's sex life (in what can be called the "forbidden fruit" principle). It is also true that there is apt to be some sexual excitement generated in an affair by having a new sexual partner, although this effect tends to wear out rather quickly for both men and women. (Men probably get more mileage from the sense of having made a "conquest," even if, in fact, it was the woman who instigated the affair.) Furthermore, two people in an affair are almost certainly more willing to experiment with a variety of sex acts, positions, and peripherals than in their marriages. (In part, this may happen because men who are sexually satisfied in their marriages, who are not looking for something new and different and exciting, are not usually the ones involved in affairs.)

However, many married women find, much to their surprise, that an affair brings them a taste of empowerment that was previously lacking from their lives. This boost to their self-esteem stems from at least four separate dynamics. First, the element of active choice replaces the sex-as-duty dullness that tarnishes many marriages. Second, and a far more powerful effect, the married woman involved in an affair is likely to be treated with attentiveness and affection that kindle a feeling of being special and being wanted that is reminiscent of one of the most positive aspects of her courtship days. This is true even if the affair is rather narrowly delineated in stark sexual terms rather than cloaked in the outward trappings of romance: it is easier to read affection into relatively uncomplicated relationships than it is when there are kids to bathe, bills to be paid, meals to be cooked, and jobs to go to. Third, an affair almost inevitably endorses a woman's sense of attractiveness and desirability. (When affairs come to an end, of course, there may be a backlash of this phenomenon, with the woman winding up feeling unattractive and undesirable if she feels that the affair was broken off unilaterally.) Finally, affairs give married women an alternate reality in their lives—a way of combating roles they have found unsatisfying and replacing them, even if only fleetingly, with new ways of self-expressiveness and different patterns of behavior.

Another source of self-empowerment for some married women in affairs is the discovery that they are more sexually responsive than they had imagined.

This is sometimes the case for women who enter affairs out of a feeling of sexual dissatisfaction in their marriages: the "is this all there is?" syndrome. Given the numerous reasons for a woman's sexual dissatisfaction—including having a sexually dysfunctional mate, having a sexually inhibited mate, having a spouse who is clumsy or inconsiderate in bed, or having a husband whose appetite for sex seems Lilliputian in comparison to hers—it is not surprising that this category is larger than many men would imagine.

That many women who opt to have affairs do so because they are sexually dissatisfied and are looking for an innovative, physically stimulating lover is neatly shown by a few comments from women we have interviewed.

A 34-year-old businesswoman: My husband thinks sex is a lot like a two-minute drill on a football field: although there's some body contact and movement, as long as he scores, he's happy—how I feel or respond doesn't seem to enter his head.

A 29-year-old physician: My husband is a really nice guy and we're basically very happy together, but when it comes to our sex life, it can only be described in one word: *boring*. No matter how many times I've tried to show him or tell him what I like, he always seems to slip back into the same old patterns, and I'm the one left high and dry. I'm sure it would be shocking to a lot of people, but I called my old college boyfriend and propositioned him, so now I get my sexual stimulation the way I like it, and I'm an easier person to be around.

A 48-year-old housewife: My husband is a successful accountant, a good father, and an all-around good guy, but when it comes to making love, it's like he's doing tax calculations in his head: he's precise, mechanical, and very unexciting. I've found that I can live with this as long as I can find a lover who can take care of my needs with a spicier kind of sexual interaction. The latest one is a kid who's almost 10 years younger than I am: I met him at a golf tournament last summer and let him think he was seducing me!

The major problem for American women when it comes to affairs is guilt, which is something of a one-sided commodity. American men generally don't view their extramarital dalliances in the same light; in fact, most of the men we've interviewed about their affairs seem to be proud of them rather than ashamed in any way. The major exception to this observation is the subcategory of men from strongly religious backgrounds who have had extramarital involvements. Although these men speak more contritely about their extramarital activities than most others do, they often sound forced and formulaic. In fact, it often sounds as if their guilt had more to do with being caught than with regret about their extramarital conduct.

Female guilt about extramarital sex is such a strongly felt emotion that in perhaps a quarter of cases it leads women to break off an affair. This finding is interesting because most of these affairs were physically pleasurable and even psychically energizing. However, the guilt and ambivalence the woman was experiencing, usually cast in terms of a sense of betraying her husband, eventually overcame her positive returns, and she ended the affair as a matter of conscience. At times, it seems that the woman's pleasure, both sexually and psychologically, itself becomes the very source of guilt. In America, women have become adept at blaming themselves for feeling good, as many feminist writers have acknowledged.

Relatively few men act in a similar vein. When men end affairs for reasons other than becoming bored or finding a new extramarital partner, it is typically because they are worried that their wives are about to discover their clandestine activities or because they are having problems meeting the demands of the extramarital relationship. Guilt rarely enters the picture: men involved in affairs may pay lip service to the notion that they are hoodwinking their wives, or may even voice dismay at being unfaithful or dishonest, but find dozens of ready explanations to justify their behavior. "It makes me feel younger." "It helps to keep my marriage together." "It helps me deal with stress." "My lover does things my wife won't do." Whatever guilt lurks in the hearts or minds of men who stray outside their marriage, it is largely counterbalanced by their libidinously lubricated pleasure. Indeed, many men regard casual extramarital flings as having about the moral equivalence of stopping for a pizza if they're hungry.

While there are many possible explanations for this difference in reactions, it is quite possible that a key factor is the old-fashioned American double standard about sex. Just as boys who are sexually active are simply considered to be "sowing their wild oats," while girls who are sexually active are loose, or "getting a reputation," in adulthood the double standard endorses the male's privilege of indulging in affairs as almost to be expected, while the woman is still seen as the one who carries the primary burden of faithfulness. A married man who is called a womanizer is not automatically considered to be morally bankrupt, but a woman who "sleeps around" is more harshly judged. It is much like the fact that in the English language there is no term applied to men that is equivalent to the derogatory word "slut."

Men who are nonmonogamous are surprisingly uniform in their motivations. With a high degree of consistency, men seek extramarital liaisons for the sexual excitement and variety they hope to find. In fact, in a survey we conducted recently of 200 married men who had had affairs, 87 percent said that their primary reason was sexual. The specific reasons given, which in some cases fell into two or more categories, broke down as follows.

To find more sexual excitement: 74 percent

To counteract sexual boredom: 67 percent

To provide better sex: 65 percent

To have greater frequency of sexual activity: 59 percent

To receive a particular type of sexual stimulation that the wife refuses to
provide: 31 percent

To have a more attractive (or younger) partner: 28 percent

To deal with a sexual dysfunction (e.g., to determine if a dysfunction was
partner-specific or to "cure" a dysfunction): 12 percent

To deal with a wife's physical incapacity: 2 percent

To have sex with another male: 2 percent

Here are some typical comments we recorded.

> *A 29-year-old stockbroker:* There's nothing wrong with my marriage, and my sex
> life at home isn't bad. It's just missing the sizzle that used to be there. Extramari-
> tal sex brings that sizzle front and center for me, and as long as my wife doesn't
> find out about it, it's actually contributing to a better marriage in a way, because
> I'm a happier, more satisfied person.
>
> *A 46-year-old attorney:* I've been married for 23 years, and for 23 years I've had a
> steady diet of exactly the same kind of sex. I finally decided that there had to be
> something more exciting, and I was right. I found exactly what I wanted: she's
> 10 years younger than my wife, 20 pounds lighter, and she gives great head, too.

Very few men deliberately turn to extramarital affairs for nonsexual
reasons alone. While men's sexual involvements may eventually lead to
emotional involvements—after all, it is not always easy to separate sex from
intimacy—the emotional bonds that form seem almost parenthetical to
what men see as "the" purpose of extramarital activities.

THE COMPLEXITIES OF EXTRAMARITAL SEX

Most married couples claim to believe in the value of monogamy, but a
sizable number of married men and women stray from this ideal. Various
estimates suggest that anywhere from 26 to 66 percent of married American
men and 18 percent to 69 percent of married American women have had
extramarital sex.[9] However, stark statistics like these don't do much to
illuminate the subject beyond suggesting that extramarital sex can hardly be
considered unusual or abnormal behavior.

Like many other aspects of sexuality, extramarital involvements cannot be considered as all alike in either form, function, or meaning. In fact, there are some intimate extramarital relationships that never include any type of sexual contact, others that involve kissing and touching but no genital stimulation or intercourse, and some that include every imaginable form of sex except intercourse. Presumably, these couples believe they are "engaged in less serious violations of the marital vows if a penis has not entered a vagina," as the marriage therapist Frederick Humphrey put it.[10]

Asexual extramarital involvements understandably hinge mainly on emotional closeness and companionship. While in one sense they are simply a type of friendship, in another sense they can arouse far more jealousy in a marriage than most relationships would, not only because the uninvolved spouse may have a hard time believing that there isn't any sex going on, but also because the potential for sexual involvement invariably lurks in the background.

At the opposite extreme from asexual extramarital involvements are the infrequent instances in which extramarital sex completely replaces marital sex. Aside from those cases where this arrangement is the result of special circumstances, such as a spouse's deteriorating health or prolonged geographic separation, there are actually marriages in which this pattern is agreeable to both spouses. The agreement can either be acknowledged openly and directly, or it may be a matter of implicit collusion. In either instance, the spouse who is not involved in the affair is often overjoyed at the prospect of being "excused" from sexual responsibilities. Sometimes this pattern is seen in couples contending with a severe sexual dysfunction such as vaginismus or primary impotence, or when one spouse has sexual aversion. In other cases, it is a simpler matter of a spouse who finds sex uninteresting and unenjoyable but recognizes that his or her partner has different feelings about it. Infrequently, both spouses agree to abstain from sex with each other and to satisfy their needs entirely via extramarital excursions.[11]

In between these two extremes—asexual extramarital involvement and extramarital sex that completely replaces its marital counterpart—one can still discover immense differences in the nature and style of affairs. Despite these differences, however, there is one relatively common feature of non-consensual extramarital sex: it almost always involves deception. This is why extramarital sex becomes problematic for many couples.

Before we address the issue of extramarital sex as cheating, deceit, or fraud, we need to comment briefly on the words people use to speak about this topic. Value-laden terms such as "infidelity" or "betrayal" automatically put a particular spin on both the meaning and merit of extramarital sex that precludes any possibility of viewing it positively. Unlike some authorities who take such a position,[12] we do not see all extramarital sex as inherently destructive. While we certainly agree that extramarital sex can be a divisive (and frequently explosive) issue, there are also many situations in which its positive aspects outweigh its negatives by a wide margin. Here are just a few examples. (1) Affairs can help keep a marriage together by a reduction in sexual tension, which in turn can lessen other forms of marital conflict. (2) Affairs sometimes turn out to be personal growth experiences. (3) Affairs don't always provide better sex or more happiness than a marriage; because of this fact, they can help a person appreciate the quality of his or her marriage at a time when this may have been in question. (4) Perhaps paradoxically, affairs sometimes lead to a rejuvenation of sex within a marriage, so in this sense they may actually contribute to marital satisfaction.

Our willingness to see that extramarital involvements can have a positive side should not be taken as a wholehearted endorsement of such behavior. We are firmly convinced that the downside of extramarital sex usually looms larger than any potential benefits that can be objectively ascribed to this situation.

We come back to a look at the innate deceit involved in extramarital dalliances. And here we find that the deceit breeds complications of numerous (and often unanticipated) sorts. Clearly, there is a sizable risk that if a person's extramarital activities are discovered, which happens in a surprisingly large number of cases, they will seriously undermine the trust and intimacy of his or her marriage. The uninvolved spouse (that is, the one who wasn't a participant in the extramarital sex) rarely reacts with casual acceptance unless he or she has had extramarital activities too. Instead, the reaction is apt to be one of shock or outrage, and it is likely to set off a cascading series of negative consequences that reverberate over time through the marriage. In fact, residual anger over a spouse's affair(s) often surfaces as a prominent feature in individual or couple therapy years or even decades after it occurred. To some individuals, extramarital sex is such a profound violation of moral and religious principles, it shatters a fundamental pillar of marital stability that can never be put back together again. In other marriages, the problems precipitated by the discovery of clandestine extramarital involvements have nothing at all to do with moral or religious beliefs but are strictly grounded in how the involvements affect the dynamics of the marital relationship. In addition, the existence of an affair, past or ongoing, sometimes becomes known by the entire family, including the children. While no formal studies have been done on the impact such a discovery has, it doesn't take a Ph.D. in child psychology to recognize that it would virtually always be damaging.

A 33-year-old husband who had been married for 5 years told us, "When I found out that Lauren had been having an affair, I felt like I had been raped." This comment points to another negative aspect of the discovery of an affair: it victimizes the uninvolved partner without giving him or her any prior warning or means of avoiding such victimization. This is not just a matter of fairness or equal opportunity—although admittedly some spouses might see it this way ("If I'd known what that bastard was doing, I would've had some fun of my own"). Uninvolved spouses may be victimized in a number of other ways beyond having their feelings hurt and their trust seriously eroded. For instance, they may have been exposed to various sexually transmitted diseases, which is neither a trivial matter nor a rare occurrence in situations of nonmonogamy. They may have been victimized economically, too: the spouse who was sexually involved with someone else may have been paying for motel rooms, candlelit dinners, weekend trysts, and little (or not so little) romantic presents, or may have even had an arrangement where substantial sums were being paid regularly for rent or other forms of support. In addition, the uninvolved spouse has been victimized in another way: he or she has had a substantial element of the balance of control in their marriage taken away in a unilateral, selfish manner.

To examine the nature of extramarital sex without recognizing its inherent selfishness (except when it is done openly and with mutual advance consent) is to miss one of its core features, one that contributes greatly to its negative impact. Selfishness is not always inimicable to a good marriage or to good sex; but selfishness played out surreptitiously, while pretending to be loving, selfless, considerate, and monogamous, is a form of theft. It is not that one spouse's affair automatically drains a marriage of its romance or its sexual vigor, since sometimes the opposite occurs, and there are certainly instances in which an affair actually improves the climate of the marriage. Instead, what is stolen is the bond of trust and its attendant consent to mutual vulnerability between spouses. Such vulnerability is based largely on the assumption that neither partner is out to hurt the other. In other words, it is not so much the extramarital sex that is destructive as it is the unprincipled deceitfulness of the behavior. Perhaps this is why in another era many wives were relatively unconcerned by their husbands' visits to brothels: not only was the risk of emotional involvement minuscule, but the nonmarital sexual activity per se wasn't threatening.

MYTHS ABOUT EXTRAMARITAL SEX

The social science literature is relatively clear on several points. Married men are less monogamous than married women are, although the difference between the sexes has narrowed considerably in the past few decades.[13] Married men have more outside sex partners than married women do. Most people go to great lengths to assure that their extramarital escapades are hidden from their spouses. And nonconsensual extramarital sex, if discovered, is generally a source of considerable anger, friction, and recriminations. Beyond this, uncertainty abounds, although you would never know it from watching the self-proclaimed experts on television talk shows who announce their theories about affairs with all the relish of a revival preacher.

To shed some additional light on the subject, we have gathered a number of common myths about extramarital sex and comment on the facts that apply to these situations.

1. Myth: *Extramarital sex is usually a sign of an unhappy marriage.* Fact: The research on this point is inconsistent. There is no overwhelming evidence that marital dissatisfaction leads people to go outside their marriages for sex, although common sense would suggest that people who have already decided to get a divorce might be considerably less likely to be monogamous than they previously had been. Thus, the absence of convincing evidence probably indicates that there is no direct cause-and-effect relationship: "bad" marriages don't necessarily trigger affairs, and "good" marriages don't always prevent them.

2. Myth: *Churchgoing couples have far lower rates of extramarital sexual involvements than nonreligious couples.* Fact: Although people who are more religious tend to have more conservative sexual values than nonreligious people and might be expected to take their marital vows more literally, there is actually no difference in their rates of extramarital sex.[14] Despite sanctimonious protests to the contrary, it appears that the flesh is indeed weaker than the spirit, or at least that the spirit is easily led into temptation. However, there is one notable difference between people who are especially religious and those who are not: those who are religious seem to experience more guilt and soul-searching as a result of their libidinous adventures.

3. Myth: *If your spouse tells you repeatedly that he or she wouldn't be terribly upset if you had an affair, you can be confident that he or she is open-minded enough to handle such a situation with aplomb.* Fact: Don't believe everything you're told. While there are certainly some people who feel this way, this sort of message may actually be an intellectualization of an issue that proves to be far more gut-wrenching if it actually happens. Furthermore, we have encountered a number of cases where such reassurances were offered in the hopes that by making extramarital sex seem less "off limits," it would actually serve as a deterrent to the deed. Marriages are certainly not immune to mixed messages.

4. Myth: *Extramarital sex occurs only if a marriage is having problems.* Fact: While many people would like to think that nonmonogamy is synonymous with marital maladjustment, there are actually many very solid marriages where one or both spouses have outside sexual partners. (Of course, there is probably no such thing as a marriage without *any* problems, so some observers would try to find a way to claim that these marriages were troubled, in order to fit their beliefs about the nature of sex outside the marital bed.) Often, these are individuals who regard their extramarital activities in casual, recreational terms, rather than as emotionally meaningful relationships, but it is certainly possible to be deeply committed to one's marriage—to be in love with one's spouse—and to have a lover as well. In addition, there are perfectly intact, solid marriages where extramarital sex occurs because of some factor unique to the individual rather than because of a relationship problem. Finally, couples who agree to a mutually "open marriage" arrangement often have particularly solid partnerships.

5. Myth: *Sex is always better with an outside lover than with a spouse.* Fact: Extramarital sex is sometimes more alluring as a fantasy than in the flesh. Although the thrill of something that is forbidden can be a powerful sexual stimulant for some people, others find that their sexual responsiveness is hampered by guilt, by anxiety over the possibility of being caught, by nagging worries about sexually transmitted diseases, or by the logistical problems of arranging clandestine meetings, alibis, and ample time. While men usually rate extramarital sex as a turn-on, many women find that it's not much different from what they experience at home, and some women are surprised to find that they are less easily orgasmic or arousable in the hands of a lover than with their husbands. Another interesting point we have noticed over the years is that many men who have little trouble with ejaculatory control in their marriage become rapid ejaculators in situations with new partners, which gives them a huge sense of inadequacy at precisely the time where they want to feel virile and in control.

6. Myth: *If you suspect your spouse of having an affair, it is probably just a sign you are insecure.* Fact: According to sociologists Philip Blumstein and Pepper Schwartz, such suspicions usually turn out to be correct.[15] They found that 90 percent of the wives in their sample who suspected their husbands of straying outside the marriage were correct, while 87 percent of the husbands who thought their wives had had extramarital experiences were accurate in their beliefs. Our own findings from doing sex therapy with several thousand couples at the Masters & Johnson Institute support these results, although we should add that there are many instances where one or more affairs have

occurred but are totally unsuspected by the spouse. In general, men tend to be less tuned in to the possibility that their wives may have been sexually active outside the marriage, while married women have a higher degree of alertness to this situation.

7. Myth: *Once a spouse has been unfaithful, the chances are he or she will have many more affairs.* Fact: Many people who have had a single episode of extramarital involvement find that it wasn't what they thought it would be. Perhaps the sex wasn't great, their guilt was more than they anticipated, or their curiosity was satisfied; in any event, they decide after such an experience that this type of behavior isn't for them. Furthermore, even individuals who have a very gratifying long-term affair sometimes never go on to other extramarital relationships after the first one ends. Our impression is that men are more likely than women to have a whole string of extramarital liaisons, but there is absolutely no way of predicting after a single episode who is going to repeat this behavior pattern and who will retire from such activities.

Notes

CHAPTER ONE: LOVE AND INTIMACY

1. See, for example, Rubin, Z., Measurement of romantic love, *Journal of Personality and Social Psychology* 16:265–273, 1970; Pam, A., Plutchik, R., and Conte, H. R., Love: A psychometric approach, *Psychological Reports* 37:83–88, 1975; Dion, K. K., and Dion, K. L., Self-esteem and romantic love, *Journal of Personality* 43:39–57, 1975; Hatfield, E., and Sprecher, S., Measuring passionate love in intimate relations, *Journal of Adolescence* 9:383–410, 1986; and R. J. Sternberg and M. L. Barnes, eds., *The Psychology of Love*, Yale University Press, 1988.
2. Walster, E., and Walster, G. W., *A New Look at Love*, Addison-Wesley, 1978, p. 9.
3. Berscheid, E., "Some Comments on Love's Anatomy," in Sternberg and Barnes, op. cit., p. 369.
4. Heinlein, Robert, *Stranger in a Strange Land*, Putnam, 1961, p. 345.
5. Hunt, M., "The Future of Marriage," in J. E. DeBurger, ed., *Marriage Today*, Wiley, 1977, p. 693.
6. Not all cultures place on romantic love the premium we do in the Western world. In many countries, arranged marriages are the norm, and love develops—if it develops at all—as an outgrowth of longevity, loyalty, parenting, and social obligation.
7. Peele, S., and Brodsky, A., *Love and Addiction*, Signet, 1976.
8. Sternberg, R. J., *The Triangle of Love*, Basic Books, 1988; ibid., "Triangulating Love," in Sternberg and Barnes, op. cit., 1988, pp. 119–138.
9. Sternberg, op. cit., 1988, pp. 43–44.
10. Sternberg in Sternberg and Barnes, op. cit., 1988, pp. 137–138.
11. Levinger, G., "Can We Picture Love?" in Sternberg and Barnes, op. cit., 1988, pp. 139–158; Williams, W. M., and Barnes, M. L., "Love within Life," in Sternberg and Barnes, op. cit., 1988, pp. 311–329.
12. Peele, S., "Fools for Love," in Sternberg and Barnes, op. cit., 1988, p. 170.

13. Shaver, P., Hazan, C., and Bradshaw, D., "Infant-Caretaker Attachment and Adult Romantic Love: Similarities and Differences." Paper presented at the 2nd International Conference on Personal Relationships, Madison, Wisconsin, 1984; idem, "Love As Attachment," in Sternberg and Barnes, op. cit., 1988, pp. 68–99.

14. Ainsworth, M., et al., *Patterns of Attachment: A Psychological Study of the Strange Situation*, Laurence Erlbaum Associates, 1978.

15. Ibid.

16. Hatfield, op. cit., 1988; Fisher, H. E., *Anatomy of Love*, W. W. Norton, 1992.

17. Peele, op. cit., 1988.

18. Dutton, D., and Aron, A., Some evidence for heightened sexual attraction under conditions of high anxiety, *Journal of Personality and Social Psychology* 30:510–517, 1974.

19. White, G. L., Fishbein, S., and Rustein, J., Passionate love and the misattribution of arousal, *Journal of Personality and Social Psychology* 41:56–62, 1981.

20. Zillman, D., *Connections between Sex and Aggression*, Lawrence Erlbaum, 1984.

21. Branden, N., *The Psychology of Romantic Love*, Bantam Books, 1981, p. 212.

22. Solomon, R. C., *About Love: Reinventing Romance for Our Times*, Simon & Schuster, 1989, p. 333.

23. Hatfield, E., "Passionate Love, Companionate Love, and Intimacy," in M. Fisher and G. Stricker, eds., *Intimacy*, Plenum Press, 1982, p. 271.

24. Millett, K., *Sexual Politics*, Doubleday, 1970.

25. Tannen, D., *You Just Don't Understand: Women and Men in Conversation*, William Morrow, 1990, p. 26.

26. Fisher, op. cit., 1992, p. 204.

27. See, e.g., Rubin, Z., and Shenker, S., Friendship, proximity, and self-disclosure, *Journal of Personality* 46:1–22, 1978; Rubenstein, C., and Shaver, P., *In Search of Intimacy*, Random House, 1982; Fisher and Stricker, op. cit., 1982; Rubin, L., *Intimate Strangers: Men and Women Together*, Harper Colophon Books, 1983; Goleman, D., "Two views of marriage explored: his and hers," *New York Times*, April 1, 1986, p. C1.; and Solomon, op. cit., 1989.

28. Hiebert, W. J., Intimacy, limits, and Lake Wobegon, *Family Therapy News* 18:7, January/February 1987.

29. Wynne, L. C., and Wynne, A. R., The question for intimacy, *Journal of Marital and Family Therapy* 12:383–394, 1986.

CHAPTER TWO: SEX AND SENSUALITY

1. Montagu, A., *Touching: The Human Significance of the Skin*, 2nd ed., Harper & Row, 1978, p. 167.

2. In case you're wondering, here are three examples of sex that doesn't involve touching, or skin to skin contact: Telephone sex (of the call-in-and-discuss-your-fantasies sort); reading erotic materials or watching erotic movies; voyeurism (what peeping Toms do). While there are undoubtedly other forms of this

sort of sexual behavior, the list is quite sparse in comparison to all of the forms of sex that *do* involve skin to skin contact. Of course, we do not mean to suggest that sex is only a matter of tactile sensations. Smell, taste, and sight also can play a role in anyone's sexual arousal.

3. Montagu, op. cit., 1978, p. 160.

4. The modifications we have made in the sensate focus program we provide in this book take into account the fact that unlike the situation in sex therapy, there won't be a therapist to talk these experiences over with day by day. Furthermore, typically sex therapy clients are contending with a great deal of sexual anxiety and performance pressures, which we do not expect to be the case for most couples using this book for guidance. Thus, sensate focus exercises as employed by sex therapists usually have a slightly different slant, although the underlying principles are basically the same.

5. Couples should never attempt intercourse in the female-on-top position by holding the penis at a 90-degree angle to the man's body and having the woman sit down on it. The weight of the woman's body and the force of her descent can injure the penis inadvertently.

6. If the man has problems maintaining erections or with ejaculatory control, it may be necessary to modify these suggestions somewhat. Some practical suggestions for dealing with ejaculatory problems are given in Chapter 5, while a discussion of erection problems can be found in Chapter 6.

CHAPTER THREE: PATTERNS OF SEXUAL RESPONSE

1. Masters, W. H., and Johnson, V. E., *Human Sexual Response*, Little, Brown, 1966.

2. Kaplan, H. S., *Disorders of Sexual Desire*, New York, Brunner/Mazel, 1979.

3. We don't, of course, mean that the basic mechanisms of excitement are predictable in every regard. For example, while virtually all healthy men will develop an erection as part of the excitement phase of the sexual response cycle, some erections occur almost instantaneously, while others may not occur for a while. A man who takes 5 minutes to become erect is not necessarily less excited subjectively than a man whose penis is rigid within seconds. Similarly, the timing of the onset of vaginal lubrication, one of the physiologic hallmarks of excitement in females, is variable. Exactly the same comments about the variability of sexual reflexes can be made in terms of quantifying these responses. Bigger is not necessarily experienced as better.

4. Penile size is less of a contributant to female coital satisfaction than is often thought, for two additional reasons. First, the width of the erect penis is not usually a key determinant of female sexual stimulation, because the orgasmic platform accommodates quite readily to the diameter of the penile shaft, receiving very adequate stimulation from even a fairly narrow penis. (In fact, the orgasmic platform can grip a finger quite tightly when sexually aroused.)

Second, and of more importance, is the fact that most women are quick to say that it is not penis size per se that makes a difference as much as it is how skillfully a man uses his penis.

5. Masters and Johnson, op. cit., 1966.

6. This sentiment is not as idiosyncratic as it sounds. The sociologists Philip Blumstein and Pepper Schwartz found that intercourse is a more essential part of sex for heterosexual women than for heterosexual men, possibly because of what it signifies to women in terms of shared intimacy and equal participation. (In contrast, in oral sex, one person usually "gives" while the other "receives"; and in solitary masturbation, one partner is excluded entirely.) (Blumstein, P., and Schwartz, P., *American Couples: Money, Work, Sex*, Morrow, 1983.)

7. Hite, S., *The Hite Report: A Nationwide Study on Female Sexuality*, Macmillan, 1976, p. 58.

8. Women from traditional, conservative, or heavily religious backgrounds are more likely to have this view than women who are more avant-garde, liberal, or nonreligious. In addition, much as in Kinsey's day, women from lower socio-economic backgrounds who have not completed at least a high school education also seem more likely to view sex as something for the man in which their own pleasure (and orgasms) is almost incidental.

9. Even when a woman is orgasmic from fantasy alone, with no physical stimulation whatever, she is likely to feel the sensation starting in her clitoris. Similarly, orgasms that occur during activities like anal intercourse or breast stimulation, where there is no genital touching at all, still have the buildup of the orgasmic platform and seem to have orgasm triggered with a sensation that is first felt in the clitoris.

10. Masters and Johnson, op. cit., 1966; Kaplan, op. cit., 1974; Barbach, L., *For Yourself: The Fulfillment of Female Sexuality*, Signet (New American Library), 1975; Hite, op. cit., 1976.

11. Robbins, M. B., and Jensen, G. G., Multiple orgasm in males, *Journal of Sex Research* 14:21–26, 1978; Dunn, M. E., and Trost, J. E., Male multiple orgasms: a descriptive study, *Archives of Sexual Behavior* 18:377–399, 1989.

12. Offit, A. K., *Night Thoughts—Reflections of a Sex Therapist*, Congdon & Lattes, 1981, p. 38.

13. Masters, W. H., Johnson, V. E., and Kolodny, R. C., *Human Sexuality*, 4th ed., HarperCollins, 1992.

14. We should point out that women are not the only ones with this complaint. There are men who also want postorgasmic cuddling and conversation and are puzzled and frustrated when their partners immediately jump out of bed and rush to clean up and get dressed. There is little doubt, however, that men with this inclination are in a distinct minority, whereas it is one of the most common complaints women voice about boorish male sexual behavior.

15. Masters, Johnson, and Kolodny, op. cit., 1992, p. 84.

CHAPTER 4: LOW SEXUAL DESIRE

1. For several detailed reviews of the hormonal regulation of sexual drive, see Kwan, M., et al., The nature of androgen action on male sexuality: a combined laboratory-self-report study on hypogonadal men, *Journal of Clinical Endocrinology and Metabolism* 57:557–562, 1983; Segraves, R. T., "Hormones and Libido," in S. R. Leiblum and R. C. Rosen, eds., *Sexual Desire Disorders*, Guilford Press, 1988, pp. 271–312; Bancroft, J., *Human Sexuality and Its Problems*, 2nd ed., Churchill Livingston, 1989; and Dixson, A. F., The neuroendocrine regulation of sexual behavior in female primates, *Annual Review of Sex Research* 1:197–226, 1990.

2. See, e.g., Berlin, F. S., and Meinecke, C. F., Treatment of sex offenders with antiandrogenic medication, *American Journal of Psychiatry* 138:601–607, 1981; and Money, J., Treatment guidelines: antiandrogen and counseling of paraphilic sex offenders, *Journal of Sex & Marital Therapy* 13:219–223, 1987.

3. Kolodny, R. C., Masters, W. H., and Johnson, V. E., "Sexual Aversion and Inhibited Sexual Desire," in R. C. Kolodny, W. H. Masters, and V. E. Johnson, *Textbook of Sexual Medicine*, Little, Brown, 1979, pp. 557–574.

4. Shearer, S. L., and Herbert, C. A., Long-term effects of unresolved sexual trauma, *AFP* 36:169–174, 1987; Wyatt, G. E., Child sexual abuse and its effects on sexual functioning, *Annual Review of Sex Research* 2:249–266, 1991.

5. We are grateful to Nancy J. Kolodny, M.S.W., Director of the Eating Disorders Program for the Behavioral Medicine Institute, who has provided us with a number of cases of this sort from her practice.

6. Lazarus, A. A., "A Multimodal Perspective on Problems of Sexual Desire," in S. R. Leiblum and R. C. Rosen, eds., *Sexual Desire Disorders*, Guilford Press, 1988, p. 155.

7. See, e.g., Laws, J. L., *The Second X*, Elsevier North Holland, 1979; Schaffer, K. F., *Sex Roles and Human Behavior*, Winthrop Publishers, 1981; Blumstein, P., and Schwartz, P., *American Couples*, William Morrow, 1983; Rubin, L., *Intimate Strangers*, Harper Perennial Library, 1984; and D'Emilio, J., and Freedman, E. B., *Intimate Matters: A History of Sexuality in America*, Harper & Row, 1988.

8. Shere Hite makes this point explicitly in her analysis of women's responses to her survey questionnaire in *The Hite Report* (Macmillan, 1976). It is interesting to note that this difference in apparent sexual goals seems to apply as well to lesbian couples compared to gay male couples. A variety of studies have found that male homosexuals have vastly greater numbers of sexual partners than lesbians do; furthermore, gay male couples have sexual activity much more frequently than lesbian couples do, as Blumstein and Schwartz (op. cit., 1983) neatly document.

9. See, e.g., Becker, J. V., "Impact of Sexual Abuse on Sexual Functioning," in S. Leiblum and R. Rosen, eds., *Principles and Practice of Sex Therapy*, 2nd ed., Guilford Press, 1989, pp. 298–318; Becker, J. V., and Kaplan, M. S., Rape

victims: issues, theories, and treatment, *Annual Review of Sex Research* 2:267–292, 1991.

10. Schwartz, M. F., and Masters, W. H., "Inhibited Sexual Desire: The Masters & Johnson Institute Treatment Model," in S. R. Leiblum and R. C. Rosen, op. cit., 1988, pp. 229–242.

11. Nichols, M., "Lesbian Sexuality: Issues and Development Theory," in the Boston Lesbian Psychologies Collective, eds., *Lesbian Psychologies: Explorations & Challenges*, University of Illinois Press, 1987, pp. 97–125, 1987; idem, "Low Sexual Desire in Lesbian Couples," in S. R. Leiblum and R. C. Rosen, eds., op. cit., 1988, pp. 387–412.

12. Kaplan, H. S., *Disorders of Sexual Desire*, Brunner/Mazel, 1979; Nutter, D. E., and Condron, M. K., Sexual fantasy and activity patterns of females with inhibited sexual desire versus normal controls, *Journal of Sex & Marital Therapy* 9:276–282, 1983; Nutter, D. E., and Condron, M. K., Sexual activity and fantasy patterns of males with inhibited sexual desire and males with erectile dysfunction versus normal controls, *Journal of Sex & Marital Therapy* 11:91–98, 1985.

CHAPTER FIVE: EJACULATORY PROBLEMS

1. In 1970, when we first reported our treatment statistics for dealing with premature ejaculation (in *Human Sexual Inadequacy*), the psychoanalytic community widely attacked us for "unattainable"—even unimaginable—claims of success. Gradually, disbelief gave way to acceptance as many psychoanalysts and psychoanalytically oriented therapists began to incorporate our rapid treatment methods into their own practices with remarkably good results. Today, virtually all sex therapists regard cases of premature ejaculation as the simplest sorts of cases to treat, but they were far from that point of view less than 25 years ago.

2. One study found that 36 percent of American men in a nonclinical sample had problems with rapid ejaculation (Frank, E., Anderson, C., and Rubenstein, D., Frequency of sexual dysfunction in "normal" couples, *New England Journal of Medicine* 299:111–115, 1978). A small study of married men in Sweden came up with a remarkably similar rate, finding that 38 percent of the men in the sample had premature ejaculation (Nettelbladt, P., and Uddenberg, G., Sexual dysfunction and sexual satisfaction in 58 married Swedish men, *Journal of Psychosomatic Medicine* 23:141–147, 1979). We have estimated elsewhere that 15 to 20 percent of American men have at least a moderate degree of difficulty controlling rapid ejaculation (Masters, W. H., Johnson, V. E., and Kolodny, R. C., *Human Sexuality*, 4th ed., HarperCollins, 1992), these figures being adjusted downward to account for those men who ejaculate quickly by preference as well as the diminishing prevalence of this dysfunction with advancing age. (This is one of the sexual benefits of aging: in men over age 60, rapid ejaculation is hardly ever a problem, even for those who had had great difficulty with this condition at younger ages.) In addition, although premature ejacula-

tion is certainly found among homosexual males, it seems to be considerably less common than among heterosexuals (Masters, W. H., and Johnson, V. E., *Homosexuality in Perspective*, Little, Brown, 1979).

3. American Psychiatric Association, *Diagnostic and Statistical Manual of Mental Disorders*, 3rd ed., revised, American Psychiatric Association Press, 1987.

4. The American Psychiatric Association apparently recognized this problem when they altered an earlier definition of premature ejaculation they had been using in their *Diagnostic and Statistical Manual*, 3rd ed. (1980). This definition couched the diagnosis in terms of "reasonable voluntary control," which left the diagnosis highly subjective. Still, Helen Kaplan states, "The essential feature of PE is that the man lacks adequate voluntary ejaculatory control with the result that he climaxes before he wishes to," and stresses that the quality of the male's ejaculatory control should be "natural, easy, and voluntary" (Kaplan, H., *How to Overcome Premature Ejaculation*, Brunner/Mazel, 1989, p. 8).

5. See, for example, Kinsey, A. C., Pomeroy, W. B., and Martin, C. E., *Sexual Behavior in the Human Male*, W. B. Saunders, 1948; and Kerchoff, A., Social class differences in sexual attitudes and behavior, *Medical Aspects of Human Sexuality* 8:10–25, 1974.

6. Masters, W. H., and Johnson, V. E., *Human Sexual Inadequacy*, Little, Brown, 1970; Kaplan, H. S., *The New Sex Therapy*, Brunner/Mazel, 1974; Levine, S. B., Marital sexual dysfunction: ejaculation disturbances, *Annals of Internal Medicine* 84:575–579, 1976; Perelman, M. A., "Treatment of Premature Ejaculation," in Leiblum, S. R., and Pervin, L. A., eds., *Principles and Practice of Sex Therapy*, Guilford Press, 1980, pp. 199–233; Assalian, P., Clomipramine in the treatment of premature ejaculation, *Journal of Sex Research* 24:213–215, 1988; Wincze, J. P., and Carey, M. P., *Sexual Dysfunction: A Guide for Assessment and Treatment*, Guilford Press, 1991.

7. Kaplan, H., op. cit., 1989.

8. Tollison, C. D., and Adams, H. E., *Sexual Disorders: Treatment, Theory, and Research*, Gardner Press, 1979; McCarthy, B. W., "Cognitive-Behavioral Strategies and Techniques in the Treatment of Early Ejaculation," in Leiblum, S. R., and Rosen, R. C., eds., *Principles and Practice of Sex Therapy—Update for the 1990s*, 2nd ed., Guilford Press, 1989, pp. 141–167.

9. In the past, many males had their first coital experiences with prostitutes, although this practice is quite uncommon today. Since prostitutes typically encouraged their customers to be quick (after all, time is money), this was another way in which some men received early conditioning that favored the development of a rapid, unbridled ejaculatory response.

10. This point was initially made by Joseph Wolpe 2 decades ago and has never been fully investigated. See Wolpe, J., *The Practice of Behavior Therapy*, 2nd ed., Pergamon Press, 1973.

11. Kaplan, op. cit., 1989, p. 20.

12. This technique works best if it hasn't been preceded by a lengthy period of sexual abstinence. If it has been, it is advisable either to have a few days of mutual

sexual activity before embarking on this program *or* to have the male ejaculate by masturbation at least twice within the 48 hours before beginning this undertaking.

13. The original work on the stop-start technique was described in Semans, J. H., Premature ejaculation: A new approach, *Southern Medical Journal* 49:353–358, 1956. Dr. Helen Kaplan's refinements and extensions to Seman's method have been presented in two of her books, *The New Sex Therapy* (Brunner/Mazel, 1974), and *How to Overcome Premature Ejaculation* (Brunner/Mazel, 1989).

14. Men whose religious or personal beliefs make them uncomfortable with masturbation may be helped by pharmacologic treatment geared at reversing rapid ejaculation. A number of prescription medications have the effect of delaying ejaculation; to be started on such a program, it is advisable to see a physician who is knowledgeable about sexual medicine. We do not recommend this approach except in selected cases because these medications involve potential side effects that may be troublesome, but we recognize that there are situations where they can be quite helpful.

15. There is no "perfect" choice for what type of lotion or lubricant you should select. While hypoallergenic lotions may be most appealing to some men (and perfumed hand lotions may be objectionable for a variety of aesthetic reasons), it may be useful to experiment with several different types or brands of lotions or lubricants before finding the one that suits you best. Dr. Helen Kaplan suggests that men try the "wet" stop-start method in a shower, using warm water and plenty of soap to act as the lubricant, but we have found that the combination of standing up and being in the shower are sufficiently unlike most sexual activity to feel very unnatural for most men, even though it may be fun.

16. Masters and Johnson, op. cit., 1970; Kaplan, op. cit., 1974; Spector, I. P., and Carey, M. P., Incidence and prevalence of the sexual dysfunctions: a critical review of the empirical literature, *Archives of Sexual Behavior* 19:389–408, 1990; Wincze and Carey, op. cit., 1991.

17. We use the term "retarded ejaculation" to mean just what it says. Others in the field sometimes use it synonymously with ejaculatory incompetence—i.e., to apply to a man who is unable to ejaculate intravaginally at all. The *Diagnostic and Statistical Manual of Mental Disorders* (3rd ed., revised) of the American Psychiatric Association uses the term "inhibited male orgasm" to apply to *either* the absence of or persistent delay in intravaginal orgasm. We think this usage is a mistake because (1) male orgasm and ejaculation are not always the same; (2) lumping the two conditions together misses some important differences in the underlying patterns of causation, most notably the fact that retarded ejaculation has a much higher likelihood of being related to a medical problem (such as being a drug side effect).

18. Apfelbaum, B., "Retarded Ejaculation: A Much-Misunderstood Syndrome," in Leiblum and Rosen, op. cit., 1989, pp. 168–206.

19. This is a problematic point in Apfelbaum's interpretation, since many men do, in fact, continue a more or less autosexual (self-centered) stimulation during any

kind of sex, including coital sex, with a partner. These men may approach intercourse as a particular form of masturbation; they experience their sexual stimulation as essentially separate and apart from their partner, who just happens to be providing the physical medium for their penis to play in. Probably all sex therapists (including Dr. Apfelbaum, for whom we have great admiration and respect) encounter men of this sort in their practices; in fact, it isn't very unusual for men to be playing out a fantasy scenario in their minds during a sexual encounter, in which their partner's identity is more or less submerged.

20. Kaplan, op. cit., 1974, p. 325.
21. Tollison and Adams, op. cit., 1979, p. 128.
22. Kaplan, H. S., *The Illustrated Manual of Sex Therapy*, 2nd ed., Brunner/Mazel, 1987, p. 151.

CHAPTER SIX: IN SEARCH OF POTENCY

1. National Institutes of Health Consensus Conference Organizing Committee, National Consensus Conference on Erectile Dysfunction (Summary Statement), Bethesda, Md., December 7, 1992.
2. Some men have told us that if their wife or partner earns substantially more than they do or if she has attained greater success in her work than they have achieved (especially if they are working in related fields), they have thought that this might have triggered their impotence. This sort of professional jealousy or rigid attitude toward stereotypical sex roles (e.g., the man should be the breadwinner in a family) is hardly apt to be "the" cause of their potency problem, although it may reflect other problems both in their relationship and in their view of themselves.
3. To be fair, some men are more concerned about the time and expense of therapy than they are about other elements, especially considering that there is no guarantee that therapy will work. Time concerns are partly a carryover from a now largely outmoded practice in which a psychoanalyst would work with a patient for years on a sexual problem, with very mixed results.
4. Masters, W. H., and Johnson, V. E., *Human Sexual Inadequacy*, Little, Brown, 1970; Kolodny, R. C., Masters, W. H., and Johnson, V. E., *Textbook of Sexual Medicine*, Little, Brown, 1979.
5. Kolodny, Masters, and Johnson, op. cit., 1979, pp. 480–481.
6. The problem is not just one of lack of access to health care, although that is a part of the explanation. Even among men who have adequate medical insurance or who are financially well off, there is considerable reluctance to seek out medical help for sexual difficulties because the man is embarrassed about his situation—and afraid of being told that his problem is "all in his mind." Another relevant point is that many, if not most, of the men who try to get medical help are brushed off by uninformed or uninterested physicians who have neither the attitudinal attributes nor the diagnostic acumen to help them. And, to take the problem one step further, some men with a medical problem that results in

impotence are afraid that they will be cheated and pushed into a treatment they don't want or need—such as surgery to implant a penile prosthesis—for the economic benefit of the doctor. (Sometimes, of course, these men are absolutely right in their suspicions.)

7. See, for example, Masters, W. H., and Johnson, V. E., *Human Sexual Inadequacy*, Little, Brown, 1970; and Kaplan, H. S., *The New Sex Therapy*, Brunner/Mazel, 1974.

8. Burgess, A., et al., Response patterns in children and adolescents exploited through sex rings and pornography, *American Journal of Psychiatry* 141:656–662, 1984; Finkelhor, D., *Child Sexual Abuse*, Free Press, 1984; Crewdson, J., *By Silence Betrayed: Sexual Abuse of Children in America*, Little, Brown, 1988; Maltz, W., Identifying and treating the sexual repercussions of incest: a couples therapy approach, *Journal of Sex and Marital Therapy* 14:142–170, 1988; Finkelhor, D., Early and long-term effects of child sexual abuse: an update, *Professional Psychology: Research and Practice* 21:325–330, 1990.

9. LoPiccolo, J., "Management of Psychogenic Erectile Failure," in E. A. Tanagho, T. F. Lue, and R. D. McClure, eds., *Contemporary Management of Impotence and Infertility*, Williams & Wilkins, 1988, pp. 133–146.

10. Kolodny, Masters, and Johnson, op. cit., 1979; Kaplan, H. S., *The Evaluation of Sexual Disorders*, New York, Brunner/Mazel, 1983; Kwan, M., et al., The nature of androgen action on male sexuality: a combined laboratory self-report study of hypogonadal men, *Journal of Clinical Endocrinology and Metabolism* 57:557–562, 1983.

11. We should point out that with any sort of treatment there can be a placebo effect that is independent of the actual drug effect. Thus, a man who strongly believes that testosterone injections or pills will boost his sexual performance *may* find that this actually happens as a result of his faith in the treatment.

12. Anderson, R. A., Bancroft, J., and Wu, F. C. W., The effects of exogenous testosterone on sexuality and mood of normal men, *Journal of Clinical Endocrinology and Metabolism* 75:1503–1507, 1992.

13. Perryman, R. L., and Thorner, M. O., The effects of hyperprolactinemia on sexual and reproductive function in men, *Journal of Andrology* 5:233–240, 1981; Prescott, R. W. C., et al., Hyperprolactinemia in men—response to bromocriptine therapy, *Lancet* 1:245–248, 1982.

14. Schover, L., and Jensen, S., *Sexuality and Chronic Illness*, Guilford Press, 1988.

15. Virag, R., et al., Intracavernous injection of papaverine as diagnostic and therapeutic measure in erectile failure, *Angiology* 35:79–87, 1984; Zorgniotti, A. W., and LeFleur, R. S., Auto-injection of the corpus cavernosum with a vasoactive drug combination for vasculogenic impotence, *Journal of Urology* 133:39–41, 1985; Sidi, A. A., et al., Intracavernous drug-induced erections in the management of male erectile dysfunction, *Journal of Urology* 135:704–706, 1986.

16. Lue, T., "Office Treatment: Papaverine Injections for Impotence," in Tanagho, Lue, and McClure, eds., op. cit., 1988, p. 162.

17. Tiefer, L., and Melman, A., "Comprehensive Evaluation of Erectile Dysfunction and Medical Treatments," in Leiblum, S., and Rosen, R. C., *Principles and Practice of Sex Therapy: Update for the 1990s*, Guilford Press, 1989, p. 229.

18. Kolodny, Masters, and Johnson, op. cit., 1979; Spycher, M. A., and Hauri, D., The ultrastructure of the erectile tissue in priapism, *Journal of Urology* 135:142–147, 1986.

19. The first drug that was used to cause erections by local penile injection—phenoxybenzamine—is banned in the United States because of concerns about its cancer-producing potential. (Zorgniotti, A. W., and Lue, T. F., "Intracavernous Injection of Papaverine and Phentolamine," in Tanagho, Lue, and McClure, eds., op. cit., 1988, pp. 160–161.)

20. Kessler, R., Complications of inflatable penile prostheses, *Urology* 18:470–473, 1981; Kaufman, J. J., Lindner, A., and Raz, S., Complications of penile prosthesis surgery for impotence, *Journal of Urology* 128:1192–1194, 1982.

21. Shaw, J., The unnecessary penile implant, *Archives of Sexual Behavior* 18:455–460, 1989.

22. Diedrich, G. K., Stock, W., and LoPiccolo, J., A study on the mechanical reliability of the Dacomed Snap Gauge: implications for the differentiation between organic and psychogenic impotence, *Archives of Sexual Behavior* 21:509–523, 1992.

23. Masters, W. H., Johnson, V. E., and Kolodny, R. C., *Human Sexuality*, 4th ed., New York, HarperCollins, 1992.

24. Kolodny, R. C., Evaluating sex therapy: process and outcome at the Masters & Johnson Institute, *Journal of Sex Research* 17:301–318, 1981.

25. If you think you'll feel less anxious if your partner starts the touching, by all means tell her this. However, keep an open mind on these matters. After all, you're going through a process that is gradually changing your ingrained reactions and responses.

26. These might not have been the initial cause of the erectile problems, but they are nevertheless important *maintaining* elements. In many cases, it may not be possible to discover what the original cause was; therapists who offer an explanation of what they think the cause might have been are usually just guessing, unless there was an extremely clearcut situation such as being the victim of childhood sexual abuse or of having no problem with erections until the patient discovered his wife was having an affair.

27. There is one exception to this statement. Persistent erections that won't go away (a condition called priapism, which we have already referred to) *do* indeed represent a medical emergency and should be treated right away. The context of our sentence should make it clear that we are not referring to medical situations.

28. Masters, W. H., Johnson, V. E., and Kolodny, R. C., "Sexual Fantasy," in *Masters & Johnson on Sex and Human Loving*, Little, Brown, 1986, pp. 263–281.

29. Masters, W. H., Johnson, V. E., and Kolodny, R. C., *Crisis: Heterosexual Behavior in the Age of AIDS*, Grove Press, 1988.

CHAPTER SEVEN: FEMALE SEXUAL DYSFUNCTIONS

1. Gagnon, J., *Human Sexualities*, Scott, Foresman and Company, 1977, p. 6.
2. Fallon, A., "Culture in the Mirror: Sociocultural Determinants of Body Image," in T. F. Cash and T. Pruzinsky, eds., *Body Images: Development, Deviance, and Change*, Guilford Press, 1990, pp. 80–109.
3. The phrase "the tyranny of slenderness" is intentionally borrowed from the subtitle of Kim Chernin's book, *The Obsession: Reflections on the Tyranny of Slenderness*, Harper & Row, 1981.
4. Roth, G., *When Food Is Love: Exploring the Relationship between Eating and Intimacy*, Dutton, 1991, p. 2.
5. Stuart, R. B., and Jacobson, B., *Weight, Sex & Marriage: A Delicate Balance*, Fireside Books, 1987, p. 56.
6. When it comes to breast size, it is not correct simply to think that bigger is better in the minds of all women. What is quite remarkable is that while females who consider themselves not well endowed often long for larger breasts, there are also tens of thousands of large-breasted women who are dissatisfied with their bust size. While this dissatisfaction is sometimes a reflection of physical factors, it is frequently a case of feeling self-conscious about having large breasts. The end result is that reduction mammoplasties—surgery to make large breasts smaller—are common operations, although not as common as breast augmentation surgery.
7. Kinsey, A., et al., *Sexual Behavior in the Human Female*, W. B. Saunders, 1953.
8. Hite, S., *The Hite Report*, Macmillan, 1976.
9. Fisher, S., *The Female Orgasm*, Basic Books, 1973.
10. Hunt, M., *Sexual Behavior in the 1970s*, Dell, 1974.
11. Tavris, C., and Sadd, S., *The Redbook Report on Female Sexuality*, Delacorte Press, 1977.
12. Wincze, J. P., and Carey, M. P., *Sexual Dysfunction: A Guide for Assessment and Treatment*, Guilford Press, 1991; Heiman, J. R., and Grafton-Becker, V., "Orgasmic Disorders in Women," in S. R. Leiblum and R. C. Rosen, eds., *Principles and Practice of Sex Therapy*, 2nd ed., Guilford Press, 1989, pp. 51–88.
13. American Psychiatric Association, *Diagnostic and Statistical Manual of Mental Disorders*, 3rd ed., rev., American Psychiatric Association Press, 1987, p. 294.
14. The exception is, of course, women who view masturbation as sinful or dirty or as a second-best type of sex. Since there are many women who do not masturbate at all, and others who rarely masturbate as adults, a direct comparison is not always possible.
15. Barbach, L. G., *For Yourself: The Fulfillment of Female Sexuality*, New American Library, 1975, p. 23.
16. Blumstein, P., and Schwartz, P., *American Couples*, William Morrow, 1983, p. 227.
17. Clearly, the cases that sex therapists see are a skewed sample. For instance, few alcoholic women come for sex therapy, and alcoholism can certainly cause

female sexual dysfunctions, as we discuss in Chapter 12. Likewise, sex therapists don't see many women with gynecologic cancers, although surgery or radiation therapy used to treat these conditions sometimes causes sexual problems. Furthermore, it is much more likely that a woman with a condition such as severe hypothyroidism would be seen by a physician because of other symptoms from this condition than it would be for her to seek evaluation primarily for a sexual problem.

18. This is not to say that such a sex-negative upbringing is restricted only to very religious families (since it clearly is not) or that it inevitably leads to adult sexual guilt, conflict, and dysfunction. In fact, while there is no way of knowing how many women who were raised in such families have gone on to fulfilling, normal sex lives, we suspect that the percentage is fairly high. Still, our point is this: although a sex-negative upbringing doesn't preordain adult sexual problems, it doesn't help matters any.

19. Masters, W. H., and Johnson, V. E., *Human Sexual Inadequacy*, Little, Brown, 1970; LoPiccolo, J., and Lobitz, W. C., The role of masturbation in the treatment of orgasmic dysfunction, *Archives of Sexual Behavior* 2:163–171, 1972; Kaplan, H., *The New Sex Therapy*, Brunner/Mazel, 1974; Riley, A. J., and Riley, E. J., A controlled study to evaluate directed masturbation in the management of primary orgasmic failure in women, *British Journal of Psychiatry* 135:404–409, 1978; Kuriansky, J. B., Sharpe, L., and O'Connor, D., The treatment of anorgasmia: long-term effectiveness of a short-term behavioral group therapy, *Journal of Sex & Marital Therapy* 8:29–43, 1982; Heiman, J. R., and LoPiccolo, J., *Becoming Orgasmic: A Sexual and Personal Growth Program for Women*, rev. ed., Prentice-Hall, 1988; Kelley, M. P., Strassberg, D. S., and Kircher, J. R., Attitudinal and experiential correlates of anorgasmia, *Archives of Sexual Behavior* 19:165–177, 1990.

20. Fisher, op. cit., 1973.

21. Kaplan, op. cit., 1974, p. 384.

22. Barbach, L., *Women Discover Orgasm*, Free Press, 1980, p. 10.

23. Women who need help in constructing their own sex fantasies can benefit from reading *My Secret Garden, Forbidden Flowers*, or *Women on Top*, by Nancy Friday, all of which contain detailed, uncensored descriptions of women's favorite fantasy scenes.

24. Masters, W. H., Johnson, V. E., and Kolodny, R. C., *Human Sexuality*, Little, Brown, 1982.

25. Our overall research population during the years that we are referring to, which included women participating in studies of hormonal changes during the menstrual cycle, contraceptive efficacy, the relationship between certain illicit drugs and sexual functioning, and control groups of "normal" women, numbered well in excess of one thousand. In addition, in screening potential research subjects, we conducted physical examinations for hundreds of other women who were ultimately not selected for these studies but for whom we nevertheless kept extensive records.

26. This observation does not apply to the cases of vaginismus that are secondary to atrophic vaginitis, which is usually a reflection of estrogen deficiency. In this subgroup of women, it is common to find that vaginismus is accompanied by depressed libido and impaired vaginal lubrication. These problems often respond dramatically to estrogen replacement therapy, although the vaginismus itself usually requires further therapy beyond hormone replacement.

27. Duddle, C. M., Etiological factors in the unconsummated marriage, *Journal of Psychosomatic Research* 21:157–160, 1977.

28. This observation is not as simple as it first appears. For one thing, women with vaginismus may be extremely grateful to their husbands for having stuck with them in light of their sexual problem, rather than deserting them. Thus, part of what is expressed as love is undoubtedly colored by a considerable quotient of guilt. Another factor to consider is that it is not unusual for the man who is married to a woman with vaginismus to have sexual problems of his own, as we discuss in the main body of the text. When both partners have sexual dysfunctions, there is often a strong emotional bonding that occurs between them as they deal together with their individual and conjoint pain and frustrations. A final point to be considered is that we are struck by the fact that many men whose wives have vaginismus seem to be relatively passive souls with low-key sexual interests. This type of personality may be somewhat self-selecting in courtship, since it is not unreasonable to think that many men would quickly walk away from a romantic involvement with a woman with whom intercourse isn't possible.

29. Kolodny, R. C., Masters, W. H., and Johnson, V. E., *Textbook of Sexual Medicine*, Little, Brown, 1979.

30. Becker and Kaplan reported that 12.7 percent of female sexual assault victims reported difficulty with intromission following the assault. Becker, J. V., and Kaplan, M. S., Rape victims: issues, theories, and treatment, *Annual Review of Sex Research* 2:267–292, 1991.

31. Masters, W. H., and Johnson, V. E., *Human Sexual Inadequacy*, Little, Brown, 1970; Tollison, C. D., and Adams, H. E., *Sexual Disorders: Treatment, Theory, and Research*, Gardner Press, 1979; Barnes, J., Primary vaginismus (Part 1): social and clinical features, *Irish Medical Journal* 79:59–62, 1986; Barnes, J., Primary vaginismus (Part 2): aetiological factors, *Irish Medical Journal* 79:62–65, 1986; Leiblum, S. R., Pervin, L. A., and Campbell, E. H., "The Treatment of Vaginismus: Success and Failure," in S. R. Leiblum and R. C. Rosen, eds., *Principles and Practice of Sex Therapy: Update for the 1990s*, Guilford Press, 1989, pp. 113–138.

32. We recognize that this may be a self-selecting feature of the types of cases seen by sex therapists. Obviously those couples who don't attempt to deal with vaginismus with any resolve to stay together break up either before marriage occurs (if they have attempted having intercourse and have thus discovered the problem) or after a brief period of marriage. Some couples succeed in having such marriages annulled on grounds of nonconsummation; others end these

marriages after a short but often turbulent period of trying to overcome this dysfunction.

33. Freud believed that girls are never fully able to compensate for their penis envy, although they partially offset this problem by shifting their focus to the wish for a baby. Many critics have debunked this portrayal of female psychosexual development, which nevertheless remains a prominent feature in modern psychoanalytic thinking. In 1926, Karen Horney pointed out rather indignantly that what women envy about men is their privileged status in a male-dominated and -organized society; she also was one of the first to note that Freud completely omitted any mention of "womb envy" in men. (Horney, K., The flight from womanhood, *International Journal of Psychoanalysis* 1:324–339, 1926.) More recent criticisms of Freud's oversimplified and often erroneous views in this area are presented in the following works: Millett, K., *Sexual Politics*, Doubleday, 1970; Tennov, D., *Psychotherapy: The Hazardous Cure*, Abelard-Schuman, 1975; Frieze, I. H., et al., *Women and Sex Roles: A Social Psychological Perspective*, Norton, 1978; and Schwartz, A. E., Freud and the feminine fallacy, *Contemporary Psychology* 33:501–502, 1988.

34. One cautionary note: in cases where the vaginismus is a result of pregnancy phobia or a phobia about sexually transmitted diseases, the involuntary spasms of the muscles around the opening of the vagina may not occur at all during a pelvic exam, since there is no trigger for the woman's phobic response. For the same reason, a few women with very severe vaginismus in sexual situations are nevertheless able to insert a vaginal tampon during menstruation, although this is an unusual pattern. Partly for these reasons, the woman's history alone cannot be used to make an accurate diagnosis of vaginismus, although it certainly can be used to provide a high index of suspicion for this condition.

CHAPTER EIGHT: COMPULSIVE SEXUAL BEHAVIOR

1. See, for example, Stoller, R. J., *Perversion: The Erotic Form of Hatred*, Pantheon, 1975; Stoller, R. J., "Sexual Deviations," in F. Beach, ed., *Human Sexuality in Four Perspectives*, Johns Hopkins University Press, 1977, pp. 190–214; Money, J., *Gay, Straight, and In-Between*, Oxford University Press, 1988; and Kaplan, L. J., *Female Perversions*, Doubleday, 1991.

2. Kleptomania, or compulsive stealing, is sometimes characterized by sexual excitement during the act of stealing; in fact, some kleptomaniac women have orgasms at the exact moment when they snatch an item off a counter or shelf and stuff it into their handbag or coat. (Current estimates suggest that there are more female than male kleptomaniacs.) However, we do not regard kleptomania as equivalent to the paraphilias, although other writers—such as Louise J. Kaplan, in her interesting book *Female Perversions* (Doubleday, 1991)—draw a close parallel (or see a virtual equivalence) between these conditions.

3. Money, op. cit., 1988; Money, J., and Lamacz, M., *Vandalized Lovemaps*, Prometheus Books, 1989.

4. Groth, N., *Men Who Rape*, Plenum Press, 1979; Finkelhor, D., *Child Sexual Abuse*, Free Press, 1984; Everstine, D. S., and Everstine, L., *Sexual Trauma in Children and Adolescents*, Brunner/Mazel, 1989.

5. Finkelhor, D., and Araji, S., Explanations of pedophilia: a four factor model, *Journal of Sex Research* 22:145–161, 1986.

6. See chap. 17, "The Varieties of Sexual Behavior," in Masters, W. H., Johnson, V. E., and Kolodny, R. C., *Human Sexuality*, 4th ed., HarperCollins, 1992.

7. Stoller, R., "Sexual Deviations," in F. Beach, ed., *Human Sexuality in Four Perspectives*, Johns Hopkins University Press, 1977, p. 196.

8. Moser, C., Sadomasochism, *Journal of Social Work and Human Sexuality* 7:43–56, 1988.

9. Maletzky, B. M., "Assisted covert sensitization," in D. J. Cox and R. J. Daitzman, eds., *Exhibitionism: Description, Assessment and Treatment*, Garland, 1980, p. 196.

10. Laws, D. R., ed., *Relapse Prevention with Sex Offenders*, Guilford Press, 1989; Furby, L., Weinrott, M. R., and Blackshaw, L., Sex offender recidivism: a review, *Psychological Bulletin* 105:3–30, 1989.

11. Carnes, P., *Out of the Shadows: Understanding Sexual Addictions*, CompCare Publications, 1983; Schwartz, M. F., and Brasted, W. S., Sexual addiction, *Medical Aspects of Human Sexuality* 19:103–107, 1985; Kasl, C. D., *Women, Sex, and Addiction*, Ticknor & Fields, 1989.

12. Earle, R., and Crowe, G., *Lonely All the Time*, Pocket Books, 1989, p. 13.

13. Carnes, op. cit., 1983.

14. Schwartz, M. F., and Brasted, W. S., Sexual addiction, *Medical Aspects of Human Sexuality* 19:103–107, 1985.

15. Kasl, C. D., op. cit., 1989, p. 50.

16. Kasl, op. cit., 1989.

17. Levine, M. P., and Troiden, R. R., The myth of sexual compulsivity, *Journal of Sex Research* 25:347–363, 1988.

18. Money, op. cit., 1988.

CHAPTER NINE: CONCEPTION AND CONTRACEPTION

1. Schatten, G., and Schatten, H., The energetic egg, *The Sciences* 23 (5):32, 1983.

2. Jones, H. W., Jr., and Schrader, C., And just what is a pre-embryo, *Fertility & Sterility* 52:189–191, 1989.

3. For a nontechnical discussion of these conditions, readers can consult chap. 7 in Masters, W. H., Johnson, V. E., and Kolodny, R. C., *Human Sexuality*, 4th ed., HarperCollins, 1992.

4. Ectopic pregnancy occurs approximately once every sixty pregnancies (Centers for Disease Control, *Morbidity and Mortality Weekly Report* 39:401, 1990). Most ectopic pregnancies abort at a relatively early stage, but when growth of the embryo, placenta, and membranes occurs, there is a substantial risk of rupture and bleeding. Because it is difficult to diagnose this condition, ectopic pregnancy is the seventh leading cause of maternal death in the U.S.

5. Wharton, C., and Blackburn, R., Lower-dose pills, *Population Reports*, Series A, Number 7, November 1988; Mishell, D. R., Jr., Contraception, *New England Journal of Medicine* 320:777–787, 1989.

6. Failure rate statistics for this and other reversible methods of birth control discussed in this chapter are from Jones, E. F., and Forrest, J. D., Contraceptive failure rates based on the 1988 NSFG, *Family Planning Prospectives* 24:12–19, 1992. These statistics are more realistic than those found in many other reports since they correctly include contraceptive failure rates for unreported abortions that certainly represent contraceptive failures, too.

7. Cancer and Steroid Hormone Study, Combination oral contraceptive use and the risk of endometrial cancer, *Journal of the American Medical Association* 257:796–800, 1987; Cancer and Steroid Hormone Study, The reduction in risk of ovarian cancer associated with oral contraceptive use, *New England Journal of Medicine* 316:650–655, 1987.

8. Spector, T. D., Roman, E., and Silman, A. J., The pill, parity, and rheumatoid arthritis, *Arthritis and Rheumatology* 33:782, 1990; Hazes, J. M. W., et al., Reduction of the risk of rheumatoid arthritis among women who take oral contraceptives, *Arthritis and Rheumatology* 33:173, 1990.

9. Vessey, M. P., "An Overview of the Benefits and Risks of Combined Oral Contraceptives," in R. D. Mann, ed., *Oral Contraceptives and Breast Cancer*, Parthenon Publishing, 1990, pp. 121–132; Panser, L. A., and Phipps, W. R., Type of oral contraception in relation to acute, initial episodes of pelvic inflammatory disease, *Contraception* 93:91, 1991; Cates, W., Jr., and Stone, K. M., Family planning, sexually transmitted diseases, and contraceptive choice: a literature update—Part II., *Family Planning Perspectives* 24:122–128, 1992.

10. Wharton, C., and Blackburn, R., op. cit., November 1988; Mishell, D. R., Jr., op. cit., 1989.

11. Enzelsberger, H., et al., Influence of oral contraceptive use on bone density in climacteric women, *Maturitas* 9:375–378, 1988; Kleerekoper, M., et al., Oral contraceptive use may protect against low bone mass, *Archives of Internal Medicine* 151:1971–1976, 1991.

12. Schlesselman, J. J., Cancer of the breast and reproductive tract in relation to use of oral contraceptives, *Contraception* 40:1–38, 1989.

13. See, for example, Carael, M., et al., Human immunodeficiency virus transmission among heterosexual couples in central Africa, *AIDS* 2:201, 1988; European Study Group, Risk factors for male-to-female transmission of HIV, *British Medical Journal* 298:411–415, 1989; Plummer, F. A., et al., Cofactors in male-female sexual transmission of human immunodeficiency virus type 1, *Journal of Infectious Diseases* 163:233, 1991; Hunter, D. J., and Mati, J. K., "Contraception, Family Planning, and HIV," in L. Chen, J. Sepulveda, and S. Segal, eds., *AIDS and Women's Health: Science for Policy and Action*, Plenum Press, 1992; Cates and Stone, op. cit., 1992.

14. Weisman, S. R., Japan keeps ban on birth control pill, *New York Times*, March 19, 1992, p. A3.

15. Wharton, C., and Blackburn, R., op. cit., 1988.

16. Mann, J. I., and Inman, W. H., Oral contraceptives and death from myocardial infarction, *British Medical Journal* 2:245–248, 1975; Jick, H., et al., Myocardial infarction and other vascular diseases in young women: role of estrogens and other factors, *Journal of the American Medical Association* 240:2548–2552, 1978; and Rosenberg, L., et al., Oral contraceptive use in relation to nonfatal myocardial infarction, *American Journal of Epidemiology* 111:59–66, 1980.

17. See, for example, Mann, D., et al., Myocardial infarction and angina pectoris in young women, *Journal of Epidemiology and Community Health* 41:215–219, 1987; Mishell, D. R., Jr., op. cit., 1989; Upton, G. V., Lipids, cardiovascular disease, and oral contraceptives: a practice perspective, *Fertility & Sterility* 53:1–12, 1990.

18. Porter, J. B., Hershel, J., and Walker, A. M., Mortality among oral contraceptive users, *Obstetrics and Gynecology* 70:29, 1987.

19. Murray, P. P., et al., Oral contraceptive use in women with a family history of breast cancer, *Obstetrics and Gynecology* 73:977–983, 1989.

20. Romieu, I., et al., Prospective study of oral contraceptive use and risk of breast cancer in women, *Journal of the National Cancer Institute* 81:1313–1321, 1989.

21. Kay, C. R., and Hannaford, P. C., Breast cancer and the pill, *British Journal of Cancer* 58:675–680, 1988; Miller, D. R., et al., Breast cancer before age 45 and oral contraceptive use: new findings, *American Journal of Epidemiology* 129:269–277, 1989; and Johnson, J. H., Weighing the evidence on the pill and breast cancer, *Family Planning Perspectives* 21:89–92, 1989.

22. See, for example, Wharton and Blackburn, op. cit., 1988, and Johnson, op. cit., 1989; and Thomas, D. B., "Oral Contraceptives and Breast Cancer: Review of the Epidemiological Literature," in Committee on the Relationship Between Oral Contraceptives and Breast Cancer, ed., *Contraceptives & Breast Cancer*, National Academy Press, 1991, Appendix B, pp. 102–142.

23. Committee on the Relationship Between Oral Contraceptives and Breast Cancer, op. cit., 1991, p. 136.

24. Wharton and Blackburn, op. cit., 1988; Mishell, op. cit., 1989; Speroff and Darney, op. cit., 1992.

25. Dyer, K. A., Curiosities of contraception: a historical perspective, *Journal of the American Medical Association* 264:2818–2819, 1990.

26. See, for example, Centers for Disease Control, Current trends—IUD safety: report of a nationwide physician survey, *Morbidity and Mortality Weekly Report* 23:225, 1974; Food and Drug Administration, Ad Hoc Ob-Gyn Advisory Committee, Report on safety and efficacy of the Dalkon Shield and other IUDs, Mimeographed report, 1974 (cited in Greep, R. O., Koblinsky, M. A., and Jaffe, F. S., *Reproduction and Human Welfare: A Challenge to Research*, MIT Press, 1976); and Tatum, H. J., et al., The Dalkon Shield controversy, *Journal of the American Medical Association* 231:716–717, 1975.

27. Unlike other IUDs, which at the time had only a single-stranded tail, the

Dalkon Shield had several strands in its tail. This unique arrangement proved to be disastrous, as it provided bacteria with a "ladder" to gain entry to the uterus, from where they had a virtually unimpeded ascent to the Fallopian tubes. One study found that Dalkon Shield users had a relative risk of PID that was 730 percent higher than for sexually active women not using contraception (Lee, N. C., et al., Type of intrauterine contraceptive device and the risk of pelvic inflammatory disease, *Obstetrics & Gynecology* 62:1–7, 1983).

28. Mosher, W. D., and Pratt, W. F., Use of contraception and family planning services in the United States, 1988, *American Journal of Public Health* 9:1132–1133, 1990.

29. Cole, H. M., Intrauterine devices, *Journal of the American Medical Association* 261:2127–2130, 1989.

30. Jones, E. F., and Forrest, J. D., Contraceptive failure in the United States: revised estimates from the 1982 National Survey of Family Growth, *Family Planning Perspectives* 21:103–109, 1989. (Note: Jones and Forrest, op. cit., 1992, do not report a specific failure rate for IUDs because the use of IUDs had declined substantially by 1988, the year this later article uses for data collection.)

31. The incidence of uterine perforation is some tenfold greater in women who are breast-feeding, so it is advisable to be especially cautious if an IUD is chosen as the contraceptive method while a woman is lactating. See, for example, Treiman, K., and Liskin, L., Intrauterine devices, *Population Reports* Series B, No. 5, 1988; and Adoni, A., and Chetrit, A. B., The management of intrauterine devices following uterine perforation, *Contraception* 43:77–82, 1991.

32. Without wishing to get overly technical in our discussion of these problems, we refer readers to our previous comments on this topic in Masters, W. H., Johnson, V. E., and Kolodny, R. C., *Human Sexuality*, 3rd ed., Scott, Foresman and Company, 1988, Research Spotlight on pp. 166–167. More recent commentaries on substantially the same issue can be found in Kessel, E., Pelvic inflammatory disease with intrauterine device use: a reassessment, *Fertility & Sterility* 51:1–11, 1989; Kronmal, R. A., Whitney, D. A., and Mumford, S. D., The intrauterine device and pelvic inflammatory disease: The Women's Health Study reanalyzed, *Journal of Clinical Epidemiology* 44:109, 1991; Petitti, D. B., Reconsidering the IUD, *Family Planning Perspectives* 24:33–36, 1992; Farley, T. M. M., et al., Intrauterine devices and pelvic inflammatory disease: an international perspective, *Lancet* 339:785–788, 1992; and Cates, W., Jr., and Stone, K. M., Family planning, sexually transmitted diseases and contraceptive choice: a literature update—Part II, *Family Planning Perspectives* 24:122–128, 1992.

33. Lee, N. C., Rubin, G. L., and Grimes, D. A., Measures of sexual behavior and the risk of pelvic inflammatory disease, *Obstetrics and Gynecology* 77:425, 1991.

34. Lee, N. C., Rubin, G. L., and Borucki, R., The intrauterine device and pelvic inflammatory disease revisited: new results of The Women's Health Study, *Obstetrics and Gynecology* 72:1–6, 1988.

35. Cole, H. M., Intrauterine devices, *Journal of the American Medical Association* 261:2127–2130, 1989; Franks, A. L., et al., Contraception and ectopic pregnancy risk, *American Journal of Obstetrics & Gynecology* 163:1120–1123, 1990.
36. Treiman and Liskin, op. cit., 1988.
37. Franks, A. L., et al., Contraception and ectopic pregnancy risk, *American Journal of Obstetrics and Gynecology* 163:1120–1123, 1990.
38. See, for example, Berger, G. S., Keith, L., and Moss, W., Prevalence of gonorrhea among women using various methods of contraception, *British Journal of Venereal Diseases* 51:307, 1975; Cramer, D. W., et al., The relationship of tubal infertility to barrier method and oral contraceptive use, *Journal of the American Medical Association* 257:2446–2450, 1987; Cates, W., Jr., and Stone, K. M., Family planning, sexually transmitted diseases and contraceptive choice: a literature update—Part I., *Family Planning Perspectives* 24:75–84, 1992.
39. See, for example, Foxman, B., and Frerichs, R. R., Epidemiology of urinary tract infection: I. diaphragm use and sexual intercourse, *American Journal of Public Health* 75:1308–1313, 1985; Fihn, S. D., et al., Association between diaphragm use and urinary tract infection, *Journal of the American Medical Association* 254:240–245, 1985; and Hooton, T. M., et al., *Escherichia coli* bacteriuria and contraceptive method, *Journal of the American Medical Association* 265:64–69, 1991.
40. Klitsch, M., FDA approval ends cervical cap's marathon, *Family Planning Perspectives* 20:137–138, 1988.
41. Boehm, D., The cervical caps: effectiveness as a contraceptive, *Journal of Nurse-Midwifery* 28 (1):3–6, 1983; Cagen, R., The cervical cap as a contraceptive barrier, *Contraception* 33:496, 1986; Powell, M. G., et al., Contraception with the cervical cap: effectiveness, safety, continuity of use, and user satisfaction, *Contraception* 33:215–232, 1986.
42. Bernstein, G., et al., "Results of a Comparative Study of the Diaphragm and Cervical Cap." Paper presented at the annual meeting of the American Public Health Association, Las Vegas, September 29–October 2, 1986.
43. Richwald, G. A., et al., Effectiveness of the cavity-rim cervical cap: results of a large clinical study, *Obstetrics & Gynecology* 74:143, 1989; and Golub, E. L., and Sivin, I., The Prentif cervical cap and Pap smear results: a critical appraisal, *Contraception* 40:343, 1989.
44. Tannahill, R., *Sex in History*, Stein and Day, 1980.
45. Centers for Disease Control, *Morbidity and Mortality Weekly Report* 38: S-8, Table 2, 1989; and Liskin, L., et al., Condoms—now more than ever, *Population Reports* Series H, No. 8, September 1990.
46. Pugh, B., "An Evaluation of the Effects of Various Lubricants on Latex Condoms." Presented at the Fifth International Conference on AIDS, Montreal, June 4–9, 1989. (Abstract W.A.P. 95, p. 135.)
47. Voeller, B., "Persistent Condom Breakage." Presented at the Fifth International Conference on AIDS, Montreal, Canada, June 4–9, 1989. (Abstract W.A.P. 99, p. 136.)

48. See, for example, Mishell, op. cit., 1989; Liskin et al., op. cit., 1990; and Speroff and Darney, op. cit., 1992.

49. Trussell, J., Warner, D. L., and Hatcher, R. A., Condom slippage and breakage rates, *Family Planning Perspectives* 24:20–23, 1992.

50. Kirkman, R., Morris, J., and Webb, A., User experience: Mates, *The British Journal of Family Planning* 15:107, 1990.

51. For example, one Danish study found that 5 percent of condoms broke (Gotzsche, P. C., and Hording, M., Condoms to prevent HIV transmission do not imply truly safe sex, *Scandinavian Journal of Infectious Diseases* 20:233–234, 1988). A U.S. study of heterosexual men found a breakage rate of 7 percent (Piedrahita, C., et al., Latex condom breakage study, Family Health International, Research Triangle Park, N.C., September 1990). Slippage rates exceeding 10 percent have also been reported in a substantial number of studies.

52. Rietmeijer, C. A. M., et al., Condoms as physical and chemical barriers against human immunodeficiency virus, *Journal of the American Medical Association* 259:1851–1853, 1988.

53. Tannahill, R., op. cit., 1980.

54. Dyer, K. A., op. cit., 1990.

55. Jones and Forrest, op. cit., 1992.

56. Speroff and Darney, op. cit., 1992.

57. North, B. B., and Vorhauer, B. W., Use of the Today contraceptive sponge in the United States, *International Journal of Fertility* 30:81–84, 1985.

58. Although there was one early study that tentatively indicated that there *might* be a heightened risk of birth defects in infants of women who had used a spermicide in the 10 months before conception (Jick, H., et al., Vaginal spermicides and congenital disorders, *Journal of the American Medical Association* 245:1329–1332, 1981), several further reports concluded that this finding was invalid, and two of the coauthors of the original study dissociated themselves from the article and its findings. See, for example, Bracken, M. B., Spermicidal contraceptives and poor reproductive outcomes: the epidemiologic evidence against an association, *American Journal of Obstetrics and Gynecology* 151:552–556, 1985; Simpson, J. L., Do contraceptive methods pose fetal risks?, *Research Frontiers in Fertility Regulation* 3 (6):8–9, 1985; Watkins, R. N., Vaginal spermicides and congenital disorders: the validity of a study, *Journal of the American Medical Association* 256:3095, 1986; Holmes, L., Vaginal spermicides and congenital disorders: the validity of a study, *Journal of the American Medical Association* 256:3096, 1986; and Louik, C., et al., Maternal exposure to spermicides in relation to certain birth defects, *New England Journal of Medicine* 317:474–476, 1987.

59. Feldblum, P. J., Bernardik, E., and Rosenberg, M. J., Spermicide use and sexually transmitted disease, *Journal of the American Medical Association* 259:2851, 1988; and Cates and Stone, op. cit., 1992.

60. Kreiss, J., et al., "Efficacy of Nonoxynol-9 in Preventing HIV Transmission."

Presented at the Fifth International Conference on AIDS, Montreal, June 4–9, 1989, Abstract MA 036; Rekart, M., et al., "Nonoxynol 9: Its Adverse Effects. Presented at the Sixth International Conference on AIDS, San Francisco, June 1990, Abstract SC36; Niruthisard, S., Roddy, R. E., and Chutivongse, S., The effects of frequent nonoxynol-9 use on the vaginal and cervical mucosa, *Sexually Transmitted Diseases* 18:176–179, 1991.

61. Faich, G., et al., Toxic shock syndrome and the vaginal contraceptive sponge, *Journal of the American Medical Association* 255:216–218, 1986.

62. In some variations on these instructions, couples are told to abstain from intercourse during the woman's menstruation (since they can't observe the woman's cervical mucus then). They are then permitted to have intercourse on alternate "dry" days only—when there is no detectable cervical mucus—so that seminal fluid doesn't build up in the vagina, where it might be mistaken for cervical mucus. As soon as cervical mucus of any consistency is identified, intercourse is again put off limits, on the premise that sperm can survive for several days in the female reproductive tract. See, for more detailed instructions, Guren, D., and Gillette, N., *The Ovulation Method: Cycles of Fertility*, Ovulation Method Teachers Association, 1984, or Cooper, S. A., *Fertility Awareness and Natural Family Planning Resource Directory*, Small World Publications, 1988.

63. Trussell, J., and Grummer-Strawn, L., Contraceptive failure of the ovulation method of periodic abstinence, *Family Planning Perspectives* 22:65–75, 1990.

64. See, for example, Bracken, M. B., and Vita, K., Frequency of nonhormonal contraception around conception and association with congenital malformations in offspring, *American Journal of Epidemiology* 117:281, 1983; and Gray, R. H., and Kambic, R. T., Epidemiologic studies of natural family planning, *Human Reproduction* 3:693, 1988.

65. Faundes, A., et al., Ovulatory dysfunction during continuous administration of low-dose levonorgestrel by subdermal implants, *Fertility & Sterility* 56:27–31, 1991; Segal, S. J., et al., Norplant implants: the mechanism of contraceptive action, *Fertility & Sterility* 56:273–275, 1991.

66. Board of Trustees, American Medical Association, Requirements or incentives by government for the use of long-acting contraceptives, *Journal of the American Medical Association* 267:1818–1821, 1992; Food and Drug Administration, The Norplant System approved as new contraceptive implant, *FDA Medical Bulletin*, 21 (1):6–7, 1991.

67. Darney, P. D., et al., Acceptance and perceptions of Norplant among users in San Francisco, USA, *Studies in Family Planning* 21:152, 1990.

68. See, for example, Food and Drug Administration, op. cit., 1974, and Speroff and Darney, op. cit., 1992.

69. Darney, P. D., et al., op. cit., 1990.

70. Church, C. A., and Geller, J. S., Voluntary female sterilization: number one and growing, *Population Reports* Series C, No. 10, November 1990.

71. Escobedo, L. G., et al., Case-fatality rates for tubal sterilization in U.S.

hospitals, 1979–1980, *American Journal of Obstetrics and Gynecology* 160:147–150, 1989.

72. See, for example, Spivak, M. M., Librach, C. L., and Rosenthal, D. M., Microsurgical reversal of sterilization: a six-year study, *American Journal of Obstetrics and Gynecology* 154:355–361, 1986; Lennox, C. E., Mills, J. A., and James, G. B., Reversal of female sterilization: a comparative study, *Contraception* 35:19–27, 1987; Dahl, C., et al., Microsurgical reversal of female sterilization, *Acta Obstetrica et Gynecologica Scandinavica* 67:223–224, 1988; Hulka, J. F., and Halme, J., Sterilization reversal: results of 101 attempts, *American Journal of Obstetrics and Gynecology* 159:767–774, 1988; and Vercruysse, P., Boeckx, W., and Brosens, I., Microsurgical reversal of female mechanical sterilization techniques, *Contraception* 38:99–107, 1988.

73. Liskin, L., Benoit, E., and Blackburn, R., Vasectomy: New Opportunities, *Population Reports*, Series D, Number 5, March 1992.

74. Alderman, P. M., The lurking sperm, *Journal of the American Medical Association* 259:3142–3144, 1988.

75. Massey, F. J., et al., Vasectomy and health, *Journal of the American Medical Association* 252:1023–1029, 1984.

76. Perrin, E. B., et al., Long-term effect of vasectomy on coronary heart disease, *American Journal of Public Health* 74:128–132, 1984.

77. Giovannucci, E., et al., A long-term study of mortality in men who have undergone vasectomy, *New England Journal of Medicine* 326:1392–1398, 1992.

78. See, for example, Honda, G. D., et al., Vasectomy, cigarette smoking, and age at first sexual intercourse as risk factors for prostate cancer in middle-aged men, *British Journal of Cancer* 57:326–331, 1988; Cale, A. R. J., et al., Does vasectomy accelerate testicular tumour? Importance of testicular examinations before and after vasectomy, *British Medical Journal* 300:370, 1990; Mettlin, C., Natarajan, N., and Huben, R., Vasectomy and prostate cancer risk, *American Journal of Epidemiology* 132:1056–1061, 1990; Rosenberg, L., et al., Vasectomy and the risk of prostate cancer, *American Journal of Epidemiology* 132:1051–1055, 1990; Giovannucci, E., et al., A prospective cohort study of vasectomy and prostate cancer in U.S. men, *Journal of the American Medical Association* 269:873–877, 1993; Giovannucci, E., et al., A retrospective cohort study of vasectomy and prostate cancer in U.S. men, ibid., 269:878–882, 1993; Howards, S. S., and Petersen, H. B., Vasectomy and prostate cancer: chance, bias, or a causal relationship?, *Journal of the American Medical Association* 269:913–914, 1993.

79. Noticeboard, Vasectomy and cancer, *Lancet* 338:1586, 1991.

80. Diaz, S., et al., Lactational amenorrhea and the recovery of ovulation and fertility in fully nursing Chilean women, *Contraception* 38:53–67, 1988; Short, R. V., et al., Contraceptive effects of extended lactational amenorrhea: beyond the Bellagio Consensus, *Lancet* 337:715–717, 1991; Perez, A., Labbok, M. H., and Queenan, J. T., Clinical study of the lactational amenorrhea method for family planning, *Lancet* 339:968–970, 1992.

81. Stone, R., Controversial contraceptive wins approval from FDA panel, *Science* 256:1754, 1992.

82. WHO Collaborative Study of Neoplasia and Steroid Contraceptives, Breast cancer and depo-medroxyprogesterone acetate: a multinational study, *Lancet* 338:833–838, 1991.

83. Leary, W., Female condom approved for market, *New York Times* May 11, 1993, p. C5.

84. Perrone, J., Controversial abortion approach, *American Medical News*, January 12, 1990, pp. 9, 18–22.

CHAPTER TEN: ABORTION

1. See, e.g., Callahan, D., *Abortion: Law, Choice, and Morality*, Macmillan, 1970; Rodman, H., Sarvis, B., and Bonar, J. W., *The Abortion Question*, Columbia University Press, 1987; Grobstein, C., *Science and the Unborn*, Basic Books, 1988; Jung, B. J., and Shannon, T. A., *Abortion and Catholicism: The American Debate*, Crossroad Publishing, 1988; Terkel, S. N., *Abortion: Facing the Issues*, Franklin Watts, 1988; Baird, R. M., and Rosenbaum, S. E., eds., *The Ethics of Abortion: Pro-Life vs. Pro-Choice*, Prometheus Books, 1989; Condit, C. M., *Decoding Abortion Rhetoric: Communicating Social Change,* University of Illinois Press, 1990; Schwartz, S., *The Moral Question of Abortion*, Loyola University Press, 1990; Tribe, L. H., *Abortion: The Clash of Absolutes*, W. W. Norton, 1990; Swindoll, C., *Sanctity of Life: The Inescapable Issue*, Word, Inc., 1990; and C. P. Cozic, and S. L. Tipp, eds., *Abortion: Opposing Viewpoints*, Greenhaven Press, 1991.

2. Terkel, S. N., op. cit., 1988.

3. Faux, M., *Roe v. Wade*, New York, Mentor Books, 1989.

4. *Roe v. Wade*, 410 U.S. 113 (1973).

5. *Webster v. Reproductive Health Services*, 492 U.S. 490 (1989).

6. Dionne, E. J., Jr., On both sides, advocates predict a 50-state battle, *New York Times*, pp. 1, 11, July 4, 1989.

7. Gianelli, D., Ruling fuels abortion debate, *American Medical News*, June 10, 1991, pp. 1, 40.

8. Annas, G. J., The Supreme Court, liberty, and abortion, *New England Journal of Medicine* 327:651–654, 1992.

9. Henshaw, S. K., Abortion trends in 1987 and 1988: age and race, *Family Planning Perspectives* 24:85–86, 96, 1992. (Note: Official U.S. government statistics, which are reported by the Centers for Disease Control, provide estimates of annual numbers of abortions in the U.S. that are consistently about 200,000 to 250,000 below estimates developed by the Alan Guttmacher Institute, which we have cited here. For a comparison, see National Center for Health Statistics, *Health, United States, 1990*, Hyattsville, Md., U.S. Public Health Service, 1991, Table 10, p. 62 [DHHS Pub. No. PHS 91-1232].)

10. Centers for Disease Control, *CDC Surveillance Summaries*, July 1991, *Morbidity and Mortality Weekly Report* 40: No. SS-2, 1991.

11. Henshaw, S. K., and Silverman, J., The characteristics and prior contraceptive use of U.S. abortion patients, *Family Planning Perspectives* 20:158–168, 1988; Henshaw, S. K., op. cit., 1992; and S. K. Henshaw, and J. Van Vort, eds., *Abortion Factbook, 1992 Edition: Readings, Trends, and State and Local Data to 1988*, The Alan Guttmacher Institute, 1992.

12. Centers for Disease Control, Abortion surveillance, United States, 1988, *Morbidity and Mortality Weekly Report* 40: SS-1, pp. 15–42, 1991.

13. Centers for Disease Control, Abortion surveillance: Preliminary analysis, 1989, *Morbidity and Mortality Weekly Report*, 40:817–818, 1991.

14. Henshaw, S. K., and Silverman, J., op. cit., 1988.

15. Quindlen, A., A time to choose, *New York Times*, p. E-21, January 28, 1990.

16. Schoenbaum, S., et al., Outcome of the delivery following an induced or spontaneous abortion, *American Journal of Obstetrics and Gynecology* 136:19, 1980; Hatcher, R. A., et al., *Contraceptive Technology*, Irvington Publications, Inc., 1982; Stubblefield, P., et al., Fertility after induced abortion: a prospective follow-up study, *Obstetrics & Gynecology* 62:186, 1984; Daling, J., et al., Tubal infertility in relation to prior induced abortion, *Fertility & Sterility* 43:389, 1985; Hogue, C. J., Impact of abortion on subsequent fecundity, *Clinical Obstetrics and Gynecology* 13:951, 1986; Marchbanks, P. A., et al., Risk factors for ectopic pregnancy, *Journal of the American Medical Association* 259:1823–1827, 1988.

17. Speroff, L., and Darney, P., *A Clinical Guide for Contraception*, Williams & Wilkins, 1992.

18. Tatum, H. L., "Contraception and Family Planning," in M. L. Pernoll and R. C. Benson, eds., *Current Obstetric & Gynecologic Diagnosis and Treatment*, Appleton & Lange, 1987, pp. 586–611.

19. Klitsch, M., *RU 486: The Science and the Politics*, Alan Guttmacher Institute, 1989.

20. Baulieu, E., RU-486 as an antiprogesterone steroid, *Journal of the American Medical Association* 262:1808–1814, 1989; Cherfas, J., The pill of choice?, *Science* 245:1319–1324, 1989; Lader, L., *RU 486: The Pill That Could End the Abortion Wars and Why American Women Don't Have It*, Addison-Wesley, 1991; Goldsmith, M. F., As data on antiprogesterone compounds grow, societal and scientific aspects are scrutinized, *Journal of the American Medical Association* 265:1628–1629, 1991.

21. Regelson, W., Loria, R., and Kalimi, M., Beyond abortion: RU-486 and the needs of the crisis constituency, *Journal of the American Medical Association* 264:1026–1027, 1990.

22. Cherfas, J., and Palca, J., Hormone antagonist with broad potential, *Science* 245:1322, 1989.

23. Data on abortion-related death rates are taken from National Center for Health Statistics, *Health, United States, 1990*, Public Health Service, 1991, Table 10, DHHS Pub. No. PHS 91-1232; data on maternal deaths are from Koonin,

L. M., et al., Maternal mortality surveillance, United States, 1979–1986, in *CDC Surveillance Summaries* July 1991, *Morbidity and Mortality Weekly Reports* 40: (No. SS-2), Table 1, p. 8, 1991.

24. Speroff, L., and Darney, P., op. cit., 1992.

25. For women between the ages of 30 and 34, the maternal death rate is 11.8 per 100,000 live births. This rises to 23.0 for women aged 35 to 39 and increases even further, to 55.9, for women in their forties. See Koonin, L. M., et al., Maternal Mortality Surveillance, United States, 1979–1986, op. cit., 1991, pp. 1–13.

26. Gold, R. B., *Abortion and Women's Health*, Alan Guttmacher Institute, 1990.

27. Mandelson, M. T., Maden, C. B., and Daling, J. R., Low birth weight in relation to multiple induced abortions, *American Journal of Public Health* 82:391–394, 1992.

28. A death associated with mifepristone/sulprostone, *Lancet* 337:969, 1991.

29. See, for example, Nadelson, C. C., "The Emotional Impact of Abortion," in M. T. Notman, and C. C. Nadelson, eds., *The Woman Patient*, vol. 1, pp. 173–179, Plenum Press, 1978; Shusterman, L. R., Predicting the psychological consequences of abortion, *Social Science and Medicine* 13:683–689, 1979; Burnell, G. M., and Norfleet, M. A., Women's self-reported responses to abortion, *The Journal of Psychology* 121:71–76, 1987; Zabin, L. S., Hirsch, M. B., and Emerson, M. R., When urban adolescents choose abortion: effects on education, psychological status and subsequent pregnancy, *Family Planning Perspectives* 21:248–255, 1989; and Adler, N. E., et al., Psychological responses after abortion, *Science* 248:41–44, 1990.

30. Holden, C., Koop finds abortion evidence "inconclusive," *Science* 243:730–731, 1989.

31. Belsky, J. E., Wan, L. S., and Douglas, G. W., "Abortion," in H. I. Kaplan, and B. J. Sadock, eds., *Comprehensive Textbook of Psychiatry*, 4th ed., Williams & Wilkins, 1985, p. 104.

32. The Boston Women's Health Book Collective, *The New Our Bodies, Ourselves*, Simon and Schuster, 1984; Winn, D., *Experiences of Abortion*, Macdonald & Co., 1988; A. Bonavoglia, ed., *The Choices We Made: Twenty-five Women and Men Speak Out About Abortion*, Random House, 1991.

33. Koop, C. E., The U.S. Surgeon General on the health effects of abortion, *Population and Development Review* 15:172–175, 1989.

34. The Human Resources and Intergovernmental Subcommittee of the House of Representatives held hearings on Koop's report and the manner in which it was developed. The subcommittee's report, *The Federal Role in Determining the Medical and Psychological Impact of Abortion on Women*, was released in 1989 and was excerpted in *Family Planning Perspectives* 21:36–39, 1990. Among other revelations of this report was the following passage: "In his private meetings with Right-to-Life advocates, Dr. Koop expressed concern about the poor quality of their research evidence and told them that they would have to provide better proof if they wanted a Surgeon General's report consistent with their point of view . . . In his public statements, he talked about how PHS [Public Health Service] scien-

tists were asked to review the major articles and found them all to be flawed; in fact, however, written reviews were only requested for the National Right-To-Life Committee's 'white paper.' No reviews were requested for the articles showing that abortion was psychologically safer than childbirth." The subcommittee report also noted various ways in which the CDC had been censored in its abortion surveillance activities, and how Dr. William Cates, Jr., who had previously been in charge of the Reproductive Health Division at CDC and was an internationally acclaimed expert on abortion, was demoted and transferred to another position at the insistence of the Reagan White House because of "what was perceived by the White House advisers to be a prochoice advocacy and bias."

35. Adler, N. E., et al., Psychological responses after abortion, *Science* 248:41–44, 1990.

CHAPTER ELEVEN: INFERTILITY

1. Mosher, W. D., and Pratt, W. D., Fecundity and infertility in the United States: incidence and trends, *Fertility & Sterility* 56:192–193, 1991.
2. American Fertility Society, *Investigation of the Infertile Couple*, The American Fertility Society, 1991.
3. See, for example, Saint Pol, P., et al., Circannual rhythm in spermatogenesis, *Fertility & Sterility* 51:1030–1033, 1989; Politoff, L., et al., New data confirming a circannual rhythm in spermatogenesis, *Fertility & Sterility* 52:486–489, 1991; and Levine, R. J., et al., Differences in the quality of semen in outdoor workers during summer and winter, *New England Journal of Medicine* 323:12–16, 1990.
4. Lamb, E. J., and Leurgans, S., Does adoption affect subsequent fertility?, *American Journal of Obstetrics and Gynecology* 134:138–144, 1979; Seibel, M. M., and Taymor, M. L., Emotional aspects of infertility, *Fertility & Sterility* 37:137–145, 1982.
5. Forrest, K. A., Vaginal douching as a risk factor for pelvic inflammatory disease, *Journal of the National Medical Association* 81:159–165, 1989; Wolner-Hansen, P., et al., Association between vaginal douching and acute pelvic inflammatory disease, *Journal of the American Medical Association* 263:1936–1941, 1990.
6. Hendershot, G. E., Mosher, W. D., and Pratt, W. F., Infertility and age: an unresolved issue, *Family Planning Perspectives* 14:287–289, 1982.
7. Syrop, C., "Hyperprolactinemia—Infertility and Beyond," in M. G. Hammond and L. M. Talbert, eds., *Infertility: A Practical Guide for the Physician*, 3rd ed. Blackwell Scientific Publications, 1992, pp. 196–209.
8. March, C., Update: home tests for ovulation and pregnancy, *Endocrine & Fertility Forum* 8 (4):2–6, 1985.
9. Moore, D. E., and Cates, W., Jr., "Sexually Transmitted Diseases and Infertility," in K. K. Holmes et al., eds., *Sexually Transmitted Diseases*, 2nd ed., McGraw-Hill, 1990, pp. 763–769.

10. Westrom, L., Pelvic inflammatory disease: bacteriology and sequelae, *Contraception* 36:111, 1987.

11. Halme, Juoko, "Endometriosis and Infertility," in M. G. Hammond and L. M. Talbert, eds., op. cit., 1992.

12. Lipshultz, L. I., and Howards, S. S., *Infertility in the Male*, Mosby-Yearbook, 1991.

13. American Fertility Society, "Varicocele and Infertility," Guideline for Practice, 1992.

14. Howards, S. S., Subclinical varicocele, *Fertility & Sterility* 57:725–726, 1992.

15. Adamson, G. D., et al., Comparison of CO_2 laser laparoscopy with laparotomy for treatment of endometriomata, *Fertility & Sterility* 57:965–973, 1992.

16. Burris, A. S., et al., A low sperm concentration does not preclude fertility in men with isolated hypogonadotropic hypogonadism after gonadotropin therapy, *Fertility & Sterility* 50:343–347, 1988.

17. Pryor, J. P., and Hendry, W. F., Ejaculatory duct obstruction in subfertile males: analysis of 87 patients, *Fertility & Sterility* 56:725–730, 1991.

18. Allen, N. C., et al., Intrauterine insemination: a critical review, *Fertility & Sterility* 44:569, 1985; te Velde, E. R., et al., Intrauterine insemination of washed husband's spermatozoa: a controlled study, *Fertility & Sterility* 51:182–185, 1989; Kirby, C. A., et al., A prospective study of intrauterine insemination of motile spermatozoa versus timed intercourse, *Fertility & Sterility* 56:102–107, 1991.

19. Seibel, M., A new era in reproductive technology, *New England Journal of Medicine* 318:828–834, 1988; Morin, N. C., et al., Congenital malformations and psychosocial development in children conceived by in vitro fertilization, *Journal of Pediatrics* 115:222–227, 1989.

20. Seibel, M., Ranoux, C., and Kearnan, M., In vitro fertilization: how much is enough?, *New England Journal of Medicine* 321:1052–1053, 1990.

21. Sauer, M. V., Paulson, R. J., and Lobo, R. A., A preliminary report on oocyte donation extending reproductive potential to women over 40, *New England Journal of Medicine* 323:1157–1160, 1990.

22. Sauer, M. V., and Paulson, R. J., Understanding the current status of oocyte donation in the United States: what's really going on out there?, *Fertility & Sterility* 58:16–18, 1992.

23. Fugger, E. F., Clinical status of human embryo cryopreservation in the United States of America, *Fertility & Sterility* 52:986–990, 1989.

24. Molloy, D., et al., The predictive value of idiopathic failure to fertilize on the first in vitro fertilization attempt, *Fertility & Sterility* 56:285–289, 1991.

25. Tan, S. L., et al., Cumulative conception and livebirth rates after in-vitro fertilisation, *Lancet* 339:1390–1394, 1992.

26. Rosenblatt, R., The baby in the factory, *Time*, February 14, 1983, p. 90.

27. Crockin, S. L., Legally speaking, *Fertility News* 25 (2):18, June 1991.

28. Lawson, C., Surrogate mothers grow in numbers despite questions, *New York Times*, pp. C1, C8, October 1, 1986.

29. Ethics Committee of the American Fertility Society, *Ethical Consideration of the New Reproductive Technologies, Fertility & Sterility* 46 (3): Suppl. 1, September 1986.
30. Chesler, P., *Sacred Bond: The Legacy of Baby M*, Times Books, 1988, p. 114.
31. Pediatricians suggest surrogacy pact conditions, *American Medical News*, August 3, 1992, p. 27.
32. See, e.g., Menning, B. E., The emotional needs of infertile couples, *Fertility & Sterility* 34:313–319, 1980; Mahlstedt, P. P., The psychological component of infertility, *Fertility & Sterility* 43:335–346, 1985; and Dunkel-Schetter, C., and Lobel, M., "Psychological Reactions to Infertility," in A. N. Stanton and C. Dunkel-Schetter, eds., *Infertility: Perspectives from Stress and Coping Research*, Plenum Press, 1991, pp. 29–57.
33. Seibel, M. M., and Taymor, M. L., Emotional aspects of infertility, *Fertility & Sterility* 37:137–145, 1982; Greil, A. L., Leitko, T. A., and Porter, K. L., Infertility: his and hers, *Gender and Society* 2:172–199, 1988; Abbey, A., Andrews, F. A., and Halman, L. J., "The Importance of Social Relationships for Infertile Couples' Well-being," in A. L. Stanton and C. Dunkel-Schetter, eds., op. cit., 1991, pp. 61–86.

CHAPTER TWELVE: SEXUAL ASPECTS OF COMMON MEDICAL PROBLEMS

1. J. H. Mendelson and N. K. Mello, eds., *The Diagnosis and Treatment of Alcoholism*, McGraw-Hill, 1985.
2. Morse, R. M., and Flavin, D. K., The definition of alcoholism, *Journal of the American Medical Association* 268:1012–1014, 1992.
3. In *Macbeth* (Act II, Scene 3), we learn that alcohol "provoketh the desire but . . . taketh away the performance." Many men who have had a bit too much to drink of an evening and then failed to stir up an erection in an amorous encounter can attest to the validity of the Bard's perceptive observation.
4. Masters, W. H., and Johnson, V. E., *Human Sexual Inadequacy*, Little, Brown, 1970.
5. Wilson, G. T., and Lawson, D. M., Effects of alcohol on sexual arousal in women, *Journal of Abnormal Psychology* 85:489–497, 1976; and Malatesta, V. J., et al., Acute alcohol intoxication and female orgasmic response, *Journal of Sex Research* 18:1–17, 1982.
6. Kolodny, R. C., Masters, W. H., and Johnson, V. E., *Textbook of Sexual Medicine*, Little, Brown, 1979; Jensen, S. B., Sexual customs and dysfunctions in alcoholics: Part I, *British Journal of Sexual Medicine* 53:29–32, 1979; Fahrner, E. M., Sexual dysfunction of male alcohol addicts: prevalence and treatment, *Archives of Sexual Behavior* 16:247–257, 1987.
7. Littleton, J., Alcohol and neurotransmitters, *Clinics in Endocrinology and Metabolism* 7:369–384, 1978; Blum, K., "Neurophysiological Effects of Alcohol," in E. M. Pattison and E. Kaufman, eds., *Encyclopedic Handbook of Alcoholism*, New York: Gardner Press, 1982, pp. 105–134.

8. This is probably an artifact of how sexual desire has been measured in typical studies, since it is common to equate sexual desire with the frequency of sexual activity. One reason this simplistic measure doesn't work very well in alcoholic women (besides the fact that it ignores the key question of whether they were really the ones who wanted to have sex) is that many of these women "buy" their husbands' covert cooperation with their abusive drinking by making themselves available to them sexually whenever the husbands are interested, without regard to whether or not these women have any sexual interest of their own.

9. Jensen, S. B., Sexual dysfunction in younger married alcoholics: a comparative study, *Acta Psychiatrica Scandinavia* 69:543–559, 1984.

10. Conington, S., Physical, emotional and sexual abuse: facing the clinical challenges of women alcoholics, *Focus on Family Medicine* 10:37–48, 1986.

11. Mendelson, J. H., and Mello, N. K., Chronic alcohol effects on anterior pituitary and ovarian hormones in healthy women, *Journal of Pharmacology and Experimental Therapeutics* 245:407–412, 1988.

12. See, e.g., Cloninger, C. R., Bohman, M., and Sigvardsson, S., Inheritance of alcohol abuse: cross-fostering analysis of adopted men, *Archives of General Psychiatry* 38:861–868, 1981; Reich, T., et al., Secular trends in the familial transmission of alcoholism, *Alcoholism* 12:458–464, 1988; Devor, E. J., and Cloninger, C. R., Genetics of alcoholism, *Annual Review of Genetics* 23:19–36, 1989; Pickens, R. W., et al., Heterogeneity in the inheritance of alcoholism, *Archives of General Psychiatry* 48:19–28, 1991; and Kendler, K. S., et al., A population-based twin study of alcoholism in women, *Journal of the American Medical Association* 268:1877–1882, 1992.

13. Kolodny, R. C., "The Clinical Management of Sexual Problems in Substance Abusers," in T. E. Bratter and G. G. Forrest, eds., *Alcoholism and Substance Abuse: Strategies for Clinical Intervention*, Free Press, 1985, p. 601.

14. Lund, D. S., Survey: many women found breast cancer "Accidentally," *American Medical News*, p. 35, June 17, 1988.

15. Shapiro, S., et al., Ten-to-fourteen year effect of screening on breast cancer mortality, *Journal of the National Cancer Institute* 69:349–355, 1982; Tabar, L., et al., Reduction in mortality from breast cancer after mass screening with mammography, *Lancet* I:829–832, 1985; Roberts, M. M., et al., Edinburgh trial of screening for breast cancer: mortality at seven years, *Lancet* 335:241–246, 1990; Frisell, J., et al., Randomized study of mammography screening—preliminary report on mortality in the Stockholm trial, *Breast Cancer Research & Therapy* 18:49–56, 1991; Day, N. E., Screening for breast cancer, *British Medical Bulletin* 47:400–415, 1991; Centers for Disease Control, Public health focus: mammography, *Morbidity and Mortality Weekly Report* 41:454–459, 1992.

16. Stomper, P. C., et al., Is mammography painful?, *Archives of Internal Medicine* 148:521–524, 1988.

17. Gail, M. H., et al., Projecting individualized probabilities of developing breast cancer for white females who are being examined annually, *Journal of the*

National Cancer Institute 81:1879–1886, 1989; Harris, J., et al., Breast cancer (first of three parts), *New England Journal of Medicine* 327:319–328, 1992.

18. King, S., Not everyone agrees with new mammographic screening guidelines designed to end confusion, *Journal of the American Medical Association* 262:1154–1155, 1989.

19. Fisher, B., et al., Five year results of a randomized clinical trial comparing total mastectomy and segmental mastectomy with or without radiation in the treatment of breast cancer, *New England Journal of Medicine* 312:665–673, 1985.

20. See, e.g., NIH Consensus Development Conference, Treatment of early-stage breast cancer, *Journal of the American Medical Association* 265:391–395, 1991; Hand, R., et al., Hospital variables associated with quality of care for breast cancer patients, *Journal of the American Medical Association* 266:3429–3432, 1991; Lazovich, D., et al., Underutilization of breast-conserving surgery and radiation therapy among women with stage I or II breast cancer, *Journal of the American Medical Association* 266:3433–3438, 1991; Tabar, L., et al., Breast cancer treatment and natural history: new insights from results of screening, *Lancet* 339:412–414, 1992; Farrow, D. C., Hunt, W. C., and Samet, J. M., Geographic variation in the treatment of localized breast cancer, *New England Journal of Medicine* 326:1097–1101, 1992; Nattinger, A. B., et al., Geographic variation in the use of breast-conserving treatment for breast cancer, *New England Journal of Medicine* 326:1102–1107, 1992; Ganz, P. A., Treatment options for breast cancer—beyond survival, *New England Journal of Medicine* 326:1147–1149, 1992; Cabanes, P. A., Value of axillary dissection in addition to lumpectomy and radiotherapy in early breast cancer, *Lancet* 339:1245–1248, 1992; Fisher, B., et al., Lumpectomy compared with lumpectomy and radiation therapy for the treatment of intraductal breast cancer, *New England Journal of Medicine* 328:1581–1586, 1993; Veronesi, U., et al., Radiotherapy after breast-preserving surgery in women with localized cancer of the breast, *New England Journal of Medicine* 328:1587–1591, 1993; and Swain, S. M., In situ or localized breast cancer—how much treatment is needed?, *New England Journal of Medicine* 328:1633–1634, 1993.

21. Greenfield, S., et al., Patterns of care related to age of breast cancer patients, *Journal of the American Medical Association* 257:2766–2770, 1987; Silliman, R. A., et al., Age as a predictor of diagnostic and initial treatment intensity in newly diagnosed breast cancer patients, *Journal of Gerontology* 44:M46-M50, 1989; Liberati, A., et al., The role of attitudes, beliefs, and personal characteristics of Italian physicians in the surgical treatment of early breast cancer, *American Journal of Public Health* 81:38–42, 1991; and Ganz, P. A., op. cit., 1992.

22. Witkin, M. H., Sex therapy and mastectomy, *Journal of Sex & Marital Therapy* 1:290–304, 1975.

23. Frank, D., et al., Mastectomy and sexual behavior: a pilot study, *Sexuality and Disability* 1:16–26, 1978.

24. Melody, G. F., Depressive reactions following hysterectomy, *American Journal of Obstetrics and Gynecology* 83:410–413, 1962; Barker, M. G., Psychiatric illness

after hysterectomy, *British Medical Journal* 2:91–95, 1968; Richards, D. H., A post-hysterectomy syndrome, *Lancet* 2:983–985, 1974.

25. Dennerstein, L., Wood, C., and Burrows, G. D., Sexual response following hysterectomy and oophorectomy, *Obstetrics and Gynecology* 49:92–96, 1977.

26. Office of Surveillance and Analysis, Centers for Disease Control, Trends in prostate cancer—United States, 1980–1988, *Morbidity and Mortality Weekly Report* 41:401–404, 1992.

27. Moon, T. D., Prostate cancer, *Journal of the American Geriatrics Society* 40:622–627, 1992; Johansson, J.-E., High 10-year survival rate in patients with early, untreated prostatic cancer, *Journal of the American Medical Association* 267:2191–2196, 1992.

28. Nelson, B. J., How to prevent impotence after prostatectomy, *Sexual Medicine Today* 2 (3):4–41, 1978.

29. Schover and Jensen, op. cit., 1988.

30. Geller, J., Benign prostatic hypertrophy: pathogenesis and medical therapy, *Journal of the American Geriatrics Society* 39:1208–1216, 1991.

31. Kolodny, Masters, and Johnson, op. cit., 1979.

32. Bruskewitz, R., and Riehmann, M., New therapies for benign prostatic hyperplasia, *Mayo Clinic Proceedings* 67:493–495, 1992.

33. Roos, N. P., et al., Mortality and reoperation after open and transurethral resection of the prostate for benign prostatic hyperplasia, *New England Journal of Medicine* 320:1120–1124, 1989; Anderson, T. F., et al., Elevated mortality following transurethral resection of the prostate for benign prostatic hyperplasia, *Medical Care* 28:870–881, 1990.

34. Blute, M. L., et al., Transurethral microwave thermotherapy for prostatism: Early Mayo Foundation experience, *Mayo Clinic Proceedings* 67:417–421, 1992.

35. Gormley, G. J., The effect of finasteride in men with benign prostatic hyperplasia, *New England Journal of Medicine* 327:1185–1191, 1992.

36. Friedewald, W. T., "Epidemiology of Cardiovascular Disease," in J. B. Wyngaarden, L. H. Smith, Jr., and J. C. Bennett, eds., *Cecil Textbook of Medicine*, 19th ed., W. B. Saunders, 1992, pp. 151–155.

37. Ueno, M., The so-called coition death, *Japanese Journal of Legal Medicine* 17:333–340, 1969.

38. Tejada, I. S. D., et al., Impaired neurogenic and endothelium-mediated relaxation of penile smooth muscle from diabetic men with impotence, *New England Journal of Medicine* 320:1025–1030, 1989; Rowland, D. L., et al., Penile and finger sensory thresholds in young, aging, and diabetic males, *Archives of Sexual Behavior* 18:1–12, 1989; Daniels, J. S., Abnormal nerve conduction in impotent patients with diabetes mellitus, *Diabetes Care* 12:449–454, 1989; Dyck, P. J., New understanding and treatment of diabetic neuropathy, *New England Journal of Medicine* 326:1287–1288, 1992.

39. Kolodny, R. C., Sexual dysfunction in diabetic females, *Diabetes* 20:557–559, 1971.

40. Jensen, S. B., Diabetic sexual dysfunction, *Archives of Sexual Behavior* 10:493–

497, 1981; Tyrer, G., et al., Sexual responsiveness in diabetic women, *Diabetologica* 3:166–171, 1983; Prather, R. C., Sexual dysfunction in the diabetic female: a review, *Archives of Sexual Behavior* 17:277–284, 1988.

41. American Psychiatric Association, *Diagnostic and Statistical Manual of Mental Disorders*, 3rd ed., rev., American Psychiatric Association Press, 1987; Goodwin, D. W., and Guze, S. B., *Psychiatric Diagnosis*, Oxford University Press, 1989.

42. Wing, J. K., and Bebbington, P., "Epidemiology of Depression," in E. E. Beckham, and W. R. Leber, eds., *Handbook of Depression*, pp. 765–794, Dorsey Press, 1985.

43. U.S. Public Health Service, *Mood Disorders: Pharmacologic Prevention of Recurrence*, Department of Health and Human Services, Public Health Monograph vol. 5, no. 4, 1986.

44. Kolodny, R. C., Masters, W. H., and Johnson, V. E., op. cit., 1979, p. 301.

45. Woods, S. M., "Sexuality and Mental Disorders," in H. L. Lief, ed., *Sexual Problems in Medical Practice*, American Medical Association, 1981, pp. 199–209.

46. Blay, S. L., Ferraz, M. P. T., and Calil, H. M., Lithium-induced male sexual impairment, *Journal of Clinical Psychiatry* 43:497–498, 1982; Ghadirian, A.M., Annable, L., and Belanger, M., Lithium, benzodiazepines, and sexual function in bipolar patients, *American Journal of Psychiatry* 149:801–805, 1992.

47. Ghadirian, Annable, and Belanger, op. cit., 1992.

48. Kolodny, Masters, and Johnson, op. cit., 1979; Segraves, R. T., et al., "Erectile Dysfunction in Association with Pharmacologic Agents," in R. T. Segraves and H. W. Schoenberg, eds., *Diagnosis and Treatment of Erectile Disorders*, Plenum Press, 1985; Jani, N. N., and Wise, T. N., Antidepressants and inhibited female orgasm: a literature review, *Journal of Sex & Marital Therapy* 14:279–284, 1988; Segraves, R. T., Psychiatric drugs and inhibited female orgasm, *Journal of Sex & Marital Therapy* 14:202–207, 1988.

49. Thompson, M., and Schwartz, D., Life adjustment of women with anorexia nervosa and anorexia-like behavior, *International Journal of Eating Disorders* 2:47–60, 1981; Pope, H. G., et al., Prevalence of anorexia nervosa and bulimia in three student populations, *International Journal of Eating Disorders* 3:45–51, 1984; Johnson, C., and Connors, M. E., *The Etiology and Treatment of Bulimia Nervosa*, Basic Books, 1987.

50. Kolodny, N., *When Food's a Foe*, Little, Brown, 1987.

51. Goldfarb, L. A., Sexual abuse antecedent to anorexia nervosa, bulimia, and compulsive overeating: three case reports, *International Journal of Eating Disorders* 6:675–680, 1987; Schecter, J. O., Schwartz, H. P., and Greenfeld, D. G., Sexual assault and anorexia nervosa, *International Journal of Eating Disorders* 6:313–316, 1987.

52. Renshaw, D., Sex and eating disorders, *Medical Aspects of Human Sexuality* 24 (4):68–77, 1990.

53. Cushman, R., Jr., Plasma testosterone levels in narcotic addiction, *American Journal of Medicine* 55:452–458, 1973.

54. Cicero, T. J., et al., Function of the male sex organs in heroin and methadone users, *New England Journal of Medicine* 292:882–887, 1975.

55. Bai, J., et al., Drug-related menstrual abnormalities, *Obstetrics and Gynecology* 44:713–719, 1974.

56. Kolodny, R. C., "Drugs and Sex," presented at the Masters & Johnson Institute Seminar on Sexual Medicine, September 10, 1982, Washington, D.C.

57. Rosenbaum, M., When drugs come into the picture, love flies out the window: women addicts' love relationships, *The International Journal of the Addictions* 16:1197–1206, 1981.

58. Gay, G. R., et al., The sensuous hippie: drug/sex practice in the Haight-Ashbury, *Drug Forum* 6:27–47, 1977; Gay, G. R., et al., Love and Haight: The sensuous hippie revisited, *Journal of Psychoactive Drugs* 14:111–123, 1982.

59. Siegel, R. K., Cocaine and sexual dysfunction, *Journal of Psychoactive Drugs* 14:71–74, 1982.

60. Cocores, J. A., et al., Sexual dysfunction in abusers of cocaine and alcohol, *American Journal of Drug and Alcohol Abuse* 14:169–173, 1988.

61. Washton, A. M., Cocaine abuse and compulsive sexuality, *Medical Aspects of Human Sexuality* 23 (12):34, 1989.

62. Macdonald, P. T., et al., Heavy cocaine use and sexual behavior, *Journal of Drug Issues* 18:437–455, 1988; Fullilove, M. T., and Fullilove, R. E., Intersecting epidemics: black teen crack use and sexually transmitted disease, *Journal of the American Medical Women's Association* 44:146–153, 1989.

63. Goldsmith, M. F., Sex tied to drugs = STD spread, *Journal of the American Medical Association* 260:2009, 1988; Chaisson, R. E., et al., Cocaine use and HIV infection in intravenous drug users in San Francisco, *Journal of the American Medical Association* 261:561–565, 1989; Fullilove, R. E., et al., Risk of sexually transmitted disease among black adolescent crack users in Oakland and San Francisco, Calif., *Journal of the American Medical Association* 263:851–855, 1990.

64. Washton, op. cit., 1989.

65. Kolodny, Masters, and Johnson, op. cit., 1979; Bush, P. J., *Drugs, Alcohol, and Sex*, Richard Marek, 1980; Halikas, J., Weller, R., and Morse, C., Effects of regular marihuana use on sexual performance, *Journal of Psychoactive Drugs* 14:59–70, 1982.

66. Kolodny, R. C., et al., Depression of plasma testosterone levels after chronic intensive marihuana use, *New England Journal of Medicine* 290:872–874, 1974; Hembree, W. C., Zeidenberg, P., and Nahas, G. G., "Marihuana: Effects upon Human Gonadal Function," in G. G. Nahas, ed., *Marihuana* Chemistry, Biochemistry, and Cellular Effects, Springer Publishing Co., 1976.

67. Bauman, J., et al., Efectos endocrinos del uso crónico de la mariguana en mujeres, in *Simposio Internacional sobre Actualización en Mariguana, Cuadernos Científicos Cemesam 10*, July 1979, pp. 85–97.

68. Wilson, J. D., Androgen abuse by athletes, *Endocrine Reviews* 9:181–199, 1988.

69. Hallagan, J. B., Hallagan, L. F., and Snyder, M. B., Anabolic-androgenic

steriod use by athletes, *New England Journal of Medicine* 321:1042–1045, 1989.

70. Washington Post, June 13, 1989, p. E1.

71. Buckley, W. E., et al., Estimated prevalence of anabolic steroid use among male high school seniors, *Journal of the American Medical Association* 260:3441–3445, 1988.

72. Newman, M., *Michigan Consortium of Schools Student Survey.* Hazelden Research Services, 1986.

73. Lamb, D. R., Anabolic steroids in athletes: how well do they work and how dangerous are they?, *American Journal of Sports Medicine* 12:31–38, 1984; Wilson, op. cit., 1988.

74. Pope, H. G., and Katz, D. L., Affective and psychotic symptoms associated with anabolic steroid use, *American Journal of Psychiatry* 145:487–490, 1988.

75. Sklarek, H. M., et al., AIDS in a bodybuilder using anabolic steroids, *New England Journal of Medicine* 311:1701, 1984.

76. Kolodny, R. C., Effects of alpha-methyldopa on male sexual function, *Sexuality and Disability* 1:223–228, 1978; Kolodny, Masters, and Johnson, op. cit., 1979.

77. Camino-Torres, R., Ma, L., and Snyder, P. J., Gynecomastia and semen abnormalities induced by spironolactone in normal men, *Journal of Clinical Endocrinology and Metabolism* 45:255–260, 1977; Soyka, L. F., and Mattison, D. R., Prescription drugs that affect male sexual function, *Drug Therapy* 11:60–76, 1980.

78. Chang, S. W., The impact of diuretic therapy on reported sexual function, *Archives of Internal Medicine* 151:2402–2408, 1991; The Treatment of Mild Hypertension Research Group, The treatment of mild hypertension study, *Archives of Internal Medicine* 151:1413–1423, 1991; Wassertheil-Smoller, S., et al., Effect of antihypertensives on sexual function and quality of life: the TAIM study, *Annals of Internal Medicine* 114:613–620, 1991.

79. The Treatment of Mild Hypertension Research Group, op. cit., 1991.

80. See, for example, Montiero, W. O., et al., Anorgasmia with clomipramine in obsessive-compulsive disorder, *British Journal of Psychiatry* 151:107–112, 1985; Segraves, R. T., Effects of psychotropic drugs on human erection and ejaculation, *Archives of General Psychiatry* 46:275–284, 1989; Herman, J. B., et al., Fluoxetine-induced sexual dysfunction, *Journal of Clinical Psychiatry* 51:25–27, 1990; Mosher, J. S., Anorgasmia with the use of fluoxetine, *American Journal of Psychiatry* 147:949, 1990.

81. [Anonymous], Prozac and premature ejaculation, *Contemporary Sexuality* 26 (11):1–3, November 1992.

82. Kolodny, Masters, and Johnson, op. cit., 1979.

83. SmithKline Beecham, the maker of Tagamet, disingenuously notes in its drug literature that "in large-scale surveillance studies at regular dosage, the incidence [of impotence] has not exceeded that commonly reported in the general population." (*Physician's Desk Reference*, 47th ed., Medical Economics Co., 1993, p. 2323.)

CHAPTER THIRTEEN: SEXUALLY TRANSMITTED DISEASES

1. Platt, R., Rice, P. A., and McCormack, W. M., Risk of acquiring gonorrhea and prevalence of abnormal adnexal findings among women recently exposed to gonorrhea, *Journal of the American Medical Association* 250:3205–3209, 1983.

2. Centers for Disease Control, Summary of Notifiable Diseases, United States, 1991, *Morbidity and Mortality Weekly Report*, 40 (53) (published October 2, 1992, for 1991).

3. This number represents a significant decline from levels reported in the 1970s and early 1980s. A significant portion of this drop has been attributed to a declining incidence of gonorrhea in homosexual and bisexual men as a result of safer sex practices linked to concerns about the HIV/AIDS epidemic.

4. Centers for Disease Control, Summary of notifiable diseases, United States, 1990, *Morbidity and Mortality Weekly Report* 39 (53) (published Oct. 4, 1991), p. 10 (Table: Summary of reported cases, by age group, United States, 1990).

5. Centers for Disease Control, Summary of notifiable diseases, United States, 1990, op. cit., p. 24.

6. Colleen, S., and Mardh, P., "Prostatitis," in K. K. Holmes et al., eds., *Sexually Transmitted Diseases*, 2nd ed., McGraw-Hill, 1990, pp. 653–661.

7. Sperling, F., "Gonococcal Infections," in J. B. Wyngaarden, L. H. Smith, Jr., and J. C. Bennett, eds., *Cecil Textbook of Medicine*, 19th ed., W. B. Saunders Co., 1992, pp. 1755–1759.

8. Washington, A. E., and Katz, P., Cost of and payment source for pelvic inflammatory disease, *Journal of the American Medical Association* 266:2565–2569, 1991.

9. Centers for Disease Control, 1989 Sexually Transmitted Diseases Treatment Guidelines, *Morbidity and Mortality Weekly Report* 38 (S-8), 1989.

10. Hook, E. W., III, and Marra, C. M., Acquired syphilis in adults, *New England Journal of Medicine* 326:1060–1069, 1992.

11. Centers for Disease Control, Table: Syphilis (primary and secondary)—by sex, United States, 1956–1989, *Morbidity and Mortality Weekly Report* 38 (54), 1989 (published Oct. 5, 1990).

12. See, for example, Goldsmith, M. F., Sex tied to drugs = STD spread, *Journal of the American Medical Association* 260:2009, 1988; Fullilove, M. T., and Fullilove, R. E., Intersecting epidemics: black teen crack use and sexually transmitted disease, *Journal of the American Medical Women's Association* 44:146–153, 1989; Rolfs, R. T., Goldberg, M., and Sharrar, R. G., Risk factors for syphilis: cocaine use and prostitution, *American Journal of Public Health* 80:853–857, 1990; and Farley, T. A., Hadler, J., and Gunn, R. A., The syphilis epidemic in Connecticut: relationship to drug use and prostitution, *Sexually Transmitted Diseases* 17:163–168, 1990.

13. Centers for Disease Control, Summary of notifiable diseases, United States, 1990, *Morbidity and Mortality Weekly Report* 39 (53), 1990 (published Oct. 4, 1991), table on pp. 10–11. See also Webster, L. A., et al., Regional and

temporal trends in the surveillance of syphilis, United States, 1986–1990, *Morbidity and Mortality Weekly Report* 40 (No. SS-3), pp. 29–33, 1991.

14. Centers for Disease Control, Summary of Notifiable Diseases, United States, 1991, *Morbidity and Mortality Weekly Report* 40 (53) (published October 2, 1992, for 1991), p. 3.

15. Wisdom, A., *Color Atlas of Sexually Transmitted Diseases*, Yearbook Medical Publishers, 1989.

16. While most people who have a sore on or near their genitals are wise enough to abstain from sex until they have the problem investigated, this isn't always true. This may be one reason for the upsurge in syphilis rates among crack users: drug addicts are unlikely to take any precautions about such problems. Many women "crackheads" are willing to have unprotected sex with any man who pays them well enough, even if he has a chancre clearly visible on his penis. And, conversely, many men who are willing to have sex with women crack-prostitutes don't bother to inspect them for the presence of genital ulcers or other signs of STDs.

17. Phillips, R. S., et al., *Chlamydia trachomatis* cervical infection in women seeking routine gynecological care: criteria for selective testing, *American Journal of Medicine* 86:515–520, 1989; Chernesky, M. A., et al., Detection of *Chlamydia trachomatis* antigens by enzyme immunoassay and immunofluorescence in genital specimens from symptomatic and asymptomatic men and women, *Journal of Infectious Diseases* 154:141–147, 1986; Handsfield, H. H., et al., Criteria for selective screening for *Chlamydia trachomatis* infection in women attending family planning clinics, *Journal of the American Medical Association* 255:1730–1734, 1986; Magder, L. S., et al., Factors related to genital *Chlamydia trachomatis* and its diagnosis by culture in a sexually transmitted disease clinic, *American Journal of Epidemiology* 28:298–308, 1988.

18. Stamm, W. E., et al., *Chlamydia trachomatis* urethral infections in men: prevalence, risk factors, and clinical manifestations, *Annals of Internal Medicine* 100:47, 1984; Stamm, W. E., Diagnosis of *Chlamydia trachomatis* genitourinary infections, *Annals of Internal Medicine* 108:710–717, 1988; Podgore, J. K., et al., Asymptomatic urethral infections due to *Chlamydia trachomatis* in male military personnel, *Journal of Infectious Diseases* 146:828, 1982.

19. Shafer, M. A., et al., Urinary leukocyte esterase screening test for asymptomatic chlamydial and gonococcal infections in males, *Journal of the American Medical Association* 262:2562–2566, 1989.

20. Centers for Disease Control, *Chlamydia trachomatis* infections: policy guidelines for prevention and control, *Morbidity and Mortality Weekly Report* 34 (Suppl.), 1985, pp. 53S–74S.

21. Sellors, J. W., et al., Tubal factor infertility: an association with primary chlamydial infection and asymptomatic salpingitis, *Fertility & Sterility* 49:451–457, 1988; Centers for Disease Control, Pelvic inflammatory disease: guidelines for prevention and management, *Morbidity and Mortality Weekly Report* 40 (RR-5), 1991, pp. 1–25; Rice, P. A., and Schacter, J., Pathogenesis of pelvic

inflammatory disease, *Journal of the American Medical Association* 266:2587–2593, 1991.

22. Centers for Disease Control, Pelvic inflammatory disease: guidelines for prevention and management, *Morbidity and Mortality Weekly Report* 40 (RR-5), 1991, pp. 1–25.

23. For a detailed review, see Kahn, R., et al., Diagnosing pelvic inflammatory disease, *Journal of the American Medical Association* 266:2594–2604, 1991.

24. Schmid, G., et al., Chancroid in the United States, *Journal of the American Medical Association* 258:3265–3268, 1987.

25. Schulte, J., Martich, F., and Schmid, G., Chancroid in the United States, 1981–1990: evidence for underreporting of cases, *Morbidity and Mortality Weekly Report* 41 (SS-3), pp. 57–61.

26. Telzak, E. M., et al., "Chancroid and the Risk of HIV Sero-conversion in Male Heterosexuals in New York City." Presented at the Seventh International Conference on AIDS, Florence, Italy, June 1991.

27. Ronald, A. R., and Albritton, W. L., "Chancroid and *Haemophilus ducreyi*," in K. K. Holmes et al., eds., *Sexually Transmitted Diseases*, McGraw-Hill, 1984, pp. 385–393.

28. Morse, S. A., Chancroid and *Haemophilus ducreyi*, *Clinical Microbiology Review* 2:137–157, 1989.

29. Jessamine, P. G., and Ronald, A. R., Chancroid and the role of genital ulcer disease in the spread of human retroviruses, *Medical Clinics of North America* 74:1417–1431, 1990.

30. Johnson, R., et al., A seroepidemiologic survey of the prevalence of herpes simplex virus type 2 infection in the United States, *New England Journal of Medicine* 321:7–12, 1989.

31. Straus, S. E., et al., Herpes simplex virus infections: biology, treatment, and prevention, *Annals of Internal Medicine* 103: 404–419, 1985.

32. Siegel, D., Prevalence and correlates of herpes simplex infections, *Journal of the American Medical Association* 268:1702–1708, 1992.

33. Middlebrooks, M., and Whitley, R. J., "Herpes Simplex Virus Infections," in Wyngaarden, Smith, and Bennett, eds., op. cit., 1992, pp. 1831–1835.

34. Levenson, J. L., et al., Psychological factors predict symptoms of severe recurrent genital herpes infection, *Journal of Psychosomatic Research* 31:153–159, 1987; Wyngaarden, J. B., Identifying factors that reactivate herpes simplex virus, *Journal of the American Medical Association* 259:1922, 1988; Kemeny, M. E., et al., Psychological and immunological predictors of genital herpes recurrence, *Psychosomatic Medicine* 51:195–208, 1989; Rand, K. H., et al., Daily stress and recurrence of genital herpes simplex, *Archives of Internal Medicine* 150:1889–1893, 1990.

35. Lafferty, W. E., et al., Recurrences after oral and genital herpes simplex virus infection, *New England Journal of Medicine* 316:1444–1449, 1987.

36. Langenberg, A., et al., Development of clinically recognizable genital lesions

among women previously identified as having "asymptomatic" herpes simplex virus type 2 infection, *Annals of Internal Medicine* 110:882–887, 1989.

37. Mertz, G. J., et al., Frequency of acquisition of first-episode genital infection with herpes simplex virus from symptomatic and asymptomatic sources, *Sexually Transmitted Diseases* 12:33–39, 1985; Rooney, J. J., et al., Acquisition of genital herpes from an asymptomatic sexual partner, *New England Journal of Medicine* 314:1561–1564, 1986; Mertz, G. J., et al., Transmission of genital herpes in couples with one symptomatic and one asymptomatic partner, *Journal of Infectious Disease* 157:1169–1177, 1988; Brock, B. V., et al., Frequency of asymptomatic shedding of herpes simplex virus in women with genital herpes, *Journal of the American Medical Association* 263:418–420, 1990; Mertz, G. J., et al., Risk factors for the sexual transmission of genital herpes, *Annals of Internal Medicine* 116:197–202, 1992.

38. Cannon, R. O., et al., "Association of Herpes Simplex Virus Type 2 with HIV Infection in Heterosexual Patients Attending Sexually Transmitted Disease Clinics." Presented at the Fourth International Conference on AIDS, Stockholm, June 12–16, 1988 (Abstract Book 2, p. 201); Holmberg, S. D., et al., Prior herpes simplex virus type 2 infection as a risk factor for HIV infection, *Journal of the American Medical Association* 259:1048–1050, 1988; Stamm, W. E., et al., The association between genital ulcer disease and the acquisition of HIV infection in homosexual men, *Journal of the American Medical Association* 260:1429–1433, 1988; Siegel et al., op. cit., 1992; Altman, L., AIDS link to V.D. becomes clearer, *New York Times* June 11, 1993, p. A6.

39. Middlebrooks and Whitley, op. cit., 1992.

40. Spear, P. G., "Biology of the Herpesviruses," in Holmes, et al., eds., op. cit., 1990, pp. 379–389.

41. Kaplowitz, L. G., et al., Prolonged continuous acyclovir treatment of normal adults with frequently recurring genital herpes simple virus infection, *Journal of the American Medical Association* 265:747–751, 1991.

42. Hirsch, M. S., and Schooley, R. T., Resistance to antiviral drugs: the end of innocence, *New England Journal of Medicine* 320:313–314, 1989; Erlich, K. S., et al., Acyclovir-resistant herpes simplex virus infections in patients with the acquired immunodeficiency syndrome, *New England Journal of Medicine* 320:293–296, 1989; Englund, J. A., et al., Herpes simplex virus resistant to acyclovir, *Annals of Internal Medicine* 112:416–422, 1990.

43. Gibbs, R. S., et al., Management of genital herpes infection in pregnancy, *Obstetrics & Gynecology* 71:779–780, 1988; Whitley, R. J., Natural history and pathogenesis of neonatal herpes simplex virus infections, *Annals of the New York Academy of Sciences* 549:103–117, 1989; Cunningham, F. G., MacDonald, P. C., and Gant, N. F., *Williams Obstetrics*, Appleton & Lange, 1989; Corey, op. cit., 1990; Gibbs, R. S., and Mead, P. B., Preventing neonatal herpes—current strategies, *New England Journal of Medicine* 326:946–947, 1992.

44. Barrett, T. J., et al., Genital warts—a venereal disease, *Journal of the American Medical Association* 154:333, 194.

45. Inoue, M., et al., Human papillomavirus (HPV) type 16 in semen of partners of women with HPV infection, *Lancet* 339:1114–1115, 1992.

46. Marx, J. L., How DNA viruses may cause cancer, *Science* 243:1012–1013, 1989.

47. Rando, R. F., Human papillomavirus: implications for clinical medicine, *Annals of Internal Medicine* 108:628–630, 1988; Reeves, W. C., et al., Human papillomavirus infection and cervical cancer in Latin America, *New England Journal of Medicine* 320:1437–1441, 1989; Marx, op. cit., 1989; Lungu, O., et al., Relationship of human papillomavirus type to grade of cervical intraepithelial neoplasia, *Journal of the American Medical Association* 267:2493–2496, 1992.

48. Reeves et al., op. cit., 1989.

49. Gissman, L., and Schwartz, E., "Persistence and Expression of Human Papillomavirus DNA in Genital Cancer," in D. Everd and S. Clark, eds., *Papillomaviruses*, Wiley, 1986, pp. 190–197.

50. Bauer, H. M., et al., Genital human papillomavirus infection in female university students as determined by a PCR-based method, *Journal of the American Medical Association* 265:472–477, 1991.

51. Kennedy, L., Human papillomavirus: a study of male sexual partners, *Medical Journal of Australia* 149:309–311, 1988.

52. Centers for Disease Control, Hepatitis A among homosexual men—United States, Canada, and Australia, *Morbidity and Mortality Weekly Report* 41, 1992, pp. 155, 161–164.

53. Alter, M. J., et al., The changing epidemiology of hepatitis B in the United States, *Journal of the American Medical Association* 263:1218–1222, 1990.

54. One of the reasons heterosexual transmission became more prominent during this period was that other mechanisms of transmitting hepatitis B were declining. Specifically, better screening of blood donors (tied in part to concerns about AIDS) reduced the number of transfusion-associated cases significantly. In addition, greater caution in the gay male community led to reductions in the rates of most STDs among the male homosexual population.

55. Rosenblum, L., et al., Sexual practices in the transmission of hepatitis B virus and prevalence of hepatitis delta virus infection in female prostitutes in the United States, *Journal of the American Medical Association* 267:2477–2481, 1992.

56. Alter, M., and Sampliner, R., Hepatitis C: and miles to go before we sleep, *New England Journal of Medicine* 321:1538–1540, 1989; Alter, M., et al., Risk factors for acute non-A, non-B hepatitis in the United States and association with hepatitis C virus infection, *Journal of the American Medical Association* 264:2231–2235, 1990.

57. Alter et al., op. cit., 1989; Benamouzig, R., Ezratty, V., and Chaussade, S., Risk for type C hepatitis through sexual contact, *Annals of Internal Medicine* 113:638, 1990.

58. Osmond, D. H., et al., Risk factors for hepatitis C virus seropositivity in heterosexual couples, *Journal of the American Medical Association* 269:361–365,

1993; Weinstock, H. S., et al., Hepatitis C virus infection among patients attending a clinic for sexually transmitted diseases, *Journal of the American Medical Association* 269:392–394, 1993.

59. Solomon, R., et al., Human immunodeficiency virus and hepatitis delta virus in homosexual men: a study of four cohorts, *Annals of Internal Medicine* 108:51–54, 1988; Weisfuse, I., Delta hepatitis in homosexual men in the United States, *Hepatology* 9:872–874, 1989; Rosenblum et al., op. cit., 1992.

60. Centers for Disease Control, Hepatitis E among U.S. Travelers, 1989–1992, *Morbidity and Mortality Weekly Report* 42 (1), 1993, pp. 1–4.

61. [Anonymous], Hepatitis A: a vaccine at last, *Lancet* 339:1198–1199, 1992.

62. Hoffnagle, J., Toward universal vaccination against hepatitis B virus, *New England Journal of Medicine* 321:1333–1334, 1989; Immunization Practices Advisory Committee, Hepatitis B virus: a comprehensive strategy for eliminating transmission in the United States through universal childhood vaccination, *Morbidity and Mortality Weekly Report* 40 (Suppl. RR13), 1991, pp. 1–25.

63. Holmes, op. cit., 1990.

64. Although high-estrogen birth control pills were clearly associated with increased rates of candidal vaginitis in the past, there is no convincing evidence that today's low-dose pills have such an action. However, there are enough cases of recurrent candidal vaginitis that are permanently cured only after a woman goes off the pill to make us feel that even low-dose birth control pills (but not the progesterone-only minipill) may be implicated at times in this annoying infection.

65. Candidal vaginitis associated with HIV infection can be especially virulent and resistant to conventional treatment, and disseminated candidiasis requires different types of drugs from those described for treating conventional vaginal infections.

66. Hilton, E., et al., Ingestion of yogurt containing *Lactobacillus acidophilus* as prophylaxis for candidal vaginitis, *Annals of Internal Medicine* 116:353–357, 1992.

67. Sobel, J. D., Bacterial vaginosis—an ecologic mystery, *Annals of Internal Medicine* 111:551–554, 1989.

68. Hill, L. H., et al., Nonspecific vaginitis and other genital infections in three clinic populations, *Sexually Transmitted Diseases* 10:114–119, 1983; Sobel, op. cit., 1989; and Hillier, S., and Holmes, K. K., in Holmes, et al., eds., op. cit., 1990, pp. 547–559.

69. A recent review of numerous studies on the best dose of metronidazole (Flagyl) found that a single 2 gm. dose is as effective as taking the drug for a week. (Lugo-Miro, V. I., Green, M., and Mazur, L., Comparison of different metronidazole therapeutic regimens for bacterial vaginosis, *Journal of the American Medical Association* 268:92–95, 1992.)

CHAPTER FOURTEEN: HIV INFECTION AND AIDS

1. Shilts, R., *And the Band Played On: Politics, People, and the AIDS Epidemic*, St. Martin's Press, 1987; Presidential Commission on the Human Immunodeficiency Virus Epidemic, *Report of the Presidential Commission on the Human Immunodeficiency Virus Epidemic*, U.S. Government Printing Office, 1988; Kramer, L., A "Manhattan Project" for AIDS, *New York Times*, July 16, 1990, p. A15.

2. Gould, S. J., The terrifying normalcy of AIDS, *New York Times Magazine*, April 19, 1987, pp. 32–33.

3. *Morbidity and Mortality Weekly Report*, 38:561–563, 1989; Eckholm, E., AIDS, fatally steady in the U.S. accelerates worldwide, *New York Times*, June 28, 1992, Section 4, p. 5.; J. Mann, D. J. M. Tarantola, and T. W. Netter, eds., *AIDS in the World*, Harvard University Press, 1992, Table 3.8, pp. 126–127.

4. Kramer, op. cit., 1990.

5. Rwandan HIV Seroprevalence Study Group, Nationwide community-based serological survey of HIV-1 and other human retrovirus infection in a Central African country, *Lancet* 1:941–943, 1989; Eckholm, E., and Tierney, J., AIDS in Africa: a killer rages on, *New York Times*, September 16, 1990, pp. 1, 15–16; Palca, J., The sobering geography of AIDS, *Science* 252:372–373, 1991; Berkeley, S. F., HIV in Africa: what is the future?, *Annals of Internal Medicine* 116:339–341, 1992.

6. Smith, D. G., Thailand: AIDS crisis looms, *Lancet* 335:781–782, 1990; Meyer, H., Prostitutes, politics heighten Thailand's AIDS dilemma, *American Medical News*, July 27, 1990, pp. 3, 26–28; Weniger, B. G., et al., The epidemiology of HIV infection and AIDS in Thailand, *AIDS* 5 (suppl 2):S71–S85, 1991.

7. Ramalingaswami, V., India: National plan for AIDS, *Lancet* 339:1162–1163, 1992; Goldsmith, M. F., Physicians at Amsterdam news seminar offer panoramic view of their varied roles in pandemic, *Journal of the American Medical Association* 268:1237–1246, 1992; Berkeley, S., AIDS in the global village, *Journal of the American Medical Association* 268:3368–3369, 1992; Brooke, J., In deception and denial, an epidemic looms, *New York Times*, January 25, 1993, pp. A1, A6.

8. Hopkins, K. R., and Johnson, W. B., *The Incidence of HIV Infection in the United States*, Hudson Institute, 1988; Laumann, E. O., et al., Monitoring the AIDS epidemic in the United States: a network approach, *Science* 244:1186–1189, 1989; Masterson, A., et al., Marked underreporting of CDC defined AIDS due to poor utilization of the HIV antibody test, Fifth International Conference on AIDS, Montreal, June 4–9, 1989. (Abstract T.A.O. 5, p. 55.); Centers for Disease Control, *HIV/AIDS Surveillance*, October 1992, Technical Notes, p. 17.

9. Centers for Disease Control and World Health Organization, AIDS Case Watch, *AIDS Clinical Care* 5 (1):1, January 1993.

10. *Morbidity and Mortality Weekly Report* 38:S-4, 1989.

11. These estimates were given by M. H. Merson of the World Health Organization in a keynote address at the Eighth International Conference on AIDS in Amsterdam, as reported in *American Medical News*, August 10, 1992, p. 31.; see also Merson, M. H., Slowing the spread of AIDS: Agenda for the 1990s, *Science* 260:1266–1268, 1993.

12. J. Mann, D. J. M. Tarantola, and T. W. Netter, eds., *AIDS in the World*, Harvard University Press, 1992, Table 2.10; Goldsmith, op. cit., 1992; World Health Organization, *The HIV/AIDS Pandemic: 1993 Overview* (document WHO/GPA/CNP/EVA/93.1), Global program on AIDS, 1993.

13. Lui, K.-J., Darrow, W. W., and Rutherford, G. W., III, A model-based estimate of the mean incubation period for AIDS in homosexual men, *Science* 240:1333–1335, 1988; Lambert, B., 10 years later, hepatitis study still yields critical data on AIDS, *New York Times*, July 17, 1990, p. C3.

14. Altman, L. K., Some optimism amid grim predictions as 87-nation AIDS meeting opens, *New York Times*, June 5, 1989, p. B4 (1989a).

15. *New York Times*, March 4, 1989, p. A20; Hopkins and Johnston, op. cit., 1988; Masters, W. H., Johnson, V. E., and Kolodny, R. C., *Crisis: Heterosexual Behavior in the Age of AIDS*, Grove Press, 1988.

16. Ades, A. E., et al., Prevalence of maternal HIV-1 infection in Thames regions: results from anonymous unlinked neonatal testing, *Lancet* 337:1562–1565, 1991; Allen, J. R., Heterosexual transmission of HIV: a view of the future, *Journal of the American Medical Association* 266:1695–1696, 1991; Banatvala, J. E., et al., HIV screening in pregnancy, *Lancet* 337:1218, 1991; Chamberlain, G., et al., HIV screening in pregnancy, *Lancet* 337:1219, 1991; Ellerbock, T. V., et al., Epidemiology of women with AIDS in the United States, 1981 through 1990, *Journal of the American Medical Association* 265:2971–2975, 1991; Forrest, B., Women, HIV, and mucosal immunity, *Lancet* 337:835–836, 1991; [unsigned editorial] Anonymous HIV testing: latest results, *Lancet* 337:1572–1573, 1991; Piribauer, F., and Zangerle, R., Heterosexual transmission of HIV-1 in Austria, *Lancet* 336:1514, 1990; World Health Organization Global Programme on AIDS, *Current and Future Dimensions of the HIV/AIDS Pandemic: A Capsule Summary, January 1992*, World Health Organization, 1992, Publication WHO/GPA/RES/SFI/92.1; Crane, L. R., Sentinel surveillance for HIV infection in Detroit: heterosexual transmission in a medium prevalence city, Eighth International Conference on AIDS, Amsterdam, July 19–24, 1992 (Abstract PoC 4013); Goldsmith, M. F., Specific HIV-related problems of women gain more attention at a price—affecting more women, *Journal of the American Medical Association* 268:1814–1816, 1992; Berkeley, op. cit., 1992; *Morbidity and Mortality Weekly Report* 48:899, 905–906, 1992; Brooke, op. cit., 1993; [unsigned editorial], Heterosexual AIDS: pessimism, pandemics, and plain hard facts, *Lancet* 341:863–864, 1993; Haverkos, H. W., Reported cases of AIDS: An update, *New England Journal of Medicine* 329:511, 1993.

17. *Morbidity and Mortality Weekly Report* 38:561–563, 1989.

18. Hilts, P. J., World AIDS epidemic draws new warnings, *New York Times*,

December 1, 1989, p. D.19; Altman, L. K., Women worldwide nearing higher rate for AIDS than men, *New York Times*, July 21, 1992, p. C3.

19. Forrest, op. cit., 1991.
20. Altman, op. cit., 1989a; *Morbidity and Mortality Weekly Report* 38:229–236, 1989; *Morbidity and Mortality Weekly Report* 39: [No. SS-3] 22–30, 1990.
21. Curran, J. W., AIDS: two years later, *New England Journal of Medicine* 309:609–611, 1983; Laumann et al., op. cit., 1989; Ellerbock et al., op. cit., 1991; Centers for Disease Control, *HIV/AIDS Surveillance*, April 1993.
22. Kolata, G., AIDS is spreading in teen-agers, a new trend alarming to experts, *New York Times*, October 8, 1989, Section 1, pp. 1, 30; Vermund, S. H., et al., Acquired immunodeficiency syndrome among adolescents, *American Journal of Diseases of Children* 143:1220–1225, 1989; Burke, D. S., et al., Human immunodeficiency virus infections in teenagers, *Journal of the American Medical Association* 263:2074–2077, 1990.
23. Centers for Disease Control, 1989.
24. St. Louis, M. E., Human immunodeficiency virus infection in disadvantaged adolescents: findings from the U.S. Job Corps, *Journal of the American Medical Association* 266:2387–2391, 1991.
25. *New York Times*, October 8, 1989, Section 1, p. 1.
26. Norman, C., Politics and science clash on African AIDS, *Science* 230:1140–1141, 1986; P. T. Cohen, M. A. Sande, and P. A. Volberding, eds., *The AIDS Knowledge Base*, The Medical Publishing Group, 1990.
27. Breo, D., AMA AIDS expert's grim message, *American Medical News*, pp. 3, 32, December 5, 1986; Kanki, P., et al., New human T-lymphotropic retrovirus related to simian T-lymphotropic virus type III (STLV III), *Science* 232:238–243, 1986; Essex, M. and Kanki, P., The origins of the AIDS virus, *Scientific American*, pp. 64–71, October, 1988; Smith T. F., et al., The phylogenic history of immunodeficiency viruses, *Nature* 333:573–575, 1988.
28. Cohen, Sande, and Volberding, op. cit., 1990.
29. Nahmias, A. J., et al., Evidence for human infection with an HTLV-III/LAV-like virus in Central Africa, 1959, *Lancet* 1:1279–1280, 1986.
30. Garry, R. F., et al., Documentation of an AIDS virus infection in the United States in 1968, *Journal of the American Medical Association* 260:2085–2087, 1988.
31. Froland, S. S., et al., HIV-1 infection in a Norwegian family before 1970, *Lancet* 1:344–1345, 1988.
32. Corbitt, G., Bailey, A. S., and Williams, G., HIV infection in Manchester, 1959, *Lancet* 336:51, 1990.
33. Redfield, R. R., and Burke, D. S., HIV infection: the clinical picture, *Scientific American* 259 (4):90–98, October, 1988.
34. Peterman, T. A., and Curran, J. W., Sexual transmission of human immunodeficiency virus, *Journal of the American Medical Association* 256:2222–2226, 1986; J. Mann, D. J. M. Tarantola, and T. W. Netter, eds., *AIDS in the World*, Harvard University Press, 1992.

35. Institute of Medicine/National Academy of Sciences, *Confronting AIDS: Update*, National Academy Press, 1989.
36. Voeller, Bruce. Personal communication, November, 1986.
37. Kingsley, L. A., et al., Sexual transmission efficiency of hepatitis B virus and human immunodeficiency virus among homosexual men, *Journal of the American Medical Association* 264:230–234, 1990.
38. Peterman, T. A., et al., Risk of HIV transmission from heterosexual adults with transfusion-associated infections, *Journal of the American Medical Association* 259:55–58, 1988; Haverkos, H. W., and Edelman, R., The epidemiology of acquired immunodeficiency syndrome among heterosexuals, *Journal of the American Medical Association* 260:1922–1929, 1988; Glaser, J. B., Strange, T. J., and Rosati, D., Heterosexual human immunodeficiency virus transmission among the middle class, *Archives of Internal Medicine* 149:645–649, 1989.
39. Perry, S., Jacobsberg, L., and Fogel, K., Orogenital transmission of human immunodeficiency virus (HIV), *Annals of Internal Medicine* 11:951–952, 1989; Spitzer, P. G., and Weiner, N. J., Transmission of HIV infection from a woman to a man by oral sex, *New England Journal of Medicine* 320:251, 1989; Staver, S., Women found contracting HIV via unprotected sex, *American Medical News*, June 1, 1990, p. 4; *New York Times* October 7, 1990, p. 37; Murray, A. B., et al., Coincident acquisition of *Neisseria gonorrhoeae* and HIV from fellatio, *Lancet* 338:830, 1991.
40. Masters, Johnson, and Kolodny, op. cit., 1988.
41. Fischl, M. A., et al., Evaluation of heterosexual partners, children, and household contacts of adults with AIDS, *Journal of the American Medical Association* 257:640–644, 1987.
42. Rozenbaum, W., et al., HIV transmission by oral sex, *Lancet* 2:1395, 1988; Piazza, M., et al., Passionate kissing and microlesions of the oral mucosa: possible role in AIDS transmission, *Journal of the American Medical Association* 261:244–245, 1989.
43. Illa, R. V., Possible salivary transmission of AIDS: case report, First International Symposium on Oral AIDS, Montreal, June 1–3, 1989. (Abstract 3.6.)
44. Institute of Medicine, op. cit., 1988; Mann, Tarantola, and Netter, op. cit., 1992.
45. Quinn, T. C., et al., Human immunodeficiency virus infection among patients attending clinics for sexually transmitted diseases, *New England Journal of Medicine* 318:197–203, 1988.
46. *Journal of the American Medical Association* 259:1048, 1988; Deodhar, L. P., and Tendolkar, U. M., Genital ulcers and HIV antibody, *Lancet* 336:112, 1989; Wasserheit, J. N., Epidemiological synergy: inter-relationships between HIV infection and other STDs, in L. Chen, et al., eds., *AIDS and Women's Reproductive Health*, Plenum Press, 1992; Altman, L. K., et al., AIDS link to V.D. becomes clearer, *New York Times*, June 11, 1993, p. A6.
47. C. F. Turner, H. G. Miller, and L. E. Moses, eds., *AIDS: Sexual Behavior and*

Intravenous Drug Use, National Academy Press, 1989; Cohen, Sande, and Volberding, op. cit., 1990; Allen, J. R., and Setlow, V. P., Heterosexual transmission of HIV, *Journal of the American Medical Association* 266:1695–1696, 1991.

48. Cohen, Sande, and Volberding, op. cit., 1990; Centers for Disease Control, op. cit., 1993.

49. Ward, J. W., et al., Transmission of human immunodeficiency virus (HIV) by blood transfusions screened as negative for HIV antibody, *New England Journal of Medicine* 318:473–478, 1988; Donahue, J. G., et al., Transmission of HIV by transfusion of screened blood, *New England Journal of Medicine* 323:1709, 1990; Busch, M. P., et al., Evaluation of screened blood donations for human immunodeficiency virus type 1 infection by culture and DNA amplification of pooled cells, *New England Journal of Medicine* 325:1–5, 1991; *Morbidity and Mortality Weekly Report* 40 (22): Figure 1d, p. 361, 1991; Conley, L. J., and Holmberg, S. D., Transmission of AIDS from blood screened negative for antibody to the human immunodeficiency virus, *New England Journal of Medicine* 326:1499–1500, 1992. (For actual data on the reported number of annual cases of AIDS attributed to the use of contaminated blood or blood products, consult the Centers for Disease Control publication *HIV/AIDS Surveillance*.)

50. Presidential Commission on the Human Immunodeficiency Virus Epidemic, op. cit., 1988; Silver, H., Autologous blood donation, *Transfusion Medicine Topic Update* 2(1):1–4, January, 1989.

51. European Collaborative Study, Mother-to-child transmission of HIV infection, *Lancet* 2:1039–1043, 1988; Cohen, Sande, and Volberding, op. cit., 1990.

52. Chiasson, M. A., Stoneburner, R. L., and Joseph, S. C., Human immunodeficiency virus transmission through artificial insemination, *Journal of AIDS* 3:69–72, 1990; *Morbidity and Mortality Weekly Report* 39:249–256, 1990; Simonds, R. J., et al., Transmission of human immunodeficiency virus type 1 from a seronegative organ and tissue donor, *New England Journal of Medicine* 326:726–732, 1992.

53. Levy, J. A., Human immunodeficiency viruses and the pathogenesis of AIDS, *Journal of the American Medical Association* 261:2997–3006, 1989.

54. Ziegler, J. B., et al., Postnatal transmission of AIDS-associated retrovirus from mother to infant, *Lancet* 1:896–898, 1985; Van De Perre, P., et al., Postnatal transmission of human immunodeficiency virus type 1 from mother to infant, *New England Journal of Medicine* 325:593–598, 1991; Dunn, D. T., et al., Risk of human immunodeficiency virus type 1 transmission through breastfeeding, *Lancet* 340:585–588, 1992; Van De Perre, P., et al., Postnatal transmission of HIV-1 associated with breast abscess, *Lancet* 339:1490–1491, 1992.

55. Pokrovsky, V. V., and Eramova, E. U., Nosocomial outbreak of HIV infection in Elista, USSR, Fifth International Conference on AIDS, Montreal, June 4–9, 1989. (Abstract W.A.O.5, p. 63); *American Medical News* July 20, 1990, p. 36.

56. Marcus, R., et al., Surveillance of healthcare workers exposed to blood from patients infected with the human immunodeficiency virus, *New England Journal of Medicine* 319:1118–1123, 1988; *Morbidity and Mortality Weekly Report* 38:S-6,

1989; Henderson, D. K., et al., Risk for occupational transmission of human immunodeficiency virus type 1 (HIV-1) associated with clinical exposures, *Annals of Internal Medicine* 113:740–746, 1990; O'Neill, T. M., Abbott, A. V., and Radecki, S. E., Risk of needlesticks and occupational exposures among residents and medical students, *Archives of Internal Medicine* 152:1451–1456, 1992.

57. Fahey, B. J., and Henderson, D. K., Minimizing risks for occupational blood-borne infections, *Journal of the American Medical Association* 264:1189–1190, 1990.

58. Vittecoq, D., et al., Acute HIV infection after acupuncture treatment, *New England Journal of Medicine* 320:250–251, 1989.

59. Tanne, J. H., The last word on avoiding AIDS, *New York*, pp. 28–34, October 7, 1985; Liskin, L., and Blackburn, R., AIDS: A public health crisis, *Population Reports*, Series L, no. 6, July–August 1986; Heywood, W. L. and Curran, J. W., The epidemiology of AIDS in the U.S., *Scientific American* 259(4):72–81, 1988; American Health Consultants, Common sense about AIDS, *AIDS Alert* 8(4): insert following p. 56, 1993.

60. Liskin, L., and Blackburn, R., op. cit., 1986; Wofsy, C. B., et al., Isolation of AIDS-associated retrovirus from genital secretions of women with antibodies to the virus, *Lancet* 1:527–529, 1986; Levy, J. A., op. cit., 1989.

61. Friedland, G., et al., Lack of transmission of HTLV-III/LAV infection to household contacts of patients with AIDS or AIDS-related complex with oral candidiasis, *New England Journal of Medicine* 314:344–349, 1986; Fischl, M., et al., op. cit., 1987; Heywood and Curran, op. cit., 1988; Bartlett, J. G., and Finkbeiner, A. K., *The Guide to Living with HIV Infection*, Johns Hopkins University Press, 1991.

62. Booth, A. W., AIDS and insects, *Science* 237:355–356, 1987.

63. Heywood, W. L., and Curran, J. W., op. cit., 1988.

64. Kish, L. S., et al., An ancient method and a modern scourge: the condom as a barrier against herpes, *Journal of the American Academy of Dermatology* 9:769–770, 1983; Conant, M., et al., Condoms prevent transmission of AIDS-associated virus, *Journal of the American Medical Association* 255:1706, 1986; Minuk, G. Y., Bohme, C. E., and Bower, T. J., Condoms and hepatitis B virus infection, *Annals of Internal Medicine* 104:584, 1986; Feldblum, P. J., and Fortney, J. A., Condoms, spermicides, and the transmission of human immunodeficiency virus: a review of the literature, *American Journal of Public Health* 78:52–54, 1988.

65. Goldsmith, M. F., Sex in the age of AIDS calls for common sense and condom sense, *Journal of the American Medical Association* 257:2261–2266, 1987.

66. Miller, L., Downer, A., and Krueger, L., Reported sexual behavior differences between heterosexual and gay/bisexual populations, Presented at the IV International Conference on AIDS, Stockholm, June 12–16, 1988.

67. Hicks, D. R., et al., Inactivation of HTLV-III infected cultures of normal human lymphocytes by nonoxynol-9 in vitro, *Lancet* II:1422–1423, 1985.

68. Much of the advice about protecting oneself against exposure to HIV hinges on establishing possible risk-factors of one's sex partner. However, as the data from 18-to-25-year-old college students summarized here show, sizable percentages of men and women lie about sex to their partners.

	MEN	WOMEN
ACTUAL EXPERIENCES	*(N=196)*	*(N=226)*
Has told a lie in order to have sex	34%	10%
Lied about ejaculatory control	38%	—
Lied about likelihood of pregnancy	—	14%
Sexually involved with more than one person	32%	23%
Partner did not know	68%	59%
Has been lied to for purposes of sex	47%	60%
Partner lied about ejaculatory control	—	46%
or likelihood of pregnancy	34%	—
HYPOTHETICAL WILLINGNESS TO LIE		
Would lie about having negative HIV-antibody test	20%	4%
Would understate number of previous sex partners	47%	42%,
Would disclose existence of other partner to new partner		
Never	22%	10%
After a while, when safe to do so	34%	28%
Only if asked	31%	33%
Yes	13%	29%
Would disclose a single episode of sexual infidelity		
Never	43%	34%
After a while, when safe to do so	21%	20%
Only if asked	14%	11%
Yes	22%	35%

Source: Cochran, S. D., and Mays, V. M., Sex, Lies, and HIV, *New England Journal of Medicine* 48:384–385, 1990.

69. Reinisch, J., and Beasley, R., *The Kinsey Institute New Report on Sex*, St. Martin's Press, 1990, p. 465.
70. *Morbidity and Mortality Weekly Report* 39:380–383, 1990.
71. Burke, D. S., et al., Measurement of the false positive rate in a screening program for human immunodeficiency virus infections, *New England Journal of Medicine* 319:961–964, 1988; McDonald, K. L., et al., Performance characteristics of serologic tests for human immunodeficiency virus type 1 (HIV-1) among Minnesota blood donors, *Annals of Internal Medicine* 110:617–621, 1989.
72. Loche, M., and Mach, B., Identification of HIV-infected seronegative individuals by a direct diagnostic test based on hybridization to amplified viral DNA,

Lancet 2:418–421, 1988; Imagawa, D. T., et al., Human immunodeficiency virus type 1 infection in homosexual men who remain seronegative for prolonged periods, *New England Journal of Medicine* 320:1458–1462, 1989.

73. Farzadegan, H., Loss of human immunodeficiency virus type 1 (HIV-1) antibodies with evidence of viral infection in asymptomatic homosexual men, *Annals of Internal Medicine* 108:785–790, 1988.

74. Consensus Conference, The impact of routine HTLV-III antibody testing of blood and plasma donors on public health, *Journal of the American Medical Association* 256:1778–1783, 1986.

75. *Morbidity and Mortality Weekly Report* 41:RR–17, December 18, 1992. (A discussion of the early impact of these revisions can be found in *Morbidity and Mortality Weekly Report* 42:308–310, 1993.)

76. Cohen, Sande, and Volberding, op. cit., 1990.

77. Cooper, D. A., et al., Acute AIDS retrovirus infection: definition of a clinical illness associated with seroconversion, *Lancet* 1:537–546, 1985; Tucker, J., et al., HTLV-III infection associated with glandular fever-like illness in a hemophiliac, *Lancet* 1:585, 1985.

78. Francis, D., and Chin, J., The prevention of acquired immunodeficiency syndrome in the United States, *Journal of the American Medical Association* 257:1357–1366, 1987; Ranki, A., et al., Long latency precedes overt seroconversion in sexually transmitted human immunodeficiency virus infections, *Lancet* 2:589–593, 1987; Imagawa, D. T., et al., op. cit., 1989.

79. Bachetti, P., and Moss, A. R., Incubation period of AIDS in San Francisco, *Nature* 338:251–253, 1989; Cohen, Sande, and Volberding, op. cit., 1990.

80. Lui, K.-J., Darrow, W. W., and Rutherford, G. W., III, A model-based estimate of the mean incubation period for AIDS in homosexual men, *Science* 240:1333–1335, 1988; Eyster, M. E., et al., Predictive markers for the acquired immunodeficiency syndrome (AIDS) in haemophiliacs: persistence of P24 antigen and low T4 cell count, *Annals of Internal Medicine* 110:963–969, 1989; Vella, S., et al., Survival of zidovudine-treated patients with AIDS compared with that of contemporary untreated patients, *Journal of the American Medical Association* 267:1232–1236, 1992; Farizo, K. M., Spectrum of disease in persons with human immunodeficiency virus infection in the United States, *Journal of the American Medical Association* 267:1798–1805, 1992.

81. Bachetti and Moss, op. cit., 1989; Lambert, B., 10 Years later, hepatitis study still yields critical data on AIDS, *New York Times*, July 17, 1990, p. C3.

82. Goedert, J., et al., Three year incidence of AIDS in five cohorts of HTLV-III infected risk groups, *Science* 231:992–995, 1986.

83. Moss, A. R., et al., Seropositivity for HIV and the development of AIDS or AIDS related condition, *British Medical Journal* 296:745–750, 1988; Goedert et al., op. cit., 1989.

84. Presidential Commission on the Human Immunodeficiency Virus Epidemic, op. cit., 1988; Cohen, Sande, and Volberding, op. cit., 1990.

85. Koralnik, I. J., et al., A controlled study of early neurologic abnormalities in

men with asymptomatic human immunodeficiency virus infection, *New England Journal of Medicine* 323:864–870, 1990; [editorial], PML: more neurological bad news for AIDS patients, *Lancet* 340:943–944, 1992; Porter, S. B., and Sande, M. A., Toxoplasmosis of the central nervous system in the acquired immunodeficiency syndrome, *New England Journal of Medicine* 327:1643–1648, 1992.

86. Brachetti and Moss, op. cit., 1989; Goedert et al., op. cit., 1989; Cohen, Sande, and Volberding, op. cit., 1990.

87. Beral, V., et al., Epidemiology of Kaposi's Sarcoma in AIDS patients: United States, Fifth International Conference on AIDS, Montreal, June 4–9, 1989. (Abstract M.A.O.30, p. 50.)

88. Liskin and Blackburn, op. cit., 1986; Gabuzda, D. H., and Hirsch, M. H., Neurologic manifestations of infection with human immunodeficiency virus, *Annals of Internal Medicine* 107:383–391, 1987; Ho, D. D., et al., The acquired immunodeficiency syndrome (AIDS) dementia complex, *Annals of Internal Medicine* 111:400–410, 1989; Dina, T. S., Primary central nervous system lymphoma versus toxoplasmosis in AIDS, *Radiology* 179:823–828, 1991; Keating, J. N., et al., Evidence of brain methyltransferase inhibition and early brain involvement in HIV-positive patients, *Lancet* 337:935–939, 1991.

89. Pantaleo, G., Graziosi, C., and Fauci, A., The immunopathogenesis of human immunodeficiency virus infection, *New England Journal of Medicine* 328:327–335, 1993.

90. Payne, S. F., et al., Effect of multiple disease manifestations on length of survival for AIDS patients in San Francisco, Fifth International Conference on AIDS, Montreal, June 4–9, 1989. (Abstract W.A.P. 80, p. 133.)

91. Fischl, M. A., et al., The efficacy of azidothymidine (AZT) in the treatment of patients with AIDS and AIDS related complex, *New England Journal of Medicine* 317:192–197, 1987.

92. Volberding, P. A., et al., Zidovudine in asymptomatic human immunodeficiency virus infection, *New England Journal of Medicine* 322:941–949, 1990.

93. Friedland, G. H., Early treatment for HIV, *New England Journal of Medicine* 322:1000–1002, 1990; Volberding et al., op. cit., 1990.

94. Collier, A. C., et al., A pilot study of low-dose zidovudine in human immunodeficiency virus infection, *New England Journal of Medicine* 323:1015–1021, 1990; Fischl, M. A., et al., A randomized controlled trial of a reduced daily dose of zidovudine in patients with acquired immunodeficiency syndrome, *New England Journal of Medicine* 323:1009–1014, 1990.

95. Cohen, Sande, and Volberding, op. cit., 1990; Friedland, op. cit., 1990; Angell, M., A dual approach to the AIDS epidemic, *New England Journal of Medicine* 324:1498–1500, 1991; Francis, D. P., Toward a comprehensive HIV prevention program for the CDC and the nation, *Journal of the American Medical Association* 268:1444–1447, 1992.

96. Larder, B. A., Draby, G., and Richman, D. D., HIV with reduced sensitivity to zidovudine (AZT) isolated during prolonged therapy, *Science* 243:1731–1734,

1989; Cohen, J., Can combination therapy overcome drug resistance?, *Science* 260:1258, 1993.

97. Aboulker, J. P., and Swart, A. M., Preliminary analysis of the Concorde trial, *Lancet* 341:889–890, 1993; [anonymous], The Concorde Study, *AIDS Clinical Care* 5(5):38, 42, 1993.

98. Nightingale, S. L., Didanosine (DDI) approved for advanced HIV infection, *Journal of the American Medical Association* 266:2528, 1991; Sachs, M. K., Antiretroviral chemotherapy of human immunodeficiency virus infections other than with azidothymidine, *Archives of Internal Medicine* 152:485–501, 1992.

99. Johnson, M. I., and Hoth, D. F., present status and future prospects for HIV therapies, *Science* 260:1286–1293, 1993.

100. Gibbs, C. J., et al., HIV immunization and challenge of HIV seropositive and seronegative chimpanzees, Fifth International Conference on AIDS, Montreal, June 4–9, 1989. (Abstract C.Th.C.O. 46, p. 541.)

101. Levine, A., et al., Immunization with inactivated, envelope-depleted HIV immunogen in HIV infected men with ARC, Fifth International Conference on AIDS, Montreal, June 4–9, 1989. (Abstract Th.B.O.44, p. 219.)

102. Haynes, B. F., Scientific and social issues of human immunodeficiency virus vaccine development, *Science* 260:1279–1286, 1993.

103. Murphy-Corb, M., et al., A formalin-inactivated whole SIV vaccine confers protection in macaques, *Science* 246:1293–1297, 1989.

104. Hilts, op. cit., 1989; Haynes, op. cit., 1993.

105. Redfield, R., and Birx, D., HIV-specific vaccine therapy: concepts, status, and future directions, *AIDS Research and Human Retroviruses*, 8 (6):1051–1058, 1992.

106. Altman, L. K., Hopes are dashed on AIDS therapy, *New York Times*, June 10, 1993, p. A16.

107. Cohen, Sande, and Volberding, op. cit., 1990.

108. *New York Times*, July 22, 1988, p. B4.

109. Siegel, K., et al., Patterns of change in sexual behavior among gay men in New York City, *Archives of Sexual Behavior* 17:481–497, 1988; Ekstrand, M. L., et al., Risky sex relapse, the next challenge for AIDS prevention programs, Fifth International Conference on AIDS, Montreal, June 4–9, 1989 (Abstract T.D.O.8, p. 699); *American Medical News*, June 29, 1990, p. 3.

110. *Morbidity and Mortality Weekly Report* 38:S-4, 1989.

111. Kelly, J. A., et al., Acquired immunodeficiency syndrome/human immunodeficiency virus risk behavior among gay men in small cities, *Archives of Internal Medicine* 152:2293–2297, 1992.

112. *Morbidity and Mortality Weekly Report* 36:S-6, 1987; Hahn, R. A., et al., Prevalence of HIV infection among intravenous drug users in the United States, *Journal of the American Medical Association* 261:2677–2684, 1989; El-Sadr, W., et al., Clinical and laboratory correlates of human immunodeficiency virus infection in a cohort of intravenous drug users from New York, NY, *Archives of Internal Medicine* 152:1653–1659, 1992.

113. *Morbidity and Mortality Weekly Report* 38:S-4, 1989, Table 6.

114. *Morbidity and Mortality Weekly Report* 38:370, 1989.

115. Masters, Johnson, and Kolodny, op. cit., 1988.

116. Fischl, M. A., et al., Seroprevalence of HIV antibody in a sexually active heterosexual population, Presented at the Fourth International AIDS Conference, Stockholm, June, 1988. (Abstract 4067, 1988a.)

117. Glaser, J. B., Strange, T. J., and Rosati, D., Heterosexual human immunodeficiency virus transmission among the middle class, *Archives of Internal Medicine* 149:645–649, 1989.

118. Ellerbock et al., op. cit., 1991; *Morbidity and Mortality Weekly Report* 40:357–363, 369, 1991; St. Louis et al., op. cit., 1991; Mann, Tarantola, and Netter, eds., op. cit., 1992; Haverkos, op. cit., 1993.

119. Weiss, op. cit., 1989.

120. Centers for Disease Control, *HIV/AIDS Surveillance*, January 1993.

121. *Morbidity and Mortality Weekly Report* 38:S-4, 1989, p. 4.

122. See, for example, *New York Times*, October 13, 1985, p. L41; Riesenberg, D. E., AIDS-prompted behavior changes reported, *Journal of the American Medical Association* 255:171, 176, 1986; Martin, J. L., Impact of AIDS on gay male sexual behavior patterns in New York City, *American Journal of Public Health* 77:578–581, 1987; Winkelstein, W., Jr., et al., Selected sexual practices of San Francisco heterosexual men and risk of infection by the human immunodeficiency virus, *Journal of the American Medical Association* 257:1470–1471, 1987; Turner, Miller, and Moses, op. cit., 1989. However, there is another side to this story, as suggested by an article describing the recent resurgence of commercial gay sex establishments in New York City [Navarro, M., In the age of AIDS, sex clubs proliferate again, *New York Times*, March 5, 1993, pp. B1, 5.]

123. Becker, M. H., and Joseph, J. G., AIDS and behavioral change to reduce risk: a review, *American Journal of Public Health* 78:394–410, 1988; Turner, C. F., Miller, H. G., and Moses, L. E., eds., *AIDS: Sexual Behavior and Intravenous Drug Use*, National Academy Press, 1989; Catania, J. A., et al., Changes in condom use among homosexual men in San Francisco, *Health Psychology* 10:190–199, 1991.

124. James, R., HIV testing and counseling: crisis and coping for adolescents and adults, In G. Anderson, ed., *Courage to Care*, Child Welfare League of America, 1990, p. 280.

125. Volberding, P. A., The clinical spectrum of acquired immunodeficiency syndrome: implications for comprehensive patient care, *Annals of Internal Medicine* 103:729–733, 1985; Bartlett, J. G., and Finkbeiner, A. K., *The Guide to Living with HIV Infection*, The Johns Hopkins University Press, 1991; N. D. Hunter and W. B. Rubenstein, eds., *AIDS Agenda: Emerging Issues in Civil Rights*, The New Press, 1992.

126. Meyer-Bahlburg, H., et al., HIV-positive gay men: sexual dysfunction, Fifth

International Conference on AIDS, Montreal, June 1989. (Abstract T.D.O. 22, p. 701.)

127. Becker, M. H., and Joseph, J. G., op. cit., 1988.

128. Linn, L. S., et al. Recent sexual behaviors among homosexual men seeking primary care, *Archives of Internal Medicine* 149:2685–2690, 1989; Ekstrand and Coates, op. cit., 1990; Kelly, J. A., et al., Situational factors associated with AIDS risk behavior lapses and coping strategies used by gay men to successfully avoid lapses, *American Journal of Public Health*, 81:1335–1338, 1991; Stone, R., Living dangerously after an AIDS test, *Science* 257:615, 1992; Navarro, op. cit., 1993.

129. Miller, Turner, and Moses, op. cit., 1990.

130. Stall, R., et al., Alcohol and drug use during sexual activity and compliance with safe sex guidelines for AIDS, *Health Education Quarterly* 13:359–371, 1986.

131. Ekstrand, M. L., et al., Risky sex relapse, the next challenge for AIDS prevention programs, Fifth International Conference on AIDS, Montreal, June 4–9, 1989. (Abstract T.D.O.8, p. 699.)

132. Siegel, K., et al., Patterns of change in sexual behavior among gay men in New York City, *Archives of Sexual Behavior* 17:481–497, 1988.

133. Kelly, J. A., et al., op. cit., 1992.

134. Martin, op. cit., 1987; Becker and Joseph, op. cit., 1988; Doll et al., op. cit., 1989.

135. Stempel, R. R., and Moss, A. R., Changes in sexual behavior by gay men in response to AIDS, Fourth International Conference on AIDS, Stockholm, June 12–16, 1988. (Abstract 6538.)

136. van Griesven, G. J. P., et al., Effect of human immunodeficiency virus (HIV) antibody knowledge on high-risk sexual behavior with steady and nonsteady sexual partners among homosexual men, *American Journal of Epidemiology* 129:596–603, 1989.

137. Masters, Johnson, and Kolodny, op. cit., 1988; van Griesven, op. cit., 1989; Kelly et al., op. cit., 1989; Linn, L. S., et al., op. cit., 1989.

138. McKusick, L., and Hoff, C. C., Relationship between HIV awareness, partner selection criteria, and early relationship formation in two groups of San Francisco bar patrons, Fifth International Conference on AIDS, Montreal, June, 1989. (Abstract W.D.O. 2, p. 704.)

139. Masters, Johnson, and Kolodny, op. cit., 1988.

140. MacDonald, N. W., et al., High-risk STD/HIV behavior among college students, *Journal of the American Medical Association* 263:3155–3159, 1990.

141. Staver, S., Women found contracting HIV via unprotected sex, *American Medical News*, June 1, 1990, p. 4.

142. Kost, K., and Forrest, J. D., American women's sexual behavior and exposure to risk of sexually transmitted diseases, *Family Planning Perspectives* 24:244–254, 1992.

143. Billy, J. O. G., et al., The sexual behavior of men in the United States, *Family Planning Perspectives* 25:52–60, 1993. (This study also found that about one-fifth of single men had had four or more female sex partners over the preceding 18 months.)

144. Catania, J. A., Prevalence of AIDS-related risk factors and condom use in the United States, *Science* 258:1101–1106, 1992.

145. *Morbidity and Mortality Weekly Report* 39:685–689, 1990.

146. Goodwin, F. K., Which kids use condoms—or don't, *Journal of the American Medical Association* 264:1389, 1990.

147. Wallace, J. I., Mann, J., and Beatrice, S., HIV-1 exposure among clients of prostitutes, Fourth International Conference on AIDS, Stockholm, June 12–16, 1988.

148. Altman, L. K., op. cit., 1989b; H. G. Miller, C. F. Turner, and L. E. Moses, eds., *AIDS—The Second Decade*, National Academy Press, 1990; *Morbidity and Mortality Weekly Report* 39:685–689, 1990; Catania et al., 1992; Anderson, J. E., and Dahlberg, P., High-risk sexual behavior in the general population: results from a national survey, 1988–1990, *Sexually Transmitted Diseases* 19:320–325, 1992.

149. Goldsmith, M. F., Sex tied to drugs = STD spread, *Journal of the American Medical Association* 260:2009, 1988; Kolata, G., AIDS is spreading in teenagers, a new trend alarming to experts, *New York Times*, October 8, 1989, Section 1, pp. 1, 30; Weiss, S. H., Links between cocaine and retroviral infection, *Journal of the American Medical Association* 261:607–609, 1989; Miller, Turner, and Moses, op. cit., 1990.

150. *Stamford Advocate*, July 16, 1989, p. B1.

151. Baldwin, J. D., and Baldwin, J. I., Factors affecting AIDS-related risk-taking behavior among college students, *Journal of Sex Research* 25:181–196, 1988; DeBuono, B. A., et al., Sexual behavior of college women in 1975, 1986, and 1989, *New England Journal of Medicine* 322:821–825, 1990; MacDonald, N. E., et al., High-risk STD/HIV behavior among college students, *Journal of the American Medical Association* 263:3155–3159, 1990.

152. Baldwin and Baldwin, op. cit., 1988.

153. Caron, S. L., and McMullen, T., AIDS and the college student: the need for sex education, *SIECUS Report* 15(6):6–7, July/August 1987.

154. *Time* March 28, 1983, p. 55.

155. Winkenwerder, W., Kessler, A. R., and Stolec, R. M., Federal spending for illness caused by the human immunodeficiency virus, *New England Journal of Medicine* 320:1598–1603, 1989.

156. Kramer, Larry, A Manhattan Project for AIDS, *New York Times*, July 16, 1990, p. A15.

157. *USA Today*, March 31, 1989, p. D1; Marshall, E., Sullivan overrules NIH on sex survey, *Science* 253:502, 1991; Moffat, A. S., Another sex survey bites the dust, *Science* 253:1483, 1991.

158. Masters, Johnson, and Kolodny, op. cit., 1988.

159. Lo, B., et al., Voluntary screening for human immunodeficiency virus (HIV) infection, *Annals of Internal Medicine* 110:727–733, 1989; Francis, D. P., et al., Targeting AIDS prevention and treatment toward HIV-1-infected persons: the concept of early intervention, *Journal of the American Medical Association* 262:2572–2576, 1989; Cohen, Sande, and Volberding, op. cit., 1990; Francis, op. cit., 1992; Quinn, T. C., Screening for HIV infection—benefits and costs, *New England Journal of Medicine* 327:486–488, 1992; Janssen, R. S., HIV infection among patients in U.S. acute care hospitals, *New England Journal of Medicine* 327:445–452, 1992.

160. Minkoff, H. L., et al., Routinely offered prenatal HIV testing, *New England Journal of Medicine* 319:1018, 1988; Angell, op. cit., 1991; Gwinn, M., et al., Prevalence of HIV infection in childbearing women in the United States, *Journal of the American Medical Association* 265:1704–1708, 1991; Brandeau, M. L., Screening women of childbearing age for human immunodeficiency virus: a cost-benefit analysis, *Archives of Internal Medicine* 152:2229–2237, 1992.

161. Gostin, L. O., Public health strategies for confronting AIDS, *Journal of the American Medical Association* 261:1621–1630, 1989; Giesecke, J., et al., Efficacy of partner notification for HIV infection, *Lancet* 338:1096–1100, 1991; [editorial], Partner notification for preventing HIV infection, *Lancet* 338:1112–1113, 1991.

162. *Morbidity and Mortality Weekly Report* 37:393–396, 401–402, 1988; Jones, J. L., et al., Partner acceptance of health department notification of HIV exposure, South Carolina, *Journal of the American Medical Association* 264:1284–1286, 1990; Ramstedt, K., et al., Contact tracing for human immunodeficiency virus infection, *Sexually Transmitted Diseases* 17:37–41, 1990; Wycoff, R. F., et al., Notification of the sex and needle-sharing partners of individuals with human immunodeficiency virus in rural South Carolina: 30 month experience, *Sexually Transmitted Diseases* 18:217–222, 1991; Landis, S. E., et al., Results of a randomized trial of partner notification in cases of HIV infection in North Carolina, *New England Journal of Medicine* 326:101–106, 1992.

163. Miller, Turner, and Moses, op. cit., 1990.

164. Presidential Commission on the Human Immunodeficiency Virus Epidemic, op. cit., 1988, p. xviii.

165. Carroll, James, Change starts with our own attitudes, In S. Alyson, ed., *You Can Do Something About AIDS*, 2nd ed., The Stop AIDS Project, 1990, pp. 20–21.

CHAPTER FIFTEEN: ADOLESCENT SEXUALITY

1. Siegel, O., "Personality Development in Adolescence," in B. B. Wolman et al., eds., *Handbook of Developmental Psychology*, Prentice-Hall, 1982, p. 538.

2. Daniel, W. A., Jr., "Obesity in Adolescence," in B. B. Wolman, ed., *Psychological*

Aspects of Obesity, Van Nostrand Reinhold, 1982, pp. 104–117; Chernin, K., *The Hungry Self*, Times Books, 1985; Mishkin, M., "The Embodiment of Masculinity," in M. Kimmel, ed., *Changing Men: New Directions in Research on Men and Masculinity*, Sage, 1987, pp. 37–51.

3. Furstenberg, F. F., et al., Race differences in the timing of adolescent intercourse, *American Sociological Review* 52:511–518, 1987.

4. See, for example, Carroll, J. L., Volk, K., and Hyde, J. S., Differences in males and females in motives for engaging in sexual intercourse, *Archives of Sexual Behavior* 14:131–140, 1985; and DeLamater, J., "Gender Differences in Sexual Scenarios," in K. Kelley, ed., *Females, Males, and Sexuality*, SUNY Press, 1987.

5. Weinstein, M., and Thornton, A., Mother-child relations and adolescent sexual attitudes and behavior, *Demography* 26:563–578, 1989.

6. Bigler, M. O., Adolescent sexual behavior in the eighties, *SIECUS Report* 18:6–9, October/November 1989; CDC, Sexual behavior among high school students—United States, 1990, *Morbidity and Mortality Weekly Report* 40:885–888, 1992.

7. Children's Defense Fund, *What About the Boys: Teenage Pregnancy Prevention Strategies*. Quoted in *SIECUS Report* 17:20, September/October 1988.

8. Nielsen, Linda, *Adolescence: A Contemporary View*, 2nd ed., Harcourt Brace Jovanovich, 1991.

9. Alexander, C. S., et al., Early sexual activity among adolescents in small towns and rural areas: race and gender patterns, *Family Planning Perspectives* 21:261–266, 1989.

10. Reinisch, J. M., et al., High-risk sexual behavior among heterosexual undergraduates at a midwestern university, *Family Planning Perspectives* 24:116–121, 145, 1992.

11. Kinsey, A. C., et al., *Sexual Behavior in the Human Female*, Saunders, 1953.

12. See, e.g., Sorenson, R. C., *Adolescent Sexuality in Contemporary America*, World Publishing, 1973; Arafat, I., and Cotton, W. L., Masturbation practices of males and females, *Journal of Sex Research* 10:293–307, 1974; and Hass, A., *Teenage Sexuality*, Macmillan, 1979.

13. Hass, op. cit., 1979; Young, M., Attitudes and behavior of college students related to oral-genital sexuality, *Archives of Sexual Behavior* 9:61–67, 1980; Newcomer, S. F., and Udry, J. R., Oral sex in an adolescent population, *Archives of Sexual Behavior* 14:41–46, 1985.

14. Sonenstein, F. L., Pleck, J. H., and Ku, L. C., Levels of sexual activity among adolescent males in the United States, *Family Planning Perspectives* 23:162–167, 1991.

15. Gagnon, J., "Sexuality Across the Life Course in the United States," in C. F. Turner, H. G. Miller, and L. E. Moses, eds., *AIDS: Sexual Behavior and Intravenous Drug Use*, National Academy Press, 1989, p. 516.

16. Centers for Disease Control, Sexual behavior among high school students—United States, 1990, *Morbidity and Mortality Weekly Report* 40:885–887, 1992.

17. Zitter, S., "Coming Out to Mom: Theoretical Aspects of the Mother-Daughter

Process," in *Lesbian Psychologies: Explorations and Challenges*, ed. the Boston Lesbian Psychologies Collective, University of Illinois Press, 1987, pp. 177–194.

18. Remafedi, G., The healthy sexual development of gay and lesbian adolescents, *SIECUS Report* 17 (5):7–8, May–July 1989.

19. Billy, J. O. G., Effects of sexual activity on adolescent social and psychological development, *Social Psychology Quarterly* 51:190–212, 1988.

20. Raymond, C. A., Cervical dysplasia upturn worries gynecologists, health officials, *Journal of the American Medical Association* 257:2397–2398, 1987; Layde, P. M., Smoking and cervical cancer: cause or coincidence, *Journal of the American Medical Association* 261:1631–1633, 1989; Wright, T. C., and Richart, R. M., Role of human papillomavirus in the pathogenesis of genital tract warts and cancer, *Gynecological Oncology* 37:151–164, 1990; Lungu, O., et al., Relationship of human papillomavirus type to grade of cervical intra-epithelial neoplasia, *Journal of the American Medical Association* 267:2493–2496, 1992.

21. Dryer, P. H., "Sexuality During Adolescence," in Wolman, et al., eds., op. cit., 1982, p. 596.

22. Erickson, P. I., and Rapkin, A. J., Unwanted sexual experiences among middle and high school youth, *Journal of Adolescent Health* 12:319, 1991.

23. Moore, K. A., Nord, C. W., and Peterson, J. L., Nonvoluntary sexual activity among adolescents, *Family Planning Perspectives* 21:110–114, 1989.

24. Warshaw, R., *I Never Called It Rape*, Harper & Row, 1988.

25. Strunin, L., and Hingson, R., AIDS and adolescents: knowledge, beliefs, attitudes, and behavior, *Pediatrics* 79:825–828, 1987; DiClemente, R., Boyer, C., and Morales, E., Minorities and AIDS: Knowledge, attitudes and misconceptions among black and Latino adolescents, *American Journal of Public Health* 78:55–57, 1988; Ku, L. C., Sonenstein, F. L., and Pleck, J. H., The association of AIDS education and sex education with sexual behavior and condom use among teenage men, *Family Planning Perspectives* 24:100–106, 1992; Reinisch, et al., op. cit., 1992.

26. Jaffe, L., et al., Anal intercourse and knowledge of AIDS among minority-group adolescents, *Journal of Pediatrics* 112:1005–1007, 1988.

27. Brown, L. K., DiClemente, R. J., and Beausoleil, N. I., Comparison of human immunodeficiency virus related knowledge, attitudes, intentions, and behaviors among sexually active and abstinent young adolescents, *Journal of Adolescent Health* 13:140, 1992.

28. Overby, C., Lo, B., and Litt, T., Knowledge and concerns about acquired immunodeficiency syndrome and their relationship to behavior among adolescents with hemophilia, *Pediatrics* 83:204–210, 1989.

29. Sonenstein, F. L., Pleck, J. H., and Ku, L. C., Sexual activity, condom use, and AIDS awareness among adolescent males, *Family Planning Perspectives* 21:152–158, 1989.

30. Trussell, J., Teenage pregnancy in the United States, *Family Planning Perspectives* 20:262–272, 1988.

31. Henshaw, S. K., and Van Vort, J., Teenage abortion, birth and pregnancy statistics: an update, *Family Planning Perspectives* 21:85–88, 1989.

32. Trussell, J., Teenage pregnancy in the United States, *Family Planning Perspectives* 20:262–272, 1988.

33. Maciak, B. J., et al., Pregnancy and birth rates among sexually experienced US [sic] teenagers—1974, 1980, and 1983, *Journal of the American Medical Association* 258:2069–2071, 1987.

34. Lewin, T., "Fewer teen mothers, but more are married," *New York Times* March 20, 1988, Section 4, p. 6.

35. Henshaw and Van Vort, op. cit., 1989.

36. See, e.g., Koenig, M.A., and Zelnik, M., Repeat pregnancies among metropolitan-area teenagers: 1971–1979, *Family Planning Perspectives* 14:341, 1982; Polit, D., and Kahn, J., Early subsequent pregnancy among economically disadvantaged teenage mothers, *American Journal of Public Health* 76:167, 1986; Mott, F. L., The pace of repeated childbearing among young American mothers, *Family Planning Perspectives* 18:5, 1986; Trussell, op. cit., 1988.

37. Upchurch, D. W., and McCarthy, J., Adolescent childbearing and high school completion in the 1980s: have things changed?, *Family Planning Perspectives* 21:199–202, 1989.

38. McLaughlin, S. D., Manninen, D. L., and Winges, L. D., Do adolescents who relinquish their children fare better or worse than those who raise them?, *Family Planning Perspectives* 20:25–32, 1988.

39. Nielsen, op. cit., 1991.

40. Dawson, D. A., Family structure and children's health: United States, 1988, *Vital and Health Statistics*, Ser. 10, No. 178, 1991.

41. Moore, K. A., and Snyder, N. O., Cognitive attainment among firstborn children of adolescent mothers, *American Sociological Review* 56:612, 1991.

42. Kahn, R. J., and Anderson, K. E., Intergenerational patterns of teenage fertility, *Demography* 29:39–49, 1992.

43. See, for example, Newcomer, S. F., and Udry, J. R., Mothers' influence on the sexual behavior of their teenage children, *Journal of Marriage and the Family* 46:477, 1984; Hayes, C., ed., *Risking the Future*, vol. 1, National Academy Press, 1987; and Furstenberg, F. F., Jr., Levin, J. A., and Brooks-Gunn, J., The children of teenage mothers: patterns of early childbearing in two generations, *Family Planning Perspectives* 22:54–61, 1990.

44. Furstenberg, Levine, and Brooks-Gunn, op. cit., 1990.

45. Hanson, S., Morrison, D. R., and Ginsburg, A. L., The antecedents of teenage fatherhood, *Demography* 26:579–596, 1989.

46. Michael, R. T., and Tuma, N. B., Entry into marriage and parenthood by young men and women: the influence of family background, *Demography* 22:515–544, 1985; and Marsiglio, W., Adolescent fathers in the United States: their initial living arrangements, marital experience, and educational outcomes, *Family Planning Perspectives* 19:240–251, 1987.

47. Marsiglio, op. cit., 1987.

48. Sonenstein, Pleck, and Ku, op. cit., 1989, Table 5.

49. Hanson, Morrison, and Gibson, op. cit., 1989.

50. Haggstrom, G. W., et al., *Teenage Parents: Their Ambitions and Attainments*, Rand Corporation, 1981.

51. Robinson, B. E., *Teenage Fathers*, D. C. Heath, 1988.

52. Marsiglio, op. cit., 1987.

53. Teti, D. M., Lamb, L. E., and Elster, A. B., Long-range socioeconomic and marital consequences of adolescent marriage in three cohorts of adult males, *Journal of Marriage and the Family* 49:499–513, 1987.

54. Hardy, J. et al., Fathers of children born to young urban mothers, *Family Planning Perspectives* 21:159–163, 187, 1989.

55. Rosoff, J. L., Sex education in the schools: policies and practice, *Family Planning Perspectives* 21:52, 64, 1989.

56. Kenney, A. M., Guardad, S., and Brown, L., Sex education and AIDS education in the schools, *Family Planning Perspectives* 21:56–64, 1989.

57. Forrest, J. D., and Silverman, J., What public school teachers teach about preventing pregnancy, AIDS, and sexually transmitted diseases, *Family Planning Perspectives* 21:65–72, 1989.

58. Zelnik, M., and Kim, Y. J., Sex education and its association with teenage sexual activity, pregnancy, and contraceptive use, *Family Planning Perspectives* 14:117–126, 1982.

59. Zabin, L. S., et al., The Baltimore pregnancy prevention program for urban teenagers: I. how did it work?, *Family Planning Perspectives* 20:182–187, 1988; and Zabin, L. S., et al., The Baltimore pregnancy prevention program for urban teenagers: II. what did it cost?, *Family Planning Perspectives* 20:188–192, 1988.

60. Howard, M., and McCabe, J. B., Helping teenagers postpone sexual involvement, *Family Planning Perspectives* 22:21–26, 1990.

61. Dawson, D. A., The effects of sex education on adolescent behavior, *Family Planning Perspectives* 18:163–165, 1986; and Furstenberg, F. F., Moore, K. A., and Peterson, J. L., Sex education and sexual experience among adolescents, *American Journal of Public Health* 75:1331–1332, 1985.

62. Peterson, L., The issue—and controversy—surrounding adolescent sexuality and abstinence, *SIECUS Report* 17:1–8, September/October 1988.

CHAPTER SIXTEEN: SEX AND AGING

1. Cantor, M. H., Family and community: changing roles in an aging society, *The Gerontologist* 31 (3), 1991.

2. See, for example, Terry, R. D., and Gershon, S., *Neurobiology of Aging*, Raven Press, 1976; Schneider, Edward L., ed., *The Aging Reproductive System*, Raven Press, 1978; and Allison, T., et al., Developmental and aging changes in somatosensory, auditory, and visual evoked potentials, *Electroencephalography and Clinical Neurophysiology* 58:14–24, 1984.

3. There is no authoritative explanation of why the need to ejaculate is reduced.

We suspect that two separate biologic processes are reflected: first, reduced production of testosterone and related androgens in the aging male may actually be accompanied by reset tissue thresholds for the effects of these hormones at the end-organ level; second, vascular changes (both the normal arteriosclerotic changes that virtually always accompany aging, and some venous leakage, as well) conspire to produce less intense vasocongestion in both the testes and the accessory male sex organs (i.e., the prostate and the seminal vesicles). The net effect is that orgasm/ejaculation does not need to be as physiologically powerful to flush out the male reproductive system and reset the tissues to their unaroused resting state.

4. Neaves, W. B., et al., Leydig cell numbers, daily sperm production and serum gonadotropin levels in aging men, *Journal of Clinical Endocrinology & Metabolism* 59:756–763, 1984.

5. Nankin, H. R., and Calkins, J. H., Decreased bioavailable testosterone in aging normal and impotent men, *Journal of Clinical Endocrinology & Metabolism* 63:1418–1426, 1986; Schiavi, R. C., Sexuality and aging in men, *Annual Review of Sex Research*, 1:227–249, 1990; and Vermeulen, A., Clinical review 24: androgens in the aging male, *Journal of Clinical Endocrinology & Metabolism* 73:221–224, 1991.

6. Vermeulen, A., and Kaufman, J. M., Editorial: role of the hypothalamo-pituitary function in the hypoandrogenism of healthy aging, *Journal of Clinical Endocrinology & Metabolism* 74:1226A–1226C, 1992; Veldhuis, J. D., Urban, R. J., and Dufau, M. L., Evidence that androgen negative feedback regulates hypothalamic gonadotropin-releasing hormone impulse strength and the burst-like secretion of biologically active luteinizing hormone in men, *Journal of Clinical Endocrinology & Metabolism* 74:1227–1235, 1992.

7. Masters, W. H., and Johnson, V. E., *Human Sexual Response*, Little, Brown, 1966.

8. Sherwin, B. B., The psychoendocrinology of aging and female sexuality, *Annual Review of Sex Research* 2:181–198, 1991.

9. Starr, B. D., and Weiner, M. B., *The Starr-Weiner Report on Sex and Sexuality in the Mature Years*, Stein & Day, 1981.

10. Schneider, E. L., and Rowe, J. W., *Handbook of the Biology of Aging*, 3rd ed., Academic Press, 1990.

11. Goldman, L., and Tosteson, A.N.A., Uncertainty about postmenopausal estrogen, *New England Journal of Medicine* 325:800–802, 1991.

12. Sullivan, J. M., et al., Estrogen replacement and coronary artery disease: effect of survival in postmenopausal women, *Archives of Internal Medicine* 150:2557–2562, 1990; Stampfer, M. J., and Colditz, G. A., Estrogen replacement therapy and coronary heart disease: a quantitative assessment of the epidemiologic evidence, *Preventive Medicine* 20:47–63, 1991; Stampfer, M. J., et al., Postmenopausal estrogen therapy and cardiovascular disease: ten-year follow-up from the nurses' health study, *New England Journal of Medicine* 325:756–762, 1991.

13. Henderson, B. E., Paganini-Hill, A., and Ross, R. K., Decreased mortality in users of estrogen replacement therapy, *Archives of Internal Medicine* 151:75–78, 1991.

14. Sullivan, J. M., et al., Estrogen replacement and coronary artery disease: effect on survival in postmenopausal women, *Archives of Internal Medicine* 150:2557–2562, 1990.

15. Ettinger, B., Genant, H. K., and Cann, C. E., Postmenopausal bone loss is prevented by treatment with low-dose estrogen with calcium, *Annals of Internal Medicine* 106:40–45, 1987; Harris, S. T., et al., The effects of estrone (Ogen) on spinal bone density of postmenopausal women, *Archives of Internal Medicine* 151:1980–1984, 1991; Consensus Development Conference: Prophylaxis and treatment of osteoporosis, *The American Journal of Medicine* 90:107–110, 1991.

16. Consensus Development Conference, op. cit., 1991.

17. Steinberg, K. K., et al., A meta-analysis of the effect of estrogen replacement therapy on the risk of breast cancer, *Journal of the American Medical Association* 265:1985–1990, 1991; Colditz, G. A., et al., Prospective study of estrogen replacement therapy and risk of breast cancer in postmenopausal women, *Journal of the American Medical Association* 264:2648–2653, 1990.

18. Whitehead, M. I., and Fraser, D., Controversies concerning the safety of estrogen replacement therapy, *American Journal of Obstetrics & Gynecology* 156:1313–1322, 1987; Ernster, V. L., et al., Benefits and risks of menopausal estrogen and/or progestin hormone use, *Preventive Medicine* 17:201–223, 1988; U.S. Preventive Services Task Force, Estrogen prophylaxis, *American Family Physician* 42:1293–1296, 1990.

19. George, L. K., and Weiler, S. J., Sexuality in middle and later life, *Archives of General Psychiatry* 38:919–923, 1981; Brecher, E. M., and the Editors of Consumer Reports Books, *Love, Sex and Aging*, Little, Brown, 1984.

20. Brecher and the Editors of Consumer Reports Books, op. cit., 1984.

21. Blumstein, P., and Schwartz, P., *American Couples*, William Morrow, 1983.

22. Starr and Weiner, op. cit., 1981.

23. George, L. K., and Weiler, S. J., Sexuality in middle and later life, *Archives of General Psychiatry* 38:919–923, 1981.

24. See, e.g., Starr and Weiner, op. cit., 1981; Brecher et al., op. cit., 1984; and Mulligan, T., and Palguta, R. F., Jr., Sexual interest, activity, and satisfaction among male nursing home residents, *Archives of Sexual Behavior* 20:199–204, 1991.

25. Catania, J. A., and White, C. B., Sexuality in an aged sample: cognitive determinants of masturbation, *Archives of Sexual Behavior* 11:237–245, 1982.

26. Diokno, A. C., Brown, M. B., and Herzog, A. R., Sexual function in the elderly, *Archives of Internal Medicine* 150:197–200, 1990.

27. See, e.g., Kaiser, F. E., et al., Impotence and aging: clinical and hormonal factors, *Journal of the American Geriatric Society* 36:511–519, 1988; Mulligan, T., and Katz, P. G., Erectile failure in the aged: evaluation and treatment, *Journal of the American Geriatrics Society* 36:54–62, 1988; Mulligan, T., et al., The role of

aging and chronic disease in sexual dysfunction, *Journal of the American Geriatrics Society* 36:520–524, 1988; and Schiavi, op. cit., 1990.

28. Bretschneider, J. G., and McCoy, N. L., Sexual interest and behavior in healthy 80- to 102-year-olds, *Archives of Sexual Behavior* 17:109–129, 1988.

29. Masters and Johnson, op. cit., 1966; Kolodny, R. C., Masters, W. H., and Johnson, V. E., *Textbook of Sexual Medicine*, Little, Brown, 1979.

30. Berger, R. M., *Gay and Gray: The Older Homosexual Male*, University of Illinois Press, 1982, p. 191.

31. Dunker, B., "Aging Lesbians: Observations and Speculations," in The Boston Lesbian Psychologies Collective, ed., *Lesbian Psychologies: Explorations & Challenges*, University of Illinois Press, 1987, pp. 72–82.

32. Retrograde ejaculation occurs because of damage to the nerves that supply the lowest portion, or neck, of the urinary bladder. Ordinarily, the neck of the bladder clamps down tightly with high levels of sexual arousal, so that when the prostate gland and seminal vesicles undergo rhythmic contractions at the beginning of orgasm, semen follows the path of least mechanical resistance, which is toward the opening at the tip of the penis. However, if the bladder isn't closed off tightly, there is less mechanical resistance flowing the short distance backward from the prostate to the bladder. Thus, the semen goes into the bladder, where it is mixed with urine.

33. Starr, B. D., "Sexuality," in G. L. Maddox, ed., *The Encyclopedia of Aging*, Springer Publishing, 1984, pp. 606–608.

34. While we certainly understand that women retire from careers, too, we haven't seen even a blip of sexual distress associated with such an event as we see among men. It looks as if retirement is apt to be more of a personal crisis for men than for women; perhaps men are more frightened about how they will respond to being retired, while women may be more confident about their abilities to relax and enjoy themselves.

35. Leiblum, S., et al., Vaginal atrophy in the postmenopausal woman: the importance of sexual activity and hormones, *Journal of the American Medical Association* 249:2195–2198, 1983.

36. Kolodny, R. C., Endocrine aspects of the "use it or lose it" phenomenon associated with male sexuality in the geriatric years, submitted for publication, 1993.

CHAPTER SEVENTEEN: AFFAIRS

1. We have not included in this chapter any discussion of sex with prostitutes, even though this is certainly a common form of extramarital sex for men. The dynamics of why men hire prostitutes are somewhat different from the other forms of extramarital sex that we consider here.

2. The term "open marriage" has a somewhat mistaken derivation. In 1972, George and Nena O'Neill wrote a widely read book called *Open Marriage* (Evans and Company) that encouraged role equality and flexibility between

spouses. The book was generally, but mistakenly, viewed as a call for consensual extramarital sex as a personal growth experience that was likely to benefit the marriage by keeping it from becoming fossilized and static. The O'Neills later voiced dismay over this reading of their ideas, and pointed out that frequently consensual extramarital sex "obscured relationship problems, became an avenue of escape, and intensified conflicts." (O'Neill, N., and O'Neill, G., "Open Marriage: A Synergistic Model," in J. E. DeBurger, ed., *Marriage Today: Problems, Issues, and Alternatives*, Wiley, 1977, p. 293.)

3. This type of threat is generally off the mark, because it's much more difficult for a man to gain entry to the swinging scene without a female partner than with one. In addition, while there may still be lots of swingers out there even in this day and age, it's doubtful that many of them are particularly interested in fostering long-term relationships or stealing someone's spouse.

4. Marriage maintenance affairs sometimes undergo subtle shifts over time as the needs of the participants change. If such an affair lasts for years, it may eventually meet totally different needs than it originally did: for example, we have seen a number of instances in which the woman began to become far more interested in the sexual side of the affair as she reached middle age, whereas the male began to rely on his female partner more for emotional support rather than simply seeing the affair in sexual terms.

5. These types of affairs should not be entirely unexpected. Middle-aged women are often first awakening to their sexuality just as their husbands are often slowing down in the intensity of their sexual interest and performance. See, e.g., Rubin, L., "Sex and Sexuality: Women at Midlife," in M. Kirkpatrick, ed., *Women's Sexual Experiences: Explorations of the Dark Continent*, Plenum Press, 1982, pp. 61–82.

6. See, for example, Reiss, I. L., Anderson, R. E., and Sponaugle, G. C., A multivariate model of the determinants of extramarital sexual permisiveness, *Journal of Marriage and the Family* 42:395–411, 1980; Blumstein, P., and Schwartz, P., *American Couples: Money, Work, Sex*, Morrow, 1983; Glass, S. P., and Wright, T. L., Sex differences in type of extramarital involvement and marital dissatisfaction, *Sex Roles* 12:1101–1119, 1985; and Glass, S. P., and Wright, T. L., "Clinical Implications of Research on Extramarital Involvement," in R. A. Brown and J. R. Field, eds., *Treatment of Sexual Problems in Individual and Couples Therapy*, PMA Publishing, 1988, pp. 301–346.

7. Grosskopf, D., *Sex and the Married Woman*, Simon & Schuster, 1983.

8. Although various writers have come to different conclusions on this topic, reflecting in part the small samples they have studied, it appears to us that those who make a case for extramarital sex being somehow freer or more creative from the woman's point of view are stretching their data. For example, two-thirds of the married women in Diane Grosskopf's study of 1,207 married women (of whom 516 admitted to extramarital affairs) said they were *not* more relaxed and sexually open with their lovers than with their husbands, and only 38 percent said that they had affairs primarily for sex (Grosskopf, op. cit., 1983).

For examples of the type of far smaller studies that reached the opposite conclusion, see Atwater, L., *The Extramarital Connection*, Irvington Publishers, 1982, which drew its conclusions from interviews with 50 women, and Heyn, D., *The Erotic Silence of the American Wife*, Random House, 1992, in which the author doesn't even describe the number of women she interviewed or attempt any statistical tabulation of her findings, yet concludes that women find far more sexual fulfillment in affairs than in marriages.

9. The original Kinsey report shocked people by noting that half of all married men had sex outside their marriages (Kinsey, A. C., Pomeroy, W. B., and Martin, C. E., *Sexual Behavior in the Human Male*, W. B. Saunders, 1948). Various subsequent reports of extramarital sex in men range from the 26 percent noted by Blumstein and Schwartz (op. cit., 1983) to a high of 66 percent found in a methodologically shakier study (Hite, S., *The Hite Report on Male Sexuality*, Alfred Knopf, 1981). The Kinsey study of females found that by age 40, 26 percent of married women had had extramarital sex (Kinsey, A. C., et al., *Sexual Behavior in the Human Female*, W. B. Saunders, 1953). Subsequent reports have generally ranged upward from this number, although Blumstein and Schwartz (op. cit., 1983) noted that only 21 percent of the wives they surveyed admitted to extramarital sex. A sampling of additional surveys includes these figures: a large-scale *Redbook* survey found a 39 percent rate of extramarital sex for women (Tavris, C., and Sadd, S., *The Redbook Report on Female Sexuality*, Delacorte Press, 1975); the Institute for the Advanced Study of Human Sexuality found that 42.7 percent of their married female respondents reported having had extramarital sex (Grosskopf, op. cit., 1983); and a study conducted by *Cosmopolitan* found that half of married women 18 to 34 years old and 69.2 percent of married women 35 or older had had extramarital sex (Wolfe, L., *The Cosmo Report*, Arbor House, 1981). While these surveys do not give a very precise view of the current status of extramarital activities, it is germane to note that the reported statistics probably underreport this behavior (see, e.g., a detailed chapter titled "Methodological Issues in AIDS Surveys," in Miller, H. G., Turner, C. F., and Moses, L. E., *AIDS: The Second Decade*, National Academy Press, pp. 359–471). People tend to be more circumspect about disclosing highly confidential material like extramarital sex than they are in giving information about birth control methods or coital frequency.

10. Humphrey, F. G., "Treating Extramarital Sexual Relationships in Sex and Couples Therapy," in G. R. Weeks and L. Hof, eds., *Integrating Sex and Marital Therapy*, Brunner/Mazel, 1987, p. 151.

11. There is one set of circumstances in which this arrangement is more common: when the husband is homosexual and the wife is heterosexual, they may agree to a more or less sexless marriage, especially after having had children. The wife permits the husband discreet homosexual contacts or relationships, and he in turn gives her carte blanche to pursue her own affairs.

12. See, e.g., Pittman, F., *Private Lies: Infidelity and the Betrayal of Intimacy*, Norton, 1989; Moultroup, D. J., *Husbands, Wives, and Lovers: The Emotional System of the*

Extramarital Affair, Guilford Press, 1990; Brown, E., *Patterns of Infidelity and Their Treatment*, Brunner/Mazel, 1991; Snarch, D. M., *Constructing the Sexual Crucible*, Norton, 1991.

13. The exact explanation for this is unclear. There is some evidence that women who work outside the home are more apt to have extramarital sexual experiences, and in the past 25 years increasing numbers of women have certainly moved into the general workforce (see, for example, Tavris and Sadd, op. cit., 1975; Thompson, op. cit., 1983; Blumstein and Schwartz, op. cit., 1983; and Humphrey, op. cit., 1987). Working women certainly have more opportunities to meet men and more opportunities to have time away from children and husband than housewives do; in addition, as Humphrey notes, working outside the home "may correlate with personality factors that reflect her increasing emancipation from traditional, double-standard, sex mores." Beyond this explanation, it has also been noted that premarital sexual behavior is one of the better predictors of extramarital sexual behavior (Thompson, op. cit., 1983), and over the last 25 years women have become more active participants in premarital sex with multiple partners (albeit primarily in a pattern referred to as "serial monogamy") than in the past, when most of those women who had premarital sex did so only with the man they were about to marry.

14. Blumstein and Schwartz, op. cit., 1983; Thompson, A. P., Extramarital sex: a review of the research literature, *Journal of Sex Research* 19:1–22, 1983.

15. Blumstein and Schwartz, op. cit., 1983, pp. 268–270.

Index